H-1

THE NEW INTERNATIONAL COMMENTARY ON THE OLD TESTAMENT

R. K. HARRISON, *General Editor*

The Books of
JOEL, OBADIAH, JONAH and MICAH

by
LESLIE C. ALLEN
Lecturer in Hebrew Language and Literature, London Bible College

WILLIAM B. EERDMANS PUBLISHING COMPANY

255 Jefferson Ave., S.E., Grand Rapids, Michigan 49502

Printed in the United States of America

Library of Congress Cataloging in Publication Data

Allen, Leslie C
The books of Joel, Obadiah, Jonah, and Micah.
(The New international commentary on the Old Testament)
Bibliography: p. 14.
1. Bible. O. T. Minor prophets—Commentaries.
I. Bible. O. T. Minor Prophets. English.
Selections. 1976. II. Title. III. Series.
BS1560.A65 224'.9 75-22484
ISBN 0-8028-2373-4

TO JEREMY, GOD'S GIFT OF A SON

AUTHOR'S PREFACE

On March 19th, 1970, I was privileged to receive an invitation from Professor R. K. Harrison to produce a volume on Joel, Obadiah, Jonah, and Micah for the New International Commentary on the Old Testament. Since then I have lived as much as possible with these books and learned to appreciate their reflection of their original environment and impact upon it, and also their relevance for the modern Christian.

The contributor to such a series as this has the difficult, not to say desperate, task of interpreting these ancient writings for the scholar and the Christian pastor and layman. He must pay due regard to "what it meant" and "what it means," to use Stendahl's classic formulation. Aiding in the latter concern, on the other side of my desk has been sitting an imaginary traditional Christian, who knows and values his New Testament, but is very hazy about the Minor Prophets and secretly doubtful as to their worth. Sometimes he has been a little bored with my emphasis on the original setting and other antiquarian matters, and I have had to tell him to be patient and to accept the necessity of hard study if these books are to display their treasures to him.

These treasures have come to us in earthen vessels, the earthen vessels of cultural orientation and expression, of ancient speech-forms and poetic and literary conventions, such as meter and structure. Our books were not produced in a vacuum nor dropped from heaven this morning. Any passage within them must be understood in the light of its literary and historical contexts. It needs to be evaluated against the general background of the OT, and then placed in a larger setting still, the total revelation that has reached its climax in the New Testament, in order to trace the recurrence and development of theological patterns. There is no shortcut from our ancient books to this year of grace: these concentric circles have to be carefully constructed if an authentic interpretation of the text is to be achieved.

Professor H. Butterfield once wrote of the need for the historian to have imaginative sympathy with the historical characters he studies. The biblical expositor has a similar need. When all possible historical and literary light has been shed upon the text there remains a gap which can be spanned only by a leap back, by an attempt to relive the human emotions expressed and the psychological effect of statements recorded on the flat written page. The men through whom God's messages came were men of flesh and blood, whose hearts pounded and lips quivered. An adequate doctrine of inspiration must take into account the personalities of the human messengers, and so must adequate exegesis.

Inevitably there is some overlapping where different books are handled in a single volume. The commentary on Micah has been taken as the basic one, with fuller treatment of recurring motifs and forms. The Introduction to Joel contains a section on canonicity which applies to all four books, and also a longer section on textual criticism.

Writing a biblical commentary is essentially a corporate effort. The insights of many scholars, past and contemporary, are reflected in the following pages. Thanks are due to Mr. Hugh Barlow, Librarian of the Bible College, for procuring microfilm and photocopies of inaccessible material, and also to the staff of Dr. Williams' Library and the British Museum. Above all my appreciation to my wife should be recorded. Often forsaken that this volume might be written, she yet labored long to make it more readable. If these prophetic books come to life for the reader and bring him nearer to God, her prayers and mine will be answered.

LESLIE C. ALLEN

CONTENTS

ABBREVIATIONS

AJSL	*American Journal of Semitic Languages and Literatures*
ANET	*Ancient Near Eastern Texts Relating to the OT,* ed. J. B. Pritchard (^{3}1969)
ASTI	*Annual of the Swedish Theological Institute*
AT	Alte/Ancien Testament
ATANT	Abhandlungen zur Theologie des Alten und Neuen Testaments
BA	*Biblical Archaeologist*
BASOR	*Bulletin of the Americal Schools of Oriental Research*
BDB	F. Brown, S. R. Driver, and C. A. Briggs, *Hebrew and English Lexicon of the OT* (1955)
BHK	*Biblia Hebraica,* ed. R. Kittel (^{3}1937)
BHS	*Biblia Hebraica Stuttgartensia,* vol. 10, *Liber XII Prophetarum,* ed. K. Elliger (1970)
BJRL	*Bulletin of the John Rylands Library*
BZ	*Biblische Zeitschrift*
BZAW	Beihefte to *ZAW*
CBQ	*Catholic Biblical Quarterly*
CBSC	Cambridge Bible for Schools and Colleges
DOTT	*Documents from OT Times,* ed. D. Winton Thomas (1958)
EQ	*Evangelical Quarterly*
ET	*Expository Times*
E.T.	English Translation
FRLANT	Forschungen zur Religion und Literatur des Alten und Neuen Testaments
G	Greek Septuagint
GK	E. Kautzsch and A. E. Cowley, *Gesenius' Hebrew Grammar* (^{2}1910) (numerals and letters signify sections)
HTR	*Harvard Theological Review*
HUCA	*Hebrew Union College Annual*
IB	*Interpreter's Bible*

ICC	International Critical Commentary
IDB	*Interpreter's Dictionary of the Bible*
IEJ	*Israel Exploration Journal*
JAOS	*Journal of the Americal Oriental Society*
JB	Jerusalem Bible (1966)
JBL	*Journal of Biblical Literature*
JJS	*Journal of Jewish Studies*
JNES	*Journal of Near Eastern Studies*
JQR	*Jewish Quarterly Review*
JRAS	*Journal of the Royal Asiatic Society*
JSS	*Journal of Semitic Studies*
JTS	*Journal of Theological Studies*
K	Kethib, the written text of MT
KAT	Kommentar zum AT, ed. E. Sellin, continued by J. Herrmann
KJV	King James Version (1611)
LBC	Laymen's Bible Commentaries
MT	Massoretic Text of the Hebrew Bible
Mur.88	Minor Prophets scroll found at Murabba'ât
NBD	*New Bible Dictionary,* ed. J. D. Douglas (1962)
NEB	New English Bible (1970)
NICNT/OT	New International Commentary on the NT/OT
NTS	*New Testament Studies*
OTS	*Oudtestamentische Studiën*
PEQ	*Palestine Exploration Quarterly*
Pss 1,2,3	M. Dahood, *Psalms I, II, III,* Anchor Bible (1965, 1968, 1970)
PTR	*Princeton Theological Review*
Q	Qere, the read text of MT
QpMic	Commentary on Micah found at Qumran
RB	*Revue biblique*
RHPR	*Revue d'histoire et de philosophie religieuses*
RHR	*Revue d'histoire des religions*
RS	*Revue semitique*
RSR	*Recherches de science religieuse*
RSV	American Revised Standard Version (1952)
RV	English Revised Version (1881)
S	Syriac Peshitta
SBT	Studies in Biblical Theology
SEA	*Svensk Exegetisk Årsbok*
SJT	*Scottish Journal of Theology*
SNT	Supplements to *Novum Testamentum*
ST	*Studia Theologica*
SVT	Supplements to *VT*
T	Aramaic Targum

TGUOS	*Transactions of the Glasgow University Oriental Society*
TTZ	*Trierer Theologische Zeitschrift*
TZ	*Theologische Zeitschrift*
V	Latin Vulgate
VT	*Vetus Testamentum*
WMANT	Wissenschaftliche Monographien zum Alten und Neuen Testament
ZAW	*Zeitschrift für die alttestamentliche Wissenschaft*
ZDMG	*Zeitschrift der Deutschen Morgenländischen Gesellschaft*
ZDPV	*Zeitschrift des Deutschen Palästina-Vereins*

Additional abbreviations are listed in the course of the individual Bibliographies.

GENERAL BIBLIOGRAPHY

G. W. Anderson, *A Critical Introduction to the OT* (1959).
P. Benoit, J. T. Milik, and R. de Vaux, *Discoveries in the Judean Desert,* vol. 2: *Les grottes de Murabbaʿât* (1961).
A. Bentzen, *Introduction to the OT,* 2 vols. (1952).
J. A. Bewer, *The Prophets in the KJV, with Introduction and Critical Notes* (1956).
L. H. Brockington, "Joel," "Obadiah," "Jonah," *Peake's Commentary on the Bible,* ed. M. Black and H. H. Rowley (1962), pp. 614–16, 626–29.
R. Calkins, *The Modern Message of the Minor Prophets* (1947).
J. Calvin, *Commentaries on the Twelve Minor Prophets,* vols. 2, 3 (E.T. repr. 1950).
A. Cohen, ed., *The Twelve Prophets.* The Soncino Books of the Bible (1948).
G. R. Driver, "Linguistic and Textual Problems: Minor Prophets II, III," *JTS* 39 (1938), pp. 260–273, 393–405.
Idem, "Hebrew Notes on Prophets and Proverbs," *JTS* 41 (1940), pp. 162–175.
S. R. Driver, *An Introduction to the Literature of the OT* ([7]1898, repr. 1957).
B. Duhm, "Anmerkungen zu den zwölf Propheten," *ZAW* 31 (1911), pp. 81–93, 175–78, 184–88, 200–204.
S. L. Edgar, *The Minor Prophets.* Epworth Preacher's Commentaries (1962).
A. B. Ehrlich, *Randglossen zur hebraïschen Bibel: textkritisches, sprachliches und sachliches,* vol. 5 (1912).
O. Eissfeldt, *The OT: An Introduction* (E.T. 1966).
H. L. Ellison, *Men Spake from God: Studies in the Hebrew Prophets* (1952).
G. H. A. Ewald, *Commentary on the Prophets of the OT,* vols. 1(1875), 2(1876), 5(1881).
G. Fohrer, *Introduction to the OT* (E.T. 1968).
R. K. Harrison, *Introduction to the OT* (1969).

F. Hitzig and H. Steiner, *Die zwölf kleinen Propheten*. Kurzgefasstes exegetisches Handbuch zum AT ([4]1881).
A. van Hoonacker, *Les douzes petits prophètes* (1908).
A. Jepsen, "Kleine Beiträge zum Zwölfprophetenbuch," *ZAW* 56 (1938), pp. 85–100.
C. F. Keil, *The Twelve Minor Prophets,* vol. 1 (E.T 1885).
C.-A. Keller, "Joel," "Abdias," "Jonas," *Commentaire de l'AT,* vol. 11a (1965).
L. Köhler and W. Baumgartner, *Lexicon in Veteris Testamenti Libros* (1953).
E. G. Kraeling, *Commentary on the Prophets,* vol. 2 (1966).
T. Laetsch, *The Minor Prophets* (1956).
J. Lindblom, *Prophecy in Ancient Israel* (1962).
K. Marti, *Das Dodekapropheten* (1904).
J. M. Myers, *Hosea to Jonah.* LBC (1960).
W. Nowack, *Die Kleinen Propheten* ([3]1922).
C. von Orelli, *The Twelve Minor Prophets* (E.T. 1893).
R. H. Pfeiffer, *Introduction to the OT* ([2]1952).
E. B. Pusey, *The Minor Prophets,* vols. 3–5 (1906, 1907).
T. H. Robinson and F. Horst, *Die zwölf Kleinen Propheten.* Handbuch zum AT ([3]1964).
W. Rudolph, *Joel, Amos, Obadja, Jona.* KAT (1971).
R. B. Y. Scott, *The Relevance of the Prophets* ([2]1969).
M. Sebök, *Die syrische Übersetzung der zwölf kleinen Propheten und ihr Verhältniss zu dem MT und zu den älteren Übersetzungen, namentlich den LXX und dem Targum* (1887).
E. Sellin, *Das Zwölfprophetenbuch.* KAT ([3]1929).
G. A. Smith, *The Book of the Twelve Prophets,* 2 vols. The Expositor's Bible (1903).
A. Sperber, *The Bible in Aramaic,* vol. 3 (1962).
K. A. Vollers, "Das Dodekapropheten der Alexandriner," *ZAW* 4 (1884), pp. 1–20.
G. W. Wade, *The Books of the Prophets Micah, Obadiah, Joel and Jonah.* Westminster Commentaries (1925).
A. Weiser, *Das Buch der zwölf Kleinen Propheten,* vol. 1. Das AT Deutsch (1949).
J. Wellhausen, *Die Kleinen Propheten übersetzt und erklärt* ([4]1963).
R. E. Wolfe, "The Editing of the Twelve," *ZAW* 53 (1935), pp. 90–129.
E. J. Young, *An Introduction to the OT* (1949).
J. Ziegler, *Beiträge zum griechischen Dodekapropheten* (1943).
Idem, "Studien zur Verwertung der LXX in Zwölfprophetenbuch," *ZAW* 60 (1944), pp. 107–131.
Idem, Septuaginta. Vetus Testamentum Graecum Auctoritate Academiae Litterarum Gottingensis editum, vol. 13: *Duodecim prophetae* ([2]1967).

The Book of JOEL

INTRODUCTION

1. DATE

Every student of the book of Joel must have sympathy with Calvin's agnostic position:

> *As there is no certainty it is better to leave the time in which he taught undecided; and as we shall see, this is of no great importance. Not to know the time of Hosea would be to readers a great loss, for there are many parts which could not be explained without a knowledge of history; but as to Joel there is less need of this, for the import of his doctrine is evident, though his time be obscure and uncertain.*

But a clue that Calvin himself favored a late date is afforded in his explanation of Joel 3:10 as a deliberate inversion of Isa. 2:4/Mic. 4:3.

Other prophetic books have editorial headings which specify to a greater or lesser degree the period of a prophet's ministry, but the heading to Joel is silent in this respect. Nor is the prophet Joel mentioned in the OT outside his book. Dating must depend on internal allusions, which are notoriously capable of multiple explanations. Apart from this, the position of Joel in the Hebrew canonical order of the Minor Prophets is in itself suggestive; Jewish tradition supports an early date, although Ibn Ezra considered that there was "no way of knowing" Joel's period.

The early view was put on a scholarly footing by K. A. Credner in 1831. He assigned it to the early part of the reign of Joash in the ninth century B.C. Many ninteenth-century scholars enthusiastically took up Credner's arguments, such as Ewald, Pusey, Keil, and von Orelli; and some more recent ones have espoused his view and dated Joel between 870 and 860 B.C.[1] The historical allusions to Egypt and Edom in 3:17, 19 are then explained by reference to Shishak's attack on Jerusalem in Rehoboam's reign (1 K.14:25f.) and to the revolt of Edom in the reign of Jehoram (2 K.8:20–22). It is assumed that citizens of Judah resident in Edom were

1. E.g., E. J. Young, *An Introduction to the OT* (1949), pp. 271f.

massacred then, and that Amaziah's savage treatment of Edom (2 K.14:7) was a reprisal for an earlier bloodbath. The nonmention of such national enemies of Judah as Syria, Assyria, or Babylon is easily explicable: Syria did not threaten Judah till later in Joash's reign, while the other two belong to a later period. On this view the reference in 3:2 to "dividing my land" also applies to Edom as part of Judah's former domain. On the other hand, the historical allusions in 3:3, 5, 7 are explained in terms of the raid of the Philistines and Arabs on Judah in the reign of Jehoram (2 Chr. 21:16f.), when the king's sons and wives were seized. It is assumed that the Phoenicians played the role of slave-traders. It is significant, however, that Keil dissented from this interpretation. He considered that the terms used in 3:2, 3 were far too strong to be interpreted thus: he took the passage as a prediction of future judgment on Jerusalem and the later dispersion of the Jews; but Keil's predictive view is exegetically doubtful, since the events do appear to lie in the author's past. The fact that a king is not mentioned in the course of Joel's oracles is explained on the early view by reference to the minority of Joash; hence his appeals to the priests are linked with the control of the high priest Jehoiada while Joash was a minor.

Credner opposed dating the book at the end of the preexilic period. But since his time yet another dating has come to the fore, and is preferred by the majority of exegetes and writers of OT Introductions: the postexilic period, especially c.400 B.C. and the following decades. This setting was first elaborated by W. Vatke in 1835.[2] Judah is called Israel in 3:1, 2 and also in 2:27; 3:16, and this suggests a date after 721 B.C. and the end of the Northern Kingdom. The great enemies of Judah are absent from the book because it belongs to a period after the fall of Babylon in 539, while the Persians would not feature as foes since Judah was on friendly terms with the Persian authorities. The historical allusions in 3:2f. are most naturally to be taken as referring to the fall of Jerusalem in 587 and the ensuing exile. The positive emphasis on the cult contrasts with the attitude of the preexilic prophets, while both the absence of the king and the dominance of the priests accord with a postexilic date. That the whole community could be summoned to the temple reflects the smallness of the population after the Exile. The allusions to cereal offering and libation in 1:9, 13; 2:14 are best understood as referring to the postexilic *tāmîḏ* or daily temple offering. The wall of 2:7 permits a more precise dating, viz., after 445 B.C. when Nehemiah completed the rebuilding of the wall of Jerusalem. The reference to the Greeks as recipients of Judean slaves in 3:6 suggests the Persian period, while the casual way they are mentioned hardly accords with their position as a world power in later times. The destruction of Sidon in 345 B.C. indicates a date earlier than this for 3:4.

Furthermore, the linguistic data favor the postexilic period, it is

2. *Die Religion des AT nach den kanonischen Büchern* (1835), p. 462, n. 1.

claimed.[3] For instance, "ministers of Yahweh," *m^e^shār^e^ṯê yhwh,* in 1:9 is characteristic of postexilic literature. Moreover, there are a host of literary allusions, e.g., to Isa. 13:6 (1:15), Ezek. 30:2f. (1:15), Zeph. 1:14f. (2:1f.), and to Mal. 3:2; 4:5 (2:11, 31). Obad. 17, which is best taken as postexilic, is explicitly quoted in 3:17.

These are the main arguments for a postexilic date. The weakness of the preexilic argument from Joel's canonical position is demonstrated by referring to the different tradition in G, where it is placed after Micah. The Hebrew position is explained on literary grounds as due to the similarities between Amos 1:2; 9:13, and Joel 3:16, 18 respectively, and to the mention of Tyre, the Philistines, and Edom in both books.

But there is also a vocal and important group of scholars who contend for a late preexilic date. A. S. Kapelrud has dated the book c.600 B.C., probably in the reign of Zedekiah. He has little to say about the chronological implications of 3:2f. The references to the Philistines he relates to the hostility evident in Zeph. 1:14–18 and Jer. 47:4. In the latter text they are significantly mentioned alongside Tyre and Sidon. The mention of the Greeks he understands as alluding to the Ionians, and he cites the preexilic trading carried on between the Ionians and Mesopotamia. Joel's call to repentance in order to avert greater danger from Yahweh's wrath is paralleled in Isa. 1:18–20; Amos 4:6–12. The failure to mention the king in Joel 1 and 2 is simply explained: the prophet did not intend to specify classes of the people. In 2:16 the people are enumerated according to age, not rank, and there was no particular reason for mentioning the king. It is significant that neither Isa. 3:1–3 nor Mic. 3:9–12 has a royal reference. The link with Zephaniah in 1:15 reflects the contemporaneity of the two prophets. Similarities between Joel and the later Isa. 13 reflect a debt to a common source.

Carl A. Keller dates the ministry of Joel between 630 and 600 B.C. 3:19 is a reference to Egyptian intervention in Palestine in the last decade of the seventh century. 3:2 says nothing about Judah; it refers to the downfall of the Northern Kingdom ("Israel") in 721. In 3:4–8 Judah, the Philistines, and the Phoenicians apparently represent independent states in control of their own political destiny, a phenomenon that fits 630–625. Like Kapelrud, Keller finds Jer. 47:4 significant, and also Ezek. 28:20–24, which mentions Tyre as among the states that were thorns in Judah's side in the late preexilic period. A reference to the Greeks is quite feasible in the seventh century. The language of Joel and links with Zephaniah, Nahum, Obadiah, Jeremiah, Ezekiel, etc. point to the end of the seventh century and the beginning of the sixth. Joel speaks the language of his time and reflects the viewpoint of his contemporaries.

3. Cf. H. Holzinger, *ZAW* 9 (1889), pp. 89–131; M. Wagner, *Die lexikalischen und grammatikalischen Aramaismen im alttestamentlichen Hebräisch*. BZAW 96 (1966), pp. 24, 29, 82f., 87.

Wilhelm Rudolph has presented the most comprehensive case for a late preexilic Joel. He dates the prophet between 597 and 587 B.C. The use of "Israel" for Judah presupposes that the Northern Kingdom has fallen and Judah is the sole representative of the old Israel. 3:2, 3, 17 refer to the Babylonian invasion of Jerusalem in 597. That the destruction of the temple is not mentioned by this temple-conscious prophet demonstrates that 587 is not in view. 3:19 probably alludes to an otherwise unattested ill treatment of Jews, who are known to have been resident in Egypt and Edom before 597 (Jer. 40:11; 44:1). 3:4–8 need have no military significance, but may refer simply to commercial transactions. Greek contacts are attested with Palestine in the seventh and sixth centuries B.C. If the king is not mentioned, neither is he in the long section Isa. 1–5. There was no reason for the prophet to refer to political issues, since his theme is essentially eschatological. The existence of cult prophets in preexilic times, which more recent scholarship has demonstrated, means that such a pro-cultic prophecy need not be postexilic. Rudolph identifies Joel with one of the optimistic prophets denounced by Jeremiah, but notes that inasmuch as the Day of Yahweh spells disaster at the outset, Joel stands with the great prophets of woe. His allusions to Amos and Zephaniah, to Ezekiel and Isa. 13 merely indicate that all are rooted in the same tradition. The vocabulary of the book may be credited to the period of Jeremiah. The summons of the whole community to the temple need not imply a small population, in the light of Jer. 26:2, 7–19; 36:6, 9. 1:9, 13 are not necessarily allusions to the postexilic *tāmîḏ*.

Three periods have been reviewed as suitable for Joel's prophetic activity, early and late preexilic and the period after 400 B.C. There remains a fourth, the final decades of the sixth century B.C. But first an exponent of an exilic dating may be considered. B. Reicke argues that in the book Jerusalem has an altar, but no temple except the porch of 2:17.[4] Cessation of sacrifice means the withholding not of expensive burnt offerings but of libations and cereal offerings. These are indications that Joel prophesied before 520 B.C., when new burnt offerings were introduced (Ezra 3:2, 10; Hag. 1:14). The locusts are in fact figurative expressions for the enemies of Judah: in light of Jer. 5:17, Joel 1:16; 2:25 allude to the Babylonian attacks of 597 and 587, while "the northerner" in 2:20 refers to Nebuchadnezzar. In 2:2 the coming of the Persians from the east is predicted; *pārûś*, "spread," may be a wordplay. A reference to the Greeks is compatible with the time shortly after the Babylonian Exile to which Joel is to be assigned.

Jacob M. Myers puts Joel c.520 B.C., the period of Haggai and Zechariah,[5] developing arguments put forward earlier by W. F. Albright.[6] He examines fully the implications of the mention of Greek traders. The gift

4. ATANT 59 (1970), pp. 133–141; cf. A. Jepsen, *ZAW* 56 (1938), p. 94.
5. *ZAW* 74 (1962), pp. 177–195.
6. *JBL* 61 (1942), pp. 120f.

of Naucratis to the Greeks by Amasis (569–526 B.C.) for commerce and colonization created one of the most important trading centers in the eastern Mediterranean. The Persian Wars against the Greeks during the fifth century B.C. rule out trade between Phoenicia and Greece then; apparently rivalry with the Phoenicians was less bitter in the sixth century. An important factor for Myers is the reference to the Sabeans in 3:8. They lost control of the eastern trade routes after the sixth century; the Mineans surged forward in the fifth century and by 400 B.C. were the dominant power in South Arabia. So Joel cannot be dated after the fifth century B.C. The combined reference to the Philistines and Phoenicians may allude to the independence of Gaza in the Persian period, while the other Philistine port, Ashkelon, belonged to Tyre. Ports in southern Palestine would be natural outlets for Judean slaves. He considers the most likely historical context of 3:4, 6 to be after the middle of the sixth century B.C., when Judah was at the mercy of neighboring states who moved into the vacuum created by the Exile and the decline of the neo-Babylonian empire, and before the Persian conquest of the West. The reference to the wall in 2:7 does not necessarily imply a post-445 B.C. dating. The fifty-two days taken to repair the wall suggests that large sections were still standing before Nehemiah rebuilt it. The literary arguments he regards as tenuous. Joel is to be placed before Malachi, whose prophecy indicates that physical conditions had improved and the priests were careless and compromising. He belongs to the period of Haggai and Zechariah, and a number of parallels may be drawn. The failure of crops recalls Hag. 1:6. The call for repentance corresponds to Hag. 2:15, 18; Zech. 1:3. Joel's judgment on the nations is comparable with Hag. 2:21f.

Gösta W. Ahlström, author of the most recent study on Joel, dates the prophet between 515 and 500 B.C. He repeats and supplements the arguments of Albright and Myers. The use of the verb *hḥzyq,* "strengthen, repair," as well as *bnh,* "rebuild," in Neh. 3 suggests that several parts of the wall did not require complete rebuilding. References to the temple indicate a time after 515, when the temple was completed. The threat to Edom in 3:19 must antedate the reference to the recent destruction of Edom in Mal. 1:3f.; and so Joel must have preceded Nehemiah.

This survey of the main chronological views and supporting arguments must leave the reader with a single clear impression: the indecisiveness of many of the arguments despite the triumphant flourish with which their proponents adduce them. But closer examination of the evidence and its interpretation creates a suspicion that certain arguments are weak,[7] while others have been ignored or handled superficially by their opponents.

7. F. R. Stephenson, *VT* 19 (1969), pp. 224–29, adduced an astronomical argument, assuming that 2:31 depends on personal observation of lunar and solar eclipses. He refers to the solar eclipses of Feb. 29th, 357 or July 4th, 336 B.C. But more probably Joel is echoing traditional material. M. Treves, *VT* 7 (1957), pp. 153–55, finds in ch. 3 references to the invasion of Ptolemy Soter in 312, but Wolff and Jones present cogent arguments against his suggestion.

For the present author the similar positions of Myers and Ahlström appear to do most justice to the evidence. 3:2f. is clearly a crucial passage: most naturally it is to be understood as a reference to the cataclysmic events of 587 B.C. Certainly in Jer. 50:17 the verb *pzr,* "scatter," is used of the Babylonian Exile, while the loss of lands and homes to foreigners mentioned in Lam. 5:2 accords with what Joel says. Rudolph's criticism that the destruction of the temple is not mentioned may be met by the observation that it is probably alluded to in 3:5. Keller's differentiation between Israel and Judah conflicts with the plain impression of 3:1f. and the use of the term "Israel" elsewhere in the book. If Obadiah is to be assigned to the early postexilic period, as the Introduction to his book will argue, then Joel can hardly be preexilic, since 2:32 is an explicit quotation of Obad. 17. It is difficult to escape this conclusion *pace* Treves, who regards Isa. 37:32 as the basis,[8] and Rudolph, who strangely considers that the reference is to Joel 2:26f.

The linguistic arguments are certainly less decisive than they were formerly assumed to be. Ahlström has a useful discussion of the issues (*JTCJ,* ch. 1) and there is no need to repeat his study.[9] Ahlström deals later in his book[10] with a form that exercised Kapelrud, the phrase *b^e^nê hayy^e^wānîm,* "sons of the Greeks," in 3:6, which accords with the Chronicler's style. Kapelrud agreed that the phrase was late, but urged that it indicated simply that the preexilic oracles of Joel were handed down orally and put into written form at a late date. More probably it reveals a postexilic date for at least the passage 3:4–8, although, as Ahlström observes, this need not imply a date as late as the Chronicler.

> *Many of the words and phrases . . . used as arguments for a late date are not late at all. On the other hand, the investigation thus far conducted shows several phenomena which have to be understood as pointing to a late period of the Biblical Hebrew. From this point of view, Joel cannot be from a time as early as Amos and Hosea or before, as has sometimes been advocated. We would rather see it as belonging to a late pre-exilic or perhaps with more probability to an early post-exilic time.*[11]

The literary arguments are another area of controversy. If one concedes with most that Obad. 17 is quoted in 2:32, then it follows that other links with Obadiah are likewise marks of dependence (Obad. 10 in 3:19; v. 11 in 3:3; v. 15 in 3:4, 14; v. 17 in 3:17). If, furthermore, Obadiah is rightly dated as early postexilic or exilic, it is quite reasonable to suppose that other prophetic echoes connote a literary dependence. It is significant that in 2:27 there occur together two expressions specially characteristic of other

8. *Loc. cit.,* p. 152.
9. It is doubtful whether the arguments that have been based on *shelaḥ,* "spear" (2:8), and *hanḥat,* "bring down" (3[4]:11), are relevant; see the commentary.
10. *JTCJ,* pp. 117f.
11. *JTCJ,* pp. 21f.

prophets: cf. Ezek. 36:11, etc.; Isa. 45:5, etc. That 1:15 is a deliberate reference to known prophetic passages (Ezek. 30:2f.; Isa. 13:6)[12] is suggested by the fact that, originally a threat to foreign nations, they are strikingly reapplied to Israel. But whether 2:11, 31 allude to Mal. 3:2; 4:5 is doubtful: the latter passages themselves have an allusive ring. Joel's knowledge of earlier prophetic writings probably accounts for his literary style. "The extent and minuteness of his acquaintance with the earlier literature are . . . quite enough to account for what has by some been felt to be a difficulty in assigning to Joel a late date, viz. the fluency of his style, which is in striking contrast to the dull—not to say stilted—style of Haggai and the semi-rabbinic periods of Malachi."[13]

2. UNITY OF COMPOSITION

Two distinct questions have been raised concerning the unity of the book, one regarding the implications of the difference of subject matter in its two halves, generally taken as 1:1–2:27 and 2:28–3:21, the other with respect to the relationship of 3:4–8 to its context. The first question was originally posed by M. Vernes in 1872 in a doctoral thesis.[14] He considered that the first half of the book speaks of a Day of Yahweh that was already come and the second of one that was still to come; therefore the two halves were to be attributed to different authors. Independently J. W. Rothstein in 1896 emphasized the radical differences between the two parts, regarding the first as preexilic and the second as postexilic.[15] He considered that in the first part a compiler added 2:20 and probably also 2:10f.

Bernard Duhm developed Rothstein's attempt to drive a wedge between the contemporary and eschatological portions of the book: Joel was the author of the prophecy only as far as 2:17, and of that portion 1:15; 2:1b–2a, 11b were the work of the apocalyptist who produced the rest of the book.[16] Duhm had a considerable influence on subsequent scholarship. E. Sellin ascribed only 1:2–2:27 to Joel, apart from the references to the Day of Yahweh. J. A. Bewer sided enthusiastically with Duhm and took his work further: Joel composed chs. 1, 2 (except for 1:15; 2:1b–2, 6, 10, 11, 27, 31b–32) and also 3:2a, 9–14a, while an editor wrote the rest, connecting the two compositions by a series of interpolations marked by dependence on earlier prophets; 3:4–8 was a still later insertion. T. H. Robinson

12. Isa. 13 is very frequently taken as a product of the mid-6th century B.C. S. Erlandsson, *The Burden of Babylon*. Coniectanea biblica, OT series 4 (1970), has argued that its historical references suggest rather the end of the 8th century. Ahlström, *JTCJ*, pp. 5f., also favors this setting.

13. G. B. Gray, *Expositor* 8 (1893), p. 223.

14. *Le peuple d'Israël et ses espérances* (1872), pp. 46–54.

15. S. R. Driver, *Einleitung in die Literatur des AT*, ed. J. W. Rothstein (1896), pp. 333f.

16. *ZAW* 31 (1911), pp. 1–43, 184–88.

differentiated between the two parts of the book on grounds of content: 1:2–2:27, which is in the main from Joel, is historically oriented, and the locusts are viewed as a harbinger of the Day of Yahweh, while the rest is apocalyptic in tone and of a much later date. He regarded 2:28–3:21 as a series of fragments from unknown authors, with 3:9–14 as the original nucleus. O. Eissfeldt, although he regarded the Day of Yahweh references in 1:2–2:27 as firmly anchored in their contexts and not conceptually out of place, took 2:28–3:21 as a collection of apocalyptic pieces mostly later than Joel.

There has been increasing opposition, however, to this radical splitting of the book into two. L. Dennefeld, A. S. Kapelrud, A. Weiser, T. Chary, J. A. Thompson, M. Delcor, and H. W. Wolff have been notable defenders of the book's essential unity. Dennefeld in a comprehensive survey of the problem contradicted Vernes' initial distinction between two Days of Yahweh; rather for him in the first part the locusts were forerunners of the coming Day which is the subject of the second part.[17] There is then a basic unity of content suggesting unity of authorship. To follow up an interpretation of the locusts as precursors of the Day with a description of the destruction the Day would cause is a natural development. Differences of style between the two parts, stressed by Rothstein and Delcor, may be explained by the fact that in the first Joel speaks as an animated eyewitness, while in the second he deals with more traditional material. Kapelrud, too, argued for continuity of thought: the so-called interpolations in chs. 1, 2 are in fact an integral part of their context.

Weiser suggested that 2:28–3:21 was an authentic addition. Joel puts into writing his oracles concerning the plague and drought after a favorable outcome and develops the theme of the Day which he had broached in his oracles by adding the present sequel. Chary reviewed the history of scholarly opinion since Dennefeld's survey.[18] He traced the return, in the main, to an affirmation of unity. He stressed that the lack of mention in the second part of the locusts which figured in the first, along with the change to an eschatological perspective, do not demand that the book be divided. To delete the "Day of Yahweh" verses from the first part is arbitrary. Joel's assurances of blessing for his people lead on naturally to a widening of perspective to the supremacy of Israel and the humiliation of other nations. Chary repeated Dennefeld's explanation for the basic difference of style between the two parts. In the first the concrete historical context shaped the style, while in the second, Joel had available an arsenal of motifs and terms upon which to draw. Bewer had exaggerated the originality of the first part.

Thompson noted the elaborate pattern of correspondences marking the two halves of the book, and drew attention to R. H. Pfeiffer's contention that a combination of a contemporary problem with an eschatological hope is

17. *RSR* 4 (1924), pp. 555–575.
18. *PC*, pp. 190–94.

by no means singular, since Haggai, Zechariah, and Isa. 13 as well as Daniel and Revelation similarly blend the present with the future. Delcor attributed stylistic differences to varying subject matter. He observed that Bewer so admired the style of 2:28–31a and 3:9b–14b that he felt obliged to attribute these passages to Joel.

Wolff is aided in maintaining the integrity of the two parts by his view that 2:1–11 is eschatologically oriented; but, like Thompson, he set down a list of verbal links between the two sections as evidence of identical authorship: 1:14 and 3:9; 1:15; 2:1b–2 and 3:14; 2:1b and 31b; 2:2 and 31 ("darkness"); 2:3 and 32; 2:10a and 3:16a; 2:10b and 3:15; 2:11a and 3:16a; 2:11b and 31b; 2:16 and 3:11; 2:17 and 3:2. W. Rudolph regards the basic unity of the book as self-evident, referring to the studies of Dennefeld and Chary. L. H. Brockington, J. M. Myers,[19] and C.-A. Keller accept the work as a unit. Ahlström does not regard the question of a literary break as worth mentioning.

To a large extent the scholarly pendulum has swung back to its position of a century ago. The bogey of a Deutero-Joel has at least prompted a deeper study of the relationship of the two parts of the book, which in turn has set on a firmer foundation its essential unity. However, mention should be made of the elaborate theory of O. Plöger.[20] He divides the book into three distinct parts, 1:1–2:27; 2:28–32; 3:1–21(except the later 3:4–8). The first part, in which the motif of the Day of Yahweh is used as a vivid metaphor, was supplied with an eschatological supplement, the third part, in order to correct the impression of the first by stressing the future reality of the Day. Both these parts come from a similar time, probably the early postexilic period. The second part, to be dated much later, is a subsequent correction of the third, applying the hopes of ch. 3 not to the empirical Israel but to an eschatological Israel which has a living faith in Yahweh's final intervention. Plöger's fascinating study depends on his evaluation of 2:28–32; it is extremely doubtful, however, whether the passage really speaks of the limiting of God's ultimate blessing to a group within the Jewish community. Moreover, he is guilty of underestimating the significance of the Day in the first part of the book.

There remains the issue of 3:4–8. The passage is considered by many scholars to be a later insertion. One reason frequently adduced is that it is in prose, while the surrounding material is in verse. *BHK* printed it as prose, and such scholars as Wade and Robinson concurred in this judgment. But *BHS* significantly sets out the piece as poetry, and Thompson and Wolff so regard it, though the latter admits a prosaic style. A more weighty objection is that it interrupts the context. 3:1–3 is resumed in vv. 9–12, and vv. 4–8 may be dropped with no loss and much gain in continuity. The theme of the climactic judgment and eventual destruction of all the nations is oddly

19. *Loc. cit.* in n. 5 above.
20. *Theocracy and Eschatology* (E.T. 1968), pp. 96–105.

broken by a noneschatological allusion to specific nations whose comparatively mild penalty is to be slavery. Wolff emphasizes the inappropriateness of the passage by contrasting "my people, my land" of vv. 2f. with "the sons of Judah/Jerusalem" and "their territory" in vv. 6, 8. The theme of the *lex talionis* in vv. 4–8 whereby the punishment fits the crime is alien to vv. 1–3, 9–12, while such rhetorical elements as a series of questions and repetition of phraseology are not found elsewhere in the book. Rudolph is less extreme: certainly the passage is an interruption, as its prose and noneschatological material reveal; but it may be viewed as contemporary with the rest of Joel and even ascribed to Joel. The small stylistic differences observed by Wolff present no obstacle to this conclusion. The oracle was placed here on the catchword principle, as many scholars point out, i.e., "sell" in vv. 3, 6–8. Originally it probably belonged after 3:21.

A difficulty expressed by many is the historical setting of the oracle. A past generation tended to be influenced by mention of the Greeks toward categorizing it as very late (e.g., Robinson), but this is no longer an obstacle. Bewer dated the underlying event in 352 B.C. But Rudolph finds no difficulty in locating it at the end of the preexilic period, while Myers dates it c.520.

Ahlström defends the authenticity of the passage by claiming that a prophet can interrupt his oracular poetic speech and switch to a prose narrative, promoted by some phenomenon or word. He gives Amos 7:10–17 as an example; that passage, however, hardly supports his thesis, since the question of editorial compilation in Amos surely complicates the issue. He observes further that two motifs of 3:1–3 are taken up, namely, selling and scattering among the nations.

Insufficient attention has been paid in the discussion to structure. It will be suggested later that 3:1–12 corresponds to the earlier section 2:18–27, and 3:4–8 is the structural counterpart of 2:21–23. In both cases there is a break from the surrounding context: the prophet's song in 2:21–23 interrupts Yahweh's oracle concerning crops and locusts in vv. 18–20, 24–27, taking up the catchword of acting mightily. 3:4–8 thus has a remarkable parallel in the earlier passage, where no one has suggested interpolation. Moreover, vv. 1–12 are bound together by a soundplay: *sh-b* runs through the whole section.[21] "Sons of Judah" (3:6, 8) significantly recurs in v. 19.[22] Rudolph is surely right in dismissing Wolff's rather fussy stylistic strictures. If Joel was as well versed in earlier prophecy as he apparently was, there can be no objection to this model prophetic piece as part of his work. The *lex talionis* motif, *contra* Wolff, does find an echo in the surrounding passages in the bringing back of the nations to the area where formerly they had committed their crime. The new battle scene reenacts the previous one, but with the opposite result. There is the same sense of

21. See n. 8 to the commentary *in loc.*

22. Wolff strangely regards vv. 18–21 as an addition, but he at least views it as an imitation of Joel's style or even composed by Joel.

grievance in vv. 4–8 and in the adjoining material, i.e., that foreigners have interfered with Yahweh's concerns. The disparity of penalty in vv. 4–8 and the context would probably have created less difficulty for an ancient hearer or reader than for a modern one, and is no barrier to taking the whole section 3:1–12 as a unit. Certainly Joel is no consistent eschatologist. It is characteristic of him to cull a variety of motifs from Judah's eschatological repertoire and to use them without constructing a systematic synthesis.

3. OCCASION AND PURPOSE

The first part of the book is concerned with a devastating plague of locusts. But are these real locusts swarming and crawling when Joel lived, or are they symbols of future foes? The history of interpretation of Joel reveals a certain leaning toward the second view. The Targum at 2:25 paraphrased the list of four locust terms as "peoples, languages, rulers, and kingdoms." The margin of a sixth-century A.D. ms. of the Septuagint, Q, more specifically interprets as "Egyptians, Babylonians, Assyrians, Greeks, and Romans." This allegorical application to future history is found also in many of the Church Fathers and was echoed by Pusey. Calvin took the locusts of ch. 1 as literal and those of ch. 2 as allegorical.

A more refined form of this allegorical view is the apocalyptic interpretation propounded by Merx, who took the locusts of ch. 1 as supernatural creatures and those of ch. 2 as symbols of the enemies of the end times. Pfeiffer and Wolff are among those who distinguish between chs. 1 and 2, the former speaking of literal locusts, the latter of apocalyptic.

But most scholars interpret the locusts in both chapters in strictly contemporary terms, and this is the most natural way of construing the material. 1:2–4 speaks of the locusts as a present threat to Joel's generation and the occasion of his summons to lamentation. 1:16 confirms this impression of direct involvement with the ravages of real locusts. The past verbs of 2:18, 19 categorize Yahweh's response to the locust crisis and the people's penitential cries as having already occurred.[23] It is significant that the locusts behave in a literal manner: they ravage fields, trees, and fruit, but do not kill or plunder, or take prisoners of war. They are indeed described metaphorically as an attacking army and are compared with soldiers,[24] but to conceive of figurative locusts who are like the soldiers they are supposed to represent is a tortuous and improbable interpretation. Moreover, the restoration promised by Yahweh in 2:18–27 concerns the material damage associated with locust attacks. In Amos 7:1–3 a locust plague is certainly a

23. Theodotion rendered with future verbs in v. 18 and was followed by Merx, who also read a jussive in v. 19 (cf. KJV); this view has rightly never met with general acceptance.
24. Cf. the ancient Near Eastern parallels adduced by Thompson, *JNES* 14 (1955), pp. 52–55, for metaphorical description of locusts and also for recourse to religious expedients.

symbol of coming destruction, and Rev. 9:3, 7–9 actually applies Joel's language to an apocalyptic event, but these passages provide no warrant for detaching the theme of Joel from its historical and literary contexts.

The description of the locusts' attacks corresponds remarkably with historical reports of their appearance and effect, and gives an impression of firsthand observation of locusts at work. Blended with this realistic eyewitness account are a number of less literal elements. "Joel's description of a locust invasion has never been surpassed for its dramatic picturesqueness combined with amazing accuracy of detail."[25] The futuristic interpretations have obviously been encouraged by such eschatological elements as the motifs of the Day of Yahweh in 1:15; 2:1, 2, 11, of theophany in 2:3, 6, and of the northerner in 2:20. It will be noted that most of these motifs occur in ch. 2, but this hardly permits a distinction between the locusts of ch. 1 and those of ch. 2. The army of 2:11 is clearly that of 1:6 over again, and 2:25 confirms this identification (Rudolph). Joel is no mere reporter, but a prophet and an interpreter of a current event in terms of its divine import. As Amos interpreted a locust plague and drought as Yahweh's means of chastising a sinful nation (4:7–9), so Joel views a series of destructive plagues and associated drought as signs that God is punishing his covenant people.

But his message goes astonishly far beyond this. Amos and later prophets had spoken of the Day of Yahweh as Yahweh's intervention in signal catastrophe against his enemies. Joel sees in the locusts the dawn of this very Day. Zephaniah had urged the people to repent and perchance avert from themselves the wrath about to be poured out upon Israel and other nations (1:14–2:3). Joel repeats his call, to which his horrified hearers respond. To interpret the Day of Yahweh and similar eschatological motifs as merely poetic and hyperbolic metaphors is to do Joel an injustice. They represent rather a conviction that the end is at hand, heralded in this unprecedented destruction caused by the locusts, which threatened the very survival of the community.

Joel had received a complex tradition of the Day of Yahweh. It was composed of a number of elements; and as Amos' audience apparently already knew, it was associated with blessing for God's people and doom for other nations. Amos had taught Israel that it spelled doom for them, too, as a sinful people, and later prophets confirmed this sinister connotation. But if the Day was averted for Joel's generation, there remained the other ingredients of the prophetic tradition to be fulfilled. Accordingly, after revealing the immediate blessing which Yahweh is to bestow on the locust-ravaged land, Joel naturally reverts to the theme of the Day. He considers its threat for the nations in reprisal for their involvement in the 587 B.C. debacle, and gives reassurance of the security and prospect of further blessing in store for the people of Judah. By their repentance they had won a reprieve from the Day: its terrors could no more appall them. Thus the first

25. B. P. Uvarov, cited by Thompson.

and second parts essentially hang together. "It was Joel's experience of the awful plagues [of locusts] that give him his intrinsic conviction that the great and terrible Day was near and impelled him to write about it. Chapters 3 and 4 [= 2:28–3:21] came from the burning heart of a poet whom we know to have experienced these depths of suffering."[26]

4. AUTHORSHIP

The tradition recorded by Pseudo-Epiphanius that Joel came from the tribe of Reuben is of little worth; it apparently emanates from a source no higher than a misapplication of 1 Chr. 5:4. He must have been a Judean, for the temple, Jerusalem, and Judah are the three concentric circles of his prophetic concern. At the heart is the temple, for his oracles have a decidedly cultic orientation. He knows well the priestly routine, he calls Judah to a penitential assembly, and he deplores the cessation of the temple ritual caused by the natural crisis. For him, the acme of Yahweh's favor is the opportunity to resume the daily offerings. The material clearly has affinity with cultic compositions such as laments, prayers, oracles of salvation, and exhortations to praise.

This close association with the cult has suggested to a number of scholars that Joel was a cultic prophet attached to the temple, a member of a prophetic group whose ministry has survived in not a few canonical psalms.[27] This identification is quite plausible. Is the book of Joel in fact a cultic liturgy?[28] Chary has observed that the book is based on a single, unique historical event and so can hardly amount to a liturgy in the usual sense of a composition to be used on a variety of occasions; besides, the eschatological emphasis of the second part of the book would strike an alien note in a cultic liturgy.[29] Rather, the prophet derived many of his forms from liturgical compositions. With their aid he challenged the people to see the hand of Yahweh in the contemporary disaster and brought them back from the brink of calamity to a right relationship with the God of the covenant.

5. CANONICITY

The canon is the traditional term for the divinely inspired, authoritative body of writings contained in the Bible.[30] The study of canonicity seeks to gather evidence for the human recognition of the authority of the scriptural books.

26. W. W. Cannon, *Church Quarterly Review* 103 (1926), pp. 46f.
27. Cf. 1 Chr. 25:3, 5; Jer. 35:4; Zech. 7:3.
28. See the concise review of scholarly opinion in Ahlström, *JTCJ*, p. 136, n. 1.
29. *PC*, pp. 209–212.
30. For further study see the OT Introductions and literature cited therein, esp. G. W. Anderson, *A Critical Introduction to the OT* (1959), pp. 10–18, and E. J. Young, "The Canon of the OT," *Revelation and the Bible*, ed. C. F. H. Henry (1959), pp. 155–168.

The canonicity of the Minor Prophets is a relatively straightforward issue. Prophets spoke with authority and claimed divine inspiration for their oracles. Their oral messages, and no less their written form, would naturally have found acceptance. But it would not be true to say of the preexilic prophets that their oracles were accepted as authoritative by the community as soon as they were delivered. In the case of Micah, his own oracles supply evidence that he belonged to a group of prophets opposed by others who regarded themselves as true prophets and who consequently dismissed the stand Micah took as mistaken. But there must have been those who accepted his messages as authoritative, and for this reason preserved his oracles for posterity. Indeed, as Jer. 26:18 remarkably testifies, at least one of his oracles was taken seriously by the king and people. A century later men had a good knowledge of his words and were ready to accord them the divine *imprimatur,* "Thus says Yahweh." The catastrophes of the fall of Jerusalem and the Exile must have been regarded as striking confirmation of Micah's prophesying, and undoubtedly commended them still further.

The present form in which Micah's oracles have come down to us is probably a postexilic edition, although there is no reason to doubt that they had previously been preserved in written form. They appear to have been supplemented with a liturgical psalm: evidently the religious community used the book at their worship as a means of confessing their sin and as an encouragement to hope for future blessing. They took to heart the penalties and promises associated with Micah, and thereby recognized the divine validity of his words.

The book of Joel contains within it a clear implication that his call to repentance was recognized as a divine summons. It is not difficult to appreciate that the associated oracles of salvation found ready acceptance among the prophet's contemporaries and succeeding generations as God's answer to their perplexed and aching hearts in difficult days. The little book of Obadiah must also have had a similar popular appeal which gave full credence its claim: "Thus says Yahweh."

The book of Jonah is quite different from the others in that it is a narrative associated with a strange prophetic anti-hero. Doubtless Jonah's name helped it along the canonical road, just as the attachment of Paul's name did to the Letter to the Hebrews. But it has a prophetic stamp of its own, which evidently was recognized as the very voice of God to the community of the old covenant.

These are reasonable reconstructions of the early process of canonization.[31] The recognition of the uniqueness of the collections of

31. A *baraitha* or unauthorized tradition preserved in the Babylonian Talmud, *Baba Bathra* 14b, 15a, attributes the writing (i.e., presumably the editing) of the Twelve and some other books to the "men of the great synagogue," a shadowy company who seem to have been regarded as an early postexilic group. Similarly according to 2 Macc. 2:13–15 (C.A.D. 50), Nehemiah "made a collection of the books dealing with the kings and the prophets." Cf. too 2 Esdras 14:18–48 (C.A.D. 100), where Ezra is said to have dictated books, including the

prophetic oracles must have been accelerated by the eventual dying out of the prophetic gift, probably by the third century B.C. The first external evidence in later times of the authority of the Minor Prophets, including our four, is dated c.190 B.C.: Jesus ben Sira mentions in his praise of famous men "the twelve prophets" (Sir. 49:12). By the beginning of the second century B.C. the works of the Minor Prophets were thus a fixed entity. His translator and grandson speaks in the prologue of "the law and the prophets . . ." (c.117 B.C.). Josephus (*Contra Apionem* i.8) writes of a limited number (22) of sacred writings, including thirteen prophetic books. The Twelve Prophets were evidently counted as one book, probably because they could be written on a manuscript about the same size as that required by each of the Major Prophets.

The Qumran community undoubtedly attached divine authority to the Minor Prophets. That they did so in the case of Micah is clear from the preservation of their *pesher* commentary on the book. In Cave Four at Qumran no fewer than eight copies of the book of the Twelve were found. Although none is complete, most probably they each originally consisted of the Twelve together.

Whatever the status and function of that vague body the Council of Jamnia c.A.D. 90, the rightful place of the Twelve in the Jewish canon did not come into the discussion. There was no need to argue about them, for their authority had evidently long been recognized and was accepted without question.[32]

But why should Christians concern themselves with the Jewish canon? The question needs to be posed and answered, for there is an implicit tendency among Christians who are otherwise most orthodox virtually to decanonize the pre-Christian scriptures and especially such books as the Minor Prophets. It needs to be understood that the Christian Church took over what we now call the OT as authoritative.[33] The motivation was its endorsement in the NT generally, and its verification in the Gospels by the testimony of Jesus Christ. Ample references are made to "the (sacred) scriptures" and to "the law and the prophets."[34] The books of Joel, Jonah, and Micah are cited in the NT. That the book of Obadiah is not explicitly quoted does not of course mean that it was not regarded as canonical. So the

---

canonical 24, for public use. The value of these traditions is uncertain; they attest a belief that the OT, including the Minor Prophets, was considered normative in matters of faith and practice for the Jewish community from its earliest period of postexilic establishment.

32. It should be mentioned that the traditional Massoretic order of the books differs from that of the Greek Septuagint. In the former the order of the first six is Hosea, Joel, Amos, Obadiah, Jonah, and Micah, but in G it is Hosea, Amos, Micah, Joel, Obadiah, and Jonah. This latter order was apparently determined by length in the case of the first five and for Jonah by the difference of content from the others.

33. There is no reason to doubt that the omission of the Minor Prophets from Origen's list (Eusebius, *Ecclesiastical History* vi. 25) was an oversight perpetrated by Origen, Eusebius, or a copyist.

34. E.g., Matt. 5:17; 21:42; Acts 8:32; 28:23; 2 Tim. 3:15.

heritage of these prophets has passed into the possession of the late twentieth-century Church, preserved by the providential control of the God who both inspired them and evoked in those who heard and read them a recognition that in them God's voice spoke and continued to speak with compelling force.

6. TEXT

The question of text is an essential concern for the exegete of a biblical book.[35] He must satisfy himself that the material he seeks to elucidate is in the earliest attainable form. The foray into the field of OT textual criticism is primarily concerned with the Massoretic Text (MT). This is the authorized Jewish text produced in consonantal form in the course of the first century A.D. by selection of older material. We are most fortunate to possess an ancient copy of the official text of the Minor Prophets dating from the early part of the second century A.D., a scroll discovered in 1955 in a cave at Murabba'ât in the Wilderness of Judah (Mur. 88). The MT was originally a consonantal text with sporadic use of consonantal signs to indicate certain vowels. A complete system of vocalization was produced by the Massoretes from the sixth century A.D. onward. The present Tiberian system of pointing with vowel signs was created in the ninth and tenth centuries; it presumably embodies the traditional interpretation of the unvocalized text. *BHK* and *BHS* print a Leningrad ms., B 19A, dated A.D. 1008, a careful copy of a model text produced by the Tiberian textual scholar Ben Asher in the tenth century.

The MT represents only a part, albeit the most important part, of the total witness to the ancient text of the OT. The extant Hebrew evidence is supplemented by that of the ancient versions, which, despite their mistranslations and accumulation of corruption and recensional adaptation in the course of their own long history, provide the discriminating textual critic with valuable pointers to their underlying Hebrew texts. Foremost among these translations is the Alexandrian Greek Septuagint (G), which in the case of the Minor Prophets most probably goes back to the first half of the second century B.C. It underwent an important revision in the first century A.D. whereby it was carefully aligned with the then current Hebrew text. This revision is contained in a leather scroll of the Minor Prophets, substantial fragments of which were discovered in 1952, including passages of Jonah and Micah. In the second century A.D. other attempts were made to render the contemporary Hebrew text into Greek. These translations are associated with the names of Aquila, Symmachus, and Theodotion.

The Syriac version, the Peshitta (S), has suffered from a confused

35. This sketch may be supplemented by reference to B. J. Roberts, *The OT Text and Versions* (1951); E. Würthwein, *The Text of the OT* (E.T. 1957).

textual history, but it probably goes back to the first century A.D. A reliable edition of S in the Minor Prophets has yet to be produced. The Latin Vulgate (V) is the work of the fourth-century Jerome. It was a replacement of the earlier Old Latin. The readings often conform to G. Jerome worked from the Hebrew text, but he was influenced by G and the later Greek texts and also by Jewish tradition.

The Jewish Targum is an official Palestinian distillation of Babylonian oral paraphrases into Aramaic, which in the case of the Minor Prophets reached final written form not before the fifth century A.D.

This is the range of the textual evidence available for the study of our prophets. The versional material provides an important means of checking the Massoretic tradition. In the case of Micah a few further rays of light are shed upon the ancient text by fragments of the Qumran *pesher* commentary.

Textual criticism obviously implies a subjective element, depending as it does on the evaluation of variant readings, but there has gradually been produced a body of controls, canons, and criteria in the textual field to which most scholars assent. In general there is at the present time a much more conservative attitude to the MT than, say, fifty years ago. This is evident from a comparison of the textual apparatus of *BHK* with that of the new *BHS*. However, there is still need for a judicious use of conjectural emendation. The OT textual critic covets the really early texts his NT counterpart has at his disposal.[36] Josephus about the end of the first century A.D. wrote of the extreme care taken in the transmission of the OT scriptures, but it is clear that in some cases corruptions antedate our earliest evidence. Yet conjectural emendation may not be resorted to in a light and arbitrary manner; it must be subject to strict controls, such as contextual, psychological, and graphic or phonetic feasibility. One difficulty in the understanding of the text is our comparatively defective knowledge of the Hebrew language of the biblical books. For example, a surprising number of words occur once or seldom in the Hebrew OT. A judicious use of comparative study in the neighboring Semitic languages has often elucidated the text and countered previous attempts to emend. A controversial tool is the use of Ugaritic linguistic phenomena, such as elements of grammar and syntax, to explain the Hebrew text.

The general reader of the OT sometimes misunderstands the textual specialist, whose task it is to concentrate on difficulties in the text. The general health of a community is hardly gauged by reference to the clinical records of its medical practitioners, who are essentially concerned with physical malfunctioning and whose very profession shields them from healthy members of society. It needs to be stressed that in the case of the prophetic material discussed in this volume, although the ravages of time

36. It is often overlooked that the NT Gk. text is generally published in a modern eclectic form, while Heb. editions of the OT apart from an apparatus are reproductions of the received text.

have caused a permanent blemish here and there, there need be little doubt concerning the preservation of the original text in the rest of the material by one or more of the extant witnesses.

The Hebrew text of Joel is well preserved. The notes will indicate the specific areas of disagreement among textual scholars. In the course of the commentary, the alteration of the MT has been judged advisable in four instances. At 2:23 *kārī'shôn* is read with one Hebrew ms. and G V S: it is assumed that in MT the first consonant has been confused with another similarly written letter (*b*). In 3(4):11, G is followed: substantially this involves a repointing of MT *hanḥat*. In 2:32 (3:5) a slight conjectural emendation has been adopted in place of the grammatically difficult *ûḇaśś*^{e}*rîḏîm* of MT; but the sense is little affected. At 2:2 *k*^{e}*shaḥar* is conjecturally repointed with many scholars to *kish*^{e}*ḥōr*, which better suits the context.

7. THEOLOGY

The theme that dominates the book of Joel and binds it together is the Day of Yahweh. By Joel's time this was a traditional complex of eschatological motifs, a cluster of ideas of varied origins to which Joel could appeal with the assurance that his audience would understand. A survey of earlier prophetic material that stresses this theme, such as Isa. 2:6–22; Amos 5:18–20; Zeph. 1, 2, indicates that it refers to a time when Yahweh would finally intervene in the world to establish his sovereignty. Hostile elements would be swept aside; the enemies of Yahweh, who were sinners against the moral God of Israel, would be exposed and punished. It was thus associated with judgment upon those who did not acknowledge Yahweh's sovereignty, especially the Gentiles, but also Israel insofar as it too was sinful. But the Day also had a positive side, abused by the people of the Northern Kingdom whom Amos criticized, but theologically valid when applied correctly. The vindication of Yahweh spelled the vindication of those who were loyal to him, and guaranteed the rehabilitation of his oppressed supporters. Essentially the Day is a two-sided phenomenon. These are the basic ideas which Joel develops and expands into a coherent synthesis with the aid of such age-old motifs as theophany, holy war, and the holy city attacked in vain by her foes.

In the first part of the book the prophet surprisingly applies one aspect of the Day to a locust plague. One might accuse Joel of debasing Israel's eschatological currency, were it not for the fact that so disastrous was the havoc caused by the locusts, in a day before pesticides were available, that the very existence of the community was at stake and the annihilation of Israel was a real possibility. This seemed to be the end. If the locusts persisted, Israel would be no more. In eschatological terms the present plague was a harbinger, or the first phase, of the Day of Yahweh. This is the terrifying theological interpretation placed upon the plague: it is

Yahweh's intervention to destroy a sinful people, his final judgment on his enemies.

Like Zephaniah in Zeph. 2:1–3, Joel summons the people to repentance, to turn back to the God of the covenant and acknowledge his lapsed moral claims (2:12f.). In fact locusts and drought are implicitly regarded as God's chastisement for breach of covenant (cf. Deut. 28:23f., 38; Amos 4:7–9). Paradoxically in the midst of judgment the prophet appeals to the covenant grace of Yahweh. As Yahweh had stated through Ezekiel in his call to Israel to repent (18:30–32), "I take no pleasure in the death of anyone. . . . Repent and live." The locusts and accompanying drought are a warning to Israel to turn back to Yahweh, as they had been to the Northern Kingdom in Amos' time. If the warning was disregarded, doom was inevitable. But what if the sinners deserted their sinful ways? Since the full onslaught of the Day is directed against sinners, will it be averted from the penitent who dissociate themselves from their sinful past? The theoretical possibility is worth putting to the test, urges Joel in conformity with the "perhaps" of Zeph. 2:3, especially in view of God's attested attribute of covenant mercy. But repentance is no guarantee of deliverance. Perhaps rather it is too late, as Amos had to learn (7:8; 8:2). Joel stresses the sovereign freedom of God: he cannot be coerced to do man's will. He does not surrender to the plausible logic of man's theology, but remains the supreme arbiter of man's destiny. "His judgments are inscrutable and his ways past finding out" (Rom. 11:33).

At first sight Joel strikes a jarring note compared with such preexilic prophets as Hosea, Amos, Isaiah, and Jeremiah, when he stresses the cultic side of Israel's life under the covenant. The religious cult obviously meant a good deal to him. Unlike the earlier Protestant-sounding prophets, he does not attack the wrong use of the cult but supports a correct one. Joel's attachment to the temple and its ritual offerings affords us a glimpse of OT faith at its highest and best within the context of a cultic system of praise and worship. But even he is aware of the possibility of abuse; for he insists that hearts and not merely clothes have to be torn in the cultic service of lamentation (2:13). For Joel the external forms of religion are, and must remain, the vehicle of the spirit and the correct expression of sincere devotion.

The people of Judah evidently acted on Joel's pleas to hold a service of lamentation and repent of their sin, and to everyone's relief the prophet is given in response a favorable oracle indicating that the danger is averted and the divine Foe is friendly toward the community, which is now submissive to his will. Covenant blessing in the form of rain and good crops is promised (Lev. 26:4f.; Deut. 28:11f.). But this is not the end of the matter. If the locusts were really heralds of the Day, the theological pattern must run its course.[37] Ahead lie contrasting fortunes for the allies and enemies of

37. For discussions of the apocalyptic dimensions of 2:28–3:21 cf. Wolff and Brockington. The passage displays several features shared by apocalyptic. Brockington rightly regards the

Yahweh, comprising the vindication of the obedient nation whose patron he is and the outworking of divine judgment upon those who have sinned against him and his. For postexilic Judah the Gentiles' major sin lay in the tragedy of 587 B.C. In tones reminiscent to the Christian of the "inasmuch" of Matt. 25:31–46, Yahweh declares that he will champion his own and wreak destruction as reprisal for these offenses. Egypt and Edom, Judah's traditional enemies, would be desolated for crimes previously committed against Judah's citizens. The destruction of Yahweh's enemies and the vindication of Israel are closely interwoven in Joel's message. God's people have passed beyond their doom. For them in the immediate future lay the prospect of material blessing which would more than compensate them for losses incurred during the locusts' depredations. This would be proof of Yahweh's presence among his people (2:27). But beyond this lay the reality of ultimate blessing, the charismatic outpouring of the prophetic spirit upon all the people, which betokens for this prophet of sacramental grace an intimate awareness of God's will as well as a new manifestation of his powerful presence. His people would be kept safe in the holy city, while the storm of his wrath raged against the nations recalled for punishment to the very scene of their crimes. Their security would be fresh proof of his saving presence (3:17). The land would blossom with evidence of God's rich blessing in the form of water, wine, and manpower. The temple, the earthly home of Yahweh, would be the fount of his benediction and the focal point of his saving presence.

Joel's comprehensive exposition of the Day of Yahweh thus reaches a climax in the fulfilment of covenant blessing of the penitent people in the land. Within the confines of the OT revelation the prophecy of Joel reaches a high-water mark of promise. Joel is a man of his time, and Yahweh speaks through him in terms of the old covenant. His book exhibits the habitual foreshortening of OT prophecy. His hearers would have been encouraged by his prophecies to believe in a Utopia round the corner which did not in fact materialize. But the NT seizes on one of his pinnacles of hope and claims its fulfilment at Pentecost. The inauguration of the eschatological scheme announced by Joel is seen in the outpouring of the Holy Spirit (Acts 2:16–21). Joel 2:28–32 gripped the minds of the early Church. Paul found the promise of 2:32 fulfilled in Christ and in the establishment of the new eschatological community (Rom. 10:13).

A temptation to which many have succumbed is to object to Joel's particularism in 2:28–3:21, especially in the light of Paul's seemingly universalistic interpretation. Certainly the outward look preserved in Gen.

---

book as essentially prophetic, in that a contemporary disaster is given a typical prophetic interpretation. If Joel gives the impression of a systematic unfolding of the future of the world, he is a veritable amateur compared with the more apocalyptically oriented tabling of Ezek. 38, 39 and Zech. 9–14. His eschatology is essentially rooted in history. His basic purpose is first to challenge and then to reassure his contemporaries, and to this end he amasses a variety of available motifs.

12:3, which held out the prospect of the blessed nation becoming a blessing to all nations, is absent from his message and so does not reflect the whole counsel of God within the OT context. But what single piece of OT literature does or can be expected to do this? Let it not be forgotten that, in the NT, Israelite particularism is from one point of view replaced by a new particularism. The principle of *extra ecclesiam nulla salus* is true, rightly understood. The overall pattern of Joel's theology strikes many a chord for those conversant with NT teaching: turning to God from sin—a call to be obeyed "now"—sovereign grace, the covenant community and its security under God, judgment to come and future bliss. NT theology builds upon a framework erected long before by Joel and his co-religionists. Joel and the follower of Jesus believe together—although their expressions and emphases may vary—in God's coming intervention in a topsy-turvy world to settle its moral accounts, to honor right and banish wrong.

8. STRUCTURE AND ANALYSIS

The book of Joel obviously falls into two parts, but there is no unanimity about where the first part ends and the second begins. There are two possibilities, one dictated by content and the other by form. Most scholars make content the criterion and distinguish between 1:2–2:27, concerned with the contemporary plague of locusts, and 2:28–3:21, the eschatological promises of blessing for Judah and judgment for the nations. But it is equally possible to differentiate 1:2–2:17, all concerned with a lament, and 2:18–3:21, which deals with the divine oracle(s) in answer to the people's lament. Keil, S. R. Driver, Wolff, and Ahlström have opted for this second division on the basis of form, and it will be shown that the overall pattern of the book favors this possibility.

Does the book have a coherent structure at all? It is a literary tapestry covered with a host of repeated motifs. Indeed it is so crammed with echoed motifs that it seems impossible to reduce their crisscross patterning into a detailed structural order. A valiant attempt to take the correspondences seriously as a major key to structure has been made by J. Bourke.[38] The first part of the book consists for him of 1:2–2:27. Its central portion is 2:2b–9, which describes an army of locusts marching on Jerusalem. This center is surrounded by the motif of the Day of Yahweh (2:1b–2, 10f.). Four other motifs are associated with the Day in varying order: (1) penitence (1:13; 2:12–14), (2) a solemn assembly to invoke the name of Yahweh (1:14; 2:15f.), (3) a lament (1:16–20; 2:17), and (4) the trumpet sounded in Zion (2:1, 15). Thus the section 1:13–2:17 is the nucleus of the first part of the book. Before and after are placed the themes of agricultural curse (1:4–12) and blessing (2:21–26). 2:18–20, concerned with Yahweh's compassion for

38. *RB* 66 (1959), pp. 11–15.

Israel and his destruction of the locust army, is evidently inserted into this concentric structure.

The recurrence of the concluding formula (2:27) in 3:17 suggests that the second part of the book, 2:28–3:21, is structurally symmetrical with the first. In fact 2:30f. and 3:14–16a again sound the Day of Yahweh motif around a long section which includes the theme of the Gentile army marching against Jerusalem (3:9–12), the counterpart of the locust army in the first section. Israel's deliverance is a motif associated with the Day references (2:28; 3:16a). The central theme of the army is immediately surrounded by the judgment and destruction of the Gentile oppressors (3:2–8, 13). Corresponding to the outer theme of curse and blessing in the first part is the outpouring of the spirit (2:28f.) and the restoration of fertility (3:18–20), motifs that are associated also in Isa. 32:15; 44:3. Bourke's complex structure is a fascinating attempt to do justice to the repetition of motifs. It is unfortunate that the fundamental passage 2:18–20 has to be regarded as a flaw in the pattern. And where does the first reference to the Day of Yahweh (1:15) fit in this structure, if correspondences are the key to structure?

If it may be assumed that 1:2–2:17 is the first half of the book, it can be divided into two parallel sections, 1:2–20 and 2:1–17, as Kapelrud observed. The first chapter may be subdivided into vv. 2–12 and 13–20. Kutsch[39] and Wolff associate vv. 5–14 as a series of parallel strophes, each with the same form of a reasoned call to lamentation, but vv. 13f. are better taken with what follows. Rudolph rightly distinguishes between vv. 5–12 and 13f., and even Wolff notes that v. 14 does not correspond to the continuation in the earlier strophes. 1:2–12 may be divided into four strophes, comprising a general appeal and explanation by way of introduction (vv. 2–4), a reasoned call to drinkers (vv. 5–7), a similar call evidently addressed to Zion (vv. 8–10), and one to farmers (vv. 11f.). The first strophe has four lines and the other three have five. 1:13–20 has a more cultic flavor. It divides into three strophes, consisting of a call to the priests to arrange a national service of lamentation (vv. 13f.), a descriptive lament (vv. 15–18), and a prayer (vv. 19f.). These strophes are of six, seven, and six lines respectively.

In 2:1–17 the first subdivision is 2:1–11, marked out by mention of the Day of Yahweh at beginning and end, as Kutsch observed. Both Kutsch and Keller consider v. 6 the central pivot of the piece. Rather, the similar Hebrew terms meaning "before them" in vv. 3, 6, 10 are to be regarded as the openings of successive strophes. There are then four strophes, comprising vv. 1f. mentioning, like 1:2–4, the unique crisis;[40] vv. 3–5

39. *TZ* 18 (1962), pp. 81f.

40. For further links see the commentary. The purpose of this section is to survey the overall structure of the various portions of the book. The commentary will often supply further details concerning the composition of the smaller units.

dealing like 1:5–7 with the locusts' destructiveness; vv. 6–9 concerned with the city of Jerusalem like 1:8–10; while by way of climax the last strophe transcends its parallel, 1:11f., and reverts to the motif of the Day in order to round off the piece. These four strophes have five, six, seven, and five lines respectively.

2:12–17 like its counterpart 1:13–20 has an intensely cultic orientation. As might be expected, it falls into three strophes, a national call to repentance (vv. 12–14), a call to the priests to arrange a communal service of lament (vv. 15f.), and a suggested prayer of lament for the priests (v. 17). The strophes have in turn seven, five, and four lines.

The second half of the book is 2:18–3:21. It has two sections, 2:18–32 and 3:1–21.[41] Kapelrud correctly noted that 2:28–32 is the continuation of the divine oracle of 2:18–27. Both passages are concerned with the chosen nation, while ch. 3 turns to the theme of the other nations. Wolff observes that in 2:32 the phrase "as Yahweh has said" is reminiscent of the initial reference to Yahweh's utterance in 2:19. He rightly points out that 2:27 does not necessarily have the ring of a conclusion. He compares 3:17 and refers to the sequence of themes in Ezek. 39:25–29 as an illuminating counterpart to 2:18–32. Keller has claimed that 2:28–32 should be separated from what precedes because the renewed crisis of 2:30 conflicts with the promises of Israel's security in 2:26f. But in 2:28–32 the prophet is at pains to stress the security of God's people amid terrors and alarms destined for others.

The first section divides into two parts, 2:18–27 and 28–32. The former deals with material and immediate promises. There are three strophes, comprising Yahweh's oracle concerning new crops and the destruction of the locusts (vv. 18–20), the prophet's exhortation to praise (vv. 21–23), and a continuation of the oracle about crops and locusts (vv. 24–27). These three strophes consist of eight, six, and six lines respectively. Verse 24 is generally attached to the preceding song, but in content it goes better with v. 25. As the commentary demonstrates, it takes up a motif found in the first part of the divine oracle, like vv. 25–27. Prophetic perfects, a stylistic feature of vv. 21–23, do not occur in v. 24, whose verbs have the same form as those in vv. 19f., 25–27.

2:28–32, an obvious unit, is concerned with less immediate and more radical blessing for God's people. It falls into three strophes. The first is vv. 28f.: it begins and ends with references to the spirit. The second, vv. 30f., deals with the cosmic signs of the Day of Yahweh. The last is v. 32, a declaration of security in Zion. It begins with the people calling upon Yahweh and ends with Yahweh calling the people. Both Keller and Rudolph draw attention to these divisions, although Keller regards v. 32 as a prose

41. A break at the end of v. 32 is presumed by the chapter divisions in G and V, followed by the English versions. The Hebrew tradition starts a new chapter at 2:28 (3:1) as well as at 3:1 (4:1).

conclusion to the two strophes. In fact the three poetic strophes each have three lines. Yahweh speaks in the first two and the prophet in the third.

The final section of the book is 3:1–21, which contrasts the fortune of Israel with the fate of the other nations. It is composed of two parts, vv. 1–12 and 13–21. The first part, spoken by Yahweh throughout, is delineated by the mention at beginning and end of the gathering of "all the nations" to Jehoshaphat Valley. As in 2:18–27, there are three strophes. The first is clearly vv. 1–3, dealing with the judgment of the nations. It is developed in the third, vv. 9–12, which begins and ends with the alerting and advance of the nations' armies. In between is the second strophe, vv. 4–8, a self-contained oracle of neatly corresponding accusation and sentence. The A-B-A′ pattern of the section matches remarkably that of 2:18–27, where the prophet's song similarly interrupted the closely related first and third strophes. These strophes have six, ten, and eight lines respectively.

The last part is 3:13–21, a series of contrasts. It consists of three strophes, in all of which both Yahweh and the prophet speak. The first, vv. 13f., issues the battle summons to Yahweh's forces and visualizes his massed foes just before the fury of Yahweh's Day is finally unleashed. Its conclusion is marked by the repetition of "Verdict Valley." Verses 15–17 contrast Yahweh's wrath issuing from Zion and his people's security within its walls. The third strophe, vv. 18–21, introduced by an opening formula, contrasts Judah's and Jerusalem's prosperity with the desolation of their foreign neighbors. Both the second and third strophes end on the same note, namely, that of Yahweh's presence in Zion. The three strophes consist of five, five, and seven lines.

The second half of the book takes up and reverses the destruction and deprivation characteristic of the laments of the first half; the locusts give way to the Gentiles as Judah's bugbear. The thread of the Day of Yahweh runs through the four sections of the composition. It occurs in the second part of each section, except in the second section, where it dominates the earlier part (2:11). The first three strophes of the former part of the first section (1:2–10) have a certain parallelism with those of the first part of the second (2:1–9). The cultic terminology and motifs of the second part of the first section (1:13–20) are clearly echoed in that of the second section (2:12–17). The correspondence of the first half of the third section with that of the fourth (2:18–27; 3:1–12) consists of their common A-B-A′ pattern. The second parts of the third and fourth sections (2:28–32; 3:13–21) both deal with foreign doom and Israel's blessing in Zion, but in reversed proportions. The whole composition has been constructed as an intricate literary mosaic with remarkable skill and care.

Heading (1:1)

I. Judah, Locusts, and God (1:2–2:17)

- A. Summons to national mourning (1:2–20)
  - 1. A call to the nation (1:2–12)
  - 2. A call to the priests and prayer (1:13–20)

B. Divine judgment and human repentance (2:1–17)
  1. Yahweh's army of locusts (2:1–11)
  2. A call for national repentance (2:12–17)

II. Divine Oracles (2:18–3[4]:21)
  A. Material and spiritual promises (2:18–32[3:5])
    1. Immediate blessings (2:18–27)
    2. Supernatural blessings (2:28–32[3:1–5])
  B. The judgment of the nations (3[4]:1–21)
    1. Charges and summonses to judgment (3[4]:1–12)
    2. The nations' fate and Judah's fortune (3[4]:13–21).

9. SELECT BIBLIOGRAPHY

G. W. Ahlström, *Joel and the Temple Cult of Jerusalem.* SVT 21 (1971). (*JTCJ*)
W. Baumgartner, "Joel 1 und 2," BZAW 34 (1920), pp. 10–19.
J. A. Bewer, "The Book of Joel," ICC (1911).
J. Bourke, "Le jour de Yahvé dans Joël," *RB* 66 (1959), pp. 5–31, 191–212.
W. W. Cannon, "The Day of the Lord in Joel," *Church Quarterly Review* 103 (1926), pp. 32–63.
T. Chary, *Les prophètes et le culte à partir de l'exil.* Bibliothèque de Théologie 3:3 (1955). (*PC*)
K. A. Credner, *Der Prophet Joel übersetzt und erklärt* (1831).
M. Delcor, "Joël," *Les petits prophètes.* La Sainte Bible 8:1 (1961).
L. Dennefeld, "Les problèmes du livre de Joël," *RSR* 4 (1924), pp. 555–575; 5 (1925), pp. 35–57, 591–608; 6 (1926), pp. 26–49.
S. R. Driver, *The Books of Joel and Amos.* CBSC ([2]1915).
T. Frankfort, "Le *kî* de Joël 1:12," *VT* 10 (1960), pp. 445–48.
G. B. Gray, "The Parallel Passages in Joel and Their Bearing on the Question of Date," *Expositor* 8 (1893), pp. 208–225.
J. Halévy, "Recherches bibliques: le livre de Joël," *RS* 16 (1908), pp. 274–284, 395–418.
H. Holzinger, "Sprachgebrauch und Abfassungszeit des Buches Joel," *ZAW* 9 (1889), pp. 89–131.
D. R. Jones, *Isaiah 56–66 and Joel.* Torch Bible Commentaries (1964).
A. S. Kapelrud, *Joel Studies.* Uppsala Universitets Årsskrift (1948).
L. Köhler, "Die Bezeichnungen der Heuschrecke im AT," *ZDPV* 49 (1926), pp. 328–333.
E. Kutsch, "Heuschreckenplage und Tag Jahwes in Joel 1 und 2," *TZ* 18 (1962), pp. 81–94.
L. Mariés, "A propos de récentes études sur Joël," *RSR* 37 (1950), pp. 121–24.
H.-P. Müller, "Prophetie und Apokalyptik bei Joel," *Theologia Viatorum* 10 (1965/66), pp. 231–252.
J. M. Myers, "Some Considerations Bearing on the Date of Joel," *ZAW* 74 (1962), pp. 177–195.
E. Nestle, "Miscellen. I. Joel 1, 17," *ZAW* 20 (1900), pp. 164f.
M. Plath, "Joel 1:15–20," *ZAW* 47 (1929), pp. 159f.

O. Plöger, *Theocracy and Eschatology* (E.T. 1968).
B. Reicke, "Joel und seine Zeit," *Wort-Gebot-Glaube*. W. Eichrodt Festschrift. ATANT 59 (1970), pp. 133–141.
C. Roth, "The Teacher of Righteousness and the Prophecy of Joel," *VT* 13 (1963), pp. 91–95.
W. Rudolph, "Wann wirkte Joel?" BZAW 105 (1967), pp. 193–98.
Idem, "Ein Beitrag zum hebräischen Lexicon aus dem Joelbuch," *Hebräische Wortforschung*. W. Baumgartner Festschrift. SVT 16 (1967), pp. 244–250.
O. R. Sellers, "Stages of Locusts in Joel," *AJSL* 52 (1935), pp. 81–85.
M. Sprengling, "Joel 1, 17a," *JBL* 38 (1919), pp. 129–141.
F. R. Stephenson, "The Date of the Book of Joel," *VT* 19 (1969), pp. 224–29.
J. A. Thompson, "Joel's Locusts in the Light of Near Eastern Parallels," *JNES* 14 (1955), pp. 52–55.
Idem, "Joel," *IB,* vol. 6 (1956), pp. 727–760.
M. Treves, "The Date of Joel," *VT* 7 (1957), pp. 149–156.
H. W. Wolff, *Joel.* Biblischer Kommentar AT 14:5 (1963).

TRANSLATION, EXPOSITION, AND NOTES

HEADING (1:1)

The message of Yahweh received by Joel son of Pethuel.[1]

This brief label attached to the book is akin in style to those found at the beginning of Hosea, Micah, and Zephaniah, except that those three set the prophets in their historical contexts by citing the kings who reigned during their ministry. The absence from this heading of any indication of time may indicate that Joel's ministry was so comparatively recent as to be well known to the readers and so not requiring specification. The formula of prophetic revelation lays the initiative and onus upon the divine side of a confrontation between man and God. Many of the pieces in the book take the form of utterances spoken by the prophet, while less than half the material is represented as coming from the divine "I." Nevertheless, in this respect form is no guide to theology, affirms the heading. The messages transmitted by the prophet, whether formally in his own name or in his Master's, bear the stamp of the divine will. Quite obviously the heading reflects a conviction that Joel's words, which comprise the "word" or *message* of Yahweh, have a continuing relevance for the people of God.

The statement that the divine word "came to" or was *received by* Joel indicates that the prophet was no mechanical medium in the process of God's communication with the religious community. He had a responsible role to play, a role no one else could discharge in exactly the same way. God was to use Joel's special gifts, insights, and background, and ally himself with this unique personality in the incarnation of truth.

Joel is given his patronymic, which demonstrates that in his lifetime he was known and accepted in the urban society of Jerusalem. His name, which like Elijah means "Yahweh is God," is Pethuel's own testimony of faith in the God of ancient Israel and the expression of his wish that his son would wholeheartedly embrace his faith and be worthy of it. His wish was granted, as this prophecy gives ample evidence.

1. G S "Bethuel" is a case of assimilation to the name of Rebekah's father (Gen. 22:23; 24:15, 24, 47).

I. JUDAH, LOCUSTS, AND GOD (1:2–2:17)

A. SUMMONS TO NATIONAL MOURNING (1:2–20)

The little country of Judah has been overwhelmed by crisis. It is Joel's responsibility to relate the human catastrophe to the purpose of God. As part of this task he interprets the crisis as constituting a dire need for divine help. He points toward the temple and so toward God. Christian countries have in the past held national days of prayer, when citizens have flocked to the churches and in earnest supplication besought God's saving mercy. So in Israel there was a tradition of holding special services of national lament in response to a variety of misfortunes. Judg. 20:26 describes such a service prompted by military defeat, a day of fasting, weeping, and sacrificing at the sanctuary of Bethel.[2] A similar service is alluded to many centuries later in Jer. 14, this time by way of reaction to a severe drought; rites of fasting, sacrificing, and prayers of lament were performed by the people gathered at Jerusalem.[3] It is Joel's conviction that the time is ripe for the community to meet in Jerusalem to hold such a service of lamentation in the temple. He reminds the people of the serious nature of the calamity that has come upon the country and makes it his basis for an appeal for a national time of lamentation.

1. A Call to the Nation (1:2–12)

Hear this, you elders;
listen, all the country's population. 3+3
Has such a thing ever happened in your lifetime
or in the lifetime of your forefathers? 3+3
3 *Tell your children all about it,*
let your children tell their children,
and their children[4] *the next generation.* 3+2+3
4 *The shearer's leavings the swarmer locust has eaten,*
the swarmer's leavings the hopper has eaten,
and the hopper's leavings the destroyer has eaten. 4+4+4

5 *Wake up, you drunkards, and weep;*
wail, all you wine drinkers,
for the sweet wine snatched from your mouths: 3+3+3
6 *because a horde has invaded*[5] *my country,*
massive and past counting. 3+3
Their teeth are lions' teeth,
they have lions'[6] *fangs.* 3+2
7 *They have wrought havoc among my vines*
and smashed my fig trees to splinters. 3+2

2. Cf. Josh. 7:6; 1 Sam. 7:6; 1 K. 8:33f.
3. Verses 2, 7–9, 12; cf. Jer. 36:6, 9.
4. The proposal to delete Heb. *liḇ^{e}nêhem ûḇ^{e}nêhem* (Robinson, following Nowack) is motivated solely by a craving for metrical uniformity.
5. Heb. *'ālâ 'al,* "go up against," is a military term: cf. Judg. 6:3; 1 K. 14:25.
6. Two words are used as poetic synonyms: cf. Mic. 5:8(7).

They have denuded them, littering the ground:[7]
their branches have turned white. 3+2

8 *Lament like a girl in funereal sackcloth*
mourning her young fiancé. 3+2
9 *Cereal offering and libation have disappeared*
from Yahweh's temple. 3+2
The priests, Yahweh's ministers,
are grieving aloud.[8] 2+2
10 *The countryside is ruined,*
the ground is grief-stricken 2+2
because the grain is ruined,
the wine is in a sorry state[9]
and the oil has feebly failed. 2+2+2

11 *Express your sorrow,*[10] *farmers,*
wail,[10] *vinedressers,* 2+2
for the wheat and barley,
because the harvest in the field is lost. 3+3
12 *The vines are in a sorry state,*
the fig trees have feebly failed. 2+2
Pomegranate tree, palm and apricot tree,
all the trees in the countryside have withered. 3+3
Joy has turned in sorrow
away from men's company. 2+2

Joel's appeal to the community falls into four stanzas. It is first issued in general terms, in vv. 2–4. Then the prophet addresses himself to three particular groups within the community, to convince each of its particular deprivation, in vv. 5–7, 8–10, 11–12. These special appeals are marked by a regular pattern of length and structure. Each of these three strophes consists of five lines of varied meter. They each comprise a sumnions to lament,

7. Lit. "It has completely stripped it (each tree) and thrown down." Wellhausen, followed by Robinson, suggested a slight textual change to *ḥ^{a}shāp̱āh ḥāshōp̱ w^{e}hashlēḵ,* "It has stripped it, throwing it down as it stripped," which is better Hebrew; the lack of suffix on the second main verb in MT may support the proposal. G. R. Driver, *JTS* 41 (1940), p. 171, replaced Wellhausen's repointing of the final word with *w^{e}hashkēl,* "causing it to lose its fruit," observing the slight awkwardness, in both MT and Wellhausen's proposal, of understanding a change of subject from tree to fragments of bark, etc. Rudolph in turn substitutes *w^{e}hashlēaḥ,* taking the verb in the Aramaic sense of "peel."
8. Baumgartner (BZAW 34[1920], p. 11), Delcor, and NEB follow G, which for MT *'āḇ^{e}lû* implies an imperative *'iḇ^{e}lû* with *priests* as vocative. The strophical pattern whereby one group is addressed per stanza, and the call to the priests in v. 13, suggest otherwise.
9. Heb. *hôḇîsh* occurs of wine, vines, and grain in vv. 10, 12, 17, of farmers in v. 11, and of joy in v. 12. It can be related either to *bûsh,* "be humiliated, express humiliation," or to *yāḇash,* "wither." It is conceivable that homonyms are used as a play on words, but it is more probable that in the first three cases mentioned a human experience of humiliation is poetically ascribed to things, since for "wither" v. 12 uses *yāḇēshû* (cf. v. 20).
10. The Heb. can be construed as imperatives or perfects. Most commentators opt for the former with T and Hebrew tradition. Bewer, Kapelrud, and Keller take as perfects with S V (G construes each verb differently).

which is backed by an explanation describing aspects of the disaster. In two cases out of the three there occurs a vocative, specifying the identity of those who are summoned. The three characteristics add up to a standard form amply represented in the prophetic literature. The prophets frequently take up what appears to be a fixed form of a call to national lament issued in times of calamity.[11] The public proclamation would have gone out to different groups in turn to ensure that all sectors of the community were covered. This is doubtless why the summons falls into a strophic pattern.[12] Like his fellow prophets, Joel is taking over the stereotyped call convening a service of lament, which generally emanated from the authorities.[13] He evidently speaks in God's name, feeling upon his own soul the divinely laid burden of pointing the people back to the paths of harmony and blessing. The attention of each group in turn is drawn to the particular seriousness of the situation for them, to impel them to humble themselves before their God.[14]

2–4 The introductory stanza, with its vocatives and its basic explanation concerning the nature of the crisis, has affinity with the next three, but it begins in typically prophetic style with imperative verbs of hearing.[15] Joel has a message that is vital for all the community. So he first addresses the representative group of civil leaders and then clarifies the all-inclusive character of his message.[16] The *elders* were ever a force in Israelite government, whether in the context of the local, tribal, or national community. A clue to their importance in the postexilic period is found in Ezra 10:8, where they appear as a legislative council or parliament alongside "the officials." What concerns the elders is naturally the interests of the rest of the community for whom they bear responsibility. In the overall context Judah is *the country* referred to here and also in v. 14 and 2:1. This is indicated by the references to the Jerusalem temple in vv. 9, 13; 2:15, etc. and also by the terms of 3:1, 18, 20. Joel's message is of national import and the whole Judean community is bidden to hang on his words.

After the imperatives he stimulates his audience further by posing rhetorical questions, a stylistic device also used by Isaiah after similar

11. Wolff, building upon the preliminary work of Baumgartner, *loc. cit.*, has reconstructed the *Gattung* from 14 passages (2 Sam. 3:31; Isa. 14:31; 23:1–14; 32:11–14; Jer. 4:8; 6:26; 7:29; 22:20; 25:34; 49:3; Ezek. 21:17; Joel 1:5–14; Zeph. 1:11; Zech. 11:2). A number of psalms which fall into the category of national laments reproduce the explanatory element in a description of calamity, but characteristically it tends to be couched in the form of a prayer to the community; cf. Ps. 74:3–9; 79:1–4.

12. So also Isa. 23:1–14; cf. 14:31; Jer. 49:3.

13. In 1 K. 21:9 Queen Jezebel issues the command, in 2 Chr. 20:3 King Jehoshaphat, in Ezra 8:21 Ezra.

14. "Throughout his poem the prophet insists that the victims of catastrophe have lost what constitutes the very essence of their existence" (Keller).

15. Cf. Isa. 1:10; 28:23; Hos. 5:1; Mic. 1:2; 3:1, 9.

16. Cf. Isa. 1:10. Commentators are divided as to whether Heb. *zᵉqēnîm* signifies *elders* or "old men." Those who opt for the latter explain it as a reference to their experience and memory in view of the question of v. 2b (cf. 2:16; Rudolph compares Deut. 32:7). But v. 14, if the text is substantially correct, points the other way, which accords with a general appeal.

invitations to listen.[17] The crisis in which the state is engulfed is unprecedented. He challenges his hearers to cull a parallel from personal experience or from the traditions of their national history. Indeed, momentous history is being written in their own times, as the prophet implies in his call to pass on an account of what has happened to their *children* for posterity to remember. "Never before and never again" is the dramatic style by which the prophet describes the exceptional nature of the tragic experience the people have been living through. His purpose is to drive them to perceive some meaning in this nadir of unique disaster and to relate it and themselves to the providential purposes of God. Their encounter with the extraordinary demands a special religious response to the divine Maker of history. Joel's words in v. 3 seem to echo the transmission of the record of God's great dealings with his people.[18] He is dropping his first hint that God has not been absent from this dynamic event.

But first Joel spells out the nature and intensity of the catastrophe, with a heavy meter and a repetitive, accumulative structure reflecting its gravity. He relieves the suspense he has created by at last explaining *this,* to which he has twice referred. The crisis concerns a plague of locusts. Interminable swarms had ravaged the countryside and systematically robbed it of all vegetable life until nothing remained to eat. Famine and death stared in the face a society not privileged to know about the can opener, let alone international relief schemes. Joel dramatically depicts how swarm after swarm diminished the potential harvest to nil, and so implicitly he reproduces the growth of despair. The prophet uses for the locusts four different terms out of a total OT vocabulary of nine. The variation has caused controversy. Is the order in which the terms are given important, relating to carefully observed stages of development? Or is Joel simply piling up various terms for locusts, using them as rhetorical synonyms?[19] The

17. Isa. 1:10f.; 28:23–25.

18. Ps. 22:30(31); 48:13(14); 78:4, 6.

19. The Semitic root of the first term, *gāzām,* signifies "cut off," and it doubtless refers to the destructive activity of the migratory locust, *Schistocerca gregaria;* cf. the context of the only other use of the noun in Amos 4:9. The same is probably true of the fourth term *ḥāsîl*; the cognate verb, actually used of locusts in Deut. 28:38, means "finish off, consume." The second term *'arbeh* is the word for locust in general use. It could be cognate with Akk. *arabu,* "devastate," but it is more probably to be related to the Heb. root *rāḇâ,* "be many," referring to the well-known gregarious habit of the locust. The third word *yeleq* used to be related to *lqq,* "lick, lap," but it is now generally taken as a reference to the first larval form of the young locust as a wingless, jumping insect: P. Haupt, *JBL* 26 (1907), p. 34, compared with it Akk. *ilqitu* and Arab. *walaqa,* which refer to the leaping gait of a camel (cf. "grasshopper"). O. R. Sellers, *AJSL* 52 (1935), pp. 81–85, developed a theory put forward earlier by K. A. Credner. He changed the order, putting the second term first, in accord with 2:25, and taking it to mean the mature locust. *Yeleq* he interpreted as above. Comparing Arab. *saḥala,* "peel," he identified *ḥāsîl* with the pupal stage which the locust reaches after several moults, when its partially developed wings are enclosed in a membrane. *Gāzām* he took to be the insect after its last moult, ready to fly as soon as its wings have dried. J. A. Thompson, *JNES* 14 (1955), pp. 52–55, also espouses the theory of stages, but keeps the present order, following the view of I. Aharoni, *Haarbeh* (1919), p. 21, that here is given the historical

majority of commentators opt for the latter explanation,[20] probably rightly in view of the paucity of etymological or literary backing for the relation of the first and fourth terms to stages of growth.

A sixteenth-century observer has mirrored Joel's description:

> *They began to arrive there one day about the hour of terce* [*nine*], *and till night they did not cease. . . . Next day at the hour of prime* [*six*] *they began to depart, and at midday there was not one there; and not a leaf remained upon a tree. At that moment others began to arrive, and they remained like the others till the next day at the same hour; and these did not leave any corn with a husk nor a green blade. In this way they did for five days one after the other.*[21]

5–7 After this general appeal and basic description of total destruction Joel is ready to deliver his first special summons for a religious response to the catastrophe. He selects a group of people who ordinarily cared little about whatever went on around them—alcoholics, who had contracted out of their environment and taken refuge in drink. With grim irony Joel observes that they will be particularly hard hit by the locust plague: once the wineskins have been emptied there will be no further supplies. A sobering thought indeed! He aims to shock them out of their escapist stupor and get them to relate to God at the point of their personal and direct need. In each of these group appeals the prophet's endeavor is to stimulate their particular sense of need and to point them to God. He calls to a service of ardent prayer, which in a culture much more demonstrative than that in the Western world would include loud sobs and wails. If, as the Hebrew world view insisted, it is God who "gives wine to gladden man's heart" (Ps. 104:15), it is peculiarly appropriate that the withholding of wine supplies should lead to sorrow on a religious plane. *Sweet wine* was evidently a delicacy among wine connoisseurs. Undoubtedly intoxicating in view of its present context and its use in Isa. 49:26, this type of wine is literally "pressed, trodden down," and so the first product of the winepress. The wine merchants of the classical world had ways of preserving the sweetness of new wine, and doubtless their Judean counterparts had the

---

order in which successive stages attacked Judah in Joel's day, and in 2:25 the more logical order beginning with the adult. So the first stage that the Judeans observed was the *gāzām*, which constitutes the two pupal forms according to Thompson, growing into the adult *'arbeh* whose eggs hatched out into the *yeleq* (the first larval form), which in turn developed into the *ḥāsîl* (the second and third larval forms). He notes that modern entomologists differentiate six stages, as does Arabic terminology, and suggests that some of the twenty names for locusts found in the Talmud include terms for various phases. L. Köhler, *ZDPV* 49 (1926), pp. 328–333, whom Keller is inclined to follow, refuses to see comprehensive references to locusts. He follows G in identifying *gāzām* with the caterpillar and takes *ḥāsîl* to be the cockroach, comparing S.

20. E.g., Keil: "One swarm of locusts after another has invaded the land. . . . The use of several different words and the division of the locusts into four successive swarms . . . belong to the rhetorical drapery and individualizing of the thought."

21. F. Alvares, cited by Pusey.

same facility.[22] Now hopes of acquiring further supplies at the next vintage were frustrated; they had, in fact, been virtually dashed from their lips.

Enemy invasion was to blame, but from no human adversary.[23] Advancing in their myriads, the locusts had done as much damage as any army could. Joel is to develop the military metaphor in 2:4–11.[24] Here he comments on their colossal numerical strength and so their enormous capacity for inflicting damage. The immense size of locust swarms is a frequent OT simile for countlessness,[25] but here it is all too real. Observers have often commented on this terrifying phenomenon, of "the myriads of insects that blot out the sun above and cover the earth beneath and fill the air whichever way one looked."[26] Judah had been overwhelmed by such a foe. But God himself is involved in the suffering of his people, for the land is his by right and they occupy it only as his tenants.[27] The prophet speaks in God's name, reassuring his hearers of his vested interest in their predicament.[28] As elsewhere in the prophets, *my country* is a phrase that carries overtones of affront and resentment.[29] It conveys a hint to the attentive ear that overtures from his people might not be unavailing, and that his passionate concern for what belongs to him might be aroused on their behalf. And so indeed it proved, as 2:18 records. Right at the beginning of his appeal through Joel, God sows the seed of hope to encourage the people that their prayers will not be in vain.

This army had no orthodox armaments: it constituted at once an enemy *horde* and savage beasts of prey, embodying the worst of both kinds of attackers. Their powerful saw-edged *teeth* were perfect weapons for destroying plants and even trees when more tender fare had been consumed. It is to this latter destruction that the prophet turns. Appealing still to those addicted to wine, he speaks of the severe damage done to the vines. Fig trees,

22. Heb. *'āsîs* is rendered by G "drunkenness" here, *glykasmos,* "sweet wine," at 3(4):18 and Amos 9:13, and "new wine" in Isa. 49:26. It invites comparison with the *gleukos* with which the apostles were accused of being drunk at Pentecost (Acts 2:13, 15), although the vintage was then some months off.

23. The explanation offered for the summons to lamentation is twofold: loss of wine which in turn is due to the locusts. The variation in form of the characteristic *kî* clause by prefixing the *'al* (for) phrase here and in v. 11 has a parallel in Isa. 32:12–14.

24. J. Bourke, *RB* 66 (1959), p. 14, observes that in the OT, locust plagues and foreign invasion featured together in lists of national misfortunes (e.g., Deut. 28:25, 38; I K. 8:37; Amos 4:9f.); thus it was a step more obvious to Joel than to us to express one misfortune in terms of the other and to discern a basic correspondence between the two. As to the metaphorical use of Heb. *gôy,* "nation," cf. *'am,* "people," of ants in Prov. 30:25 and of locusts in Joel 2:2.

25. Judg. 6:5; 7:12; Jer. 46:23; 51:14.

26. J. Bryce, cited by G. A. Smith.

27. Cf. the comment on Mic. 2:2.

28. It is possible that the whole of the section vv. 2–12 is a *Jahwerede,* in which case the phrases in v. 9 are stereotyped expressions (cf. the note on Mic. 3:7). However, the next section, vv. 13–20, is definitely a *Prophetenrede* in light of vv. 13, 16, 19.

29. Cf. Jer. 2:7; Ezek. 36:5; 38:16. Cf. Ehrlich.

which often grew in vineyards,[30] had also suffered. Mention of vines and fig trees constitutes a grim reversal of the usual tenor of their association, for often in the OT they are symbols of peace and prosperity. But now the leaves of the latter, and even bark and twigs, had been torn off by the voracious insects as *leavings* for the next batch. All that remained of shady, fruit-laden bowers were skeletonized wrecks of trees with their barkless branches gleaming white. What looked "like a birch tree forest in winter"[31] rose from ground strewn with a rough carpet of debris. Once again Joel is God's voice in speaking of *my vines* and *my fig trees*: they are gifts which God has given to his people.[32] Here is another hint that holds out hope amid the desolation, if only appeal is made to the Lord of the trees.

8–10 The second group addressed by the prophet is left unspecified, except that the imperative verbs are feminine singular. This suggests that Jerusalem is in mind, especially as the term "maiden, virgin" in the simile seems to evoke the standard personified appellation of the capital, "virgin daughter Zion."[33] The cultic context suits a reference to Zion. It is noteworthy that in ch. 2, which has many parallels with ch. 1, the counterpart to 1:8–10 is 2:6–9, where the invasion of a city is described. Moreover, the reference to "sons of Zion" in a song of encouragement at 2:23 implies that Zion has been addressed earlier in the course of Joel's summons to lament. The section again falls into the pattern of a short appeal and an extended explanation to lend psychological support to his appeal.

Joel claims that a tragedy has befallen the city which must evoke a demonstration of bitter grief. The tragedy is comparable with a personal bereavement. In the ancient Near East, marriage took place in two stages, the first of which was betrothal, an act more binding than the modern engagement. Although the consummation of marriage was delayed till after the second stage, so close a bond did betrothal create that the betrothed man could be called "husband," as more literally here,[34] and the betrothed woman could be called "wife."[35] One can imagine the anticipation of a betrothed girl as she looked forward to the wedding and life shared with the man who was already her own—and the bitter frustration of his being snatched from her waiting arms by death. The poet depicts a scene of acute pathos. Instead of donning the customary embroidered, gaily colored wedding robes and enjoying the usual merrymaking, she puts on her

30. Cf. 1 K. 4:25 (5:5); Mic. 4:4; Luke 13:6.
31. From an account cited by S. R. Driver.
32. Cf. Hos. 2:8f. (10f.).
33. Ewald; cf. 2 K. 19:21; Lam. 2:13. For a similar nonspecified address to Zion cf. Mic. 1:16. A. Jepsen, *ZAW* 56 (1938), p. 89, and Rudolph insert *tsiyyôn*. Commentators who retain MT generally interpret as a call to the land or the people: cf. T's addition of "Israel." Others change or reinterpret the verb *'ᵉlî*. Duhm read a plural *'ᵉlû* and Robinson and Wolff *hêlîlû*. Bewer and Baumgartner read *'ēḇel*, "mourning"; Keller takes *'ᵉlî* as a noun.
34. Heb. *ba'al*; cf. Matt. 1:19.
35. Gen. 29:21; Deut. 22:24; Matt. 1:20. However, G. J. Wenham, *VT* 22 (1972), p. 345, urges that the reference is to a girl widowed shortly after marriage.

widow's weeds of *sackcloth* and wails a dirge. Amos had drawn a similar analogy of wearing sackcloth in mourning for an only son to illustrate intense grief.[36]

To such deep mourning does Joel summon the citizens of Jerusalem. Their world, orbiting as it did around the temple, the cultic center of Judah, had been shattered. Normal temple services had been suspended. Although various rites of sacrifice would be affected, principal reference is probably being made to the traditional daily ritual in which every morning and evening the sacrifice of a lamb as a burnt offering was accompanied by an *offering* of meal moistened with oil and by a *libation* of wine.[37] Shortage of supplies of important ingredients made these divinely ordained services impossible. The clock of religious routine, which it was the duty of each generation of Israelites to keep ticking, had to be allowed to run down and stop. Members of other cultures in which ritual traditions do not play a compulsive part can hardly understand the overtones of emotional horror with which the simple statement is invested for Joel and especially for the inhabitants of Jerusalem, across whose lives fell the shadow of the adjacent temple.[38] For Joel shock is not enough: he calls for a service of a different kind, of ritual lamentation by which his hearers may bring their problem to God. This was already being done on a small scale. The *priests,* prevented from fulfilling the normal rites, were engaging in cultic lamentation.[39] Their reaction to the religious significance of the catastrophe set an example which the laity of Jerusalem ought to follow.

The clergy were in tune with nature, which had donned its own pall of mourning. As the result of the locust plague *the countryside* wore a woe-begone look as if in its desolation it too was pleading with God to intervene and restore its productiveness.[40] Where the priests of Jerusalem and the personified country outside the capital have led the way, it is clear that the lay citizens of Zion should follow. Priests and fields alike were mourning the loss of *oil, wine,* and *grain.* The priests were particularly concerned because of the disastrous effect on the cultic routine, in which all three products played a vital role. They were the principal crops of

36. Amos 8:10; cf. Jer. 6:26; Zech. 12:10. In light of these parallels, attempts to see in Joel's analogy a reference to the fertility cult (Kapelrud, endorsing a suggestion made by Hvidberg; Ahlström, *JTCJ,* pp. 48–51) are unnecessary.

37. Exod. 29:38–40; Num. 28:3–8. The combination of cereal offering and libation featured in other sacrificial rituals according to Lev. 23:18; Num. 6:15, 17; 15:24; 29 *passim*; cf. Ezek. 45:17. But these were occasional rituals; it was the daily offerings that would be chiefly affected. The *tāmîḏ* or daily offering is not to be regarded as a solely postexilic phenomenon; cf. 2 K. 16:15; Ezek. 46:14f. (Ahlström, *JTCJ,* pp. 15–17; cf. R. J. Thompson, *Penitence and Sacrifice in Early Israel Outside the Levitical Law* [1963], pp. 129f.).

38. Cf. Josephus, *Jewish War* vi.2.1, where the Jews are described as "terribly despondent" at the suspension of daily sacrifices in A.D. 70.

39. *Yahweh's ministers, mᵉshārᵉṯê yhwh,* especially used appositionally as here, is a phrase characteristic of postexilic writings (cf. Chary, *PC,* pp. 197f.). However, Kapelrud and Rudolph find significant the use of the phrase in the singular at 1 Sam. 2:11, 18; 3:1.

40. Bewer aptly contrasts the jubilant singing of the fertile fields in Ps. 65:13(14).

Palestinian farmers and are celebrated in the OT as generous gifts of God.[41] Joel employs a traditional formula in referring to these products,[42] but he puts it to sinister use. The fertility hailed in OT times as a pledge of the harmony between Israel and its God has disappeared. With his terminology of feebleness and humiliation the prophet almost personifies what are normally tokens of Yahweh's blessing. It is as if by their very absence they were engaging in some mute mourning rites of their own. He intends to perturb his hearers and to suggest that they in turn resort to the temple nearby and get this sad reversal resolved.

George Adam Smith finely comments on "the rapid series of short, heavy phrases, falling like blows" in vv. 9b–10. "Joel loads his clauses with the most leaden letters he can find, and drops them in quick succession, repeating the same heavy word . . . , as if he would stir the senseless people into some sense of the bare, brutal weight of the calamity which has befallen them"; and, one might add, provoke a religious response.

11, 12 If the townsfolk should be reflecting the grief of clergy and countryside, how much more should the sector of the community whose livelihood depended on harvests of grain and fruit? Joel passes naturally to the third of his selective appeals. He challenges workers in agriculture and viticulture, backing up his call with reasons applicable to each in turn. He takes up the verb just used of the wine crop and applies it to the countryfolk, calling on them to take a cue from their environment and match its mood with a demonstration of their own humiliation in wailing cries. Again he has a religious connotation in mind, and again he supports his appeal with compelling evidence. He reminds first the *farmers* of the failure of their *wheat* and *barley* crops. These were the most important of the Palestinian cereals. Wheat, requiring richer soil and making better bread, was the more valued of the two, while barley was the staple diet of the poorer people. But now there were no cereals to sell, or seed to sow next season, and the economic consequences for the farmer were disastrous.

Nor were the prospects of the viticulturalist any brighter, for his *vines* looked very *sorry* for themselves. Indeed, the other fruit trees had fared no better. No pomegranates nor dates, which were produced especially in the Jordan valley,[43] would be sent to market, nor apricots.[44] Without exception *the trees* were shrivelled and barren. One might regard the calamity as solely the effect of the plague of locusts, but vv. 18–20 mention a drought, with

41. Deut. 7:13, etc.; Hos. 2:8(10); cf. Ps. 104:15f.

42. Heb. *dāḡān* is the general term for cereal from which bread is made; *tîrôsh* is probably the archaic Semitic word for wine, which the foreign loanword *yayin* generally replaced; *yitshār* is a descriptive term for *shemen,* "oil," as shining (*ṣhr*) (Köhler, *ZAW* 46 (1928), pp. 218–220; J. P. Brown, *VT* 19 (1969), pp. 147f., 168f.).

43. Deut. 34:3; Judg. 1:16.

44. Heb. *tappûaḥ* has been variously identified as apple, apricot, citron, or quince. H. N. and A. L. Moldenke, *Plants of the Bible* (1952), pp. 184–88, call it "one of the most perplexing problems of biblical botany." After reviewing the requirements of the OT references and the range of suggested identifications they conclude that the apricot, *Prunus armeniaca,* is the only one that seems to meet all the requirements.

which a locust attack not infrequently coincides.[45] The trees stood gaunt, lacking moisture at their roots to replenish the damage sustained from the locusts.

Joel gives a final compelling reason why the countryfolk should engage in rites of lamentation.[46] Good crops were usually celebrated with happy harvest festivals which were bywords for joy. The psalmist praises God that:

You have put more gladness in my heart
than people have when their corn and wine have yielded well.
(Ps. 4:7[8])

The vintage especially was an occasion for festivity,[47] but, as Moab was once threatened,

Joy and gladness are taken away from the fertile field.
In the vineyard there is no singing nor festive shout.
In the presses no one treads out wine. (Isa. 16:10)

So Judah enjoyed no prospect of harvest merrymaking. *Joy* had been overwhelmed by *sorrow* in *men's* hearts. "Joy hides herself in shame" (Bewer). But now that the harvest festival was cancelled, was there not place for a festival of a different kind? Amos had spoken of the farmers being called to mourning and of wailing in every vineyard (5:16f.) as part of a general response of the community to disaster. Was not the time ripe for such lamentation before God?

The prophet has gradually been building up a picture of ghastly desolation. Between his appeals have been interspersed grim cameos of the contemporary scene depicted with heavy brushstrokes. He has spoken of what his audience already knew and probably were loath to be reminded, but he has so analyzed the disaster as to present a series of arguments to bring them to their knees.

2. *A Call to the Priests and Prayer (1:13–20)*

Tie on sackcloth,[48] *priests, and lament;*
wail, ministers of the altar. 3+3
Go in and spend the night in your sackcloth,
ministers of my God, 3+2
because offering and libation
are denied the temple of your God. 3+2
14 *Order a sacred fast,*
proclaim a special service. 2+2

45. Thompson refers to B. P. Uvarov, *Locusts and Grasshoppers* (1928), p. 146.

46. The last sentence of the piece begins with Heb. *kî,* which Bewer, Thompson, Wolff, and Rudolph take as asseverative "yea." T. Frankfort, *VT* 10 (1960), pp. 445–48, observing the frequency of *kî* in a causal sense in ch. 1, has explained the link with the preceding theme of aridity in terms of human neglect: men are so demoralized that they have failed to irrigate the fruit trees. More probably Joel is giving the last of a series of reasons why the peasantry should engage in lament (Wade). This may also be the role of *kî* in v. 10.

47. Cf. Judg. 9:27; Isa. 9:3.

48. Heb. *ḥgr* is used absolutely only here and in Isa. 32:11. *Sackcloth* may easily be understood from v. 8.

Assemble the elders,
all the country's population 2+2
to the temple of Yahweh your God,
and cry to Yahweh. 3+2

15 *Alas, it is the Day,* 2
Yahweh's Day will soon be here,
it is coming with mighty ruin from the Almighty. 3+3
16 *Before our very eyes*
food has disappeared, has it not? 3+2
So have joy and gladness
from the temple of our God. 2+2
17 *Shrivelled seeds*
lie under their shovels. 2+2
Granaries are ruined,
barns[49] *dilapidated,*
because the grain is in a sorry state. 2+2+2
18 *What groans the animals raise!*[50]
Herds of cattle wander in distress 3+3
because they have no pasture;
and flocks of sheep waste away.[51] 3+3

19 *To you, Yahweh, I call* 3
because fire has consumed
the prairie pastures, 2+2
flames have burned
all the trees in the countryside. 2+2
20 *Even*[52] *the wild beasts*
cry[53] *to you* 2+2

49. Heb. *mammᵉgūrōṯ* is an anomalous form; *mᵉgūrōṯ* is expected from the root *gûr* (cf. *mᵉgûrâ,* Hag. 2:19). The initial *mem* has been explained as a partitive *min* (i.e., *mimm-*), "some of," by Ehrlich and Rudolph (cf. Sprengling, *JBL* 38 [1919], p. 138), following Aquila. Bewer, Delcor, and *BHS* (*prb*) disregard it as due to dittography. Most interestingly T. H. Gaster, *JQR* 37 (1946/47), p. 65, n. 32, and H. D. Hummel, *JBL* 76 (1957), p. 95, explain in terms of enclitic *mem* and false word division: *neherᵉsû-m mᵉgūrōṯ.*
50. For Heb. *mah-ne'enᵉḥâ ḇᵉhēmâ,* G implies *mah-nnannīḥâ bāhēmâ* (or *bāhem*), "What shall we put in them?" which Wellhausen, Sellin, Bewer, and Robinson prefer. But as G. R. Driver (*JTS* 39 [1938], p. 400) observed, it destroys the balance of thought in the line, where two parallel statements are expected as in v. 17b.
51. Heb. *ne'shāmû* is here evidently not related to *'šm,* "be guilty." Rendered "perish" by G S V T (cf. KJV, NEB), it is a variant form of *šmm.* G. R. Driver, *Occident and Orient* (1936), pp. 75f., compares another byform *yšm* and cites Hos. 13:6 (14:1); Ps. 34:21f. (22f.); similarly M. Dahood, *Pss 1,* pp. 35f., and *BHS.*
52. Against Dahood's proposal to equate Heb. *gam* with Ugar. *gm,* "aloud" (*Pss 2,* p. 14), see C. J. Labuschagne, "The Emphasizing Particle *Gam* and Its Connotations," *Studia biblica et semitica Th. C. Vriezen dedicata* (1966), pp. 193–203.
53. Heb. *ta'ᵃrōg* has been related to Ethiop. *'arga,* Arab. *'araja,* "ascend." But S "call" is supported by rabbinic tradition and was followed by Luther, Calvin, KJV, RSV; it is suggested by the parallelism with v. 19a. It may well correspond to the onomatopoeic *'ajja,* "cry aloud," in Arabic (Ehrlich, *Die Psalmen* [1905], p. 95; Bewer; Dahood, *Pss 1,* pp. 255f.).

because river beds
are dry of water 2+2
and fire has consumed
the prairie pastures. 2+2

In this next section Joel intensifies his appeal for a service of lamentation. He addresses the priests (vv. 13, 14) and then goes on to give a lead to the community by engaging first in a descriptive lament, which begins and ends with an exclamatory cry (vv. 15–18), and then in prayer to Yahweh (vv. 19, 20). The three parts are marked by a strongly religious emphasis: mention of Yahweh and his concerns are intensified to a final point of direct supplication. Links with the first section are provided by the continuation of the selective appeals in the first part and by renewed description of the catastrophe in the second.[54] The second and third parts both begin with a short, striking line.[55]

13, 14 In the light of v. 9 the prophet's appeal to the *priests* is to be considered as an encouragement to continue in the rites of lament in which they are already engaged.[56] But he urges an amplification of their present lamentation in two ways: first that it should be intensified, and then that it should be extended to form the prelude of a public service of humiliation and mourning. The coarse *sackcloth* mentioned in v. 8 as funeral garb had another use as clothing suitable for ritual lamentation.[57] It took the form of a strip tied around the thighs. Fresh allusion to wearing sackcloth is made in the second line, which probably represents Joel's suggestions for intensifying the cultic rites, after his endorsement in the first line of their present measures. Only in instances of exceptional distress was sackcloth kept on day and *night*. Such a custom is mentioned as part of Ahab's response to the bloodcurdling threats of the prophet Elijah.[58] The priests are bidden to report to the sanctuary[59] and engage in a night of prayer and supplication. So

54. Kapelrud rightly divides the chapter into vv. 2–12 and 13–20. Rudolph recognizes vv. 2–12 as a unit, noting that *men,* v. 12, summarizes the various groups specified in earlier verses. *Contra* Wolff and Keller, vv. 13f. are not to be taken with the previous section despite their formal similarity. Rather the form of the verses has the effect of bridging the sections. This part is differentiated from what has gone before in consisting of six lines instead of five and in including more exhortation. The parallelism of chs. 1 and 2, to be demonstrated later, also suggests a break after v. 12. Cf. also n. 28 above.

55. Cf. *BHS*.

56. Ahlström, *JTCJ,* pp. 52f., speculates that the priests' activities in vv. 9 and 13f. should be differentiated by interpreting the former as "a non-Yahwistic ritual." "Instead of continuing their mourning rites they are to begin a fast and lament and cry to Yahweh." But if *Yahweh's ministers* were thus engaged in v. 9, it would surely have been made clearer. Verse 9b is not concerned with "cultic wrongdoing" but serves as an inducement to the people of Jerusalem to share the reaction of the temple staff to the cessation of ritual offerings.

57. Cf. 2 K. 19:1, 2; Lam. 2:10.

58. 1 K. 21:27; cf. 1 Sam. 12:16.

59. *Go in* may refer to a ritual procession, but it more naturally implies undertaking temple duties, as in Ex. 28:29, etc.; cf. Luke 1:9.

serious was the situation that nothing less was sufficient to procure its alleviation.

Warrant for this extreme advice is provided in the phrase *my God.*[60] As God's prophet, Joel has the right to speak thus and direct the rites of humiliation. The prophet claims special insight into God's will, just as Paul did when he reported a surprising revelation from "the God to whom I belong and whom I serve" (Acts 27:23). He reminds them of the suspension of the daily offerings already mentioned in connection with the appeal to Jerusalem (v. 9), but this present reference has a more intimate ring: it is the house of *your God* that is being deprived. The priests had responsibility for the maintenance of the ritual system whereby due praise was ascribed to God and his name was honored. Now the system of worship had broken down and they were obliged to cancel the traditional rites for which the missing ingredients of grain, oil, and wine were necessary. In this emergency a new obligation was imposed on them by virtue of their sacred rank, namely, to intercede with their God in prayers of mourning day and night.

Joel urges the religious leaders to set in motion the machinery for a period of national lament. It has already been observed that fasting played an important part in such services. It provided a physical expression of the earnestness of the people in abasing themselves before God.[61] The term rendered *special service* means a public holiday from normal work to be devoted to religious use.[62] There were a certain number of holy days in the Hebrew calendar, but extra ones could be arranged in times of national emergency. One of the first steps in making such arrangements was to convene a meeting of *the elders*. As elsewhere, they are probably the ones whom Joel envisages as actually responsible for organizing the public assembly.[63] The representatives of the nation along with those whom they represent are to be summoned *to the temple,* where *Yahweh* gives audience. There in the name of the congregated community the priests in his service are to fulfil their responsibility to act as mediators by addressing to him their fervent appeals for help, their agonized cries of distress to one who has the ability to deliver.[64]

15–18 In speaking of the elders and the citizens of Judah, Joel has

60. Cf. Mic. 7:7 and comment. Sellin, Bewer, Wolff, *et al.*, read simply "God" with G, but MT seems to have point. G probably took the suffix *-î* as an abbreviation for *-îm,* as elsewhere.

61. The usual expression is "proclaim a fast" (e.g., 1 K. 21:9; Jon. 3:5), but Joel uses the verb "sanctify" to stress the religious nature of the activity.

62. Heb. *'ªtsārâ,* literally "stoppage"; cf. "order a sacred *'ªtsārâ,*" 2 K. 10:20.

63. Cf. 1 K. 21:8. Chary, *PC,* p. 202, is correct both in condemning the deletion of *elders* recommended by Bewer, Weiser, Baumgartner, and Rudolph, following Wellhausen, and in differentiating the use of Heb. *zᵉqēnîm* here and in 2:16 to mean *elders* here and *old men* there, *contra* Robinson and Kapelrud. Sellin, Delcor, *et al.* take the word as vocative (so JB, NEB), but this is unlikely since the priests are addressed in the context.

64. Heb. *za'ªqu;* cf. Mic. 3:4 and comment. The verb is regularly associated with public laments; cf. Judg. 10:10; 2 Chr. 20:9; Isa. 14:31.

come full circle to his starting point in 1:2, where the nation and its representatives were addressed before appeal was made to various sectors of the community. Now the prophet addresses again the whole community to whom he has just urged that a general summons should be given. Just as earlier the different groups within society were given appropriate reasons for religious lament, so now he has to provide compelling cause for the nation to break into mourning before God. At the same time he offers an appropriate lament which the people may use in their wailing. This section moves much closer to the form of the descriptive lament found in the lamenting psalms than did the descriptions earlier in the chapter. The first person plural is characteristic of the descriptive lament,[65] but it is generally couched in the form of direct prayer to God. In view of the third person references in v. 15, necessitated, it is true, by the factor of quotation, vv. 15–18 represent a transition from the description of the call to lament into the description to be found in an actual psalm of lament.

Joel achieves his ends by first uttering a cry of alarm in which he interprets the present dire situation in terms of *the Day,* which he goes on to elucidate as *Yahweh's Day*. He appears to fuse two prophetic passages doubtless well known to his audience. Ezekiel had enjoined at God's behest:

> ''*Wail 'Alas for the Day!'*
> *for the Day will soon be here,*
> *Yahweh's Day will soon be here.*'' (Ezek. 30:2, 3)[66]

Moreover, Isa. 13:6 had warned:

> *Wail, because Yahweh's Day will soon be here,*
> *it is coming with mighty ruin from the Almighty.*[67]

Both passages had used this ominous language to threaten foreign nations,[68] but Joel turns the dire warning of disaster against his own people, just as Amos had done long before.[69] In the course of his prophecy Joel draws heavily upon the complex of ideas and vocabulary associated with the Day of Yahweh. Historically it first appears on the pages of the OT in Amos 5:18, but even there it is obviously an accepted term whose original significance the prophet did not need to stop and explain. It is portrayed as an event in the future, when Yahweh is to intervene against his enemies. Whether or not it was originally a term associated with the Israelite concept of holy war,[70] it eventually appears invested with military trappings and is associated with battles and conquest. These associations Joel is to exploit later. But a phenomenon important for the present verse is the way the theme oscillates in the prophets between woe and weal for God's people. Joel's combination

65. Cf. Ps. 44:9–14(10–15).
66. Joel uses *'ᵃhāh,* Ezekiel *hāh*.
67. Joel inserts ''and'' before the final clause.
68. Cf. Obad. 15.
69. Amos 5:18–20; cf. Zeph. 1:7–13.
70. Cf. G. von Rad, ''The Origin of the Concept of the Day of Yahweh,'' *JSS* 4 (1959), pp. 97–108; *OT Theology,* vol. 2 (E.T. 1965), pp. 119–125.

of prophetic language directed against Gentiles with the anti-Israelite meaning of Amos is deliberately designed to shock his audience. In fact he creates a double shock, for his use of the Day of Yahweh motif is surprising. Were not plagues of locusts commonplace in the experience of Israel? And was not the Day a mighty manifestation of eschatological wrath against his own nation or other nations? Indeed, there were those who interpreted the downfall of Jerusalem in 587 B.C. as so shattering that it constituted realized eschatology, the fulfilment of that terrible Day.[71] With reference to the first question, Joel had stressed in 1:2, 3 the unique nature of this particular locust plague and hinted that it was a new act of Yahweh comparable with his great deeds in former days. So horrifyingly abnormal does the prophet feel it to be, that in response to its impact upon his soul he ransacks the prophetic literature for terms adequate to explain its significance. He is aware that a locust plague often has the role of a divine visitation, as retaliation for breach of covenant.[72] In this outstanding plague he sees the first signs of Israel's eschatological day of judgment at the hands of its covenant God. The nation stands on the brink of ultimate disaster unless it draws back by turning to God. The point need not be labored; there is much that the prophet can leave unsaid, for the very mention of the Day would open the floodgates of association with former prophecies:

> *"Soon I shall pour out my wrath upon you and vent my anger against you and judge you. . . ."* (Ezek. 7:8)
> *I shall bring distress upon men . . .*
> *because they have sinned against Yahweh.*
> *Their blood will be emptied out like dust,*
> *and their flesh like dung.* (Zeph. 1:17)

But two prophetic statements concerning Yahweh's Day he does echo, the first because of its fitting tone of lament, and the second because of its strong language of ill omen. *Mighty ruin from the Almighty* is an attempt to render a striking play on words, *shōḏ—shadday*. The second term is an ancient title for God associated with the patriarchs and taken up in Israel's psalmody.[73] Its meaning is unknown, although there is an exegetical tradition preserved in the Septuagint and Vulgate that it signifies "omnipotent." But here it is related to *shōḏ, ruin*. The venerated, comforting title of the God of help in ages past is turned into a negative expression for dread and alarm, "destroyer," which in its original context spells disaster for a foreign nation, but here for Israel itself. The Hebrew ear was sensitively attuned to associations of sound, and this emotional effect was not infrequently exploited by the prophets.[74] Joel has subtly created a strong sense of shock by suddenly transposing the natural plague to a higher plane of supreme judgment, and heightening the effect by producing a wordplay which is

71. Cf. Obad. 11–14 and comment.
72. See the references in n. 24.
73. E.g., Gen. 17:1; 43:14; 49:25; Ex. 6:3; Num. 24:4; Ps. 68:14(15); 91:1.
74. Cf. Mic. 1:10–15 and comments.

rendered more frightening by its new context. Here the presence of *ruin* in the quotation is particularly apt since it recalls the ruin of countryside and grain in v. 10.[75]

The prophet wisely rests the whipped emotions of his audience. He turns to remind them of the plain evidence *before* their *eyes* and to appeal to the reasoning powers of their minds. He takes his place alongside the people as a fellow sufferer, as he analyzes the situation. He points to various features to show that the scene is indeed one of *ruin*. Joel's contemporaries have only to look around to be convinced that starvation faces the community.[76] The locusts have eaten up the products that would eventually have fed the Judeans, who have had to look on, powerless to prevent it.[77] The situation also had religious consequences, which Joel spells out. "For him man does not live by bread alone, but by communion with God" (Keller). It was impossible to celebrate at the temple the customary festivals of firstfruits and harvest, which meant so much to the Judean, who lived in a culture heavily weighted on the religious side. Sounds of joy could no longer echo in the courts of the sanctuary, concerning which it had been commanded in the holy law:

> "*There you shall eat in the presence of Yahweh your God, and you and your families shall rejoice over every asset with which Yahweh your God has blessed you.*" (Deut. 12:7)[78]

In v. 17 Joel returns to a description of the terrible conditions on the farms. This is clear at least from v. 17b, but the first line is enigmatic, since three of the four words occur only here in OT literature. Presumably they were common enough to Joel's audience, but because of the scantiness of ancient Hebrew literary material which has survived the centuries the line is little more intelligible to us than Lewis Carroll's: "All mimsy were the borogoves,/ and the mome raths outgrabe." An amazing variety of suggestions have been offered,[79] but none has the clear ring of certitude. Consequently, until further evidence turns up, any proposed rendering remains conjectural. At least one expects in v. 17a a couplet dealing with different aspects of a single subject,[80] and in the light of v. 17b it is feasible that the first line concerns the loss of grain.[81] The rendering above, that of S.

75. Heb. *shuddaḏ*.

76. Cf. Deut. 3:21; 6:22; 1 Sam. 12:16.

77. Cf. Deut. 28:31; Isa. 1:17; 13:16 for the suggestion in the first phrase of being helpless spectators.

78. Cf. Deut. 16:10, 11; 26:10, 11.

79. E.g., RSV "The seed shrivels under the clods" (cf. KJV, RV, JB, Wolff); Rudolph, "Stores have rotted under their covers"; Kapelrud, "The grains have shrunk; their irrigation-spades are disheartened"; Sprengling, *loc. cit.*, "The watercourses have dried up under over-hanging banks"; NEB "The soil is parched, the dykes are dry."

80. Cf. vv. 7, 10, 12, 18.

81. Heb. *pᵉrūḏôṯ*, from a root signifying "separate," probably means "seeds" in view of Syr. *perdâ/pᵉrāḏâ*, "grain of corn or sand, seed, berry," and Jewish Aram. *pᵉrîḏâ*, "pebble, berry" (so KJV, RV, RSV, JB). NEB interprets as grains of soil. Sprengling compares the use of the

R. Driver, is the best compromise between the demands of suggested etymology and the context.[82] Allusion is evidently made to drought conditions. When ground in which seed had been sown showed no sign of green life, investigating *shovels* had uncovered the ungerminated grain. With no prospect of harvest, routine maintenance of flimsy storage buildings had evidently not been carried out. They had been allowed to fall into disrepair because there was nothing to store in them: the cereal crops had failed. Joel repeats terms already used in v. 10 in a kind of sad refrain.[83]

The prophet moves from failure of the crops to a poignant description of farm *animals* in *distress*. His heart goes out in remarkable tenderness to the thirsty, starving creatures in response to their piteous lowing. He interprets their noise in human terms as *groans*. As he had imaginatively depicted the countryside as mourning in vv. 10, 12, so now he fancies that the very animals join in the lament. The whole creation seems to be groaning, as Paul was to affirm in another age (Rom. 8:22). And if brother ox and brother sheep are responding in this way, implies the prophet, ought not we ourselves join in unison? There is an implicit contrast between the response of brute animals and the people's insensitivity. He observes with compassionate eye the weary wandering of *cattle* in search of *pasture*, driven by the hunger pangs of empty stomachs. His sympathetic eye has also seen the *sheep* suffering from lack of grass and whole *flocks* dying off.

19, 20 Finally the prophet turns to God in prayer. The prayer falls

---

verb in Gen. 2:10 concerning rivers, and takes as "rifts, watercourses." Rudolph, comparing Theodotion, interprets as "what has been put aside, kept for later," and so "supplies, stores." G S V construe as animals, either *p^{e}rāḏôṯ*, "female mules," or *pārôṯ*, "cows"; but as Bewer and Rudolph observe, mention of animals is premature and unsuitable before v. 18.

82. The verb *'āḇ^{e}shû* has been compared with Arab. *'abisa*, "contract, be dried up." A strong Jewish tradition, represented in V T Symmachus and the expositions of Ibn Ezra and Kimchi, interpreted as "rot, decay," relating it to postbiblical Heb. and Aram. *'pš*, "rot." Heb. *megr^{e}p̱ōṯêhem*, "their . . . ," was understood as "clods" by Ibn Ezra and Kimchi, whence it has come into the English translations. It makes good sense, but is probably a guess from the context; there is no etymological justification for it (Merx, S. R. Driver). The verb and related nouns in Hebrew, Aramaic, and Arabic signify "sweep away" (e.g., Judg. 5:21) and tools for this purpose such as "shovel, hoe, broom," e.g., Syr. *magrap̱tâ*, "shovel, ladle," *magrûp̱îṯâ*, "fire shovel." Kapelrud cites from Dalman an Arab. cognate referring to a mattock for controlling water channels. G "stalls" evidently relates to Heb. *r^{e}p̱āṯîm* (Hab. 3:17). Robinson emended to *gor^{e}nōṯêhem*, "their threshing floors," which *BHS* favors. Rudolph proposes either to emend to *m^{e}gûp̱ōṯêhem*, which apparently underlies T, relating to postbiblical Heb. and Aram. *m^{e}gûp̱â*, "lid, cover" (cf. *gûp̱*, "close [doors]," Neh. 7:3), or to take MT as a form with an infixed *resh*. Sprengling interprets as banks washed by torrents: cf. Arab. *gurf*, "water-worn bank"; similarly NEB. For *taḥaṯ*, "beneath," Robinson read a verb *ḥattû*, "are dismayed" (cf. Jer. 14:14), while Kapelrud repoints as *tēḥēṯ*, Niphal imperfect, with the same sense; NEB appears to do similarly. G "upon" is a loose rendering, as E. Nestle, *ZAW* 20 (1900), pp. 164f., showed in a careful correlation of G and MT in this line.

83. Sprengling takes *dāg̱ān*, *grain*, as "rainclouds," the NEB as "rains," both depending on Arab. *dajn*, "copious rain, rainclouds." But the same meaning as in v. 10 is expected, especially as repetition is a hallmark of Joel's style. Sprengling also refers the earlier part of the line to lack of water storage: "Reservoirs are desolate, disintegrated; pools have crumbled into ruins" (or "stores have vanished from reservoirs").

into two parallel parts. Each consists of a line of petition and two lines of descriptive lament, bound together by repetition of a line in the lament. The first part reads like an individual lament, which is marked by a first singular subject; otherwise the piece could be a communal lament, which like this one is characterized by address, petition, and description.[84] In fact Joel is probably speaking in the guise of the cultic leader of the national lament, who at times would doff his representative mantle and allow his own personality to dominate the lament.[85] This explains how easy it is for Joel to switch from the first plural of v. 16 to the singular here. His prophetic imitation of the ritual form corresponds to his own strong desire to bring the people to God, as well as to the duty of intercessory prayer which was included in the prophetic office.[86] It is designed to act as a stimulus to the community, inciting the members to respond to his pleas and hold such a service. Like a teacher with a child, he guides them through the proper motions and encourages them to do likewise.

Joel is very conscious of the correct forms of lament at this point. This is evident from his use of traditional language in his words of lament,[87] as he lays the dire situation before God, who alone can help. The cultic theme of *pastures* suffering from drought is also echoed in Jer. 9:10(9); 23:10.[88] Originally it was probably a lament uttered at the height of summer in response to the scorching heat of the sun, but Joel can strikingly reapply it to a period earlier in the year because the drought had created abnormal conditions, dehydrating not only grazing land[89] but also *the trees* with which ancient Judah abounded. Like some forest fire it had swept over the countryside and left destruction in its wake.

As in vv. 17, 18, the prophet is sensitive to the fact that not only vegetation has been victim of catastrophe. He returns to the theme of suffering animals. As earlier he interpreted the noise of domestic animals in terms of groans, now he goes further and hears those of *wild beasts* as a prayer to their Creator in animal language.[90] "Was it not such a calling upon God as their nature admitted? As much then as the nature of brute animals allows they may be said to seek their food from the Lord" (Calvin). Joel is probably echoing Ps.42:1(2), where the same verb is used of the deer as it searches for water,[91] and it is from the same source that he derives the

84. Cf. C. Westermann, *The Praise of God in the Psalms* (E.T. 1965), pp. 52f., 64, 66.
85. Cf. Ps. 44:4, 6, 15f. (5, 7, 16f.); 74:12; 83:13(14). Cf. H. Gunkel and J. Begrich, *Einleitung in die Psalmen* (1933), p. 124.
86. Cf. Jer. 42:1–4; Amos 7:1–6.
87. The words of the prayer in v. 19a are also traditional: cf. Ps. 28:1; 30:9; 86:3.
88. Cf. Ps. 65:12(13).
89. Heb. *midbār*, traditionally rendered "wilderness," is more strictly an area where cattle are led out (*dbr*) to graze, as distinct from cultivated parts.
90. Cf. Job 38:41; Ps. 104:21, where lions' roars and the squawking of baby ravens are interpreted as prayers for food.
91. This is the only occurrence of the verb in the Heb. OT apart from Ps. 42:2(3). The singular verb, retained despite the plural subject, is permissible (GK 145k).

expression *river beds*. The prophet follows the pattern of v. 19, i.e., petition and descriptive lament. Pride of place in the lament is given to a new factor relevant to the needs of wild creatures, namely, the drought-dry river beds. The second line of v. 19 is taken up as a doleful refrain in the third line, rounding off the passage. Appeal to scorched *pastures,* the traditional basis of prayers pleading for rain, is echoed by prophet and beast. Joel yearns for the people to take their cue from the rest of animate creation, and to engage themselves in earnest prayer to God in the sanctuary. His desire is that they may share his heightened sensitivity to his environment and relate it to the God of creation and covenant.[92] Joel's knowledge of God enabled him to evaluate the scene around him. His eyes were open to God and to God's world.

B. DIVINE JUDGMENT AND HUMAN REPENTANCE (2:1—17)

Joel renews his appeal to the community with greater intensity. Whether a fresh attack of locusts prompted this fervent outburst, or whether a cool response to his earlier appeals simply provoked a more impassioned attempt it is not possible to decide.[1] In many respects this second challenge forms a parallel to the first in ch. 1. The impression given is that earlier motifs are taken up and transposed into a higher key, a more strident setting and a faster pace. The prophet replaces the recital of the destruction caused by the locusts with a depiction of the locusts themselves in lurid colors, carefully chosen for their impact on his audience. Having conditioned them with culturally coercive language, he urges them afresh to turn to God and to use a national service of lamentation as a vehicle of repentance and throwing themselves upon divine mercy.

1. Yahweh's Army of Locusts (2:1–11)

"Blow the horn in Zion,
sound the alarm in my sacred mountain." 3+3
Let all the country's population quake
because Yahweh's Day is coming,[2] *will soon be here,* 3+3
2 *a gloomy, dark day,*
a cloudy, lowering day.[3] 3+3
Like blackness covering the mountains
is the vast, massive horde. 3+3

92. Keller is doubtless correct in finding in the appeal to drunkards in v. 5 a hint of the indifference to Yahweh of the community as a whole.

1. The increase in momentum and tension renders unlikely Bewer's view that 2:1–14 was delivered earlier than 1:2–20 and that the present placing represents only literary arrangement.
2. Heb. *bā'*, theoretically either perfect or participle, is evidently the latter: cf. 1:15 *yāḇô'*, "will come."
3. The sense suggests that the *soph pasuq* at the end of v. 1 in MT should be moved here.

Their like has never appeared before
nor ever will again
for years and years to come. 3+3+3

3 *Ahead of them fire consumes,*
behind them flames burn. 3+3
Land ahead of them is like Eden's garden,
behind them a desolate heath.
In fact nothing escapes them.[4] 3+3+3
4 *They look like horses*
and charge just like cavalry. 3+3
5 *With a noise like chariots*
they leap over the mountain tops. 2+3
The noise is like fiery flames
consuming stubble. 3+2
They are like a massive horde
marshalled for battle. 2+2

6 *At their advance peoples writhe in terror,*
every face is flushed.[5] 3+3
They charge like soldiers,
scale walls
like men at war. 2+2+2
They each move straight ahead
without overlapping[6] *their tracks.* 3+3
8 *Never jostling each other,*
they each follow their set paths. 3+3

4. Heb. *lô* generally refers to that which escapes (Judg. 21:17; 2 Sam. 15:14; Ezra 9:13). Accordingly Keil and Wade refer it to the land, the latter comparing Gen. 13:6 for the masculine reference to *hā'ārets*. But this is set in a chain of suffixes referring to the locust horde of v. 2. The force of the preposition invites comparison with Ugar. *l,* "from."
5. The exact meaning is uncertain. The clause occurs also in Nah. 2:11 in a similar context and obviously describes the expression on the faces of the panic-stricken. The noun *pā'rûr,* not found elsewhere, has plausibly been related to an assumed root *pûr,* from which also is derived *pārûr,* "pot," cognate with Arab. *fāra* and Syr. *pûr,* "boil," "be excited"; then it refers to a red flush of passion (P. Haupt, *JBL* 26 [1907], p. 43). For the resultant meaning "gather a flush" cf. Isa. 13:8 in a similar setting: "their faces will be aflame," i.e., with excited agitation. Some, e.g., Keil and A. Haldar, *Studies in the Book of Nahum* (1946), p. 59, find a reference to paleness (cf. RV and Jer. 30:6). The noun can be related to the Heb. root *p'r,* "be beautiful, glorious," assuming a derived meaning "brightness"; the verb *qibbēts* is then interpreted as "take away" on the analogy of Ethiop. *qabatsa,* "fail," and the double meaning of Heb. *'āsap̱*. KJV "gather blackness" follows G S V T in ascribing to the noun a derived meaning from *pārûr,* "pot." J. J. Glück, *Ou-Testamentiese Werkgemeenskap van Suid-Afrika* 12 (1969), pp. 21–26, defends the association with pottery, rendering "greyness," the pale color of a clay pot, and comparing *'ēp̱er,* "dust, soil."
6. The sense in the light of the context is obvious, the etymology less so. Heb. *y^{e}'abb^{e}ṭûn* is hardly from *'bt,* "take a pledge" in a derived sense of trespassing upon a course intended for another (Ehrlich), which would be "a very forced metaphor" (S. R. Driver). The text is often changed either to *y^{e}'abb^{e}ṯûn* (cf. Mic. 7:3) or to *y^{e}'aww^{e}ṯûn,* "bend, make crooked" (Wellhausen, Sellin, Bewer, *BHK*), or to *yaṭṭûn,* "turn aside" (Robinson, following Grätz). But in justification of MT, G. R. Driver, *JTS* 34 (1933), p. 378, has plausibly compared

They press headlong through the aqueduct
without halting their course.[7] 3+2
9 *They rush into the city,*
running up the wall. 2+2
They climb into the houses;
in through the windows
they come like burglars. 2+2+2

10 *Ahead of them the earth quakes,*
the sky vibrates, 3+2
sun and moon grow dark
and stars stop shining, 3+3
11 *as Yahweh thunders*
at the head of his army.[8] 3+2
For vast is his battalion
and massive the force that executes his orders.[9] 3+3
Yahweh's Day is momentous,
terrible indeed.
Who can withstand it? 2+2+2

Joel issues to the people a dire warning, which he proceeds to justify by describing the locust attack in terms of divine judgment. The brief warning cry in v. 1a comes from Yahweh himself; it is followed in vv. 1b–11 by the prophet's description of the locusts, interspersed with dramatic allusions to Yahweh's Day and to a hostile theophany. The passage is a closely knit unit. The theme of the Day of Yahweh, used already in 1:15, now appears in the form of two resounding echoes at beginning and end, in vv. 1f., 11.[10] Within this evocative framework is set the complex description of the locusts as an army, which develops the hint of 1:6. The unit falls into four parts, just like 1:2–12; in fact there is a close correspondence between the two passages, which will be traced in the course of the exposition. After the introductory section the other three divisions, vv. 3–5, 6–9, 10f., are marked by similar

Arab. *'abaṭa,* "tear (a garment), disturb (dust)," from a basic meaning "spoil what is sound, intact." Van Hoonacker's appeal to Syr. *'abbîṯ,* "dense, overgrown," used of trees and paths, is less convincing. J. C. Greenfield, *JAOS* 82 (1962), pp. 295f., is unable to elucidate the present usage but relates the verb to a proto-Semitic *'bṭ,* "tie." Ahlström, *JTCJ,* pp. 11f., builds upon his analysis by taking *lō'* as emphatic and interpreting in terms of closed ranks, "almost 'tied' to each other."

7. Heb. *yiḇtsā'û* means "cut off, break off," sc. their course. Kapelrud interprets as "break away from one another." Kimchi and some other Jewish commentators took the basic meaning to be "cut," comparing the similar sounding *pṣ'*, "wound"; hence KJV "are not wounded" (similarly Keil and von Orelli). Ahlström, *JTCJ,* pp. 11f., who relates the three instances of *lō'*, "not," in vv. 7f. to the emphatic *lameḏ,* compares Arab. *baḍa'a,* "cut into pieces," and Isa. 38:12, and finds here the idea of cutting down (the people) as an irresistible force.

8. For the syntax of vv. 10–11a see E. Kutsch, *TZ* 18 (1962), pp. 87f. *For* explains v. 10a.

9. The singular *'ōśeh* does not refer to Yahweh but agrees with *ḥêlô*. For the phrase cf. Ps. 103:20; 148:8.

10. Kutsch, *loc. cit.,* p. 83.

openings:[11] compare the similarity of the last three parts of 1:2–12 after the introductory general summons of 1:2–4, each of the three consisting of a special appeal to a certain group. Just as the beginning of the piece puts the locusts into eschatological perspective by reference to Yahweh's Day, so the beginning of the second stanza significantly uses the language of theophany (v. 3); that of the third creates a similar effect by using universal terms (v. 6), and that of the fourth refers to cosmic disturbances (v. 10). These various motifs constitute a recurring drumbeat of dread, for they all have prior associations with Yahweh's Day. Verse 11 marks a climax by reverting to explicit mention of the Day. The whole passage is suffused with tones that heighten the locust plague to a macabre religious pitch. The armory of eschatological prophecy is ransacked in order that, under a barrage of its themes, the religiously insensitive community may be compelled to react aright to the seriousness of the present situation and its critical significance in terms of their relation to Yahweh.

1, 2 The wall-towers of an ancient city were manned by guards alert for enemy attack. Upon their keen eyes the security of the community within the walls depended. Should they spy a hostile force appearing, it was their duty to *sound the alarm* on a curved *horn* of ram or cow:

> *"Their sentry . . . sees the sword attacking the area and blows on the horn and warns the people. If anyone who hears the sound of the horn pays no attention to the warning and the sword comes and takes his life, the responsibility for his death will be his own."* (Ezek. 33:2–4)

The horn blast was thus the ancient equivalent of the modern air raid siren blaring its alert. Here God himself acts as watchman for his people, and through the prophet orders the alarm to be sounded so that due precautions may be taken in Jerusalem. As Joel has already made clear and will later repeat more precisely, God does not look for a reaction of military defense such as manning the ramparts, but manning the temple for special services of humiliation before him. There is in fact a play on ideas, which v. 15 later clarifies.[12] The horn was also blown by way of invitation to temple services, like the tolling of church bells.[13]

The priests are evidently addressed, as earlier at 1:14 and later in 2:15, 16. His ministers are to heed this warning and publicize a service to be held for the whole community in the temple at *Zion,* God's *sacred mountain,*

11. Verses 3 and 10, Heb. *lᵉp̱ānāyw,* v. 6, *mippānāyw,* "before them." Cf. too the occurrence of *kᵉ*, "like," twice in v. 2, six times in vv. 3–5, and twice in v. 7, and the similar sounding *kî,* "for," twice in v. 1 and thrice in v. 11. Keller's analysis of the passage into eight stanzas symmetrically grouped around a central pivot, v. 6 (cf. Kutsch, *loc. cit.*, p. 88), ignores these strophic guides and the links with ch. 1, and overestimates the importance of v. 6, which in thought, function, and initial wording is parallel to vv. 3a, 10a.

12. Cf. H.-P. Müller, *Theologia Viatorum* 10 (1965/66), p. 235.

13. Keller and Ahlström, *JTCJ,* p. 58, find especially significant the references to the horn and Yahweh's Day in the same context, since the former was associated with the coming of Yahweh in the theophany (cf. Ps. 47:5[6]; 81:3[4]).

the seat of his special revelation. The phrase is intimately associated with the OT theme of the inviolability of Jerusalem,[14] and thus in the midst of the distress adds another hint to those in 1:6, 7 concerning Yahweh's vested interest in the situation, and his deep desire to bring his people through to an experience of renewed worship and blessing. There the people were to flock to meet with God in the time of dire need. The sound of the alarm horn would send a stab of fear into the hearts of the people:

> *"Is a horn blown in a city without the people being scared?*
> *Is a city victim of calamity and Yahweh not responsible?"*
> (Amos 3:6)

Here the calamity was on a national scale. Joel, who as it were takes over from Yahweh as speaker after the initial line,[15] can leave unspoken the conclusion so often drawn in OT thinking that Yahweh himself was punishing the people for their sin. The people might well *quake,* for the locust plague constituted a signal that they stood at the brink in the ultimate of divine punishment, the *Day* of Yahweh. The prophet probably again echoes Isa. 13 (vv. 6, 9), as he often does in this chapter. He follows up the quotation with another, word for word from Zeph. 1:15. He sees an adumbration of Zephaniah's words coming true; for it was Zephaniah who developed into a somber melody the motif of darkness which Amos had so inexorably attached to the Day (Amos 5:18–20). Joel cites it, doubtless knowing that it would bring to his hearers' minds the whole gamut of associations that belonged to the *Dies Irae*. It is essential to Joel's purpose that he should not be original. His deliberate aim is to make a deep impression by using stereotyped, well-known language to show that in the present situation venerated prophecies were on the verge of fulfilment.[16] His newness lies in the application of the old words.[17]

The prophet sees the shadow of this Day looming over his contemporaries in the phenomenon of the plague of locusts. They have spread a pall of darkness over the hills around Jerusalem. A plague on Lebanon in 1845 was described in similar terms: "Their number was astounding; the whole face of the mountain was black with them."[18] Indeed, Ex. 10:15, which is probably in Joel's mind, reports that in the great Egyptian plague "they covered the surface of the whole land, and the ground was

14. Cf. the comments on Obad. 16f.
15. Cf, the same phenomenon in vv. 12f.
16. Cf. Bourke, *RB* 66 (1959), p. 29.
17. Ezek. 34:12 applies the same text to the downfall of Jerusalem in 587.
18. W. M. Thomson, *The Land and the Book* (1905), pp. 416f. It is possible that Joel's audience would also connect the first line with black clouds of flying locusts. Cf. a report cited by S. R. Driver: "In the heat of the day they formed themselves into large bodies, appeared like a succession of clouds and darkened the sun." MT *shaḥar,* "dawn," has been compared with observers' reports of the sun's rays reflected in the wings of the locusts in flight. Then they are not on the ground but glinting swarms in the sky, seen against the background of the mountains (so, e.g., S. R. Driver, von Orelli, Smith). Kutsch (*loc. cit.*, p. 83), Keller, Wolff, and Rudolph interpret MT in terms of suddenness and ubiquity. Kapelrud,

darkened.'' The uncanny sight of normal scenery obliterated by these teeming legions of dark-bodied insects is heightened by Joel into an adumbration of the all-engulfing Day of darkness.[19] Realistic description and transcendental interpretation are intertwined throughout this passage. The military reference takes up a motif that was used before in 1:6 and is to be developed extensively in the course of this passage and finally explained in v. 11. The prophet closes this section with a pointed reference to the abnormality of the plague. Locusts were no uncommon phenomenon, but this visitation stood out from previous experiences. Joel's hearers would catch the intended reminiscence of Ex. 10:14. The plagues of Egypt which preceded the Exodus were remembered as divine wonders of exceptional severity: the size of the locust swarms was ''such as had never been before nor ever will be again.'' The comment is here reapplied to the contemporary situation with fearful implications. It is a reversal typical of the OT prophets. The great God of the Exodus, who had intervened to strike down the enemies of his people in signal acts of judgment, was at work again. But now were not his own people at the receiving end of his outstretched hand of judgment?[20] Joel sows the terrible hint in order that it may grow into a harvest of contrition in his hearers' hearts and lives.

This first stanza is obviously intended as a counterpart to that in the first poem. The appeal to *all the country's population* in 1:2 reappears in 2:1. The reference in 1:4 to swarm after swarm of locusts is taken up in 2:2 by the mention of their vast quantity. The note of unique crisis in 1:2 sounds out again here. Joel rhetorically repeats his earlier message in order to convict the community. He underlines it with frightening allusion to the Day of Yahweh and to the Exodus. He invests the plague with an aura of divine hostility. As Jacob had learned from his dream the terrifying truth, ''Surely Yahweh is in this place and I did not know'' (Gen. 28:16), so Joel intended to startle Judah into seeing God's presence in the plague.

3–5 The second stanza also combines the factual and the interpretative. It begins by recording the effect of the locusts' devastation in terms of conflagration. The description accords remarkably with the reactions of many an observer. ''Bamboo groves have been . . . left standing like saplings after a rapid bush fire. . . . And grass has been devoured so that the bare earth appeared as if burned.'' ''It looks as if the country had been burnt by fire.''[21] But there is an unusual ring about the first line. The second one

---

followed by Keller, finds a mythological allusion in MT ''dawn,'' comparing Ps. 110:3; Isa. 14:12. But MT is to be repointed *sh^eḥōr,* ''blackness,'' with Duhm, Bewer, Robinson, Sellin, and Thompson (so RSV, NEB), which better suits the sequence of thought. The implicit link between the locusts and the darkness of the Day is clearly the darkness of Ex. 10:15; cf. the allusion to Ex. 10:4 in v. 2b.

19. Cf. the use of *'ānān,* ''cloud,'' of Gog's advancing army in Ezek. 38:9, 16: ''like a cloud covering the ground''; cf. too Jer. 4:13.

20. Cf. Isa. 1:24f.; 28:21.

21. Cited by S. R. Driver.

expresses the expected theme of beauty replaced by barrenness, which at first sight the first line virtually contradicts. One could explain the burning that preceded the locusts in terms of the drought both mentioned and implied in ch. 1, but this explanation only reinforces the rift between the two lines. It is almost as if a fiery aura emanating from the advancing locusts sweeps ahead of them. Joel appears to be tingeing his sober observation with a numinous hue. The description of Yahweh's kingly majesty and holiness in Ps. 97 includes a reference to the "clouds and lowering darkness" that envelop him—itself an impressive link with v. 2[22]—and crowns it with a line strikingly akin to the present one:

Fire goes before him and burns his enemies round him.[23]

The echo of these dynamic terms puts the locusts on the side of divine reality. Joel's daring application of the language of theophany interprets them as a manifestation of the destructive wrath of God.

The prophet passes to a more ordinary observation, but even this has overtones for the listening ear. The stark contrast of the scene before and after the locusts' ravages finds an echo in reports of the substitution "in the twinkling of an eye" of "the dreary spectacle of winter for the rich scenes of spring." "Fields which the rising sun beheld covered with luxuriance are before evening a desert."[24] Joel phrases the reversal in dramatic terms of Paradise and a desert. The figurative contrast is not unparalleled in the prophets,[25] except that it is associated with the gracious assurance of God's turning curse into blessing for his people. Here, as elsewhere, Joel startlingly reverses the pattern of usage. God had withdrawn his blessing and put in its place a curse wrought by agents of divine wrath upon human sin. Joel preaches as powerfully in his unspoken hints as in his plain speaking. A master in the craft of suggestion, he provokes the attentive mind to produce within itself conclusions more shattering than if he had voiced them openly.

The desolation the locusts have caused is total. Ex. 10:15 is another biblical witness to this well-attested truth. "Where these destructive swarms alight, not a leaf is left upon the trees, a blade of grass in the pastures nor an ear of corn in the field."[26] Joel's word for *escapes* is one that is associated with survivors from the hazards of war,[27] and his use of it is designed to take up the theme of the locust army introduced by *horde* in v. 2, in preparation for the next verses. He alludes first to the appearance of the locust, whose head bears a startling resemblance to that of a horse.[28] Not only their

22. Heb. *'ānān wa'ᵃrāpel* in both cases.
23. Heb. *lᵉpānāyw, tᵉlahēṭ,* as here. Cf. Ps. 50:3; Hab. 3:5. *Fire* is associated with the Day of Yahweh in Zeph. 1:18.
24. Quoted by Pusey.
25. Isa. 51:3; Ezek. 36:35 (cf. Gen. 2:8; 13:10).
26. Quoted by Pusey.
27. Heb. *pᵉlêṭâ*: e.g., 2 Sam. 15:14; 2 Chr. 20:24.
28. Cf. German *Heupferd,* Italian *cavaletta*. Keller finds in Heb. *kᵉmar'ēh,* "like the appearance of," an allusion to the supernatural (cf. Judg. 13:6; Ezek. 1:13, etc.) and compares the idea of celestial horses in 2 K. 2:11; Zech. 1:8; 6:2–8.

physical appearance but their massed swiftness suggests a *cavalry charge*.[29] Joel is gradually building up a frightening picture of military invincibility.[30] His emotional appeal to the senses continues with a description of the effect of the locusts upon the ear of an observer. He compares the *noise* they made, as they came foraging across the hills toward Jerusalem, with the clatter and thudding of *chariots*.[31] It has also been described as like "a heavy shower on a distant forest."[32] The prophet goes on to echo the dread theme of *fire* mentioned at the head of the stanza.[33] Their feeding has likewise been compared to "the crackling of a bush on fire" (G. A. Smith) and "the rushing of flames driven by the wind."[34] Here again there are sinister overtones: the seemingly homely metaphor of the burning of *stubble* after harvest has associations of divine wrath which would not be lost on Joel's audience.[35] The alternating themes of God's wrath and the locust army are eventually to be explicitly resolved toward the end of the fourth stanza.

The last in this present series of comparisons appeals to the strangely military impression the locusts give, like a countless army, seeming to "march in regular battalions,"[36] ready to engage their enemy. With the words *massive horde* Joel reverts to a phrase used already, in v. 2, but the addition of his final phrase looks forward to its expansion in the next stanza.[37] Thus the last line serves to bind together this stanza artistically with what precedes and follows. A further example of the prophet's artistry is the way he has provided here a parallel to the second stanza of the first poem. The themes of agent, victim, and effect are echoed in the repetition of the vocabulary *massive, land,* and devastation.[38]

6–9 The third stanza, like the second, prefaces a straightforward description of the locusts with a statement suggestive of a higher realm of thought. It relates the reaction to the locust army, the apprehension and alarm they evoke from their victims.[39] But a hint that the prophet is transcending the plane of the commonplace is contained in the plural *peoples*. This is no prosaic encounter between Judah and a mass of insects.

29. Cf. the reverse metaphor in Job 39:20. For Heb. *pārāsh* and cavalry in the ancient Near East see D. R. Ap-Thomas, "All the King's Horses?" *Proclamation and Presence*. G. H. Davies Festschrift (1970), pp. 135–151.

30. Bewer refers thus to the Heb. archaic imperfect forms ending in *-ûn* in this and the following verses: "They are used purposely to bring out the whole weight and power of the attack, they deepen the impression of terror and awe."

31. The reference is not, as many commentators suggest, to the locusts' flight, in view of the second half of the line, which as Bewer rightly notes can hardly refer to the chariots.

32. Thomson, *op. cit.*, p. 417.

33. Heb. *'āḵ^{e}lâ 'ēsh . . . lehāḇâ* becomes *lahaḇ 'ēsh 'ōḵ^{e}lâ*.

34. Cited by S. R. Driver.

35. See the comment on Obad. 18.

36. Cited by S. R. Driver.

37. Kutsch, *loc. cit.*, p. 84.

38. Heb. *'ātsûm* 1:6; 2:5; *'artsî* 1:6, *hā'ārets* 2:3; *shammâ* 1:7, *sh^{e}māmâ* 2:3.

39. For the motif of the reaction to bad news see the sketch by D. R. Hillers, *ZAW* 77 (1965), pp. 86–90.

As in v. 3, Joel seems again to be using the language of theophany:

Writhe in terror before him, all the earth. (Ps. 96:9)[40]

This warning heralds the coming of the universal Judge. In Ps. 99:1 the reaction to Yahweh's manifestation of his kingly might is that "peoples tremble," while in Ex. 15:14 the response to his victorious championing of Israel is that "peoples . . . tremble and writhing seizes the inhabitants of Philistia."[41] The widespread range of the reaction in these texts reflects the terrible and sublime power of Yahweh over the nations of Palestine and of the world.[42] All cower in panic before him; such is his overwhelming grandeur that no less an effect is adequate. Joel transfers such a response from the context of Yahweh's appearing to that of his instruments through whom he reveals his will.[43] Their vehement visitation he implicitly traces back to the empowering impulse of God. His heightened, loaded language serves to reflect the awe-inspiring role of the locusts as Yahweh's plenipotentiaries. They come not in their own name, for behind them stands the might and majesty of God. This is the perspective that sets the tone for Joel's description of the locusts' irresistible onslaught in vv. 7–9. The theme of the advancing army, introduced in the previous stanza, is developed further. Joel's imagery has often suggested itself to observers. "On they came like a disciplined army. . . . They charged up the mountainside and climbed over rocks, walls, ditches, hedges, those behind coming up and passing over the masses already killed."[44] Like some infantry corps charging with high morale,[45] like commandos assaulting some fortress, on they press with remorseless purpose. "The roads were covered with them all marching in regular lines, like armies of soldiers." "They seemed to be impelled by one common instinct and moved in one body, which had the appearance of being organized by a leader. . . . They seemed to march in regular battalions, crawling over everything that lay in their passage, in one straight front."[46] Joel and his contemporaries witnessed a similar phenomenon. With uncanny parade-ground precision they made their steady advance, undeterred by any obstacle. Such was their ruthless enterprise that they even attacked via the Siloam *aqueduct,* which brought water from the Gihon spring into the city on the southeast side.[47] The reference admirably paves the way for the locusts' invading and pervading the city in v. 9. So Jerusalem falls victim to these

40. Heb. *ḥîlû mippānāyw;* here *mippānāyw yāḥîlû.*

41. Cf. too Hab. 3:10: "Mountains writhe in terror" at the hostile theophany of Yahweh.

42. Cf. the use of "peoples, nations" in wisdom contexts at Job 17:6; Prov. 24:24 to reflect the enormity of an attitude or state.

43. Cf. the similar adaptation in Ex. 15:4; Deut. 2:25.

44. Cited by S. R. Driver from Thomson.

45. For *soldiers* cf. the same Heb. term in Isa. 13:3 (Wolff).

46. Cited by S. R. Driver. Cf. Prov. 30:27.

47. Heb. *shelaḥ* has traditionally been rendered "weapons," but a missile or javelin, which the word strictly means, is hardly a likely deterrent to be tried against locusts nor is it supported in historical reports. S. E. Loewenstamm, *Leshonenu* 26 (1961/62), p. 62, interprets the phrase as "attack (cf. Job 1:15) the outer rampart (= Akk. *shalḥu*)." But better is Rudolph's

invading forces which storm its walls. They take over the city and make it their own. "They flood through the open, unglazed windows and lattices; nothing can keep them out" (G. A. Smith). They loot and forage where they will, irresistible conquerors to whom every house in their path must surrender. To illustrate from a nineteenth-century report, they "entered the inmost recesses of the houses, were found in every corner, stuck to our clothes and infested our food."[48] With this excited portrayal of the conquest of Jerusalem, Joel brings his description to a vivid close.[49] The prophet is still tracing a course parallel to that of the first poem. This third stanza he has planned as the counterpart of the corresponding stanza in the first poem (1:8–10), where Jerusalem was addressed.

10,11 In the fourth strophe Joel brings the first half of the poem to an impressive climax. Hitherto he has been mixing factual description with metaphysical comment, but now he drops the role of observer of the locusts' movements and concentrates on their religious significance. He begins the stanza with a cosmic motif akin to the themes of theophany at the head of the second and third stanzas (vv. 3, 6), and then rounds off the passage by returning to the motif of Yahweh's Day which he had proclaimed in v. 2.

One of the standard effects of a theophany reflecting the majesty of the God who breaks into history is earthquake, along with similar disturbances in nature.[50] Yahweh's intervention in past history to aid his people is pictured as an occasion when

> *Seeing you, the waters writhed in terror. . . .*
> *The noise of your thunder was in the whirlwind,*
> *your lightning flashes lit up the world,*
> *the earth trembled and shook.* (Ps. 77:16, 18[17, 19])[51]

The victorious God is magnificently described as Lord of the storm, who convulses the elements as he demonstrates his almighty power. So sublime is he and so abject are all who incur his wrath, is the poet's affirmation stripped of its vivid imagery. If God's theophany in the past could be described thus, so also could his appearing in the future. Cosmic convulsions became part of the trappings of the Day of Yahweh.

> *The stars in the sky . . . will not be bright with their light,*
> *the sun will be dark at dawn*
> *and the moon's light will fail to shine. . . .*

---

explanation, since it relates to a Heb. word attested elsewhere: in Neh. 3:15 it stands for *shīlōaḥ*, Siloam (cf. Isa. 8:6). Rudolph argues that the term indicates the time of Hezekiah as a *terminus post quem* but it could refer to an earlier aqueduct (cf. Isa. 8:6).

48. Cited by S. R. Driver.

49. Regarding the 2+2 rhythm in v. 9 (cf. v. 7 at the beginning of the description) Bewer comments: "The staccato character of the rhythm brings out the movement of the advancing and attacking hosts with great realism. The rhythmic tone corresponds exactly to the graphic description and heightens its effect."

50. Cf. Mic. 1:4 and comment.

51. Heb. *rgz* and *r'š* as here; cf. Ps. 18:7(8).

I shall make the sky tremble,
and the earth will be shaken out of its place[52]
at the wrath of Yahweh of hosts,
on the day of his fiery anger. (Isa. 13:10, 13)

This is the ideological climate in which these two verses move. The daring innovation Joel makes is to transfer the cultic language of theophany and the imagery of eschatological prophecy to the contemporary event of the locust plague. The notion of the earthquake is probably based on the visual effect of the locusts covering the ground: "The whole earth seemed to be creeping and jumping," reported Thomson.[53] The idea of preternatural darkness is suggested by their flight. "In the heat of the day they formed themselves into large bodies, appeared like a succession of clouds and darkened the sun," stated one observer.[54] But the locusts are nightmarishly endowed with divine significance, as in vv. 3, 6. Here the prophet takes his cue from the cultic representation which poetically surrounded historical events with a chaotic aura in order to stress their earth-shattering significance. As the world quakes in alarm at God's appearing, so the locusts to Joel's mind have the same effect. For they represent him and come as emissaries of his wrath. They constitute an epoch-making crisis for the people of God—a people whose world is turned upside down, for in the semblance of the locusts their mighty God is in their midst, present to judge and to destroy.[55] They confront his people with a dire message of God's intentions, a message as loud as theophanic thunder[56] to those with ears to hear it.

With the reference to God's *army* the prophet moves from one strand of the bundle of traditions around the Day to another:

I have issued orders to my crusaders
and summoned my heroes to wreak my anger. . . .
Yahweh of hosts is mustering a host for battle. (Isa. 13:3, 4)

This motif, by now an ingredient of the Day of Yahweh but originally independent of it,[57] is echoed here in order to gather up all the martial allusions of vv. 2–9 and crown them with a tremendous crescendo of interpretation. The role assigned by Hebrew eschatology to the agents of God's final wrath is played by the locusts in Joel's presentation. A hostile, irresistible *army* is on the march. The reason why all attempts to check it have failed is because none other than Yahweh leads them in judgment upon his own

52. The same two Heb. verbs are used.
53. *Op. cit.*, p. 419. Cf. J. D. Whiting, *National Geographic Magazine* 28 (1915), p. 525.
54. Cited by S. R. Driver.
55. Kutsch has revealed great insight into Joel 2, but he has failed to see the subtle nature of this allusion when he makes Yahweh the antecedent of *lᵉpānāyw* (*loc. cit.*, p. 88); the prophet goes on to define it as *lip̄ᵉnê ḥêlô,* "before his army."
56. For this significance of *nāṯan qôl,* "produce sound," cf. Ps. 18:13(14). This was another theophanic element that was taken over as a motif of the Day; see J. Jeremias, *Theophanie*. WMANT 10 (1965), pp. 99f.
57. Cf. Isa. 5:26–29; Jer. 5:15–17; Amos 6:14; Hab. 1:5–11.

people. Numerically this force is amazingly strong. Overwhelming armies are traditionally compared with locusts, and so it is an artistically apt reversal to give the locusts a military connotation.[58] They are loyal to Yahweh and storm the capital only at his bidding. Joel uses the theme of the storming of Jerusalem as a recognized part of the ancient tradition enshrined in the Songs of Zion, which doubtless had already been made into an eschatological feature.[59] The strategy of the divine General is directed against his covenant people. Their great Ally against foreign foes in ages past is portrayed as Abyssinia's Mussolini, England's Napoleon, and the Sennacherib of an earlier Judah. God is present indeed among his people, but for bane and not for blessing. Nor was this a normal chastisement from the Lord of history, but the first telltale signs of the End. Here was the inauguration of Judah's Armageddon. Here was prophecy coming true before the eyes of Joel and his contemporaries.

This is the theme to which the prophet is returning at the end of the piece. The Day, announced in v. 2, is now explicitly mentioned after a series of hints throughout the passage. He enhances a reaction of dire alarm by calling the Day "great" or *momentous,* an adjective derived from the classic description of Zeph. 1:14. To it he attaches another, *terrible,* thus making a traditional pair associated with Yahweh's mighty activity on Israel's behalf, which evoked awesome worship.[60] But now Israel is victim of Yahweh's dealings and takes the place of Israel's foes. Joel endeavors to challenge his audience with this shattering perception by posing a final question of despair. God's people are powerless in the face of his wrath,[61] helpless before the onslaught of his forces of final retribution.

This last stanza, though formally a parallel to 1:11f., breaks the bounds of parallelism in the interests of development and climax. The failure of the crops is heightened to a cosmic crisis, while the emotion of sorrow is replaced by helpless fear. Its more obvious function is to round off the piece by reusing the theme of the opening stanza of this second poem, 2:1f. It echoes and intensifies the note of alarm in the light of the significance of the locust-event as the Day of Yahweh in embryo.

Joel has been building up gradually a tremendous interpretation of the sinister reality behind the locust plague. He has taken up the natural impressions of wondering apprehension made upon the observers of the locusts and, by interspersing these impressions with images known to them from eschatological prophecy, he has created a religious nightmare. The

58. Cf. Judg. 6:5; 7:12; Jer. 46:23. For the representation of the locusts as God's instruments of judgment, Thompson, *JNES* 14 (1955), pp. 54f., compares a traditional saying of Mohammed: "Do not kill the locusts, for they are the army of God the Almighty."

59. Cf. Zech. 12:2, 3; 14:1, 2. In Ezek. 38, 39 the land of Israel is threatened. Cf. H.-M. Lutz, *Jahwe, Jerusalem und die Völker*. WMANT 27 (1968), p. 37.

60. Cf., e.g., Deut. 7:21; 10:21; Ps. 106:21f. The use of the phrase in Mal. 4:5 (3:23) and of the later question in Mal. 3:2 is most probably to be regarded as an echo of Joel: in their context they have a secondary ring.

61. Cf. Jer. 10:10.

whole piece is shot through with preternatural coloring. Simple reflections upon the army-like character of the locust masses are turned into somber hints of the divine warfare against sin which marked Israel's Day of Judgment. The transposition is reminiscent of the Elisha story in 2 K. 6, in which his servant's eyes are opened to a metaphysical reality of "horses and chariots of fire" protecting the prophet against his foreign foes. Similarly in Eph. 1:18, 19 Paul prayed that the spiritual eyes of his readers might be enlightened so that they might know the infinite greatness of God's power. With similar yet contrasting purpose Joel seeks to rip away the veil of normal perception and reveal a new dimension of divine power at work in the locusts. His aim has been gradually to arouse in his hearers' insensitive minds and consciences a sense of utter foreboding and a state of intolerable tension. Having strung his hearers to the pitch of feverish excitement warranted by the occasion, he is ready to channel their emotions to a point of spiritual release.

2. *A Call for National Repentance* (2:12–17)

"Now is the time,"
runs Yahweh's oracle; 2+2
"return to me wholeheartedly
by fasting, weeping, and lamenting." 3+3
13 *Tear not just your clothes*
but your hearts, 2+2
and return to Yahweh your God,
because he is kindly and compassionate, 3+3
so patient,
lavish in loyal love,
ready to relent over punishment. 2+2+2
14 *He may turn and relent—who knows?—*
and leave a blessing behind him, 3+3
offering and libation
for Yahweh your God. 2+2

15 *Blow the horn in Zion,*
order a sacred fast,
proclaim a special service. 3+2+2
16 *Assemble the people,*
arrange a religious meeting, 2+2
gather the old men,[62]
assemble the children,
even breastfed babies. 2+2+2
Let the newlywed leave his bedroom,
the bride her place of honeymoon.[63] 3+2

62. See the note on 1:14.
63. Heb. *ḥuppâ,* the room, originally tent, in which the marriage was consummated (cf. 2 Sam. 16:22; Ps. 19:5). Today it is the canopy under which the couple stand at a Jewish wedding.

17 *Between porch and altar*
let the priests weep, 3+2
Yahweh's ministers, and say,
"Take pity, Yahweh, on your people. 3+3
Do not permit your possession to be ridiculed,
a swear word bandied about by the nations.[64] 3+2
Why should it be asked among the peoples,
'Where is their God?' " 3+2

Joel has prepared the people for a summons to repentance in Yahweh's name (v. 12). This he follows with a prophetic exposition of the summons and its grounding in the character of God, expressed in traditional language (vv. 13, 14). These three verses, which comprise the first of three stanzas, contain a motif amply represented in the prophetic literature.[65] A typical example occurs in Amos 5:4–6:

Thus has Yahweh said to the community of Israel:
"Seek me and you will live,
do not seek Bethel. . . ."
Seek Yahweh and you will live,
or else he will attack like fire the community of Joseph.

There the summons is found in a basic pattern of an appeal in the form of the messenger-formula and an admonition, and a motivation made up of the elements of promise, accusation, and threat. This summons partially repeats that structure, omitting the latter two elements. In fact, the threat has been amply represented earlier in his interpretation of the locust plague. At a previous stage in its history the summons to repentance was associated with the covenant mediator in the making and renewal of the covenant.[66] The prophet, in taking up the form as a vehicle of moral challenge, would appear to his hearers in the role of a covenant mediator; and indeed there are a number of allusions to the covenant in the summons.

In the second stanza the priests are urged to call the whole community to a service in which national repentance is to be demonstrated (vv. 15, 16). Finally in v. 17 Joel suggests a form of lament which the priests

64. KJV and RV followed G S V T in taking Heb. *m^eshol* as "rule." While this is linguistically possible, the context does not favor a reference to Gentile domination. Wolff so renders at the expense of interpreting 2:1–11 in terms not of the locusts but of an apocalyptic army. The preceding and following references to ridicule, and the telescoped allusion to the third line of v. 17 in the phrase at the end of v. 19, point rather to a denominative verb from *māshāl,* "byword." Bewer, Wolff, and Ahlström, *JTCJ,* pp. 20f., object that *māshal b^e* elsewhere means either "rule over" or "mock among"; but for *bām,* lit. "against them," cf. the common use of this preposition to introduce the object of other verbs of mocking, as in 2 K. 2:23; 2 Chr. 30:10; Job 17:6 (cf. BDB, p. 89a). There is no need to change to *l^emāshāl baggôyīm,* "to a byword among the nations," with Bewer, Ehrlich, and (similarly) G. R. Driver, *JTS* 39 (1938), p. 400.

65. See T. M. Raitt, "The Prophetic Summons to Repentance," *ZAW* 83 (1971), pp. 30–49, for an analysis. He lists 29 passages, including Jon. 3:7–9.

66. Cf. Ex. 19:5, 6; Deut. 28:1–15; Josh. 24:14, 15; 1 Sam. 7:3 (*ibid.,* pp. 40–42).

may pray in the service. The whole passage forms a conscious counterpart to the three stanzas of 1:13–19, where, first, the priests were similarly challenged to arrange a service for the people, and then Joel engaged in a communal lament, leading in prayer.[67] In this second poem these themes are handled in a heightened, starker form,[68] just as the material earlier in the chapter represents an intensifying of the motivation of 1:2–12.

12 As the climax to all his psychological and theological conditioning the prophet calls for decision. Judah's doom has been inaugurated by the locusts. The divine avalanche has started in the form of the locusts, and if they have had such a devastating effect on the people's fortunes, what hope does the future hold? There is only one way the avalanche may be stemmed. On the people's side it requires immediate action. *Now* is the psychological moment. It signifies both a consequence and a caution; since the people are in their present circumstances of distress, they must respond before it is too late. The immediacy of the challenge represents an element occasionally encountered in the biblical summonses to repentance.[69] It is from this source that its firm place in evangelistic hymnology and preaching is derived.

The prophet stresses that this is no wishful human expedient, no worldly-wise recourse to parry merited punishment. It is Yahweh's own summons that Joel presents, and so it may be acted upon with confidence. The prophets often presuppose that the proclamation and inauguration of punishment for God's people are interim, *ad hoc* measures, closely related to the present state of their hearts and lives.[70] Yahweh's desire was ever that threat and chastisement would make his covenant people think again and come back to him.[71] But so often he was disappointed, as for instance the pathos of the refrain in Amos 4:6–11 attests:

"Yet you did not return to me," runs Yahweh's oracle.

In echo of that refrain exactly the same terminology is used in this positive challenge. Here is their last chance. The call to *return* presupposes the covenant relationship.[72] Joel's contemporaries had evidently strayed from their Shepherd, turning to their own way. Now comes the rallying call to retrace their steps. The people's true habitat is at Yahweh's side, within the sphere of his moral requirements and material blessing. To stray morally is to leave the place of blessing and stumble into the electrified fence of the covenant curse. But as yet there is still time to turn back. Yahweh's voice rings out in tones of warning and concern.

67. Cf. too the repetition of the vocabulary of 1:13, 14 in 2:12–17.

68. Mention of fasting, sanctifying, assembling, and of the phrase *Yahweh your God* (1:14) now occurs twice in the course of 2:12–16.

69. Josh. 24:14; Jer. 26:13; cf. Acts 17:30. Readers of KJV, RV, and RSV are warned that in Jer. 25:5; 35:15 "now" is not temporal nor logical but represents a particle emphasizing the imperative.

70. Cf. Jer. 26:2–6; 36:2, 3.

71. "God . . . speaks in our conscience, but shouts in our pains: it is his megaphone to rouse a deaf world" (C. S. Lewis, *The Problem of Pain* [1940], p. 81).

72. Cf. W. L. Holladay, *The Root Shûbh in the OT* (1958), *passim*.

He will not be satisfied with a perfunctory show of repentance,[73] prompted by a shrewd and selfish desire to save their skins. On one occasion the complaint was made that Judah had not returned to him *wholeheartedly,* but in pretense (Jer. 3:10). Now it is to be sincere and heartfelt. The heart is here the source of "moral purpose and resolve" (S. R. Driver); the reference is to a determined act of will. The change of heart was to be revealed in outward symbols by this people whose culture taught them to wear their hearts on their sleeves. When deep repentance welled up within, it would gush out in demonstrations of humiliation and distress. Yahweh called for the performance of ritual actions to serve as signs of true repentance. Joel had earlier appealed for *fasting* in the context of a national service of humiliation (1:14), and it is to this regular feature of Israelite religious response to a communal crisis that renewed reference is made here. It was regarded as a vehicle of self-renunciation and submission to God, and also as a proof of the earnestness of the accompanying lament and petition. *Weeping and lamenting* were likewise expected as evidence of renouncing a sinful past and turning to God in penitence. Strangely there is no explicit reference to the sin of the people: the rhetorical form here used certainly has room for an accusation in which wrongdoing may be elaborated. Joel's whole interpretation of the locust plague does presuppose serious sin in the life of the community. It is evidently left to the people and priests to search their own hearts and habits for evidence of the sin that God's reaction proved to be there. Self-criticism could be an aid to true repentance, as Lam. 3:40 indicates:

> *Let us test our ways and examine them,*
> *and return to Yahweh.*

13, 14 The prophet now expounds Yahweh's summons and its implications. His homiletical amplification is threefold, like many a good sermon. First he underlines the necessity for sincere repentance and then he holds out the incentives to repentance to be found both in the character of their covenant God and in the prospect of consequent blessing. It was a feature of the lamentation service to strip off or *tear* one's *clothes* as an act of self-despair before donning sackcloth.[74] Joel issues a striking warning against a dichotomy of purpose and performance, of motive and the mechanics of repentance. Yahweh's appeal had been for penitence within the cultic sphere, neither conscience nor cult being sufficient without the other. Joel knows too well the duplicity of the human heart to let the occasion pass without stressing the necessity for both, and cautioning against a hollow ritualism.[75] He urges literally, "Tear your hearts and not your clothes." He does not hereby speak of alternatives, any more than John in counselling, "Do not love in word and speech but in deed and truth" (1 John 3:18) was

73. Cf. Hos. 6:1–3 in the light of 6:4.
74. Isa. 32:11; cf. 2 K. 19:1; 22:11.
75. Cf. Isa. 29:13; 58:1–5.

deprecating loving words.[76] The prophet calls for "a broken and contrite heart" (Ps. 51:17[19]) as the inspiration of the ritual acts. The people's *hearts* are stony and hard, "like adamant, refusing to hear the law . . . and so great wrath has been shown by Yahweh of hosts" (Zech. 7:12).[77] They need to be shattered into tender sensitivity to God's will.

Joel reissues the challenge to repentance on Yahweh's behalf,[78] grounding it in the theological truth that he is *your God,* the God of the covenant, who both claims his people's allegiance and cares for them with a forbearing love which "is not willing that any should perish but that all should come to repentance" (2 Pet. 3:9). *Your God* reflects one side of the traditional formula of the covenant.[79] A longer formula is echoed in the hymnlike recital of proven beneficent attributes of the covenant God, which Joel's audience must often have heard in the cultic poetry of the temple.[80] In its full form it was intimately associated with Yahweh's renewal of the covenant on Sinai after the golden calf incident (Ex. 34:6, 7). From there this "perfect example of propositional theology,"[81] in which the character of God is described without reference to his mighty acts on Israel's behalf, had a profound influence on the OT writings. It is quoted as a credal statement in eight passages[82] and echoed in a number of others. Joel takes up this familiar language to explain the surprising about-face from a depiction of Yahweh as dire enemy of his people (2:1–11) to an invitation to repentance (2:12). He need not quote the second half of the formula concerning the divine judgment upon sinners, for this theme he has already stressed at length.[83]

The invitation is a corollary of Yahweh's goodness, his forgiveness of repentant sinners. The very context indicates that this is no offer of grace to the sinful that they may go on sinning with impunity; it presupposes a change of heart and life. To the repentant, Yahweh shows compassion like a father to his child who is sorry for his misbehavior.[84] His people had often provoked him, yet still he cared and yearned to show them that kind of covenant love which would not let them go.[85] His stern threats were not

76. For this well-attested biblical idiom of relative negation whereby "not merely . . . but also" is rhetorically expressed for emphasis, especially in prophetic statements concerning sacrifice, such as Hos. 6:6, see C. Lattey, *JTS* 42 (1941), pp. 155–165.

77. Cf. Ezek. 11:19; 36:26.

78. Heb. *shûḇ 'aḏ,* "return to" (v. 12), is stylistically varied as *shûḇ 'el*. Both occur together elsewhere; cf. Deut. 30:2, 10; Hos. 13:1f.(2f.).

79. Cf. Gen. 17:8; Lev. 26:12; Jer. 7:23; Hos. 5:4.

80. Cf. J. Scharbert, "Formgeschichte und Exegese von Ex. 34, 6f und seiner Parallelen," *Biblica* 38 (1957), pp. 130–150; W. Beyerlin, *Origins and History of the Oldest Sinaitic Traditions* (E.T. ²1965), pp. 136–138, 164; R. C. Dentan, "The Literary Affinities of Exodus xxxiv 6f.," *VT* 13 (1963), pp. 34–51.

81. Dentan, *loc. cit.*, p. 36.

82. Num. 14:18; Neh. 9:17; Ps. 86:15; 103:8; 145:8; Joel 2:13; Jon. 4:2; Nah. 1:3.

83. Dentan's claim that Joel's replacement is "more congenial" (*loc. cit.*, p. 39) ignores the context.

84. Ps. 103:13; cf. Luke 15:20.

85. Heb. *ḥeseḏ;* cf. the comment on Mic. 6:8.

inflexible, but subordinate to the higher purpose of his people's welfare.[86] This divine relenting is not to be regarded as fickleness or an irresolute retraction of a formerly absolute decree, as if God dillydallies or cannot make up his mind. The emphasis here is on the personal relationship of God with his people and his varying attitude toward them according to their sensitivity to his will.[87]

Joel's theology is not theoretical but based on the past experiences of the covenant people time and time again. Yet past experience is not an infallible guide to God's future action. Lest his audience shrug off the seriousness of the situation and think in terms of an easy solution, the prophet stresses the mere possibility of Yahweh's pardon in response to his people's repentance. There is a reserve about his reaction that is beyond man's ken, an element of mystery which is the safeguard of his sovereignty. The OT periodically witnesses to this divine trait which made agnostics out of men who were closest to Yahweh's counsels.[88] The prophet's overall aim is to create in his hearers "a desire for the grace of God that they might by degrees gather courage and yet not immediately rise to confidence but that they might come anxiously to God and with much deliberation, duly considering their offences" (Calvin). Men may not presume upon God and take him and his grace for granted; they are called to cast themselves upon his inscrutable will with a conviction of their utter unworthiness and leave the rest to him. Joel is issuing a call to faith not in a doctrinal system, but in an intensely personal God, a faith that is only partially sighted and trusts in the transcendent God, who alone can see what lies around the corner. Contrast the spurious words of repentance in Hos. 6:1–3, which represent Yahweh in terms of Canaanite fertility religion as a metaphysical machine under human control, which automatically delivers the goods when the money is put in and the button is pressed.

But the hope was that Yahweh would *turn* from his present dire policy as the people turned in faith to him. He had been set on a path of judgment, marching at the head of the locust battalions. His mighty anger

86. Here and in Jon. 4:2 the last clause concerning relenting replaces a standard phrase "and faithfulness" because of the specific needs of the context and situation.

87. "The purpose of anthropomorphisms is to make God accessible to man. They hold open the door for encounter and dialogue between God's will and man's will. They represent God as person. They avoid the error of presenting God as a careless and soulless abstract Idea or fixed Principle standing over against man like a strong, silent battlement. God is . . . offended at men's sins yet with a ready ear for their supplication, and compassion for their confession of guilt. In a word, God is a living God" (L. Köhler, *OT Theology* [E.T. 1957], pp. 24f.). "By contrast, however, when certain anthropopathisms are endangering the idea of God, [the prophets'] voice is heard in clear condemnation. 'God is not a man that he should lie; neither the son of man that he should repent'; the purpose of both Num. 23:19 and 1 Sam. 15:29 in making this declaration is to combat the erroneous idea that it is easy to talk God round, and that his threats and promises are not to be taken seriously" (W. Eichrodt, *Theology of the OT*, vol. 2 [E.T. 1961], p. 216).

88. Ex. 32:30; 1 Sam. 6:5; 2 Sam. 12:22; Lam. 3:29; Amos 5:15; Jon. 3:9; Zeph. 2:3; cf. Acts 8:22; 2 Tim. 2:25.

had been brandished against Judah in a special intervention. If the people repented, there was a chance that he would withdraw at this eleventh hour and demonstrate his abandonment of punishment by tokens of *blessing*. Blessing is here viewed in terms of material symbols of divine favor: Joel supplies his own commentary on the word in vv. 19–27. When there was harmony between Yahweh and his people, it was revealed in a harmony between people and land resulting in good crops:[89] "He will bless the fruit . . . of your ground, your grain, wine and oil . . . upon the land which he promised on oath to your forefathers to give you" (Deut. 7:13). The prophet had a concern for Judah's religious responsibility to God as a not unimportant part of the covenant relationship; this material harmony would be used to demonstrate the renewal of spiritual harmony that would occur when the lapsed temple routine had started up again and was running its sweet, uninterrupted course. The covenant would thus come to its intended fruition in fellowship, as the repeated covenant term *your God* implies. His people would give back to him what they had first received. The beautiful cycle of provision and praise, of divine blessing and human worship, would be re-created. His gifts were by no means to be taken and dissipated in any selfish spirit, but used for his glory. There is in this religious concern of Joel and his community fine evidence of a sense of stewardship as upholders of the cultic obligations inherent in the covenant. Its spirit finds an echo in the prayer attributed to David in 1 Chr. 29:14 concerning gifts for the new temple:

> *"Who am I and what is my people that we are able to make voluntary contributions on this scale? It all comes from you, and from your own hand have we given it to you."*

15, 16 The next stanza moves briskly to the practical implementation of the attitude of repentance just counselled. Joel views religious organization as the necessary means of attaining spiritual ends. The urgency of the situation is reflected in the staccato way he raps out instructions. He takes up the divine call of 2:1, now making it quite clear that it is to a temple festival that the blast of the *horn* is to summon the people.[90] He evidently addresses his instructions to the priests. The orders for a *special service* of fasting and lamentation are repeated from 1:14 and then expanded in greater detail. The people are to be bidden to a great penitential assembly to which they will gather as the covenant community at worship.[91] It is stressed that none is exempt from the summons. The intensity of the people's repentance in vv. 13f. is to be matched by its extensiveness (Weiser). Graybeard and youngster are to gather at the temple; not even the youngest members of the theocracy may stay at home. So important is the meeting that all the shareholders in the covenant, as it were, must be present. The entire

89. Contrast the cursed ground which produces reluctantly as a corollary of sin in Gen. 3:17–19.

90. Cf. Lev. 25:9; Ps. 81:3(4).

91. Heb. *qāhāl*.

community stands under the shadow of divine judgment, and so must meet with God, every face turned heavenward in appeal against his wrath. The most helpless through old age or youth must parade, symbolizing the helplessness of the whole people.

So serious is the crisis that a normal privilege is temporarily withdrawn. A bridegroom was usually given compassionate leave from military and other public duties: "He is to stay at home free of obligation for a year, to make happy the wife he has married" (Deut. 24:5). Since military service was a religious undertaking, it is feasible that the young couple would generally be released from cultic requirements for a period. At a later period newlyweds were excused from reciting the set daily prayers on their wedding day and, if the marriage was not consummated, up to the end of the next sabbath.[92] But for once such a privilege is withdrawn. At the moment there is no place for normally legitimate human joy. The atmosphere of mourning must pervade every quarter in the hope that Yahweh will heed the concerted pleas of his people and turn away from wrath.

17 It was the priests' task to offer up prayers on behalf of the assembled community, as their representatives before God. In this final stanza Joel urges them to occupy what was evidently a customary position. If the temple of which Joel speaks was that built by Zerubbabel, it was presumably based on Solomon's in design. In front of the temple building was an open forecourt, divided by a wall from an outer court. It was in the inner court that the priests were to congregate, while the laity would be assembled in the outer one. On the west side of the inner court were the temple steps, at the top of which were situated two free-standing pillars and the doors into the vestibule or *porch*.[93] In the inner court stood the *altar,* the large altar where burnt offerings were sacrificed.[94] It was in this area, on the west side of the inner court, that the priests were to perform their intercessory ministry; in 2 Chr. 4:9 the inner court is in fact referred to as "the priests' court." Ezekiel mentions the position designated by Joel as the one where he saw the abominable sight of "about twenty-five men . . . bowing down to the sun in the east" (Ezek. 8:16).[95] This place was thus the traditional site where the priests were to stand and engage in lamentation as Yahweh's ordained ministers.

Joel suggests a pattern of prayer suitable for the occasion. Its form and generalized nature are typical of the communal lament. Two petitions are followed by a plaintive question which presents the main basis of the appeal for divine intervention. There are interesting parallels with Ps. 79, a lament over enemy invastion and destruction of the sanctuary:

> *May your compassion come quickly to meet us.* (v. 8)
> *We have become the object of our neighbors' ridicule.* (v. 4)

92. *Berakoth* 2:5.
93. 1 K. 6:3; 7:21.
94. 1 K. 8:22, 64. In Herod's temple the altar was 22 cubits from the porch (*Middoth* 5:1).
95. Cf. 1 Macc. 7:36; Matt. 23:35.

Why should the nations ask,
"Where is their God?" (v. 10)

The lament form had standardized elements which could be used whatever the precise cause of distress might be.[96]

The prophet does not wait till the end to adduce reasons for Yahweh to act. The references to his strong links with Judah in the petitions also have this purpose. Yahweh is appealed to as having a vested interest in the community: it is *your people, your possession*. This was the basis of the plea of Moses in Deut. 9:26, 29. A similar motif appears in a psalm of lament at Ps. 74:2.[97] Disloyal though they have been, the community still regard themselves as under Yahweh's patronage and protection. To him they appeal as a powerful Being who is both able to intervene to alter the situation and, in view of his covenant character outlined in v. 13, predisposed to accept Israel's urgent pleas as their covenant Partner. Joel's exhortation to them in v. 13 to honor their covenant responsibility to their God is here matched with a plea to God to honor his covenant obligations to his people. The two halves of the traditional covenant formula are echoed as the expression of Joel's desire for a renewed fellowship of harmony.

A sensitive shrinking from the taunts of foreign observers is a regular motif of the national lament.[98] In an environment where each people attributed its well-being to the blessing of its deity, the conclusion would be drawn from Judah's plight that their God was weak, and powerless to defend his nation from humiliation. The sneering question is brought to God in another, deprecating question, as often in the lament.[99] The honor of Yahweh was at stake, and it is this plea that the prayer emphasizes in order to encourage his intervention. "For thy name's sake" is the burden of the appeal. The beseeching cry of Ps. 79:9 is implicit here:

Help us, O God our Savior,
for the glory of your name.
Rescue us and forgive our sins
for your name's sake.

Joel has been laboring to wean the people away from indifference and insensitivity to the things of God. This suggested prayer marks the climax of his endeavors: the people's desperate flinging of themselves upon Yahweh as the one who is able to save those who otherwise are helpless, a recognition of the close ties that bind them to him, and a concern for his glory.

96. Cf. A. Weiser, *The Psalms* (E.T. 1962), p. 67, commenting on psalms of lament: "The similarity of the phrases used in these psalms, phrases which are couched in general terms and often give the impression of being stereotyped . . . can probably be traced back to the fact that the laments originated and were used in the cult, where the general predominates over the particular."

97. For Israel as Yahweh's *possession* see also Deut. 32:9; 1 Sam. 10:1; 2 Sam. 14:16; 20:19.

98. Besides Ps. 79:4 cf. Ps. 44:13f.; 89:41(42); 109:25.

99. Besides Ps. 79:10 see Ps. 42:3, 10(4, 11); 115:2; Mic. 7:10.

II. DIVINE ORACLES (2:18–3[4]:21)

Laments in the OT are sometimes followed by a divine oracle in which Yahweh, through a prophet, assures his people that their prayers will be answered (or sometimes rejected). In 2 Chr. 20 a great penitential assembly is held in reaction to news of enemy invasion. King Jehoshaphat addresses a lament to God, while all the men of Judah stand listening with their wives and children. After the lament, a Levite is inspired to give an answer of reassurance and promise of victory, which he delivers partly in Yahweh's name and partly in his own by way of amplification. Then the community worship and offer praise. Such a response must have been a regular sequel to the communal lament. Although evidence for it is scanty in the Psalms, there are examples in the prophetic literature that clearly follow an established cultic pattern.[1] It is this pattern that is exemplified in the second part of the book, which comprises a series of divine oracles in encouraging response to the people's lament.

A. MATERIAL AND SPIRITUAL PROMISES (2:18–32[3:5])

1. Immediate Blessings (2:18–27)

Then Yahweh showed passionate concern for his country
and spared his people. 3+2
19 *Yahweh said*
in reply to his people: 2+2
"I am soon going to supply you with grain,
wine, and oil, as much as you want. 4+4
I shall no longer allow you
to be ridiculed by the nations. 3+2
20 *Of the northerners I shall relieve you, sending them far away.*
I shall drive them to a country parched and waste, 4+4
their front ranks to the sea in the east,
their rear ranks to the sea in the west. 3+3
The stench of them will rise,
their foul smell[2] *will rise*
because of their high and mighty deeds." 2+2+2

21 *Do not fear, ground,*

1. Cf. Ps. 12:5(6); 60:6–8(8–10); Isa. 33:10–13; Jer. 4:1, 2 (cf. 3:21–25); Hos. 14:4–7(5–8); Mic. 7:11–13.

2. Heb. *tsaḥ*ᵃ*nāṯô* is a *hapax legomenon,* but the root appears in Aramaic and later Hebrew, and indeed in Sir. 11:12. It has been suggested that the previous clause is a later gloss, inspired by Isa. 34:3, to explain the rare word, especially in view of the syntactical irregularity of *w*ᵉ*ṯa'al* after *w*ᵉ*'ālâ* (Merx, Smith, S. R. Driver, *et al.*). G. R. Driver, *JTS* 39 (1938), p. 400, noted that the clause should be retained as necessary to the rhythm of 3+3 varied by 2+2+2: he proposed transposing to *w*ᵉ*'ālāṯ* or *w*ᵉ*'āl*ᵉ*ṯâ*. But probably MT should be retained as the more difficult reading.

rejoice and be glad
because of Yahweh's great and mighty deeds. 2+2+3
22 *Do not fear, wild beasts:*
the prairie pastures will turn green, 3+3
the trees will bear fruit,
fig tree and vine will yield a maximum crop. 3+4
23 *And you, sons of Zion,*
rejoice and be glad
because of Yahweh your God: 2+2+2
for he will give you
the autumn rain in token of covenant harmony 2+2
and send you down the rain,
the autumn and spring rains as before. 3+3

24 *Threshing floors will be crammed with wheat*
and vats will overflow with wine and oil, 3+4
25 *and so I shall give you back the years*
eaten by the swarming locusts, 3+3
by the hopper, the destroyer, and the shearer,
my great army
that I launched against you. 3+2+3
26 *You will eat your fill*
and praise the name of Yahweh your God, 3+4
who has worked wonders for you,
and never again will my people be humiliated. 4+4
27 *Then you will know that I am here in Israel,*
that I am Yahweh your God and there is no other,
and never again will my people be humiliated. 4+4+4

After a short narrative introduction the first divine oracle comes in two parts, vv. 19, 20 and 24–27. It is split by a prophetic song of encouragement which applies God's promises to the hearts of his hearers, and calls for a joyful response (vv. 21–23). Both the two-part oracle and the song present a glorious reversal of the grim situation of distress depicted in 1:4–2:17. Earlier motifs are deliberately taken up and put in a new setting of salvation. It is mainly the factually descriptive phraseology of 1:4–20 that is echoed, but elements from 2:3, 11, 17 are also repeated in these promises of victory and blessing.

18–20 We are intended to assume that Joel's appeals preserved in the preceding part of the book were successful. Evidently the people did gather to a national service of fasting and lamentation, and the priests duly offered prayers on behalf of a genuinely repentant community. It was Joel's privilege, of which his earlier efforts surely made him worthy, to be the bearer of an oracle of salvation. The crisis was to be averted; the tide of calamity that threatened to engulf the community was to turn. The priests' prayer of v. 17 was to be answered. It is to this prayer that both the prophetic introduction and the divine oracle allude. The introductory narrative reports Yahweh's reaction and interprets it in terms of covenant devotion. The narrative form is used by other prophets to describe Yahweh's intervention in place of an oracle,[3] but Joel combines the two forms.

The prayer that pleaded that Judah was the *people* of God is shown to have been effective. Yahweh did honor the obligations his grace had laid upon him, and twice Joel takes up the term, savoring the faithfulness of God. Lest the people congratulate themselves on their sincerity and success, the prophet also twice mentions pointedly that *Yahweh,* to whom was addressed the prayer for his intervention, was alone the great agent of salvation. The prayer for clemency is noted as answered by the use of a verb of similar meaning. Yahweh has proved himself to be a faithful God who is not deaf to pleas for mercy. At the last moment a reprieve has come from the Judge, and he has given a fresh opportunity to live aright, to go and sin no more. In 1:6 the statement that locusts had invaded God's land was intended as a hint that, despite his obvious hostility to his sinning people in this use of locusts to chastise them, yet in a sense he was disposed to act otherwise because it was his own property that was being damaged. This note is struck again here. He intervened to protect the land that was *his* and which he had entrusted to *his people,* "a land," we are told elsewhere, "which Yahweh your God cares for" (Deut. 11:12). When either suffered, it aroused strong and deep emotions in his heart. He had now rushed to show his *passionate concern,* his keen ardor which would not allow his rights to be infringed. This zealous or jealous love is a passion that in the OT can show itself in judgment upon Israel, but here it is protective, and is to cause Yahweh to drive away the trespassers from his property (v. 20).[4]

The divine proclamation begins with a typical formula pledging God's imminent intervention in a situation of distress or disorder.[5] In view of the people's repentance, his attitude toward them has necessarily changed, and once again they may enjoy the material good of the covenant relationship. Joel had recorded in 1:10 the sorry state of the three traditional products of the land of promise, *grain, wine, and oil,* as a result of the locusts' depredations. They were tokens of harmony between Yahweh and his people, his blessing upon an obedient partner in the covenant. Judah has now stepped back into the place of blessing. The promise of plenty to eat falls with little impact on the ears of an affluent society, but to a community that had struggled against famine and economic hardship and had seen pests destroying the result of laborious toil, it was a promise of life itself. The promise of these essential crops is combined with one of plentiful food in Deut. 11:13–15, a passage that contains many of the motifs found in vv. 19–26:

> *"If you obey my commands which I am giving you today, by loving Yahweh your God and serving him with all your heart and soul, I shall give your land rain in its season, the autumn*

3. Isa. 59:13–17; Hab. 3:3–6.
4. Cf. Ezek. 39:25; Zech. 1:14; 8:2.
5. Heb. *hin*ᵉ*nî* + participle; see the comment on Mic. 2:3.

rain and the spring rain, to enable you to harvest your grain, wine, and oil. I shall provide grass in your fields for your cattle, and you will eat and have plenty.''

These are covenant promises proffered to those mindful of covenant obligations.

The oracle then takes up the specific prayer of v. 17, just as the prophetic introduction did. To a people now at last sensitive to Yahweh's will comes the assurance that they will cease to be subjected by Yahweh to the ridicule of foreigners. His forceful intervention will alter the humiliating situation and restore their fortunes so that other nations will no longer have occasion to jeer. The instruments of his wrath, now needed no more, will be swept away. The locusts, subject of the appeals of lamentation in the earlier part of the book, had constituted a scourge laid across the people's backs, an oppressive burden which had sapped their strength,[6] but soon they would know the sweet relief of freedom from this affliction.

The locusts are referred to collectively as ''the northerner.'' The insects normally attack Judah from the south or southeast, borne by the prevailing winds, but cases are known of approach from the north. The plague that hit Jerusalem in 1915 came from the northeast.[7] Presumably in Joel's time the onset had come from the north; the ensuing references to geographical features in the other three directions support this inference. But as in 2:1–11 the locusts were seen through psychic spectacles, so here the present term has a numinous dimension superimposed upon the natural. Earlier prophets had given dread description of the ''enemy from the north.'' The phrase has something of the flavor of Tolkien's grim hosts of Mordor. In Ezek. 38:15; 39:2 the apocalyptic hordes of Gog come from the farthest north to destroy Judah, only to be smashed by Yahweh's counterattack. Even before Ezekiel's time Jeremiah had made the theme his own, using it repeatedly to describe the uncanny forces of evil that Yahweh would employ as his agents to punish sinful Judah:

''I am bringing disaster from the north
and great destruction.
The lion has left his lair,
the destroyer of nations is on the march.
He has set out from his home
to lay your country waste.''[8]

The motif of the enemy from the north is clearly related to that of the attacking army used in 1:6; 2:2–11, and it is employed in the oracle as an echo of the earlier theme. Joel treats as grist for his mill all manner of older prophetic concepts. Here he applies to the locusts an eschatological notion

6. Heb. *mē'alêkem*, ''from upon you,'' is used in a similar context in Ex. 10:17.

7. Whiting, *loc. cit.*, p. 513.

8. Jer. 4:6, 7; cf. 1:13–15; 6:1–5, 22–26, etc. It is probable that Jeremiah took up an existing popular notion apart from the historical connotation of the north as the frequent source of invasion. See A. Lauha, *Zaphon. Der Norden und die Nordvölker im AT* (1943), pp. 75f., 79–89, and the discussions of Kapelrud and Ahlström, *JTCJ*, pp. 32–34. The north is not only

colored by both Jeremiah's and Ezekiel's usage. The insects had been the dire instruments of divine wrath for the people's sin; now that they had repented, Yahweh would turn against the locusts and drive them out of his land.

The implicit means by which he was to destroy them may be discerned from the description of the ending of the locust plague in Ex. 10:19:

> *Yahweh made a very strong west wind veer round so that it lifted the locusts and thrust them into the reed sea; not one locust was left on Egyptian territory.*

Here we are to envisage a strong wind rising in the northwest and veering round to the northeast. Those at the head of the swarm would be dashed into the Dead Sea and the last ones into the Mediterranean,[9] while the main body would perish in the desert to the south of Judah, where nothing grew for them to eat.

A realistic touch is added in the gruesome reference to the decomposition of the drowned insects washed up on the shores. Jerome mentions that he had witnessed locust swarms over Judea driven by winds into the Dead Sea and the Mediterranean, and had observed the beaches filled with stinking heaps of dead locusts which endangered the health of man and beast. The intention in emphasizing to the people this offensive phenomenon was "to assure them of the total destruction of the locusts" (Bewer). It is significant that *stench* in its other two uses in the OT occurs in a military setting of corpses on the battlefield.[10] Probably such an association is intended, and the locusts are viewed still in military guise.[11] The invaders will meet with a resounding defeat at the hands of Judah's great Ally, invincible though they were in 2:2–11. Yahweh, formerly at the head of this army (2:11) and enemy of his people, is now on their side again as a result of their change of heart and life. The curse passes to the locusts, which are to be repulsed and destroyed.

The reason given for their destruction is that "they have done great things," in the bad sense of acting in a highhanded manner.[12] There is

---

the Semitic mythological location of the home of the gods (cf. Ps. 48:2[3]; Isa. 14:13), but also apparently the source of baleful powers. Rudolph marries the two uses by interpreting here as "divine messengers."

9. Cf. Deut. 11:24; Ezek. 47:18; Zech. 14:8. There are no grounds for postulating with Kapelrud and Keller a mythological reference to the cosmic ocean surrounding the earth. For the effect of changing winds on flying locusts cf. the report cited by S. R. Driver: "The wind was blowing from the north-east and they were borne along upon it. Afterwards the wind veered round, and the locusts turned with it."

10. Heb. *bᵉʾōsh*: Isa. 34:3; Amos 4:10.

11. Heb. *pānāyw,* "their front," has a martial ring: cf. 2 Sam. 10:9; 11:15.

12. Keil compares German *grosstun.* There is no necessity to delete this clause as a doublet of that in v. 21 (*BHK,* Delcor); nor to insert "Yahweh" (Weiser, *BHS*), since a third person reference would be out of place in this *Jahwerede;* nor even to read a first person *'agdîl* (Bewer, Ehrlich, Sellin). For the contrast between vv. 20 and 21 cf. Ps. 35:26 *hammagdîlîm 'ālay,* "who do great things against me," of the psalmist's enemies, and v. 27 *yigdal yhwh,* "let Yahweh be great."

probably a reminiscence here of the proclamation of the failure of Assyria's attack on Judah in Isa. 10. The Assyrian was not his own master but "the rod of (Yahweh's) anger," used against Judah, "the people of (his) wrath." But he had overstepped the divine mandate and indulged in arrogance and brutality. Let those whom God uses beware lest they turn their service into a platform for egotism! Yahweh would show who was in control, promised Isaiah, by cutting down to size the power-inflated Assyrian. This theme Joel appears to echo, rhetorically deducing motive from effect.[13] His aim is to stress Yahweh's overall control and the subjection of the locusts, all-powerful though they seem, to his will. Now that Judah had repented there was no place in Yahweh's purposes for the locust army. They were doomed as surely as the Assyrians of old. Yahweh viewed with abhorrence the violation of his territory[14] and gladly took the opportunity to evict the invaders.

21–23 Joel breaks into the oracle with a prophetic song of praise. This well-established form is an adaptation of a cultic hymn, used by the prophets in order to convey God's message by means of its enthusiastic and informative motifs. It follows the cultic pattern by issuing a call to praise. But whereas in the Psalms the accompanying reason for praise might lie in a succinct description of God's attributes and general dealings with men, or in a specific act already done on his people's behalf, the prophets sang of an event that God was about to create.[15] The community members are bidden to respond to God's promise of salvation. They are urged to take a joyous leap of faith and to transcend the dismal present by praising him for what is as good as done, since his word guarantees its fulfilment. A decisive change has occurred and a new situation has been brought about. Thus the "prophetic" perfect is not infrequently found in this speech-form.[16]

This use of the perfect is also characteristic of another form that the prophet echoes.[17] The cry *Do not fear* has its home in the oracle of salvation delivered at the sanctuary, which gave assurance that a prayer of lament had been answered:

> *"You drew near when I called on you;*
> *you said, 'Do not fear.'* " (Lam. 3:57)

Accordingly it normally comes direct from Yahweh, backed by some such divine substantiation as "I shall help you," or "I am with you";[18] but it can also be used in an authoritative report by a priest or other cultic official concerning divine response to a lament.[19] It is quite appropriate that the prophets took over this declaration of good news to the sufferer who had

13. Compare *l^ehagdîl,* "to act greatly," with *gōḏel l^eḇāḇ,* "greatness of mind," Isa. 10:13, and *yiṯgaddēl,* "show oneself to be great," Isa. 10:15.
14. Cf. Isa. 14:25, "I shall break the Assyrian in *my land.*"
15. Cf. Westermann, *The Praise of God in the Psalms* (E.T. 1965), pp. 142–44. See Deut. 32:43; Isa. 44:23; 49:13; 52:9f.; 54:1–3; Jer. 31:7; Zeph. 3:14f.; Zech. 2:10(14); 9:9f.
16. E.g., Isa. 44:23; 49:13; Zeph. 3:15.
17. See Westermann, *Isaiah 40–66* (E.T. 1969), pp. 67–73.
18. Cf. Isa. 41:10; 43:1, etc.
19. Cf. Deut. 20:3; 2 Chr. 20:17.

made supplication out of the depths of his humiliation.[20] In view of the military allusions of earlier verses, it is noteworthy that the cry that commands an end to fear occurs frequently in a context of enemy attack.[21]

The passage is a deliberate reversal of the bad news Joel was forced to deliver in the earlier part of the book. The terms of his lament and prayer in 1:15–20 are reused with a new air of exhilaration. Joy and gladness need be absent no longer (1:16), urges the prophet on two occasions. To the drought-dry countryside (1:17–20) rain is to bring new life. The *wild beasts,* whose whimpering prayers Joel had earlier brought to Yahweh (1:20), are told to take heart, for he is to intervene to change the situation. The *prairie pastures,* though still brown and barren (1:19, 20), are to be *green* once more. The *trees,* though still like relics of some great conflagration (1:19), are to become alive again and *bear fruit.* The prayer to Yahweh who is "our God" (1:16, 19) is to be answered by mighty acts of blessing accomplished by Yahweh who is *your God,* and this is made clear in the song both at the start and finish. "Repentance has made such a revolution possible; divine grace has made it actual" (von Orelli)—or rather, certain to be enacted.

The threefold calls to lament and accompanying reasons in 1:5–12 stressed that the whole community was to lament; they find their counterpart in these individualizing threefold reasoned calls to joy, addressed to the community and its environment. Human, animal, and plant life is to be re-created with a glorious total harmony of divine blessing, a striking contrast for the reader of the OT to the threefold effect of the Fall in Gen. 3:14–19. Curse is to give way to blessing. It is not surprising that the motifs representing the divine curse in 1:5–20 are echoed here. The *fig tree* and *vine,* hard hit by the plague (1:7, 12), are to yield bumper crops.[22] *Zion* should not *rejoice* instead of mourn (1:8–10). The *ground,* clad in its shroud of woe (1:10), is told to take heart in anticipation of the *great deeds* of Yahweh. He is to effect a transformation in keeping with the transformed hearts of his people and the restored spiritual harmony. "Rain and harvest are not merely physical benefits but religious sacraments: signs that God has returned to his people and that his zeal is again stirred on their behalf" (G. A. Smith).

In lyrical tones the prophet invites the people to take to heart God's promises by changing their mood of fear and despair to one of joy. His specific appeals and promises of individual blessings to each group in turn are rhetorical devices used to impart the message that everybody and everything are to enter into the good of God's outpoured grace. Joel urges a response of thanksgiving and praise from the community, such as the return from exile called forth:

20. Cf. Isa. 51:7; 54:4.
21. Num. 21:34; Josh. 8:1, etc.
22. This is strictly irrelevant to the present context, but Joel deliberately adds it as a poetic contrast to ch. 1. Heb. *ḥêlām,* "their strength," signifies their utmost, "all they are capable of producing" (Wade).

Yahweh has done great things for us;
we are glad. (Ps. 126:3)

As in earlier passages the locust plague had been described in terms evocative of God's *mighty* acts of old, so the promised deliverance is to be a demonstration of his power exerted on Judah's behalf. A new chapter was in process of being written in the salvation history of Israel. Joel has a tremendous sense of being involved in a wonderful work of grace. The God of past glories was to reveal himself again. He bears glad and excited testimony to a living and powerful God who is to work in the lives of his people. There is a pointed contrast to the greatness of the locust plague and the threat it constituted to Judah.[23] Great as the danger was, Yahweh is greater still. Joel's song is a prelude to Paul's cry of confident faith in the triumph of God's salvation: "If God is for us, who is against us?" (Rom. 8:31–39). For both prophet and apostle the greatness of the opposition is bound to shrink as they contemplate the greatness of their God, and fear evaporates. God's renewed provision of earthly necessities is for Joel no mundane thing but a seal of divine faithfulness to be hailed with festal glee and praise.

Joel comes to a plain statement of his meaning in his appeal to the *sons of Zion,* evidently the national community congregated in the temple area for the service of lamentation.[24] The verbs now have their full cultic flavor as expressions of fervent ritual praise at the sanctuary. The prophet calls his audience to anticipate by faith the future blessings of Yahweh.[25] He selects as the climax of joy the gift of *rain,* upon which depend the earlier gifts of green pastures and fruit-laden trees. The mention of rain accords with the promise of Deut. 11:13–15, cited above. There is a close link too between the motifs of this passage and the form of the covenant promise in Lev. 26:3, 4:

"If you walk in my statutes . . . , I shall give you your rains in their seasons, the land will yield its produce and the trees in the countryside will yield their fruit."

Joel seems to be echoing both passages. While Deut. 11 mentions grass and Lev. 26 fruit, both are combined here. Like Deut. 11, the prophet specifies the traditional two parts of the rainy season, the *autumn rain*[26] and the *spring*

23. See n. 12 above.
24. Cf. the parallelism in Ps. 149:2.
25. The verbs with Yahweh as subject are still prophetic perfects, as in vv. 21f., in harmony with the form employed. For the future sense of *wayyôreḏ* cf. Mic. 2:13 and note.
26. Deut. employs the usual form *yôreh,* Joel uses *môreh,* which probably occurs in this sense at Ps. 84:6(7). Since this must be the meaning at the end of the verse, it is natural to take it in the same sense here (Kapelrud, Thompson). Duhm, Bewer, G. R. Driver (*loc. cit.*), and Rudolph read *yôreh* for *môreh*[2] with 34 Heb. mss., but this is surely a standardizing secondary reading. Driver, *loc. cit.,* pp. 400f., endorsed van Hoonacker's suggestion to read *marweh,* "saturation," for *môreh*[1]. G S "food" apparently misread *mwrh*[1], relating it to *brh,* "eat": cf. the same equivalent in G at 2 Sam. 13:5, 7, 10 for *biryâ* and in Ps. 69:21(22) for *bārûṯ* (K. A. Vollers, *ZAW* 4 [1884], p. 14). Bewer, Wolff (*ma'ᵃḵāl*), and NEB ("good

rain. The former normally began in October or November, and was vital for giving the ground a good soaking before plowing and sowing. The latter refers to the lighter rainfall of March and April which brought the growing crops to maturity.[27]

The prophet piles up and partially repeats various terms for rain.[28] He revels in the idea of rain, lovely rain. Undernourished prisoners of war in the Far East daydreamed constantly of food, we are told; certainly the minds of Joel's contemporaries must often have lingered on the theme of rain. He takes up this wistful craving and echoes it in his heartening promise. All around the landscape is still parched, but in their hearts he bids the people praise God for the rains that are now sure to come. The covenant relationship is restored; they are right with God once more. They can expect the rain as a sign of this rightness or covenant "righteousness" in accord with the ancient promises of Deut. 11 and Lev. 26. When all was well between God and his people, the physical blessings, including rain, were sure to follow. Judah is once more in this happy state of normal relations with Yahweh and can expect the rain *in token of covenant harmony*.[29]

---

food") accept G's reading. Weiser is among those who have seen here a wordplay, taking this and the next word as "that which points to, indicates [Hiphil participle] prosperity." Ehrlich repointed the prefixed object sign *'eṯ-* as *'ōṯ*, "sign," and has been followed by Sellin, Rudolph, and NEB mg. ("a sign, pointing to prosperity"). A personal version of this view, "teacher of righteousness," was evidently the standard early Jewish interpretation. It is found in V T and Symmachus and supported by Rashi. In fact the Qumran sectaries derived a title for their leader from the present phrase understood as "the true teacher," in association with Hos. 10:12 *wᵉyôreh tseḏeq* (cf. J. Weingreen, *JSS* 6[1961], pp. 162–174; C. Roth, *VT* 13[1963], pp. 91–95; Wolff, however, denies the influence of Joel 2:23). A similar individual exegesis has been espoused in more recent times by Pusey, Merx, and van Hoonacker, interpreted in a messianic sense, following the Jewish exegete Abarbanel. Keil, observing that *môreh/yôreh* in the sense of rain never has the article, took the phrase collectively concerning all God-given teachers from Moses to the Messiah. Von Orelli interpreted of the prophet who has summoned the people to repentance. Ahlström, *JTCJ*, pp. 98–110, emphasizes what some earlier exponents have mentioned, that correct teaching in cultic matters is the prelude to rain in 1 K. 8:36; Isa. 30:20, 23 (cf. Zech. 10:1f.; 14:17). Relating this instruction to royal responsibility, he suggests that this is a veiled promise of a new Davidic leader and teacher, politically unintelligible to the Persian authorities at the time of Joel's postexilic ministry after the disappearence of Zerubbabel. Ahlström has presented an impressive case for a personal interpretation and shown that it need not strike a discordant note in a list of physical blessings culminating in rain, as many commentators categorically claim. But it is significant that in both of the two Pentateuchal passages whose data this piece takes up with remarkable consistency, *ntn*, "give," is used with rain as object (Lev. 26:4; Deut. 11:14). This fact strongly suggests that here the object of *nāṯan* has to do with rain.

27. One must not, however, think of a period wet at beginning and end and dry in the middle. The two terms stand for the whole rainy season; this is a case of *merismus* (A. M. Honeyman, *JBL* 71 [1952], p. 15; D. Baly, *The Geography of the Bible* [1957], pp. 47–52).

28. There is no need to delete *môreh*² as otiose with Wellhausen and S. R. Driver.

29. For this use of Heb. *litsᵉḏāqâ*, lit. "according to righteousness," cf. K. H. Fahlgren. *Ṣᵉdāḳā, nahestehende und entgegengesetze Begriffe im AT* (1932), pp. 88f.; Wade; Kapelrud ("according to the claims of the covenant, according to the norm of fellowship"); Delcor. Cf. the interpretation "justification" of Ewald, Wellhausen, *et al*. (cf. Knox "proof of . . . your restoration to favor," RSV "for your vindication"), so that the rain is a sign that their sin is

The covenant community would enjoy afresh that blessedness which once they knew before the sweet relationship with God was disrupted by their sin.[30] The psalmist's testimony of God's bounty to a repentant people would be Judah's experience:

> *You care for the ground by watering it. . . .*
> *You soak its furrows, level its ridges,*
> *soften it with showers*
> *and bless its growth.* (Ps. 65:9f.[10f.])

Joel's song throbs with assurance and praise. He has been calling the community to share his conviction that God's face is now turned toward them in favor and that he will shower upon them the blessings promised in the covenant documents. Outwardly nothing has changed, but he has a song in his heart which he would have them share. They may face the future with lighter hearts, knowing that their God is with them. With faith's Hallelujah they are to give him the glory for the covenant gifts they will receive.

24–27 The prophetic song of encouragement and praise has been an interlude in the divine proclamation so that the people may think upon its message and thank God for his promises. This section has two purposes: to develop the former half of the oracle, and to continue the contrast with the cursing of 1:2–2:17. As to the first, the motifs of vv. 19, 20 sound out again. *Wine and oil* echoes v. 19, *wheat* taking the place of grain for stylistic variation. The plentiful supply of food in v. 26 also echoes v. 19.[31] The sending of gifts in that verse is now enhanced by contrasting it with the erstwhile sending of locusts (v. 25).[32] The divine "no" to Judah's humiliation in v. 19 twice rings out again in vv. 26, 27. The welcome reiteration that Judah is God's *people* in the introduction of vv. 18, 19 now features in the oracle and receives stress from Yahweh himself in vv. 26, 27.

The difference that sensitivity to Yahweh's will can make in the life of the people is emphasized. In v. 24 the motif of bumper harvests presents a contrast with the famine of 1:10–12, 17. The recital of locust terminology and their voracity in v. 25 is a poignant reminder of 1:4, while the reference to Yahweh's *army* takes up 2:11. Judgment is past, and now salvation is to be Judah's happy lot since the community has repented and softened their hearts before God. Verses 26, 27 hark back to that humiliation of the people which was reflected in their environment (1:10–12, 17) and insist that this is a thing of the past.[33] The pleading reference to the community as God's *people* in 2:17 finds its counterpart in the reiterated acknowledgment of vv. 26, 27, for God now lays claim to them and pledges his support. The prayer that

---

forgiven. In addition to the explanations mentioned in n. 26 above, others take it as "according to the normal amount of rain" (cf. Calvin "according to what is fit," KJV "moderately," RV "in just measure," Moffatt "amply," NEB "in due measure").

30. MT *bārī'shôn,* apparently "at first" (or with T "in the first month"), can hardly be a contrast with "afterward," v. 27 (Ewald, Keil, *et al.*). In accord with one Heb. ms. and G S V, *kārī'shôn* is generally read (for the masculine cf. *mērī'shôn,* Jer. 17:12).

31. Heb. *ûśᵉḇa'tem—wᵉśāḇôa'.*

32. Heb. *shōlēaḥ lāḵem—shillaḥtî bāḵem.*

33. Heb. *hôḇîsh,* etc.*—yēḇōshû.*

reported to Yahweh the taunting question of Judah's neighbors, "Where is your God?" is decisively answered: Judah would experience his presence among them in power and blessing.

The continuation of the oracle looks forward to a bountiful harvest in terms that would make any farmer's eyes glisten. It was the practice to spread *wheat* over the *threshing floor,* which was set in a high open spot, ready for the oxen to go round and round loosening the grain and chopping the stalks.[34] Grapes and olives were taken to troughs cut out of rock where they were trodden[35] to extract the juice, which flowed into *vats* below. These were happy scenes, which made all the previous toil worthwhile. Welcome indeed would be the event when Yahweh crowned the year with his generous bounty. Where sin abounds, grace superabounds: God would make up for the produce lost in the years when locusts had ravaged the crops. He would give full compensation, although Judah could make no formal claim. A legal term for indemnifying is ironically used[36] in a manner that recalls Paul's offer to Philemon concerning his runaway slave: "If he has wronged you or owes you anything, charge it to my account. . . . I shall pay it back—to say nothing of your owing me your very self!" (Philem. 18, 19). Apparently the locusts' attacks were not confined to a single year, but had occurred several years in succession. The bad *years* would be compensated by an especially good year.[37] The whole sorry tale of the locusts' depredations is brought to mind with the catalog repeated from 1:4, together with a somber reminder of the holy war that through them Yahweh had waged against his people in judgment for their sin. This sobering thought is a warning of the penalty that disobedience can bring. It also provides a measure of the blessing of God: "so great was the disaster that also the restoration will be correspondingly great" (Kapelrud).

Instead of the locusts' eating, the theme is now the people's eating the abundance of Yahweh's provision. Thanksgiving would rise to the covenant God, who lived up to his *name* and its associations of faithfulness and greatness. Once again he would prove himself a wonder-working God, just as the temple hymns celebrated him to have been in the past. The Song of Moses could be sung with a new relevance:

> *"Who is like you majestic in holiness,*
> *awesome for praiseworthy deeds, working wonders?"*
> (Ex. 15:11)[38]

The OT abounds in the reapplication of ancient themes. In Israel's experience, past events seem to come alive in new demonstrations of God's

34. See the comment on Mic. 4:13.
35. See the comment on Mic. 6:15.
36. Cf. Ex. 22:1 (21:37); Lev. 24:18.
37. Heb. *shānîm* is evidently used as a poetic metonym for the crops harvested in the course of years. Kapelrud compares Prov. 5:9 and Wolff Ps. 90:15. Sellin, Robinson, and Rudolph consider MT an unnatural development, or question so long a plague, and read some expression for "double" (*sh^{e}nayim* or *mishneh*).
38. Cf. Ps. 77:14(15); 78:12, etc. and the reapplication of this motif in Ps. 98:1; Isa. 25:1; 29:14.

power and love, just as the NT proclaims in Christ a new passover and a new promised land. Here was material crying out to be incorporated into a new song of praise.[39] The covenantal reference to *Yahweh your God* is capped by mention of *my people*. The bond is intact once more, and the cycle of blessing and praise will soon be turning in land and temple.[40] No longer will they experience the humiliation of suffering such as they have recently undergone, nor will it be their lot again. With touching faith in the continued obedience of his people, Yahweh pledges his continual upholding in an affirmation that takes up a standard theme of lament.[41] Here is expressed divine desire, an implicit wish that the people for their part may be ever mindful of their obligations in return:

> *"Oh that they always had such an attitude as this, reverencing me and keeping my every command, so that it might go well for them and their children for ever."* (Deut. 5:29)

Judah's renewed prosperity would constitute a vital proof to them of Yahweh's active presence to aid his people,[42] of his fellowship with them (*your God*) and of his uniqueness. Their experience would lead to a fresh awareness of his omnipotent reality and an appreciation of his covenant grace,[43] and would create confidence in his power to keep those whom he had saved from destruction. Other nations had mocked Judah, believing their gods to be superior to Yahweh; but Israel would learn from her rescue the lesson of a convinced faith in her God, which none could shatter.[44] This would be "the finest fruit" of God's enabling (von Orelli). The promise of v. 26 rings out again in a reassuring refrain.[45] For an obedient people there is only the prospect of well-being, as long as they abide near the Fount of every blessing.

2. *Supernatural Blessings (2:28–32 [3:1–5])*

Afterward
I shall pour out my spirit upon everybody:
your sons and daughters will prophesy, 3+3

39. The third person references in a *Jahwerede* allude to this hymn (Keller). Yahweh composes a call to praise and a cause for praise, ready for the people to sing; cf. Ps. 148:5, 13.
40. Cf. Deut. 8:10; Ps. 22:26(27).
41. Cf. Ps. 25:2; 31:1(2); 71:1; Jer. 17:18.
42. Cf. Num. 14:42; Josh. 3:10; Jer. 14:9; Mic. 3:11.
43. Notice the continued covenantal emphasis, *your God, Israel,* which occurs here for the first time, *my people*; there may be in this verse a reminiscence of Ex. 6:7. For the formula of self-revelation in v. 27a, used typically at the end of a speech unit or subunit, see W. Zimmerli, *Erkenntnis Gottes nach dem Buche Ezechiel. Eine theologische Studie*. ATANT 27 (1954), esp. pp. 32f.; "Das Wort des göttlichen Selbsterweises (Erweiswort), eine prophetische Gattung," *Mélanges bibliques . . . André Robert* (1957), pp. 154–164. It is used extensively by Ezekiel: cf. esp. Ezek. 36:11. Heb. *w*^{e}*'ên 'ôḏ, and there is no other,* echoes the refrain of Isa. 45. The self-predication *I am Yahweh* is an ancient formula associated with the covenant (cf. Ex. 20:2; Ps. 50:7; 81:10[11]).
44. Cf. Deut. 4:35.
45. Many scholars, e.g., Wellhausen, Ehrlich, *BHK,* Delcor, Wolff (cf. NEB), delete one or other of the promises. For the rhetorical rounding off of the passage in this way cf. 1:19, 20.

while your old men will have dreams
and your young men will see visions. 3+3
29 *Even upon your slaves and slave-women*
in those days shall I pour out my spirit. 3+4

30 *I shall set portents in sky and earth,*
blood, fire, and columns of smoke. 4+4
31 *The sun will be turned into darkness,*
the moon into blood, 3+2
before the Day of Yahweh comes,
that momentous, terrible Day. 3+2

32 *But everyone who calls*
on Yahweh's name will be safe, 3+3
because on Mount Zion people will find security,[1]
as Yahweh has promised, 3+3
and in Jerusalem will be survivors
whom Yahweh has called. 3+3

After the first oracle of material blessing in answer to the immediate problems of the locusts and drought, there follows a series of more profound promises, such as only men who can look forward to having empty stomachs filled would be ready to receive. The passage falls into three strophes, each of three lines, which deal with the outpouring of God's spirit in prophecy (vv. 28, 29), the cosmic signs heralding the Day of Yahweh (vv. 30, 31), and the security of his people (v. 32). The first and second are spoken by Yahweh, the third by his prophet.[2] The first and third are marked by the device of inclusion,[3] the first beginning and ending with the spirit's outpouring and the third with a call associated with Yahweh. As before, earlier motifs are taken up in a glorious reversal of the situation of disaster. The enumeration of groups within the community in vv. 28, 29 echoes in happier vein the call for everyone to flock to the service of lamentation in 2:16. The motifs of fire, darkness, the veiling of sun and moon, and the great, terrible Day of Yahweh are taken up afresh, but in a new context.[4] Verse 32 makes it abundantly clear that the threat is directed elsewhere and constitutes instead a demonstration of the supremacy of Israel's God active in the world. While before there seemed no escape from the locusts which marked the outbreak of Israel's Day till God's grace averted them, now escape is guaranteed.[5]

28, 29 The bestowal of material blessing, which carries with it proof of Yahweh's gracious presence in Israel, is but the first stage. Further, deeper gifts of God's grace were in store, to be dispensed at a subsequent

1. More literally "there will be those who escape."
2. In v. 31 the *Day of Yahweh* is used as a stereotyped expression; "my Day" never occurs in the OT.
3. See n. 27 on Mic. 2:3.
4. Cf. 1:15, 19f.; 2:1–3, 5, 10.
5. Heb. *p*ᵉ*lêṭâ* in 2:3, 32.

stage.[6] His indwelling of his people would be revealed in a clearer way than by rain and crops, through the charismatic flow of a divine spirit of prophecy throughout the community. In this way the promise of God's presence in 2:27 would be more abundantly fulfilled. Joel evidently ministered in an age when prophecy was in little evidence in Judah. This constituted a state of spiritual deprivation in OT thinking. The narrator at 1 Sam. 3:1 commented pityingly on a period when "the word of Yahweh was rarely given . . . ; visions were uncommon." In the NT Paul declares that if all the church prophesy, a non-Christian visitor will be constrained to "declare that God is really among you" (1 Cor. 14:24). The theme of Yahweh's presence, with which the previous promise ended, is now taken up and amplified.[7] Here is a spiritual counterpart to the rain, this outpouring of a higher gift.[8]

The recipients of this blessing are said to be "all flesh," which has a variety of meanings in the OT but "comes to mean simply *everybody,* as the French *tout le monde*" (Bewer).[9] Here the following elaboration of the term, as well as the whole context of ch. 3, makes it clear that Joel is referring to the community of Judah. "The gift of prophecy would be common and prevail everywhere among all the Jews in a new and unusual manner" (Calvin). It was obviously in this sense that Peter understood it in his exposition of the passage in Acts 2, especially in light of the amazement expressed at the "Gentile Pentecost" in Acts 10:45. The present phrase invites comparison with the promise through Ezekiel that Yahweh would pour out his spirit "upon the house of Israel" (Ezek. 39:29).[10]

"Flesh" essentially distinguishes man as belonging to an order of being other than that of God. It stands over against the almighty power and perfection of God as that which is fragile, creaturely, and fallible. The Egyptian military supplies upon which Judah in an earlier age placed so much store were only "flesh and not spirit" (Isa. 31:3). *Spirit* refers to God in relation to mankind, communicating himself to his creatures.[11] As in Mic. 3:8, the divine spirit is the medium of prophetic inspiration by which God reaches down to his prophet and gives impulse and authority to his oracles.

6. Metrically the expression is in anacrusis. It is a general temporal adverb linking what precedes with what follows, but Joel presumably regards this next stage as imminent by a foreshortening typical of the prophets.

7. Wolff helpfully refers to 2 Chr. 15:1; 20:14, where spirit-filled prophets declare "Yahweh is with us."

8. P. Reymond, *L'eau, sa vie, et sa signification dans l'AT*. SVT 6 (1958), p. 235, objects that Heb. *špk* is not used of rain and that the unction of oil underlies the metaphor. But it is significant that the verb is used freely with water in literal and metaphorical senses: see esp. Isa. 44:3; Hos. 5:10; Amos 5:8; 9:6.

9. It is used of animate life, including animals, in Gen. 6:17; Lev. 17:14; of mankind in Gen. 6:12; Num. 16:22; of Israel in Jer. 12:12 and perhaps Ps. 65:2(3).

10. Accordingly "all mankind" (JB, NEB) is out of place in the primary interpretation of the passage.

11. D. Lys, *Bâsâr: Le chair dans l'AT* (1967), p. 91. "The activity attributed in the OT to the spirit of God . . . may be taken as indeed the action of the Third Person of the Eternal Trinity in unity; the personality, not to say deity of the Spirit was not known to the writer, the prophet

The immanence of Yahweh in Israel's ongoing history would be manifested in a special way, by the charismatic endowment of every member of the community with this prophetic gift. The promise takes up the wistful longing of Moses expressed in Num. 11:29:

> *"Would that all Yahweh's people were prophets, that Yahweh would put his spirit upon them,"*

and stamps it as a definite part of Yahweh's program for the future. It is comparable with Jeremiah's great prophecy of the New Covenant in which an intimate knowledge of the Law and of Yahweh is promised to all the people, "from the least of them to the greatest."[12] The stress upon the external phenomena of the prophetic gift by no means excludes the thought of moral transformation.[13] Joel himself is a living example of sensitivity to the divine will for the moral and spiritual life of the community.[14] The prophetic privilege of standing, as it were, among Yahweh's council and hearing his word at first hand (Jer. 23:18) would be the personal experience of every member of the religious community.

The elaboration of the basic first clause poetically combines a variety of ecstatic media of God's truth with an enumeration of the constituent parts of the community.[15] *Dreams* and *visions* were regarded as legitimate channels of divine revelation, although there was an awareness that counterfeit claims to them could be made.[16] Distinctions of age, sex, and social class would be swept away in this common spiritual endowment. *Even slaves,* who though they might be of foreign origin were counted as part of the religious community and took part in Israel's festivals,[17] were to be included. The wideness of God's endowment of his people prepares the way for Paul's even greater declaration of blessing in Christ: "There is neither Jew nor Gentile, neither slave nor free, neither male nor female" (Gal. 3:28).[18] Important though these natural distinctions remained in the rest of life, in the sphere of spiritual capacity they would not be relevant.

30, 31 The second stanza of this piece takes up the theme of God's demonstration of astounding power on his people's behalf in v. 26. It has

---

or the person acted upon but only to the Eternal God himself. . . . In the fullness of time the Spirit whom men in ignorance had been groping after, him the NT religion declared" (R. S. Cripps, *Theology* 24 [1932], p. 280). Cf. further the comment and note on Mic. 3:8.

12. Jer. 31:33f.; cf. Isa. 54:13.

13. L. Dennefeld, *RSR* 5 (1925), p. 593, *contra* Bewer.

14. Cf. Ezek. 36:26f.

15. Von Orelli's comment betrays a lack of understanding of the poetic style: "*dreams* are ascribed to slumbering age, *visions* to youths with their eager receptiveness."

16. Cf. Gen. 28:12–17; Num. 12:6; 1 Sam. 28:6. Jeremiah (23:25–32; 27:9, etc.) was opposed not to the form but to the content of dream communications, according to T. W. Overholt, *The Threat of Falsehood*. SBT 2:16 (1970), pp. 66–68.

17. Cf. Deut. 5:14; 12:12; 16:11. Bourke, *RB* 66 (1959), pp. 198f., considers the description of the community to be a trait borrowed from the Deuteronomic tradition.

18. In view of Paul's association of this theme with a quotation from v. 32 in Rom. 10:12f., it is quite likely that his statement was modelled on the present passage. That the gift of the Spirit was not far from his mind is clear from Gal. 3:3–5; 4:6.

been noted how Joel at times alludes to the story of Israel's redemption from Egypt, and sees both in the locust plague and in its removal the mighty hand of the God of the Exodus at work again in Israel. Now that the matter of the people's sin has been dealt with, it is possible to envisage Yahweh in the role of mighty champion with which the ancient traditions endowed him. Ps. 105:5 combines the vocabulary of vv. 26 and 30:

> *Remember the wonders he has wrought,*
> *his portents and the judgments of his mouth.*[19]

In light of v. 26 it is quite clear that the present declaration constitutes no threat to God's people. In the heritage of the prophetic teaching handed down to Joel, the Day of Yahweh had a double, even a triple function. Zeph. 1f. presents the Day as a threat to Judah and foreign neighbors alike. As Amos had declared before him, no nation would escape its disastrous judgment (Amos 5:18–20; 9:7, 8a). Yet Joel also knew of promises of salvation which would follow the judgment upon Israel. They were an ancient element of the Day before the prophets took over the theme (Amos 5:18). The next verse makes it clear that Joel had heard and taken to heart the message of Obadiah in this respect. For Obadiah the Day had already come upon God's people; for Joel it had come in the terrible experience of the locust plague, which put the very existence of the community in jeopardy. For both there remained to be fulfilled prophecies concerning the other nations. Judgment Day for them was still to come, while Israel awaited only eschatological bliss. The time had come—and gone—for judgment to begin at God's household. The message of the next stage of Yahweh's dynamic intervention in the world can hold no terrors now for Joel's hearers.

The Day was traditionally accompanied by strange upheavals in the world of nature as Yahweh was to step into the arena of history in theophany. These upheavals Joel had earlier in this chapter interpreted in a nonliteral fashion while describing the macabre dawn of the Day in the locusts. Now he presents the traditional motifs anew in a manner more akin to standard eschatological usage.[20] These cosmic signs heralded the Day for the nations as surely as the locusts did for Judah. Terrestrial *portents* too are to inaugurate the Day. There is a chiastic order: the signs in the *sky* are mentioned first and expounded last, while those of *earth* are artistically selected for immediate elaboration. The eschatological teaching of Jesus applied these phenomena to the future, partly the time of Jerusalem's destruction (A.D. 70) and partly that of the final judgment: then "nation will rise against nation" and there will be "great signs from heaven."[21] The bloodshed mentioned is evidently the carnage associated with the Day in Zeph. 1:17, when men's "blood will be poured out like dust." The *fire* and

19. Cf. Neh. 9:10, 17; Ps. 78:32, 43. Heb. *môp̄ᵉṯîm, portents,* is especially associated with the Exodus: cf. also Ex. 4:21; 7:9.
20. Cf. Isa. 13:10, 13; 34:2–4, 10; Ezek. 32:3–8; Amos 8:9.
21. Luke 21:10f., 25; cf. Matt. 24:6–8, 29; Mark 13:7f., 24f.

columns of smoke, traditionally signs of theophany,[22] are now interpreted in terms of destruction of war and the burning of cities.[23]

Reverting to the celestial signs, the prophet takes up the terrifying traditional motif of the disfigurement of sun and moon, which would cause men to "faint from fear and anticipation of what is to befall the world" (Luke 21:26). The tokens of a smiling providence would be startingly taken away. For a prescientific age a solar eclipse was not a matter of scientific observation but an uncanny happening, as indeed it still is for ordinary folk, and thus it was a fitting precursor of God's catastrophic intervention into the orderliness of normal life. Rev. 6:12 employs as signs of "the great day of wrath" of God and the Lamb these very portents, including the full moon becoming "like blood." Joel's terminology for the latter portent significantly echoes that used of an Exodus plague in Ex. 10:17, 20. It alludes to a reddish obscuring of the moon through sandstorms and the like, whose color ominously suggested bloodshed. These phenomena proclaim with awful certainty the dawning of the *Day of Yahweh.* Judah had already seen its own version of the harbingers of doom (2:11); as ch. 3 will teach, the cup of eschatological wrath snatched in time from Judah's lips will be handed to the nations to drain.

32 Before this theme is developed the prophet supplements Yahweh's message with a reassuring word to his people.[24] They have nothing to fear. Gathered in the sanctuary, had they not been engaged in invoking Yahweh and bringing him their prayer and praise?[25] For all such there is no danger: they will be kept *safe.* To use the language of Zeph. 2:3, they would be "hidden on the day of Yahweh's wrath" as a consequence of their coming to "seek" him. In Isa. 26:20, 21 Yahweh issues an invitation in similar vein:

"Come, my people, . . .

22. Cf. Ex. 19:18; Ps. 18:8(9).
23. For *fire* cf. Num. 21:28; Ps. 78:63; for *smoke* cf. Josh 8:19f.; Judg. 20:38, 40. S.R. Driver interprets of abnormal atmospheric phenomena, including columns of sand and dust, on the ground that "wars are not suggested in the context." But they are a firm feature of the ideological context.
24. *Contra* Bewer, who thought of a Jewish elite surviving, Dennefeld, *loc. cit.*, pp. 596f., was surely correct in stressing the demands of the context. The promise is as wide as v. 28. All the people are to become prophets, and so they are all envisaged as being faithful to Yahweh; there is no notion of a new remnant saved out of the Jewish nation. The promise is also as narrow as v. 28. Since the nations are represented in ch. 3 as destroyed, and aliens are to be debarred from Jerusalem (3:17), no substantial inclusion of Gentiles can be inferred from the oracle in its primary sense. Cf. Obad. 17 and comment. The postexilic community was at times regarded as the remnant. Here there is a contrast between the nations who are to perish and Israel which is to survive.
25. Heb. *yiqrā' bᵉshēm yhwh* literally means "call (upon God) by the name Yahweh," i.e., by calling out the name; cf. 1 K. 18:24, 26, 36f., 39 (A. R. Johnson, *The Cultic Prophet in Ancient Israel* [²1962], pp. 55f.). "The name of Yahweh is a strong tower; the righteous person runs into it and is safe up there" (Prov. 18:10).

hide yourselves for a little while
until the wrath is past.
For Yahweh is soon to come out from his place
to punish the inhabitants of the earth."

As divine warrant for this promise of comfort Joel gives a formal quotation from an older oracle, Obad. 17a. In fact he cites one half of a line and is to echo the second half in 3:17. The passage from which he quotes is explicitly concerned with Yahweh's Day for the nations, from which Judah is now exempt, having already experienced it. The citation is thus contextually apt, for Joel has a similar message to proclaim. The focal point symbolizing the community's *security* is *Mount Zion,* since there it is that Yahweh dwells, as 3:17 will explain. His home is open to his people. While the stormclouds gather, he will call them in tender invitation, as in Isa. 26:21 cited above.[26] In the place he has prepared he will receive them, that where he is they may be also. He has a continuous welcome for them.[27] They will survive the coming destruction safe in the eye of the storm, in the presence of their God, which casts an aura of inviolability around *Jerusalem.*[28]

Like so many OT promises, this passage bursts its original wrappings and leaps into the NT with wider and deeper significance. Peter cited vv. 28–32 at Pentecost and claimed their fulfilment. "This is what was spoken through the prophet Joel" (Acts 2:16–21).[29] The experience of the hundred and twenty who constituted the total nucleus of the new Christian community, whereby they were "all filled with the Holy Spirit" (Acts 2:4), was understood as the fulfilment of Joel's promise about the community of Israel. Their speaking "in other languages," an ecstatic endowment of a special type, was hailed as the realization in principle of the charismatic gifts enumerated in this ancient oracle. The Pentecost sermon proceeds to relate

26. For this use of *qr'* cf. Isa. 54:6, where it means "call to oneself, welcome"; it is associated with gathering, taking to oneself in Isa. 54:7.

27. This seems to be the force of the Heb. participle.

28. MT places *ûḇîrûshālayim* after Zion and later reads *ûḇaśśᵉrîḏîm,* "and among the survivors ([there will be those?] whom Yahweh calls)." Most probably the latter word resulted from accidental telescoping of an original *ûḇîrûshālayim śᵉrîḏîm* (Sellin, Delcor, Jones, JB, NEB). This conjectural emendation (1) removes the unnecessary "among" and the uncertain construction; (2) makes the earlier clause conform to the quotation in Obad. 17, where there is no mention of Jerusalem; and (3) gives the external parallelism expected in view of the balance between *pᵉlêṭâ* and *śᵉrîḏîm*. Presumably *ûḇîrûshālayim* was put in the margin by way of correction and subsequently misplaced.

29. The Gk. version cited in the speech is based on G. Proof of this may be found in two factors: (1) the inserted preposition "of/from" in Acts 2:17f. (under the influence of G in Num. 11:17, 25), upon which Calvin passed scathing comment: "The Greek interpreter diminishes this promise . . . , as though God promised here some small portion of his Spirit, while on the contrary the prophet speaks of abundance"; and (2) the rendering *epiphanē* for Heb. *nôrā'*, which *contra* F. F. Bruce (*The Book of the Acts*. NICNT [1954], p. 18, n. 47) does not imply a variant reading *nir'eh,* since it is a frequent equivalent of *nôrā'* in the Gk. OT. But upon this basic textual stratum have been set two further layers. The first is a closer approximation to MT. Heb. *wᵉgam,* "and indeed," is rendered *kaíge* in Acts 2:18, a telltale sign of the first-century A.D. recension of the Gk. Minor Prophets discovered by D.

portions of the oracle to the career of Jesus and derives from it an invitation to the assembled Jews of the Diaspora and proselytes to enlist in the young community. Evidence of the promised outpouring now confronts the audience (Acts 2:33), and it may be experienced by them on certain conditions (2:38). This promise comes to "you and your children" (2:39); probably an allusion to *your sons and daughters* in the basic text. The *wonders* and "signs" are related to the miracles performed by Jesus as divine attestation of his mission.[30] There may well be a reference to the uncanny happenings in sky and earth some seven weeks before, which Jewish pilgrims to the Passover would have witnessed. "The people in Jerusalem had indeed seen the sun turned into darkness, during the early afternoon of the day of our Lord's crucifixion. And on the same afternoon the paschal full moon may well have appeared blood-red in the sky in consequence of that preternatural gloom."[31] "The name of Jesus Christ," in which the hearers are invited to be baptized (2:38), is an interpretation of *the name of Yahweh* which is typical of early Christian exegesis. The rendering of Yahweh as "the Lord" in the Greek OT[32] facilitated the reference of many OT passages to Christ; here in Acts it is explicitly claimed on the evidence of two psalms that God made "this Jesus both Lord and Christ" (2:25ff.). The appeal to "be saved" (2:40) echoes the promise of salvation given in the Joel oracle to those who *call on* the *name* of "the Lord." On the other hand, the quotation of Joel 2:32b, which is fused with part of Isa. 57:19 in Acts 2:39, interprets "the Lord" who calls in effectual grace as "your God."

Luke's abbreviated form of the Pentecost sermon (cf. Acts 2:40)

Barthélemy (*Les devanciers d'Aquila*. SVT 10 [1963]). Also Heb. *qōrē', calls,* taken as *qārā'*, "has called," in G is rendered more exactly by a subjunctive (cf. the future in Aquila and Theodotion). The second layer imposed upon G is of quite a different nature, consisting of exegetical amplifications. *Afterward* becomes "in the last days," an interpretation of Joel's general phrase in eschatological terms of the dawning of a new age (G. W. Buchanan, *JNES* 20[1961], p. 190, compares the different renderings in G and Theodotion respectively at Dan. 2:29, 45). *Slaves and slave-women* are graced with the epithet "my," which gives the social terms a new religious orientation. "Above" and "beneath" are added, a well-attested type of liturgical expansion (cf. J. S. Sibinga, *The OT Text of Justin Martyr,* vol. 1 [1963], pp. 90f.). The insertion of "signs" recalls the translation of the preceding *wonders* in T in this very way. Less significant changes are the addition of an introductory formula, the inversion of the clauses in v. 28b, the addition of "and they will prophesy" after v. 29, which conforms to v. 28a, and the replacement of the accusative case of "dreams" by the dative. It is strange that the NT does not take up G *euangelizomenoi*, "bearers of good news," read for *baśś*^{e}*rîḏîm* (yet not by way of reading *m*^{e}*ḇśś*^{e}*rîm, contra BHK,* Wolff, *et al.*, but simply picking out the letters *bśr* and relating them to the verb "bring good news").

30. Verse 43 is significant as Luke's interpretation of the continuing fulfilment of the oracle. It is possible that the references to eating bread and praising God in v. 46 are intended as an echo of Joel 2:26 (cf. too the link between the "gladness" of this group in Jerusalem and Joel 2:23).

31. Bruce, *op. cit.*, p. 69.

32. At first the divine Tetragrammaton appeared in Heb. script in G mss., and "the Lord" was an oral substitute.

contains hints of Peter's appreciation of the overall context of the passage.[33] The appeal for repentance in Acts 2:38 has an obvious affinity with Joel's call in Joel 2:12f., the sacrament of baptism replacing the mourning rites. The reference to wonders performed "in the midst of" the "men of Israel" (Acts 2:22) takes up the theme of the divine promise attested "in the midst of Israel" (Joel 2:27). Mention of "the crooked generation" from which Peter's audience are urged to "be saved" (Acts 2:40) indicates that it is ripe for the judgment associated with the Day, a judgment that the citation of Ps. 110:1 in Acts 2:34f. specifies as certain to be inflicted on the enemies of the exalted Christ.

In the fact of Christ and the experience of his followers at Pentecost, Peter found inaugurated eschatology.[34] According to rabbinic teaching, the activity of the Holy Spirit was both relegated to the past and expected in the Age to Come.[35] God was working in a way consonant with the hopes of devout Jews. He had poured out his Spirit and revealed in Christ the saving name. Thus was established the new community of his people: inside it lay salvation, but outside, the wrath of the Day of Judgment.

Paul in Rom. 10:13 cites Joel 2:32a. In fact the descriptive clause was evidently used in the Church as a synonym for a Christian.[36] The apostle finds warrant for the inclusion of Gentiles in the comprehensive character of the Joel quotation, arguing from it that "there is no distinction between Jew and Gentile." He is obviously extending the bounds of the original force of Joel's message. Those commentators who scan it for universalistic hints are in danger of misrepresenting its primary meaning. To this Peter is obviously closer, although it is doubtless true that for Luke "an adumbration of the worldwide Gentile mission" was implicit in the phrase "all flesh."[37] It was Paul's task to be pioneer in the theological rationalization of that hybrid entity, the Christian Church; and this was one of his prime concerns in his letter to the Romans. His exposition of Joel 2:32 in Rom. 10 depends heavily on his earlier argument in Rom. 4. This is evident from his appeal to faith in 10:11, which, although explicitly referring back to Isa. 28:16, is inextricably linked with the doctrine of justification in his complex theology (Rom. 10:3–6, 10). Underlying the concept of faith in Rom. 10 is the analysis of the implications of Gen. 15:6, a basic text for the doctrine in Rom. 4. There he argued the legitimacy of regarding Abraham as "father" of a spiritual

33. C. H. Dodd, *According to the Scriptures* (1952), p. 126, stressed that NT exegesis majored in the selection of certain large sections "as *wholes,* and particular verses or sentences were quoted from them rather as pointers to the whole context than as constituting testimonies in and for themselves. . . . In the fundamental passages it is the *total context* that is in view, and is the basis of the argument." He found Joel 2, 3 to be one such passage (pp. 62–64) and gave a fascinating survey of its echoes in the NT, finding it "probable that it played a significant part in moulding the language with which the early Church set forth its convictions about what Christ had done and would yet do."

34. Cf. F. Mussner, *BZ* 5(1961), pp. 263–65.

35. Cf. W. D. Davies, *Paul and Rabbinic Judaism* (1955), pp. 208–217.

36. Acts 9:14, 21; 22:16; 1 Cor. 1:2; 2 Tim. 2:22.

37. Bruce, *op. cit.*, p. 68.

community of believing Gentiles and Jews. For the apostle the concept of God's people received in Christ a wider meaning than that latent in the OT. "All flesh" for him is still Israel, but a greater Israel. Unbelieving Jews and Gentiles stand outside the community, which comprises the new people of God.[38] He was shortly to claim that believing Gentiles were included in the "olive tree," a metaphor for God's people borrowed from Jer. 11:16 (Rom. 11:17–24). While indeed there was a new universalism, it was by no means total but bound up in a new particularism. Paul defined those who would not be ashamed as all who believe in Christ, while in Joel 2:26f. God significantly declares that those who would not be ashamed are *my people*.[39]

The last strand in the skein of NT references to this passage was mentioned earlier, namely, its echo in apocalyptic material such as Mark 13:24; Luke 21:25; Rev. 6:9; 9:2 and the like. This is the simplest application: Joel's words are referred forward to an eschatological event endorsed by Christ and entailing his return to this world. The different types of NT application reveal an amazing richness of interpretation and a keen desire to relate the passage to the great phenomenon of Jesus Christ.[40] What will be true of the End was true also of God's great year of the Christian Passover and Pentecost. What was true of Jewish converts to Christianity is by a deeper insight true also of a worldwide Church. The Church's birthday marked the coming of age of God's people. The Lord who is the object of faith is also the hope of the Church, the guarantee of a full and final salvation.

B. THE JUDGMENT OF THE NATIONS (3[4]:1–21)

The last unit continues the theme of the Day of Yahweh and makes clear what was implicit in 2:28–32: now that the Day which threatened Judah has been averted, it is the turn of the other nations to face its terrors. Again, as in 2:28–32, intertwined with this theme is Yahweh's concern for Judah and Jerusalem, which are mentioned together in vv. 1, 6, 20.

1. Charges and Summonses to Judgment (3[4]:1–12)

For take note that in those days,
at that time 3+2

38. Cf. Calvin, who after stating that "Paul appears to misapply the prophet's words, for Joel no doubt addresses here the people to whom he was appointed as a teacher and a prophet," claimed that Joel had in mind the principle "that the blessing in the seed of Abraham had been promised to all nations."

39. B. Lindars, *NT Apologetic* (1961), p. 244, has helpfully pointed out the implicit link that Joel 2:26f. provides between 2:32 and Isa. 28:16.

40. Cf. also Rom. 5:5, which reapplies the terminology of Joel 2:28 to love, the Spirit's greatest endowment, outpoured via Pentecost into all believers. In Tit. 3:6 the outpouring of the Spirit "through Jesus Christ" is likewise a basic act into the good of which Paul and his associates had entered. Acts 2 is the counterpart of the beginning of Luke's first volume, where the activity of the Spirit in the life and mission of Christ is stressed (Luke 3:22; 4:1, 14, 18).

when I reverse the fortunes
of Judah and Jerusalem, 3+2
2 *I shall bring all the nations together,*
take them down to Jehoshaphat Valley
and put them on trial there 3+3+3
for their treatment of Israel, my people and possession,
scattering them among the nations, 3+3
sharing out my country among themselves,
3 *throwing lots for my people,* 3+3
selling boys as the price for prostitutes,
and bartering girls for wine and then drinking it. 3+4

4 *Furthermore,*
what were your intentions with me, Tyre and Sidon
and all the districts of Philistia? 4+3
Were you paying me back for something
or[1] *initiating an attack on me?*[2] 4+3
I shall quickly, rapidly,
make your actions recoil on your own heads. 2+3
5 *You took my silver and my gold*
and carried home my finest treasures to your own temples. 4+4
6 *The young people*[3] *of Judah and Jerusalem*
you sold to the Greeks 4+3
so as to take them far away
from their own territory. 2+2
7 *I am soon going to enable them to leave*
the place to which you sold them,
and also make your actions recoil on your heads. 3+3+3
8 *I shall sell your own sons and daughters*
into the possession of the Judeans, 4+3
and they will sell them to the Sabeans,
a distant nation. 2+2
So Yahweh has spoken. 3

9 *Make this proclamation among the nations:*
prepare a holy war, 2+2
alert the soldiers,
let all the troops
advance for attack. 2+2+2
10 *Beat your hoes*[4] *into swords,*
your pruning tools into spears. 3+2
Let the weakling
think himself a fighter. 2+2

1. Heb. *we'im* is better taken as an introduction to the second half of a double question with G (cf. NEB) than as "and if" with S V (cf. KJV, RSV, JB). The poetic parallelism and the usage in 1:2 support the former interpretation.
2. For Heb. *gōmelîm* see K. Seybold, *VT* 22 (1972), pp. 114–17.
3. Heb. *benê* is taken up in *benēkem*, *your sons*, v. 8 (Ehrlich).
4. See the note on Mic. 4:3.

11 *Hurry*[5] *and come,*
all nations around; 2+2
let them gather there.[6]
Let the timid man become a hero.[7] 2+3
12 *Let the nations be alerted to advance*
to Jehoshaphat Valley. 3+2
For there I shall sit in judgment
on all the nations around. 3+2

The bounds of this penultimate section of the book are indicated by the device of inclusion: it opens with Yahweh's pronouncement of his intention to judge all the nations in Jehoshaphat Valley, and in v. 12 returns to this very theme.[8] In this respect it is the counterpart of the corresponding section in the first half of the book, 2:1–11, which began and ended with a reference to the Day of Yahweh. This present section also has affinity with the opening one of the second half, 2:18–27: they both have an A-B-A′ structure. There the prophet's song marked an interlude between the two parts of the divine oracle, both of which dealt with the motifs of crops and locusts. Here also there are three stanzas (vv. 1–3, 4–8, 9–12); the general theme of the nations' judgment is interrupted by a specific indictment of

5. The translation of the *hapax legomenon ʿûshû* as "assemble yourselves" in G S T, KJV has no known etymological basis. It is often rendered "help" (BDB, NEB) on the basis of Arab. *ǵwṯ,* but a Hithpael would then be expected. Rudolph, who makes this point, compares Arab. *ǵashāshan,* "speedily," from a root *ǵšš* and considers it cognate with the present verb. Rashi mentions a view that the verb had this meaning. It is not then necessary to emend to *ḥûshû* (S. R. Driver, *BHK,* Köhler, Robinson, *et al.*) or *ʿûrû* (Wellhausen, Sellin, *et al.*).
6. MT links *there* with what follows, but it is metrically preferable to follow G and take it with the previous verb. The third person form *w^eniqbātsû* is a little strange. It has been explained as an unusual form of the imperative (GK 51o); indeed an emendation to *w^ehiqqāḇ^etsû* is often proposed (e.g., Sellin, Robinson, Wolff, *BHS*). Dahood, *Biblica* 52(1971), pp. 342f., finds here one of his precative perfects. It is tempting to view the clause as misplaced from a position after v. 12a (cf. NEB's wholesale rearrangement), which would provide an antecedent for *there* as well as preceding jussives, but it would create metrical difficulties. Moving the last five words of v. 11 to a position after v. 12b (Rudolph, following Procksch) ruins the inclusion.
7. MT *hanḥaṯ yhwh gibbôreyḵā,* "send down, Yahweh, your troops," is apparently a reference to heavenly warriors, a theme not inappropriate in a conflict of this type; cf. Ps. 68:17(18); 103:20; Zech. 14:5 (cf. P. D. Miller, Jr., *VT* 18 [1968], p. 103). It is the form that strikes a wrong note: a prayer is out of place in this *Jahwerede* (Mowinckel, cited by Kapelrud), and so is an appeal for forces belonging to the other side in this battle summons to the nations. Accordingly the reading implied by G is preferable: *hanniḥāṯ y^ehî gibbôr.* Moreover it links well with v. 10b. For *yhwh* and *y^ehî* as variants see 2 Chr. 36:23 and Ezra 1:3. *Hanniḥāṯ,* Niphal participle of *ḥtt,* "he who is frightened" (G. R. Driver, *JTS* 39[1938], p. 401), is better than postbiblical *hannôaḥ* (Sellin), *haḥāṯ* (Bewer), or *hannāḥ* (Procksch), none of which does justice to the letters of MT. Presumably the suffix was added to the third word after the misunderstanding of the first two in terms of v. 13; other suggested expedients are to take the final *yk* as originally *kî,* "for," before the next clause (Bewer) and to read by transposition *kaggibbôr,* "like a hero" (G. R. Driver).
8. The sound of Heb. *'āshûḇ/'āshîḇ,* v. 1, is echoed in *'ēshēḇ,* v. 12, and in the course of the piece by *'āshîḇ,* v. 4, and *wah^ashîḇōṯî,* v. 7.

Tyre and Sidon. Verses 1–12 are distinguished from the rest of the chapter in consisting completely of *Jahwereden*.

There are a number of echoes of the first half of the book. The clearest is the repeated mention of war in v. 9, corresponding to that in 2:5, 7. What was there the lot of Judah in the form of locust attack is now to be the fate of the nations in this counterpart to Judah's experience of the dawn of the Day of Yahweh. The change of fortune in v. 1 corresponds to the people's change of heart in 2:12f. *My country* in v. 2 has the same aggrieved air as in 1:6. Just as eventually the locusts were annihilated for despoiling God's property, so would be the nations. The smirks would be wiped off the nations' faces (2:17), as they in turn became victims of the Day. *My people and possession* takes up terms used in the model lament of 2:17. The summons to the nations in vv. 9–11 echoes that issued to Judah in 1:14; 2:15f., in a deliberate contrast. The people, weaklings and all, were summoned to Jerusalem to avert Yahweh's wrath by repentance; the other nations are now summoned in total mobilization to the environs of the city to face Yahweh's wrath in judgment.[9]

1–3 The first two lines serve as an introduction and make explicit what has just been implied, that the judgment of the nations, signalled by the wonders of 2:31, is the necessary complement to the blessing of *Judah and Jerusalem* recorded in 2:28f., 32. The outworking of the Day upon *all the nations* inside Judah's horizon is now developed in this important pronouncement.[10] The time reference[11] harks back to those of 2:28f. and makes it clear that the world judgment is essentially linked with the events of the preceding five verses as their continuation. The promised attesting of the presence of God in the prophetic spirit and in the security of his people is a contrast indeed with their hapless state from which the absence of Yahweh in blessing was only too evident. But Yahweh had already promised rehabilitation, a radical change in the people's fortunes to correspond with their change of heart and so with his change of policy toward them.[12]

The gathering of the nations is for the purpose of judgment, in the adverse sense of punishment. Joel is once more developing a theme contained in Zephaniah's exposition of the course of the *Dies Irae:*

> "*My decision is to assemble nations,*
> *to gather kingdoms,*
> *to pour out upon them my anger.*" (Zeph. 3:8)

In Ezek. 38f. the theme was amplified into a detailed apocalyptic scheme, but Joel is content to speak in more general terms. He does name the place of

9. Cf. the contrast of Zeph. 2:2f.; 3:8.
10. *Take note* is an attempt to render Heb. *hinnēh,* traditionally rendered "behold." As often, it calls attention to an announcement of a new, momentous intervention of Yahweh. The preceding *for* develops v. 31, just as in Isa. 66:15 it refers back to v. 6 (C. Westermann, *Isaiah 40–66* [E.T. 1969], p. 421).
11. The double phrase occurs also at Jer. 33:15; 50:4, 20.
12. Heb. *sh*ᵉ*ḇûṯ* is most probably to be derived from *šwb* (cf. *l*ᵉ*zûṯ* from *lwz*) and regarded as a cognate accusative, "turn with a turning (with regard to)." K *'āshûḇ* is to be read. For a

judgment. It is doubtful, however, whether he thinks in terms of a definite place on the map. In light of v. 16 and in view of the age-old motif of the nations' attack upon Jerusalem which was echoed in 2:9, it was probably envisaged as in the vicinity of the city. But the change of name to *Verdict Valley* in v. 14 suggests that the present name is intended as a theological symbol rather than a topographical identification: "the place where Yahweh is to judge."[13] *Jehoshaphat* means "Yahweh judges," and it was evidently selected for use here because of this meaning. The place is referred to as a (wide) *valley* because large numbers of people are involved and the judgment is conceived as a battle which requires for its venue such a wide depression between the hills of Judah.[14]

The announcement of a trial leads logically to a list of charges in a series of historical references. The crimes for which the nations are to stand trial have been committed against God's people and so against their God. This passage was echoed by Jesus in the Matthean description of the return of the Son of man: before him would "be gathered all nations" for a trial based on the treatment of his brothers and so of himself (Matt. 25:31–46).[15] It was noted above that *my people and possession* harks back to the lament of 2:17. This part of Yahweh's oracle is intended to be one of his answers to the communal prayers: in the terms of Eph. 3:20 he is "able to do so very much more than all we ever ask." There was a history of ill treatment which went far beyond the taunting of other nations. When that was dealt with (2:19), there remained a backlog of other, more serious incidents. Yahweh champions his people's cause on the principle, "Hurt my people, hurt me." It was his rights of ownership that were infringed, and for this reason he promises vindication. *Judah and Jerusalem* are no ordinary country and capital: they constitute the contemporary expression of *Israel,* Yahweh's covenant people. As in 2:27, the term is loaded with theological import, which spells the inheritance of promises of divine aid made in ancient times. The charges levelled against the nations are threefold, with an elaboration of the third. The *scattering* of Judah is evidently a reference to the Babylonian

---

review of suggested explanations see W. L. Holladay, *The Root Shûbh in the OT* (1958), pp. 110–14. Although in certain contexts return from exile may be involved, the phrase is quite general in meaning: cf. its use in Job 42:10; Ezek. 16:53; Hos. 6:11.

13. Theodotion so understood it, rendering "place of judgment." Cf. NEB "the Valley of the LORD's Judgment." Zech. 14:4 speaks of a valley specially created for the purpose. Cf. Isa. 22:1, 5 "the valley of vision." There appears to be no reference to King Jehoshaphat. He did fight in a valley, but its distance from Jerusalem militates against equating the two; the Valley of Berakah seems to be a different place from the battlefield (2 Chr. 20:20–28). Since the time of Eusebius and the Pilgrim of Bordeaux early in the fourth century A.D. the Kidron Valley on the east of Jerusalem has borne the name, and there are Jewish, Christian, and Muslim traditions that this would be the place of final judgment. But probably it received the name "on the basis of our passage rather than on any other ground" (Bewer) and because in the OT the area is associated with the burning of idols. For the role of *Jehoshaphat Valley* in later Jewish apocalyptic see L. Krinetzki, *BZ* 5 (1961), p. 215.

14. Cf. Gen. 14:8; 1 Sam. 17:19.

15. Cf. R. T. France, *Jesus and the OT* (1971), pp. 158f.

deportations in 597 and 587 B.C., which involved many thousands.[16] Similar phaseology is used in Ezek. 12:15; 22:15; 36:19 concerning these events.

The sense of outrage conveyed by *my people and possession* shouts out again at the hearer and reader in *my country,* and once more in the repeated *my people*. Yahweh as owner of the promised land and patron of Israel resents the commandeering of his private property entrusted to Judah.[17] The land-grabbing that occurred is mentioned in Lam. 5:2:

Our property has been turned over to aliens,
our homes to foreigners.

The regular policy after conquering an area was to divide it among new occupants.[18] The Babylonians did not in fact deport new people to Judah; presumably the reference is to seizure by neighboring states.

Not only was land lost by the Judeans, but their very liberty was forfeited. They were regarded as loot to be apportioned, as slaves in a lottery. Joel's phrase takes up Obad. 11, which applies it to the fall of Jerusalem in 587 B.C.[19] The life of a Judean was held so cheap that a boy slave was sold as payment for the use of a prostitute and a girl slave was exchanged for *wine* in the impromptu market doubtless set up by camp-followers trading in such commodities. The hope of Judah's destiny was degraded into currency for debauchery and drunkenness. The sensual revelry of conquering soldiers is depicted with horror from the standpoint of the losing side. The phrase *and then drinking it* is the final bitter touch. It epitomizes the callous disregard for the future mothers of the chosen people, that they were rated as worth no more than a moment's gratification. Judean bystanders doubtless shook impotent fists beneath their cloaks, but Yahweh is to step in and exact compensation. Champion of these war victims, he will ensure that the swaggering perpetrators are brought to justice. "Inasmuch as you did it to one of the least of these, you did it to me" (Matt. 25:40).

This list of offenses to be judged in Judah, the scene of the war crimes, at God's Nuremberg trial, serves to pinpoint the historical period to which Joel looks back, the identity of the nations involved, and the reason for their punishment. *All the nations* are in fact those who participated in and benefited from the conquest of Judah, i.e., those who lay within Judah's horizon of hostility at a certain point in her history. Among them would be Chaldeans, Arameans, and Moabites, to cite the list in 2 K. 24:2. Ps. 137:7f. accuses the Edomites and Babylonians. Ezek. 25 enumerates Ammonites, Moabites, Edomites, and Philistines. The oracle is set against the background of a particular crisis in the history of Judah in conflict with

16. See 2 K. 24:14, 16. Jer. 52:30 gives much smaller numbers. For a discussion of the discrepancy see J. Bright, *History of Israel* ([2]1972), p. 330; *idem, Jeremiah*. Anchor Bible (1965), p. 369.

17. The paradoxical fact that Yahweh commissioned these enemies (cf. Ezek. 12:15; 39:28) could be held in tension with their own guilt: cf. the classic case of Assyria in Isa. 10.

18. Cf. Josh. 13:6f.; Amos 7:17.

19. Note the quotation from Obad. 17 in v. 5. The Heb. phrase for *threw lots* occurs elsewhere only in Nah. 3:10.

Babylon and her satellites. And if any should take offense at this particularistic presentation of divine providence, let him ponder upon the survival of the Jewish nation to be hosts of their Messiah and first messengers of the Christian faith in which we now glory, while those other nations waned into insignificance.

4–8 The theme of judgment upon the nations is set aside until v. 9. The intervention singles out the reprehensible part played by the Phoenicians and Philistines in respect of their traffic in Judean slaves. In Amos 1:6, 9 the Philistine city of Gaza and the Phoenician state of Tyre are condemned for slave-trading, but there they acted as middlemen for Edom. Here their dealings are oriented in a westward direction. The mention of the Sabeans in v. 8 indicates their control over the South Arabian trade routes, which was lost after the sixth century B.C.[20] Palestinian trade with the Greeks was carried on over a long period; a date in the late seventh or sixth century B.C. would be the most likely.[21] The oracle appears to be intended as an expansion of vv. 1–3, taking up the motifs of scattering Judeans and selling their youth, and Yahweh's championship of his oppressed people. In view of the literary association it is most natural to relate this happening to the Babylonian conquest of Jerusalem, and there are no good arguments against this ascription. Ezek. 25:15–17 mentions vengeful destruction exacted by the Philistines from Judah in a context that refers back to this period, while in Ezek. 28:20–24 Sidon is named as one of the hostile neighbors who proved to be a thorn in Judah's side. Such an active involvement in Judah's affairs at this time would help to explain the vehemence with which Ezekiel denounces in chs. 26–28 the great commercial city of Tyre, and would be a manifestation of Tyre's malicious delight in Jerusalem's fall and of the material advantages thereby accruing to Tyre (Ezek. 26:2).[22] If the Edomites exploited Jerusalem's downfall by looting (Obad. 13), it is reasonable to suppose that traders from the coast did not pass by this golden opportunity.[23]

This artistically constructed piece is presented in a more vigorous manner than vv. 1–3. Yahweh plays the part of a plaintiff in a lawsuit who opens his speech by firing a series of indignant questions at the defendants. Then in the role of judge he announces swift retribution. The pattern of vv. 2, 3 is reproduced in that the announcement of judgment is followed by a recital of the charges.[24] Then in classic prophetic fashion Yahweh's imminent intervention is proclaimed in a punishment that fits the crime.[25] The oracle is

20. See Myers, *ZAW* 74(1962), pp. 186–88.

21. Cf. Kapelrud; Myers, *loc. cit.*, pp. 178–185; D. Auscher, *VT* 17(1967), pp. 8–30.

22. Nebuchadnezzar's siege of Tyre after the fall of Jerusalem indicates an anti-Babylonian stance, but not a pro-Judean one.

23. It is noteworthy that in the second half of the fifth century Tyrian fishmongers and other merchants had shops in Jerusalem (Neh. 13:16).

24. In the Hebrew each set of charges is put in an extended relative clause.

25. Cf. Mic. 2:1–5 and comment. The *ius talionis* is vigorously applied in both passages. As in Mic. 2:3, Heb. *hinᵉnî* is used with a participle referring to the imminent future.

rhetorically rounded off by repeating the promise of retribution and by taking up the second of the accusations and reversing it into a retaliatory punishment.[26] The piece closes with a final short line attesting the divine authority of the oracle.[27]

As in vv. 2f., Yahweh identifies himself wholeheartedly with his people. What the accused have done to Judah they have done to him. Here his championship is shown emotionally in a passionate quickfire of objections to Judah's undeserved ill treatment. Implicitly the passage is an assurance that Yahweh is on the side of his people and will see that justice is executed in their favor. It is intended to inspire such a conviction as the Servant had: "My vindication is near" (Isa. 50:8). The first question has the force of "How dare you interfere with me and mine?"[28] The contrasted pronouns set the pattern of personal affront and challenge which marks the whole passage. Yahweh refuses to recognize any right they may claim to lay hands on his people and property. The targets of his questions are *Tyre,* the giant of maritime commerce, and its sister seaport of *Sidon,* along with the *districts of Philistia,* presumably a reference to the traditional federation of five cities, each with its own ruler.[29] The accusation of slave-trading is doubtless directed primarily against Gaza, the Mediterranean outlet for the South Arabian trade and so equipped with a commercial pipeline along which to pass Judean slaves, but the charge of looting would of course apply to any Philistines.

Further questions are fired out, inquiring after the defendants' motivation, whether they considered their outrages against Judah and so against Yahweh to be reprisals, or whether they admitted them to be unprovoked and so morally reprehensible. In powerful personal contrasts, Judah's enemies are rhetorically brought face to face with Judah's patron to account for their crimes against God's people. They will find that their *actions* ricochet back upon themselves in a process accelerated by Yahweh.[30]

The grave charges levelled against the people of the coast are twofold. The first is of taking *gold, silver,* etc. which belonged to Yahweh. No doubt temple equipment and ornamentation are primarily meant, in view of the pointed reference at the end of the line.[31] These holy things, treated as

26. The verbal correspondence is matched by the metrical repetition of consecutive lines of 4+3 and 2+2 in accusation and punishment.
27. This closing formula also occurs at Obad. 18 in the same metrical role; see the comment there. Elsewhere it is found in this form at the end of an oracle only in 1 K. 14:11; Isa. 22:25; 25:8.
28. Heb. *māh-'attem lî*, "What you to me?" appears to be a variant of the idiomatic formula of repudiation *mah-llî w^{e}lāḵem,* "What to me and to you? What have you to do with me?" (2 Sam. 16:10; 19:23; cf. John 2:4).
29. The phrase also occurs in Josh. 13:2.
30. In light of the echoes of Obad. 11, 17 in the preceding passage, the phrase is probably a reminiscence of Obad. 15, where it is used of a natural process to befall Edom.
31. Instead of *temples,* "palaces" is also possible, but the other translation is more pointed and so in accord with the tone of the context.

common currency by the troops, were recognized by the traders as having an aura of sanctity and later reverently installed in their own shrines, not without an implication of the weakness of Yahweh.[32] The second charge is of slave-trading in Judean prisoners of war. It represents a climax of wickedness, worthy of more censure even than the misappropriation of temple property, that members of the chosen nation should be deprived of God-given liberty and land. This impression is reinforced in that the announcement of punishment takes up a reversal of this second charge and passes over the first. People matter more than things! The youngsters of *Judah* and *Jerusalem* belonged there; the foreign traders had received no mandate from Yahweh to remove his own servants from his domain given to them as a promise kept and a possession held in trust. By sending them so *far away,* they had minimized their chances of return, and so the magnitude of the crime is enhanced.[33] There is probably a glance back at v. 3, which mentions the enslavement of Judean *boys* and *girls*.

The charges take up three interconnected themes dear to Joel's heart: temple, people, and land. Yahweh's will was that his people should live in peace in their own country, tilling its soil and bringing to his temple praise for God's bounty. This divine plan for Israel had been scandalously thwarted. Doubtless Joel was fully aware of the factor of Judah's sin and in common with Obadiah viewed the exile as divine punishment. But there has never been a truly righteous war: outstanding accounts remained to be settled. It is these moral debts to Yahweh that are now served on the Philistines and Phoenicians.

Yahweh pledges his intervention to redress the situation. He would ensure that those members of his people who now languished in foreign slavery far from home would find their way back. It is apparently presupposed that the way had already been opened up for the exiles in Babylonia to return. But those sold into slavery in the west were obviously in more awkward circumstances. The promise comes that they would be given the opportunity to return. The means is not stated; the fact is enough. Not only would the wrongs done by the peoples of the coast be righted, they would be avenged. The clause used at the end of v. 4 is repeated and explained. The measure they got would be the very measure they had given. On this principle the only prospect for the slave-traders was a taste of their own medicine: they in turn would experience the bitter grief of losing their own children into slavery. In exquisite irony the *Judeans* are represented in the role of middlemen which the Phoenicians and Philistines had played, while the part of the Greeks would be taken by the *Sabeans,* the great traders of Sheba in Southwest Arabia who controlled the eastern trade routes by their caravan routes in North Arabia.[34] The slave traffic that had flowed to the

32. Cf. 1 Sam. 5:2; Dan. 1:2.

33. Heb. *l^e^ma'an* is strictly telic, "in order to (take)," and seems to imply a malicious design.

34. Cf. Jer. 6:20; Ezek. 27:22.

northwest would move southeast instead; the distance from home that the Judeans had journeyed into slavery would be matched in the experience of the accused.[35]

The oracle closes with a solemn formula of divine attestation. It was no wishful thinking on the prophet's part nor a mere echo of the dreams of his contemporaries, but an expression of the very mind of God and so certain to be fulfilled. Indeed, the very fate of these peoples has a startling correspondence to Joel's oracle. The people of Sidon were sold into slavery by Antiochus III in 345 B.C., while the citizens of Tyre and Gaza were enslaved by Alexander in 332 B.C. Thompson comments that no doubt Jews were among the buyers.

The destiny of enslavement pronounced upon these specific nations at first sight strikes a discordant note when in the surrounding oracles the eschatological fate of all the nations is nothing less than destruction. There is no hint that the people of the coast are being let off lightly. However, in view of the many links between vv. 1–3 and the present oracle it is clear that the composer was not aware of any grave inconsistency between the passages. Joel characteristically does not venture to draw up a comprehensive apocalyptic scheme of history in advance,[36] but is content to spell out Yahweh's judgment of the nations in terms of two separate prophetic traditions—that of precise compensation exacted for crimes committed, and that of the destruction of the Day of Yahweh. To expect him to coordinate these traditions is to turn Joel into a prophet of a different kind from what he was. Under cross-examination he might have suggested that the enslavement was preliminary to destruction, but clearly the inconsistency did not bother him. His main purpose is to highlight Yahweh's moral providence in human experience and the rehabilitation of the chosen people. His purpose is admirably served, though from a different perspective, in both this oracle and the surrounding material.

9–12 The last section resumes vv. 1–3 and so rounds off the unit. Yahweh carries a stage further his declaration in v. 2 of his purpose to gather all nations to Jehoshaphat Valley for trial. He orders messengers to summon them to battle. Verses 9–11, after the initial command, comprise a speech-form found frequently in the prophets.[37] Originally a call to Israel to engage in holy war, this battle summons is here put to different use by its application not to those whom Yahweh aids to victory, but to the victims, as in Jer. 46:3–6, 9f. The summons is characteristically followed in v. 12 by an

35. Duhm, von Orelli, Bewer, Wade, and Rudolph differentiate between *the Sabeans* and *a distant nation* on account of the change of preposition from *l^e* to *'el*. However, this upsets the artistic balance of the oracle. The combination also occurs in Gen. 37:36. In Jer. 6:20 Sheba is in parallelism with "a distant country." Merx and Robinson changed *lish^eḇā'îm* to *lashsh^eḇî*, "to captivity," with G, but a precise counterpart to *the Greeks* is required.

36. Cf. Weiser on 2:28f.

37. Cf. R. Bach, *Die Aufforderungen zur Flucht und zum Kampf im alttestamentlichen Prophetenspruch*. WMANT 9 (1962), pp. 51–104; H.-M. Lutz, *Jahwe, Jerusalem und die Völker*. WMANT 27 (1968), pp. 56–62; Obad. 1, 2; Mic. 4:13 and comments.

ill-boding statement which supplies the reason for it. The section is artistically tied together by the repetition in the final verse of the two verbs used at the beginning of the summons and of *all nations around* (v. 11).

God's voice rings out with orders for a state of war to be declared *among the nations*. His heralds are not identified, but are evidently members of the divine council in the role of angels (= messengers).[38] The basic call to *prepare a holy war* is an expression derived from Israel's wars under Yahweh's command.[39] Here it is ironically used of Yahweh's enemies in a divinely instigated war. The elaborations of the first command in vv. 9b, 11a, ordering the levy of the national armies and their advance, include vocabulary typical of the OT battle summonses.[40] All the hectic arrangements for a military campaign are evoked by a brusque, staccato meter. Verse 10 deals with the equipping of the international army with weapons for the battle. So serious is the coming conflict that as many weapons as possible are to be procured. The standard call for armaments[41] here takes the form of a parody of Isa. 2:4 (= Mic. 4:3). That passage spoke of universal peace; by reversing the old words Joel implies widespread involvement in this war of judgment.[42] Farmers called up for military service are to bring with them their agricultural implements refashioned into swordblades and spearheads. All available manpower is needed in this total war against God. Even the physically weak and psychologically unsuited are not to be exempted.[43] The last and least reserves would have to be drawn upon. Verse 11 is marked by some awkwardness: *there* has no antecedent, and one might expect vv. 10b, 11b to be adjacent for parallelism. There may be a deliberate intention to evoke a chaotic air of disorder. The nations are urged to converge on an area in the distance to which the speaker points. The end of the summons is linked to the projected trial of v. 2. Battle and trial are one. In OT thinking the two ideas are closely connected, war being regarded as a medium of divine justice, the execution of God's sentence.[44] The reason for the battle summons in v. 12b is an explanation of the name *Jehoshaphat,* reinforcing that given in v. 2b. To "judge" means not only to hear the evidence and deliver the verdict but also to carry out the verdict, which would be done in

38. Sellin; P. D. Miller, *loc. cit.*; Rudolph; cf. 1 K. 22:19–21; Amos 3:9.

39. Hitler uttered a grim parody of the underlying concept in one of his pre-war speeches: "I believe that I act today in unison with the Almighty Creator's intention: by fighting the Jews I do battle for the Lord."

40. Cf., e.g., Jer. 46:3 (*ngš*), 9 (*'lh*); 49:14 (*bw', qbṣ* Hithpael [here Niphal]). The first two terms are military terms for advancing to battle. Wade, Keller, and Wolff interpret *'lh* as going up to Jerusalem, but this sense does not apply to 1:6, which is here echoed. G reads imperatives for the two jussives in v. 9, but the juxtaposition of imperatives and jussives in Jer. 46:9 supports MT.

41. Cf. Isa. 21:5; Jer. 46:3f.; 51:11 (Bach, *op. cit.*, p. 63).

42. Bach, *op. cit.*, p. 72, n. 1, considers that the present sense is a survival of the original one and that the other passages reverse it. This view is less likely in light of the frequency of Joel's deliberate echoes of older scriptures, sometimes with a contrary nuance.

43. Contrast Deut. 20:8; Judg. 7:3.

44. Cf., e.g., Deut. 32:41; Judg. 11:27; 2 Sam. 18:19.

the final battle. Joel is taking up a motif familiar to the OT reader. The Songs of Zion celebrate the victory of Yahweh against his enemies who attack Jerusalem,[45] and Isa. 8:9f.; 17:12–14 are echoes of this cultic theme. Zech. 12 and 14 develop it in apocalyptic fashion, and so does Ezekiel's account of Gog's invasion, although in that case it is the country that is attacked rather than the capital. Here the Valley is envisaged as in the vicinity of Jerusalem, although Joel places no emphasis on this factor.

The reason given in v. 12b is the climax of the piece for which the battle summons has prepared as "a monumental introduction" (Lutz). So strong is Yahweh's providential control over the nations that the very summons comes from the Enemy and, as in Mic. 4:12f., the nations gather to be destroyed. Here the warrant is that they themselves had earlier gathered to destroy. The *ius talionis* so explicit in the intermediate section is hardly less evident in vv. 1–3, 9–12: the nations whose crime was their attack of Judah and Jerusalem would be brought back to the same venue to receive their sentence. The scene of the humiliation of Yahweh's people would fittingly become that of the downfall of foes who were both theirs and his.

2. *The Nations' Fate and Judah's Fortune* (*3*[*4*]:*13–21*)

Wield the sickle:
the harvest is ripe. 2+2
Get in and tread the grapes:
the press is full. 2+2
The vats are overflowing,
so great is their wickedness. 2+2
14 *Crowd upon noisy crowd*
fills Verdict Valley, 2+2
because Yahweh's Day is soon to come
in Verdict Valley. 3+2

15 *Sun and moon grow dark*
and stars stop shining, 3+3
16 *as Yahweh roars from Zion*
and thunders from Jerusalem;
and sky and earth vibrate. 3+3+3
But Yahweh proves a shelter for his people,
a stronghold for the Israelites. 3+3
17 *Then you will know that I am Yahweh your God,*
whose home is in Zion, my sacred mountain; 4+3
and Jerusalem will be made sacrosanct,
never having aliens pass through it again. 3+3

18 *On that day*
mountains will flow with sweet wine
and hills will run with milk; 3+3

45. See the comments on Mic. 4:1–5.

all the river beds of Judah
will run with water. 3+2
A spring will issue from Yahweh's temple,
watering Acacia Gorge. 4+3
19 *Egypt will become a desolation,*
Edom will become[46] *a desolate heath* 3+4
because of their violent treatment of Judeans,
spilling innocent blood in their country. 3+3
20 *But Judah will never lack inhabitants,*
nor will Jerusalem for generations to come. 3+3
21 *And shall I leave their bloodshed unpunished? I will not,*[47]
as surely as Yahweh has his home in Zion. 3+3

The book draws to a close by concluding its theme of the Day of Yahweh and its repercussions upon the chosen nation and the rest. This section dovetails artistically into the previous one by means of a new battle summons, addressed to the other side, together with an associated statement. This natural subunit forms the first of three stanzas, vv. 13f., whose close is marked by the repetition of *Verdict Valley.*[48] Verses 15–17 are interlocked as the second stanza by double references to Zion and Jerusalem; its conclusion is marked by the formula of self-revelation of Yahweh as Judah's covenant God. It is a description both of the cosmic disturbances set off by Yahweh's intervention in judgment, and of Judah's preservation. The third stanza, vv. 18–21, introduced by an opening formula, is a promise of fertility for Judah, enhanced by reference to the desolation of her neighbors' territory. The speakers change at the end of each stanza. In the first Yahweh

46. MT *tihyeh, will become,* may be a copyist's addition from v. 19a (Robinson, cf. *BHS*); it gives a weak ending to the line. Its omission, supported by S, would provide a 3+3 meter, in which the piece majors.
47. Verse 21 is a notorious crux. The solution adopted is that of H. Steiner: to take the first clause as a question, which characteristically lacks the interrogative particle when preceded by the conjunction (GK 150a), and the second clause as the reply with a perfect of certainty. Cf. Jer. 25:29, which actually uses the same verbs. Alternative proposals are as follows: (1) To take MT as "I shall declare/show to be innocent their blood (which) I have not (hitherto) shown to be innocent" (S. R. Driver). (2) To take the negative as a miswriting of the emphatic *lameḏ*: "Je déclare que leur sang est innocent, oui je le déclare" (Keller; Ahlström, *JTCJ,* p. 96; cf. Kapelrud). (3) To render the verb as "cleanse" (RV) or "expiate" (Keil, Weiser) with V; this interpretation in terms of punishment gives a hardly permissible meaning to the verb. (4) G. R. Driver, *JTS* 39(1938), pp. 401f., followed by NEB and Rudolph, has assigned to the verb a primary meaning "pour out," comparing Akk. *niqu* and Syr. *naqqî*: "I shall pour their blood (which) I have not (hitherto) poured out." (5) To emend, reading *w^eniqqamtî* for *w^eniqqêṯî*: "I shall avenge (their blood)." For this the support of G S is claimed, but the use of *ekdikein* for *nqh* in Zech. 5:3 renders this claim unlikely. This emendation is usually accompanied by one of two others: (a) *w^elō' 'ᵃnaqqeh* for *lo niqqêṯî*, "and I shall not leave unpunished," for which again appeal is made to G S, which read a future prefaced with the conjunction (*BHK,* RSV, Thompson, JB, cf. *BHS*); or (b) another *niqqamtî* for the second verb, "(which) I have (not) (yet) avenged" (Wellhausen, Bewer, Wade, Robinson).
48. Cf. 2:26f. for this pointer to the end of a strophe, and also 3:11f.

presumably issues the battle summons, but the prophet adds a crucial comment in v. 14. In the second the prophet continues, but Yahweh breaks in to point the moral at the end (v. 17). In the third stanza there is a similar pattern to that of the second: the final verse is spoken by Yahweh.

The whole piece is resonant with echoes of earlier parts of the book, which will be noted as they occur. Two purposes are intended by this parallelism. First, the prophetic Day of Yahweh, which Judah underwent in a kind of trial run in the form of the locust plague, is to be unleashed in its full force upon the nations, according to Joel. The curtailed prototype of Judah's experience is now built into its fully developed counterpart. Secondly, Judah is to experience a reversal of the devastation caused by the locusts and drought. The curse will be no more: it is to give way to a wealth of blessing.

13, 14 One might have expected the preliminary military instructions to the nations to culminate now in an order for them to attack. Surprisingly the command is given to Yahweh's army to attack the nations: they have been mustered to lose, not win, his holy war. The identity of Yahweh's forces is not revealed. Most probably we are to think in supernatural terms such as are explicit in the fiery chariots and horses seen around Elisha (2 K. 6:17) and "the ten thousands of holy ones" of Deut. 33:2.[49] Two orders are given, each with an encouraging reason. Orders and reasons employ two metaphors for judgment, both borrowed from farming. The first is a picture of cereal crops harvested with *the sickle,* as in Isa. 17:5, while the second alludes to the vintage, like Isa. 63:3. All is ready:like a field of ripe corn the nations are gathered in the valley, crying out to be cut down. Their armies are packed like so many grapes in the hollowed *press,* waiting to be trodden.[50] The third line of the verse amplifies the second reason and translates its metaphor into moral terms. Such a mass of grapes was piled in the press that its own weight was forcing the liquid down the channels into the nearby *vats,* which were spilling over and clamoring for attention. What a harvest! How ripe for judgment were the assembled nations who overflowed the boundaries of the broad valley! Yes, indeed, for it was only the enormity of their own *wickedness* that had brought them here to receive the annihilating judgment of God. So vital is the connection between the mass guilt of the nations and their massed presence that they can be run together poetically. There is a glance back at the accusations of vv. 2f. as the verdict is delivered, and, as it were, the hangman is instructed to do his grisly work.

Verse 14 gives a snatch of commentary on the scene from the prophet. A feature sometimes associated with the prophetic battle summons is a report of a vision of the armies in auditory and visual terms.[51] This report

49. Cf. Zech. 14:15; Matt. 26:53. Yahweh's people do not fight: cf. v. 16.
50. Heb. *rᵉḏû* could be taken as "go down," i.e., into the vat, from *yrd*; V, KJV, BDB, S. R. Driver, and Smith so interpret. But G S T "tread" from *rdh* accords well with the context. Only here does the verb bear this primary meaning, but it is present in its Arab. cognate.
51. Cf. Isa. 13:4; Jer. 46:5; and cf. Bach, *op. cit.*, p. 68.

is couched in terms reminiscent of Isa. 13:4, where in preparation for the imminent Day of Yahweh (v. 6, cited by Joel in 1:15) the prophet warns:

Hark, a tumult in the mountains,
like a great mass of people.
Hark, a din of kingdoms,
of nations mustering.

There the army which was to implement Yahweh's vengeance was meant. If, in view of the Day of Yahweh context and the similar language, Isa. 13:4 is here echoed, it serves as a gateway to reach the theme of Isa. 17:12:

Oh, the tumult of many peoples,
like tumultuous, crashing seas.

The "many peoples" were the Assyrian army, with its national brigades, which was attacking Judah. Isaiah forecast their doom for all their frightening din. In Joel's commentary on the call for judgment, he applies the thought of Isa. 17:12 to the Day of Yahweh via the language of Isa. 13:4. He repeats their key noun, "tumult," which appeals to both ear and eye. Literally "crowds, crowds," his phrase includes in its sound the effect of noisy commotion crowds sometimes make.[52] The quotation of Isa. 13:6 in 1:15 is taken up again with all its grim foreboding. This time it is no longer a cry of warning to Israel: Israel's Day has been averted by God's graciously heeding their repentant cries. Now it is the nations' turn. As Yahweh gives the signal for action, the prophet has glanced at the crowds gathered in the *Valley* and comments that the *Day* is now so *soon to come* for them in the form of their destruction.[53] Jehoshaphat Valley is given a new name, *Verdict Valley,* which is repeated with climactic emphasis at the end of the stanza. The different name reinforces the significance of the Valley as the place where God carries out his judicial sentence upon the nations' war crimes against his people.[54]

Mention of the Day is not the only echo of material found earlier in the book. Overflowing vats figured in 2:24 in the literal sense of the abundant fertility Judah was to enjoy after the locust plague. The deliberate repetition of happenings that were to take place on Judean soil stresses the gulf that lay between the fate of the nations and the blessing of Judah. It is not surprising that Joel's impressive language in v. 12 was reused in the NT. In Rev. 14:15, 18, 20 it is employed to describe the harvest of judgment. In

52. Heb. *hᵃmônîm hᵃmônîm.* The noun appears in the singular at Isa. 13:4; 17:2 and is backed by two verbal forms in the latter verse. The repetition is a characteristic Heb. device to express intensification; cf. Ex. 8:14(10); 2 K. 3:16 (GK 123e).

53. A revocalizing of *qārôḇ,* "near," to *qᵉrāḇ,* "war" (Rudolph, Sellin), on the ground that the Day was present, is pedantic and spoils one of the backward-pointing allusions of which this passage is so deliberately full.

54. Heb. *ḥārûts* can also mean "threshing sledge," since the root meaning "cut" develops both in a literal sense and in a metaphorical one of a binding, irrevocable decision (the English word comes from Latin *decido,* "cut off"). Calvin, Merx, and von Orelli prefer the agricultural meaning in view of the harvest metaphor in v. 13. Keller and Ahlström, *JTCJ,* p. 81, see here a *double entendre.*

Mark 4:29 Jesus uses it to describe the dynamic manifestation of the kingdom of God.[55]

15–17 The first stanza has represented the scene just before the Day of Yahweh; this second one describes conditions during the Day, while the third is to depict the situation when the Day's conflict is done. Now the moment of truth has arrived for the nations. In 2:10 the eschatological motif of the darkening of *sun, moon,* and *stars* was used to convey the terrible fact that in the locust plague Judah was undergoing the first hours of the Day of Yahweh.[56] In the second phase of the Day, experienced by nations other than Judah, the motif fittingly reappears as the horrifying reaction of nature to the theophany of Yahweh in judgment wrath. The thunder of Yahweh's voice, which sounded in 2:11 via the locusts, breaks out again. Now it is the final verdict on the assembled nations, the order to administer the *coup de grâce*. A new feature, so far as Joel is concerned, is the source of the thunderclap of wrath and the angry roar that spells disaster: it is *Zion, Jerusalem*. Such a location is very old. The book of Amos opens with this very line (Amos 1:2) to represent the dire message for the Northern Kingdom given through Amos from the God who had revealed himself in the temple at Jerusalem. The line has a cultic ring, and Jeremiah, who often echoes cultic themes, uses very similar expressions in 25:30 concerning the judgment that is to fall upon all, Israel and other nations alike. Joel cites it probably from Amos in view of the word-for-word correspondence between the two: the book was by now doubtless taken up into the cult.

Our prophet had a spiritual purpose in referring to the capital at this point. The stanza gradually moves from the theme of the terrifying phenomena of the nations' Day to the comforting message of the safety afforded to Israel in Jerusalem. The first four lines have an alternating progression: cosmic signs–Yahweh in Zion–earthquake–Yahweh's protection of Israel. Accordingly, although Zion is the Lion's lair and the source of the thunder, its mention also functions as "a favorable omen" (S. R. Driver) for his own people, which the stanza is soon to develop. Zion and its environs, including Verdict Valley, are places of terror only for the enemies of Judah and of Judah's God; Judah herself has nothing to fear. The motif of earthquake was used in 2:10 as a reaction to the theophany on the Day of Yahweh when he makes his presence known in judgment. It now appears again as a further parallel between phases one and two of the Day.

Joel draws a veil of reticence over the carnage. In place of the details

55. "As seedtime is followed in due time by harvest, so will the present hiddenness and ambiguousness of the kingdom of God be succeeded by its glorious manifestation" (C. E. B. Cranfield, *The Gospel According to St. Mark.* Cambridge Greek Testament [1959], *in loc.*, *q.v.* for discussion). The textual relationships between the OT and NT passages are discussed by R. H. Charles, *The Revelation of St. John.* ICC, vol. 2 (1920), *in loc.*; and France, *op. cit.*, pp. 242, 247.

56. In 2:31 these celestial phenomena are precursors of the Day, but here and in 2:10, as in Isa. 13:10, 13, they occur on the Day.

of the destruction, which occurs offstage, as it were, he describes the concomitant sounds and sights of cosmic upheaval and the divine cry. If the stable bodies of the natural world were convulsed at Yahweh's appearing, it can be taken for granted that mere mortals had little chance of escape. This very fact places a question mark against the position of the people of God, so close to the Hiroshima blast of judgment. It is necessary for the prophet to reassure them as soon as he has dealt with the terrifying topic of the nations' doom. The same compulsion was discernible in 2:30–32, to which this stanza is, and must be, so similar. So far Joel has been deliberately reusing 2:10f., but now he draws from a happier section, 2:27, which gave promises to *Israel* as the covenant *people* of Yahweh. He first amplifies the former promises with an element derived from cultic psalmody, namely, Yahweh as the *shelter* and *stronghold* in whom his people may find security in time of danger. Such psalms of assurance as Ps. 46, a Song of Zion, are echoed here:

> *God is our shelter and stronghold,*[57]
> *ever ready to help in times of trouble.* (Ps. 46:1[2])

In fact there are a number of links between the context and this psalm: cf. Ps. 46:3(4) and 6(7). Further links will be evident later. Joel is echoing not necessarily this particular psalm but a whole bundle of cultic concepts to many of which this psalm gives expression.

So much of Joel's eschatology is but the themes of Judah's worship projected on the screen of Israel's future, a fact also true of Isaiah in his qualified application of Zion theology to the Assyrian crisis. Joel and Isaiah were in this respect saying little that was new. Their novelty lay in their specific application of perennial ideas celebrated in the temple songs of praise. Joel is eschatologically oriented: he claims the fulfilment of a sacred theme for this Day of days. Yahweh would not fail his people, but would live up to his merited reputation as the God of help in ages past. They would be kept safe in the center of the raging storm. Their refuge would lie in the very person of their Lord: they could rest secure in the truth of what he was. He would protect them in accordance with the bond of covenant fellowship between them: the divine name and the traditional name for the people significantly frame the line.

This theme is taken up in the next line. Just as in the near future Judah was to deepen her understanding and appreciation of Yahweh from his wonder-working power in dealing with the enemy army of locusts and in restoring fertility (2:27), so at a later time she would glean from his display of ultimate might against her human enemies a fresh insight into the great reality of God in her midst. The covenant formula would find a new relevance in this demonstration of his championship of their survival. Moreover, an age-old truth celebrated in Israel's hymns would strike them with new impact: what a privilege was theirs in that their capital was his earthly residence. Isaiah had echoed this devotional theme when he spoke of

57. Heb. *'ōz* in the psalm, *mā'ōz* here.

"Yahweh of hosts" as the one "whose home is on Mount Zion" (Isa. 8:18). The *sacred mountain,* which their neighbors located elsewhere as the home of the gods,[58] was in reality Jerusalem. It was none other than

> *the city of God,*
> *the holy habitation of the Most High.* (Ps. 46:4[5])

There it was that the people had gathered to the temple to seek Yahweh's face in supplication (2:1), and the fact that they had not been disappointed had confirmed his holy presence "in the midst of Israel" (2:27). The divine holiness, which usually has something of a physical quality about it in the OT, spreads out from the temple and envelops the city with its sacred aura. Unhappily history had dealt a cruel blow to the long-cherished theme of Zion's inviolability. But the promise given through Obadiah, of which Joel reminded his audience in 2:32, had gone on to give a new assurance of the old doctrine (Obad. 17), and this assurance is re-presented here: *Jerusalem will be made sacrosanct* once more. Mount Sinai was put out of bounds to unauthorized persons on pain of death (Ex. 19:12, 23); so now no access would be permitted *aliens* "who have no share in Israel or its privileges and do not care for them" (S. R. Driver). Despite the teeming thousands on Jerusalem's doorstep on the nations' Day, not one would be allowed to trespass inside and desecrate it as once they had done. Yahweh's protection of his people would be extended to all that both they and he held sacred. A people whose hearts still bled and eyes still watered at the memory of the profanity of the Babylonians and their allies are given the promise they crave in their devout faith. "Never again" is the welcome word to a faithful people whose hearts are turned back to God. The city of Jerusalem had a sacramental significance in the spiritual relationship between Judah and her God. Its function and associations in Joel's present message are captured for the Christian reader in the vision of "the holy city, the new Jerusalem" and the report of the "great voice" explaining,

> *"Behold, God's home is with men. He will make his home with them and they will be his people, and God himself will be with them. He will wipe away every tear from their eyes, . . . for the former things have passed away."* (Rev. 21:3)

18–21 When the drama of the nations' Day is over, there remains a final scene in which Judah will feature. Judah is to enjoy God's richest blessing. The book closes with a description of the salvation Yahweh is to bring about for his people. The promises of material plenty are pledges of the spiritual presence of Yahweh *in Zion*. It is significant that the phrase in v. 17 crowns this piece in v. 21, so that all between is a commentary on its implications. There is an intimate link between the temple and the land: Yahweh's presence in Zion was the key to the blessing of the whole land.[59] From his throne in the temple he will distribute gifts to the surrounding

58. See the comment on Mic. 2:3 and n. 27 there.
59. Cf. Ex. 15:17; Ps. 78:54, 67–72; Isa. 57:13, where Zion and the land are closely related. See the analysis of the theme of these texts by R. E. Clements, *TGUOS* 19(1961/62), pp. 16–28.

countryside. Good crops were ever dependent in Israelite thinking upon harmony between God and his people, as Ps. 65 so beautifully illustrates. The relationship between Yahweh and his own would be so close that the land would be laden with lavish fruits of grace. But there is a more subtle intention than to close the book with happy thoughts of Paradise, wonderful though they are. Joel's purpose is to take up key phrases used to describe Judah's disastrous condition in the first half of the book and to weave them into a grand finale of reversal.[60] In those very areas where sin and wrath had left their black marks of destruction, grace would make new life blossom for Judah.

The opening temporal phrase serves as both an introduction to the new piece and a link with the preceding. The traditional association of the Day with prosperity and blessing was a theme Amos' northern contemporaries had stressed so exclusively as to merit the prophet's ire (Amos 5:18–20). But it had its place alongside the themes of judgment for Israel and the nations in Joel's synthesis, and now he spells it out in a way especially attractive to his hearers. He brings the promise of *sweet wine* galore to an audience who had experienced the lack of it during the locust plague (1:5). So abundant a crop would the vineyards yield upon the terraced hillsides, such rivers of grape juice would *flow* from the presses nearby that the memory of Judah's deprivation would be lost beneath the deluge. Joel has clearly selected the line from a fund of cultic material. A similar line occurs in Amos 9:13, but Joel's addition of *milk,* which is not for him an essential element,[61] seems to indicate that both passages depend on a cultic tradition whose roots stretch wide and deep into ancient Near Eastern lore. An Ugaritic text speaks in similar terms of prodigious fertility associated with general rehabilitation after conflict:

> *The skies will rain oil,*
> *the wadis run with honey.*[62]

The reference to milk indicates such rich highland pastures that the cattle would produce a surfeit of milk: it would be as if it ran from the very ground. The poetic hyperbole recalls the stock description of Canaan as "a land flowing with milk and honey." Hebrew eschatology very often applies ancient promises to a future time.

In 1:20 Joel's plaint had been that the *river beds* were dry of *water* as a result of the drought. The torrents produced in the rainy season tended to dwindle till only dry beds were left in summer. Now the promise is given that they will flow all the year round. The lament recorded in ch. 1 would be removed from the people's lips as they received divine blessing in place of a curse.

A related promise follows, again dealing with water and again

60. A similar purpose underlies Amos 9:11–15; see L. C. Allen, *Vox Evangelica* 6 (1969), pp. 51, 53.

61. Wolff finds a contrast with 1:18.

62. C. H. Gordon, *Ugaritic Handbook* (1947), text 49:iii, 6f., 12f. Cf. J. Gray, *The Legacy of Canaan*. SVT 5 (^{2}1965), p. 70; Ahlström, *JTCJ*, p. 87.

alluding to the reversal of an earlier deprivation. Because of the locusts' ravages, cereal offering and libation had been withheld from *Yahweh's temple,* and therefore joy and gladness as well (1:9, 13, 16). Even the temple had been victim of the infertility caused by the locusts and drought. But Joel can promise a time when the very sanctuary would be the source of amazing fertility. The eschatological concept of a river issuing from the temple was already in existence by Joel's time, and Ezek. 47:1–12 furnishes a detailed description.[63] Eschatology had taken it over from religious tradition. Ps. 46:4(5) speaks of a "river whose streams gladden the city of God." The little stream flowing from the Gihon spring is invested with the majesty of the vitalizing river of Paradise as symbol of the nearness and blessing of Yahweh.[64] Ancient lore placed the divine dwelling place by a river. In an Ugaritic text, El's residence is "at the spring of the rivers in the middle of the stream of the two deeps," that is, at the place where the subterranean flood wells up; and the Akkadian mountain of the gods was situated "in the mouth of the rivers."[65] The Christian seer adds another chapter to this Near Eastern saga when in his vision of the new Jerusalem he describes "the river of the water of life flowing from the throne of God and of the Lamb" and providing water for the perennially fruiting varieties of the "tree of life" on the river banks, whose very leaves had healing power (Rev. 22:1f.). Joel by this symbol speaks of God's presence as the means of transforming barren aridity into newness of life. *Acacia Gorge* represents what is dry and infertile, for on such soils acacias manage to grow.

Unmentioned elsewhere in the OT, the symbolic value of this gorge seems to transcend any literal placing on a map, like Jehoshaphat Valley and Verdict Valley.[66] If a definite place was in Joel's mind, it was probably that deep and rugged part of the Kidron Valley which runs down to the Dead Sea.[67] In this lower stretch it is called Wadi en-Nar, "wadi of fire," because of its intense heat. According to Thompson, acacias grow there still. Certainly this was the direction in which Ezekiel's river flowed on its way down to the Dead Sea.

63. Cf. Zech. 14:8.

64. Cf. Weiser, *The Psalms* (E.T. 1962), *in loc.*; Clements, *God and Temple* (1965), pp. 72f.

65. H.-J. Kraus, *Worship in Israel* (E.T. 1966), p. 202; Gray, *op. cit.*, p. 113; Ahlström, *JTCJ*, p. 87.

66. Wade; Kapelrud, who finds here a guarantee of the supply of acacia wood for temple furniture; Dennefeld, *RSR* 5 (1925), pp. 601f.; Chary, *PC*, pp. 215f.; Rudolph.

67. This identification is followed by Credner, Hitzig, von Orelli, Thompson, Wolff, and Keller. There are two less likely proposals. (1) Wadi es-Sant, to the southwest of Jerusalem, was named identically in later times. Whereas in Ezek. 47 the river flows east, in Zech. 14:8 it flows both east and west; it is suggested that the conceptions of both Ezekiel and Joel have there been combined (Wellhausen, Bewer, Delcor). (2) The name is related to Abel-Shittim (Acacia Meadow, Num. 33:49), the eastern part of the broad valley around the south end of the Jordan; it is also called Shittim (Acacias) in Josh. 2:1; Mic. 6:5; etc. (Keil; van Hoonacker; cf. Ahlström, *JTCJ*, pp. 92f.). But difficulties are raised not only by the name Gorge or wadi, but also by the necessity of envisaging the stream crossing the Jordan.

So drastic had been the locusts' depredations that they transformed a veritable garden of Eden into a *desolate heath* (2:3). Accordingly v. 19a follows smoothly v. 18b, not merely by virtue of the link of Paradise but as a further reversal of Judah's experience.[68] Now it was the turn of the lands of Judah's enemies to lie waste. Moreover, 2:20 had promised that the locusts would be driven into a desolate land,[69] making for a fitting correspondence between the fate of the two sets of Judah's foes. Joel reverts to the black side of the Day in order to enhance the security and fertility of Judah: he sets its splendor against the dark fate of traditional enemies. Just as the prophet had one eye on Judah while he related the outworking of the nations' Day in vv. 15–17, so his treatment of Judah's blessing is balanced by reference to the destiny of her foes' territories. *Egypt* could boast of an abundant water supply in the Nile, while Judah often suffered from drought: thus the present contrast with Zion's spring and Judah's perennial rivers is all the more pointed. Joel is probably influenced by Ezekiel, who had spoken of both Egypt and Edom as a desolation.[70]

The Hebrews could never resist in the midst of new-found prosperity a side-glance at the downfall or chagrin of their foes, as Ps. 23:5 illustrates; and certainly it serves as a final vindication of their cause. This factor is stressed in the next line. The *Judeans* had suffered *violent treatment* at the hands of both nations to the extent of unnecessary loss of life. Suggested identifications of the incidents to which the prophet refers vary according to the date to which he is assigned and according to whether *their country* is interpreted as that of the foes or Judah. In exilic and postexilic times the Edomites are the object of particular resentment for the part they played in 587 B.C. after the downfall of Jerusalem. If, as seems likely, Joel is echoing Obadiah at this point,[71] there is added reason for locating Joel's grievance in this period. Then Egypt's murderous violence might well be Pharaoh Neco's killing of Josiah and imprisonment of Jehoahaz (2 K. 23:29–34),[72] which brought to an abrupt and shocking end a reign that had been marked by religious reformation and territorial gains, and on which the editor of Kings had bestowed the accolade "right in Yahweh's eyes."

Against the curse on the countries of Egypt and Edom, there stands out in clear relief the blessing of *Judah and Jerusalem,* to which the prophet now reverts. The present theme follows on naturally from the catastrophe of 587 B.C. to which Joel has just alluded. Never again would capital and country see that draining of the population which had occurred in the exile to Babylon. Rather, the union between people and promised land is sealed afresh with a pledge of perpetual occupation and enjoyment of new

68. Cf. too 1:7, 17f.
69. Heb. *'erets . . . sh^emāmâ*; here *sh^emāmâ, miḏbar sh^emāmâ*.
70. Ezek. 29:9 (*lish^emāmâ*, as here), 12; 32:15; 35:3f., 7, 14f. Cf. too Ps. 46:8(9).
71. Heb. *mēḥ^amas* appears to be an echo of Obad. 10, especially in view of the earlier links with Obadiah.
72. Wade, Delcor, *et al.*; cf. Wolff.

prosperity.[73] A grand word for the future, but what of those citizens who were cut off in their prime, whose eyes saw Judah's ruin and would never see her rehabilitation? The minds of Joel's audience cannot help lingering on the rankling acts of foreign injustice. The spilled blood cried out to Yahweh in a lament like that of the Christian martyrs in Rev. 6:10:

> *"How long will it be, Lord holy and true, before you pass sentence and avenge our blood?"*

Yahweh breaks in with a final word of assurance to the sorrowing.[74] They receive the glad promise that he will not leave the debt unpaid, but will exact punishment for the last dark drop. The promise is appropriately reinforced by a solemn pledge.[75] The fact of Yahweh's presence in Zion, celebrated in v. 17, is the guarantee of vindication. Yahweh had already heard the cry of lament from their hearts concerning the locusts. Now the book closes with the promise that he would champion anew his chosen people and see that justice was done on this long-standing issue.

> *Sing praises to Yahweh, enthroned in Zion. . . .*
> *For he, the avenger of blood, remembers them;*
> *he does not forget the appeal of the afflicted.*
> (Ps. 9:11f.[12f.])

God is on the throne: the reminder of his sovereignty is balm for the wounds of injustice and the basis of his people's hope for the future.

73. Cf. Jer. 17:25; Zech. 12:6.

74. Wolff deletes v. 21a as a later comment on *innocent blood* in v. 19. Sellin, Bewer, Moffatt, and NEB place v. 21a after v. 19. Rudolph puts the whole of v. 21 there. Certainly that order would be more logical, although the splitting of the two halves of v. 21 would spoil the existing metrical scheme, if all the wording of MT in vv. 19, 21 is retained. The alternation of theme is not impossible (cf. vv. 15f.); Robinson perceived a chiastic order in the section (v. 18 = 20 = 21b; v. 19 = 21a). *Contra* Merx, von Orelli, Wolff, and Keller (cf. Rudolph), the present order need not indicate that the pardon of bloodguilt attaching to Judah is meant: the expression *niqqeh dām* obviously picks up *dām nāqî'*, "innocent blood," in v. 19b and refers back to it. As Rudolph observes, the book nowhere mentions Judah's bloodguilt.

75. The conjunction is to be taken as introducing an asseveration (BDB, p. 253b; Ewald, Smith, S. R. Driver, Wade, Rudolph), and thus the change to the third person is not so abrupt as it would otherwise be.

The Book of OBADIAH

INTRODUCTION

1. DATE AND HISTORICAL BACKGROUND

Jerome was the first to observe that the difficulties presented by the short book of Obadiah are in inverse proportion to its size. To add to its complexity the various problems tend to be interrelated. The chronological discussion to a certain extent runs on a parallel course to that concerning the dating of Joel. As with Joel, one factor is the significance of the canonical position of the book as the fourth of the Minor Prophets.[1] If on other grounds Obadiah is not to be placed early, it is possible to regard its position after Amos as a thematic sequence: the book may have been viewed as a virtual commentary on Amos 9:12.

There are a series of historical references to the overthrow of Jerusalem in vv. 11–14. Taking their cue from the canonical order, Keil, von Orelli, and Young[2] are representative of those who have appealed to the Philistine and Arabian attack in the reign of Jehoram c.850 B.C. (2 Chr. 21:16f.) and related it to the revolt of Edom in his reign (2 K. 8:20–22; 2 Chr. 21:8–10). But it is questionable whether an attack on Jerusalem is envisaged in 2 Chr. 21, and certainly the Edomites are not mentioned in connection with it. Accordingly, most refer the strong terms of vv. 11–14 to the fall of Jerusalem in 587 B.C. Some indeed who opt for the early date regard the verses as predictive.[3] But this is to ignore the rhetorical nature of the passage as a dramatic representation of a past event, as the plainer language of vv. 11, 15b reveals. The Edomites were certainly associated with the events of 587, as later recriminations attest, e.g., Ps. 137:7; Lam. 4:21f.; Ezek. 25:12–14; 35:5f. 1 Esdras 4:45 preserves a tradition that "the Edomites burned the temple when Judah was devastated by the Chaldeans."

1. G makes Obadiah the fifth, after Joel, perhaps because of the affinities between the two prophecies.
2. *An Introduction to the OT* (1949), p. 277.
3. E.g., F. Gaebelein, *The Servant and the Dove* (1946), p. 5: "The capture by the Chaldeans most nearly fits the picture."

This historical passage with its passionate tone and vivid detail has seemed to many to indicate that its author was an eyewitness of the 587 B.C. tragedy.[4] His work, the extent of which has yet to be determined, has accordingly been dated early in the exilic period and regarded as comparable to the outbursts of Lamentations. Calvin must evidently be listed among this group.[5] He explicitly stated: "They seem to be mistaken who think that Obadiah lived before the time of Isaiah." In fact it is implied throughout his commentary that the Jews are in exile.

But it may be questioned whether so early a date does justice to vv. 1, 7. Rudolph admits that there is no occasion that fits these allusions in the period immediately after 587, but he claims that none is necessary. Obadiah's message is a theological necessity of reprisal for what the Edomites did to the people of Judah and Jerusalem. Sufficient warrant for his words is found in the justice of God. Other scholars have found it necessary to specify a historical setting for v. 1 and a feasible occasion for v. 7 within the period of Obadiah's ministry. Mal. 1:3 in the middle of the fifth century announced that the land of Edom, that rugged and mountainous terrain lying to the south of Moab between the Dead Sea and the Gulf of Aqaba, had been devastated beyond hope of recovery. In 312 B.C. the capital of Edom was firmly in the hands of the nomadic Nabatean Arabs, and the army of Antigonus fought two campaigns against them at Petra (Diodorus Siculus xix.95). This process of Arab occupation evidently had already reached a climax by the time of Malachi. Wellhausen was apparently the first to date Obadiah in terms of Arab invasion from the desert in the south and east, and to place him shortly before Malachi.[6]

His conclusion was determined by his view of vv. 2–9 as a description of a past event. But are not the Hebrew perfect verbs to be regarded as "prophetic," and the imperfects to be given their normal future role? Subsequent scholarship has tended to disagree with Wellhausen, and to place the fulfilment of the passage in a period later than Obadiah. Rudolph observes that the divine message of v. 1 obviously looks forward to a future defeat, as does the statement that nations are summoned to battle against Edom. The passage announces that Edom is to be overthrown in the future.

With Arab pressure on Edomite territory is to be linked to some extent at least the Edomite occupation of the Negeb to the south of Judah. Apparently the Negeb was removed from Judah's control in 597 B.C.,[7] and

4. J. Morgenstern has related Obadiah to a postulated occupation of Judah and siege and capture of Jerusalem in 485 B.C. by a coalition of Edomites, Moabites, and Ammonites, with the support of Persia (*HUCA* 27 [1956], pp. 114f.). See the criticisms by H. H. Rowley in *Men of God* (1963), pp. 238–242.

5. J. M. P. Smith, Rudolph, Weiser, Ellison, Myers, and Eaton are among those who date Obadiah in the (early) exilic period.

6. Pfeiffer and Thompson follow Wellhausen.

7. Cf. Jer. 13:19, and H. L. Ginsberg, *Alex Marx Jubilee Volume* (1950), pp. 363f.

whether or not the Babylonians formally handed the region over to the Edomites or merely filled the vacuum left by Judah, they were certainly the beneficiaries. According to 1 Esdras 4:50, by the time of Darius I, Edomites had occupied Jewish villages, and the postexilic province of Judah extended only as far south as Beth-zur, north of Hebron. To what extent was this infiltration due to Arab pressure upon the Edomite homeland? A seal of a local Edomite official of Ezion-geber, Qaus'anal, was assigned by Albright to a probable date after 600 B.C., while an ostracon from there which he dated in the first half of the sixth century lists names of which four are specifically Edomite and none is definitely Arabic.[8] Evidently the Edomites were still in control of their native land until after 550 B.C. However, by the fifth century Arab names had appeared at Ezion-geber.

In the Persian period the land of Edom had no sedentary occupation.[9] The Edomites were displaced by nomadic Arab tribes. The Nabateans, who controlled Petra by 312 B.C., and by Roman times had developed into a prosperous and highly cultured state, were eventually to emerge as dominant.[10] But the initial onslaughts upon Edom were due to a coalition of Arab tribes, led doubtless by Qedar, whose king Geshem was to be one of Nehemiah's adversaries c.440 B.C.[11] Obad. 1b seems to suggest that already in Obadiah's time the position was unstable, and plans were afoot for attacking Edom. Probably the prophet is to be dated in the early postexilic period.[12] Since Joel 2:32 quotes Obad. 17 and echoes the prophecy in a number of other places, Obadiah preceded Joel. If Joel was rightly assigned to the last part of the sixth century, such a dating for Obadiah is feasible, since it allows him to be contemporary with early Arab infiltration into Edomite territory and also to be an eyewitness of the 587 B.C. disaster.[13]

There is another factor which at first sight looks promising for the dating of Obadiah.[14] Verses 1–9 have so many terminological and thematic links with Jer. 49:7–16 that there is obviously a close relationship of some kind between the two passages. Can it be established whether Obadiah followed or preceded Jeremiah? Unfortunately the issue is too complex to

8. Albright, "Ostracon No. 6043 from Ezion-geber," *BASOR* 82 (1941), pp. 11–15.
9. N. Glueck, *Annual of the American Schools of Oriental Research* 15 (1935), pp. 138–140; *idem, The Other Side of the Jordan* (1940), p. 128.
10. Cf. J. Starky, "The Nabataeans: A Historical Sketch," *BA* 18 (1955), pp. 84–106.
11. Cf. I. Rabinowitz, *JNES* 15 (1956), pp. 5–9.
12. Deissler and G. W. Ahlström, *Joel and the Temple Cult of Jerusalem*. SVT 21 (1971), p. 120, date him between 550 and 500, Watts at the end of the sixth century or the first half of the fifth.
13. Cf. Ezra 3:12.
14. The language of the book is hardly a decisive factor, though Deissler strives to prove its affinities with exilic and postexilic literature. There is one Aramaism, *qṭl* (v. 9), which Rudolph finds consistent with a late preexilic dating; Dahood, *Pss 3*, p. 297, denies that the root is an Aramaism.

give a straightforward answer.[15] The parallels are obvious enough.[16] Obad. 1b–4 is more or less parallel with Jer. 49:14–16, and Obad. 5 with Jer. 49:9. The heading and introduction to the oracle against Edom in Jer. 49:7 reappears in Obad. 1, while the motif of Edom's loss of wisdom in that verse emerges in Obad. 8. There is no parallel for the distinctive Obad. 7, but Obad. 6 is related to Jer. 49:10a.

Caspari argued that Jer. 49 is dependent on Obadiah, and to this priority von Orelli, Keil,[17] Deissler, Eissfeldt, Rudolph, Keller, and others have given assent. Bewer, however, urged that the Obadiah passage is secondary. A third position, that both passages depend on a common source, has been taken by a number of scholars.[18] The primary nature of Obadiah is suggested by the orderly and compact arrangement; the material in Jer. 49 appears disorganized in comparison. Caspari considered that the Obadiah piece had a bolder, starker air, whereas Jer. 49 smoothed and simplified. On the other hand, signs are not lacking that Jer. 49 is more primitive. The feminine suffix in v. 1 ("against her") is most unusual. Aalders has noted that in Jer. 49:14 it has Bozrah as its antecedent, which is lacking in the selective Obadiah material.[19] Moreover Jer. 49:14 can easily be scanned as two lines of verse, but its counterpart in Obad. 1 is reduced to prose by the variant form of the second line. Jer. 49:15 begins with Heb. *kî*, "for," giving a more closely structured relationship with v. 14, which is quite in keeping with the form of the passage; Obad. 2, however, lacks the conjunction and its contents have a different purpose.[20] This formal degeneration has a secondary ring. Obad. 3 suspiciously lacks the difficult *hapax legomenon* that occurs at the beginning of its parallel, Jer. 49:16.

It hardly seems possible to trace a direct line from Jer. 49 to Obadiah or the reverse. It is unlikely that the problem may be solved by recourse to textual criticism, as if one can pick and choose among the two recensions and blame subsequent copyists for what one considers inferior readings. Both

15. The issue is further complicated by the fact that very many scholars do not regard Jeremiah as the author of parts or the whole of Jer. 49; rather, Jer. 49:7–22 is a compendium or anthology of assorted anti-Edomite material. Cf. Rudolph, *Jeremia*. Handbuch zum AT 12 (^{3}1968), pp. 268f., who claims that since Jer. 49 is partially dependent on Obadiah, it cannot wholly be attributed to Jeremiah. He attributes very little of the section to him: v. 12, for instance, written after 587, assumes that the destruction of Jerusalem was undeserved, but this viewpoint is untypical of Jeremiah. J. Bright, *Jeremiah*. Anchor Bible (1965), p. 307, regards Jer. 46–51 as an amplification of genuine utterances of Jeremiah by numerous anonymous sayings.

16. For a list of the textual variation between the two passages, see the apparatus of *BHS* (in its n. 5a-a it misquotes Jer. 49:9b) or Bewer.

17. Keil argued that the parts of Jer. 49 that have no counterparts in Obadiah contain expressions used by Jeremiah elsewhere, while the material in Jer. 49 shared by Obadiah does not appear in the rest of the book.

18. E.g., Ewald, Sellin, J. M. P. Smith, Bewer, Wade, Cannon, Robinson, Pfeiffer, Thompson, Eaton, and Watts.

19. G. C. Aalders, *The Problem of the Book of Jonah* (1948), p. 18.

20. See n. 10 in the commentary.

Obad. 1–9 and Jer. 49 seem to have preserved separately features derived from a third source. Is Obad. 1–9 a deliberate updating of an older oracle, adapting it to the sixth-century circumstances and claiming its contemporary and imminent fulfilment?[21] Possibly the plural "we have heard" in Obad. 1 (cf. "I heard," Jer. 49:14) is a reference to the community's inheritance of a venerated oracle.[22]

2. UNITY OF COMPOSITION AND PURPOSE

Apart from the question whether an older oracle has been used in Obad. 1–9, there tend to be two major views current concerning stages of composition. The first, adduced by Wellhausen, attributes to Obadiah vv. 1–14, 15b, and assigns the rest to one or more later hands.[23] Representative of this literary position are Bewer, Pfeiffer, Eissfeldt, Myers, Deissler, and Keller. The reason for denying vv. 15a, 16–21 to Obadiah is the difference of theme. The first part of the little book deals with concrete situations, the fall of Jerusalem and the impending conquest of Edom, while the rest is eschatologically oriented toward the Day of Yahweh and the destruction of all nations save Judah. "We pass from the realm of historical events to that of apocalyptic fancies" (Pfeiffer). Moreover, the change of address in v. 16 is so abrupt that "the same author can hardly be credited with it" (Bewer). The second part of the book is generally divided into vv. 15a, 16–18 and 19–21. The latter portion is differentiated from the former as a subsequent prose appendix or appendices commenting on v. 17b; v. 19 especially has been heavily glossed with explanatory material.

There are varying views within this general position. Deissler grants that the later supplement, vv. 19–21, may be from the same author as vv. 15a, 16–18, while Myers affirms the unity of vv. 15a, 16–21. Keller considers vv. 16–18 the work of a contemporary of Obadiah. Eissfeldt does not quickly dismiss the possibility that Obadiah was the author of vv. 15a, 16–18, in which Edom is involved, as in earlier verses. But he notes a tendency to fill out with subsequent eschatological material older oracles that refer to concrete events, citing the book of Joel as an example, and he puts the present book in this category.

The second main position[24] is that of von Orelli,[25] Rudolph, Weiser,

21. Cf. the probable use of an older oracle against Moab in Isa. 15f.

22. Thompson suggests that the historical background of the traditional preexilic oracle lay in the recurrent pattern of Arab raids on Edom. He cites Judg. 6:1–6; 2 Chr. 21:16, and a seventh-century B.C. Assyrian reference to Arabs invading lands to the west of the North Arabian desert (*ANET*, pp. 297–301).

23. Earlier attempts to divide the book otherwise, such as by J. G. Eichhorn in 1824 and Ewald in 1840, have been abandoned. Wellhausen's exclusion of vv. 6, 8, 9, 12 has also not found favor. On the reversal of the two halves of v. 15 see n. 16 on that verse.

24. Mention should also be made of Robinson's view that the book is an anthology of eight anti-Edomite sayings from different periods, vv. 1–5, 6, 7, 8–11, 12–14, 15f., 17f., 19–21.

25. Not in the English edition but in *Die zwölf Kleinen Propheten* ([3]1908), *in loc.*

Fohrer, and Brockington, who deny to Obadiah only the third part of the book, vv. 19–21. Rudolph, who is followed closely by Weiser, is careful to distinguish authorship from continuity, regarding vv. 15a, 16–18 as an independent oracle of Obadiah. He has given a classic definition of the differences between the first and second parts of the book. In the first part the nations are the agents of Yahweh's punishment of Edom, in the second victims along with Edom, while Israel is his agent; in the first part Edom is addressed, in the second the Jews. But he notes that the second part has the same historical background as the first, namely, the fall of Jerusalem (v. 16), and both concentrate on Edom. He dates the first part soon after 587 B.C. and finds in the second no eschatological concepts inappropriate to that period: the motifs of the nations' destruction, the cup of wrath, and the return of the northern exiles all have counterparts in contemporary or older prophecy. He has no hesitation in ascribing both units to Obadiah. As for vv. 19–21, he observes the sobriety of their content: far from being Utopian, they merely promise that Israel's land would be restored to its natural limits. In this last part he considers the possibility that v. 21, which can be scanned as poetry, was the original conclusion to Obadiah's work. But vv. 19f., which he assigns to different hands qualifying v. 17b, are later than the previous verses, since v. 20 assumes widespread deportation.

Fohrer splits vv.1–18 into independent, nonconsecutive units to be assigned to Obadiah. He finds five separate sayings, self-contained units which form an anthology of Obadiah's work. Verses 19–21 he considers a typical eschatological addition to prophetic sayings. At this point he argues like Eissfeldt, but his application differs. This last part he significantly denies to be prose; when the glossed elements have been removed he discovers poetry, even if it lacks sparkle.

Brockington differs from Rudolph and Fohrer, claiming continuity for vv. 1–18 as well as common authorship. He finds no urgent reason to dissociate the two parts, vv. 1–14, 15b and 15a, 16–18. He compares the book of Joel for the development of thought: in both cases a contemporary situation is seen as a token of the coming of the Day of Yahweh, and as soon as this latter theme is introduced it naturally brings in its train a worldwide eschatological event. But vv. 19–21 are a prose appendix to the foregoing.

A third critical position is maintained by Thompson, who ascribes the whole book to Obadiah. He follows older commentators such as Keil and van Hoonacker. In favor of its literary unity he notes the consistent background of its progressive parts. He adduces the argument which he elaborated in his introduction to Joel, that many prophets combine historical and eschatological elements. He dates the whole c.450 B.C., and *contra* Pfeiffer's ascription of vv. 19–21 to a century later, considers hopes of reconquest of the land just as feasible at the earlier date. Changes of person and time in vv. 10–21 are admittedly sudden, but he claims parallels in other emotional prophetic writings.

This comprehensive review of various standpoints concerning the composition of the book has a blurring effect upon the rigid distinctions between the parts made by this scholar and that one. Rudolph's chronological objection to taking vv. 19–21 with the preceding is of his own making. If Obadiah is placed toward the end of the sixth century he could have been an eyewitness of the fall of Jerusalem, which he so vividly describes, and still speak of Jewish exiles far away. If Sepharad is indeed Sardis, there is evidence of the presence of Jews in the area in the second half of the fifth century, and their earlier settlement there by the time to which Obadiah has been assigned is quite plausible. A historical setting in the latter part of the sixth century suits the whole book. The change of address at v. 16 is not unnatural. As in all foreign oracles, the apostrophizing of the nation under attack is a rhetorical device in an overall oracle addressed in fact to the people of God for their encouragement. Obadiah at v. 16 directly addresses the audience who have been listening all the while to his tirade against Edom. Stylistic assessments to the detriment of vv. 15a, 16–21 leave out of account the different mold created by new subject matter and the echoing of traditional material. Fohrer's demonstration that vv. 19–21 need not be regarded as prose serves to demolish a frequent argument against authenticity.

The positive parallel with Joel drawn by Thompson and Brockington deserves to be taken seriously. Joel saw in an exceptionally severe locust plague a sign of Judah's impending doom, the dawn of the Day of Yahweh; the theme sets in motion a recital of the various events traditionally associated with the Day, especially its consequences for the nations involved in the 587 B.C. tragedy. It is probable that Joel is reapplying a pattern of thought created by his predecessor Obadiah. Insufficient attention has been paid to the theological progression of the book. Like the author of Lamentations, Obadiah sees in the fall of Jerusalem an outworking of the wrath of the Day of Yahweh upon his people; but he has left a remnant who have a right to capital and country, while the merited lot of the nations who attacked Jerusalem is to perish. There is a natural development throughout the book: from the forecast of Edom's downfall to a passionate delineation of its crimes on Judah's Day, then to the wider theme of the nations' Day of doom and the rehabilitation of God's people. But in passing from the particular to the general Obadiah still keeps Edom to the fore: Edom is one of the nations to suffer, Edom's annexing of Israelite territory is to be reversed. In this way the pronouncement of Yahweh the sovereign Lord (v. 1) would be substantiated in actuality by a demonstration of his kingly power (v. 21). The logical progression whereby sentence (vv. 2–9) passes to accusation (vv. 10–14, 15b) is repeated in a theological progression whereby Judah's experience of the *Dies irae* (vv. 10–14, 15b), summarized in the comparison of v. 16, passes to the nations' version and the twin vindication of Yahweh and his people (vv. 15a, 16–21).

To a people still smarting from the 587 B.C. catastrophe and, though restored to the land, few in number and confined to a pitiable fragment and hemmed in by foreign squatters on territory traditionally their own, Obadiah brings the divine assurance that Yahweh has not forgotten their plight and will intervene to redress the situation. The book takes up and answers what was doubtless a perennial theme of communal laments. Edom, the special object of Judah's resentment, would be signally punished for its part in Jerusalem's downfall, as would the other powers who had participated. Yahweh would gather home the rest of his people and correct the present travesty of ancient promises concerning Israel's possession of the land.

3. AUTHORSHIP

Nothing is known about the prophet who delivered this prophecy apart from his name. Even about the form of his name there is some uncertainty. MT reads *'Ōḇaḏyâ,* but G *Abdiou* and V *Abdias* imply a different vocalization for the first element: *'Aḇdīyâ(hû),* "servant of Yahweh," rather than "worshipper, devotee of Yahweh." It has even been suggested that the term does not represent the name of a prophet but is simply symbolic. But it is a fairly common name, borne by about a dozen men in the OT. A tradition in the Babylonian Talmud (*Sanhedrin* 39b), known to Jerome, identified the author with Ahab's steward (1 K. 18:3–16). But there are no grounds for identifying our prophet with any of the other Obadiahs in the OT.

It is often suggested that he was a cult prophet attached to the staff of the Jerusalem temple and that the book represents a cultic composition. Its main ingredient, an oracle directed against Edom, is a frequent feature of the OT prophets. Foreign oracles are associated with the books of Isaiah, Jeremiah, Ezekiel, and Amos, and in each case Edom is one of the nations denounced. An oracle against a foreign nation is not necessarily cultic. But the overall composition, in which the basic reasoned judgment progresses to Edom's inclusion in a wider judgment and to coming vindication and blessing for the people of God, may have been designed for use at temple services.

The motif of the demonstration of Yahweh's kingship in v. 21 is reminiscent of a group of "enthronement" psalms (Pss. 47, 93, 96–99) often associated with the New Year Festival, and the theme of the nations' judgment echoes a note struck in these psalms.[26] Bič calls the book an oracle for the enthronement festival,[27] while Watts defines it as a single part of the judgment of Israel and the nations proclaimed in a festival of covenant judgment. These classifications must be regarded as doubtful. The strongly historical emphasis in the book (vv. 1, 11–16) militates against an originally liturgical composition, which tends to be more general in tone.[28] The piece

26. E.g., Ps. 96:10, 13.
27. SVT 1 (1953), p. 16.
28. J. L. Mays, *Amos* (1969), p. 27, rightly urges that there is no need to search for a cultic background to Amos 1f.

evidently arose out of a concrete political situation of widespread Edomite agitation (v. 1). It is safer to conclude that Obadiah borrowed cultic and traditional themes in developing his prophecy.

4. TEXT

See the basic section in the Introduction to Joel. The Hebrew text of Obadiah has been fairly well preserved. Commentators frequently emend those portions parallel with Jer. 49 in accordance with the latter. But one must respect the recensional form in which the text has come down, and the present author has found no reason to judge that Obadiah has suffered any textual corruption which may be corrected from Jer. 49 or which has been contaminated by that text.

At v. 6 a singular *niḥpaś* has been read with G S V for the plural of MT. Revocalization has been deemed necessary at vv. 7 (*lōḥ^ameyḵā* with V T, Symmachus and the Lucianic text of G), 17 (*môrīshêhem* with G S V T, cf. Mur. 88 *mwryšyhm*), 21 (*mûshā'îm* with G S Aquila and Theodotion), and also conjecturally at v. 13 (*tishlāḥannâ*). In v. 20 the awkward relative has been conjecturally emended with many scholars to *yīr^eshû*.

There is reason to believe that at several places the text has suffered dislocation. Transposition has been affected at vv. 5 (*'êḵ niḏmêṯâ* to a position after *dayyām*), 15, reversing the two halves, and 21, placing before v. 18. Throughout v. 19 and at the beginning of v. 20 it is generally concluded that historical and topographical annotations were added to the text at an early stage.

5. THEOLOGY

The theological emphases of Obadiah are a direct response to the historical setting of the book. Just as the book of Joel meets national disaster with an appropriate divine undertaking, so this one, its predecessor and in some respects its model, provides balm to the remnant of Judah, as it licked its wounds and lamented past catastrophe and present impotence. Was this the pattern set for succeeding years? Were God's great promises to his people doomed never to come true? Was Edom to get away with its perfidy scot-free, and the other nations too? Obadiah's ministry was to take seriously these burning questions of the hour and deliver a reassuring oracle from Yahweh in response to the laments of his contemporaries.

Essentially it is lopsided and hardly a presentation of God's whole counsel, even by OT standards. But the early postexilic period was a "day of small things" (Zech. 4:10), even necessarily of what we in more relaxed times might glibly call smallmindedness. The nation, a shadow of preexilic glory, was struggling for its very existence and fighting overwhelming problems on political, territorial, and economic fronts. A hasty condemnation of the later leaders Ezra and Nehemiah must give way at least to a resigned admission that under the circumstances there was little alternative to their policies. Their religious community on the verge of extinction had to be nationalistic or perish, particularistic or disappear. Through Obadiah, Yahweh understandingly gives a word for the times. He soothes festering mental sores which developed from national humiliation, and yet he lifts the issues to a higher plane than mere resentment and revenge.

George Adam Smith could dismiss the book with peremptory rhetoric: "It seems but a dark surge staining the stream of revelation, as if to exhibit through what a muddy channel these sacred waters have been poured upon the world." Bewer was fairer to the little book when he spoke of the triumph of justice vouchsafed by it and the consolation of God's ultimate purposes: "It made it possible for many Jews to go on believing in the moral government of the world, in the justice of their God." Promise of eventual vindication and victory is given to the defeated, demoralized community. Their feeble, seemingly ineffectual protests against the wanton violence of strangers and especially against the brutal treachery of their half-brothers, the Edomites, do not fall on deaf ears but find a divine answer for faith and hope to grasp.

Compensatory judgment is promised. To the balance sheet doubtless frequently drawn up in the bitter memories of surviving victims of the tragedy of 587, Obadiah adds another column, detailing the price to be exacted to clear the moral debts of Edom. Verses 2–9 are the new entries made against the items of complaint echoed in vv. 10–14, and v. 15b is the notice demanding that Edom eventually pay the price for its crimes against Judah and against a moral God.

With this motif of justice, the principle of an eye for an eye extended to a nation's wrongdoing, is interwoven another, equally traditional, the Day of Yahweh.[29] It is possible to trace a developing sequence in three OT books: Joel builds upon Obadiah, while Obadiah in turn develops a theme broached in the book of Lamentations. Lam. 1:21; 2:21f. speak of two phases of the Day, the first already past in the fall of Jerusalem and the dissolution of the state of Judah, and a second in store for the gloating enemies of God's people. This double-edged motif is the heritage Obadiah brings afresh to a later generation in his message of encouragement. The conquest of their capital was itself the reprisal of a just God for Judah's own rebellion, his cup of wrath which a sinful nation had to drink, to be sent reeling into exile and political extinction (v. 16). The people of Judah had only themselves to blame. But had not the other nations committed sin? Indeed they had, and Yahweh's Day against them had been "proclaimed" long before (Lam. 1:21). Their exploitation, especially Edom's, of Judah's chastisement now constituted a final debt, a last straw, which merited Yahweh's coming

29. See the discussion of this motif in the Introduction to Joel.

intervention. Their day of doom is announced, not now as a far-off eventuality but as "near" (v. 15). "Here is something more than mere vengeance; it is the protest of outraged justice. It is not denied or in any way excluded that the fall of the city was a bona fide judgment of Yahweh, but it is felt that the chastisement of Judah did not fully rectify the injustices of history. There is an increment of justice still to come."[30]

This is not the facile optimism of Amos' unrepentant audience, who regarded the Day of Yahweh as all sweetness and light (Amos 5:18–20). Obadiah addresses a chastened community, whose stiff neck had been bent by the divinely imposed yoke of catastrophe and who cried to God, "How long?" and looked to him for salvation to succeed the judgment. The yearning prayer, "Renew our days as of old" (Lam. 5:21) must often have been echoed by the returned exiles, who after their second Exodus found their promised land a sad travesty of their hopes. The answer comes through Obadiah to such a prayer. The ancient promise of possessing the land is no dead letter; it is renewed to the "remnant," the survivors of tragedy's toll (vv. 17–21). The pitiable number of present returnees from exile would be swollen by an influx of others, stranded though they be at earth's remotest bounds (v. 20). So the nation would be healed and made whole again, worthy representatives of the supremacy of Yahweh their God.

Divine sovereignty is the audacious, historically unlikely theme Obadiah stresses. To all the world around, Judah's weakness must have seemed a mirror of the weakness of Yahweh, surely a subordinate deity who had yielded to the pressure of the stronger gods of Babylon, Edom, and the like. At the outset the prophet corrects such a conclusion from appearances. His message comes from "the Lord Yahweh" (v. 1), from Edom's judge and overlord. No matter that Edom boasted of being inaccessible, of wealth, of manpower native and allied, of expertise—Yahweh was more than a match for them; his power would bring them tumbling down from their lofty perch (vv. 2–9). Even now, reported Obadiah, there was news of a coalition of neighboring tribes mustering to march against Edom. This was no coincidence, but Yahweh's providential manipulation of history. His was the master mind, intent on Edom's downfall, behind the machinations of men. Obadiah's God is the Lord of history, working out his purposes via the vicissitudes of past and present events.[31]

He is also the Lord of the future. It is Obadiah's privilege to announce the coming kingdom of God, his vindication through the exaltation of his people as a theocracy which executed his own rule in the world around (v. 21). Mount Zion, ancient seat of Yahweh's sovereignty over Israel, would be rehabilitated as the proud capital of a glorious nation worthy of its God, cleansed forever of the pagan defilement that had sullied it in 587 B.C. (v. 17).

30. N. K. Gottwald, *Studies in Lamentations*. SBT 14 (1954), p. 88, commenting on Lam. 1:21.

31. Cf. the discussion of this theme by H. Butterfield, *Christianity and History* (1954), ch. 2.

These pledges, which must have put new luster into the downcast eyes of contemporary believers and sustained them through life's rigors, have passed, through Christ, into the possession of the Christian Church. They require translation into the language of the new covenant to be meaningful today. The book of Obadiah offers the assurance of a God of moral justice who will restore the moral equilibrium and right the blatant wrongs of this wicked world. God is in control, at work behind the scenes, working out his own plans through the chaos of human moves and countermoves. The Church triumphant is our destiny, and toward this end we are to work with confidence, however much Christian communities here and there seem to shrink and be ineffective. With hope that matches Obadiah's we can look forward to a new Jerusalem, and with faith akin to his declare: "The kingdom of the world has become the kingdom of our Lord and of his Christ, and he will reign for ever and ever," and his servants with him (Rev. 11:15; 22:5).

6. STRUCTURE AND ANALYSIS

The little book of Obadiah cries out to be considered as a model upon which to demonstrate structural and strophical theories, and accordingly it has received a good deal of attention. A. Condamin worked out a strophical structure based on the chorus theory of P. Zenner.[32] Basically he found five strophes: vv. 1–4, which begin and end with "Yahweh," 5–7, 8–10, and 11–14, marked by repetition of "day" and having a refrain "in the day of distress" at vv. 12 and 14, and 15–21, which again begin and end with "Yahweh." J. M. P. Smith[33] dissected the work into three independent units: vv. 1–7c, 10f., 15b as five six-line strophes, vv. 12–14 as a six-line strophe, and vv. 15a, 16–21 + 8f. as three strophes of four, eight, and eight lines. This result required a considerable amount of rearrangement and emendation.

Coming to more recent times, Keller finds four units in the book apart from the heading (v. 1a) and the final series of prose comments (vv. 19–21). They are (1) a prophetic vision in v. 1b, (2) a divine oracle in vv. 2–9, consisting of two strophes (2–4, 5–7) and an *envoi* (8f.), (3) a prophetic accusation in vv. 10–15, consisting of three strophes (10f., 12–13a*a* 13a*b*–14) and a concluding couplet serving as an *envoi,* (4) a divine declaration to Israel (vv. 16–18) in two strophes (16–17a, 17b–18).

Fohrer has provided a useful survey of previous work on the constituent units of the book,[34] and has devised a scheme based upon both the study of strophical devices and form criticism. He discovers six units of varying length, deleting and emending rather freely in the process.

32. *RB* 9 (1900), pp. 261–68.
33. *AJSL* 22 (1906), pp. 131–38.
34. *Studia biblica et semitica T. C. Vriezen dedicata* (1966), pp. 81–93.

(1) Verses 1b*b*–4, closed by a typical concluding short line which is also a final formula, "oracle of Yahweh." (2) Verses 5–7, a threat which stands out as a unit since a new saying begins in v. 8. He reverses vv. 6 and 7 since the former gives the impression of a final statement. (3) Verses 8–11, with an initial formula "oracle of Yahweh" and a final short line. (4) Verses 12–14, 15b which after an accusation give eight uniform warnings; v. 15b is clearly a conclusion. (5) Verses 15a, 16–18, threats around a promise, concluded by a formula, "for Yahweh has spoken." (6) Verses 19–21, a promise with a final short line.

Watts has simply divided the book according to form and content. After the heading and an audition in v. 1 comes a divine announcement of judgment of five lines, vv. 2–4, at the head of which he sets "Thus says the Lord Yahweh to Edom," moving it from v. 1. Next comes a second divine announcement of judgment in vv. 5–10, ten lines grouped in pairs; "oracle of Yahweh" in v. 8 is moved to the end of v. 10. Verses 11–14 are a ten-line prophetic indictment and deprecation. Four lines of theological explanation follow in vv. 15f. Finally, vv. 17–21, after removal of glosses in v. 19, comprise eight lines of Mount Zion-oriented promises.

Most recently Rudolph has divided vv. 2–14, 15b into two coordinated parts, vv. 2–9 an announcement of punishment to Edom, and vv. 10–14, 15b which level accusations against Edom. The first part consists of three strophes of four lines each: vv. 2–4, 5f., 7–9. To achieve this result he makes deletions in vv. 4, 7, 8. The first strophe ends with the formula "oracle of Yahweh," which he avers *contra* Fohrer can close a subsection. He criticizes Fohrer's independent unit, vv. 5–7, arguing that there is no indication in v. 5 as to who is addressed. By deleting v. 8a he dispenses with the need to begin a new saying there. The second part also has three strophes of four lines (vv. 10f., 12–13a*a*, 13a*b*–14) and a concluding line, v. 15b. The remaining unit, vv. 15a–18, he splits into two strophes of four lines, 15a, 16, 17a and 17b, 18.

It was made clear at the end of the second section of the Introduction that the present author divides the book into three, vv. 2–9, 10–14 + 15b, and 15a + 16–21.[35] The first and second parts consist of sentence and accusation (Rudolph, Weiser, Eissfeldt), while the second and third contrast the manifestation of the Day of Yahweh in the past and the future. After the heading and prose introduction of v. 1, the first part is an announcement of punishment to Edom. It falls into four strophes. The first is a divine oracle of four lines, vv. 2–4 (Watts, Rudolph). It is closed by the oracular formula and a short line (Rudolph, cf. Fohrer). The second is a prophetic saying of four lines, vv. 5f. (Rudolph), consisting of two parallel parts, a threat and a mock lament. Fohrer rightly stated that v. 6 looks like a final statement, but was wrong to move it. The third strophe is a four-line prophetic announcement of

35. D. Deden, *De Kleine Profeten,* vol. 1 (1953), *in loc.,* also divided the book into these three parts. Myers finds a final unit vv. 15a, 16–21, but for him it is independent of the preceding material.

punishment (v. 7); its close is marked by a short line. Each of the three long lines ends with a rhyme *-e(y)ḵā* (cf. the endings of the half-lines). The fourth strophe rounds off the section by reverting to a divine oracle announcing punishment (vv. 8f., cf. Smith). It has an initial oracular formula (Fohrer) and consists of three lines, the last two of which have a refrain "from Mt. Esau."

The second part is a series of prophetic statements, consisting of accusations and a final announcement of punishment. The first strophe, vv. 10f. (Rudolph), consists of four lines; its close is indicated by a final short line (Fohrer). The second, v. 12, is three lines long; it is marked out by its identical line openings (Heb. *w^{e}'al,* "and not") and similar endings, "on the day of" plus a synonymous noun of disaster lacking a suffix (contrast v. 13). The third strophe, v. 13, is distinguished by its near-identical refrain at the end of each of its three lines. In the fourth, vv. 14, 15b, the content of the third and final line represents an obvious ending (Fohrer).

The third part of the book, like the other two, falls into four strophes. First is a three-line divine announcement of punishment for the nations (vv. 15a, 16),[36] the first two lines of which have a refrain "all the nations." The next strophe is made up of vv. 17 and 21,[37] four lines of promise concerning Mount Zion; its end is marked by a final short line (cf. Fohrer). Verse 18 is the four-line third strophe, a divine announcement of punishment; it is bounded by a final formula (Fohrer). The last strophe consists of vv. 19f., a three-line prophetic promise concerning Israel. It begins and ends with mention of the Negeb; Hebrew *w^{e}yār^{e}shû,* "and they will possess," occurs in it three times.

All three sections of the book and the individual strophes are tied together by various interlocking devices, which will be noted in the course of the commentary.

Heading (1a)
Introduction (1b)
I. The Destruction of Edom (2–9)
  A. Edom's downfall (2–4)
  B. The completeness of Edom's overthrow (5, 6)
  C. The treachery of Edom's allies (7)
  D. Edom's loss of wisdom and warriors (8, 9)
II. The Wrongdoing of Edom (10–14, 15b)
  A. Edom's unbrotherliness (10, 11)
  B. Edom's mockery (12)
  C. Edom's trespassing (13)
  D. Edom's collaboration and coming retribution (14, 15b)
III. Edom on the Day of Yahweh (15a, 16–21)
  A. The Day of Yahweh (15a, 16)

36. "The Day of Yahweh" is a stereotyped expression.
37. For the association of these two verses see the commentary.

B. The role of the remnant (17, 21)
C. Judean fire and Edomite stubble (18)
D. The land regained (19, 20)

7. SELECT BIBLIOGRAPHY

M. Bič, "Zur Problematik des Buches Obadja," *Congress Volume, Copenhagen 1953*. SVT 1(1953), pp. 11–25.
W. W. Cannon, "Israel and Edom: The Oracle of Obadiah," *Theology* 15 (1927), pp. 129–140, 191–200.
C. P. Caspari, *Der Prophet Obadja* (1842).
A. Condamin, "L'unité d'Abdias," *RB* 9 (1900), pp. 261–68.
A. Deissler, "Abdias," *Les petits prophètes* 8:1. La Sainte Bible (1961).
J. H. Eaton, *Obadiah, Nahum, Habakkuk, Zephaniah*. Torch Bible Commentaries (1961).
G. Fohrer, "Die Sprüche Obadjas," *Studia Biblica et Semitica T. C. Vriezen dedicata* (1966), pp. 81–93.
N. Glueck, "The Boundaries of Edom," *HUCA* 11 (1936), pp. 141–157.
J. Gray, "The Diaspora of Israel and Judah in Obadiah v. 20," *ZAW* 65 (1953), pp. 53–59.
W. Kornfeld, "Die judaische Diaspora in Ab., 20," *Mélanges bibliques rédigés en l'honneur de André Robert* (1957), pp. 180–86.
W. H. Morton, "Umm el Biyara," *BA* 19 (1956), pp. 26–36.
T. T. Perowne, *Obadiah and Jonah*. CBSC (1883).
W. Rudolph, "Obadja," *ZAW* 8 (1931), pp. 222–231.
J. M. P. Smith, "The Structure of Obadiah," *AJSL* 22 (1906), pp. 131–38.
J. A. Thompson, "Obadiah," *IB*, vol. 6 (1956), pp. 855–867.
J. D. W. Watts, *Obadiah: A Critical Exegetical Commentary* (1969).

TRANSLATION, EXPOSITION, AND NOTES

HEADING (1a)

The revelation to Obadiah.

The overall brevity of the book, the shortest in the collection of the twelve Minor Prophets and indeed in the whole OT, is matched in the brevity of its title. In the other prophetic books the editors have supplied some information concerning the period or place of origin of the author of the oracles, but in this case not even the name of the prophet's father, frequently used as the equivalent of a surname, has been preserved. The name *Obadiah* is relatively common in the OT. Signifying "one who serves or worships Yahweh," it was an obvious choice for parents as a means of expressing their own faith and their expectations for the child. This particular Obadiah lived up to his name in a special way as a man in the prophetic service of his God.

His prophecy is described as a *revelation,* a technical term which has to do primarily with seeing a vision, but widened to mean simply a divine communication to a prophet.[1] In 1 Sam. 3:1 it is used in parallelism with "the word of Yahweh." The prophet was credited in Israel with the gift of inspired insight into the purposes of God.

INTRODUCTION (1b)

This is what the Lord Yahweh has said about Edom. We heard a message direct from Yahweh, while an envoy was being sent[2] *among the nations, urging, "Let us move and march to battle against her."*[3]

1. Cf. Mic. 1:1 and comment. Heb. *ḥāzôn* is cognate with *ḥōzeh,* "seer"; cf. T "prophecy."
2. In light of the Qal passive participle *shālûaḥ* in Jer. 49:14, *shullāḥ* is to be taken as a Pual participle without its preformative *mem* (cf. GK 52s).
3. In view of the masculine references to Edom in the rest of the book, *'ālāyw* is expected. Cf. Mal. 1:4, where the verb with Edom is feminine.

The first clause of this prose introduction[4] functions as a preface not so much to the divine oracle of vv. 2–4 as to the prophecy as a whole. This more general purpose is suggested by the similar role in the parallel Jer. 49. There this opening sentence substantially reappears in v. 7, while the oracle corresponding to vv. 2–4 does not feature until vv. 15f.[5] Obadiah uses the typical messenger formula of the prophets, which serves at once to affirm the divine authority and to specify the target of his prophetic pronouncements.[6] The prophet does not speak in his own name or right, but introduces himself as a messenger from one whom he regards as the Overlord of the nations. His message concerns Edom, Judah's eastern neighbor and longstanding rival. Judah had recently been given fresh and terrible cause to resent the Edomites because of their role in the events of 587 B.C., which Obadiah is vividly to relate in vv. 12–14.

Before launching into the substance of his declaration, he pauses to explain the events that occurred at the time he received it from Yahweh. He judges them to be important as hints at the means whereby God's purposes for Edom are initially to be fulfilled. The prophet's identification of himself with his Judean audience (*we heard*) stresses the significance of the divine communication for Obadiah's own nation. Strictly the message came to the prophet, but it reached him as representative of his people and was not for his ears alone.[7] The rest of the introduction is best understood as an allusion to a local event that impressed the prophet as striking confirmation of his message.[8] Probably a coalition of neighboring Arab tribes was conspiring against Edom. To the prophet it was no coincidence that divine oracle and human machinations occurred at the same time; the latter were regarded as proof that God was moving among men, working toward the accomplishment of his sovereign will and making "the wrath of men" to "praise" him (Ps. 76:10[11]). The God who had made Cyrus his anointed king and Nebuchadnezzar his servant[9] was using as the instruments of his ire nations who evidently had grievances of their own against Edom. The *Lord* who is author of the oracle was already taking steps to carry out its message in clear demonstration to the faithful that he was Lord of history, disposing while man proposed.

The final words of direct speech are a typical summons to battle.[10]

4. It is better taken as prose. It is possible to scan the central portion as a line of poetry, but hardly what precedes or follows it.
5. Heb. *le'ᵉḏôm* is better taken as *about Edom,* as in Jer. 49:7, rather than as "to Edom."
6. Cf. the comment on Mic. 2:3.
7. The parallel text in Jer. 49:14 reads *shāma'tî,* "I heard." G sides with Jer., but its agreement is probably due to contamination from a better-known text.
8. It is then a circumstantial clause. It is also possible, though less likely, to regard the second clause either as a definition of the message ("that an envoy . . ."; cf. GK 120f. and, e.g., Gen. 30:27) or as an independent clause "and . . . was sent," in which case the message is the summons to war and the envoy is to be taken as angelic.
9. Isa. 45:1; Jer. 43:10.
10. Cf. R. Bach, *Die Aufforderungen zur Flucht und zum Kampf im alttestamentlichen*

Little did the circle of Edom's enemies know that included in their number and supreme above them all was Yahweh, and that the coming battle was his and not merely their own. The prophet delights in the divine irony, in a manner akin to that made explicit in Mic. 4:12.

I. THE DESTRUCTION OF EDOM (2–9)

A. EDOM'S DOWNFALL (2–4)

I am soon going to make you the tiniest of nations,
you will become utterly despised.
3 *Your proud attitude of mind has misled you.* 3+3+3
Living in crevices among the rocks,
in your[11] *home on high,*[12] 3+2
you think in your mind
that nobody can bring you down to earth. 2+3
4 *Though you soar high as the eagle,*
though your eyrie is placed[13] *among the stars,*
I shall bring you down even from there. So runs Yahweh's oracle. 3+3+3

The poem proper opens with an oracle which the prophet delivers in Yahweh's name. The four-line announcement of punishment for Edom concludes with a typical asseveration of divine origin, "oracle of Yahweh."[14] Repetition is used with artistry to reinforce the thought and to mark its progression. The arrogant mentality of the Edomites is specified at the beginning and end of v. 3. The challenge closing that verse is finely capped by the divine assertion that repeats the verb *bring down* at the end of v. 4. Metrically the piece is irregular: it exhibits an intriguing chiastic order.

Prophetenspruch. WMANT 9 (1962), pp. 62–65. Cf. the comments on Joel 3:9–13; Mic. 4:13. For the cohortative form cf. Jer. 6:4f.; for the verb *qûm*, "arise," i.e., "advance," cf. also Isa. 21:5; Jer. 49:28, 31; Mic. 4:13. In Jer. 49:14f. the summons is closely linked with the following announcement of punishment ("for . . .") according to a frequent formal pattern (cf. Joel 3:12; Mic. 4:13) in which the summons comes from God. Bach, *op. cit.*, p. 68, regards the present passage in this light, noting that the conjunction is often absent. But the Obad. recension appears to interpret the summons as issued within the context of an international coalition.

11. Lit. "his." Cf. Isa. 47:8; 54:1 for this common change to a third person after a vocative (GK 144p).

12. Heb. *m^{e}rôm* is often emended to a participle *mērîm*, "making high (your home)" with G V to improve the parallelism. But MT is quite explicable: the force of the preceding preposition carries over (cf. GK 119hh). MT provides an expected link with Jer. 49:16 *tōp^{e}shê m^{e}rôm*, exhibiting a shorter text, as earlier in the verse.

13. Heb. *śîm*, a passive Qal as in Num. 24:21, which may have been in the prophet's mind (cf. the links between Num. 24:18f. and Obad. 17f.), is preferable to the easier—and so inferior—reading *tāśîm*, "you place," which many read on the basis of G S V T. Keller construes *śîm* as an infinitive absolute.

14. Cf. the comment on Mic. 4:6.

As is generally the case with oracles against foreign nations in the prophetic literature, the form of the oracle is dramatically presented as a direct communication from God to the nation concerned, although in fact Obadiah is not confronting the Edomites face to face but delivering the oracle among his own nation. Its implicit aim is to encourage and reassure God's people, reminding them of his purpose and power to cut down to size their high and mighty rivals.

The oracle begins in a characteristic way by Yahweh's announcing his purpose of imminent intervention in Edom's affairs. The first word *hinnēh,* traditionally rendered "behold," is designed to arrest the hearers and focus their attention on God's coming involvement in the affairs of men.[15] The verb is a prophetic perfect: God's deed is as good as done, and the fate of Edom is sealed. Their destiny is to be one of utter insignificance. It will be all the more shocking to the Edomites because they have been the victims of self-deception. They shrug off any suggestion of invasion and defeat with a confident denial, thinking themselves safe in their rocky bastion. The Hebrew *sela',* *rocks,* does not refer merely to the rugged terrain of Edom in general but alludes specifically to Sela, Edom's capital, which was situated on the high plateau of Umm el-Biyara.[16] This formidable rock mass could be ascended only from the southeast, the other faces consisting of perpendicular cliff-walls. Perched on the top of this natural fortress, the Edomites assimilated from their habitat a superior attitude of impregnability, which represented a defiant challenge: "Who can bring me down to earth?" This description of arrogant supermen serves as a stark prelude to the shock of their imminent downfall.[17] In their presumptuous pride they have reckoned without God. Over these puny creatures, sadly mistaken in their illusions of superhuman invincibility, looms the majestic figure of Yahweh. Like the eagle they are denizens of rocky heights, but were they likewise to *soar* into the sky above,[18] they could not get beyond the reach of the long arm of divine justice. The reference to flying high in the sky and to roosting *among the stars* paints a vividly imaginative picture, which serves to stress the power of God and the powerlessness of the Edomites. Earthbound mortals as they are, they present an easy prey for Yahweh despite their boasts.

The oracle, which began with one statement of God's purpose, ends

15. Cf. the comment on Mic. 2:3.
16. W. H. Morton, *BA* 19 (1956), pp. 26–36.
17. Fohrer finds in v. 3 an implicit reason for divine punishment, but Rudolph and Deissler, following van Hoonacker, are more probably correct in interpreting as above and finding no *Strafgrund* in this oracle. The OT motif of blasphemous arrogance (see the useful sketch in B. S. Childs, *Isaiah and the Assyrian Crisis.* SBT 2:3 [1967], p. 88) often presents an attitude of defiance as the motivation for divine punishment (cf., e.g., Isa. 10:5–19; Ezek. 28:1–10; 35:10–15), and it is probably employed with this significance in the parallel Jer. 49:15f. But in this larger composition its role is reduced to a mere description in order to increase the impression of a tremendous fall.
18. Cf. Job 39:27f.; Prov. 23:5.

with another, both enhanced by the intervening description of Edomite power, which is dismissed as insignificant in the face of God's might. The mighty will become little and belittled; the high in habitat and in flight of fancy will be brought low. The oracle concludes with a formula representing a solemn pledge that the foregoing is indeed Yahweh's word and will.

B. THE COMPLETENESS OF EDOM'S OVERTHROW (5, 6)

When thieves visit you
or marauders by night, 3+2
they will steal all they want, won't they?
How completely you are to be ravaged! 3+2
6 *When men come to gather your grapes,*
they will leave only gleanings behind, won't they? 3+3
How thoroughly Esau is to be ransacked,[19]
his hidden hoards rifled! 3+2

Like the preceding stanza this next unit is an announcement of the punishment to which Edom is to fall victim. But in form it is evidently a prophetic rather than an explicitly divine declaration.[20] It is a lively piece, with its metaphors, rhetorical questions, and expressions of mock despair. Two parallel statements are made concerning invaders and the havoc they will cause. In each occurs first a metaphorical statement composed of a temporal clause and a question expecting an affirmative answer; then each is concluded with an exclamation of pseudo-lament.[21] Strict uniformity is avoided by lengthening the first clause of time and the second exclamation.

Metrically this four-line piece is more uniform than the preceding one, consisting mainly of a 3+2 rhythm. There are links of style and content between this stanza and the first. The conditional clauses of v. 4 are echoed in the temporal ones here.[22] Edom's inaccessibility (v. 3) is to be proved false when *his hidden hoards* are *rifled* (v. 6). Moreover there is a link with the introduction: the agents of Yahweh's destruction whom the prophet

19. MT *neḥpᵉśû,* a plural verb, is possible with a collective subject, but in view of the later singular suffix it is probably a copyist's error for *neḥpaś,* assimilated to the following plural verb *nib̲ʿû* (Ehrlich, *BHS,* etc.). G S T have a singular verb.
20. See the note on Mic. 2:3.
21. In MT *How completely you are to be ravaged!* occurs awkwardly after the first temporal clause. Comparison with the construction of vv. 5b–6 suggests that it belonged originally after the main clause and has been accidentally misplaced (Sellin, Rudolph, *BHS*). Probably *'k . . .* was omitted before *'m* by homoeoarcton because of their visual similarity in the ancient Heb. script, and the omitted words were subsequently supplied in the margin, only to be incorporated in the wrong place. This same argument could be used to justify a position at the head of v. 5, where a number of scholars, including Bewer, Brockington, and Watts, place it; but parallelism with vv. 5b–6 and metrical considerations render this possibility less likely.
22. Heb. *'im,* "if, when," occurs twice in v. 4, thrice in v. 5.

revealed to hearer and reader in his whispered aside of v. 1b now come to the fore.

Thus the unit develops the thought of its preceding context. Edom is addressed still as the victim of coming destruction. Unfortunately the piece contains two ambiguities. The first concerns its aspect in time. The Hebrew verbs in the exclamations are in the perfect state, as are those in the temporal clauses. Does this piece look back to an overthrow that has already taken place? This is a problem that poses itself again in v. 7. Verse 1 speaks of preparations for an attack. So it seems more likely that the perfect verbs are to be construed like the verb in v. 2 as prophetic perfects and that the imperfect verbs in the two main clauses of v. 5 are normal futures. The second problem concerns the nature of the reference to thieves and grape-gatherers. Has the prophet a contrast in mind: both leave behind pieces of property and odd grapes respectively, but Edom is to be cleaned out? Or is the point a double comparison: a reckless, ruthless stripping of house and vineyard which bodes ill for Edom's wealth? The latter interpretation is more realistic in view of the wording in the first comparison.[23]

If the first stanza stressed the inevitability of destruction, this next one emphasizes its thoroughness. Metaphors are used to describe the utter desolation that will be theirs. The raiders are represented first as burglars who raid a house and leave nothing of value, free in the owner's absence, or while he sleeps, to make off with anything they fancy. The invaders will come like *thieves* who have no regard for rights of ownership. The prophet breaks out into a shocked exclamation which had its provenance in a funeral lament and similar expressions of grief, and was then applied satirically to add weight to prophetic denunciations.[24] Remorselessly the prophet pursues his theme with a second metaphor, derived from the grape harvest. Busy hands plucking impatiently at the vines till they are virtually denuded are used as dread symbols of the enemy ravaging the well-stocked cities of Edom and leaving behind only bits and pieces of no real worth. This second metaphor is apt, since the mountainous slopes of Edom provided a good location for vines.[25] Esau or Edom[26] is to know no merciful alleviation, but is to be exposed ruthlessly to the greedy hands of enemy looters. The warehouses of this trading center, crammed with valuable goods, are to be broken open, and the safes of its wealthy merchants are to be left empty. With solemn effect the prophet finally turns from direct address of Edom to a mournful soliloquy, as if Edom is already dead and gone, unable to hear this pronouncement of its doom.

23. Heb. *dayyām,* "their sufficiency," is more naturally to be taken to mean "as much as they want," i.e., "to their hearts' content" (JB), than "only as much as they need" (von Orelli, *et al.*). Then the end of v. 5 signifies that *only* gleanings are left (Fohrer). Rudolph deletes the negative in v. 5b as a case of mechanical assimilation to the preceding one: "Do they leave gleanings?" implying that nothing is left; but this is not necessary.

24. Cf. 2 Sam. 1:19; Isa. 14:12; Jer. 9:19(18); Zeph. 2:15.

25. Cf. Num. 20:17.

26. For the use of the synonym cf. Gen. 36:1, 8, 19.

C. THE TREACHERY OF EDOM'S ALLIES (7)

They will send you back to the frontier,
all those allies of yours. 2+2
They will mislead you, do you down,
those confederates of yours. 2+2
Your guests[27] *will lay*
snares[28] *for your feet,*[29] 2+2
without your knowing it.[30] 3

This third stanza unfolds still further the theme of Edomite destruction. The prophet speaks again, giving a threefold, matter-of-fact, taunting description of the circumstances of Edom's coming downfall, outlined in a metrically uniform composition of three double lines of 2+2 and a final short line of three beats, which is not infrequently used to round off a poetic unit.[31] The first two lines are marked by external parallelism and by a common rhyme in the middle and at the end of each line, and so is the third line to a lesser extent. They repeat the contrasted themes of treaty and treachery. Verbal echoes of the preceding stanzas are sounded here. The sending of v. 1 is repeated in the first verb and the deception of v. 3 in the second, while the nest-building of v. 4 finds its tragic counterpart in the

27. MT *laḥmᵉḵā,* "your bread," is hardly intelligible in the context: presumably the Massoretic pointing implies that the force of *'anᵉshê,* "men of," carries over to this word (so S) or else that it is somehow an object of the following verb, either as "make your bread into a snare/wound (?)" or "make a snare/wound your bread." It is best to revocalize as a plural participle *lōḥᵃmeyḵā* in the sense "those who eat with you," assuming a loose use of the suffix and the verb *lāḥam,* "eat," which occurs in Deut. 32:24; Ps. 141:4; Prov. 4:17; 9:5; 23:1, 6 (Halévy, Sellin, Weiser, Deissler, Keller, Rudolph, with the support of the Lucianic text of G and V T and Symmachus). G. R. Driver's objection that this could only mean "those who eat you" (*JTS* 35 [1934], p. 391) is invalid in the light of GK 116h. Wellhausen, G. A. Smith, J. M. P. Smith, Robinson, Fohrer, and Watts delete with G, either as a pseudo-dittograph of the preceding *(š)lmk* or as a variant of it.

28. Heb. *māzôr* means "wound" in Jer. 30:13; Hos. 5:13, which *contra* Calvin, KJV, Keil, and Halévy is here contextually incongruous. G S V "ambush," T "stumbling block," Aquila and Theodotion "bond" all suggest some such meaning as "rope, snare, net," which indicates a connection with the root *mzr,* in postbiblical Heb. "twist, weave" and in Syr. "bind, stretch out." A conjectural emendation *mātsôḏ,* "net" (*BHK,* following Vollers), is less likely.

29. Lit. "under you."

30. Heb. *bô* is conceivably a reference to Edom ("there is no understanding in him"; cf. G "in them"); cf. the change from second to third person at the end of the preceding stanza. It is more naturally taken as "concerning it," referring to *māzôr* earlier (cf. *bîn bᵉ, hēḇîn bᵉ* Ezra 8:15; Neh. 8:12; Dan. 9:23, etc.). Some of those who adopt the former interpretation, including J. M. P. Smith, Rudolph, Fohrer, and Keller, follow Wellhausen in deleting the phrase as a gloss on v. 8, while G. R. Driver, *Orientalia et biblica lovaniensia* 1 (1957), p. 161, ingeniously takes it as a gloss on the unknown *māzôr*: "it makes no sense." But the phrase is quite intelligible and relevant to the context, since it functions as a typical link with the next stanza.

31. Cf. Fohrer, *ZAW* 54 (1966), p. 210, for the phenomenon, although in this case he deletes.

snare-laying mentioned here.[32] Such verbal allusions serve to unify the pieces and tie them together in an intricate pattern of verbal artistry.

Once again the problem of timing arises. Of the four verses of the piece, the first three are in the perfect state and the fourth in the imperfect. In light of the overall context it is preferable to regard the perfects as again prophetic, referring to the future, and to take the final verb as a simple indication of the future fulfilment of the prophet's words.

The human element, mentioned by the prophet at the outset and developed in vv. 5f., comes to the fore again. The *allies* are probably to be distinguished from the enemies of the preceding material, lending no support when those enemies invade. The first verb, an intensive form of a verb that has a basic meaning "send" but also a wide semantic range, is ambiguous. Does it here mean "escort," "send away," or "drive away"? The first sense could refer to a courteous farewell to be given to Edomite envoys, sent home again with their appeal for help against their foes refused. Or does the verb describe a later stage in the struggle, the sending away of Edomite refugees who have no alternative but to face the onslaught of their enemies? This explanation has the merit of corresponding to the Edomites' treatment of the Judeans mentioned in the next section (v. 14), which tends to match crimes previously committed by Edom to the punishment predicted in the first section. Another possible interpretation is that their enemies are to be assisted by Edom's former allies in driving out the Edomites from their ancestral territory.[33]

The prediction is a shocking one. Agreements between groups, as between individuals, were held to be sacrosanct and breaking them was viewed with abhorrence. Amos delivered an oracle promising divine retribution to those who forget "the covenant of brotherhood" (Amos 1:9), while the psalmist deplored the treachery of his friend who "violated his covenant" (Ps. 55:20[21]). By dint of repetition the poet savors the stark contrast between obligations of fidelity and the eventual stab in the back. Deception is stressed again, as previously in v. 3. Edom's security, based both on impregnable position and on international alliance, will prove equally ill-founded. The emphasis upon deception appears to be a taunting allusion to the famed wisdom of the Edomites, to which v. 8 explicitly refers. The ironic truth is that those who know so much are to come to their downfall by their lack of knowledge.

The third line of the stanza is textually and exegetically difficult, although it is clear that in some way it must amplify the sentiments of the two preceding lines. It probably refers to abuse of the honor of hospitality, which in the Semitic world ever created a solemn bond of loyalty, as the psalmist's words of aggrieved shock attest:

32. Heb. *śîm, yāśîmû*.

33. For this sense of the Piel *shillaḥ* cf. Lev. 18:24; Jer. 28:16. Robinson and Fohrer take the clause as a reference to deportation.

Even my friend whom I trusted,
who ate my bread, has kicked me. (Ps. 41:9[10])

The final line underscores Edom's uncharacteristic lack of discernment. So unexpected will be this turn of events that they will be unable to anticipate it.[34] They are to be taken completely by surprise and so will fall an easy prey to their foes.

D. EDOM'S LOSS OF WISDOM AND WARRIORS (8, 9)

I intend on that day,
runs Yahweh's oracle, 3+2
to destroy the wise out of Edom
and knowledge out of Mount Esau. 3+3
Your soldiers, Teman, will be demoralized
so that every single one may be destroyed
out of Mount Esau by slaughter. 3+3+3

The first part of the composition closes with a supplementary oracle from Yahweh. It matches and reinforces the oracle at the beginning, in vv. 2–4, and so brings the first series of pieces to a fitting close. In fact the word *oracle,* which ended the first stanza, stands artistically near the start of this one. Two parallel statements are made concerning Edom's twin assets of wisdom and military strength. Their parallelism is indicated by the repetition of *out of Mount Esau* at the end of the second line and toward the end of the third. The oracle is closely integrated with the preceding stanza by the way it picks up the thought of lack of knowledge and develops it.

Throughout vv. 1b–9 the themes of divine and human action are closely intertwined, first one and then the other coming to the fore. Here in this fourth stanza it is finally stressed that the nations of v. 1b, the invading thieves and harvesters of the second stanza, and the ex-allies of the third are subservient to the sovereign will of Yahweh concerning the destruction of Edom. An element that frequently appears in the concept of holy war in Hebrew thinking is the notion of Yahweh as a secret ally, creating havoc in the enemy ranks by confusing their reactions and robbing them of morale and confidence.[35] It is this motif of divine help against the adversaries of Israel that is here reused concerning the war against Edom, Judah's archenemy. But now it is not Israel but other peoples whose efforts are reinforced by Yahweh's aid. He is to strike a mysterious blow against the expertise for which Edom was famed.

In the book of Job, Eliphaz, whose traditional wisdom is attacked, is

34. Keil and Wade interpret not of lack of foresight but of bewilderment, not knowing what to do, which is certainly the case in v. 8, but not necessarily here.
35. Ex. 23:27; Deut. 7:23; Josh. 10:10.

stated to have come from Teman in Edom.[36] To Edom's bazaars thronged peoples of the east, who brought with their wares travellers' tales of learning and lore. It was probably this byproduct of its being a center of trade and travel that gave rise to Edom's awesome reputation for wisdom.[37] Here its wisdom takes the form of skill in military strategy. But the God who had overthrown the counsel of wise old Ahithophel (2 Sam. 17:14) is to intervene now to distort the thinking of Edom's military and political advisers. Their shrewdness will be no match against foes on whose side Yahweh fights. Edom is here referred to in parallelism as *Mount Esau,* a term not found apart from Obad. 8f., 19, 21. It doubtless refers to the mountainous terrain of the country of Edom/Esau.

This secret weapon of bewilderment which causes incompetence is to be wielded against the Edomite troops. *Teman,* an important city of Edom,[38] is here used poetically as a part for the whole. The nation's army, losing their sense of morale and *esprit de corps,* would flee in panic, easy victims for their pursuing foes. God's purpose is nothing less than the complete annihilation of Edom's forces.[39]

This first section of the composition in vv. 2–9 has analyzed from various angles the theme of the destruction of Edom. Beginning and end have stressed that neither natural impregnability nor native wisdom nor national manpower can provide adequate defense against the set purpose of Yahweh to overthrow the Edomites. Edom will come tumbling down from its proud position, deprived of wit and warrior. Its rich warehouses are to be looted and left bereft of spices and gold. Its allies will turn traitor against it. Such is to be the punishment for Edom. Dire indeed must be the sins that earn such wages, and it is to an accusation of Edom's crimes that the prophet turns in the second part of his composition.

36. Job 2:11; cf. Jer. 49:7; Baruch 3:23.

37. Cf. 1 K. 4:30 (5:10).

38. N. Glueck, *The Other Side of the Jordan* (1940), pp. 25f., plausibly identified it with modern Tawilan, 5 miles east of Petra. For *gibbôreyḵā,* "your warriors," some follow Marti in reading *gibbôrê,* "warriors of (Teman)," in view of the third person references elsewhere in the stanza. Dahood, *Pss 2,* p. 147, considers that this interpretation may be obtained from the consonantal text, regarding the *kaph* as an emphatic *kî* interposed in a construct chain, comparing esp. Ezek. 27:8. But in view of the direct address of Edom in the earlier verses it is not out of place here; cf. the oscillation in vv. 5f.

39. G S V link *miqqāṭel, by slaughter,* with v. 10 and have been followed by Wellhausen, Rudolph, Weiser, Brockington, Deissler, Keller, Fohrer, *et al.* Keil and Bewer considered the order to be then rather inept, a stronger term preceding the weaker. Others, such as *BHK* and Thompson, delete the word as a gloss explaining in less vague terms, or citing a variant to, *mēḥᵃmas, because of violence,* in v. 10. Better motivation for a gloss would be provided by regarding it as a comment on the two forms of the verb *krt* in vv. 8f., distinguishing their meaning from the apparently nonfatal use of the verb in v. 14. However, MT can be justified metrically as a triple line of 3+3+3 (Robinson, Watts, cf. Bewer). Poetically it might appear more probable that the two adjacent lines would end with *mēhar 'ēśāw,* but vv. 15a, 16 provide a convincing parallel to the present arrangement.

II. THE WRONGDOING OF EDOM (10–14, 15b)

A. EDOM'S UNBROTHERLINESS (10, 11)

Because of violence done to your brother Jacob
you will be covered with shame and destroyed for ever. 3+4
11 *On the day when you stood aloof,*
the day when aliens carried away his property[1] 3+4
and foreigners entered his gate[2]
and drew lots for Jerusalem– 3+4
you *behaved like one of them.* 3

This first stanza of the new division of the poem falls into two parts. First it announces Edom's punishment for good and all as the express consequence of its ill treatment of Judah. Secondly it points the finger of accusation at Edom by defining what this ill treatment was and when it occurred. Metrically it consists of three uniform lines, brought to a close by a short line, as in v. 7. Like the opening stanza of the first section, this one has an introductory function. It acts as a bridge between the first section and this one, as the repetition of the motif of destruction makes plain.[3] The initial words of v. 10 stress that the punishment related in vv. 2–9 is not arbitrary but provoked by cause enough. The basic charge of v. 11 sets the scene for the more specific accusations which are to follow. The repeated mention of *on the day* jerks the listener and reader back to v. 8, where the *day* of Edom's punishment was mentioned. That day is the grim, inexorable echo of this one.

The prophet, who apparently speaks throughout vv. 10–14, 15b as the interpreter of God's will, places side by side in sharp relief two words opposed in meaning: *violence* and *brother*. The kinship of the two national groups of Edom and Israel, and its corresponding obligation, are stressed in Deut. 23:7: "You must not regard an Edomite with abhorrence, because he is your brother." This kinship is grounded in the patriarchal traditions of Gen. 25–29; 32f., which present in prototype the history of rivalry and suspicion subsequently experienced by the two nations. Judah is expressly called *Jacob* in order to bring out this relationship. Whatever the rights and

1. Bewer follows Duhm in emending MT, objecting that in the present text the order is illogical: the carrying off of property must have followed the entry of Jerusalem. The difficulty is hardly resolved by interpreting solely of possessions in Judah outside Jerusalem (Keil), nor by rendering "captured his fortifications" (Watts), since although Heb. *ḥêlô* can be derived from *ḥêl*, "rampart," the verb is never used thus. The earlier clause gives the main point, while the rest supplies details (Sellin, Rudolph). *Ḥêlô,* from *ḥayil,* "power, wealth, army," is here evidently not "army" (G V, von Orelli, Robinson, Deissler, Rudolph) but *property,* as in v. 13. It is true that the verb *shāḇâ* generally has a personal object, but 2 Chr. 21:17; Jer. 43:12 are significant exceptions.
2. Q "his gates" or "his towns," but v. 13 supports K *his gate.*
3. Heb. *yikkāreṯ, may be destroyed,* v. 9—*wᵉniḵrattâ, and you will be destroyed,* v. 10.

wrongs of this habitual hostility, the prophet can see no sufficient warrant for this unforgettable instance of Edom's treatment of a brother nation already overwhelmed by crisis. Kinship creates obligation, which cannot be neglected with impunity.

Edom's *violence,* a basic disregard for human rights, will prove the prelude to its inevitable humiliation, and indeed to its permanent dissolution. So certain is the prophet of God's justice and its outworking in the world of men. In fact the mills of God's judgment ground slowly but inexorably to this very destiny. Taking advantage of Judah's downfall and pressing into the west, the Edomites eventually proved natural victims to a resurgent Judah in the second century B.C., when John Hyrcanus conquered them, and, compelling them to be circumcised, deprived them of their nationhood.

Obadiah thinks back to the tragic day when Judah stood alone, exposed to the fury of an enemy invader. Where was Edom then? Did the Edomites rally round, family squabbles forgotten in the face of a common enemy? No. Like the priest and Levite in the parable of the Good Samaritan who "passed by on the other side" and failed to help the bandits' victim lying wounded in the road (Luke 10:31f.), the people of Edom refused to become involved on Judah's side.[4] The prophet proceeds to give a poignant description of the calamity that had befallen his people. His mention of *aliens* and *foreigners,* instead of specifying them by name, is intended to bring out Edom's heartlessness in failing to come to the aid of their kinsmen. He has in mind a foreign invasion of Judah, clearly the one perpetrated by the Babylonians in 587 B.C. Thinking back to the calamitous day when the capital's peace and independence were desecrated by ruthless trespassers, he concentrates on their plundering and looting, grabbing what was not their own and vying with one another over the allocation of the citizens of Jerusalem as slaves.

The final statement constitutes a climactic punch line. The people of Edom did not maintain their neutrality for long. Hesitant to enter the lists on Judah's side, they were not averse to exploiting the situation for their own ends. With all the force of *et tu, Brute,* the exclamation rings out with profound horror. So far from presenting a united front with Judah against the outsider, they made common cause with the enemy. Here is the acme of unbrotherliness, that he who should have regarded himself as "one of us" behaved *like one of them.* Whether Obadiah is referring to formal Edomite contingents in the Babylonian army, or merely to private individuals and groups sorting over soldiers' leavings, is uncertain. The accent on plundering and looting is deliberate. Its purpose is to take up the brutal theme of vv. 5f. as cause and effect. The punishment predicted there is to the prophet's mind no arbitrary one, but a natural corollary of what the Judeans themselves had suffered at the hands of their enemies and also of the Edomites, who had not only supplied no help but—and this was the last

4. For *stood aloof* cf. the similar phrase in 2 Sam. 18:13.

straw—actually derived gain from their kinsmen's misfortune. But right would eventually be done, he was sure. Edom would be forced to pay compensation, as it were, for the callous part played in the tragic events of 587.

B. EDOM'S MOCKERY (12)

But do not gloat over your brother's day
on the day of his misfortune. 3+2
Do not jeer at the Judeans
on the day of their ruin. 3+2
Do not talk so big
on the day of distress. 3+2

This stanza is the first of three with a similar construction. In highly imaginative fashion the prophet speaks of events in the past as if they were still present.[5] The rhetorical nature of his speech is disclosed in v. 15b, where he abandons this device and speaks plainly of Edom's activities as in the past. Moreover, v. 13 clearly harks back to v. 11, which is firmly placed in the past. Dramatically reliving the dire experiences of 587, Obadiah puts his indictment of the Edomites in the form of a series of protests, which are full of pathos because they are necessarily unavailing. This section and the next have three lines constructed in the form of external parallelism, each synonymously consisting of a warning and a reference to the tragic happening. In this first stanza each of the three lines starts in the same way[6] and ends in a synonym. It is associated closely with the previous stanza by the echoing and reechoing of the repeated *day* of v. 11[7] as well as by the allusion to *foreigners* in the word at the end of the first line.[8] These three lines by their uniformity of meter and similarity of form build up a powerful theme which the next two sections are to develop in slightly different ways. This stanza constitutes a series of verbal hammerblows designed to drive the message vigorously home.

The narration of bare facts given in the heart of v. 11 now yields to an excited elaboration of the heartless behavior of the Edomites. The prophet shouts as if in the grip of a nightmare. He feels afresh the emotions of resentment and loathing as in his mind's eye he sees again the leering, loutish folk of Edom. In his anguish he screams out "No, no, no!" protesting with all his being against their revelling in the situation that spelled the end of Judah. Again the keynote *your brother* sounds out in condemnation of their

5. Cf. GK 109e.
6. Heb. *w*[e]*'al*, "and not."
7. Heb. *b*[e]*yôm* twice in v. 11 and four times in v. 12.
8. Heb. *nokrîm*, v. 11—*nokrô*, "his misfortune."

lack of concern. The usage of *day* in its first occurrence is strikingly similar to that in Ps. 137:7:[9]

> *Remember, Yahweh, against the Edomites*
> *Jerusalem's day.*
> *They it was who said, "Level it, level it*
> *down to its foundations."*

It refers to the day of disaster, the fatal day of Jerusalem's capture and destruction. It is not a literal day but rather the period of a month or so in the summer of 587, which commenced with the first breakthrough of the besieging Babylonians and culminated in the burning down of the temple and other important buildings. Stunned into unbearable grief, the prophet's melancholy is disturbed by the memory of the shocking blatancy of the Edomites who gathered like so many greedy vultures around the scene of doom. He tries in vain to shut out from his ears these voices which haunt him with the echo of malicious chuckles and jeers. He screams at them to keep their big mouths shut.[10] How dare they add their supercilious insults to the injuries of body, mind, and spirit already inflicted upon the people of Judah?

The attitude of arrogant superiority revealed in this gloating and taunting sounds like a deliberate reminiscence of the description of Edom's mentality in v. 3: Edom's pride was there used as a contrast to emphasize their coming fall. The link is significant: it makes a fall from greatness an appropriate retribution for the Edomites' big talk when Jerusalem fell. The repetition of *your brother* from v. 10 also seems to have a significance greater than its immediate context. The treachery of Edom in its treatment of Judah is to be echoed in the betrayal of Edom by its own allies and confederates. The traitor will be betrayed in turn, and the unfaithful will discover how bitter is the taste of infidelity.

C. EDOM'S TRESPASSING (13)

Do not enter my people's gate
on the day of their calamity. 3+2
Do not gloat like the rest over their trouble
on the day of their calamity. 3+2
Do not lay hands[11] *on their property*
on the day of their calamity. 3+2

9. Cf. too Job 18:20; Ps. 37:13. Many scholars, including J. M. P. Smith, Robinson, Weiser, Deissler, and Fohrer, read *bᵉ'āḥîḵā,* "over your brother," for *bᵉyôm 'aḥîḵā,* regarding *yôm* as an anticipation of the next phrase and observing that *your brother* is the expected external parallel to *Judeans* later. But the usage of *day* is fitting; cf. the second line of v. 13.
10. Lit. "make your mouth big."
11. MT *tishlaḥnâ,* an incongruous feminine plural, is to be repointed as a second masculine singular form of the energic imperfect *tishlāḥannâ* with the ellipse of *yâḏ,* "hand," as at 2 Sam. 6:6; Ps. 18:16(17) (von Orelli; G. R. Driver, *JTS* 39 [1938], p. 398; Dahood, *Pss I,* p. 49). There is no need to emend to *tishlaḥ-nā'* (J. M. P. Smith, Bewer, Wade, Keller) or to *tishlaḥ yāḏ* (Ewald, Wellhausen, *BHK,* Robinson, Weiser, Rudolph, *BHS,* Watts, Fohrer).

This next stanza is obviously the second of a structural triad. As before, warnings are linked with temporal refrains; the recurrent motif of gloating provides continuity of theme. These next three lines, again of a regular 3+2 meter, are bound together as a small unit by the near-identical refrain that ends each line.[12] Mention of entering the gate harks back to the action of the foreign enemy in the introductory piece of vv. 10f.; the Edomites follow in their wake, aligning themselves with Judah's enemies. A similar echo is sounded in the reference to *property* and in the phrase "you too."[13] There is a trace of a larger artistic network of connected themes and sounds in the repetition of the verb "send" of vv. 1, 7 in this unit.

The strophe presents a reaction to further links in the chain of events of 587 B.C. The Edomites who stood gloating outside the fallen city now venture inside on the heels of the Babylonian troops. The ghostly voices that haunted the prophet's imagination in the previous stanza have died away. His mind's eye is now assaulted by vivid scenes of horror. He shouts in vain, "Keep out"; still the Edomites press through the ruined gate and look brazenly around at the smoldering remains of their rivals' capital. *My people* is a sob of pathos mingled with indignant passion, as Obadiah recalls the blatant trespass.

Edom's stock of guilt is growing in the prophet's eyes. The first instance of *their calamity* is a play on Edom[14] which the listener would not miss and from which he would rightly glean a suggestion of ill omen. Probably they were not the only ones to find malicious satisfaction in Jerusalem's downfall, but it was especially unworthy of them. "If other neighbors do it, yet abstain yourself, seeing you are of one blood. If you cannot render assistance, at least show some sign of sorrow and sympathy" (Calvin). But not content with trespass and gloating, the Edomites engaged in covetous theft. Taking their cue from the Chaldean victors (v. 11), they looted like any foreigner.

But God is not mocked. Edom's greedy outstretching (lit. "sending") was fated to end in the sending of a messenger to arouse the nations to do battle against Edom (v. 1) and in the sending away of Edomite refugees unhelped (v. 7). The prophet does not lightly repeat his vocabulary; as will be later made explicit, all these things are bound together in divine providence by an inevitable chain of cause and effect.

12. Absolute symmetry is avoided; the first case has a plural suffix, while the other two have collective, singular suffixes.

13. Heb. *gam 'attem,* rendered 'you' and *like the rest* respectively.

14. Heb. *'êḏām,* cf. *'ᵉḏôm,* Edom. The play also occurs in Ezek. 35:5. Deissler observes that *'êḏ* tends to be a stereotyped term referring to the fall of Jerusalem.

D. EDOM'S COLLABORATION AND COMING RETRIBUTION (14, 15b)

Do not stand at the crossroads,[15]
ready to intercept their fugitives. 3+2
Do not hand over their survivors
on the day of distress. 3+2
15b *As you have done, so will be done to you:*
your deeds will recoil on your own heads.[16] 4+3

This final stanza of the second part of the composition has a dual role. It continues the series of impassioned accusations against Edom[17] and draws the overall unit to a close with a threat of punishment. That threat suitably rounds off this section, reverting to a note struck at the very beginning in v. 10a.[18] The stanza conforms to the pattern of the preceding ones in this section by consisting of three lines. The similarity of theme of the first two lines to the earlier indictments is echoed in the continued use of a 3+2 meter. But the final line, in keeping with its solemn change of subject, changes the tempo to a weightier rhythm.

The grim saga continues, with the Edomites plunging ever deeper into guilt as they interfere further in Judah's affairs. In this next cameo which the prophet dramatically reveals, they have left the city and are thronging the roads to the east. They are not the only travellers, for refugees from Jerusalem are trying to escape from the Babylonians. It is significant that in 587, when the wall of Jerusalem finally crumbled before the Chaldean onslaught, King Zedekiah fled to the east with his army under cover of darkness, only to be overtaken on the plains of Jericho. Many an aristocrat as well as less elevated citizens must have had a similar notion, but evidently their hopes of escape were dashed by roadblocks set up by Edomites. They collaborated with the enemy, and simply handed back those who fell into their hands.[19] As a consequence the Judeans endured more suffering.

15. Heb. *pereq* occurs only here and at Nah. 3:1, where it apparently means "plunder." But here it seems to refer to a place where roads divide. The basic meaning of the root is "tear apart, tear away."

16. Most scholars since Wellhausen reverse the two halves of v. 15 on the ground of content. Verse 15b uses second singular verbs and pronouns like the preceding material, and refers to Edom. Verse 15a introduces the theme of universal judgment which occupies the next section, in the course of which the Jews are addressed with a plural verb (v. 16a). The change of order may be explained simply as due to a copyist's oversight. Since both vv. 15a and 16a begin with *kî*, his eye slipped by homoeoarcton and v. 15a was temporarily omitted. It was doubtless added in the margin or squeezed in between the lines, but was unfortunately misplaced before the *ka'ᵃsher* of v. 15b instead of before the *kî ka'ᵃsher* of v. 16.

17. Heb. *bᵉyôm tsārâ, on the day of distress,* echoes v. 12.

18. Heb. *lᵉhakrîṯ*, "to cut off," subtly paves the way for the motif of precise retribution by harking back to *wᵉnikrattā*, v. 10, and *yikkāreṯ*, v. 9. Many interpret this instance in terms of extermination, but that would turn the following accusation into an anticlimax.

19. Sellin and Thompson interpret in terms of enslavement in view of the use of the verb *hisgîr* in Amos 1:6, while von Orelli and Watts take as "imprison" (cf. Job 11:10); but the context suggests simply *hand over,* "betray" (cf. Deut. 32:30; Amos 6:8).

Obadiah and his fellow Jews never forgot such a festering memory. Here is the climax of treachery and vindictiveness; it is such perverseness as this that is here revealed as justification for the betrayal of Edom by her own allies and her coming failure to find refuge in neighboring territory (v. 7).

A belief that the world is under the control of a moral God permits a much more positive reaction to the prophet's historical analysis than wringing one's hands or shrugging one's shoulders. Obadiah passionately believed in God's providence as a powerful factor, which would eventually right wrongs or at least compensate in some way for wrongs committed. History was for him the continual adjustment of a set of moral balances, a view the Church has partly taken over and partly projected into the future context of judgment after death and the punishments and rewards of eternity. The core of the prophet's conviction was the *lex talionis*. God's intervention was the law of an eye for an eye writ large on the tablet of world history. Destiny would mirror deeds committed earlier. *As you have done, so will be done:* the passive, as often, alludes to divine agency.[20] The next clause speaks of a natural boomeranging of events as consequences. For Obadiah the orientation of judgment was centered firmly in this world and this life upon earth. Therefore God's moral sovereignty meant that God had so ordained the constitution of the world and the movement of its history that the principle of retribution was written into life. God ruled and overruled through a natural law at work in the world so that equilibrium was achieved. "Whatever amount you measure out for others will be measured back for you" (Matt. 7:2). Justice would be done, the prophet assured his contemporaries. How it would be done he had already revealed in part in vv. 2–9.

III. EDOM ON THE DAY OF YAHWEH (15a, 16–21)

The final portion of the poem sets the downfall of guilty Edom within a wider perspective. A substantial part of the prophetic literature of the OT is concerned with eschatological expectations, in which the themes of the Day of Yahweh and his people's domination of other nations come to the fore. It is to this larger hope that our prophet now not unnaturally turns in climactic conclusion. Relating his own theme to the great traditional framework of the future, he is still much concerned with Edom but shows how his special message fits into the eschatological pattern of God's final triumph. The conquest of Edom already predicted is now presented as a signal inaugurating that traditional widespread demonstration of divine justice and grace which is associated with the Day of Yahweh. Behind the fate of the nations,

20. Cf. Mic. 1:7 and comments.

as behind that of Edom alone in the preceding part of the book, stands the fall of Jerusalem in 587 as the crime that sets the wheels of divine retribution in motion.

A. THE DAY OF YAHWEH (15a, 16)

The Day of Yahweh certainly[1] *looms near*
for all the nations. 3+2
16 *The cup that you have drunk on my sacred mount*
all nations will drink without respite.[2] 4+3
They will drink it and swallow it down,[3]
and become as though they had never been. 2+3

This first piece is a divine pronouncement of coming punishment *for all the nations,* i.e., excluding the Jewish nation. Its three lines are metrically diverse but are obviously bound together by their common theme. The word *day,* which was the keynote struck no less than ten times in the second part of the poem, has a fresh, single mention in this third part, corresponding to its initial single occurrence in the first (v. 8). In fact this latter correspondence is not only stylistic but thematic: allusion is made in both the first and third parts to a future day, while the middle part is concerned with that terrible day in 587 when Jerusalem fell. For the prophet there is an intimate link between that day of oppression and the coming day of judgment.[4] But the future day of v. 8 is not simply to be equated with the Day of Yahweh now mentioned, although they clearly have common features. The prophet broadens the dimensions of his thinking and ranges further afield to the traditional horizons of Israel's hope.

The OT looked forward to a time when Yahweh would finally intervene in human affairs and set right the wicked world, a time when man's day of self-sufficiency and oppression would be brought to a close. This future period, when moral debts would be settled and Yahweh openly revealed to all as the upholder of right and justice and the victor over sin and violence, was called the Day of Yahweh. A basic and traditional part of this eschatological motif was the participation of the people of God in his victory.[5] It is with the former of these twin ideas that the first piece is concerned.

1. Heb. *kî* is emphatic.
2. Some Heb. mss. read *sāḇîḇ,* "around," for MT *tāmîḏ,* "continually," evidently influenced by the similar context of "all peoples around" in Zech. 12:2. G "wine" presupposes not *ḥemer,* which Robinson adopted, but a repointing in terms of postbiblical *temeḏ* (E. Nestle, *ZAW* 23 [1903], p. 345; J. Ziegler, *ZAW* 60 [1944], p. 112).
3. Heb. *lāʿû* from a root associated with *lōaʿ,* "throat," Prov. 23:2, and related to Syr. *laʿ* or *lāʿ,* "lick, sip." Some relate it to a homonym, "talk wildly," which occurs in Job 6:3; Prov. 20:25. There is no need for Wellhausen's emendation *nāʿû,* "stagger."
4. Cf. the repeated *ka'ᵃsher,* "as," in vv. 15b, 16.
5. Cf. Amos 5:18–20, where the popular view is criticized.

Over against the day of disaster endured by Jerusalem in 587 stands another Day, a day of vindication and judgment in Israel's favor. Edom's defeat is but the prelude to the overthrow of all the powers who pit themselves against Yahweh and do not acknowledge his sovereignty. Verse 16 contrasts the Jews and *all the nations;* the punishment of these nations is evidently grounded in the crisis of 587. It seems therefore that Obadiah is thinking specifically of the many nations represented in the attacking armies; these would have included detachments of regional troops loyal to Babylon. The Day is to be a time of reprisals against savage, wanton destruction. The seer offers as some consolation for the shattered survivors of that catastrophe the prospect that justice would certainly be done and those nations involved in the guilt of that international crime would be brought to book.

The figure of the cup of wrath is one used in Hebrew literature to express God's judgment:

> *In Yahweh's hand is a cup*
> *of foaming wine, heavily spiced.*
> *From it he pours*
> *for all the wicked in the world to drink,*
> *draining it right down to its dregs.* (Ps. 75:8[9])

For the Christian the figure has a specially sacred significance because Jesus used it in the garden of Gethsemane in his poignant prayer, "Take this cup away from me. Yet not what I want, but what you want" (Mark 14:36; cf. 10:38f.). Whether the metaphor had a cultic basis in the temple ritual is unknown. Did a cup of strong wine feature in some ceremony to symbolize God's judgment against sinners?[6] There is no evidence for this; but, if so, the reference in the present context to Jerusalem would be very apposite. The point of the illustration is that the victim of divine wrath is sent reeling, as helpless under its potent influence as a drunken man.

> *"You have given your people a bitter drink,*
> *you have given us wine to drink that made us reel."*
> (Ps. 60:3[4])

As in that psalm, the affliction of the people of God is here in view.[7] The prophet addresses his sorrowing audience with a word of implicit comfort direct from Yahweh. The community had indeed been punished for its sin, and from this point of view the fall of Jerusalem was God's own reprisal against a rebellious people. But as a loving cup is passed from hand to hand, so it was to be with this cup of wrath. It would in due course be the turn of the other nations. Isa. 51:17–23, a fine commentary on this present verse, includes a promise:

6. Cf. H. Ringgren, *Israelite Religion* (E.T. 1966), pp. 78f.

7. Heb. *shᵉtîtem,* "you have drunk," a plural verb, is clearly differentiated from the preceding second singular verbs and pronouns addressed to Edom. The next words make it clear that the drinking signifies defeat and destruction and so can hardly refer to the carousing of the Edomites in Jerusalem (von Orelli, Watts), nor to the revelling of all the nations in Edom in return for their revelling in Jerusalem (König).

"You will drink it no more.
I shall put it into the hands of your tormentors."

(Isa. 51:22f.)[8]

A charge of sacrilege is levelled against the oppressing forces. Agents of God's own wrath though they were, they were not themselves guiltless. Jerusalem the golden, set apart for the worship of Yahweh, had been vilely desecrated. No respect had been paid to this blessed sanctuary. God's honor had been besmirched in the ruthless trespass upon holy ground and in the looting of temple ornaments and vessels.[9] Obadiah echoes the age-old Zion theology, which had been reflected in the oracles of Isaiah long before.[10] On its basis he can affirm that the nations represented in the sack of the holy city would not go unpunished. Their turn would come. But for them the experience of punishment would be intensified. What had been a temporary experience for God's people was to be echoed in a catastrophe of greater severity and longer duration. God in his mercy had left survivors of the 587 B.C. crisis, as the next stanza affirms; but the rest of the nations were to suffer a fate of total destruction. Such was the enormity of the outrage they had committed that nothing less could be punishment adequate for it. In this drastic way the honor of God would be vindicated. As long ago Uzzah had profaned the holiness attaching to the ark and provoked the anger of Yahweh, which destroyed him,[11] so the powerful holiness of God which enveloped Jerusalem must lash out and take a terrible toll of its profaners. They were to be destroyed so utterly that they would leave no trace of their former existence, so awesome is the holy power of God, and so lethal to those who pit themselves against it.

B. THE ROLE OF THE REMNANT (17, 21)

But on Mount Zion
those who escaped will continue,
and it will be sacrosanct. 2+2+2
The community of Jacob will regain territory
from those who took it from them.[12] 3+2
21 *Then those saved*[13] *on Mount Zion will go up*
to govern Mount Esau, 4+3
And so the sovereignty will be Yahweh's. 3

8. Cf. Lam. 4:21f., where interestingly the cup is to pass to Edom.
9. Cf. 2 K. 25:13–15.
10. Cf. G. von Rad, *OT Theology*, vol. 2 (E.T. 1965), pp. 155–58.
11. 2 Sam. 6:7.
12. MT *môrāshêhem*, "their possessions," is a minority reading. It is generally repointed *môrīshêhem*, "their dispossessors," with G S V T and Mur. 88 *mwryšyhm*. Pointed thus, it provides a better link with the reference to the nations in the previous stanza and to Edom in the next. Cf. the similar phrase in Jer. 49:2.
13. MT *mōshī'îm*, "saviors," is to be revocalized with a number of scholars as a Hophal participle *mûshā'îm* in accord with the passive in G S Aquila and Theodotion. This is preferable to postulating a Niphal *nôshā'îm* with *BHK*, Deissler, etc. That a Hophal is not found else-

This next stanza is a promise, which provides a counterpart to the threat against the other nations in the previous one. The prophet presents the second stage in the divine plan for the future. The *sacred mount* of v. 16 features again, split into its two component parts in the first line.[14] The term *those who escaped* reaches back into the previous main section and echoes the *fugitives* of v. 14.[15]

There are indications that v. 21 should be taken with v. 17 to form a single stanza. The combination provides a unit conforming to the pattern of three or four-line stanzas that runs right through this little book.[16] The theme of Zion dominates both verses. Verse 21 takes up the phrase *on Mount Zion* which begins v. 17.[17] It is not difficult to appreciate that later ignorance of the strophic structure led to its being displaced to the end of the book in order to obtain a more impressive finale.

The prophet proceeds to the next stage in his unfolding of the divinely ordained future. The desecration of Jerusalem having been avenged, the next step is obviously a positive one, the rehabilitation of the sacred site. Moreover, mention of the complete overthrow of the nations is followed naturally by contrasting the fortunes of the Jews, who after the Babylonian onslaught and its aftermath were left as a comparatively small remnant. That Obadiah is thinking in terms of the survivors of the earlier conflict rather than of some distant event in the future is suggested by his taking up the term of v. 14. The survivors are invested with theological significance as those who inherit the old prophetic promises concerning the remnant. Jerusalem had passed through her own version of the Day of Yahweh,[18] and its destiny was to inherit the salvation of God which in the prophetic scheme follows on the heels of judgment. There is consolation and hope for the future in that some were left to form a nucleus for God's plan of blessing to come.[19] Obadiah looks forward to the time when Jerusalem would become demonstrably free from violation, immune from a repetition of the previous outrages deplored earlier in the poem. Joel 3:17 in citing this verse correctly interprets the sanctity of Jerusalem as the prospect that "aliens will never again pass through it."[20] It is said elsewhere of "Jerusalem, the holy city":

---

where probably encouraged the interpretations of its letters as a Hiphil. The following phrase *on Mount Zion* qualifies the passive participle (Halévy, Rudolph, Weiser) and is intended as a recapitulation of the first clause in v. 17.

14. Heb. *har qoḏshî*, v. 16—*har . . . qōḏesh*, v. 17.

15. Heb. *pᵉlîṭāyw*, v. 14—*pᵉlêṭâ*, v. 17.

16. For the concluding short line cf. vv. 7, 11, 18.

17. The phonetic reversal of *wᵉlā'û*, v. 16, into *wᵉ'ālû*, "and they will go up," v. 21, is apparently intended to express further the contrast already observed between the previous stanza and this one.

18. Cf. Lam. 1:12; 2:1, 21f., where for Israel the day of Yahweh is past in the fall of Jerusalem, while for the nations it is still future according to 1:21 (N. K. Gottwald, *Studies in Lamentations*, SBT 14 [1954], pp. 84f.).

19. Cf. Ezra 9:7–9.

20. It is sometimes urged that *wᵉhāyâ qōḏesh, and it will be sacrosanct,* is a later addition (*BHK*, cf. *BHS*) as metrically superfluous, having been inserted from Joel. But the meter is

There will enter you no more
the uncircumcised and the unclean.[21]

This hope of a future for Jerusalem befitting its special status in the purpose of God fills the hearts of the post-587 generations of the covenant community.

The fortunes of Jerusalem and the land of Israel are inextricably linked together. Worship in the temple of the holy city was the key to the blessing of the whole land.[22] "The possession of Mount Zion as Yahweh's abode is very closely connected with the right to dwell on the land.... Yahweh's holy hill was a symbol of Yahweh's land, and to worship on the one carried with it the privilege of dwelling on the other."[23] With the reversal in the capital's fortunes it is therefore only to be expected that the land too will be restored to its rightful owners. The prophet subtly expresses the natural link between the city of Jerusalem and the nation's inheritance by a play on words. The Hebrew *wᵉyārᵉshû* deliberately evokes the sound of the name of the capital *yᵉrûshālēm*.[24] Moreover the new thought provides a simple development from the theme of the preceding stanza. The nations under Babylon had commandeered Judean territory, and the decimation and deportation of Jews from their homeland had led to neighbors' encroachment upon their territory. Now the tables would be turned. The new Israel, graced with the traditional title *community of Jacob,* which here harks back to the ancient antipathy alluded to in v. 10, would be enabled to claim back possessions once wrested from their hands. The nations, erstwhile victors, would appropriately become victims. They would lose their ill-gotten gains to the legitimate owners, whose right of occupation went back to the age-old divine covenant that promised the land to Israel.

The time is now ripe for Obadiah to integrate his recent theme of the Day of Yahweh and attendant events with his earlier motif of Edom's downfall. Having linked his specific burden with the traditional general theme dear to the prophets and so underscoring it with extra significance, he has carefully steered his pronouncements around to the point where he can revert to his main message. But he stays within the thematic bounds of the stanza, drawing together the threads of Mount Zion, the remnant, and territory regained. It is those who have survived the catastrophe of Jerusalem whose role it will be to venture forth from the capital, ancient seat of Israel's theocracy, and annex the territory of Edom, incorporating it into Yahweh's kingdom. Once again the term *Mount Esau* is used, echoing the refrain of vv. 8f., where it occurred in the context of Yahweh's purposes. Here it is chosen as a dramatic counterpart to Mount Zion. The two rivals are brought together

---

adequate as a tricolon (2+2+2 according to Robinson and Watts) and the Joel reference is sufficiently different to suggest that Joel echoes Obad., as in 2:32 (3:5).

21. Isa. 52:1; cf. Zech. 9:8.

22. Cf. R. E. Clements, *TGUOS* 19 (1961/62), pp. 16–28. He does not cite this passage, but refers *inter alia* to Ex. 15:17; Ps. 78:54; Isa. 57:13; Ezek. 47. Cf. Joel 3:17 and comment.

23. *Ibid.*, pp. 22, 24.

24. Cf. the explicit play in v. 20.

again, but now the loser is on the winning side. Yet the true victor is to be not Israel but Yahweh. His will be the enabling and so his the credit. The prophet looked for a revival of the grand old days of David, when he reigned in Jerusalem as God's viceroy and Edom lay within the empire of Israel. Just as David did not rule in his own right, so again true theocracy would be manifested, with the community of God serving as the agents of his will. The nation would be a window through which the power and presence of the divine Monarch could be glimpsed.

Here is the great motivation which sets in a better light what might appear to be merely a nationalistic craving for revenge. The prophet's great passion is for Yahweh's sovereignty to be made evident. God and his people were bound together in the bundle of covenantal life, and so his supremacy would be mediated through his earthly representatives. But the prayer of Obadiah is "Thine be the kingdom, the power and the glory." His vision is of a sovereign God, and by implication an obedient people, who exist only to do his bidding and enhance his glory. The prophet's aspiration is akin to Peter's:

> *The God of all grace, who has called you to his eternal glory in Christ, will restore you, after you have suffered a little while; he will give you firmness and strength and a secure foundation. To him be the power for ever and ever. Amen.* (1 Pet. 5:10f.)

C. JUDEAN FIRE AND EDOMITE STUBBLE (18)

The community of Jacob will become fire,
the community of Joseph flame, 3+3
and the community of Esau stubble–
they will set them ablaze and consume them. 3+3
Not a survivor will be left
for the community of Esau. 3+2
So Yahweh has spoken. 3

This stanza is at once a reassuring promise of Judah's future destructive power and a grim pronouncement of Edom's punishment. The unit of three double lines plus a short line is presented as a divine oracle culminating in a formula of attestation, which like a signature marks the end of the stanza. The visible strand linking it to the previous strophe is the mention of *the community of Jacob*. The onslaught upon Edom is an unfolding of one aspect of their reclamation of territory from those who dispossessed them (v. 17). The general theme of reinstatement is applied specifically to the region of Edom. Like the last stanza this one echoes the previous section in its use of the term *survivor,* which significantly was used of Judeans suffering at the hands of Edomites in v. 14.

The superficial reader will view this piece as a simple statement of Judah's destruction of Edom. A knowledge of the usage of the key terms *fire, stubble* in the OT reveals a far deeper level of theological content than appears on the surface. Over and over again, separately and together, they connote God's judgment of the wicked. The ancient Song of Moses already reflects this usage in describing the defeat of Pharaoh's army:

"You released your fury
and it consumed them like stubble." (Ex. 15:7)

Isaiah applied this imagery to the cosmopolitan Assyrian army which threatened Jerusalem in 701 B.C.: it would be reduced to "drifting chaff" (Isa. 10:17)[25] and Yahweh would visit them with "the flame of a devouring fire" (Isa. 29:5f.).[26] John the Baptist similarly defined the role of the Messiah as agent of divine judgment: "He will burn the chaff with unquenchable fire" (Matt. 3:12; Luke 3:17). The present pronouncement stands firmly within a consistent biblical tradition in its use of the metaphor of fire and stubble. Judah is represented not as a people who will act on their own initiative in working out their own questionable desires for revenge, but as the instrument of God by which his just verdict is to be executed. The import of this declaration is brought out plainly in Ezek. 25:14, which may be regarded as a commentary on the stanza:

"I shall inflict my vengeance upon Edom by means of my people Israel. They will treat Edom as my anger and my wrath dictate, and the Edomites will experience my vengeance."

There is a hint, to be expanded in the next stanza, that Judah, here called *Jacob* as in v. 10, is not to be alone in wreaking divine retribution on the Edomites. *The community of Joseph* could be merely a poetic echo of the previous phrase in synonymous parallelism.[27] But the frequent usage of *Joseph* in the OT to stand for the northern tribes suggests a wider significance. Compare, for example, Ps. 77:15(16):

You redeemed with your arm your people,
the sons of Jacob and Joseph,

and the promise in Zech. 10:6:

"I shall make the community of Jacob strong
and save the community of Joseph."[28]

The prophets viewed the little remnant of Judah as incomplete in representing the covenant people, and frequently transmitted the hope of replenishment from members of the other tribes of Israel, most of whom had been exiled in the eighth century B.C.[29]

The theme of total destruction is an application to Edom of the fate of *all the nations* in the introductory stanza of this final section. The term

25. Heb. *qash* means both "stubble" and "chaff."
26. Cf. further Nah. 1:6, 10; Mal. 4:1 (3:19); 1 Cor. 3:12f. Deissler finds in Obad. 18 an adaptation of Isa. 10:17, with Yahweh replaced by his people.
27. But Rudolph notes that it is difficult to believe that *Joseph* can stand for Judah since Judah, one of Jacob's sons, was Joseph's brother.
28. Cf. too Ezek. 37:16–19; Amos 5:6.
29. Cf. Mic. 5:3 and comment.

survivor reveals the motivation of such destruction; it is no accident that it has occurred in v. 14 to describe the Judean refugees of 587 B.C. whom the Edomites mercilessly handed over to the Babylonian forces. The inexorable principle of an eye for an eye, stated at the end of the preceding section of the poem (v. 15b), is to operate against Edom. That this is no mere spiteful desire of Judah but the very decree of Yahweh is attested by the final oracular formula. The God who vindicates the oppressed rules that Edom's war crimes could be expiated by no lesser punishment.[30]

A slight awkwardness arises at first sight from the fact that in the early part of Obadiah's poem it is a league of nations who are evidently to act as the agents of Yahweh's destruction, whereas here it is the people of God who wage this holy war. Both themes are at home in Israelite tradition, however. Yahweh sometimes uses his own people and sometimes foreign nations to wreak his judgments. The community that first received Obadiah's prophecy would probably not have been so aware of the apparent inconsistency as more logical Western commentators are. Doubtless, if pressed, the prophet would have regarded Israel as having the honor of applying in God's name the *coup de grâce* to a people and a country crippled earlier by foreign attacks.

D. THE LAND REGAINED (19, 20)

They will regain the Negeb [from Mount Esau] and the
Shephelah [from the Philistines].
They will regain the region of Ephraim [the region
of Samaria] and Gilead [Benjamin]. 3+3
20 *The exiles of the people of Israel [this army]*
will regain Canaanite territory as far as Zarephath. 3+3
The exiles of Jerusalem who are in Sepharad
will regain the Negeb towns. 4+3

These two verses are best taken as the fourth stanza of the third movement in Obadiah's poetic symphony, which thus matches the two preceding movements. In our present Hebrew text the passage is in tortuous prose, which contains difficulties so great that it cries out to be regarded as originally a piece of three lines of verse, which has not only been overlaid with explanatory material but has suffered corruption in the course of transmission.

The general tenor of the composition shines through clearly. It is a promise of the territorial expansion of God's people in all directions until they regain their ancient territory. The old promise of the land is reaffirmed as the implicit corollary of the restored covenant and God's renewed blessing. The role of this stanza within the last movement is to develop the

30. Cf. Amos 1:3–2:3.

theme mentioned in the second stanza as the subsequent, positive stage of God's purposes, following on from the first and negative stage elaborated in the first stanza. The third stanza has just taken up the first stanza's general theme of the nations' destruction in specific terms of Edom. Indeed, the last line of the second stanza (v. 21) narrowed the theme of conquest to Edom's territory, and the third strophe may be regarded as serving to amplify this positive theme. This final piece marks a broadening of the perspective closer to the note of *all nations* struck at the beginning of the section (vv. 15a, 16). It expands the virtual promise of Paradise regained, but in such a way as to make it clear that land occupied by the Edomites will be reclaimed. Those nations which have encroached on the territory of God's people will be forced back. The passage is a tremendous echo of the initial occupation of Canaan when with God's aid the nations were driven out and Israel took possession.[31] That glorious achievement would come alive again in Israel's experience. What looks to the modern reader, even in a less full form, like a dull catalog must have been music to the ears of a people crammed into a small area and overshadowed by powerful neighbors occupying land they had once called their own.

But if this passage is a recital of the various tracts of territory to be reclaimed on all sides, great care has been taken to put Edom in a prominent position. Reference to the Negeb begins and ends the stanza. This area to the south of Judah with its northern boundary in the area of Beersheba had been infiltrated by Edom, its eastern neighbor, after the deportation of the Judeans in 587.[32] In fact, Hebron to the north of the Negeb was still held by Edomites in Maccabean times, according to 1 Macc. 5:65, when the whole area was known as Idumea. This process had begun by the time of the poet and it is for this reason that he concludes as he began. Edom is to lose the territory it was filching from Judah. In thus giving prominence to Edom, the seer appears to view it as the key to the prophetic program in the manner outlined in Amos 9:12, whereby Israel would

> *"regain the territory of Edom's remnant and of all the nations called by my name."*[33]

The conquest of Edom thus played an important role as the initial factor which would trigger off a whole series of victories restoring Israel's ancient bounds.

The traditional form of the Hebrew text is a morass of difficulty, especially in v. 19. It is not clear whether *the Negeb* and *the Shephelah* should be regarded as the subject of the verb[34] or as the object.[35] Both possibilities are unsatisfactory. The former expedient runs into the grammat-

31. The verb *yrš*, "gain, regain," is frequently used in Deut., Josh., Judges.
32. Cf. Ezek. 36:5; 1 Esdras 4:50. Jer. 13:19 suggests that in 597 Nebuchadnezzar removed the Negeb from Judah's control; he may have entrusted it to the Edomites.
33. Cf. the importance of Edom in the divine judgment on the nations in Isa. 34:1–7; 63:1–6.
34. So G V "the men [i.e. Jews] in the Negeb will regain Mount Esau, . . . the men in the Shephelah . . ."; similarly RSV, JB.
35. I.e., "they will regain the Negeb, namely Mount Esau"; cf. Moffatt, NEB.

ical difficulty that, of the four clauses, the third one strangely fails to specify a subject.[36] In the latter interpretation mention of *Benjamin* is anomalous. In addition to the grammatical problems, strophical considerations place a further question mark against the passage in its present form. One expects it to fit into the poetic structure exhibited in the preceding material. The poetic jigsaw tantalizingly has a missing piece; the misshapen piece available already fits at one point, v. 20b, which has a 4+3 rhythm. The combination of these two factors strongly suggests that the text has been amplified by means of explanatory notes, and was not always composed of such difficult and heavy prose.[37]

Doubtless the poet still has in mind the combined elements of old Israel mentioned in the preceding stanza (v. 18). The thrust southward to regain control of the Negeb, and that westward into the lowlands in the southwest of Judah, would presumably be tasks falling to the lot of representatives of the tribe of Judah. Meanwhile members of the northern tribes would return, as the next line is to make clear, and not only take over the central area of Palestine, *Ephraim,* but also press eastward into Transjordan. In view of v. 20b it appears that Jerusalem was already occupied by returned exiles, and doubtless that is why no reference is made to this area. A final push into the far north remains to be mentioned in the next line to complete a campaign of reoccupation on all four sides.

The last pair of lines deal with a dual attack to north and south launched by two groups of returned exiles, survivors of the old Northern and Southern Kingdoms.[38] The Phoenicians who presumably had trespassed on

36. Rudolph overcomes this obstacle by the expedient of lengthening the second *wyršw* into *wyrwšlm,* "and Jerusalem."

37. So many scholars since Wellhausen have concluded. Heb. *'et-har 'ēśāw, Mount Esau,* was probably added as a historically correct gloss identifying the inhabitants of the Negeb as Edomites in terms of the appellation in vv. 8f., 21. Grammatically it stands as a second object of the verb (cf. Deut. 9:1). Similarly *'et-pᵉlishtîm, from the Philistines,* is a not incorrect amplification. The third case, *'ēṯ śᵉḏēh shōmᵉrôn, the region of Samaria,* is a gloss of a different kind, identifying Ephraim with the province of Samaria. The gloss was evidently eased into the text at some stage by adding the copulative. G reads "mountain" for region, yielding the familiar phrase "Mount Ephraim" for an unfamiliar combination; but this smacks of an easier reading, prompted by the earlier gloss *Mount Esau.* The significance of *Benjamin* is not clear: Duhm's suggestion that *bnymn* was earlier *bny 'mn,* "Ammonites," is plausible, in which case it was intended as a gloss of the same type as the first two (Sellin, Bewer, *et al.,* cf. *BHK, BHS*; cf. Isa. 11:14). But it may have originated in a comparative marginal note alluding to the fact that in Jer. 32:44; 33:13 Benjamin features in a list along with the Negeb and the Shephelah.

38. The significance of *this army* is unknown. Heb. *haḥēl* looks like "the fortress," but it is better taken as *army*; cf. *ḥêl* for *ḥayil* in 2 K. 18:17; Isa. 36:2. Since the parallelism suggests a reference to a place of exile, Cheyne, Bewer, Robinson, Brockington, *et al.* have viewed MT as a corruption of *baḥᵃlaḥ,* "in Halah," an area in Northern Mesopotamia to which the northern exiles were deported in 721 (2 K. 17:6). Sellin did more justice to the consonantal text by reading *ḥᵃlaḥ zeh,* "this is (a reference to) Halah," a gloss defining the place of exile; then the following *lameḏ* was doubtless added to make sense after the gloss had been interpolated. G S "this beginning" obviously reflects MT, relating *hḥl* to *hēḥēl,* "began,"

old Israelite territory in the north would be forced back *as far as Zarephath*, a town near the Mediterranean coast some 10 miles south of Sidon, which features in a story of Elijah in 1 K. 17:9f. Thus the ideal northern border of Josh. 19:28f. would be attained.

The northern expansion would be matched by one to the south, and here the prophet returns to the theme laid upon his heart, namely that of Edom. Judeans returning from exile to Jerusalem would penetrate southward and wrest *the Negeb towns* from Edomite interlopers. One might have expected a reference to Babylon as the domicile of Jewish exiles, but instead a mysterious *Sepharad* is named. The various identifications assigned to the place underscore the uncertainty of present knowledge. Most impressive is the case that can be made for Sardis, as the Greeks called it, capital of Lydia in the west of Asia Minor.[39] A Lydian-Aramaic bilingual inscription refers to the capital as *sprd* in Aramaic. It is dated in the tenth year of King Artaxerxes and so, if Artaxerxes I is meant, 455 B.C.[40] Since Aramaic is rare in the inscriptions of Asia Minor, it may indicate a sizable colony of Arameans or Jews. Moreover, an Aramaic inscription discovered at Daskyleion on the coast to the north of Sardis, and variously assigned by scholars to a date c.450 or c.400 B.C., gives evidence of the presence of a rich Jewish family there.[41] The intention in mentioning *Sepharad*[42] is to give an assurance that, far away though the exiles may be from their native Jerusalem, they are not too distant for their God to restore them to their homeland.

The territorial and imperialistic emphasis of the passage is embarrass-

---

and seeing a reference to the deportation of 721 B.C. Later in the line a verb is required for the incomprehensible *'ᵃsher*, "which," of MT. G "land" may presuppose *'erets*, but it looks like an attempt to get sense out of an already corrupt text. Many read *yīrᵉshû*, "will dispossess," in accord with v. 20b; and this word could have become distorted after *yiśra'el* and in view of *'ᵃsher* in the next line.

39. W. Kornfeld, *Mélanges bibliques . . . André Robert* (1957), pp. 180–86.

40. C. C. Torrey, *AJSL* 34(1917/18), p. 192; Thompson, Myers. Kornfeld prefers Artaxerxes II or III: 395 or 349 B.C.

41. Cf. E. Lipiński, "Obadiah 20," *VT* 23 (1973), pp. 368–370.

42. The two other main suggestions for the location of Sepharad should be mentioned. (1) J. Gray, *ZAW* 65 (1953), pp. 53–59, following N. Slouschz, favors an equation with the Hesperides, islands off Libya near Benghazi, and sees a parallelism between a return of Israelite exiles from Mesopotamia by way of the north to occupy the north of Canaan, and, from North Africa by way of the south, the return of Judean exiles to occupy the Negeb, an argument Watts finds convincing. (2) An inscription of Sargon II mentions a place Shuparda in southwest Media, which some, e.g., G. A. Smith, have considered to be the import of Sepharad. People of the Northern Kingdom were exiled to Media (2 K. 17:6) and the assumption is that Judeans were too. But, as Gray observes, there is a phonetic discrepancy between the two names. S T render "Spain," which is reminiscent of the medieval Jewish designation that led to Spanish Jews being called Sephardim (cf. D. Neiman, "Sefarad: The Name of Spain," *JNES* 22 [1963], pp. 128–132, who explains the name in terms of Etruscan colonization). V "Bosphorus" may be simply a confusion of the Heb. prefixed preposition *b-sprd* (von Orelli), but it is possible that Jerome followed an exegetical tradition passed on by his Jewish mentor (Rudolph).

ing to the Christian reader, but it is of a piece with general OT theology whereby the blessing of God was intimately bound up with material possession of the land of promise. Accordingly the land had a sacramental significance: spiritual restoration to divine favor is inextricably linked with material restoration to Palestine.

Many an observer of modern history has been so impressed by the establishment of the state of Israel as to hail it as the long-awaited fulfilment of prophecy of the present type. Unfortunately this relation of ancient hope to modern happenings labors under the theological difficulty that, in its contemporary form, Israel is a secular state inspired by nationalism rather than by religion. Diverse eschatological expectations among Christians are influenced by presuppositions concerning the relation between the old covenant and the new. Certainly the NT transmutes the territorial into the celestial, the material into the supernatural. It holds forth the hope of a heavenly country, Jerusalem, and a temple which Christ has entered and to which the Christian already has some access. "Here we have no permanent city, but we look for the one that is to come," wrote a Jewish Christian in Heb. 13:14. Since it is Christians, whether of Gentile or Jewish stock, who are henceforth the heirs of Abraham and the promises made to him, according to Paul's teaching in Galatians and Romans, it is difficult to see how any Christian can contemplate turning the theological clock back to a limited, pre-Christian point of expectation.

The Christian is handed the book of Obadiah as part of the OT heritage he has received with Christ. He will interpret the hope of territorial expansion in terms of his inspired teachers of the NT, finding in it encouragement to possess the land whose horizons he can now understand to be far wider and higher than Obadiah was privileged to grasp. But his interpretation will be no more spiritual than the literal one of Obadiah, for whom matter was ideally the incarnation of spirit.

The Book
of
JONAH

INTRODUCTION

1. LITERARY GENRE

It is obvious to the most casual reader of the Minor Prophets that the book of Jonah is quite different from the rest. The others are collections of oracles; in Jonah there occurs only one prophetic oracle, consisting of five words in the original. It is a different kind of literature from the others. There are many different literary types in the OT, including laments, love songs, parables, apocalypses, and histories. Into what category does Jonah fall? This is not a purely academic question, but basic to one's understanding of the book. The modern reader can read it aright only if he understands it as it was originally intended.[1]

The first step toward categorizing it is to define it as a prophetic narrative. The commentary will note how, for instance, 1:1–3a and 3:1–3a follow the stereotyped norms of such narrative material as it appears elsewhere in the OT, for example in the Elijah stories. Moreover it begins as if it were an extract from a longer narrative: "*And* the word of Yahweh came. . . ."[2] But this is a most unusual prophetic narrative. Generally the prophetic stories in the OT seek to glorify the man of God in the sense that he is revealed as a noble mediator of God's own power and glory. But Jonah is no hero: he is deliberately portrayed in a very poor light.[3] The concern of a number of OT prophetic narratives is to trace the process whereby a divine oracle was fulfilled.[4] This book, on the contrary, breaks the pattern surprisingly by showing how and why a divine oracle, concerning the destruction of Nineveh, was not fulfilled.

1. Cf. Bird: "The question is not whether what is related could possibly have taken place, but rather in what genre of literature the author is writing."
2. Cf. 1 Sam. 15:10; 1 K. 17:2, 8.
3. G. von Rad defined the difference thus: "God is here glorified not through his ambassador, but in spite of his ambassador's complete refusal" (*OT Theology*, vol. 2 [E.T 1965], p. 291).
4. Cf. B. O. Long, *VT* 23 (1973), pp. 337–348, analyzing what he calls an oracle-actualization narrative, 2 K. 3.

This element of surprise is a key factor throughout the book. A prophet's journeying to Nineveh to deliver his message is an extraordinary phenomenon. Prophetic oracles against the nations are commonplace, but they were normally spoken on the prophet's native soil for the benefit of his fellow nationals. The political mission of Elijah and Elisha to Damascus (1 K. 9:15; 2 K. 8:7–13) is the nearest parallel, but Jonah's journey is of a different nature.

Another surprise, a shocking one, is Jonah's refusal to shoulder his prophetic burden. Moses, Elijah, and Jeremiah indeed shrank from their assignments, but Jonah's blunt refusal goes far beyond their hesitation. In fact this little book is a series of surprises; it is crammed with an accumulation of hair-raising and eye-popping phenomena, one after the other. The violent seastorm, the submarine-like fish in which Jonah survives as he composes a song, the mass conversion of Nineveh, the magic plant—these are not commonplace features of OT prophetic narratives. While one or two exciting events would raise no question, the bombardment of the reader with surprise after surprise in a provocative manner suggests that the author's intention is other than simply to describe historical facts. Bold would be the man who ventured to say that this series of happenings was impossible, for who can limit the omnipotence of God and say categorically that any could not happen? Not impossible but improbable is how they strike the ordinary reader. What if the author meant to arrest our attention and focus it on his message by means of a string of improbabilities?[5]

A further interesting feature of the book is its "old world" air. The overturning of Nineveh (3:4) sounds like a recapitulation of Sodom and Gomorrah (Gen. 19:25, 29). The theme of collective punishment is reminiscent of the destruction of those cities, and of the Flood.[6] The moral charge of "violence" is one that features in Gen. 6:11, 13. Jonah's role is that of the divine messengers sent to announce the destruction of Sodom (Gen. 19:1, 15). This rather than any previous prophetic experience is the precedent for Jonah's mission. This modelling of the story upon the old Genesis narratives leads one to question the nature of its links with the

5. It is worth noting that the miracles do not fall into the landmark pattern, whereby biblical miracles tend to cluster around crucial points of history, the Exodus, the ministry of prophets engaged in repelling Baalism or secular involvement in power politics, and the inauguration of Christianity (cf. L. Sabourin, "OT Miracles," *Biblical Theology Bulletin* 1 [1971], pp. 227–261). It was unfortunate that A. J. Wilson, "The Sign of the Prophet Jonah and its Modern Confirmations," *PTR* 25(1927), pp. 630–642, espoused the dramatic story of James Bartley's fall overboard from the whaling ship *Star of the East* in 1891 and his survival after a day and a night inside the sperm whale which swallowed him. The captain's widow affirmed that no sailor fell overboard during the period of his captaincy of the vessel (*ET* 17 [1905/6], p. 521; 18 [1906/7], p. 239). G. C. Aalders, *The Problem of the Book of Jonah* (1948), pp. 1f., takes over the story from Wilson.

6. Cohn, *JLBE*, pp. 75, 96f. Y. Kaufmann, *The Religion of Israel from Its Beginnings to the Babylonian Exile* (1961), p. 283, compares the reaction of the sailors and Ninevites with the pagan "fear of God" found in the early narratives (Gen. 20:11; 39:9; 42:18).

prophetic narratives of 1, 2 Kings and elsewhere. Did the author intend to set forth an imitation of a prophetic narrative, presenting it *as if* it were an old story culled from a prophetic collection? If so, it would explain both the echoing of prophetic motifs and the way the narrative consistently pushes beyond anything that has gone before. It is significant that the elements of surprise and hyperbole are characteristic of the parable.

> *The realistic* [*is combined*] *with the extraordinary and the improbable. The behavior of the prodigal's father and of the vineyard owner is not what we would expect under the circumstances. The debt which the unforgiving servant owed was fantastic, and the commending of the dishonest steward surprises us. . . . Such features burst the limits of the probable but are kept locked into the narrative frame and hence are rendered possible and convincing.*[7]

Another pervasive element highlighting the degree of literary creativity is the apparent echoing of experiences or statements of particular prophets in a different key from the original. In 4:4, 8 Jonah is portrayed as a parody of Elijah (1 K. 19:4); he apes Elijah's words but by so doing shows himself to be far inferior to his model[8]—and so the author intended. Jon. 3:9; 4:2 look suspiciously like quotations from the probably postexilic Joel 2:13, 14, and so surely they are intended. The author strikingly reapplies the accepted passage to a non-Israelite setting and extends God's characteristic love for Israel to cover pagans.[9] Jon. 3:9, 10 is dependent on Jer. 18:7, 8, 11 in theme and terminology—designedly so, for the author is implicitly appealing to Jer. 18 as an accepted prophetic principle and claiming it as the warrant for an incident the audience would otherwise have found much harder to swallow than the fish found Jonah to be. In these and other cases which the commentary will disclose, the narrator is copying not because of his deficiency in narrative skill, still less as an act of plagiarism, but in order to create a contrast with the past or to use accepted truth as a religio-psychological stepping stone to an unwelcome revelation.

This trait, like those mentioned earlier, suggests strongly that the author is less concerned with a bare recital of historical facts than with his Jewish audience and their reception of an important truth, which would revolutionize both their understanding of the nature of God and their attitude toward pagans.

If it is correct to describe the literary genre of the book of Jonah by the loose designation of parable, as the majority of commentators conclude,

7. D. O. Via, Jr., *The Parables: Their Literary and Existential Dimension* (1967), pp. 105f. R. W. Funk has stressed the elements of exaggeration and shock in the parables of Jesus (*Language, Hermeneutic and the Word of God* [1966], ch. 5).
8. "He has Elijah's despondency without Elijah's excuse" (S. R. Driver, *An Introduction to the Literature of the OT* [[7]1898, repr. 1957], p. 325).
9. Van Hoonacker, Delcor, and Cohn, *JLBE*, p. 99, consider that Joel is later and borrows from Jonah, but the extension of meaning in Jonah's case is a secondary feature which fits well into the book's general surprise pattern.

then it is possible to add that its literary tone is that of parody or satire.[10] Jonah is made to appear a ridiculous figure whose part none would be prepared to defend. With his narrow pretensions and uncharitable grudges he pits himself against the very will of God, only to be cut down to size and exposed as self-centered and self-righteous. Behind him must stand a group of people whose mouthpiece Jonah is or whom Jonah caricatures, as surely as the Pharisees stand behind the Elder Brother of Lk. 15:11–32. The function of the final question of the book is surely to challenge the attitude of this group among the author's contemporaries. It is true that a parable is generally less complex than the book obviously is,[11] but parables do vary in their degree of complexity, just as they vary in length from a simple comparison to a short story. Now that Jülicher's dictum that a parable has but a single point is no longer being regarded as axiomatic for the study of parables,[12] the complexity of this story is no barrier to its classification as a parable. The two-part nature of the story is paralleled in the parable of the Unforgiving Servant, who is forgiven a huge sum only to deny forgiveness to a colleague over a trifling debt (Matt. 18:23–35). Jonah too is a sinner saved by divine grace, who will not allow that pagan sinners may be recipients of the compassion to which he owes his own life. If it is claimed that elsewhere in the OT parables are accompanied by an explicit indication of their meaning,[13] comparison with the parables of Jesus demonstrates that this is no *sine qua non* of the parabolic technique, since sometimes his parables are left unapplied (e.g., Luke 13:6–9). There are extensive parallels between the parable of the Prodigal Son and our story. Nineveh's sin is confronted by the great love of God; Nineveh's repentance is met by the forgiveness of God, while misunderstanding of God's forgiveness is challenged by a reasoned reprimand. All these facets find easy counterparts in the parable that Jesus told against the scribes and Pharisees.[14]

For a long time the book of Jonah was interpreted in a strongly historical vein. Yet although the Church Fathers, who mostly used Jonah symbolically, admitted its historicity, there were those who doubted it, including in the fourth century Gregory of Nazianzus and in the eleventh, Theophylact. Luther viewed the story as nonhistorical. Today there are both Roman Catholic and Protestant circles that maintain the historicity of the

10. Cf. esp. M. Burrows in *Translating and Understanding the OT* (1970), pp. 95–97.
11. Aalders, *op. cit.*, p. 13.
12. Cf. E. J. Tinsley's discussion and documentation in "Parable, Allegory and Mysticism," *Vindications. Essays on the Historical Basis of Christianity*, ed. A. Hanson (1966), pp. 153–192; J. Drury, "The Sower, the Vineyard and the Place of Allegory in the Interpretation of Mark's Parables," *JTS* 24 (1973), pp. 367–379. It may be noted that even Jotham's short fable impinges upon the real situation at several points. It compares kingship unfavorably with more worthwhile religious and social service, denounces the worthless and baneful character of Abimelech, forecasts the disastrous result of such kingship, and questions the good faith of his supporters.
13. Aalders, *loc. cit.*
14. J. Alonso Díaz, *Biblica* 40 (1959), pp. 632–640.

book with a fervor that assumes that its inspiration and authority depend upon it: "If the book of Jonah is history, it is part of the evidence for the most important truth imaginable, namely that the Almighty God seeks to bring men to repentance and will pardon those who truly repent. But if the book is not historical, then it is only the opinion of some singularly broadminded Jew that God ought to pardon even Gentiles if they truly repent."[15] But is it inconceivable that "some singularly broadminded Jew" was inspired to teach this much-needed lesson? Such a viewpoint is in danger of restricting the Spirit of God and belittling the value of the parable as a genuine scriptural medium.

Certainly the story is set out in a narrative form, but "all parables resemble a record of historical events. . . . It is impossible to argue from the form of the book of Jonah that it must have been meant as a record of historical events."[16] Another factor to be taken into account is the obviously intended identification of the hero or anti-hero with the prophet of 2 K. 14:25. Here at least is a historical basis, which suggests that the incidents related in our book are historical. There may well be a historical nucleus behind the story,[17] but this is not relevant to its understanding in its present form. Behind the parable of the Good Samaritan (Luke 10:25–37) lies 2 Chr. 28:15. Behind the parable of the pounds (Luke 19:11–27) lies the visit of Archelaus to Rome to get his succession to Herod authorized. Behind the parable of Dives and Lazarus may well lie the rabbinic tale of how Abraham's steward Eliezer, of which Lazarus is the Greek form, was sent to Sodom to test the hospitality of its citizens.[18] But no one would fail to differentiate these parables from a straightforward recital of events. In each case an older theme has been used as raw material for the creation of something new and contemporary.

There is shrewd psychological insight in the choice of Jonah as the key figure. Nothing was known about him apart from the information in 2 K. 14:25, and no writings derived from him have been received into the Judean collection of holy books. 2 K. 14:25 sets him in the reign of the eighth-century B.C. king Jeroboam II as a nationalistic prophet who forecast the extension of the frontiers of the Northern Kingdom. He is thus ideal as the butt for an attack on religious nationalism. The author's Judean hearers would accept the fact of a prophetic revelation through Jonah, but Jonah's

15. F. A. Molony, *Journal of the Transactions of the Victoria Institute* 69 (1937), pp. 246f.
16. Aalders, *op. cit.*, p. 12.
17. Cf. S. Talmon, *VT* 13 (1963), p. 453: "A precarious balance between underlying traditional motifs and a possible historical actuality is maintained." The mythical parallels that have been drawn with the book are unconvincing. Trible, *SBJ*, pp. 141f., is skeptical: "Most myths adduced are not genuine parallels to *Jonah*. The fish in *Jonah* is not an enemy: it is not the chaos-dragon. . . . Thus to say that the author of *Jonah* is deliberately borrowing from any myth or group of myths is to exceed the evidence. He is not using myth, but rather he is utilizing a theme common in both the mythical and non-mythical literature of the world."
18. Cf. J. D. M. Derrett, *Law in the NT* (1970), pp. 86–92.

nationalistic sentiments would cause a natural resentment in minds that cherished a longstanding antipathy against the people of the north. Thus right from the start there is created a tension, which the book goes on to exploit, between the word of God to which the listeners will pay respectful heed, and the unpopular figure of a prophet whom they will be more prone to condemn than to applaud. Jonah is damned from the start in the prejudiced eyes of a Judean audience—and so some are trapped into damning themselves as latter-day Jonahs.

Yet does not the statement of Jesus concerning Jonah in Matt. 12:39–41 constitute a testimony to the historicity of our book? Von Orelli, who himself interpreted the story thus, admitted: "It is not indeed proved with conclusive necessity that, if the resurrection of Jesus was a physical fact, Jonah's abode in the fish's belly must also be just as historical." In this regard it is important to note a feature which will be shown in the later section on the sign of Jonah, that it is not strict exegesis that is reflected in Jesus' use of the narrative of Jonah and the fish, but the popular Jewish understanding, which the Lord took up and employed as a vehicle for truth concerning himself. If this is so, it is quite possible to maintain that his reference merely reflects the contemporary view without necessarily endorsing it for the student of the OT. Moreover, allowance must be made for a figurative element in the teaching of Jesus, an element Western literalists have notoriously found difficulty in grasping. If a modern preacher would not be at fault if he challenged his congregation with a reference to Lady Macbeth or Oliver Twist, could not Jesus have alluded in much the same manner to a well-known story to reinforce his own distinctive message?

Some unsuccessful attempts have been made to specify the nature of the parable of Jonah. Several scholars have defined it in terms of a Jewish category, midrash. Midrash was a typically rabbinic method of instruction which used a scriptural text as a peg upon which to hang some moral or psychological observation in what strikes us as a fanciful manner. It was "the rabbi's tool for making sermons and for enhancing moral lessons and increasing faith."[19] Karl Budde first considered Jonah a midrash on 2 K. 14:25.[20] He has been followed by Wellhausen, Loretz, Delcor, Knight, and Trible. However, it is doubtful whether the midrashic method is as old as Jonah appears to be. The Chronicler mentions a midrash of kings (2 Chr. 24:27), but it appears to be of a different nature from what is known in the rabbinic literature. Moreover, on what text is Jonah a midrash? On 2 K. 14:25 (Budde), or on Jer. 18:8 (Brockington), or on parts of Jeremiah and the second half of Isaiah (Knight), or on Ex. 34:6 (Trible)? It is impossible to pinpoint a single text to which the book was linked.

The story has also been regarded as an allegory. Parables vary in the amount of allegorical material they contain.[21] It is extremely difficult to

19. *Ibid.*, p. xxxvii.
20. *ZAW* 11 (1891), pp. 37–51.
21. See the documentation of n. 12.

categorize Jonah as a thoroughgoing allegory, a literary code in which every detail stands for something else in reality. Such scholars as Cheyne, G. A. Smith, Knight, and Smart have lent their names to this interpretation.[22] "Jonah" means "dove" in Hebrew, a symbol for Israel. He is son of truth, faithfulness (Heb. *'ᵉmeṯ*), satirically an orthodox son of the faith. Jonah's stay in the fish, in light of Jer. 51:34, 44, is the period of punishment in exile when Babylon swallowed Israel. Even the plant, according to Smith, stands for Zerubbabel. This approach has generally been abandoned, if only because some parts of the story do not fit into any allegorical framework. In any event, it is doubtful whether "dove" is a symbolic name for Israel in the OT.[23] If Amittai had been intended as allegorical, the author missed a golden opportunity to reveal that fact.[24] The fish is not an instrument of punishment but a vehicle of deliverance from drowning.[25] If the fish stands for anything, it represents the *Heilsgeschichte* of Israel, the acts of grace and power demonstrated by Yahweh on Israel's behalf in her past history.

It is best to confine the definition of the literary form of the book to that of a parable with certain allegorical features. Rabbinic parables sought not only to interpret OT texts but to explore God's dealings with man,[26] and in this second regard the little book of Jonah stands out as an illustrious ancestor.

2. UNITY OF COMPOSITION

The question as to whether the book is a literary unit intact from the author's pen, or a compilation of sources of different origins and periods, centers nowadays on the prayer of Jonah in ch. 2. There was a time, however, when wider areas of the book were called in question. W. Böhme, taking his cue from Pentateuchal analysis, discovered from the use of different divine names in the book the products of no fewer than four hands: a Yahwistic narrator of the core of chs. 1–4, an Elohistic author of a parallel narrative in chs. 3 and 4, a redactor who united both sources, and an amplifier in chs. 1 and 4 who also inserted the psalm in ch. 2.[27] H. Schmidt viewed 1:1–10 as a separate narrative from the rest of the book and detected substantial insertions made for religious reasons in 1:13f.; 2:2–9(3–10); 3:6–9.[28] It was

22. Cf. too P. R. Ackroyd, *Exile and Restoration* (1968), pp. 244f. The first English scholar to develop this interpretation at length was C. H. H. Wright, "The Book of Jonah Considered From an Allegorical Point of View," *Biblical Essays* (1886), pp. 34–98.
23. Cf. Aalders, *op. cit.*, pp. 24f. In Jer. 48:28 it is used of Moab; in Nah. 2:7 of Ninevite women.
24. Heb. *we'ᵉmeṯ,* the standard ending to the formula used in Jon. 4:2, is replaced by another phrase here and in Joel 2:13.
25. Cf. Wade; Feuillet, *RB* 54 (1947), p. 182; Trible, *SBJ*, p. 157.
26. Cf. R. A. Stewart, "The Parable Form in the OT and the Rabbinic Literature," *EQ* 36 (1964), pp. 133–147, esp. pp. 143f.
27. *ZAW* 7 (1887), pp. 224–284.
28. *ZAW* 25 (1905), pp. 285–310.

Gunkel who wrote the obituary for these and similar ventures: "The attempt to discern different sources in Jonah has failed."[29]

As for the psalm of 2:2–9(3–10), two objections to it as an original feature of the book are based on structure. First, without the psalm, the context can be viewed as having a chiastic structure with four parts. Yahweh is the subject in the outer clauses, Jonah in the inner: 1:17a and 2:10, 1:17b and 2:1 correspond. This artistic structure is broken by the psalm.[30] Secondly, it has been claimed that the overall symmetry of the book is badly damaged by the insertion of the psalm: the counterpart of Jonah's prayer in 4:2 is not 2:2–9 but the sailors' prayer in 1:14.[31] The later section on structure will be the best place to discuss these objections.

The general objection to the prayer of ch. 2 is that its content ill fits the context. Recourse to poetry is unexpected in an otherwise consistently prose narrative. Verse 1 states that Jonah prayed, but what follows is not a prayer in the normal sense of a plea for help, but a song of thanksgiving for deliverance already granted. Yet Jonah in his dire state could hardly have uttered such praise until after v. 10, where it would fit much better. Some have regarded the psalm as misplaced. Calvin's comment is noteworthy: "Jonah relates now, after having come forth from the bowels of the fish, what had happened to him and he gives thanks to the Lord."[32] Ibn Ezra interpreted the past verbs of deliverance in the song as prophetic perfects so that Jonah looks forward to deliverance, while Cohn and apparently Ellul interpret in the same way. But this does violence to the basic form of the unit as essentially a psalm of thanksgiving for help already received.

Form-critically, 2:2–9 is a composition such as a grateful worshiper might use in the temple, and the "drowning" vocabulary is a standard metaphor for deliverance from any plight. Yet Jonah's location is quite different, namely inside a fish, and the figurative expressions are reinterpreted with a crude literalism. The parallels with other psalms in respect of motifs and vocabulary suggest that this one has been taken from a cultic collection by a reader who wished to supply the missing prayer (Bewer).[33]

The language of the psalm departs awkwardly from that used in the preceding narrative. The adjective "great," which occurs fourteen times in the book, nowhere appears in it,[34] nor does the variously used term *rā'â* (evil, plight, etc.). A different term is used in v. 3(4) for "throw" from that in 1:12, 15.[35] "Sea," used so often in the first chapter, here becomes a plural. "From the face" of Yahweh (1:3, 10) becomes "from before the

29. *Die Religion in Geschichte und Gegenwart,* vol. 3 (²1929), p. 369. See Bewer's detailed criticism.

30. N. Lohfink, *BZ* 5 (1962), p. 196, n. 37, p. 200.

31. Trible, *SBJ,* pp. 76, 185–202.

32. Josephus (*Ant.* ix.10.2) placed a prayer for pardon after v. 10.

33. The argument that an interpolator would have done a better job by inserting it in a more fitting place (Feuillet, *loc. cit.,* p. 169) or by relating its terminology more closely to that of its context (Aalders, *op. cit.,* p. 21) is not convincing.

34. Wolff, *SJ,* p. 61, n. 82.

35. Heb. *hēṭîl-hišlîḵ.*

eyes'' (2:4[5]).[36] ''Perish'' (1:6, 14) could easily have been used in the psalm, but it is not. These are indications that the psalm is a foreign body, for had it been an integral part of the book, surely the author would have made the terminology match. Of course it was not Yahweh who threw Jonah into the sea (2:3[4]), but the sailors at Jonah's request, according to the narrative (1:15).[37]

Nor do the expressions of gratitude in the psalm fit the psychological character of the prophet as the surrounding narrative presents it. He is a surly, unappreciative fellow who resents being drafted into Yahweh's service and objects in every conceivable way. ''He is not a creature of gratitude and thanksgiving.''[38] The emphasis on drowning in the psalm has no counterpart in the preceding story. The impression has been given that the fish swallowed Jonah as soon as he was thrown overboard. No time is allowed for the experience so elaborately depicted in the psalm.[39]

Such is the apparently damning case that can be brought against Jonah's thanksgiving. In fact most scholars dismiss Jon. 2:2–9 as a later interpolation. G. M. Landes has boldly endeavored to meet the detailed arguments of Trible and others and to defend the psalm as an integral part of the book. The ensuring discussion is indebted to his labors,[40] as the frequent acknowledgments will indicate, although not all his arguments have been accepted.

The position taken in the commentary is that the narrator himself selected the psalm from an existing collection and inserted it to give voice to Jonah's sentiments. It is of a definite type known to us from numerous examples in the canonical Psalms. It is a thanksgiving of an individual, the glad counterpart to an individual lament.[41] Many commentators regard the psalm disparagingly as a hotchpotch of fragments of other psalms, but Bewer had a truer insight: ''The phrases it has in common with other psalms were the common property of the religious language of the author's day.''[42] The motifs and metaphors of this psalm are stereotyped vehicles of devotion used by spiritual folk in many a situation of distress.[43] The advantage of this

36. Heb. *millip̱ᵉnê—minneg̱eḏ ʿêneyḵā*.
37. Trible, *SBJ*, p. 78.
38. *SBJ*, p. 80; cf. Wolff, *SJ*, p. 61.
39. *SBJ*, p. 78.
40. *Interpretation* 21 (1967), pp. 3–31.
41. Other examples are Ps. 18; 30; 34; 40:1–10(11); 66:13–20; 116; 118:5–21; 138. Cf. C. Westermann, *The Praise of God in the Psalms* (E.T. 1965), pp. 102–117. In his terminology it is a declarative psalm of praise of the individual.
42. Cited with approval by Johnson, *Studies in OT Prophecy* (1950), p. 83, n. 8; cf. Kaufmann, *op. cit.*, p. 310. A. Weiser, *The Psalms* (E.T. 1962), constantly makes this point concerning the affinity between psalms, e.g., *ad* Ps. 86: ''We are here dealing with a liturgical style which is deliberately used to incorporate the personal concern in the larger context of the cult community and of the speech-forms and thought-forms proper to it'' (p. 576).
43. ''The psalmist does not intend to relate what happened to him but to testify what God has done for him'' (Westermann, *op. cit.*, p. 109). That this statement is not true of Jon. 2 reveals a major difference its new setting has brought about.

generalization was that such a psalm, once composed, might be drawn upon by any sufferer, whatever his precise affliction. The theme of the descent to the underworld is a constant feature of Hebrew psalmody to express the psalmist's brush with death encountered in one form or another. "To be in sickness of body or weakness of circumstance is to experience the disintegrating power of death and to be brought by Yahweh to the gates of Sheol."[44]

Yahweh, you have brought me up from Sheol,
restored me to life from among those gone down to the Pit.
(Ps. 30:3[4])

So one song of thanksgiving expressed the relief of recovering from distressing circumstances. One of a number of standard poetic metaphors used of the psalmists' various misadventures was drowning:

The currents of perdition overwhelmed me. . . .
He drew me out of deep water. (Ps. 18:4, 16[5, 17])[45]

Generally the psalm would be recited at the sanctuary before the offering of a sacrifice of thanksgiving.[46] This present psalm fits perfectly into the pattern of the thanksgiving songs extant in the Psalter. The author evidently selected it from the temple repertoire of cultic praise, as an apt vehicle for his theme. He exercises in an unusual way every believer's right of reuse, whatever his particular circumstances. But in the setting into which he introduces it the metaphor of drowning becomes literal, and the ex-victim celebrates his deliverance not in the temple but in a fish. The psalm was chosen because of its appropriateness to Jonah's situation. It was used as it stood; no matter that the vocabulary varies from that of ch. 1. That the author did not take liberties with the psalm shows his respect for the original composition and for conventional psalm language. Does a modern preacher, citing a hymn in a sermon, regularly change words here and there to conform more exactly to the precise point he is making? The psalm is obviously not made to measure, but as a secondhand article it is a remarkably good fit.[47] With the psalm the author took over the tradition of voicing thanksgiving in poetry.

A straightforward reading of ch. 2 indicates that the psalm was meant as praise for deliverance not from the fish but from drowning.[48] A number of scholars have perceived that the fish was not a means of punishing Jonah but a means of deliverance. "It is a beneficent device to return Jonah to the land where he had previously abandoned his commission."[49] It is in fact more than this: the sailors in 1:13 could have done this just as well, but were

44. Johnson, *loc. cit.*, p. 100.
45. Cf. Ps. 42:7(8); 69:2, 13–15(3, 14–16); 124:4, 5; 144:7; Lam. 3:54.
46. Cf. Ps. 116:19; 118:20; 138:1, 2.
47. Note *qr'*, "call," 1:6, 14; 2:2(3); *nep̱esh,* "life," 1:14; 2:5, 7(6, 8); "Yahweh his/my God," 2:1, 6(2, 7); and the motifs of sacrificing and vowing in 1:16; 2:9(10). Links with ch. 4 will be mentioned in the section on structure.
48. See n. 25 above and also E. J. Young, *Introduction to the OT* (1949), p. 281.
49. Landes, KBJ, p. 12; cf., e.g., van Hoonacker; Wade; Feuillet, *RB* 54 (1947), p. 344; Delcor; Trible, *SBJ,* p. 157.

deliberately foiled. Jonah deserved to die, and the fish is Yahweh's last-minute device to save him from merited death by drowning. The charge of irrelevance to its context is the creation of those who level it. It reflects a failure to read the account as it stands. The sea is the enemy, the bearer of death; the fish is Jonah's ally by divine provision.

The verb "pray" is used in 2:1(2) in accordance with the function of the passage as a structural counterpart to 4:2 where this verb appears. Compare the use of the verb of an utterance other than lament and supplication in 1 Sam. 2:1.[50] Landes observes that the parallelism with 4:2, "and he prayed to Yahweh and said," suggests that the content of the prayer should follow, just as it does there. In reply to the objection concerning the apparently superfluous drowning experience, Landes has referred to the narrator's well-attested device of deliberately omitting certain events from their proper chronological sequence in order to introduce them later for greater impact (cf. 1:10; 4:2). The previous prayer for divine assistance mentioned in the song of praise at vv. 2, 4, 7, 9 logically belongs immediately after he was thrown overboard.[51]

Nor is the charge of psychological inconsistency in the portrayal of Jonah justified. Landes has pointed out that the characterization in the prose parts of the book is equally inconsistent, since in 4:6 he rejoices in response to God's act of deliverance (*l^ehatstsîl,* "to deliver"). "When God acts beneficently on his behalf, his mood can and does change."[52] The psalm's ascription to Yahweh of responsibility for throwing Jonah into the sea is hardly a contradiction of 1:15. Yahweh is recognized as having been in providential control of the human situation, and indeed the sailors' survival is proof that they were agents of the divine will in light of the prayer of 1:14.[53]

The fish episode stands for divine grace; the end of the psalm, "Salvation belongs to Yahweh," is an apt commentary on the significance of the adjacent narrative. This commentary, which the whole psalm eloquently amplifies, is basic to the meaning of the book. The psalm plays its part in demonstrating an overall theme, depicting the inconsistency of one graciously brought back from the brink of deserved destruction churlishly resenting the divine right to rescue other sinners from perishing.

3. DATE AND PURPOSE

The date of the book of Jonah is by no means easy to determine. The period of the prophet of 2 K. 14:25, c.780 B.C., is not necessarily the time when the book was produced. Although it has often been assumed that Jonah was the

50. Landes, KBJ, p. 17, n. 51, pp. 30f.
51. *Ibid.*, pp. 13–15.
52. *Ibid.*, pp. 18f.
53. *Ibid.*, p. 24.

author, the narrative is in fact anonymous and has no direct reference to its author. There are some clues that point to a later date. The reference to Nineveh in 3:3 seems to indicate that the city was only a distant memory in the author's time.[54] Nineveh fell in 612 B.C. B. Eerdmans has argued that to make sense of the story Nineveh must still have been in existence when it appeared, because a fallen Nineveh contradicts its being spared in the story.[55] But his conclusion is invalid, for it can easily be imagined that a later generation slipped back into bad ways and incurred a fresh demonstration of divine wrath. There is no suggestion in ch. 3 that Nineveh was to be immune from judgment for all time. The way in which the city is spoken of appears to reflect the period when Nineveh was capital of Assyria, a role it played in the last century of its existence. Its colossal size in 3:3 reflects the exaggerated tradition echoed by the fourth-century Ctesias rather than literal fact. The reference to the "king of Nineveh" in 3:6 instead of to the standard "king of Assyria" betrays a remoteness from historical actuality. The Assyrian annals never use this title. It is quite unlike such titles as "king of Damascus," since Nineveh was not a city-state. These phenomena are all quite consistent with a later author who had no intention of teaching a history lesson but employed contemporary tradition as basic material for a didactic parable.

The echo of Persian customs in the book suggests that the author wrote in the Persian period, between the mid-sixth century B.C. and the mid-fourth. The participation of domestic animals in mourning ceremonies (3:8) is mentioned by Herodotus as a Persian practice. The linking of king and nobles in the decree of 3:7 is a characteristic Persian trait rather than Assyrian.[56]

The apparent use of Jer. 18 and Joel 2 in the last two chapters similarly labels the book as postexilic, especially if the book of Joel is rightly located in the postexilic period.

A further argument for a comparatively late date is of a linguistic nature. The assessment of the language of the book calls for great care. Scholars are now much more guarded and hesitant in their appraisal of Aramaisms than many of their predecessors were. "Study of the relations of Aramaic to the Canaanite group of tongues in the light of the increased comparative material has shown that many of the alleged Aramaisms of the Hebrew Bible, on which occasionally far-reaching critical conclusions have been based, are in fact pure Canaanitisms or common North-west Semitic."[57] A. Hurvitz has laid down careful guidelines for assessing linguistic peculiarities that have often been regarded as late Aramaisms.[58] To be a clear

54. See the note in the commentary. R. D. Wilson suggested that 3:3b is a later note interpolated by an editor or copyist (*PTR* 16 [1918], pp. 455f.).
55. *The Religion of Israel* (1947), p. 176.
56. Cf. Ezra 7:14; Dan. 6:17; and extrabiblical references cited by E. J. Bickerman, *RHPR* 45 (1965), p. 250.
57. A. M. Honeyman in *The OT and Modern Study* (1951), p. 278.
58. "The Chronological Significance of 'Aramaisms' in Biblical Hebrew," *IEJ* 18 (1968), pp. 234–240.

pointer to lateness of composition they must appear in concentration rather than as isolated elements. They should be characteristic of assuredly late Hebrew sources and obvious replacements of vocabulary used in preexilic Hebrew literature. Alternative explanations need to be considered. Does the language merely echo such Aramaic elements as are clearly present in early biblical Hebrew? Is the text written in northern dialect, which included Aramaic features? Is the terminology a mark of special coloring, such as a stylistic device in a foreign setting?

At least seven Aramaisms have been detected in the book: *mallāḥ,* "sailor" (1:5); *s^epînâ,* "ship" (1:5); *'št,* "think" (1:6); the relative *š* in 1:7, 12; 4:10; *minnâ,* "appoint" (2:1; 4:6, 7, 8); *ṭa'am,* "decree" (3:7); and *ribbô,* "myriad" (4:11).[59] Moreover, *q^erî'â,* "proclamation" (3:2), has been regarded as a late Hebrew formation, while the divine title "God of the heavens" (1:9) has been noted as typical of the postexilic period. O. Loretz has challenged a number of these claims.[60] *Mallāḥ* is more probably Phoenician: Ezek. 27:9 uses it concerning Tyre; so too is *s^epînâ* more naturally to be taken.[61] The relative *š* accords with Phoenician *'š* and *š,* as Kautzsch admitted,[62] and is an old Canaanite element. It occurs in early narratives emanating from the Northern Kingdom. Loretz explained *ribbô* by reference to Ugaritic *rbt,* and in fact a merely late use in Hebrew is ruled out in the light of Ps. 68:17(18) and Hos. 8:12 Kethib (Rudolph). Loretz concluded from the combination of the sea motif and of language at home in Phoenicia and/or Northern Israel that the author derived his material from a milieu where both were at home, perhaps the Phoenician coast or an adjacent area.[63] His researches raise an interesting question concerning the antiquity of the narrative. But maritime terminology would naturally be Phoenician, irrespective of the chronological origin of the story. And it may be that the nonmaritime instances are merely features of postexilic Hebrew, since they permit rather than demand a preexilic provenance. In any case there are a number of linguistic phenomena left unaccounted for by Loretz. *Hith'ashshēṯ* looks like an Aramaizing replacement of the earlier Hebrew *ḥšb*. A noun *'eshtōnôṯ* occurs in Ps. 146:4;[64] the verb occurs in Dan. 6:4 (Aramaic), the Elephantine papyri, and the Targums, and also in earlier Aramaic material.[65] The root *mnh* is well attested in preexilic Hebrew, but the Piel in the sense of the normal Hebrew *tsiwwâ* or *pāqaḏ* corresponds to the Aramaic Pael in biblical Aramaic (Ezra 7:25; Dan. 2:24, 49; 3:12) and in

59. E. Kautzsch, *Die Aramaismen im AT* (1902).
60. *BZ* 5 (1961), pp. 19–25.
61. Cf. Wilson, *loc. cit.*, p. 282.
62. *Op. cit.*, p. 87.
63. Eerdmans, *op. cit.*, p. 177, had earlier suggested that *b^eshell^emi* (1:7), *s^epînâ,* and *mnh* were indications of a North Israelite story.
64. Cf. Sir. 3:23.
65. Dahood, *Pss 3,* p. xxxvii, notes that it occurs in the mid-eighth-century Aramaic Sefire inscription and also in the Sayings of Ahiqar, which although a late fifth-century document contains older material. This rules out Wilson's claim that it came into Aramaic from Hebrew (*loc. cit.*, pp. 282f.).

the Targums. In Hebrew it occurs significantly in Job 7:3; Dan. 1:5, 10, 11; and in the passive at 1 Chr. 9:29. Its presence in Ps. 61:7(8) is disputed.[66] Hebrew *ta'am* usually means "taste, discretion." The meaning "decree" accords with the usage of the Aramaic counterpart, *ṭᵉʿēm, ṭaʿmâ* in the postexilic Ezra 6:14; 7:23; Dan. 3:10, etc. It should be noted that Pusey, Keil, von Orelli, Wilson,[67] and Aalders[68] refer to the Akkadian *têmu,* "command," and imply that this is an echo of Assyrian usage.

The form of the *hapax legomenon qᵉrîʾâ* certainly has preexilic precedents, such as *ḥᵃlîp̄â* and *hᵃlîḵâ,* but it may be significant that later Hebrew used this noun form much more commonly.[69] The title "God of the heavens" may be an archaism, echoing Gen. 24:3, 7, but its widespread usage in the Persian period[70] is a factor to be reckoned with.

These are the linguistic phenomena commonly adduced as marks of the postexilic period. Although it is possible to counter a number of them, their cumulative effect conveys an impression of lateness.

It used to be an axiom of critical orthodoxy to regard the book as propaganda directed against the work of Ezra and Nehemiah. But this view has rightly fallen into disfavor. "We have no knowledge of a 'universalistic' opposition to the 'particularistic' measures taken by Ezra and Nehemiah, and the book itself contains no evidence to support such a theory."[71] Moreover, the oft-repeated contention that the book is dependent on Isa. 40–55 is equally questionable.[72]

The book of Jonah was certainly known and accepted by 200 B.C. according to Sir. 49:10. It is a moot point whether Jonah is cited in the fourth-century Tobit 14:4, 8.[73] Probably the book is best assigned to the fifth or fourth century B.C.

The book of Jonah is like some ancient pot spirited away from its stratum and site and presented to a curator as an archeological conundrum. A knowledge of the original situation is necessary for the interpretation of any parable addressed to its contemporaries. "It must be observed what ideas, images and evaluations were at work in the hearers of the parable, in what the opposition between the narrator and his listeners consisted and how accordingly his words must have acted upon them."[74] Yet the investigation

66. Heb. *man* is notoriously difficult. G. R. Driver's endorsement of Perles' explanation of *mn* as an annotation, an abbreviation of *mālēʾ nûn* with reference to the unassimilated *nun* in the following *ynṣrw* (*Textus* 1 [1960], p. 125), is plausible. Wilson, *PTR* 16 (1918), pp. 645–654, leaned heavily on the presence of this form in a preexilic psalm.

67. *PTR* 16 (1918), p. 289.

68. *Op. cit.,* pp. 9f.

69. P. Joüon, *Grammaire de l'hébreu biblique* (1923), section 88b.

70. See the commentary and note.

71. Von Rad, *OT Theology,* vol. 2 (E.T. 1965), p. 291; cf. Loretz, *loc. cit.,* p. 28; Eissfeldt, *The OT: An Introduction* (E.T. 1965), p. 405; Trible, *SBJ,* pp. 262f.

72. Cf. Trible, *SBJ,* pp. 111f.

73. While Codex S reads "Jonah," Codex B reads "Nahum" in v. 4 and lacks a name in v. 8. See the discussion in *Biblica* 33 (1952), p. 363.

74. E. Linnemann, *The Parables of Jesus. Introduction and Exposition* (E.T. 1966), pp. 22f.

of the purpose of Jonah is handicapped at this very point. An attempt has been made in the course of the commentary to assess the impact of the narrator upon his audience, on the assumption that postexilic Judah is the historical setting. To ascertain the purpose of the story one can rely only on internal evidence. Obviously the question in 4:11 is the climax of the book and the key to its understanding. It is generally concluded that the narrator is combatting Jewish particularism by emphasizing the all-inclusive nature of the love of God. But there have been a surprising number of variations and permutations in evaluating the purpose and nuance of the book.[75] One variety of interpretation denies that the foreignness of Nineveh has any relevance. For Kaufmann the book says nothing of Israel's quarrel with the Gentiles, and he compares the non-Israelite setting of the book of Job. Rather it is concerned with the wholly moral problem of justice *versus* mercy.[76] Similarly Trible sees no mirror of particularism in Jonah. Jonah's complaint is about God's repenting of evil, and the salvation of a foreign city is the occasion for, and not the cause of, Jonah's attitude. Jonah cannot bear a love that repents of evil, be it extended to foreigners or to himself.[77] Keller too is opposed to the portrayal of Jonah as the incarnation of a particularistic Jew. Nineveh is merely a great sinful city, and there is no antipagan emphasis. The book is a challenge to all to hear God's appeal to be like the sailors and the Ninevites in their submissiveness to Yahweh.

Another line of interpretation is concerned with the nonrealization of prophecy. For Hitzig the book had an apologetic aim of showing the divine justification for unfulfilled prophecies. Feuillet developed this viewpoint further. Decrees of destruction against foreign nations, even if they carry most certain marks of divine origin, remain always conditional, though they are pronounced by God in an absolute manner. Belied prediction need not be false but can be truly inspired.[78]

At the other extreme is the interpretation of Cohn, who divorces the book from any purely Jewish background. Jonah does not represent a prophet or Israel. The story is concerned with the problem of the direction of man's life and contrasts the way of God with the way of man. God's word alone indicates the right direction and is the essence of life.[79] Cohn presents the book from the standpoint of religious existentialism. A similar temptation to which many interpreters have succumbed is to view the book through Christian spectacles as a missionary tract. Robinson and Weiser speak loftily of the missionary message of the book and of the obligation of mission which devolves upon God's people. It is common to relate this view to OT data by dramatizing the author as a defender of the world-embracing

75. For a useful survey of older interpretations of the book and its parts see Bickerman, *RHPR* 45 (1965), pp. 232–264.
76. *Op. cit.*, p. 283.
77. *SBJ*, pp. 262–65.
78. *RB* 54 (1947), p. 345.
79. *JLBE*, p. 102.

message of the noble Second Isaiah over against the introverted bigotry of Ezra and Nehemiah.

At which of a variety of targets was the author aiming? To deny the foreignness of Nineveh is surely to underestimate the religious and psychological impact of the old Assyrian capital upon a community that had received the book of Nahum as part of its religious heritage.[80] Comparison with Job is hardly valid since that book lacks the Jew-Gentile confrontation of the Jonah story. A question of unfulfilled prophecy is a conceivable concern. Delcor develops this interpretation by regarding the book as a damper upon the zeal of those who awaited the arrival of the Day of Yahweh and the fulfilment of associated prophecies of doom for foreign nations. But if 4:11 presents the message of the book, its burden must rest upon a broader basis.

To view the author as a latter-day disciple of the message of Isa. 40–55 is to overlook that idolatry is not the charge levelled against Nineveh or the sin of which its citizens repent. The sin of Nineveh is the violation of that moral law of Yahweh which foreign nations were obliged to keep, and disregarded at their peril. In this respect the book presents again the message of Amos 1f., where man's inhumanity to man (not necessarily to the Israelite) is promised divine retribution. Universalism is an ambiguous term: it may denote the universal power and concern of Yahweh, as Amos construed it (cf. Amos 9:7); or it may mean something quite different, such as the personal self-revelation and grace of Yahweh, who throws open to Gentiles the covenant relationship that hitherto was Israel's privilege. The book of Jonah is universalistic in the former sense.[81] Neither the sailors nor the Ninevites are converted to Jewish monotheism; they do not become Gentile proselytes to Judaism.

Jonah 4:11 is a restatement of 4:2, which itself is a reinterpretation of an old Israelite credal statement along new lines. The author does not stand alone in broadening the concept of *ḥeseḏ,* usually Yahweh's covenant-love for Israel, to cover his care for all his creatures. Some of the Psalms exhibit this widening and weakening trend, which the book develops.[82] The parallel of the Elder Brother of Luke 15 and the Laborers of Matt. 20, where Jesus glances at the resentful opposition his gospel encountered, suggests that the book of Jonah is challenging its audience to face up to the unwelcome truth of God's sovereign compassion for foreigners and beasts. Rebellious Israel, who has in her history seen the forbearance, compassion, and help of God

80. Cf. T. F. Glasson, "The Final Question in Nahum and Jonah," *ET* 81 (1969), pp. 54f.
81. Cf. R. Martin-Achard, *A Light to the Nations* (E.T. 1962), pp. 52f.; H. M. Orlinsky, "Nationalism-Universalism and Internationalism in Ancient Israel," *Translating and Understanding the OT*. H. G. May Festschrift (1970), pp. 206–236; H. L. Ellison, "Is the Book of Jonah a Missionary Pamphlet?" *Evangelical Fellowship for Missionary Studies Bulletin* 1 (1972), pp. 31–36.
82. Especially Ps. 145:8–21. Cf. Feuillet, *RB* 54 (1947), p. 355; E. Jacob, *Theology of the OT* (E.T. 1958), pp. 106f.; W. Eichrodt, *Theology of the OT,* vol. 1 (E.T. 1961), p. 239.

carried to such amazing lengths on her behalf, dare not take up a purely negative attitude toward non-Jews. The author deliberately gives a sympathetic representation of Gentiles, clearly to counter an opposite conviction among some at least of his contemporaries. In this respect Jesus' parable of the Good Samaritan comes to mind as a NT counterpart. The target was evidently a community embittered by its legacy of national suffering and foreign opposition. The postexilic Jews are challenged to rise above their antipathy and see the world through the eyes of their Creator God, whose care and compassion are as great as his power. The Gentiles' obligation to obey God's moral law need not apply only negatively. The audience is asked to ponder a theological riddle: what would have happened if no less a den of foreign devils than Nineveh had repented? God's primary providential concern is to preserve life, human and animal, not to destroy.

There is much one would like to know about the background of the book. Part of the problem is the paucity of information concerning the postexilic period and the crosscurrents of religious controversy. Perhaps eschatological enthusiasts needed to be reminded of Jonah's simple but profound lesson. A plausible source for the book has been suggested in the wisdom movement. Certainly the international interest of the wisdom teachers, their concern with natural phenomena, and their use of dialogue constitute affinities with our book.[83] As the wisdom teachers challenged self-righteous Israel with the devastating book of Job, so perhaps they produced the little book of Jonah as another shock for a self-centered community. Haller has plausibly suggested that the narrator told his tale at the *sôḏ,* which Köhler has defined as "the free meeting together in time of leisure of the adult men."[84] It may well be that the book of Jonah was born at this Israelite equivalent of a campfire scene. Its preservation and survival among the sacred literature of the OT are an indication that its message was heeded by that listening circle long ago.

4. TEXT

The Hebrew text has been exceedingly well preserved. The most comprehensive and recent comparative textual study of the MT and the ancient versions is that of Trible, *SBJ,* pp. 1–57. Apart from this unpublished work, Bewer's notable contribution in the ICC must be mentioned. Snaith's small book is an introduction to the subject.

Textual questions are regularly discussed by commentators at eight places: concerning the unusual use of the verb *ḥishshᵉḇâ* at 1:4, the

83. Trible, *SBJ,* pp. 249–259; cf. Haller, Kraeling.
84. *Hebrew Man* (E.T. 1956), pp. 102f. Note his imaginative reconstruction of the setting and significance of the *sôḏ* on pp. 99–106, especially as a center of wisdom teaching. Cf. Trible, *SBJ,* pp. 259–261.

authenticity of a clause of five Hebrew words in 1:8 and of the last clause in 1:10, the overloaded line in 2:3(4), the pointing of *'k* (*'aḵ* or *'ēḵ*?) in 2:4(5), the unusual word *qits*^{e}*ḇê* at 2:6(7), the transposition of 4:5 to a position after 3:4, and the *hapax legomenon h*^{a}*rîshîṯ* in 4:8.

Mur. 88 contains no significant variants; it supports MT at all the points listed above, except of course where a vowel sign is concerned, at 2:4(5). *BHS* reflects the modern respect for MT among textual critics: while listing various proposals, Elliger recommends only a deletion at 2:3(4), a ("probably") change and transposition at 2:6(7) and a ("perhaps") insertion in 2:4(5).

Only one departure from MT has been deemed necessary in the commentary, namely, the conjectural deletion of *m*^{e}*tsûlâ* (2:4) as an annotation, on syntactical and metrical grounds.

5. THEOLOGY

The theological orientation of the book has already been broached in the discussion of its purpose. In a game of word-association "Jonah" would undoubtedly prompt the reaction "whale," but obviously a subject that takes up only three verses out of a total of forty-eight can hardly be regarded as the narrator's main concern. G. Campbell Morgan uttered a wise word: "Men have been looking so hard at the great fish that they have failed to see the great God."[85] It is the greatness of Israel's God that is the burden of the book. Very much of its theology radiates out from the two credal confessions of Jonah in 1:9; 4:2. The narrative is largely an application of the significance of this traditional material in easily digestible form.

Yahweh is the Creator of the world, Maker of land and sea; in Hebrew thought this implied that he was the providential controller who held the world in his grasp and manipulated its phenomena, manifesting his powerful presence via the natural world in order to achieve his purposes among men. This universal sovereignty is displayed in the first two chapters, where the hurricane, the tempestuous sea, and the enormous fish are represented as but minions in the service of the divine will (1:14). The uselessness of pitting oneself against it is dramatically portrayed: it is irresistible. And what is the divine will? It is presented first in traditional terms as the condemnation of a foreign city for flouting a natural law, God's moral law. The divine power is used for a moral end. Yahweh is "the Judge of all the earth" (Gen. 18:25), and upon the nations is placed the obligation of moral obedience. If Nineveh, former hub of the world, was great, Yahweh is greater as its Overlord to whom it must give account. The God of universal power is the God of moral order in the world. These truths are

85. *The Minor Prophets* (1960), p. 69.

nothing new: the Genesis narratives and the prophetic oracles against the nations, especially Amos 1 and 2, are old witnesses to these divine themes to which a forgetful generation needed to be recalled.

Yahweh is also the God who delivers. First the Gentile seamen are saved from perishing in the storm. There is no wanton destruction, no waste of valuable human life. Yahweh is no arbitrary Herod who slew all to slay one. He derives no pleasure from the death of anyone; he is no sadist, as Ezek. 18:32 testifies. He is the God of the living world: it is his prime concern to sustain the lives of his creatures. This is a natural corollary of the doctrine of creation. But the author takes his representation of God a significant step forward in introducing the deliverance of Jonah. Justice demanded the death of Jonah for rebellion and desertion; mercy prevails and grants a new lease on life. The amazing grace of Yahweh, typified in the fish, would be no theological novelty to the listening circle, for his forgiveness and forbearance are attested throughout the OT, especially in the Psalms.

But if the juxtaposition of justice and mercy in the story creates no surprise from a theological point of view, the author is to apply it to a less acceptable situation in the second half of the book. The first two chapters are a rehearsal for the second two, a preliminary scene in which certain theological themes are introduced as the real *dramatis personae* of the story.

The repentance of the Ninevites is an unexpected and disturbing feature, for it places a question mark against the destruction of Nineveh. The author guards carefully against the charge of making God the automatic reactor to human activity, as if man could be the arbiter of his own fate. The "who knows?" of 3:9, taken over from Joel 2:14, is a declaration of the sovereignty of God, whose mysterious will cannot be manipulated by man for his own ends. Behind the last few verses of ch. 3 lies not only the possibility of reprieve which Joel had preached to Judah, but also the theology of divine pardon which Jeremiah had applied not merely to Israel but to all nations. This was the principle that Yahweh is characteristically prepared to qualify a death sentence passed upon any nation if there is a radical change in the moral situation (Jer. 18:7, 8). These implicit appeals to former prophecies are an important element in the message of the book. By superimposing the essentially Israel-oriented appeal of Joel upon the explicitly international setting of the declaration in Jer. 18, the author has presented to his hearers a highly significant synthesis.

He continues this disturbing process in the use of the old covenant formula in 4:2: God is good, compassionate, and kind, and hesitant to punish. In origin this formula belongs firmly to an Israelite setting of application, but there are signs that it gradually lost this exclusiveness and was applied to the providential goodness of God toward all his creatures. The author exploits this trend. The God of the covenant has never ceased to be the God of creation. Other nations are objects of his providential care besides Israel, as Amos declared long before (9:7). The rival claims of mercy and justice, the nations and Israel—these are the theological questions which the book raises and dares to answer on the basis of former revelation and acknowledged truths.

The final question of the book challenges every hearer and reader to appreciate God's care for all creatures great and small. His is a heart that yearns, a hand that tends. The doctrine of divine providence is presented as no theological abstraction, but concerns the intensely personal nature of God. Israel has no monopoly of his loving care. "Is he only the God of the Jews? Is he not also the God of the Gentiles?" (Rom. 3:29). Paul goes on to draw a more radical conclusion than did the author of the book of Jonah. But if the book is no missionary tract, it is an important contribution to the prolegomena of a theology of mission.[86] As so often, the effect of this OT book is to lay a foundation upon which the NT can build. "God so loved the world" is its basic affirmation, which the NT is to conclude with the message of the gift of his Son.

Throughout the story the figure of Jonah is a foil to the divine hero, a Watson to Yahweh's Holmes, a Gehazi to Yahweh's Elisha. The greatness and the goodness of God are enhanced against the background of Jonah's meanness and malevolence. Look out at the world, pleads the author, at God's world. See it through God's eyes. And let your new vision overcome your natural bitterness, your hardness of soul. Let the divine compassion flood your own hearts.

6. THE SIGN OF JONAH

For many Christians the significance of the book of Jonah is determined by Matt. 12:40:

> *"For as Jonah was in the belly of the sea monster three days and three nights, so will the Son of man be in the heart of the earth three days and three nights."*

This text has often been hailed as a guideline, and it is possible to let one's exposition of the whole book be governed by the basic and important supposition that Jonah is a type of Christ. J. Ellul's *The Judgment of Jonah* is a distinguished example of this hermeneutical position. A warning against the assumption that the book has this exclusive significance has been issued by the conservative writer J. Stek.[87] He observes that if its purpose was simply to provide a prophetic type of Christ, it remained an enigma until the antitype appeared, and the Israel to whom the book was originally addressed was doomed to misunderstand it. An OT commentator will take to heart this plea for an understanding of the book in terms of its own milieu.

86. Ellison, *loc. cit.*, pp. 34–36. He derives from the book a warning against racism and other divisive factors in society, and a challenge to Christian involvement in social service and in relief and medical work not simply as a means to an evangelistic end.
87. *Calvin Theological Journal* 4 (1969), p. 37, n. 29.

Nevertheless, since the book is part of the Christian heritage, he must take seriously its reflection on the pages of the NT and especially on the lips of Christ.

The "sign of Jonah" is mentioned three times in the Gospels, twice in Matthew (12:39; 16:4) and once in Luke (11:29). In the last reference the counterpart to Matt. 12:40 is, "For as Jonah was a sign to the Ninevites, so also will the Son of man be to this generation." Luke 11:31, 32 contrasts the Jews' reaction to the preaching of Jesus with both the readiness of the Queen of the South to hear Solomon's wisdom and the repentance of the Ninevites after Jonah's proclamation. Matt. 12:41, 42 presents the same material but in the reverse order. Matt. 16:4 simply repeats 12:39: Jesus refuses to give any sign on demand except Jonah's. All this material bears some relation to Mark 8:12, where a sign is categorically refused. One may interpret this varied evidence in terms of redaction criticism, as has been done thoroughly by R. A. Edwards,[88] and seek to unpeel layers of interpretation imposed upon a basic saying by subsequent Christian teachers, but this is only one of a number of possible approaches to the Gospels.

A basic question which the very alignment of the material poses concerns the authenticity of Matt. 12:40.[89] A popular view is to prefer the less specific Lukan version and to interpret the sign in terms of Jesus' preaching of repentance.[90] The verse has been regarded as an interpolation after the book was completed; Justin Martyr omits it in his exposition.[91] Others have considered it an expansion in line with the Matthean predilection for scriptural proof-texts. Certainly the text falls into the pattern of emphasis upon OT fulfilment evident both in the selection of dominical teaching and in the commentary on events. But it is difficult to believe that it represents a *vaticinium ex eventu;* the nonliteral realization of the "three days and three nights" motif raises a barrier against such a supposition.[92] Justin Martyr's omission of the verse has been explained plausibly on grounds other than its absence from the Gospel as he knew it.[93] The separation of the sign from the preaching of Jonah in the Third Gospel suggests that Luke did not interpret the sign simply in terms of the preaching of Jesus. Moreover, the importance of the book of Jonah for contemporary Judaism lay in the first two chapters rather than in his preaching.[94]

Joachim Jeremias laid stress on the future tense of the verbs in Matt. 12:40 and Luke 11:30 as a pointer away from a preaching interpretation. He

88. *The Sign of Jonah in the Theology of the Evangelists and Q*. SBT 2:18 (1971).

89. See esp. R. T. France, *Jesus and the OT* (1971), pp. 80–82.

90. Cf., e.g., A. D. Martin, *The Prophet Jonah: The Book and the Sign* (1926), pp. 70–85; R. B. Y. Scott, *Interpretation* 19 (1965), pp. 17f.

91. K. Stendahl, *The School of St. Matthew* (1954), pp. 132f.

92. M.-J. Lagrange, *Évangile selon St. Matthieu* (1923), pp. 249f.; O. Cullmann, *The Christology of the NT* (E.T. ^{2}1963), pp. 62f.

93. Cf. Lagrange, *ibid.*; Edwards, *op. cit.*, p. 97; France, *op. cit.*, pp. 81f.

94. P. Seidelin, *ST* 5 (1951), p. 130.

interprets the sign in both the First and Third Gospels as the miracle of Jonah's deliverance from the fish.[95] In Luke, Jonah constituted a sign to the Ninevites as one who had been delivered from the belly of the fish; and likewise Jesus would be displayed to the contemporary generation as one who was raised from the dead. Accordingly the sign both old and new stands for "the authorization of the divine messenger by deliverance from death." Jeremias suspects that the explicit time reference in Matt. 12:40 is secondary, but B. Gärtner has drawn attention to the parallel of the well-attested tradition that Jesus would destroy the temple and rebuild it in three days, a reference to his rising from the dead.[96] The implication of the time reference appears to be that Jonah would spend only "three days and three nights" in Hades; after a short stay Jesus too would return to life.[97] The terminological relationship between Jonah and Jesus lies in the sending of a preacher of repentance whose mission is attested by a miraculous act of deliverance.

This negative interpretation of Jonah's stay in the fish, which underlies Matt. 12:40, is an old one. It is implied in the Septuagint. In Jon. 2:6f. (7f.) past verbs of deliverance are there invested with a future significance; and the use of *koilía,* "belly," for both the fish and Sheol in Jon. 2:1f. (2f.) accords with the Matthean typological equation of the belly of the fish and the heart of the earth. 3 Macc. 6:8 (first century B.C.) and Josephus *Antiquities* ix.10.2 agree with rabbinic evidence[98] in interpreting the fish as a threat to Jonah. Accordingly Matt. 12:40 is firmly grounded in the current Jewish interpretation of the incident.

A comprehensive study of Jon. 2 suggests, however, that the primary and precise function of the fish was to be an instrument not of punishment or death, but of deliverance from a watery grave; but this basic meaning is irrelevant to the usage in Matt. 12:40.[99] Essentially Jesus referred to Jonah and the fish as a means of communicating the significance of his own mission. His fundamental concern was not to expound the book of Jonah but to reveal truth concerning himself in terms his Jewish audience acknowl-

95. *Theological Dictionary of the NT,* vol. 3 (E.T. 1965), pp. 406–410. He finds no discrepancy between Matthew, Luke, and Mark: God will not give any sign that is abstracted from the person of Jesus and that does not give offense.

96. *The Temple and the Community in Qumran and the NT.* SNTS Monograph series 1 (1956), p. 112. Cf. Matt. 26:61; 27:40; Mark 14:58; 15:29; John 2:19–22. There is an interesting terminological link between the two sayings in the references to the temple in Jon. 2:4, 7(5, 8). J. W. Doeve, *Jewish Hermeneutics in the Synoptic Gospels and in Acts* (1954), p. 149, has noted the parallels between Jon. 2:2, 6(3, 7) and Ps. 16:10, Heb. *sheʾôl* and *shaḥaṯ*.

97. Edwards, *op. cit.,* p. 98.

98. Cf. H. L. Strack and P. Billerbeck, *Kommentar zum NT aus Talmud und Midrasch* (³1926), pp. 645–49.

99. E. J. Young, *op. cit.,* pp. 280f., who rightly interpreted ch. 2 as a psalm of thanksgiving for deliverance from drowning uttered from inside the fish, related Matt. 12:40 to Jonah's being cast into the depths of Sheol, the sea, and being brought up alive. This faithfully reflects the OT record but at the expense of the explicit NT reference.

edged and could understand. The best of teachers, he argued from what was accepted to what was as yet unknown. He turned to good use the current interpretation of Jon. 2 and made it the vehicle of vital truth. A greater phenomenon than that of Jonah was here. Prophet *par excellence,* he was to conquer death in a reality that transcended the symbolic shadow of Jonah's survival.[100]

7. STRUCTURE AND ANALYSIS

The book of Jonah is a model of literary artistry, marked by symmetry and balance. That it falls into two parts is obvious from the parallelism of 1:1–3 and 3:1–3. This parallelism extends beyond the openings of the two parts. Of the four episodes in the overall plot of the story, the first and third and the second and fourth correspond to each other. In chs. 1 and 3 Jonah is set in a social situation, in which a pagan group under their leader appeal to God for help; in chs. 2 and 4 Jonah is devoid of human company and speaks with God. The analysis at the end of this section shows the close correspondence that may be traced between the two major divisions of the book.[101]

The author's concern with structure extends beyond correspondence between different sections of the book to the composition of the actual sections. An exception proving the rule is 1:1–3, which by contrast with 3:1–4 has a deliberately defective structure. The verb "arise" in the divine command is repeated, but the following material is alien to what has gone before. The aim is to stress the disobedience of Jonah by this discord. As if to balance this intentional jarring, v. 3 is carefully structured as a subunit of narrative.

1:4–16 exhibits a fine concentric structure. R. Pesch[102] has analyzed it thus: A, A′. Narrative and response of fear (4–5a, 15–16a); B, B′. Sailors' prayer (5b, 14); C, C′. Narrative (5c–6a, 13); D, D′. Captain's/Jonah's speech (6b, 12); E, E′. Sailors' speech (7a, 11); F, F′. Narrative (7b, 10c); G, G′. Sailors' speech (8, 10b). These elements cluster around a nucleus of Jonah's statement and the response of fear in vv. 9, 10a. This structural view necessitates taking v. 11b as a continuation of direct speech instead of narrative, as it is usually construed. This is quite feasible: v. 12b is then the answer to v. 11b. The last two clauses of v. 16 lie outside the concentric

100. It is a moot point whether 1 Cor. 15:4 refers to Jon. 2:1. See the discussions of B. M. Metzger, *JTS* 8 (1957), pp. 118f.; B. Lindars, *NT Apologetic* (1961), p. 60; France, *op. cit.*, pp. 54f.; H. K. McArthur, *NTS* 18 (1971), pp. 81–86. Hos. 6:2 is a more likely basis, but Jon. 2:1 probably played a supporting role.

101. Cf. Trible's detailed chart in *SBJ,* pp. 186–192. The scheme presented here differs from hers mainly in the retention of the psalm of ch. 2 and in not moving 4:5 to a position after 3:4.

102. *Biblica,* 47 (1966), pp. 577–581. He is followed by Cohn, *JLBE,* pp. 51f. Pesch's scheme is a refinement of that suggested by N. Lohfink, *BZ* 5 (1961), p. 201, with which Trible, *SBJ,* pp. 207–209, rightly takes issue.

structure as a supplementary amplification. The section is dominated by key terms: throwing, the sea, and fear.

Lohfink argued that 1:17–2:10 without the psalm exhibited a chiastic structure.[103] But his structural analyses are suspect: not only does his view of 1:4–16 require correction, but his suggestions that 4:5 begins the fourth and last episode of the book and that 3:1–4:4 has a concentric structure[104] are questionable.

The psalm in 2:2–9 (3–10) consists of three stanzas (vv. 2–4, 5–7, 8f.). The first two are marked by a refrain and by parallelism of motifs. They contain four motifs, answered prayer, crisis, banishment, and assurance. The first occurs at the start of the first strophe and the end of the second, while the other three occur in the same order in both.[105] 2:9 takes up the theme of sacrifices and vows with which the first chapter ended: Jonah is brought to the same situation as the sailors. Landes traces in both ch. 1 and the psalm a general parallelism, consisting of the themes of crisis, prayer, deliverance, and worship.[106] The relevance of the psalm to the overall structure of the book will be discussed later.

3:1–4, the counterpart of 1:1–3, is marked out as a unit by careful repetition of vocabulary: the terms of the divine commission in v. 2, arise—go—proclaim, are taken up stage by stage in vv. 3f.

3:5–9 falls into three parts, the people's response to Jonah's preaching (v. 5), the king's (v. 6), and the royal decree reinforcing the people's response (vv. 7–9). Sackcloth is mentioned in all three parts as a key term. The first and third parts are parallel: fasting, sackcloth, and total involvement figure in both. The third part not only repeats but develops the first. It is clear that the whole section, dealing with Nineveh's repentance, is intended as a parallel to ch. 1, which narrates the sailors' homage. 3:9 corresponds to 1:6 in its tentative expression of hope and its identical final clause.

A key word in chs. 1 and 3 is *qārā'*, "call." It occurs in the prophetic introductions (1:2; 3:2, 4) and also in the ensuing narratives concerning the reactions of pagans (1:6, 14; 3:5, 8). Another key word in the book is *rā'â,* which is used in various senses in 1:2, 7f.; 3:8, 10 (*bis*); 4:1f.

The demonstration of divine grace in 3:10 is the intended parallel to that in 1:17; Jonah's deliverance from deserved destruction has a sequel in the sparing of Nineveh.

The prophet's complaint in 4:1–3 is in stark contrast to his song of praise in 2:1–9 (3–10). It is highly significant that they each have a similar introduction, "And Jonah prayed to Yahweh and said." The conclusion drawn by E. J. Young from this repetition is correct: "The removal of 2:2–9 . . . destroys the symmetry of the book."[107] It does not appear to have

103. *Loc. cit.*, p. 196, n. 37, followed by Trible, *SBJ*, pp. 218f.
104. *Loc. cit.*, pp. 198f., 202.
105. See the commentary for further details.
106. KBJ, p. 26.
107. *Op. cit.*, p. 281; cf. Landes, KBJ, p. 17.

been noted before that three key words in the psalm, referring to God's steadfast love and Jonah's life, find an echo in 4:2.[108] The themes that drew forth Jonah's praise in the psalm are ironically the very ones that cause him grief in his second prayer. The claim that 1:14 is the intended counterpart of 4:2f.[109] ignores the balance of the narrative introductions. The limited similarities to 1:14 certainly call to mind the sailors' prayer, just as the mention of fleeing to Tarshish recalls 1:3, 10, but to claim more is to confuse formal parallelism and the overall interlocking of the whole narrative. Landes pertinently observes that the inclusion of traditional cultic material in both Jonah's song and his complaint suggests that the author was consciously balancing the two utterances.[110]

The last section is 4:4–11, which is parallel to 2:10 (11), Yahweh's reply by his word and use of nature.[111] Obviously the two sections are ill-matched, if length is the criterion. But Trible has called attention to the "symmetriphobia" displayed in the book as justification for the inequality of length in parallel sections.[112] Landes has turned this factor into a weapon against Trible's contention that 2:2–9 (3–10) damages the symmetry of the book by disproportionately increasing the length of the first half.[113] In fact in the second and fourth episodes the greater length of 4:4–11 over against 2:10 (11) is finely balanced by the greater length of 2:1–9 (2–10) by comparison with 4:2.

In 4:4–11 the purpose of vv. 4f., 9–11 is to function as a framework for the nucleus of vv. 6–8, which relates three divine acts. The theme of the surrounding framework is the unreasonableness of Jonah's anger concerning the city of Nineveh.[114] This concluding section deliberately harks back to earlier material, just as 4:2f. recalled 1:3, 14. The triple use of *wayᵉman,* "and he appointed," recalls the former expressions of divine wrath and grace, the sea and the fish, chiastically now replaced by the plant and the insect, while the wind echoes that which caused the storm. Verse 10 repeats the verb "perish" of 1:6, 14; 3:9. The final verse artistically reuses in a surprising way the key phrase "Nineveh the great city," which opened both parts of the book (1:2; 3:2). So the threads of the story are drawn together in a climax that stamps the story as a carefully structured composition.

108. Heb. *ḥasdām,* 2:8(9)—*ḥeseḏ; ḥayyay,* 2:5(6); *napshî*, 2:7(8).
109. Wolff, *SJ,* p. 60; Trible, *SBJ,* p. 229, n. 1. Trible notes that both prayers commence with the same invocation; the divine name occurs in similar places throughout. Their content is parallel; invocation, petition, and motivation in 1:14 are amplified by the insertion of a complaint in 4:2f. Both are concerned with the life, *neḇesh,* of Jonah and with the nature and activity of God. Yet it is significant that in her chart (pp. 190f.) 4:2f. is not formally matched with 1:14, but with 2:1(2), while 1:14 is made part of a portion 1:7–16 which corresponds to 3:10.
110. KBJ, pp. 17f.
111. Trible, *SBJ,* pp. 191f.
112. *SBJ,* pp. 199f.
113. KBJ, p. 18; *SBJ,* p. 75.
114. The anger, *ḥrh,* of vv. 4, 9 is subtly echoed in sound by *hšḥr,* "dawn," *lmḥrt,* "on the morrow," and *ḥryšyt,* "hot(?)," in vv. 7, 8.

- **I. A Hebrew Sinner Saved** (1:1–2:10[11])
  - A. Jonah's disobedience (1:1–3)
  - B. Jonah's punishment; heathen homage (1:4–16)
  - C. Jonah's rescue (1:17–2:10 [2:1–11])
    1. God's grace (1:17 [2:1])
    2. Jonah's praise (2:1–9 [2–10])
    3. God's last word (2:10 [11])
- **II. Heathen Sinners Saved** (3:1–4:11)
  - A. Jonah's obedience (3:1–4)
  - B. Nineveh's repentance (3:5–9)
  - C. Jonah's rebuke (3:10–4:11)
    1. God's grace (3:10)
    2. Jonah's plaint (4:1–3)
    3. God's last word (4:4–11)

8. SELECT BIBLIOGRAPHY

J. Alonso Díaz, "Paralelos entre la narrácion del libro de Jonás y la parábola del Hijo Pródigo," *Biblica* 40 (1959), pp. 632–640.

E. J. Bickerman, "Les deux erreurs du prophète Jonas," *RHPR* 45 (1965), pp. 232–264.

T. E. Bird, *The Book of Jona*. Westminster Version of the Sacred Scriptures (1938).

S. H. Blank, " 'Doest Thou Well To Be Angry?' A Study in Self-Pity," *HUCA* 26 (1955), pp. 29–41.

W. Böhme, "Die Composition des Buches Jona," *ZAW* 7 (1887), pp. 224–284.

L. H. Brockington, "Jonah," *Peake's Commentary on the Bible*, ed. M. Black and H. H. Rowley (1962), pp. 627–29.

K. Budde, "Vermutungen zum 'Midrasch des Buches der Könige,' " *ZAW* 11 (1891), pp. 37–51.

M. Burrows, "The Literary Category of the Book of Jonah," *Translating and Understanding the OT*. H. G. May Festschrift (1970), pp. 80–107.

T. K. Cheyne, "Jonah (Book)," *Encyclopedia Biblica* (1901), pp. 2565–2571.

B. S. Childs, "Jonah: A Study in OT Hermeneutics," *SJT* 11 (1958), pp. 53–61.

G. H. Cohn, *Das Buch Jona im Lichte der biblischen Erzählkunst* (1969). (*JLBE*)

M. Delcor, "Jonas," *Les petits prophètes* 8:1. La Sainte Bible (1961).

R. A. Edwards, *The Sign of Jonah in the Theology of the Evangelists and Q*. SBT 2:18 (1971).

J. Ellul, *The Judgment of Jonah* (E.T. 1971).

A. Feuillet, "Les sources du livre de Jonas," *RB* 54 (1947), pp. 161–186.

Idem, "Le sens du livre de Jonas," *RB* 54 (1947), pp. 340–361.

E. M. Good, *Irony in the OT* (1967). (*IOT*).

E. Haller, *Die Erzählung von dem Propheten Jona. Theologische Existenz heute* 65 (1958), pp. 5–54.

D. E. Hart-Davies, *Jonah: Prophet and Patriot* (1925).
J. Jeremias, "*Iōnas,*" *Theological Dictionary of the NT,* vol. 3 (E.T. 1965), pp. 406–410.
A. R. Johnson, "Jonah ii, 3–10: A Study in Cultic Fantasy," *Studies in OT Prophecy.* T. H. Robinson Festschrift (1950), pp. 82–102.
G. A. F. Knight, *Ruth and Jonah: The Gospel in the OT.* Torch Bible ([2]1966).
G. M. Landes, "The Kerygma of the Book of Jonah," *Interpretation* 21 (1967), pp. 3–31. (KBJ)
N. Lohfink, "Jona ging zur Stadt hinaus (Jon. 4, 5)," *BZ* 5 (1961), pp. 185–203.
O. Loretz, "Herkunft und Sinn der Jona-Erzählung," *BZ* 5 (1961), pp. 18–29.
A. D. Martin, *The Prophet Jonah: The Book and the Sign* (1926).
H. Martin, *The Prophet Jonah* ([2]1877).
R. Pesch, "Zur konzentrischen Struktur von Jona 1," *Biblica* 47 (1966), pp. 577–581.
T. T. Perowne, *Obadiah and Jonah.* CBSC (1883).
H. Schmidt, "Die Komposition des Buches Jona," *ZAW* 25 (1905), pp. 285–310.
J. Schreiner, "Eigenart, Aufbau, Inhalt und Botschaft des Buches Jonas," *Bibel und Kirche* 17 (1962), 8–14.
R. B. Y. Scott, "The Sign of Jonah," *Interpretation* 19 (1965), pp. 16–25.
J. D. Smart, "Jonah," *IB,* vol. 6 (1956), pp. 869–894.
N. H. Snaith, *Notes on the Hebrew Text of Jonah* (1945).
J. H. Stek, "The Message of the Book of Jonah," *Calvin Theological Journal* 4 (1969), pp. 23–50.
P. L. Trible, *Studies in the Book of Jonah.* Columbia University Ph.D. dissertation, 1963 (unpublished). (*SBJ*)
A. J. Wilson, "The Sign of the Prophet Jonah and Its Modern Confirmations," *PTR* 25 (1927), pp. 630–642.
R. D. Wilson, "The Authenticity of Jonah," *PTR* 16 (1918), pp. 280–298, 430–456.
Idem, "*Mnh,* 'To Appoint', in the OT," *PTR* 16 (1918), pp. 645–654.
H. W. Wolff, *Studien zum Jonabuch.* Biblische Studien 47 (1965). (*SJ*)

TRANSLATION, EXPOSITION, AND NOTES

I. A HEBREW SINNER SAVED (1:1–2:10[11])

A. JONAH'S DISOBEDIENCE (1:1–3)

A message from Yahweh was received by Jonah son of Amittai: 2 "Go off and visit the vast city of Nineveh and denounce it, because their wickedness down there has come to my notice." 3 Jonah did go off—in the direction of Tarshish, running away from Yahweh.

The story opens with a time-honored expression for the communication of the divine will to a prophet.[1] It has an awesome aura about it, and deliberately evokes such prophetic narratives as 1 K. 17:8; Jer. 1:4; Hag. 1:3. The Judean circle of hearers would respond affirmatively to this statement of prophetic revelation, and by it would be conditioned psychologically to open their minds to the narrative and to assimilate it favorably into their religious frame of reference. Their emotional compliance receives a jolt, however, with the mention of *Jonah son of Amittai*. Old political feelings ran deep in their souls. Was not this a prophet of the Northern Kingdom, which had seceded from Judah and Davidic rule? Moreover, far from fulminating against the sins of this rebel state, like such fine prophets as Amos and Hosea, had he not forecast the extension of its frontiers under King Jeroboam II (2 K. 14:25)? True, Yahweh in his mysterious providence had inspired the prophecy and its fulfilment, but the nationalistic sentiments have for Judeans something of the flavor Hitler's *Lebensraum* policy has for non-Germans. A shadow of prejudice has been cast over the initial favor with which the story was first received. If Jonah is to be the hero of this prophetic narrative, he will be an unpopular one, whom it will be easier to condemn than to applaud. This reaction is one the narrator has intended. In the course of his story he is to exploit the emotional tension created by his

1. Cf. O. Grether, *Name und Wort Gottes im AT*. BZAW 64 (1934), pp. 67f.; he observed that the formula is used of prophets 112 times.

opening statement, a tension between saying "yes" to God's message and "no" to God's messenger.

The divine commission is presented in orthodox fashion. It follows a familiar pattern, such as is represented in 1 K. 17:8, "Arise, go to Zarephath."[2] The task of denouncing *Nineveh*[3] is in line with the tradition of Judean prophecy represented by Zephaniah (2:13) and Nahum. Here surely was a task more worthy of Jonah than the jingoistic pronouncement of 2 K. 14:25. In the minds of the listening circle Nineveh stood for the essence of human self-exaltation and anti-God power. Was it not from the time of Sennacherib the capital of Assyria? And did not Sennacherib call himself "the great king"[4] and think of himself as the great "I am" in his program of world conquest?[5] These are the associations that would come crowding into the minds of those who heard mention of *the vast* (lit. "great") *city of Nineveh*. It corresponds to that cipher for Rome which throbs through Revelation: "Babylon the great." This phrase, too, tolls like a bell through the book of Jonah (1:2; 3:2, 3; 4:11), to be given a twist in its last occurrence. But at the moment it connotes what is big and bad, an intolerable affront to God.

In accord with the best prophetic tradition Yahweh is represented as the Lord of the nations, to whom the whole world is held morally accountable. If Nineveh is great, God is greater, for he speaks from heaven above. The simple way in which the reason for denouncing Nineveh is expressed recalls the divine statement in Gen. 18:20, 21 concerning Sodom and Gomorrah, an allusion that is to reappear in 3:4. Nineveh is another Sodom, an unhallowed haunt of *wickedness* meriting destruction. Perhaps the listening circle would be reminded too of Nahum's last words about Nineveh's downfall in 612 B.C.

> *All who hear the news about you*
> *clap their hands at you.*
> *For who has not experienced*
> *your unremitting wickedness?* (Nah. 3:19)

True, there it was seventh-century imperialistic oppression and here it is immorality within the city walls, but mental association transcends such barriers. What a privilege for Jonah to be selected for such a role as the two angels played who visited Sodom as agents of divine destruction (Gen. 19:1, 13)! This was an honor that fell to few prophets, since they mostly prophesied their oracles of doom against foreign nations within the safety of Israel's own frontiers.

Jonah did not go. He went off on a journey of his own devising instead of where God sent him. By comparison with 1 K. 17:10 the story was

2. Heb. *qûm lēḵ,* as here; cf. Jer. 13:6.
3. Assyria's capital for nearly a century before its fall in 612 B.C. It was sited on the left bank of the Tigris opposite present-day Mosul in Iraq. See the comments on 3:3; 4:11.
4. 2 K. 18:28. The phrase corresponds to the Akkadian royal title.
5. Cf. Isa. 10:12–14. Heb. *gōḏel,* "arrogance," in v. 12 is lit. "greatness."

expected, according to the norms of prophetic narrative, to continue: "He set off and went to Nineveh," as in fact 3:3 does.[6] The pattern is broken by deliberate discord, and a strong sense of shock is created. There were precedents indeed for protest at a divine command,[7] for natural shrinking at the first hearing of an overwhelming summons, but who had dared disobey the call of God?

"The lion roars—who does not fear?
The Lord Yahweh has spoken—who can but prophesy?"
(Amos 3:8)

Those semiconscious feelings of distasteful resentment aroused by v. 1 now have fuel to feed on and can flare up in open shock. The prophetic hero becomes the villain, despised and degraded. A murmur would go round the listening circle: "Just what you would expect of a northern prophet." Nineveh, the erstwhile villain, fades into the background by contrast with this new effrontery. No reason is given for the disobedience.[8] Jonah is simply stamped as a deserter from God's army, running as hard as he can away from the enemy's direction.

Verse 3 is cleverly structured by means of repetition to make the narrator's point, as a more literal rendering and a layout of the various elements disclose:

Jonah rose to run away to Tarshish from Yahweh's presence
and he went down to Joppa
and he found a ship
going to Tarshish
and he paid its fare
and he went down into it
to go with them to Tarshish from Yahweh's presence.[9]

Jonah does the exact opposite of what he is told. The narrator makes him act out a defiant "no" to Yahweh's call to Nineveh. *Tarshish* was at the other end of the world from Nineveh.[10] It was the *ultima Thule* of the OT

6. Cf. 1 K. 18:2; 19:7; Jer. 13:2, 5, 7.
7. Ex. 4:10, 13; Jer. 1:6.
8. Jonah is punished because he disobeys, not because of his lack of compassion (4:2; Cohn, *JLBE,* p. 55). One must respect the narrator's sequence: there is a time to explain, but it is not yet.
9. N. Lohfink, *BZ* 5(1961), p. 200; P. L. Trible, *SBJ,* p. 206.
10. It is usually identified with Tartessos in southwest Spain near the mouth of the Guadalquivir. In Jer. 10:9 Tarshish is a source of silver and in Ezek. 27:12 of tin, iron, and lead. This information accords with Pausanias' reference to Tartessos as a source of metal and to Pliny's description of Spain as rich in lead, iron, bronze, silver, and gold. R. D. Barnett, *Journal of Hellenic Studies* 73 (1953), p. 142, n. 3, and *Antiquity* 32 (1958), p. 226, identifies with Tarsus in Cilicia, following Josephus *Ant.* ix.10.2; but the narrative seems to require a location in the far west (cf. Dahood, *Pss 1,* p. 292, *ad* Ps. 48:7[8]). W. F. Albright, *BASOR* 83 (1941), pp. 17–22, and *The Bible and the Ancient Near East.* Albright Festschrift (1961), pp. 347, 360f., referred to a ninth-century Phoenician inscription found at ancient Nora in Sardinia which mentions Tarshish, probably as the Phoenician name of Nora. Although he claimed that phonetic objections that have been raised against relating Tarshish and Tartessos

(Robinson), one of those far-off places where Yahweh had not revealed himself, "which have not heard my fame or seen my glory" (Isa. 66:19). As such, it is an ideal destination in the escape plan Jonah devises.[11] His rejection of the divine commission is shown in concrete terms as a desire to put as much distance as possible between himself and the place where Yahweh revealed his word to him, "that he might withdraw himself from the service of God" (Calvin).[12] The plethora of verbs indicate the hustle and bustle in which he engages in order to achieve this self-centered end. At the harbor of Joppa he boards a Phoenician cargo ship[13] to travel all the way to Tarshish in the west, instead of starting out on the eastward trek by land to Nineveh.

The Hebrews were landsmen with little experience of the sea. That Jonah was prepared to entrust himself to an ocean-going boat rather than face up to God's call must have struck the hearers as proof positive of his mad determination. Surely no good can come of this foolhardy venture. Jonah will not be allowed to snap his fingers at Yahweh and get away with it. In his hasty plans he has reckoned without the Hound of Heaven. It is as the psalmist said:

Where could I run away from your presence. . . ?
If I . . . lived far across the sea,
even there your hand would . . . take hold of me.
(Ps. 139:7, 9)

B. JONAH'S PUNISHMENT; HEATHEN HOMAGE (1:4–16)

But Yahweh hurled a strong wind onto the sea: so violent was the storm at sea that the ship thought it would break up. 5 The sailors grew frightened

---

are not cogent, he located the biblical Tarshish in Sardinia. He defined it as "smelting plant, metal refinery," a *taf'îl* form from a root *ršš*, "smelt," used as a place name. "There were doubtless at least as many Phoenician settlements which bore the name *Tarshish* as there were 'New Towns' [= Carthage]."

11. The infinitive of purpose introduces the narrative device of *erlebte Rede* (M. Weiss, *VT* 13 [1963], p. 460; Cohn, *JLBE*, p. 73), whose purpose has been defined as "direct introduction of the reader into the interior life of the character, without any interventions in the way of explanation or commentary on the part of the author" (R. Wellek and A. Warren, *Theory of Literature* [³1966], p. 244, citing E. Dujardin).

12. Cf. T "from prophesying in Yahweh's name" and the regular idiom for prophetic service, "stand before Yahweh" (1 K. 17:1; Jer. 15:19). "Jonah is aware he cannot escape Yahweh's power (1:9), but thinks he can avoid another confrontation" (G. M. Landes, KBJ, p. 20; cf. Keil; von Orelli; Delcor; Trible, *SBJ*, p. 267; Rudolph). Yahweh's localized presence and universal power are twin tenets of OT faith: cf. Ps. 95:2–5.

13. During the Persian period Tyre and Sidon controlled Joppa (Y. Aharoni, *The Land of the Bible* [E.T. 1967], pp. 17f., referring to *ANET*, p. 505). On the basis of Assyrian reliefs at Nineveh depicting the flight of King Luli from Tyre, a Tarshish ship (cf. Isa. 2:16; 60:9, etc.) can be described as a long bireme with a pointed ram, having a complement of some 15 or 25 oars a side in two banks, i.e., a total of 30 or 50 oars, with a hurricane deck and a single mast carrying a square sail (Barnett, *Antiquity* 32 [1958], pp. 226f.).

and each of them appealed to his god. They hurled the cargo overboard to lighten the ship, so that it would not weigh them down.[14] *Meanwhile Jonah had gone down into the hold below deck and fallen fast asleep. 6 The captain came across him and said, "What are you doing fast asleep?*[15] *Get up and call upon your god. Perhaps that god*[16] *will pay heed to us and stop us from perishing."*

7 The crew said to one another, "Come on, let's throw lots to find out who is to blame for this plight we are in." They did throw lots, and Jonah's lot came up, 8 whereupon they said to him, "Tell us, please. Who is to blame for this plight we are in? What is your business and where do you come from? What is your country and of what nationality are you?" 9 "I am a Hebrew,"[17] *he told them, "and I worship Yahweh, the God of heaven, maker of land and sea." 10 The men were filled with fearsome awe. "What is this you have done!" they said to him, knowing that he was running away from Yahweh because he had just told them. 11 "What shall we do with you to make the sea stop attacking us*[18] *and grow calm, because the sea is getting roughter?" 12 "Pick me up," he told them, "and hurl me over the side, and then the sea will stop attacking you and grow calm. I know I am to blame for this violent storm that has hit you." 13 However, the men rowed for the shore, to get the ship back. They failed, finding the sea getting rougher and resisting their efforts. 14 So they called upon Yahweh, "We implore you, Yahweh, please do not let us perish to pay for this man's life. Do not punish us for murder.*[19] *You have acted in accord with your own will, Yahweh." So saying, 15 they picked Jonah up and hurled him overboard. Thereupon the sea stopped its raging. 16 The men were filled with fearsome awe of Yahweh, and they offered him sacrifice and made vows.*

4, 5 The listeners' morbid foreboding and pious craving that sin should not go unpunished are soon satisfied. Yahweh, the passive victim of Jonah's tactics, now intervenes in activity of his own.[20] Verse 4 and the first clause of v. 5 introduce the key words which the new passage is to develop: throwing, the sea, fearing. Yahweh throws down upon the sea a gale so furious that even these experienced sailors are frightened:

Behold, the tempest of Yahweh: wrath has appeared,
a whirling tempest which bursts over the heads of the wicked.

14. Lit. "from upon them," implying an irksome burden.
15. For the Heb. construction see GK 120b.
16. Heb. *hā'ᵉlōhîm*—not "God" (KJV, RV); the captain would not regard Yahweh in this absolute way.
17. G "a servant of the Lord," a misreading of *'bry* as *'bdy,* taking the *yoḏ* as an abbreviation for the Tetragrammaton. The change took place under the influence of 2 K. 14:25. All other textual evidence supports MT, which the context requires.
18. The same compound preposition as in v. 5, which here suggests the sea "towering up and crashing down on their decks" (Horton).
19. Lit. "Do not put upon us (the responsibility for) innocent blood," i.e., the death of an innocent man.
20. *Yahweh* ends v. 3 and begins v. 4.

Yahweh's anger will not turn back
until he has accomplished and carried out
the purpose of his mind. (Jer. 23:19, 20)

Yahweh will not be brushed aside and ignored. He sets in motion a series of violent actions: the gale hits the sea, the resultant storm well nigh shivers the timbers of the poor old ship,[21] and the sailors' reaction is one of panic.

Benighted heathens as they are, they resort to S.O.S. prayers. They are doomed to obtain no help from that expedient, because the cosmopolitan crew worship various gods of their own and not Yahweh. It is a case of "All lost! To prayer, to prayer! All lost!"[22] but the situation is too serious for false religion to solve. Yet it is to their credit that even they can see that this is no ordinary storm, but betrays a divine reaction to some grave sin. Their fear is an uneasy feeling that, as they would put it, one of the gods is responsible.[23] Still the storm rages: they can't have called on the right god yet. The listening circle know that this is so. Thrown back on their own resources, the seamen jettison *the cargo,* with which the ship was "filled and heavily laden on the high seas" (Ezek. 27:25). They try to deal with the storm God had thrown upon the sea with a counter-throw. But if religion was no solution, neither is the way of works. The problem lies elsewhere, beyond the sailors' knowledge. One feels sorry for them, caught up unawares in the consequences of the sin of that wretch Jonah, and so the narrator intends.

Where was Jonah all this time? The narrator has a surprise for us. Jonah is sound asleep, lying in a corner of the hold below the busy deck.[24] The storm that so alarmed the crew served only to rock Jonah into deeper slumber, blissfully unaware of all the trouble he is causing. The shock of being called to Nineveh and the journey to the coast have taken toll of his nerves and physique, and he is glad to relax, safe on the ship that would carry him far away, as he thinks, from that appalling experience. Little does he know what has just been told to the listening circle. He is due for a rude awakening.

6–8 The ship's captain, evidently going down into the hold to fetch up the cargo, discovers the sleeping figure among the jars and bales, to his extreme annoyance. This is no time for rest. *Get up and call . . .* —Jonah must have thought he was having a nightmare: these were the very words

21. Heb. *ḥishshᵉḇâ, thought,* has been explained in terms either of personification or of semantic development to "was about to," comparing Aram. and Syr. *bʿh,* "seek, be about to" (used by T here), and French *penser*. G. R. Driver, *Studies in OT Prophecy*. T. H. Robinson Festschrift (1950), pp. 69f., repointed to a Pual *ḥushshᵉḇâ,* "was reckoned." D. N. Freedman, *JBL* 77 (1958), pp. 161ff., followed by Wolff, *SJ,* p. 84, appeals to G "was in danger" and postulates an original *ḥāḇâ,* "was sentenced, was in jeopardy," observing that *ḥûḇ* apparently underlies G's equivalent in Dan. 1:10; the *shin,* he considers, came in from the following *lhšbr*. But G in Jonah does paraphrase on occasion. MT can be retained as exhibiting rhetorical animation and assonance.

22. Shakespeare's *The Tempest,* Act I, Scene i, cited by Perowne.

23. S. Plath, *Furcht Gottes. Der Begriff* yr' *im AT* (1963), pp. 21f.

24. Heb. *sᵉp̱înâ* is a ship covered with a deck, from the root *spn,* "cover."

with which God had disturbed his pleasant life a few days before.[25] They have come back to haunt him and remind him reproachfully of his dastardly desertion from his prophetic duty. Rubbing his eyes, Jonah can see that it is not an irate God standing over him, but the captain. He means something else: he is telling Jonah to pray to his God. Pray! If only the captain knew how far spiritually Jonah was from God and what little claim he had upon Yahweh! For the captain, Jonah's God was possibly the one behind the storm. Here was one god not represented among the crew, and it was essential to tap every divine possibility. "That way we must hit the right god sooner or later, and he'll stop the storm."[26] Or rather, he *may* graciously "spare us a thought" (JB, NEB) and come to our aid,[27] for the captain is too good a theologian, polytheist though he is, to make man the master of such a situation. If Yahweh had sent the storm, they were all in his hands: it was not for Jonah to dictate to him to stop it. He at least is alive to the sovereignty of Yahweh and the need for a tentative, submissive approach to his inscrutable will. Grudgingly one has to admire this enlightened pagan who outshines Jonah in his grasp of divine truth.

Jonah doesn't pray. Doubtless he murmurs something and lurches after the captain up to the rolling deck. There they find the captain's men discussing a further way of resolving their religious problem, for that is what the storm is to them, as it is to the circle around the narrator. The men have by now thrown the cargo overboard, but although there is less chance of the ship sinking, the storm shows no sign of abating. They are sure that among their number is a guilty individual who, like a magnet, has attracted to the ship this demonstration of divine anger. For heathen and Hebrew alike there was a sure way of finding the culprit, a way the listeners would approve as fair, according as it did with their own highest traditions. When Jonathan inadvertently violated Saul's oath in the Michmash campaign against the Philistines, was it not the sacred lot that eventually found him out?[28] When lots were thrown, "the result comes wholly from Yahweh" (Prov. 16:33). By this means of providential guidance the person whose guilt had unleashed destructive force upon them all could be isolated.

Of course, Jonah won the lottery—or lost it.[29] As soon as he is singled out as the culprit, the crew want to know the whys and wherefores of the affair. They bombard the mysterious passenger with religiously loaded questions.[30] First, in order to make quite sure that no mistake has been made,

25. Heb. *qûm lēḵ*, both here and in v. 2.
26. W. Mankowitz, "It Should Happen to a Dog," *Religious Drama 3*, ed. M. Halverson (1959), p. 128.
27. Cf. Ps. 40:17(18). G S correctly paraphrase as "save." T "have compassion" is closer, for *'št* connotes "kindly interest" (H. L. Ginsberg, SVT 16 [1967], pp. 81f.).
28. 1 Sam. 14:40–42; cf. Josh. 7:16–18; 1 Sam. 10:20f.; Acts 1:26.
29. For lottery methods in the OT see Mic. 2:5 and the appended note.
30. Cohn, *JLBE*, p. 91. Good, *IOT*, p. 44, has missed the point in imagining here the "wildly incongruous" situation of a request for "a thumbnail biography in the midst of a howling storm."

they ask him to confirm the way the lot went, for they must be sure and will not condemn him before he has given evidence on his own behalf.[31] They inquire why he is taking the sea trip, for that will afford a clue to explain the storm. Jonah will shortly give the significant answer that he is *running away from Yahweh* (v. 10). They ply him for information concerning his nationality, for from that they may deduce which god is responsible, since nationality and religion went together in the ancient Near East. The barrage of questions fired in quick succession are psychologically true to life as an outlet for emotions aroused by the implacable storm.

9–12 Jonah's reply goes to the heart of the matter. Verses 9, 10a represent the focal point of the section. The whole section, vv. 4–16, has a concentric structure, with vv. 9, 10a as the nucleus; the elements leading up to it are supplied with matching counterparts in the sequel.[32] This core takes up the motifs expressed at the outset in vv. 4, 5a—Yahweh, the sea, and fear— and develops them. Jonah answers the last question first, explaining that he is *a Hebrew,* the term generally used by the people of Israel in describing themselves to foreigners.[33] Since Yahweh was "the God of the Hebrews" (Ex. 3:18), this means that Jonah is a worshipper of Yahweh. *Worship* is literally "fear," but its use on Jonah's lips contrasts starkly with its meaning in vv. 5, 10. Jonah's fear is a feeble thing, for all its orthodoxy, compared with the numinous awe of the seamen, which Jonah is deliberately not recorded as sharing. The runaway prophet is shown in a bad light: crew and captain can teach him many a lesson about his own faith.

The epithet *God of heaven* which Jonah appends to the divine name, although an ancient one (Gen. 24:3, 7), sprang into popularity in the Persian period after the exile. It identified Yahweh as the supreme deity, the ultimate source of all power and authority. Jews used it especially in contacts with Gentiles, who it was assumed possessed a knowledge of Yahweh's universal sovereignty as distinct from the Jews' insight into the purposes of Yahweh as

31. Most scholars delete the first question because (1) it is superfluous since the lot has already answered it; (2) the Heb. interrogative compound reads like a rather awkward rendering of *b^e^shell^e^mî* in v. 7 and so the question appears to be a marginal gloss incorporated into the text; and (3) it is omitted in G codices B and S and in several Heb. mss. Ehrlich retained MT by understanding *mî*, "who?" in a relative sense: "you on whose account." P. Joüon, *Biblica* 10 (1929), p. 418, read *mâ* for *mî* with T: "for what reason this disaster has befallen us." But MT is permissible in the normal sense. Non-Septuagintalists tend to take the oddities of B and S too seriously: here both Ziegler and Rahlfs in their editions judge that the clause has been dropped by homoeoteleuton. The Heb. mss. probably attest nothing more than the omission of an 18-letter line for the same reason. Keil, Perowne, and von Orelli justify the question as seeking confirmation. Such caution accords with the sailors' reluctance to take an irrevocable step in v. 13. R. Pesch, *Biblica* 47 (1966), p. 579, followed by Cohn, *JLBE,* p. 14, argues that the concentric structure of the passage demands the retention of the question as a counterpart to that in v. 7: the similarity of phrase in the sailors' speeches in vv. 7, 8 matches that of *What is this you have done!* and *What shall we do with you?* in their speeches of vv. 10, 11.

32. See the Introduction.

33. Gen. 40:15; Ex. 1:19.

"God of our fathers."[34] By this title Yahweh is presented as no mere local deity, but one to whom all peoples may look for help.[35] This universalistic note is reinforced by the claim that Yahweh is *maker of land and sea*. It is a credal confession which echoes such cultic statements in the Psalms as

> *The sea belongs to him, for he made it;*
> *so does the dry land, which his hands molded.* (Ps. 95:5)

The implication of the confession of faith is that the source of the storm is none other than Yahweh who made the sea. The wonder is that Jonah can recite such a creed and yet show disrespect to the commands of the God whose sovereignty it celebrates.

The narrator brings out the poor nature of Jonah's fear by jumping immediately to the sailors' reaction. If the storm created in them a numinous dread, identification of the God who was responsible fills them even more with holy fear. *The men* realize their humanity in the face of such divine power.[36] As Jonah answers their questions and tells them the sorry tale of his flight from this very God,[37] they become more and more horrified. No wonder Yahweh has sent such a father and mother of a storm, for so grave a sin deserves no less a show of wrath.[38] "How could you do such a thing!" they exclaim, aghast at Jonah's insolent temerity. They go on to make another vocal contribution, so that their pair of speeches in vv. 7, 8 correspond with a further pair. Since it is Jonah's God who is behind the worsening storm, he ought to know how best the tempestuous sea can be calmed.[39] So they ask him what should be done with him, for Jonah is the key not only to the storm but to its stilling, and they cannot withstand the sea's attack much longer. Jonah's reply is the counterpart to the captain's outburst in v. 6 and is a crucial step forward in the development of the plot. The captain had posed the stark alternatives: "Pray or we perish," but Jonah knows that the upshot must be that he should perish. He is the target of Yahweh's weapon and sooner or later it will catch him. He accepts his fate and is prepared to face it at once. He replies at last to a question put to him by the sailors earlier. Yes, he admits his responsibility for the storm. The piety

34. D. K. Andrews, "Yahweh the God of the Heavens," *The Seed of Wisdom*. T. J. Meek Festschrift (1964), pp. 45–57. The title occurs in the Elephantine papyri. Most of the OT instances appear in 2 Chr., Ezra, Neh., Ps. 136, and Daniel.

35. Wolff, *SJ*, p. 81.

36. Cohn, *JLBE*, pp. 70, 91.

37. Some scholars, e.g., Wellhausen, Sellin, Bewer, Weiser, Smart, Trible (*SBJ*, p. 89), delete the final clause in v. 10 as a gloss. But most agree that "the narrative hurries along and the author summarizes the full conversation" (Bird; cf. Calvin, Delcor, Knight, Keller, Wolff [*SJ*, p. 42], Rudolph). Lohfink, *loc. cit.*, pp. 193–95, stresses that this is one of a number of cases in the book where the religious category is put first and other considerations are relegated to second place; the double causal *kî*, to which objection has been raised, has many parallels as "the proximate and ultimate cause respectively" (BDB, p. 474a).

38. Plath, *op. cit.*, p. 105, compares Isa. 25:3; Zech. 9:5, for fear as the response of observers of Yahweh's wrath.

39. Bewer compares 2 K. 17:26. Myers suggests that the sailors requested an oracle (cf. Judg. 13:8; 1 Sam. 6:2).

of the seamen has evidently banished his nonchalant indifference and touched his conscience. By now he has realized how terrible is the sin that has provoked this terrible storm. The only way to appease the tempest of Yahweh's wrath is to abandon himself to it as just deserts for his sin. His willingness to die is an indication that he realizes his guilt before God.[40]

13–16 The *men,* overawed at the power of Jonah's God, are unwilling to take the possibly fatal step of committing Jonah to a watery grave, as their apprehensive prayer in v. 14 reveals. But they do want to rid themselves of his malignant presence. Jonah's diagnosis is certainly correct, but is his prescription the right one? Since the storm had hindered their voyage, perhaps Yahweh wanted Jonah returned to shore. Just as in the corresponding part of the concentric narrative (v. 5), they resort to their own efforts to escape the peril of the sea. "All these aids had to be shattered, all solutions blocked and man's possibilities hopelessly outclassed by the power of the challenge" (Ellul). So it is of no avail when they brave the dangerous reefs[41] in an attempt to land Jonah and thus to bring him back to the place where he can obey Yahweh's command. Why? Was not the fish merely Yahweh's alternative device to do the very thing the sailors were trying to do? No, their failure indicates the narrator's conviction that it was not sufficient to put the clock back to a time before Jonah's rebellion. Jonah deserves to die, and he has himself shown his awareness of this in his plea to the sailors to throw him into the sea. He is ready to surrender to the divine wrath. In fact Jonah is to be saved—yet his life can only be saved by a signal demonstration of the grace of Yahweh. But this lies in the future. The message of vv. 13f. is that nothing less than death is Jonah's deserved fate. "The soul that sins will die" (Ezek. 18:4, 20).

The crew, realizing that they cannot evade Jonah's drastic solution, are properly aware that they may face a new danger by so doing: they may incur the curse of bloodguiltiness.[42] They are outsiders, and not a properly constituted court which can sift the total evidence at length. If there is a shadow of doubt, Jonah's patron may make reprisals for the death of his devotee. So they are driven to pray to his God and plead their warrant for dropping Jonah to certain death. They have a commendable respect for Yahweh and his power. Their passionate prayer, formally a lament consisting of an invocation, a doubly formulated petition, and a motivation, is the structural counterpart of the earlier one to their assorted deities in v. 5. Clearly they have taken to heart a great deal of truth about Yahweh since then. In a sense they pray the prayer that Jonah would not pray at the captain's bidding; the wish not to perish ends one and begins the other. Their warrant is based on Yahweh's own actions:

40. Verse 12 is neither Jonah's final solution to evade his mission (Trible, *SBJ,* p. 80, following Haller) nor a gallant bid of vicarious sacrifice (Smart, Brockington, Keller, Ellul), which would upset the psychological tone of the chapter, since Jonah is the villain, not the hero.

41. Bewer observed that the open sea is safer in storms along the Palestinian coast.

42. Cf. Deut. 21:8; 2 Sam. 1:6; 14:7; Jer. 26:15.

For he commanded, and raised the stormy wind
which lifted up the waves. (Ps. 107:25)

The onslaught of the storm, which had moreover prevented them from reaching the coast, and the verdict of the lot were indications of Yahweh's purpose. Jonah, sinful victim of Yahweh's wrath, seemed doomed to die. So, viewing themselves as agents of divine justice, they tossed Jonah into the raging sea below. They thus achieved the intent for which Yahweh had first tossed the gale upon the sea; v. 15 forms the counterpart to v. 4.

The result was dramatic: the storm was switched off and the sea became docile. Its fury, eloquent symbol of Yahweh's anger,[43] subsides now that Yahweh's dire will is done. Thereby also the sailors have the answer to their prayer. The narrative deals with this reaction before turning to poor Jonah, exhibiting the author's principle of giving priority to religious themes.[44] If their awe at the storm was great, no less so was their reaction to its cessation. "Who is this that even wind and sea obey him?"[45] Moreover, they have escaped both the storm and their disposal of Jonah, scot-free. Both the justice and the power of Yahweh command their reverence. They give vent to their relief and gratitude by sacrificing to Jonah's God.[46] Their *sacrifice* and *vows* to offer him still more later are a typical Israelite response to Yahweh's deliverance from danger and distress:

I shall offer to you a sacrifice of thanksgiving. . . .
I shall pay my vows to Yahweh. (Ps. 116:17f.)

They offer to Yahweh their Hallelujah in devout recognition of his saving power. How amazing that these heathen play the part of pious Israelites! The listening circle have been given much food for thought. The prophet, usually hero of prophetic narratives, has turned into the villain of the piece and is now disposed of—good riddance! Beside the Gentile sailors Jonah had cut a sorry figure. These paid extras in Jonah's story have drawn nearer to Yahweh as Jonah's sinfulness and liability to punishment have been gradually exposed. Some stereotyped conventions of the Hebrew religious ideology have been thrown overboard with Jonah. The listeners have been induced to turn completely against an Israelite prophet and to view Gentile dogs with increasing admiration and respect. These attitudes are seeds the narrator has sown to harvest later.

If Jonah has sunk in the hearers' estimation and the seamen have risen, the author has remained true to a basic tenet: Yahweh has emerged as the hero. The story begins with his word of moral rule and ends with his worship. His almighty power and inexorable justice have been demonstrated. He has the sea in his hand; he controls the destiny of those who venture upon it. In fact the sea, a perpetual menace throughout the narrative,

43. Heb. *z'p* is commonly used of divine and human anger.
44. Cf. v. 10 and n. 37.
45. Mark 4:41 and parallels.
46. "How the detail of sacrifice was handled on board was a detail outside the range of the author's interest" (Brockington).

mentioned ten times in the Hebrew text, has had two vital roles, first as instrument of Yahweh's wrath against Jonah's rebellion and secondly as the means of revealing his might to the Gentile crew.[47] Above all, the story thus far extols the fact that sin does not pay and that, try as the sinner will to escape, he is God's marked man. The wages of sin are death.

C. JONAH'S RESCUE (1:17–2:10[2:1–11])

1. God's Grace (1:17[2:1])

Meanwhile Yahweh arranged for an enormous fish to swallow Jonah. He stayed inside the fish for three days and three nights.

The gracious gift of God is life. He does not abandon his servant to death, but snatches from its clutches the drowning man. To the thrill of the hearers the key figure is saved at the last moment from a seemingly inescapable plight. Yahweh mounts a special rescue operation: *an enormous fish*[48] plays the astounding part of a submarine to pick up Jonah from the murky seaweed at the bottom of the ocean and transport him safely to the mainland. The fish stands for the amazing grace of Yahweh, which came down to where he was and lifted him to new life. The Lord of the sea is Lord also of its creatures, and his providential control extends over both. Contrary to all expectation Jonah does not die. He is spared the due reward of his sins. The deliverance of Jonah is a prime factor in the story as a whole, not only for its own sake but for its implications in the later part of the narrative. It is a theme the author means to stamp upon the minds and memories of the listening circle, and it is for this reason that a wonderful device is employed, the use of a giant fish by which to effect not only Jonah's rescue but also his conscious preservation inside it. The significance of the period of *three days and three nights* is uncertain.[49] Is it to enhance the miraculous nature of the episode, implying a far longer period than Jonah might have been expected to survive?[50] G. M. Landes, noting the many OT cases where *three days* is used of a journey, has compared the use of the present phrase in a Sumerian myth apparently to denote the time it takes to travel to the underworld. Accordingly in the context of the following psalm he has interpreted it as the period of a journey back from Sheol to the world of the living represented by the dry land.[51] If his interpretation is correct, the motif emphasizes the great

47. Cohn, *JLBE,* p. 92.
48. "It is idle to seek its name or to consider zoological possibilities with a view to identifying the species. It is idle to ask whether the Mediterranean could have contained such a monster. That is not the question. The real question is: Of what is this fish the sign?" (Ellul). G *kētos,* echoed in Matt. 12:40, is any sea monster or large fish.
49. For the NT application of the motif see the Introduction.
50. J. B. Bauer, *Biblica* 39 (1958), p. 356.
51. *JBL* 86 (1967), pp. 446–450.

gulf between death and life and the difficulties God gloriously overcame in rescuing his servant from his merited doom.

2. *Jonah's Praise (2:1–9[2–10])*

He prayed to Yahweh his God from inside the fish:
2 *"I called out of my distress*
to Yahweh and he answered me. 3+2
From Sheol's belly I cried for help,
you heard my voice. 3+2
3 *You threw me into the heart of the seas,*[1]
the current[2] *overwhelmed me.* 3+2
All your breakers and billows
passed right over me. 3+2
4 *I said, 'I have been banished*
out of your sight.' 3+2
But I shall look once more
at your holy temple. 3+2

5 *Water was all round me up to my neck,*
the ocean overwhelmed me. 3+2
Seaweed was wrapped round my head
6 *at the bases*[3] *of the mountains.* 3+2
I went down to the underworld,[4]
its bars closed behind me for ever. 2+3
But you brought me up alive from the Pit,
Yahweh, my God. 3+2
7 *As I was losing consciousness*
I remembered Yahweh.[5] 3+2

1. MT has *m^e^tsûlâ*, "depth," before this phrase. It is probably to be deleted with *BHK*, Bewer, etc. (cf. *BHS*), on both grammatical and metrical grounds. A. R. Johnson, *Studies in OT Prophecy*. T. H. Robinson Festschrift (1950), p. 84, n. 9, explains it well as a gloss not on the following phrase, which hardly requires explanation, but on the next word *nāhār,* here used in a specialized sense. Dahood, *Pss 1,* p. 202, pleads for MT as an instance of a double-duty preposition, but in the example he calls "equally good," Hab. 3:8b, the preposition occurs with the first word, unlike here.
2. This meaning accords with Ps. 24:2 and Ugar. usage (Johnson, *loc. cit.,* p. 84; Dahood, *Pss 1,* p. 151).
3. Heb. *qits^e^ḇê* recurs in Sir. 16:19 in parallelism with "the foundations of the world." An emendation to *qats^e^wê,* "ends" (*BHS*), is thus unwarranted, as Bewer realized. Its precise significance is not clear. Most infer from the root meaning "cut (off)" a sense "extremity" (BDB) and so "bottom." G. R. Driver, *JTS* 35 (1934), p. 382, rendered "crevasses," comparing G and a cognate Arab. term meaning "channel, duct." The first two words of v. 6 are generally taken with v. 5 for the sake of meter.
4. Heb. *hā'ārets,* "earth," occasionally has this connotation (e.g., Ex. 15:12; Isa. 29:4), like its Akk. and Ugar. counterparts (Bewer; F. M. Cross, Jr., and D. N. Freedman, *JNES* 14 [1955], pp. 247f.; Dahood, *Pss. 1,* p. 106; N. Tromp, *Primitive Conceptions of Death and the Underworld in the OT*. Biblica et Orientalia 21 [1969], pp. 23f.).
5. Dahood, *Pss 3,* p. 270, revocalizes the object sign as *'attā,* "you," which he claims can be used as a pronominal object; this expedient would eliminate the unique *'ēṯ* and avoid the jarring shift from second to third person (*Ephemerides theologicae lovanienses* 44 [1968], p.

and my prayer reached you
in your holy temple. 3+2

8 *Those who pay court to*[6] *false idols*
spurn God's grace to them; 3+2
9 *but I with praising voice*
shall sacrifice to you. 3+2
What I have vowed I shall pay.
Salvation belongs to Yahweh.'' 3+2

Sensing himself to be safe in his odd conveyance, Jonah prays. It is a prayer of thanksgiving for deliverance from a watery grave. The narrator has evidently selected it from an existing collection and inserted it to give voice to Jonah's sentiments.[7] It was remarkably fitting, although its present use is rather different from its original setting. Doubtless it was known to the listening circle and its inclusion lent verisimilitude. It related the story to real life—in the religious community—and would strike a spiritual chord in the listeners' hearts as they heard God's goodness sincerely praised.

Four typical elements of the psalm of thanksgiving are reproduced: an introductory summary of answered prayer, reports of the personal crisis and divine rescue, and a vow of praise.[8] These elements are woven into a composition of three stanzas, the first and second of six lines (vv. 2–4, 5–7), and a short one of three.[9] The first two, whose conclusions are marked by a refrain *(to) your holy temple,* are parallel in thought.[10] Apart from the motif of answered prayer which opens the first and closes the second, the other themes occur in the same order: the overwhelming crisis,[11] the consequent banishment from Yahweh's sight to Sheol, and the assurance of new life with God.[12] The psalm is bound together by an intricate pattern of recurring motifs and phraseology.[13]

---

37). But the shift is paralleled in the report of prayer in v. 2; a ''unique *'ēṯ*'' occurs too in Ps. 53:3 (contrast vv. 6, 7); 100:2 (contrast v. 4); finally, the meter does not support Dahood's suggestion. The particle has point in its wider context: listeners would be reminded of *'eṯ-yhwh* in 1:9, 16, where Yahweh's power over the sea was first affirmed and then confirmed.

6. The Qal occurs in Ps. 31:6(7). For the Piel here G. R. Driver, *loc. cit.*, pp. 384f., compares Akk. *shummuru,* ''carefully regard (the name or deity of a god).''

7. See the Introduction.

8. C. Westermann, *The Praise of God in the Psalms* (E.T. 1965), pp. 103f.

9. Cf. the strophic structure of Mic. 1:10–16.

10. Cohn, *JLBE*, p. 93.

11. Heb. *y^{e}sōḇ^{e}ḇēnî* closes the initial lines in vv. 3, 5(4, 6).

12. This structure depends on retaining MT in v. 4b(5b); see n. 17 below.

13. Apart from the repetition already mentioned, note the occurrence of *Yahweh* at beginning and end and twice in the second strophe, and of *voice* at beginning and end. *But I (wa'^{a}nî)* begins the last pair of lines in the first and third strophes, and *'ālay,* ''upon me,'' occurs in the first and the second (vv. 3, 7[4, 8]). *Nep̱esh, neck,* ''life,'' appears twice in the second strophe. This study of structure and distribution is necessary as ''an attempt to appreciate concisely, abstractly and rather woodenly the unconscious and intuitive perfection of a poet's rhythm and a master's style'' (J. D. Crossan, *NTS* 18 [1972], p. 294).

2–4 Jonah recalls his earlier prayer offered in the sea—so different from this one—in which he poured out his perilous need in entreaty. He mentions it as a thing of the past: now he can rejoice that his prayer has been answered.[14] His plight had threatened his very existence: he had been in *Sheol's belly*. Sheol, the world of the dead, is depicted as a monster in whose maw Jonah was trapped.[15] He was as good as dead before Yahweh graciously answered his appeal. He had no claim upon God, for he acknowledges that his very plight was the result of Yahweh's own action, divine punishment for his sin. The listening circle know that the sailors who had prayed in 1:14 for their action to coincide with Yahweh's will were actually agents of that will. The sea, like the sailors, had been God's instrument in inflicting upon Jonah his punitive purpose. Another psalm brings out this implication:

The weight of wrath lies upon me
and you have afflicted me with all your breakers.

(Ps. 88:7[8])

The rescued prophet remembers his erstwhile lament whose actuality, thank God, has now passed. It had seemed that he was exiled from the living world upon which God looked down in favor.[16] Jonah's self-willed flight from Yahweh's presence in ch. 1 had been ratified by Yahweh's "so be it" in banishment from life. The alternative to saying to God "Thy will be done" is to hear him say eventually, "*Your* will be done." The awful significance of being rejected by God had dawned upon him.

Jonah can voice his despair as the prelude to an expression of confidence,[17] for now he is safe. He has the sure prospect of renewed

14. Reference is made to *Yahweh* in both the second and third persons. This is a feature of thanksgiving psalms, relating to the singer's twofold task, to praise Yahweh and to testify to the congregation of his saving help. In the new use to which the psalm is put, the third person presumably indicates Jonah's musing to himself: cf. Ps. 27:14 after the prayer of vv. 11f.

15. Cf. Prov. 1:12, 15; Isa. 5:14, and the representation of Mot (= Death) as a monster in Ugaritic literature (cf. Tromp. *op. cit.*, p. 26; yet on p. 124 he sees here a reference to mother earth).

16. "Although one tradition represented by Ps. 86:6 and Jon. 2:5 holds that God is absent from Sheol, another school of thought confesses Yahweh's presence even in the realm of the dead [e.g., Ps. 95:4; Prov. 15:11; Amos 9:2]" (Dahood, *Pss 3*, p. 289).

17. An imposing list of scholars, including Wellhausen, *BHK*, Bewer, Sellin, Wade, Weiser, Robinson, and Aalders (cf. RSV, JB, NEB), read *'ēḵ*, "how," with Theodotion for MT *'aḵ*, *but*, "however," thus securing a despairing question in accord with the former line. The lines of the psalm are mainly arranged in synonymous pairs—but note v. 6(7). Similarly Calvin and Rudolph interpret the clause as a wish. An element of assurance is judged premature. But this is to overlook the structure. Johnson, *loc. cit.*, p. 85, refers to van Hoonacker's scheme of three strophes, vv. 2–4, 5f., 7–9(3–5, 6f., 8–10), the first two concluding in joy and the third consisting of joy throughout. Although this scheme is not entirely correct, it is true that the first is rounded off with a reference to Jonah's deliverance, a note struck again in the course of the second. All the ancient evidence supports MT (G *ara* turns the line into a question, "Shall I indeed . . . ?"), which is retained by Keil; Trible, *SBJ*, p. 36; Cohn, *JLBE*, p. 16; Landes, KBJ, p. 6; Keller. The contrasted lines are paralleled in Ps. 31:22(23); Isa. 49:4, where previous short laments are echoed only to be pitted against a new confidence, except that *'āḵēn* stands in the place of *aḵ*. Cf. Ps. 82:6f.; Lam. 3:54; Zeph. 3:7.

fellowship with God in the sanctuary. This is a new Jonah. He is soon to demonstrate a willing spirit by accepting the commission he formerly had rejected. In line with this change of heart, even now in this testimony to God's grace he looks forward to seeking the special presence of God to offer his praise and utter such a cry as the pilgrim's:

How I love your dwelling place, Yahweh of hosts.
My soul longs and pines
for Yahweh's courts.
My heart and flesh sing for joy
to the living God. (Ps. 84:1f.[2f.])

5–7 The second stanza begins by dwelling again on the greatness of the past peril in order to enhance the magnitude of his present salvation and of his saving God. So he goes back to the moment when he was thrown overboard and his head sank beneath the waves,[18] to be entangled among the marine growth at the bottom of the ocean, down at the very roots of *the mountains.*[19] This surely meant the end of him; his descent constituted a journey to *the underworld.* At the very point where in the previous stanza the psalm looked back to Jonah's willful behavior before the storm, there is a further backward glance in this stanza. The narrative at the outset had twice stressed Jonah's going down: his own downward course had proved the start of a slippery slope, ending in the fate that endorsed what Jonah himself had done.[20]

He found himself at death's door. The gates of hell prevailed against him, clanging shut with a terrible finality—or so it seemed.[21] He had reached the land of no return: what awaited him but inescapable death? But God has wrought a miracle. He is the the one "who lifts me up from the gates of death" (Ps. 9:13[14]). Jonah anticipated the apostle's sense of relief and gratitude:

We despaired of life itself. But we had had a death sentence passed against us in order that we might rely not on ourselves but on God.... From so awful a death he rescued us. (2 Cor. 1:8–10)

Up from the virtual grave[22] Jonah was brought by his God, a phrase that expresses a new sense of reliance. As a prophet he has a special relationship with God, which he had spurned.[23]

Now the prodigal returns, drawn closer to him than ever before by the

18. "Verses 5 and 6 form a repetition, in general, of verse 3" (Myers). Cf. A. R. Johnson, *The Vitality of the Individual in the Thought of Ancient Israel* (^{2}1964), p. 93, n. 1. For the rendering *neck,* "throat," cf. Ps. 69:1(2); Isa. 5:14, and Akk. *napishtu* and Ugar. *npš* (L. Dürr, *ZAW* 43 [1925], p. 264; Johnson, *op. cit.,* pp. 4–6; Dahood, *Pss 3,* p. 212).
19. Cf. the note on Mic. 6:2.
20. Cf. Cohn, *JLBE,* p. 93; Landes, KBJ, p. 25.
21. Johnson, *Studies in OT Prophecy,* p. 84, n. 14, renders "whose bars *were to be* about me for ever." The Hebrew lacks a verb.
22. *Pit* is part of the rich OT vocabulary for the world of the dead.
23. Prophetic and cultic usage are combined here, as in Mic. 7:7: see the comment there.

cords of redemptive love. Just as dire physical extremity forced the Prodigal Son to a decision to return home in penitence, so Jonah in his last moments thought of the one who alone could help him as Creator and controller of the sea. Indeed his plight was due to his deliberately forgetting Yahweh and his claims upon him. His remembering takes the active form of prayer.[24] He returns to the opening theme of the song, the boon of answered prayer. His request was accepted; it penetrated to Yahweh so far above the depths of Jonah's underworld experience in his heavenly sanctuary. The last phrase takes up the motif at the end of the first stanza in a final refrain, but now the sense has shifted from earthly model to heavenly prototype of the temple, an easy movement for the Hebrew mind.[25] Jonah avails himself of that help which Yahweh makes available to everyone in covenant relationship with him, his covenant *grace* (v. 8), which is "the looking into the depths by the one who is enthroned in the heights."[26] Thus is demonstrated "the necessity and efficacy of prayer" (Bewer). As in 1:6, prayer is presented as the key to the salvation of the one who would otherwise have perished. Yahweh is both ready and able; so often the fault lies in human stubbornness. "Let us approach confidently the throne of grace to receive mercy and find grace in the form of timely help" (Heb. 4:16).

8, 9 The final, short stanza promises praise. To accentuate the wholeheartedness of his devotion to Yahweh and his awareness of indebtedness to divine grace, the psalmist prefaces his avowal with a reference to idolaters. Bewer correctly saw that v. 8 is prompted not only by the intended contrast with v. 9 but by the personal conviction of Yahweh's readiness to help voiced in v. 7. To ally oneself with idols is folly, for they can give no help. Other gods are contemptuously dismissed as useless idols, worthless nonentities. The contrast in ch. 1 between the ineffectual prayer *each to his own god* and the answered prayer to Yahweh, sovereign over the sea, is echoed in the declaration and denial of vv. 7, 8. In its original setting this section of the psalm envisaged Israelites who betrayed the covenant by resorting to the worship of other gods, and recorded the speaker's dissociation from them in a profession of complete loyalty and so accessibility to Yahweh's favor.[27] Cutting themselves off from Yahweh's aid, they only "multiply their sorrows" (Ps. 16:4). His *grace,* the loyal love that rushes to the aid of his own at their first cry, in the psalm's present context not only glances back to Jonah's deliverance but hints at that of the

24. Cf. B. S. Childs, *Memory and Tradition in Israel*. SBT 37 (1962), pp. 49, 65.
25. "The temple is the place on earth where God rests his foot—it still belongs to the heavenly sphere: Yahweh sits on his throne in heaven as well as in the temple" (R. Knierim, *VT* 18 [1968], p. 52).
26. Westermann, *op. cit.*, p. 121.
27. Cf. Ps. 31:6f.(7f.), where the poet's trust "rests on a firm foundation and cannot come to nought, as is the case with those who rely on 'vain idols' " (Weiser, *The Psalms* [E.T. 1962], p. 277). Renunciation of foreign gods is a feature of many of the Psalms.

sailors who abandoned their own gods and relied upon Yahweh.[28] This hint is to be taken up in ch. 4.

Jonah promises to sing praises to Yahweh in the sanctuary on his return. His song will be accompanied by sacrifices tangibly expressing his thanks for the signal favor shown to him. His present prayer looks back to the past prayer of affliction and forward to his future song of praise. Cultic thanksgiving will be the fulfilment of his vows, for deliverance creates the obligation of worship. The vows link together the previous prayer for help to be given and the praise for help actually received. Customarily made in time of distress, these promises sought a relationship with God which the votive sacrifice and song acknowledged and confirmed:[29]

> *What can I give to Yahweh in return*
> *for all his dealings with me? . . .*
> *Yahweh, I am your servant. . . .*
> *You have loosed my fetters.* (Ps. 116:12, 16)

In a final exultant shout Yahweh is acknowledged as Savior. This is the climax of the psalm. Jonah is now supremely a saved man who has tasted the grace of Yahweh, and who has been delivered from the just reward of his disobedience. It is in this radically new role that he is soon to be addressed by Yahweh again.

Both chs. 1 and 2 end with the theme of sacrifice and vows. The narrator by his inclusion of the psalm immediately after ch. 1 slyly intends his audience to draw a parallel between Jonah's experience and that of the seamen. Both faced a similar crisis, peril from the sea; both cried to Yahweh, acknowledging his sovereignty. Both were physically saved; both offered worship. Ironically Jonah is at last brought to the point the Gentile seamen have already reached. In his supreme devotion he is still only following in the wake of the heathen crew. He who failed to pray, leaving it to the pagan sailors, eventually catches up with their spirit of supplication and submission. "One of the most important things the author would have us see is that when faced with similar perils there is no significant difference between pagans and Jonah concerning prayer, deliverance received and the type of response to the source of salvation. A sincere cry to Yahweh is efficacious whether from a pagan . . . or from one of his own rebellious prophets."[30]

28. Heb. *ḥasdām*. In light of the use of *ḥeseḏ* in the intended parallel 4:2, the suffix is not subjective, "their loyalty" (RSV, NEB), "their devotion" (Johnson), but objective: the divine *ḥeseḏ* previously shown and still available to them (cf. S "your *ḥeseḏ*"). Many, including Sellin, Wade, Delcor, Kraeling, N. Glueck (*Ḥeseḏ in the Bible* [E.T. 1967], p. 67), take the term as a metonym for Yahweh, "their own good God" (A. D. Martin), comparing Ps. 144:2; similarly L. J. Kuyper, *VT* 13 (1963), p. 490, and Rudolph, who, however, assign to *ḥeseḏ* the meaning "strength."
29. Cf. Westermann, *op. cit.*, pp. 77f.
30. Landes, KBJ, p. 26.

3. *God's Last Word (2:10[11])*

Yahweh said the word to the fish and it vomited up Jonah onto the shore.

Reverting to narrative, the storyteller draws the first half of his tale to a close. All this time Jonah has been in the fish travelling back to dry land. Now the journey is over. Yahweh speaks to the fish, his instrument of salvation for Jonah. It obediently and doubtless gladly spews up this indigestible object and swims off with a flick of its tail, its distinguished mission accomplished.

II. HEATHEN SINNERS SAVED (3:1–4:11)

A. JONAH'S OBEDIENCE (3:1–4)

Jonah received Yahweh's message again: 2 "Go off and visit the vast city of Nineveh and proclaim to it the announcement I tell you." 3 Jonah did go off and came to Nineveh, obeying Yahweh's message. Now Nineveh was a vast city, even by God's standards: it took three days to cross. 4 Jonah began crossing the city and after travelling for a day he proclaimed, "Another forty days and Nineveh will be overthrown."

Jonah has been brought back to his point of origin—in place but not in experience. He is now "a new man, a new creature like the one who has passed through baptism" (Ellul). He is fortunate to be reprieved. Had not the disobedient prophet in 1 K. 13 been mangled by a lion? Jonah has been face to face with death—and with exceptional grace which saved him from death. He who had run away from Yahweh met him in the sea and in the fish as Judge and Savior. Paul urged his baptized converts to present themselves in obedience to God "as men once dead and now alive" (Rom. 6:13). Jonah needs no urging: with open ears he listens to the commission he shunned before.[1] For Yahweh patiently gives Jonah a second chance. Like Simon Peter, whose forgiveness for denying Jesus was sealed by the repetition of his initial summons "Follow me,"[2] Jonah is called *again* to be the divine messenger to Nineveh. He has learned his lesson. This time the traditional formula can run its course: *Jonah did go off and came to Nineveh.*[3] The following phrase "according to Yahweh's word" is another ancient element in prophetic narratives.[4] It traces an artistic arc between the original proclamation of the word and its positive implementation. Along with the

1. Cf. Haller.
2. John 21:19; cf. Mark 1:17.
3. Cf. the comment on 1:3.
4. Cf. 1 K. 17:5; Jer. 13:2.

repeated verbs it stresses that the divine will finds fulfilment. Jonah is now as compliant as those other servants, the wind, the sea, and the fish.

The narrator interrupts the flow of the story to tell his audience something about Nineveh. His manner of referring to the city indicates that for him it belonged to the past.[5] Tradition had imparted to him an impression of its colossal size. He elaborates its extent, which the second divine command had mentioned like the first, by describing it as "great to God." This is a striking biblical way of expressing a superlative by bringing into relation with God.[6] Men have their ways of assessing size, but what are they but grasshoppers in his eyes (Isa. 40:22)? God's idea of greatness must be on quite a different scale, yet Nineveh could be called God-sized, for had not Yahweh himself designated it "great"? Nineveh had been so completely destroyed in 612 B.C. that in 401 Xenophon walked past the site without noticing it (*Anabasis* ii.4.28). In the first century B.C. Diodorus Siculus (ii.3) relates with awe the information received from the fourth-century Ctesias that Nineveh's longer pair of walls were 150 stades and the shorter two were 90, a total circumference of 480 stades, about 55 miles. He fittingly commented: "No one afterward built a city of such compass or with walls so magnificent." The narrator's conception of Nineveh was on a similarly grand scale. "Three days' journey," which in light of v. 4 represents the city's diameter,[7] would amount to some such length as 450 stades or over 50 miles, if Herodotus' reasonable definition of a day's march as 17 miles (v. 53) is followed.

This image of Nineveh must have originated in its magnificence during the last eighty years of its existence. Sennacherib early in the seventh century B.C. made it the capital of Assyria and embarked on an extensive building program, enlarging and beautifying it like an ancient Versailles.[8] An inscription of his mentions that formerly the circumference of the city was 9300 cubits, less than 3 miles, but he added 12,515 cubits. This information accords with a survey of the site, which revealed that the city's circumference was 7½ miles, an extraordinary size for an ancient city.[9] The oblong area had on its widest axis a diameter of 3 miles, not 50. It is possible

5. Heb. *hāyᵉṯâ, was,* indicates that the situation came to an end before the time of the author's statement. Cf. G. S. Ogden, "Time and the Verb *hyh* in OT Prose," *VT* 21 (1971), pp. 451–469, who establishes the principle that in direct speech the perfect can appear in a "stative" sense to indicate a present situation, more precisely a situation that arose in the past and persists into the speaker's present time, but in past narrative its usage reveals that a statement about the past is being made.

6. Cf. D. W. Thomas, *VT* 3 (1953), pp. 210–16.

7. Rudolph observes that a circumference of three days' journey, as some have interpreted, is untenable in the context: it would mean a diameter of one day's journey (cf. 1 K. 7:23), but in v. 4 this is only the first stage of crossing the city.

8. See R. C. Thompson and R. W. Hutchinson, *A Century of Exploration at Nineveh* (1929), pp. 120–25.

9. F. Jones, *JRAS* 15 (1855), p. 324.

that the conception of its much greater size was due to a reminiscence of a vast administrative complex, a triangle stretching from Khorsabad in the north to Nimrud in the south and Nineveh in the west.[10] But there remains a lack of harmony with the datum of 4:11.[11] The city which took three days to cross had for the narrator a population of over 120,000, yet that is a reasonable figure for the historical city 3 miles wide.[12] The narrator's intention in recording the colossal dimensions of the city was to convey the magnitude of the prophet's task—and to enhance the sequel.

Jonah trudges for a whole day and yet he has not reached the heart of the city. He feels small, one man against a vast metropolis. Lost like a needle in a haystack inside this gigantic Vanity Fair, this Sodom of a city, the tiny figure feels he can go no further. He stops and shouts out the laconic message with which he has been entrusted. Nineveh's days are numbered: it is to be *overthrown* soon.[13] The verb recalls the overthrow of Sodom and Gomorrah,[14] and once more the narrator dresses Jonah in the garb of the angelic messengers of Gen. 19:1, 13. But there is a difference. Lot's family had only a few hours' notice of Sodom's destruction, dusk to dawn. Nineveh is allowed *forty days'* grace.[15] Why forty? Conceivably as a typical waiting and testing period: compare Israel's forty years in the wilderness and Jesus' forty days. Is there a hint of Moses' forty days of supplication before God in Deut. 9:18, 25? Mention of the delay builds a bridge between the decree of destruction and the surprising narrative that follows. The "tension-laden interval" between the delivery of the message and its fulfilment was to be understood by the Ninevite listener as "a time when it would be possible for him to bend himself to the will of the one who sends the message."[16]

B. NINEVEH'S REPENTANCE (3:5–9)

The people of Nineveh believed God; calling for a fast, they dressed themselves in sackcloth, from noble down to pauper. 6 When the message

10. A. Parrot, *Nineveh and the OT* (E.T. 1955), pp. 85f.; Trible, *SBJ*, pp. 175f.
11. Cf. J. Simons, *The Geographical and Topographical Texts of the OT* (1959), p. 527.
12. See the comment and notes on 4:11.
13. "The author did not concern himself with the detail of language" in which Jonah prophesied (Smart).
14. The verb *hpk,* here only in the Niphal in this sense, occurs for their destruction both in the Qal and as a noun *mahpēḵâ* (e.g., Gen. 19:25; Deut. 29:22; Amos 4:11). Good, *IOT,* pp. 48f., reviving an ancient view (cf. Bickerman, *RHPR* 45 [1965], p. 255), finds here a double meaning, overturn and turn to God, but this is oversubtle.
15. G's reading "three days," followed by Duhm, *BHK,* Bewer, and Smart, is a blatantly inferior reading under the influence of v. 3. Cf. a possibly intermediate reading *šlšym,* "thirty," in a de Rossi ms.
16. W. Zimmerli in *Essays on OT Hermeneutics,* ed. C. Westermann (E.T. 1963), pp. 101f.

reached the king of Nineveh, he got up from his throne and, exchanging his royal robes for sackcloth, sat in ashes. 7 He had an announcement made in Nineveh: "By order of the king and his nobles. No man or animal, cattle or sheep, is to taste anything. They are not to feed or drink water. 8 Man and animal alike are to wear sackcloth and call on God with all their might. Every one is to turn from his wicked ways and meddling in violence. 9 Who knows, God may turn around and relent; and then, if he gives up his fierce anger, we shall not perish."

The response to Jonah's preaching is astounding. The news of it spreads like wildfire throughout Nineveh. Its citizens make good use of the breathing space allotted to them. They accept *en masse* the divine source of Jonah's message,[17] believing its author has the power to carry out his threat. The previous mention of the city's colossal size lingering in the minds of the listening circle now has a different nuance: it enhances the miraculous nature of the reaction to the prophecy of doom, that so vast a population should turn instantly to God as one man, imploring his mercy.

Their reaction to the warning of destruction follows a pattern typical of Israel in the OT. The three elements of threat of disaster, acts of penitence, and eventual divine intervention to avert disaster constitute a scheme illustrated in 1 Sam. 7:3–14; 2 Sam. 24; Ezra 8:21–23; Esther 3:7–4:17; Jer. 36; and, not least of the parallels, Joel 1:1–2:27. This section is concerned with the phenomena and theology of repentance. Its motifs fall with reassuring familiarity on the ears of the narrator's audience, for they are just what Israel would have done in the same circumstances.[18] These wicked barbarians react in quite a normal and commendable manner. The designed impact is similar to that of the sailors' behavior in ch. 1. In fact, v. 5 echoes 1:10, 13, 16: the *men* of Nineveh are starkly contrasted with *God,* to stress their creaturely subordination. The author "strips his country's foes of everything foreign or provocative of envy and hatred, and unfolds them to Israel only in their teeming humanity" (Smith).

The section falls into three parts: the religious activities of the people, the personal reaction of the king, and the official decree which reinforces and amplifies the people's response. The third part takes up the first in parallelism and progression: fasting and mourning-garb feature again. The comprehensiveness in v. 8 echoes that at the end of v. 5. *Sackcloth,* mentioned in all three parts, is the emphatic symbol of Nineveh's repentance. The mass proclamation of a *fast* would remind the listening circle of Jer. 36:9, the only other occurrence in the OT, where a fast was proclaimed in Jerusalem by the people of the capital and pilgrims from Judah. This most orthodox expedient of self-abasement before God[19] is

17. T correctly paraphrases *God* as "the word of God." For the construction cf. Jer. 12:6.
18. In fact these motifs are characteristic of the ancient Near East. Cf. J. B. Schaumberger, *Miscellanea biblica* 2 (1934), pp. 123–134, for Assyrian parallels.
19. See the comments on Joel 1:14; 2:15.

accompanied by the donning of sackcloth, another traditional symbol of mourning or penitence.[20] The efficacy of their measures depended on complete participation, as Joel 2:16 illustrates well. So the whole community responded, regardless of social distinctions.

Even *the king of Nineveh,* sitting in his palace, was overcome when he heard *the message*. He is obviously the counterpart of the ship's captain in ch. 1, a leader in different dress and setting. His position in the story is partly dictated by a desire for symmetry; just as the captain emerged from the crew to play his role in the narrative, so the figure of the king emerges from the Ninevites.[21] The narrator's psychological purpose in drawing this and other parallels with ch. 1 is to induce his hearers to transfer their kindly attitude toward the ship's captain and crew to the king and citizens of Nineveh. Had he begun his story with ch. 3, his aim in telling it would have had no hope of fulfilment. Chapter 1 has served the purpose of softening the reaction of the listening circle toward comparatively innocuous foreigners before confronting them with an odious community of hardcore heathens.

The king at once abdicates his high position in face of the sovereign power of God revealed through Jonah's words. His *throne* and *royal robes* are exchanged for *sackcloth* and *ashes*.[22] The narrative now moves from his personal reaction back to the subject of the communal response to the crisis, via a royal edict which regularizes the spontaneous reaction of the populace in the manner of officialdom the world over. After he has hastily conferred with his privy counsellors, the edict is promulgated with the authority of the court behind it. A touch of exotic color is added in the inclusion of domestic animals in fasting and donning of penitent garb; it was a Persian custom for animals to participate in mourning ceremonies.[23] Although alien and odd, the gesture would impress forcibly upon the listening circle the sincerity of Nineveh's repentance. The community was threatened with the destruction of all animate life; it was fitting that animals who were to share the fate of their human masters should join in the appeal. The section builds up an impression of the totality of Nineveh's repentance by mentioning the mourning of great and small, king and commoner, man and beast.[24] The

20. Cf. 2 Sam. 3:31; Joel 1:17 and comment.
21. Trible, *SBJ*, p. 188. Wolff, *SJ*, pp. 46f., followed by Cohn, *JLBE*, p. 57, and Rudolph, suggests that, as elsewhere, the narrator has detached information from its chronological sequence and presented it after a religious reaction. The first verb in v. 6 then has the force of a pluperfect, and the order "from the greatest to the least" in v. 4 has special point. The order of presentation he explains as a device to set last the climactic v. 9 to prepare for the divine response in v. 10. This view was held by Calvin and is implied in KJV ("For . . .").
22. Cf. Job 12:7; Isa. 58:5. It was a Semitic practice to mourn seated on the ground. Notice the chiastic order here.
23. Cf. Herodotus ix.24; Plutarch, *Alexander* 72; Judith 4:10. In Western society horses were commonly caparisoned in black till the black motor car replaced them. The proposal to delete *wᵉhabbᵉhēmâ* in v. 8, advocated by Bewer, Snaith, Rudolph, and JB, like the more widespread one to delete *hā' āḏām wᵉhabbᵉhēmâ* (e.g., Wellhausen, Sellin, Keller, NEB), is prompted by modern judgment of the tale's propriety at this point.
24. Wolff, *SJ*, pp. 109ff.

summoning of animals to prayer would doubtless remind the audience of Joel's poetic interpretation of the cries of thirsty beasts as fervent prayers to God.[25]

The king is not satisfied with a cultic show of penitence. He demands in addition a change of moral behavior, a personal turning from *wicked ways,* lest penance be a cloak for persistence in sin. The listening circle would nod their heads in approval. In this confession of guilt and call for genuine repentance it is as if the king had shared with them the advantage of Joel's ministry, for had not he stressed the necessity for rites to be matched by a wholehearted turning to God (Joel 2:12f.)? Furthermore, the king describes the needed personal reformation in acceptable Jeremian language.[26] *Violence,* the arbitrary infringements of human rights,[27] is a term that occurs in the OT prophets especially in connection with cities: urban conglomeration encourages scrambling over others, like caterpillars in a jar.[28] Although the tale deals with moral misbehavior in an Assyrian city, the listeners would recall that Assyria's aggressive violence toward other nations was condemned by the prophets as a national characteristic, and so by association it has special point.[29]

Of such social injustice Nineveh was blatantly guilty, and this the king confesses on behalf of the community. With the humble earnestness of the prophet Joel, the royal decree holds out the bare possibility of God's turning away from his *anger* in response to their turning away from the sin that had aroused it. If man's inhumanity to man is halted, there may be an exercise of divine clemency. The phraseology of Joel 2:14 is reproduced, the foreign king being portrayed as an impeccable exponent of orthodox Jewish theology. His sentiments would fall like music on the ears of the audience. The "perhaps" in this call to repentance[30] corresponds to the cautious reference to God's mercy in the captain's speech (1:6). Both these foreign leaders acknowledge the sovereignty of God. Men cannot twist his arm; even genuine repentance is no virtue by which to win his approval. His reaction lies hidden behind the clouds of mystery and glory that surround his throne, until it emerges into human experience. The prospect of avoiding destruction closes both the decree and the section, challenging the proclamation of Nineveh's overthrow at the end of the previous unit of the narrative (v. 4).

25. Joel 1:20: *bahᵃmôṯ* corresponds to *bᵉhēmâ* here.
26. Notably Jer. 18:11.
27. See the comment on Mic. 6:12.
28. Jer. 6:7; Ezek. 7:23; Amos 3:10; Mic. 6:12; cf. Ps. 55:9(10).
29. Isa. 10:13f.; Nah. 2:11f.; and esp. 3:1; in 3:19 *rāʿâ,* "wickedness," corresponds to the adjective *wicked* here.
30. The element of contingency is a typical ingredient of the prophetic summons to repentance. The summons in its present form consists of an admonition, which includes an accusation of wrongdoing, and a promise which includes a threat (T. M. Raitt, *ZAW* 83 [1971], pp. 35f.). See the comment and note on Joel 2:12–14, where the motif of divine repentance is discussed.

C. JONAH'S REBUKE (3:10–4:11)

1. God's Grace (3:10)

> *When God saw their reaction, how they had turned from their wicked ways, he relented and did not carry out the punishment with which he had threatened them.*

No fire and brimstone fell on this latter-day Sodom after all. There was a venerable precedent for such reversal of divine policy. Moses had prayed that Israel might not be destroyed despite the sin of making and worshipping the golden calf: "Turn from your fierce anger, relent and do not punish your people" (Ex. 32:12). And it is duly recorded that "Yahweh did relent over the punishment with which he had threatened his people." That was Israel, it is true, but had not Nineveh reacted in a typically Israelite way? Moreover, there was warrant for clemency to be shown to foreigners, provided they repented. Jeremiah had been the bearer of a divine oracle whose thesis was very relevant to the narrator's theme:

> *"At times I threaten some nation or kingdom that I shall tear it up, break it down, and make it perish; then the threatened nation turns from its wickedness and I relent over the punishment I intended to carry out."* (Jer. 18:7f.)

That oracle culminated in a (fruitless) call to Judah and Jerusalem to "turn every one from his wicked ways" (v. 11). It was this call that the narrator had put into the royal edict, and so predictably God's reaction accords with the quite general affirmation contained in the same oracle. This is another psychological ploy which the narrator has used in order to force the listening circle to assent to a course of action that of themselves they would have rejected out of hand. He has subtly made his tale comply with accepted prophecy and deliberately echoed its phraseology so as to induce a favorable response. Our story-teller is a master of persuasion.

The original has a wordplay difficult to reproduce in English. *Wicked,* which takes up the same word rendered *wickedness* in 1:2, now recurs as *punishment.*[31] Bad behavior should lead to a bad end. The logic of the multiple term is broken by a higher logic, the exercise of the divine compassion laid down in the book of Jeremiah.[32] A divine prophecy of doom is not necessarily absolute, but—who knows?—may turn out to be conditional if it creates in the recipients a change of heart and life.[33] Justice is better served by reformed characters than by corpses. God's deepest intent is

31. Heb. *rā'â.*

32. We are meant to assume that the Ninevites complied with the summons to true repentance.

33. This is "offensive to those who seek to glorify God by so exalting his power that there is no possibility of choice left to his creation," and "infuriating to those who . . . wish to show their importance by knowing the working out of God's plans in detail" (H. L. Ellison, *EQ* 37 [1965], p. 154).

thus achieved, for "he does not want any to perish, but wants all to come to repentance" (2 Pet. 3:9).

The story of the sparing of Nineveh is ch. 1 all over again: just as the praying sailors were delivered from the fatal effect of the storm, so now is Nineveh from the realization of Yahweh's prophecy of doom.[34] It is even more a repetition of Jonah's experience. Jonah had been the object of divine anger, symbolized in the fury of the storm (1:15). He too had been under sentence of death and conscious of his guilt (1:12). He had been saved from drowning at the last moment by a signal act of grace shown by his sovereign God. Divine inactivity is here the counterpart to the divine activity in rescuing Jonah at 2:1. The parallelism of the narrative creates a logical presupposition that Jonah would hail with joy this new demonstration of divine goodness. The saved sinner is surely glad to see others saved—or does he sometimes resent sharing his privileges?

2. *Jonah's Plaint (4:1–3)*

> *Jonah was terribly upset, and angry too. 2 He prayed to Yahweh, "I implore you, Yahweh. Was not this what I said while I was still in my own country? That is why I ran away to Tarshish earlier—I knew you were 'a kindly and compassionate God, so patient and full of grace, ready to relent over punishment.' 3 So now, Yahweh, please take my life away because I would rather die than go on living."*

Jonah finds that the time-fuse does not work on the prophetic bomb he planted in Nineveh. Evidently the time limit has expired by now. He considers it intolerable that Israel's experience of Ex. 32 should be mirrored in Nineveh; he cannot stomach Yahweh's cheapening his mercy by offering it to all and sundry. The wordplay continues. Bad behavior should lead to a bad end, and Jonah takes it very badly that it does not.[1] The cessation of God's anger is the signal for Jonah's to start.[2] He fails to take a cue from God. His reaction strikes a wrong note in the logic of the story, as in 1:3. Who is Jonah to complain, especially since he himself was recently so glad to be saved from destruction? In the parallelism of the narrative, 4:2–3 is the counterpart to 2:1–9. He who praised the gracious mercy of God in ch. 2 turns around and deplores it in ch. 4![3] Jesus was later to tell a parable of grace gladly received for oneself but selfishly denied another: the courtier had his colossal debt annulled only to clap into prison a fellow courtier who could not repay a trifling sum (Matt. 18:23–35). "Ought you not have shown mercy to your fellow servant as I showed mercy to you?" was the king's

34. *Plight,* 1:7f., is the same word as *wicked,* 3:8.

1. Heb. *wayyēra' . . . rā'â.*
2. Heb. *wayyiḥar* corresponds to *ḥ^a^rôn,* 3:9.
3. Feuillet, *RB* 54 (1947), p. 347, following L. Gautier. "He has already forgotten the grace which was lavished upon him. He has already lost the mystery of the pardon by which he lives again in newness of life" (Ellul).

indignant question. In Jonah's case the logic of grace was broken in a similar way. The listening circle, after the build-up of chs. 2 and 3, must have winced at the jarring note of Jonah's reaction. Their antipathy to the prophet, encouraged in ch. 1, returns with a new vehemence. How dare this man quarrel with God? Emotionally they stand firmly on the divine side of the ensuing discussion, and small-minded Jonah damns himself more in their eyes with every syllable he utters. And so they fall into the narrator's trap.

Jonah brings his prayer to God, but it is the very opposite of the prayer of praise and thanksgiving. Its key terms, Jonah's *life* and Yahweh's *grace,* are indeed echoed, but in quite different tones. This is not the new Jonah who followed with firm tread the signpost pointing to Nineveh, but a reversion to the "old man" who ran away from God's will and service. The prayer begins with a particle of entreaty, but the petition does not appear till the end. First Jonah brings a complaint that his worst fears have been realized. He reveals that his flight to Tarshish was motivated by a bitter knowledge of the characteristic clemency of Yahweh.[4] Jonah is a specialist in credal confessions: he made one in 1:9 which was the central feature of the initial chapter, and now he makes another, no less crucial in its context. He flings in Yahweh's face an orthodox summary of his attributes of patience and mercy, which appears in a basic form in Ex. 34:6f.[5] Jonah cites it in the distinctive form it took in Joel 2:13; the identity of citation is significant in view of the parallel with Joel 2:14 in 3:9. The book of Joel was obviously known and revered in the community the narrator addressed, and he quoted it deliberately, to win acceptance for his message.

But if the words are cited, the meaning is changed subtly. The credal statement is essentially concerned with the opening of the divine heart to Israel. The key word *ḥeseḏ, grace,* especially arises out of Yahweh's covenant relationship with his chosen people. The narrator ironically makes Jonah take it for granted that Yahweh's concern is universal. It is probable that this interpretation was already gaining ground among the author's contemporaries, in the light of Ps. 145:9, where the credal confession concludes:

> *Yahweh is good to all*
> *and his compassion extends to all his creatures.*[6]

It is unlikely, however, that the community as a whole would accept the implications the narrator drew from this Israelite creed. Jonah complains bitterly. "I *knew* it right from the beginning," he says. He could see it

4. Compare and contrast Matt. 25:24.

5. See the comment and notes on Joel 2:13. For the use of Joel in the book of Jonah see Wolff, *SJ,* pp. 68–71. He notes that only in these two passages does divine repentance conclude the formula. Unlike Joel 2:13, a variant form of the tradition is here followed by the use of *'ēl, God.*

6. Cf. the use of *ḥeseḏ* in Ruth 1:8; 2 Sam. 15:20; Ps. 33:5; 117:1f.; 119:64. Its expansion paves the way for the *charis* of the NT.

coming, and had done all he could to avert what was to him a theological embarrassment and a divine *faux pas,* of which he had been compelled ignominiously to be the instrument.[7] The listening circle, having already condemned Jonah's initial disobedience, are induced to condemn too the cause for his flight, which is now revealed. This is the psychological reason why the prophet's desertion is mentioned, to remind the audience of both it and their negative reaction. Moreover, words that elsewhere in the OT call forth men's praise are here offensively made a cause for complaint. So the dice are loaded against Jonah and in favor of the author's thesis.

What I said is literally "my word," with which Jonah brashly counters "Yahweh's word" of 1:1. "My word" was correct, claims Jonah, and God's was ill-advised. The egocentricity sets a keynote for the prayer as a whole: "I" or "my" occurs no fewer than nine times in the original.[8] Jonah's prayer is reminiscent of the expostulation of the Elder Brother with its similar selfish emphasis and tone of bitter complaint (Luke 15:29). Appointing himself theological adviser to the Almighty, Jonah pronounces himself completely out of sympathy with divine policy. As Ahithophel, Absalom's counsellor, reacted to his master's mistaken strategy by suicide (2 Sam. 17:23), so Jonah feels that he can no longer represent the deity, and prays for death. "Over my dead body" is his vehement reaction to God's grace. Himself forgiven, he cannot accept that non-Israelites should be forgiven too.

The prophet strikes a noble pose by echoing the prayer of Elijah in 1 K. 19:4: *Take my life away.*[9] Instead of continuing "for I am no better than my fathers," Jonah adapts it to "for my death is better than my life."[10] The pose is a parody. Elijah, wearied with his endless struggle with Baalism, was convinced that he would not succeed where his fathers had failed, and so felt that it was time to join them in death. Jonah is peevishly disappointed with the very success of his mission. He is unworthy of the mantle of Elijah, who had not disdained doing miracles for his Phoenician hostess (1 K. 17:8–24). Jonah is no Elijah, as the listening circle are well aware: the echo of Elijah's prayer is but another nail in the coffin of Jonah's reputation. What religious monster is this?[11] This living miracle of God's grace disdains his new lease

7. His complaint is not that he has lost his prophetic reputation (Philo, Rashi, Weiser, Myers, *et al.*) but that God's behavior does not conform to Jonah's theology (Wolff, *SJ,* p. 113; Good, *IOT,* p. 51).
8. Wolff, *SJ,* p. 118.
9. The tradition of the weary prophet begins with Num. 11:11–15; cf. Jer. 15:10; 20:14–18. Cf. D. Daube, "Death As a Release in the Bible," *Donum Gratulatorium E. Stauffer* (1962), pp. 82–104, esp. pp. 94–98.
10. Heb. *w*^{e}*'attā, so now,* which opens the petition, is a typical introduction to the main point of a speech, prayer, or letter after the preliminaries; cf. Gen. 44:33; 1 Sam. 25:7; Isa. 5:3, 5 (H. A. Brongers, *VT* 15 [1965], pp. 296f.).
11. G. von Rad, *Der Prophet Jona* (1950), p. 11, called Jonah a "religionspsychologisches Monstrum."

of life. Praise has given way to dispute and despair, as Jonah contemplates others enjoying honey from the Jewish hive. This nationalistic prophet is running odiously true to type.

3. *God's Last Word (4:4–11)*

> *"Have you any right to be angry?" asked Yahweh. 5 Now Jonah had left the city and sat down to the east of it. There he made himself a shelter and sat under it in the shade, waiting to see what would happen in the city. 6 Yahweh God arranged for a ricinus to grow up over Jonah to provide shade for his head and give him relief*[12] *from his distress. He was terribly pleased with the ricinus. 7 But at dawn the next day God arranged for a weevil to attack the ricinus, and it withered. 8 Then, as the sun rose, God arranged for a hot(?)*[13] *east wind to come. The sun beat down on Jonah's head until he felt faint and wished he were dead. "I would rather die than go on living," he thought. 9 God said to Jonah, "Have you any right to be angry about the ricinus?" "I could die," replied Jonah, "of righteous indignation." 10 Said Yahweh, "You have shown concern for the ricinus, which you did not toil over to make it grow, which grew one night and was gone the next. 11 So should not I too have shown concern for the vast city of Nineveh, with its population of over 120,000 who cannot tell their right hand from their left, as well as animals galore?"*

In 2:10 Yahweh's word had been a straightforward one of command to his huge but docile instrument of salvation, a word that had resulted in the fish's landing Jonah. Yahweh replied to Jonah's prayer both by his word and by his use of nature. This section has the same function, but its points of divergence highlight the difference in the situation. Yahweh now has a rebel on his hands: his agent of salvation, though compelled to do his will, is by no means convinced of its correctness. Accordingly God's last word and the accompanying actions require to be more lengthy in order to bring this refractory servant to his senses. It starts as a question, which Jonah is in no mood to answer. By exposing him to a series of overwhelming experiences, Yahweh conditions the prophet to a point where he can hear the question afresh, and is given the opportunity to use his own self-centeredness as a window upon the very heart of God.

This final section begins as the previous one did, with the theme of Jonah's anger. Yahweh's question is an answer to Jonah's prayer, which bypasses the explicit petition and goes to the heart of the problem. The

12. G "give shade" presupposes *l^{e}hātsēl* for MT *l^{e}hatstsîl*. Cohn, *JLBE*, pp. 64, 100, finds a *double entendre* here.

13. Heb. *ḥ^{a}rîshîṯ* occurs only here, apart from its occurrence in a Qumran hymn, *Hodayoth* 7:5, which is no help toward elucidating it but does indicate that the word should not be emended. G S render "burning," V "hot and burning," and T "quiet," i.e., presumably "sultry." T derived from the root *ḥrš*, "be silent"; the other versions may have guessed, perhaps linking with *ḥeres*, "sun."

question intends to elicit from Jonah a negative reply. Yet God does not condemn, but invites Jonah to condemn himself and admit that his anger was not good.[14] There is an implicit play on v. 1, where Jonah took God's forbearance very badly and was angry; now this anger is characterized as morally bad.[15] Yahweh's actions whereby he turns Jonah's justification of this self-destructive anger to good account are prefaced by mention of Jonah's movements in v. 5. The narrative had diverged at the end of 3:4 where we last heard of Jonah delivering his message of doom. The story concentrated on the religious reaction of the Ninevites, and then on Jonah's own religious reaction to Yahweh's sparing Nineveh. Now there is opportunity to relate more mundane details about the prophet in order to set the scene for the final act.[16]

After his preaching Jonah *had left the* doomed *city,* glad to shake its dust off his feet. The sentence stresses the city, mentioning it no fewer than three times. Verses 4f. thus enunciate the vital concerns of this closing passage, i.e., the unreasonableness of Jonah's anger concerning the city of Nineveh. These are the themes to which the passage will revert in vv. 9–11 and which thus act as a framework for the three divine acts. Awaiting Nineveh's destruction and safe outside its walls, Jonah had constructed a rough and ready *shelter* from the sun by day and the chill by night. The same word is used for the structures of leafy branches made for the Feast of Tabernacles.[17] The shelter proved inadequate, its shade being insufficiently dense to keep the sun off Jonah's head (v. 6). The situation is ideal for Yahweh to play a trick on Jonah. Actions speak louder than words: he teaches Jonah (and the listening circle) a practical lesson likely to have more impact than just verbal reasoning.

14. Heb. *hêṭēḇ,* lit. "well," i.e., with good reason. An alternative rendering is "very, exceedingly" (G S T). Most scholars and modern translations reject this possibility in light of the context here and in v. 9.

15. Jonah's assessment of good in his prayer, that death was "good" for him rather than life, is also implicitly challenged.

16. This literary forking, whereby the religious category is given pride of place, is matched in 1:15, where Jonah is left drowning while the sailors' awe and sacrifices and vows in reaction to the ending of the storm are described, and Jonah is picked up (literally) only in 1:17. Many, including Sellin, Robinson, Weiser, and Trible, *SBJ,* pp. 100–102, have followed H. Winckler, who suggested a whole series of transpositions including moving 4:5 to a more logical position after 3:4 on the ground that it did not fit its present setting ("Zum Buche Jona," *Altorientalische Forschungen* 2:2 [1900], pp. 260–65). More recently there has been a tendency to revert to an older explanation, favored by the medieval Jewish commentators Kimchi and Ibn Ezra and also by some early Christian commentators (see Lohfink, *BZ* 5 [1961], p. 191, n. 23), namely to take the verse as a flashback and the verb as a virtual pluperfect. Lohfink, *loc. cit.,* pp. 185–203, has demonstrated that v. 5 thus understood fits into a pattern of jumps in the narrative in order to highlight religious reactions; he compares 1:10, 17. His view has been espoused by Wolff, *SJ,* pp. 44–48; Cohn, *JLBE,* p. 57; and Rudolph. Landes, KBJ, p. 27, n. 65, retains 4:5 in its present position on the grounds of unanimous textual evidence and the difficulty of explaining why it was moved. Bewer and Smart refrain from moving it on similar grounds, although they delete part as a gloss.

17. Heb. *sukkâ*: Lev. 23:40–42; Neh. 8:14–18; cf. Mark 9:5.

The God of the sea, who can produce a fish to swallow Jonah, is also the God of the earth and its plants. He produces a plant which grows Jack-in-the-beanstalk fashion[18] and is soon high enough to shade Jonah's head with its huge leaves. The narrator specifies the plant as a *qîqāyôn;* its identity is uncertain, but it is probably the quick-growing *ricinus* or castor-oil plant, which in hot climates grows like a tree and gives ample shade with its palmate leaves.[19]

There is a subtle change in the divine names at this point. In 4:2–4 Jonah has been talking to Yahweh and Yahweh has replied, but in vv. 6–9 it is God who acts and speaks until he reappears as Yahweh in v. 10. Actually in v. 6 the transition is bridged by the use of both titles, evidently to indicate the identity of the doubly named deity. In fact the general term *God* was used earlier, in 3:5–10, in the description of his dealings with the Ninevites and their reactions. For a while Yahweh shelved his function, which in Jonah's eyes he ought always to exercise, as the exclusive, gracious God of Jonah the Jew[20] and acted as the Creator of all men, the God who has kindly dealings with foreigners. In 4:6–9 he plays the role of Creator, using the world of plants and insects, sun and wind, to fulfil his purposes. He is also acting as Jonah expects the God of the Gentiles to act: as one who indeed creates and yet is disposed to inflict sudden destruction upon his creatures. Then in vv. 10f. he reappears synthesized as Yahweh, the God of compassion, endorsing that characterization to which Jonah objected in v. 2, as a God who desires to reveal his mercy consistently not only to Israel but to the whole world of men and animals.[21]

18. Note v. 10 and *the next day,* v. 7.

19. The meaning of Akk. *kukkanitu,* evidently the same plant, is unknown. Most identify the present term with *Ricinus communis,* the palm-christ, which according to Perowne can grow 8 feet in five or six months. Aquila and Theodotion rendered thus, and it corresponds to the Egyptian *k'k' (kiki)* (Herodotus ii.94; Pliny *Naturalis Historia* xv.7) and also to Talmudic *qîq.* Symmachus and Jerome rendered "ivy," envisaging a trailing plant to cover the shelter; similarly G translated "gourd," a vine *Cucurbita lagenaria.* See the discussion in H. N. and A. L. Moldenke, *Plants of the Bible* (1952), pp. 203f.

20. Cf. 2:1, 10; 3:1–3; 4:1–4.

21. In 1:14, 16 *Yahweh* stands primarily for Jonah's God, yet 4:10f. casts new light on its use, just as it does on the significance of "the great city," 1:2. For this explanation of the use of the divine names cf. Wolff, *SJ,* pp. 81f., 120; Cohn, *JLBE,* p. 72. The attempt of W. Böhme, *ZAW* 7 (1887), pp. 224–284, to solve the problem by means of source criticism has found little favor. Bewer, adapting an idea put forward by Marti, resorted to a text-critical solution: on the basis of S, which has "Yahweh God" throughout, and of a few variants in mss. of G and in the Old Latin and V, he claimed that the author originally wrote "Yahweh" all the way through. J. Möllerfeld, *Geist und Leben* 33 (1960), pp. 324–333, considers that the use of *God* is a sign that the relationship between Yahweh and Jonah has cooled and that Yahweh is offended. But as F. D. Kidner observes (*Tyndale Bulletin* 21 [1970], p. 127), *Yahweh* is used in v. 10, yet one might have expected increased estrangement after Jonah's second, stronger outburst. Kidner (pp. 126–28) finds here an element of stylistic variation, "a responsible but not hidebound attitude to distinctions," suggesting that this explanation of literary freedom is relevant to the usage in Gen. 2f. A similar view was earlier espoused by Trible, *SBJ,* p. 86, who however agreed with Eissfeldt that a satisfactory explanation of the problem had not yet been found.

Jonah is delighted with the ricinus. God has rescued him from *distress,* which represents the same term as that rendered *wickedness* in 1:2 and *punishment* in 3:10. It recalls the theme of Nineveh repentant and reprieved. Viewing the situation as a parable of God's dealings with his non-Jewish creatures, however, God ought not act in a kindly way: Jonah's attitude demands of God that he destroy. So God does just that, to see how Jonah likes his theology coming true in the physical realm. Early next morning along comes a *weevil* by special arrangement, and chews its way through the stem of the ricinus so that the leaves shielding Jonah's head droop and shrivel.[22] Nor has God finished his destructive activity. Along comes the sirocco at his command and blows its hot breath through the loosely woven shelter till it feels like an oven. The blazing sun beats down on Jonah's poor head, now bereft of the friendly ricinus. Enervated by sunstroke and exasperated by the loss of his plant,[23] Jonah's recent zest for life shrivels like the ricinus leaves. The shoe Jonah wanted Nineveh to wear was on his foot now, and it pinched.

He cannot tolerate the situation any longer and thinks he would be better off dead. By so thinking he does not advance his cause in the eyes of the listening circle. The words rendered *wished he were dead* occur in only one other place in the OT, in 1 K. 19:4, concerning Elijah's death-wish. Indeed Elijah was sitting under a broom tree when he said it, while Jonah had lately been sitting under the shadow of a ricinus. The narrator's echo of the Elijah story is here, as in v. 3, a deliberate anti-Jonah device. Jonah may mouth Elijah's words, but against that giant of a prophet this squirming victim of his own ideology cuts a pitiable figure.

The narrative appears to have gone around in a circle and reached the point of v. 3 as a preface to another question about Jonah's anger, as in v. 4. But by inducing Jonah's identical reaction in a new, specially engineered situation, the story-teller has paved the way for a devastating denouement. The prophet's own frustration and fury are turned into weapons against him. The divine question, which Jonah did not deign to answer before, now stings him into a vehement reply, by which he unwittingly plays into Yahweh's hands. For now the question is asked not about Nineveh's reprieve but about the shrivelled ricinus. The innocent-sounding query as to the rightness of the prophet's anger, which in v. 4 clashed with Jonah's conviction by inviting a negative reply, now cunningly elicits a positive protest. Of course he was right to be angry, damned angry.[24] His shocked anger was such that he could see no sense in living. How could he live in a world so constituted as to allow the ricinus affair?

"Let us analyze this anger of yours, Jonah," comments Yahweh. "It

22. The ricinus has little resistance to even slight damage.

23. "Sirocco days are particularly trying to the temper. They tend to make even the mildest people irritable and fretful" (D. Baly, *The Geography of the Bible* [1957], p. 68).

24. Heb. *'aḏ-māweṯ,* "as far as death," partly has the force of an expletive; cf. D. W. Thomas, *VT* 3 (1953), p. 219.

represents your *concern* over your beloved ricinus—but what did it really mean to you? Your attachment to it could not be very deep, for it was here one day and *gone the next*. Your concern was dictated by self-interest, not by a genuine love. You never had for it the devotion of the gardener. If you feel as badly as you do, what would you expect a gardener to feel like, who tended a plant and watched it grow only to see it wither and die, poor thing? And this is how I feel about Nineveh, only much more so. All those people, all those animals—I made them, I have cherished them all these years. Nineveh has cost me no end of effort, and they mean the world to me. Your pain is nothing to mine when I contemplate their destruction."[25]

The argument is an *a fortiori* one.[26] If Jonah could show concern, how much more would Yahweh! The vastness of Nineveh, reprehensible in 1:2 and formidable in 3:2, now takes on a new meaning: a teeming population,[27] myriads of creatures for whom God cared, and dumb *animals galore*. It was this same divine compassion that Jesus reflected in his reaction to crowds of people.[28] The final verse is a revelation of what God was thinking when he observed the royal edict being carried out by man and beast (3:7–10). He is the God who notices when a sparrow falls to the ground (Matt. 10:29); he is the God who saves man and beast (Ps. 36:6[7]). By borrowing the verb "show concern" (*ḥûs*) from Joel 2:17 the narrator makes blatantly obvious his insistence that Yahweh cares not only for Israel but for all men.

The Ninevites deserve compassion not only as creatures for whom God cares but also as virtual children compared with the Jews.[29] They know no better, for they have not had the spiritual advantages of Israel, and so it is necessary to make allowances for them. This is a theme Jesus took up in his

25. Cf. S. H. Blank, *HUCA* 26 (1955), pp. 29–41. He compares Jer. 45, where again the thought is, "What is your hurt compared with mine?" and Hos. 11:8. He observes that God's toil is the missing term to be understood in v. 11; "Nowhere in the Hebrew Bible do the 'personhood' of God and his entanglement in the human situation stand more clearly revealed" (p. 41). "A man's troubles are matched and dwarfed by God's own hurt" (p. 36).
26. Cf. Matt. 7:11.
27. 120,000 is a reasonable figure for the population of Nineveh. M. E. L. Mallowan, *Iraq* 14 (1952), pp. 20–22, has published an inscription on a stele of Ashurnazirpal II found at Nimrud (Calah), which states that he invited 69,574 people to a feast there to commemorate the building of his palace. Mallowan suggests a figure of 65,000 as a minimum for the population of Calah when it was settled and observes that this figure of 120,000 is moderate in comparison. D. J. Wiseman, *ibid.*, p. 28, concurs, noting that Nineveh's walls enclose an area twice that of Calah. However, Rudolph finds here merely a round number, "a dozen myriads."
28. Matt. 9:36; Mark 6:34; 8:2.
29. Cf. Deut. 1:39; 9:36. "They might be adult in years, but in character they were children—wilful, passionate, perishing without vision yet not without value . . . , undisciplined and overgrown children yet also the work of God's hands" (A. D. Martin, *The Prophet Jonah: The Book and the Sign* [1926], p. 87). Many commentators take the number as referring to literal children, but in recent years the tendency has been to interpret more widely: Brockington; Wolff, *SJ*, pp. 51, 124; R. B. Y. Scott, *Interpretation* 19 (1965), p. 24, who compares Luke 12:48; Kraeling; Ellul. Heb. *'āḏām*, "men, human beings," echoes 3:7, 8; the relative clause is not restrictive. Cf. n. 27.

cry from the cross: "Forgive them, for they know not what they do" (Luke 23:24). Paul claimed that he received mercy because he acted in ignorance before he became a believer (1 Tim. 1:13).[30] Sympathetic overtures were what these spiritual minors needed, not aloofness and hatred.

Jonah and his self-pity fade away, and the Jonahs among the listening circle feel that Yahweh is putting the question to them personally. The story is deliberately left open-ended and the listeners are brought face to face with the existential challenge of the story, just as in the parable of the Prodigal Son the appeal to the Elder Brother was really addressed to the religious snobs of Jesus' day (Luke 15:2, 31, 32).[31] Did those scribes and Pharisees slink away into the spiritual night, or did some at least greet the prodigal tax-collectors as long-lost brothers? And whose side did the listening circle take? Jonah's, whose petty attitude they had constantly been invited to condemn? Or did they identify themselves with the divine Hero, whose love "is broader than the measures of man's mind"?

A Jonah lurks in every Christian heart, whimpering his insidious message of smug prejudice, empty traditionalism, and exclusive solidarity. He that has ears to hear, let him hear and allow the saving love of God which has been outpoured in his own heart to remold his thinking and social orientation.

30. Lack of understanding was regarded as a mitigating circumstance when there was a chance that encouragement would bear fruit (D. Daube, *Studia Patristica* 4. Texte und Untersuchungen 79 [1961], pp. 58–70). He also cites Acts 3:17; 13:27; 17:23, 30.

31. Cf. the final question in Luke 10:36, outside the structure of the parable of the Good Samaritan.

The Book of MICAH

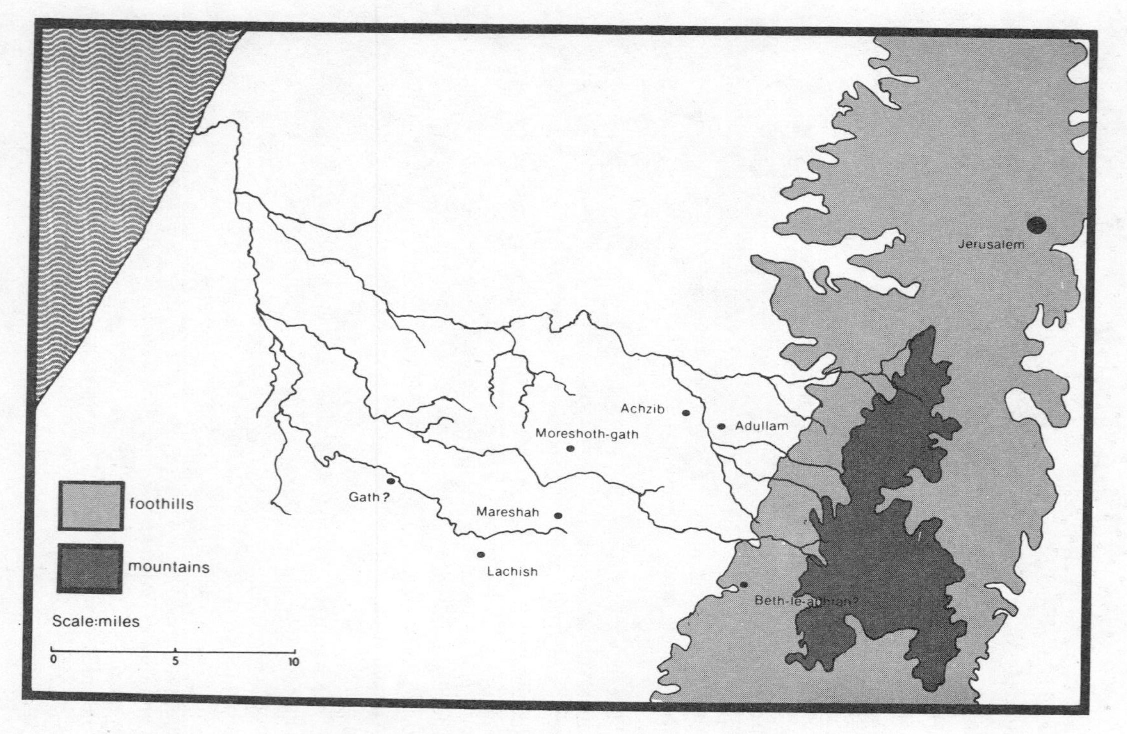

(The Southern Shephelah. See pp. 279–280.)

INTRODUCTION

1. HISTORICAL BACKGROUND TO MICAH'S MINISTRY

The heading to the book assigns the prophet's ministry to the reigns of Jotham, Ahaz, and Hezekiah. For the reader who has a basic knowledge of the history of Israel and Judah, this reference to the second half of the eighth century B.C. speaks volumes. By collating references to the period in the religious histories of Kings and Chronicles and in the Assyrian records, and by comparing social allusions in both Isaiah and Micah, a good deal of the social and political history of the period can be reconstructed. Micah's oracles, therefore, may be considered in the light of their environmental context.

The heyday of Uzziah (767–739 B.C.) was over. In his reign the imperialistic thrust of Assyria westward and southward had been temporarily halted by internal dissension, but not before the powerful Aramean state of Damascus to Israel's north had been crippled. Benefitting from the lull and the economic opportunities it presented, Jeroboam II of the Northern Kingdom, and in alliance with him his contemporary Uzziah of Judah, had surged forward and won territorial and commercial gains. Uzziah's death marked the end of an era, as decisively as did Queen Victoria's. The old world was no more, though for a time men basked in the last rays of its lingering light.

The reign of Jotham, Uzziah's successor, coincided with fresh Assyrian campaigning under the vigorous Tiglath-pileser III, Assyria's Napoleon. Damascus and Israel, by now tributary to Assyria, chafed under their vassalage and together put pressure on Ahaz, the young crown prince of Judah who had just succeeded Jotham as king, to support their rebellion. Ahaz's appeal to their overlord certainly relieved that pressure, but at the cost of enmeshing Judah itself in the Assyrian net. First Damascus and then Israel were removed from the political scene, paying the ultimate price for their continued lack of cooperation with Assyria. Samaria, Israel's capital, fell to Assyrian besiegers in 722 B.C., and deportation of the people of the Northern Kingdom, begun some ten years before, was rigorously resumed.

Undeterred by this demonstration of the iron fist of his suzerain, Hezekiah later attempted to secede from the empire, heading an anti-Assyrian coalition of Palestinian and Syrian subject states. Judah might have suffered the fate of its northern neighbor, but although in reprisal the country was overrun by Assyrian troops in 701 B.C., Jerusalem itself was not taken, and Hezekiah was let off with payment of a fine and loss of part of his territory to the Philistines.

Micah lived in a period of economic revolution, which was proving a mixed blessing. Unfortunately the influx of material prosperity had spawned a selfish materialism, a complacent approach to religion as a means of achieving human desires, and the disintegration of personal and social values. Wealth was invested in land, with the result that the traditional system of agricultural small holdings collapsed with the growth of vast estates, and material and emotional distress ensued. Age-old sanctions associated with the divine covenant were shrugged off, and social concern was at the bottom of the list of priorities of national and local government officials. Even religious leaders—priests and prophets—did little more than echo the spirit of the period, buttressing the society that gave them their livelihood.

Micah's role was to act as religious commentator in Jerusalem on the contemporary social scene. As a prophet, one of God's men in Judah, he spoke as a representative of the divine will. It fell to him to deliver Yahweh's stern warning. As a countryman from the fertile lowlands of southwest Judah, doubtless he had firsthand knowledge of the sufferings of the rural proletariat and was thus providentially prepared to voice God's own indignation. This Amos of the Southern Kingdom realized that the God of the nation could not lightly be brushed aside. Though hailed as the great standby of his people, he would in fact intervene in terrible judgment, and only after they had been diminished and refined in the crucible of divine chastisement would he rescue and rehabilitate.

Addressing himself to the nominal theocracy of Judah, the prophet attacked the establishment for abandoning divinely ordained standards in favor of self-interest, to the point of neglecting or actively illtreating the underprivileged. He saw Judah to be on the brink of disaster, whose causes he interpreted in typical prophetic fashion not as solely political but as theological at heart. Claiming God-given insight, he discerned a close link between the social and economic abuses of the Judean lawcourts and general civil administration on the one hand, and the irresistible, glacier-like menace of Assyria on the other.

Jer. 26:18f. records a fascinating tradition of the stirring effect the bluntness of Micah's fatal diagnosis and prognosis had upon King Hezekiah and his subjects. It is probably not going too far to say with A. F. Kirkpatrick that "Hezekiah's reformation was due to the preaching of Micah."[1] In fact Judah staggered on after the 701 B.C. crisis for another century or so before

1. *The Doctrine of the Prophets* (^{3}1915), p. 208.

God's dire threats through Micah materialized in all their starkness. After 587 B.C., when Jerusalem fell and the Judeans were deported to Babylon, men must have looked with new eyes at Micah's reasoned oracles of doom, bordered by hope on the farther side.

In OT study Micah has tended to be overshadowed by Amos and Hosea and especially by his great contemporary Isaiah, whose prophetic material has been preserved in much greater quantity. Stylistically, to be sure, he sometimes has more of the qualities of an orator than of a poet. But his message is proclaimed with no uncertain sound, as with passionate forthrightness he attacks the social evils of his day. His stubborn refusal to float on the tide of his social environment, and his courageous stand for his convictions of God's truth, must commend Micah to believers in every age.

2. DATING, AUTHORSHIP, AND COMPOSITION

The heading in 1:1 attributes the prophetic ministry of Micah to the period of the second half of the eighth century B.C. An external indication of date occurs in Jer. 26:18f., where 3:12 is assigned to Hezekiah's reign. Apart from these explicit chronological pointers, the historical circumstances of each prophetic oracle can be constructed only from internal evidence. The authenticity of each oracle is bound up with its applicability to, and reflection of, its historical setting. Over the past century, scholars have been prone to assign to periods after Micah's lifetime the following oracles: 2:12, 13, all or some of those in 4:1–5:9, and 7:8–20. Do we in fact have in the book of Micah an amalgam of oracles, i.e., Micah's own supplemented with later ones? The answer must lie in an investigation of the contents of the material from a chronological viewpoint.

The oracles of chs. 1–3 are almost universally assigned to Micah apart from 2:12, 13. The first unit is 1:2–9. The fall of Samaria evidently lay in the future, to judge from vv. 6, 7. Accordingly this message was given before the city fell to Sargon II in 722 B.C. after a three-year siege, which represented a death-blow to the Northern Kingdom. Was it as early as the Syro-Ephraimite War of 734 B.C., after Damascus and Israel, rebelling against their Assyrian overlord, unsuccessfully urged first Jotham and then Ahaz to join in a western uprising? It was in that period that Isaiah predicted that an Assyrian flood would not only overwhelm the two northern states but would also "sweep on into Judah, it will overflow and pass on" (Isa. 8:6–8). There is a striking similarity to vv. 5 and 9 here, where the overthrow of Samaria is made a warning to Jerusalem to prepare for a like fate. Micah's concentration on Samaria does not necessarily presuppose that Samaria was already suffering siege. Isaiah had singled out Samaria during the Syro-Ephraimite War: "The head of Ephraim is Samaria and the head of Samaria is the son of Remaliah" (7:9). Any time between 734 and 722 B.C. would be possible for the content of this oracle.

The date of 1:10–16 is circumscribed by two references in the course of the oracle, to Gath in v. 10 and to Israel in vv. 13–15.[2] The mention of Gath implies that this Philistine city has not yet fallen to the Assyrians, as it did in 711, but is still free. Israel is evidently used of the Southern Kingdom, and this probably indicates that the Northern Kingdom has already fallen, so that the year 722 lies in the past. The oracle may well have been provoked by Sargon's campaigns against Philistia in 720 or 714–711 B.C., when the danger that overwhelmed Judah in 701 cast a warning shadow.

2:1–5 and 6–11 obviously belong together, and no one has found reason to doubt their ascription to Micah. They reflect a settled background in which the economy was flourishing, and look forward to an invasion of Judah; but there are no indications of a particular period.

The promise of 2:12, 13 was assigned to an exilic hand by Stade in 1881 and to a postexilic origin by Wellhausen. Most scholars have followed them and denied it to Micah. But the piece is strikingly similar to part of another oracle which is set in a collection of prophetic narratives concerning Isaiah and which on a number of counts may with confidence be credited to him:[3]

> *"For from Jerusalem will issue a remnant,*
> *survivors from Mount Zion.*
> *The zeal of Yahweh [of hosts] will accomplish this."*
> (2 K. 19:31=Isa. 37:32)

Isaiah's oracle is linked with the 701 B.C. disaster of the Assyrian invasion of Judah and its attendant disruption of the agricultural calendar. He promises the reestablishment of the farming routine of sowing and harvest, and makes it a parable and pledge of the regrowth of the nation. As a prelude to this eventual hope is given the promise of deliverance from the immediate crisis. Those who have had to flee into Jerusalem from the areas of Judah overrun by the enemy will be able to leave safely and so, it is implied, return home to resume normal life. The links between Isaiah's oracle and the present one are the occurrence in both of the term *remnant* and the verb *go out* and the emphasis, expressed in different ways, upon the certainty of the prediction, apparently made in view of the seriousness of the crisis. Accordingly it is possible not only to find a historical setting for this oracle within the period of Micah's prophetic ministry but also, in the light of Isaiah's explicitness, to identify the venue of salvation as Jerusalem.[4] It is feasible to proceed on the reasonable assumption that this oracle may be assigned to Micah, unless one has an *a priori* objection to Micah's ever having uttered prophecies of

2. Cf. Lindblom, Robinson, Bentzen, and Fohrer, BZAW 105 (1967), p. 80. On pp. 77–79 Fohrer disputes the dating and setting ascribed to the oracle by Elliger, *ZDPV* 57 (1934), pp. 81–152, who has had many followers in seeing here a lament after the separation of the specified area from Jerusalem in Sennacherib's campaign of 701.

3. For the period of three years cf. Isa. 7:14–16; 20:3. For the motif of a future sign cf. Isa. 7:14. The remnant is a characteristic theme of Isaiah. The final clause recurs in Isa. 9:7.

4. Sellin; cf. Robinson, who finds here a reference to an apocalyptic deliverance from a siege of Jerusalem. "The similarities between the three hope sections in the book make it likely that 'fold' . . . here refers to Zion or Jerusalem. See Mic. 4:8. Compare 7:14 . . . with Isa. 1:8" (Willis, *SEA* 34 [1969], p. 26 and n. 49).

salvation. Micah spoke with two voices, and was by no means the only prophet to do so. His task was not just to afflict the comfortable but also to comfort the afflicted. It is the second role that he plays in this short oracle, bringing a message of hope to those for whom his message of chastisement had come or was coming true.

3:1–12 is made up of three oracles with a similar setting. As in 2:1–11, there is an atmosphere of external calm and national security (cf. v. 11), which leaves men free to pursue their chicanery and moneymaking. Micah interrupts their profiteering with forecasts of disaster which doubtless came like bolts from the placid blue. Since in the light of Jer. 26:18f. the final oracle is to be dated in Hezekiah's reign, it is probable that the two earlier ones come from the same period, pre-701; the similarity of the introductions to the first and the third confirms the contemporaneity of these two at least.

4:1–5 raises a special problem in that it appears also in Isa. 2:2–4.[5] What is the explanation of this double occurrence? There are four main possibilities: (1) Isaiah composed the oracle and Micah quoted it; (2) Micah composed the oracle and Isaiah quoted it; (3) both are quoting from an earlier composition; or (4) it is a later composition inserted subsequently into the works of both prophets. There is no certain proof that any one of these answers is the correct one, but there are considerations supporting some over against others. An important factor is the age of the motifs found in the so-called Songs of Zion, Pss. 46, 48, 76, which this oracle appears to be taking up.[6] Did the victory won over Jerusalem's enemies, which these Songs celebrate, allude originally to its reprieve from Assyrian conquest in 701? Or do they commemorate an earlier historical event,[7] or a religious drama enacted in the temple?[8] Does the associated theme of Jerusalem's importance go back to early times, perhaps even to the era of Jebusite rule before David's capture of the city?[9] That in the eighth century Jerusalem was already invested in men's minds with an aura of inviolable sanctity is suggested by Isaiah's frequent use of Zion ideology in tones that suggest he is echoing rather than creating.[10] If so, it is likely that this oracle builds upon sacred traditions already established in the period of Isaiah and Micah.[11] In

5. Apart from small textual variants the differences in Isa. 2 lie in its supplementary conclusion (Isa. 2:5, contrast Mic. 4:5) and in its omission of Mic. 4:4.
6. H. Wildberger, *VT* 7 (1957), pp. 73–75, lists the links, most of which are cited in the course of the exposition.
7. Such as David's victory over the Philistines in 2 Sam. 5 (A. Weiser, *The Psalms* [E.T. 1962], p. 525).
8. *Ibid.*, pp. 50f. H.-M. Lutz, *Jahwe, Jerusalem und die Völker*. WMANT 27 (1968), pp. 171–77, regards the theme of the nations' battle against Jerusalem as a pre-Israelite cultic tradition.
9. Cf. Ps. 110:4; J. H. Hayes, "The Tradition of Zion's Inviolability," *JBL* 82 (1963), pp. 419–426, esp. p. 424; G. von Rad, *OT Theology*, vol. 2 (E.T. 1965), pp. 156f.
10. Isa. 8:9f.; 14:32; 28:16; 29:5–8. Cf. Hayes, *loc. cit.*
11. H. H. Rowley, *The Biblical Doctrine of Election* (1950), p. 64, and J. Gray, *VT* 11 (1961), p. 15, assume from its presence in both prophetical books its genuine currency in the eighth century B.C. H. Junker, "Sancta civitas, Jerusalem nova," *Ekklesia*. M. Wehr

recent years it has been strongly urged that this oracle emanates from Isaiah. In favor of this solution is the evidence that Isaiah took a great interest in the theological tenets he apparently found attached to Jerusalem. Moreover, a number of the terms used in this poem recur in his oracles.[12] The weak link in this argument is the nonoccurrence of Mic. 4:4 at the end of the Isaianic piece. Verse 4a forms a fitting positive sequence to the previous negative sentiments, while v. 4b rounds off the poem well with an oracular formula found elsewhere only in the book of Isaiah.[13] The verse has an original ring and suits Isaiah's style. Did it fall out of Isa. 2?[14] This supposition is difficult to substantiate. Are not the links with Isaiah rather to be explained by his frequent practice of taking over terminology already associated with Zion and temple worship? If so, he may be quoting part of an existing piece, his own contribution being merely to add an exhortation to challenge his hearers to "walk worthy of the gospel" of God's future plans for Jerusalem. On the other hand, Micah or possibly his editor cites the traditional piece in its entirety and adds a separate affirmation.[15] Its position next to the oracles of disaster for Jerusalem is not intended to represent an original oral context. Here and in 2:12, 13 we are rather to think of the editorial arrangement of oracles from different times and situations into an artistic pattern.[16]

The original setting of 4:6–8 is difficult to determine, and doubtless this very feature encouraged its preservation, as a message that could easily be reapplied to Israel's recurring periods of weakness. It was likely placed here as a deliberate reminiscence of the similar oracle of hope at the end of the first main section of the book (2:12, 13). Both employ the motifs of the remnant, sheep, and divine kingship. Have they sprung from the same background? It was claimed that the earlier oracle fits the period of Assyrian invasion. Can the same original setting be substantiated for this one? The reference to limping and straying sheep would be an appropriate description of Judean refugees fleeing in panic from their town and villages before the enemy invader and collecting in the capital, where it was claimed Yahweh would demonstrate his kingly power. The description of Jerusalem as a sheep-tower may then be an allusion to the city's isolation, like the similes in Isa. 1:8 referring to this period of history. The weakness of Jerusalem at that time would constitute a poignant contrast with the old Davidic empire, now that the ten tribes had gone and even Judah was overrun. Or were these lost

---

Festschrift. Trierer Theologische Studien 15 (1962), pp. 17–33, esp. pp. 29f., finds a fitting *Sitz im Leben* in Hezekiah's cultic reformation, which he thinks encourages Isaiah to adopt an old temple promise dating back to the time of Solomon.

12. Wildberger, *loc. cit.*, pp. 69–75.
13. Isa. 1:20; 40:5; 58:14.
14. Wildberger, *loc. cit.*, pp. 75f.
15. Cf. E. Nielsen, *Oral Tradition*. SBT 11 (1954), p. 93.
16. Time was when a commentator could write that "it is now admitted by almost all expositors that Isaiah borrowed from Micah" (C. W. E. Nägelsbach, *The Prophet Isaiah* [E.T. 1878], p. 54), mainly on the grounds of a better text and closer contextual links in Micah. But textual superiority is not necessarily a proof of originality (Chronicles sometimes preserves a text better than Kings), nor is literary dovetailing.

sheep of the house of Israel intended to be a reference to the northern tribes now in Mesopotamian exile? In either case the oracle could be given an eighth-century provenance. The obstacle to these historical reconstructions is the usage of the term *remnant* in v. 7.[17] It is employed in a different sense from the reference in 2:12. There it was a negative term, alluding to the weakness with which God's people had been overwhelmed. Here, however, as the poetic parallelism indicates, it is a positive term, alive with potential. The prophet addresses an audience who readily associated the word with great expectations of future good rather than with dread and disaster, who apparently prized old prophetic promises and looked for their fulfilment. From our present knowledge it is difficult to view eighth-century B.C. Judah as the home of such accepted hopes.[18] The oracle is generally assigned to the exilic or postexilic period; the era of Jeremiah would appear to be the earliest to provide an appropriate setting, by which time Isaiah's teaching on the remnant would have had time to take root in the popular mind by long familiarity. Since in Jer. 23:3 the imagery of scattered sheep is apparently applied to the hope of restoration of the Judean exiles of 597 B.C., it is not unlikely that a similar hope of restoration from Babylonian exile is the original basis for this oracle.[19]

The theme of 4:9, 10 accords well with the Mican expectation of the fall of Jerusalem (3:12) and the prospect of deportation which he glimpsed (1:16). However, a substantial obstacle to Mican authorship has generally been seen in the reference to Babylon, which appears to have no relevance to Micah's situation at the end of the eighth century. Accordingly the oracle would be more obviously fitting on the lips of a contemporary of Jeremiah, and many have dated the oracle in 597 or 587 B.C.[20] The other expedient frequently adopted is to regard the third line of v. 10, either the second half or the whole, as a later addition to the text. The conservative Jewish scholar Y. Kaufmann describes the half-line as "one of the few instances in the whole corpus of prophecy of a genuine revision in the light of later events. It is characteristically obvious, no exegetical subtlety being required to detect it. The glossator doubtless imagined that he was doing no more than making explicit the vague terms of ancient prophecy."[21] Kaufmann speaks for many who are willing to ascribe the oracle to Micah apart from this intrusion.[22] He may have been influenced by an observation often made that the deletion

17. Wellhausen, J. M. P. Smith, Willi-Plein, *et al.*

18. Contrast the sinister use of the idea in Lev. 26:36, 39; Isa. 10:20; Amos 5:15. It is sometimes urged that the use of Aram. *tĕ'ṯeh, come,* in v. 8 indicates lateness, but cf. its use in such early literature as Deut. 33:21; Ps. 68:31(32).

19. Cf. Zeph. 3:19, which echoes the language of this present oracle. Ezek. 34:16 uses similar terms in a passage that develops the sheep-shepherd imagery at length.

20. E.g., J. M. P. Smith, Wade, Robinson, Deissler, Marsh, Thomas.

21. *The Religion of Israel from Its Beginnings to the Babylonian Exile* (E.T. 1961), p. 352.

22. E.g., Sellin, S. R. Driver, G. A. Smith, George. It is sometimes claimed, e.g., by Cheyne and Bewer, that G's addition "from Babylon" in v. 8 (see the textual note on that verse) confirms a tendency to historicizing accretions of this type. The Gk. addition does not necessarily imply amplification in MT, for which there is no textual evidence.

would remove an exegetical difficulty which the present text raises in addition to the historical one: v. 13 speaks of the defeat of the foes who in the full text of v. 10 are blatantly victorious. However, since each of the three adjacent oracles has a different tone and emphasis, it is perhaps too facile to resort to deletion as a means of harmonization.

With regard to the historical objection it is not beyond possibility that we should think in terms of a subsequent amplification, although it would be preferable to think of its being made on the occasion of the oracle's reissue and reapplication in the reign of Zedekiah than to regard it as a *vaticinium ex eventu*.[23] But how incredible is a Mican reference to Babylon? Appeal may be made to two pieces of biblical evidence that may justify mention of Babylon as the place of exile by a prophet in whose times Assyria dominated the political horizon.[24] The first is 2 K. 17:24, which specifies Babylon as one of the places from which deportees were brought to colonize the new Assyrian province of Samaria after the fall of the city in 722 B.C. The second and more important passage is 2 K. 20:16–18, where in reaction to the visit of Merodach-baladan's envoys to Hezekiah, presumably to coordinate anti-Assyrian uprisings in the east and west of the empire, Isaiah is said to have delivered an oracle forecasting the time when the treasures shown to the envoys would be carried off to Babylon, along with some of Hezekiah's own family. Doubt is frequently cast on the authenticity of this oracle for the same reason as in the case of Mic. 4:10, but certainly the oracle gives the impression of a typical Isaianic reaction condemning would-be cures like foreign alliances as the cause of worse ills.[25]

If the oracle attributed to Isaiah is authentic, there is hardly reason to question the authenticity of this one as it stands. It must be remembered that the specific background of the oracle is unknown. It may be that Micah was addressing a situation in which hope had been expressed of Babylonian backing. For his hearers his meaning need be no more than a prospect of Assyrian deportation to the city whose envoys Hezekiah welcomed with such expectation; and this would imply the extinction of these hopes, since first of all Babylon would necessarily be conquered and brought back into the Assyrian sphere of power. If so, the plain meaning of Micah's words was doomed to nonfulfilment, as was his evident fear in 3:12 that Assyria would capture Jerusalem. But they both represent a remarkable presentiment of the future doom of Jerusalem and the Judeans, and would so increase Micah's stock in the sixth century as to guarantee the preservation and continued study of his oracles.

Two questions are posed by 4:11–13, one concerning the date of the oracle and another regarding its authorship. The question of date is linked with the discussion already broached in connection with vv. 1–5, since the motif of foreign attack upon Jerusalem is a major one in the Songs of Zion.

23. Cf. Stade, Wellhausen, Wolfe.
24. Cf. Schwantes, van der Woude, Kapelrud, Vuilleumier.
25. Cf. Isa. 30:3, 16; 31:3.

For many commentators the question of date is easily solved by reference to the recurrence of the nations' attack in such passages as Ezek. 38f.; Joel 3; Zech. 12; 14, and this oracle is accordingly labelled late apocalyptic.[26] Those who judge the Songs of Zion to be a later theological reflection upon Jerusalem's 701 B.C. experience naturally regard this oracle as of a similarly late origin. G. Wanke has compared the vocabulary with usage elsewhere in the OT and concluded that it can hardly have originated before the exile.[27] As to the parallels adduced from Ezekiel, Joel, and Zechariah, Lindblom has questioned their relevance: those prophets issue apocalyptic promises of salvation, but this oracle is firmly tied to contemporary history. The significance of *many nations, many peoples* he takes to be not a vague apocalyptic allusion but a precise reference to the various national units that made up the Assyrian imperial army.[28] He has no hesitation in ascribing the oracle to the year 701 B.C. during the period before the Assyrian withdrawal.

Adam S. van der Woude has criticized Wanke's vocabulary test on the ground of the fragmentary nature of Hebrew literature.[29] Certainly to conclude that vocabulary typical of later times does not have roots in an earlier period is unwarranted if on other grounds this passage can be credited with an early date. Wanke's treatment of the *Völkerkampfmotif* is vitiated by his cavalier dismissal of the relevance of the admittedly early Ps. 2, which he sharply differentiates from the nonroyal Pss. 46, 48, 76. But he underestimates the similarity of Ps. 2 to the Songs of Zion, with its mention of "Zion" as Yahweh's "holy mountain." Although the foes are subject kings, they are also "nations" and their rebellion constitutes a threat to divinely favored Zion. Moreover, Isaiah appears to echo this motif in Isa. 17:12–14; 29:5–8 (cf. 8:8, 9), and to historicize it in the events of 701.[30] Indeed, he delivered a number of oracles remarkably similar to this present one in their theme of God's last-minute intervention to ward off Assyrian attack.[31]

As to date, then, it is feasible to attribute it to the 701 B.C. crisis. The question of authorship is a separate issue. Lindblom and van der Woude[32] credit it to a different prophetic source representing a nationalistic and optimistic attitude, on the ground of its completely opposite tone from that of the previous oracle. Certainly the present stark literary continuity can hardly represent a historical, oral one. But the ambivalence to be found in Isaiah's prophetic ministry[33] warns against forbidding too hastily the presence of

26. E.g., by Stade, Wellhausen, J. M. P. Smith, Robinson, Marsh, Thomas.
27. *Die Zionstheologie der Korachiten in ihrem traditionsgeschichtlichen Zusammenhang*. BZAW 97 (1966), pp. 82f. H.-M. Lutz, *op. cit.*, pp. 213–16, criticizes Wanke's conclusions. Cf. the discussion of 4:1–5 earlier.
28. He compares Isa. 22:6; 29:7f. Cf. Hos. 10:10.
29. *VT* 19 (1969), p. 260.
30. Cf. Wildberger, *VT* 7 (1957), pp. 69f.
31. Cf. Isa. 10:24–27; 14:24–27 referring to Yahweh's "counsel"; 31:5, 8f.
32. He places vv. 11–13 within a debate between Micah and his prophetic rivals, regarding vv. 9, 11–13 as their statements and vv. 10, 14 as Micah's retorts.
33. Cf. von Rad, *op. cit.*, p. 164.

both dark and light tones in Micah's. Our ignorance of the background to his oracles means that we are uninformed concerning any winds of change that might have blown across the historical scene. Obviously a change in the circumstances or the attitude of the prophet's hearers lies like a chasm between the end of v. 10 and the beginning of v. 11. One must not ignore the possibility of two Assyrian campaigns against Judah, one in 701 and the other in the early 680's.[34] Or did a change of heart among Micah's shocked audience warrant a change of message? Whatever the explanation, it is methodologically unsound to deny that a prophet who in so many respects stood shoulder to shoulder with his greater contemporary Isaiah could speak like him of the triumph of God's grace.[35]

In 5:1–6 there seems to be little reason to take *Assyria* (vv. 5f.) as other than literal.[36] The resultant period can be narrowed down by the reference in v. 1 to the state of siege Jerusalem was undergoing.[37] Accordingly 701 B.C. appears to be the year when this oracle was delivered. Micah's authorship is suggested by a number of factors. The mention of a mourning rite is characteristic of Micah: compare 1:8, 10, 16; 3:7; 4:9. The wordplay in v. 1 accords with a propensity profusely illustrated in 1:10–16. The links between this oracle and the teaching of Isaiah are in line with the many other parallels to be found in the ministries of these contemporary prophets. The implicit warning against trusting in armaments and military leadership in the last part of the oracle echoes the theme of the Mican piece, 5:10–15.

5:7–9 is generally denied to Micah, along with the other remnant passages, 2:12, 13; 4:6–8, and given a postexilic dating. In fact it is a timeless piece which must have proved relevant to many generations of God's people in circumstances of need. It must have had an appeal for the struggling postexilic community and this appeal undoubtedly encouraged its preservation. But there is nothing in the oracle to rule out an eighth-century provenance. The basic twin idea of the piece is very old. The double promise "I shall bless those who bless you and him who curses you I shall curse" has been handed down as one of the fundamental assurances given to Abraham (Gen. 12:3). There is no barrier to seeing here a primary reference to the circumstances of Micah's own times when various national units in the

34. Cf. J. Bright, *History of Israel* (^{2}1972), pp. 296–308.

35. Cf. G. A. Smith; George; Sellin, who attributed v. 11 to Micah; Weiser; von Rad, *Der heilige Krieg im alten Israel* (^{4}1965), p. 64. Lutz, *op. cit.*, p. 96, assigns the oracle to an early date, but leaves open the question of authorship.

36. *Contra* Robinson, Weiser, George, Thomas. Older scholars, such as Calvin, Pusey, Keil, and also van Hoonacker and Deissler, took *Assyria* as a general label for the enemies of God's people on the practical ground that the Messiah did not materialize in the Assyrian period. It is a fact that the name is used of later Mesopotamian heirs of the Assyrian empire, such as Babylon (Lam. 5:6) and Persia (Ezra 6:22). But it is difficult to see how it could refer to Syria here, as J. M. P. Smith, Wolfe, and Marsh suppose.

37. Robinson and Thomas find a reference to Nebuchadnezzar's siege. On the bounds of the oracle see the exposition.

Assyrian army threatened the capital,[38] although the oracle must indeed have come alive again in the experience of many a future generation.

An eighth-century date for 5:10–15 is suggested by its links with the teaching of Isaiah in Isa. 2:6–8, 15, verses most scholars consider authentic, where amassing of military materials and recourse to occult practices and religious fetishes are similarly attacked (cf. 17:7, 8); in 30:15, 16, where military defeat is predicted for those who do not trust in Yahweh; and in 29:5–8, which promises God's sudden intervention to deal with "the multitude of nations that fight against Jerusalem" (cf. 17:12–14). This similarity provides a strong argument for Mican authorship, since it matches the general affinity to be found between the ministry of these two prophets. The passage echoes sentiments to be found in other oracles of Micah. The denunciation of Samaria's image-based religion in 1:7 is applied to Judah here in vv. 13f. A note struck before in 1:13 is repeated in vv. 10f., where an emphasis on fortresses and chariotry is deplored. The reliance on oracular devices attacked in v. 12 has been mentioned in 3:6, 7, 11. Historically the oracle fits the period before the religious reformation with which Hezekiah is credited in 2 K. 18:4.[39] A large number of scholars, including Wellhausen, Weiser, George, Marsh, and Deissler, consider vv. 10–14 authentic and v. 15 secondary, but rightly understood v. 15 is a necessary and integral part of the oracle.[40]

In date, 6:1–8 is certainly preexilic. Its disparagement of sacrifice as an easy answer to the problem of the people's sin echoes the criticisms of Amos, Hosea, and Isaiah. Verse 3 strikes a note of divine pathos which has already sounded in 2:9 and has been echoed in the prophet's sentiments expressed in 1:8f. Verse 8 reveals the influence of Hosea,[41] not for the first time in the book, for at 1:7 Micah was evidently depending on the earlier prophet in his delineation of Samaria's cultic sins. The comprehensiveness of the reference to the Exodus and related traditions in vv. 4f. can hardly be a barrier to an eighth-century dating. The use of deuteronomic language raises questions in commentators' minds, but they are not sufficient to overthrow the tradition of Micah's authorship to which very many scholars assent.[42] It is hardly possible to date the oracle precisely, such as soon after 701 (Weiser) or during the 701 crisis (Willis). Ewald's assignment of the oracle to the reign of Manasseh, favored by not a few, rests on a misunderstanding of v. 7. The view of J. M. P. Smith, Horton, and Wade

38. Sellin. Deissler suggests that a Mican fragment has been amplified.

39. "There is no good reason to deny him the credit of the reformation described in this verse" (Gray, *1 and 2 Kings* [^{2}1970], p. 670). Cf. H. H. Rowley, "Hezekiah's Reform and Rebellion," *Men of God* (1963), pp. 98–132.

40. See the well-documented and ably argued article of J. T. Willis, *ZAW* 81 (1969), pp. 353–368.

41. Hos. 12:6. Willi-Plein demonstrates the similarity of vv. 2–5 to Hos. 4:1–3; 12:2–4, 7–9(3–5, 8–10).

42. E.g., Sellin, Lindblom, Weiser, Wolfe, George, von Ungern-Sternberg, Marsh, Beyerlin, Deissler.

that v. 8 is not addressed to Israel but represents an individualizing and universalizing religious standpoint typical of the postexilic period, is exegetically unsatisfactory and receives little support today.[43]

Most scholars accept 6:9–16 as Mican.[44] Its date can hardly be determined beyond the probability that it was delivered after 722 and before 701.[45] Like a number of oracles in the book, it presupposes a period of peace. The commercial accusations suggest a time when the economy was buoyant. A crucial factor is the identity of the unspecified city of v. 9. Most take it as Jerusalem but a few scholars, notably Lindblom, following a fashion set by Jerome, interpret it as Samaria and accordingly date it before 722 B.C. The reference to the northern kings Omri and Ahab in v. 16 could be cited in support. But if Micah refers to a tribe in v. 9, he probably means Judah, and then the southern capital must be in view.

7:1–7 reveals "no features which do not fit with Micah and his time,"[46] and most scholars accept its authenticity. But within Micah's period it is not possible to date the oracle. Accusations of decadence are to be found in the literature of every age; their essential relativity hampers chronological pinpointing, especially in the absence of a detailed social history of Judah. Many have thought of the period of Manasseh and some of Ahaz, but such precision is unwarranted, as is an ascription to the postexilic period.[47] The general description fits the mood of the foregoing oracle; and it is reasonable to assume that the doom of which v. 4 speaks is, as elsewhere in Micah's oracles, a presentiment of the catastrophe of 701 B.C.

The historical situation in view in 7:8–20 is one of calamity. The *havoc* envisaged in the previous piece (7:4) has apparently now occurred. There is obvious warrant for Micah's lament of vv. 1–7 to be taken up afresh. Jerusalem has *fallen* and sits in darkness, enduring God's punishment, which is evident in its shattered walls. A small population, cooped into a narrow, infertile area, looks with longing at regions beyond the Jordan that once were theirs but are no longer. Attempts have been made to relate the liturgy to the fall of Samaria and to see here the "swansong of Northern Israel."[48] In such a case it could hardly be Micah's, although its

43. T. Lescow, *Micha 6, 6–8. Studien zu Sprache, Form und Auslegung* (1966), p. 57, and G. Fohrer, *Introduction to the OT* (E.T. 1970), p. 446, interpret in terms of universality or individualism.

44. Deissler and Willi-Plein regard v. 16 as a later addition.

45. Wolfe suggests a date after 701, comparing the thought of Isa. 1:2–9. His dating depends upon accepting in v. 13 an emendation that many favor.

46. O. Eissfeldt, *The OT: An Introduction* (E.T. 1965), p. 411.

47. Fohrer, *op. cit.*, p. 446, suggests that the passage is an elaboration of Isa. 57:1f., yet he calls Isa. 58:1b an echo of Mic. 3:8 (p. 386).

48. F. C. Burkitt, "Micah 6 and 7 a Northern Prophecy," *JBL* 45 (1926), pp. 159–161. Cf. O. Eissfeldt, *ZDMG* 112 (1962), pp. 259–268; J. Dus, "Weiteres zum nordisraelitischen Psalm Micha 7, 7–20," *ZDMG* 115 (1965), pp. 14–22. *Assyria* in v. 12 is sometimes cited in favor of an early date, but this is to misunderstand its geographical and traditional function.

composition would fall within the period of his prophetic ministry: its tone labels its author as a member of the suffering community. Eissfeldt regards the speakers as "the inhabitants of the northern kingdom of Israel or of the truncated kingdom of Ephraim left after 732 or—and this is the most likely—of the territory of the Assyrian province left after its removal in 722," but goes on to regard Micah as author, expressing on their behalf the expectation of a future salvation for this part of Israel.[49] But one would hardly expect Micah to celebrate Yahweh as patron of a sanctuary on Mount Carmel, to whom Eissfeldt finds reference in v. 14 as a crucial ingredient of his view. More likely the unnamed speaker in vv. 8–10 and the addressee in vv. 11–13 is Zion, and God's people in v. 14 are the early postexilic community. Most commentators take the piece either as exilic or as postexilic before the advent of Nehemiah, in view of v. 11.

It is possible therefore to defend the Mican origin of most of the book apart from 4:1–4, 6–8; 7:8–20, if one's guiding principle is "to accept the tradition for those parts of the book where no compelling reasons can be urged against their authenticity."[50] The content of the latter two passages appears to point to a later date, while 4:1–4 probably antedates Micah. There are no compelling grounds for denying the authenticity of further material. The claim is often made on the basis of Jer. 26:18 that Micah was remembered only as a prophet of disaster and not as also the bearer of a positive message. But this is an unwarranted conclusion: it lays too much stress on an isolated incident relating to Jeremiah which recalled a parallel in the case of Micah. The later reminiscence by no means excludes the possibility that Micah also saw beyond destruction.[51] The prophetic material ascribed to Micah is too scanty to provide sure canons concerning what he could or could not say. An expression of hope is not necessarily a pointer to nonauthenticity. Certainly a message of comfort would weaken one of condemnation if both were uttered in the same situation to the same audience, but literary juxtaposition is no proof of contemporaneity. Oracles collected from years of prophetic ministry and different spiritual climates can reasonably range over a host of prophetic moods from stormy to fair. When promised judgment comes near enough for all to see, a prophet can safely bring remorseful hearers comfort concerning the future without compromising his earlier stand.

The earlier detailed study of oracles provokes a new question, one concerning the divinely guided composition of the book in its present form. How soon Micah's oracles were committed to writing is unknown, but a study of the structure will reveal an artistic arrangement of the total material in which the later pieces are firmly embedded as essential structural ingredients. Skill in the literary composition of the book in its

49. *Op. cit.*, p. 412.
50. E. Hammershaimb, *Some Aspects of OT Prophecy From Isaiah to Malachi* (1966), p. 29.
51. See A. S. Kapelrud, *VT* 11 (1961), pp. 392–94; Hammershaimb, *op. cit.*, pp. 29, 41–50.

final form is further revealed in the recurring motifs. References to the remnant feature in 2:12 and 7:18, in the first and last sections of the book; and in the second section they surround the heart of the book, at 4:6 and 5:7. Sin and rebellion are a pair of words that figure in all three sections, at 1:15; 3:8; 7:18f. The metaphor of sheep and shepherd to describe the covenant relationship between Yahweh and his people occurs similarly in 2:12; 4:6–8; 7:14 and is also applied to his royal representative in 5:4.

The structural patterning and the deliberate and symmetrical echoing of motifs yield clues to the concerns of the editor of the book and to his conception of the relevance of the material to his own times. The latest datable material in the book, 7:8–20, fixes the probable time of composition. Standing doubtless in the postexilic era before the appearance of the dynamic Ezra and Nehemiah, who set the struggling community on its feet,[52] the editor presented a composition whose intention was to serve as a digest of the counsel of God for his generation. The past history of his people, culminating in the exile, is interpreted as a time when God's wrath was at work, in reprisal for the sins of leaders and people. The phenomenon represents an implicit warning that the path of disobedience leads to disaster for Jerusalem and Judah. The centrality of the capital in the Mican material strikes a chord especially relevant to those early postexilic days when attempts were made to rebuild the temple and the capital was viewed as the key to the destiny of God's people as a whole.[53] As in Micah's days the promise was given of Yahweh gathering his people to the capital as a prelude to leading them out to victory and rehabilitation, so the new people of God are reminded of the promise in 2:12, 13 that it may be claimed afresh. The threat that Jerusalem would be reduced to scrubland (3:12) had been fulfilled, and those who view it thus (7:14) pray that in turn the gracious side of Micah's ministry may be their lot. Their hope is to radiate out from the central area to repossess the ancient realm under a new Davidic king, as God had promised of old through his prophet. The strong messianic interest evinced by making 5:1–6 the pivot of the book is reminiscent of the ministry of Haggai and Zechariah. The book was evidently issued for use in temple worship, and supplied with an introductory heading and with fitting responses in 6:9, and also at the end of the book, whereby the congregation might voice their prayers.

Thus centuries later Micah's message came alive in a new environment for a fresh generation of God's people. Reapplied to a quite different historical situation, it spoke to the hearts of a later audience as the very

52. The Aramaisms *'iyyîn* 3:12 (an Aram. plural; contrast *'iyyîm* in Jer. 26:18) and *'ar'ēnû* (see n. 43 on 7:15) favor a postexilic date for the edition. Von Ungern-Sternberg and Willis, *SEA* 34 (1969), pp. 40–42, place it in the period immediately after the fall of Jerusalem in the sixth century. Willis views it as emanating from Judeans left in Palestine, but von Ungern-Sternberg considers its provenance Babylonian. B. Renaud, *Structure et attaches littéraires de Michée iv–v* (1964), regards 2:12f.; chs. 4–5; 7:8–20 as the literary production of a priestly scribe in the fifth century; he allows only 5:5b–6a, 10–14 to be earlier units.

53. Cf., e.g., Zech. 8:1–8.

word of God for themselves and drew forth the prayer that God's prophetic truth would find fulfilment in their own context. So the prophet's message spanned the centuries and imparted to many a weary believer holy awe and confidence to face the future. May we in turn appropriate the divine challenge and comfort mediated through this ancient prophet.

3. TEXT

See the basic section in the Introduction to Joel. The Hebrew text is fairly well preserved. The time is past when a textual scholar could write: "The first three chapters of the Book of Micah, in which only 32½ lines are genuine, are more corrupt than any other Old Testament text I ever studied."[54] Mur. 88, which apart from minor variants reflects MT, and the fragments of the Qumran commentaries 1QpMic and 4QpMic, are of little importance for improving the text.[55]

The ancient versions, especially G, play a valuable role in attesting the original text in places where MT has suffered in transmission. There are three blocks of material where MT appears to have lost the thread of the original meaning: 2:7–10; 6:9–12; 7:11, 12. Many scholars would include 1:10–15 in a list of corrupted areas, but there it is quite possible to justify MT in most cases.

Vowel letters in MT require to be changed or omitted in four cases, all with versional support: 1:6, 9; 3:10, 12. Repointing has been resorted to in five cases, two with versional support (3:6; 7:14) and three simply according to the demands of the context (1:13; 2:6; 7:15). Apart from vocalization, emendation has been judged advisable in a number of instances. Of the damaged blocks, in 2:7–10 of seven changes deemed necessary four have versional support (vv. 7, 9, 10); in 6:9–12 one out of four changes is partially supported by G (6:9f.); in 7:11, 12 two out of three changes have the backing of V, both in 7:12. The slight emendations, supported and conjectural, are easily explicable according to standard text-critical principles. Outside the blocks, in 1:5, 10; 3:3; 5:5; 6:16; and probably 7:19, superior readings are represented in one or more of the old versions and in the last case also in Hebrew mss. Minor conjectural emendations are required in 1:14, 15 (metathesis); 2:4, 5 (haplography), 12 (word division); 4:8 (transposition).

4. THEOLOGY

Micah's God was no less than *the Lord of the whole earth* (4:13). The prophet evidently takes up a term current in the language of public worship

54. P. Haupt, *JBL* 29 (1910), p. 95.
55. See the detailed study of M. Collin, *VT* 21 (1971), pp. 281–297. His work is vitiated by a wooden attitude in reconstructing the Heb. *Vorlage* of G.

and proclaims its imminent demonstration in the contemporary experience of God's people. The nations gathered around Jerusalem in 701 B.C., already savoring its downfall, have walked into a trap (4:12). Arrayed against God's people, and so against God, they have played into the hands of a master Strategist who is in control of the situation and will turn defeat into victory. God has his plan and also the power to effect it. Mighty as the nations are, Jerusalem's God is mightier still.

The process illustrated in 4:13 whereby the content of traditional worship bursts its cultic bounds and comes alive in a new act of God recurs in 1:2–4, where the vocabulary of theophany, replete with the age-old motifs of earthquake and fire, is used to describe the intervention of Yahweh, who comes to destroy the northern capital of Samaria, descending from heaven and striding the hilltops as a giant figure. It was no little God who was worshipped in Jerusalem. Faith's potential, ascribed to their God by the devout at worship, is reaffirmed by Micah as true and about to be demonstrated in visible fact. The intervention is local, but it is expressly described as part of a greater judgment which is only beginning at the house of God. All the nations of the world are summoned to judgment on serious charges which Yahweh is to bring. This theme occurs afresh in 5:15, where Yahweh, the Overlord of the nations, is described as about to make reprisals upon his disobedient vassals.

In the hymn of bright-eyed hope which Micah takes over in 4:1–4, there is a positive outworking of the universality of Yahweh. The ideal pattern of Israel's visiting the sanctuary as pilgrims and returning home to live out the lessons of faith is expanded to international dimensions. Other nations are to visit the temple at Jerusalem, and this acknowledgment of Israel's God is to be accompanied by communal living ordered according to his revelation.

The God of Micah is supremely the covenant God. He bears the covenant name of Yahweh. The Judean community among whom Micah ministered in Jerusalem is described by the traditional covenant terms, *(house of) Israel* and *Jacob*. They are *his people* and *my people* to Yahweh (2:8, 9; 6:2, 3, 5). Micah reminds the community of the debt they owe to the grace of Yahweh, which is exemplified in the series of saving acts that commenced at the Exodus and culminated in their arrival in Canaan (6:4f.). These basic deeds of grace they all knew well from their recital in services of worship, but they had ceased to be moved by them sufficiently to shoulder the social and moral obligations laid down in the terms of the covenant. The *good* had been revealed (6:8), but there was little sign of the fellowship of the covenant being worked out in the community (2:2, 8f.; 6:10f.). The justice of God and the loyalty of God were not being reflected in dealings between those who shared in the covenant relationship with God. It was against the absence of justice, both in its forensic sense and in its wider meaning as a comprehensive term for the fulfilment of the covenant's demands, that Micah inveighed (3:1–3, 9; 6:8). He stood out against his environment as a courageous, passionate champion of justice (3:8).

He is particularly shocked at the perversion of true religion. God was being represented onesidedly as a benevolent and forgiving deity, perpetually blessing in grandfatherly fashion. Sinners were being comforted by such easy doctrines (2:6–9). Exodus theology was being greedily appropriated as a pledge of redemption from political misfortune (4:10). The doctrine of Yahweh's special revelation of himself at Jerusalem was turned into a guarantee of security for those who lived in this sacred city (3:11). Religious leaders in the community were misrepresenting God and so leading their flock astray (3:5). Faith was perverted into a presumptuous, cocksure leaning upon God (3:11) or was adulterated with ventures into the occult, or flirtation with syncretism, or else exchanged for the self-help associated with armaments (5:10–14). Micah himself is revealed as a living illustration of true faith, as for example in 7:7, where he makes the language of pious psalmists his own. God was going to strike away such false props as his contemporaries preferred, in a signal demonstration of the truth.

They needed to be reminded of the implications of covenant disloyalty. There were covenant curses which covered this eventuality, and they would have to be applied in a coming crisis of enemy invasion (6:14f.). Yahweh was not feeble, as he was to show and did show in the doom of the northern capital—and how could the southern capital hope to escape, since Jerusalem was equally reprehensible? God's blow had to fall, and soon it would (1:9, 12; 2:1, 3; 6:13). The present willful alienation from Yahweh of Zion's leaders merited the destruction of Jerusalem, temple and all (3:12). For if the most sacred institution was not serving its purpose but in the hands of religious perverts was acting as a barrier to God, of what further use could it be to him?

So God must punish, provoked by the sin and rebellion of his covenant partner (1:5; 3:8; 6:13). An interesting feature of the punishment pronounced by Micah is its continual correspondence to the *lex talionis,* the principle of sacral law that demanded an eye for an eye. For example, evil plotting would be answered by divine plotting of an evil fate (2:1, 3). Those who had misappropriated the ancestral property of others would lose their own right to a foothold in the promised land (2:2, 4f., 9f.). Civil leaders who had turned a deaf ear to appeals for help would find God equally deaf to their entreaties (3:4). The dimensions of punishment vary in Micah's oracles. Sometimes it is the individual leaders of society who by their antisocial behavior forfeit their membership of the covenant community and are doomed to excommunication from God's land, or are otherwise afflicted (2:4f., 9f.; 3:4, 6f.). At other times, by virtue of that solidarity which so often in human experience has dragged down a whole society along with its immoral government, the punishment falls upon a broader grouping (1:16; 3:12; 4:10; 6:13–16; cf. 7:4).

But the God who destroys is also the God who delivers. To a community experiencing the judgment of God, Micah can bring a word of hope which would have been utterly inappropriate in pre-judgment days. In a historical context of chastisement there is room for a message of comfort without fear of a presumptuous misunderstanding that Yahweh shrugs off his people's rebellion. In one phase of Micah's ministry of consolation there does enter a satirical note warning Jerusalem against too quick a shift from judgment to salvation in Yahweh's dealings (4:10). In another phase he can promise beleaguered Jerusalem and its provincial refugees a prospect of rescue and release at the hands of their royal Shepherd (2:12f.). Their role, reduced though they are to a pitiful remnant (cf. Isa. 1:9), is to be the traditional, paradoxical dual function of Israel as agent of the baneful and beneficial power of God (5:6f.). The stirring challenge to the ancient tradition of holy war can ring out afresh to a city at last convinced of its own weakness and lack of resources (4:13). To a people who have lost faith in their anti-Assyrian sovereign (4:9; 5:1) can be offered the promise of a king to come who would be God's own answer to the problem of Assyria, now that the people's self-confident hopes have been proved ill-founded (5:5f.). A Davidic prince, he would be the embodiment of theocratic power and peace, and his coming would spell the creation of a new, united Israel (5:2–4).

Such is the theology of Micah's oracles. The prophetic material of 4:6f. has been included as a supplement which builds upon the themes of 2:12f. and matches 5:6f., its structural counterpart. The role of Yahweh as Israel's Shepherd-King is echoed, and the concept of the remnant is reinterpreted as a promise for the postexilic community. The importance of Jerusalem as the scene of God's royal victory (2:12f.; 4:13) is underlined: it is to be the capital of a divine monarchy. The people's merited judgment is to be succeeded by salvation, and Israel is to be a theocracy wherein is revealed God's greatness.

In 7:8–20 the book is brought to a triumphant climax echoing and endorsing the hopes of the postexilic nation. The passage resounds with the conviction of a divinely guided future. The judgment of which Micah had spoken is interpreted as the sixth-century B.C. destruction of Jerusalem and the deportation of the Judeans. The contemporary people of God have taken to heart the somber message of the judgment prophesied through Micah, and now they look for the ensuing salvation. They await that renewal of salvation history—the Exodus and the reoccupation of the land of promise—which Micah had rightly declared premature in the eighth century (4:10). Their hopes are ratified by the divine assurance that now is the time for their God to work again, granting the rebuilding of walls and the rehabilitation of Israel. Their fervent longing is that Yahweh their covenant God will shepherd his people anew. The proof of divine forgiveness is sought, not now in any facile manner, but from hearts that have been chastened and know the exceeding sinfulness of sin. The ancient promises of God, which stretch back to patriarchal times, are claimed again for his covenant people. A hard lesson has been learned from the twin textbooks of Micah's message and national experience. It is a humbled people who, pinning their faith on Yahweh alone, look into the future with assurance.

5. STRUCTURE AND ANALYSIS

"They have a queer way of talking, like people who, instead of proceeding in an orderly manner, ramble off from one thing to the next, so that you cannot make head or tail of them or see what they are getting at." So commented Martin Luther[56] on the impression given by the prophetic books. The book of Micah is a blatant example of this seeming jumble, so that a search for a literary structure is at first sight an impossible task. But if the book is accepted on its own terms, hints of artistic patterning emerge for the careful reader. Unfortunately they have led scholars to follow a variety of structural trails. A basic problem is that of the major divisions of the book. Chapters 1–3 are composed for the most part of material quite similar in tone and apparently in chronological period. Is that therefore to be regarded as the first main part of the book?[57] Only if one is prepared to detach 2:12f., which rises like an oasis of hope from a desert of doom. It appears to spoil the uniformity of its context. One could argue, as a number have done, that it belongs elsewhere in the book and has suffered transposition, but it is obviously better to try to find a structural framework that does justice to the present order of oracles than to resort to the theory of a scheme that was subsequently sabotaged. Its present position is certainly a strong argument against a first main section of chs. 1–3 in the absence of a similar doom–hope–doom structure elsewhere in the book.

The first chapter reveals a remarkable parallel with ch. 6, which appears to go beyond coincidence. In each the first oracle begins with the summons *Hear* (1:2; 6:1) and borrows heavily from the language of the lawcourt, as Yahweh levels serious accusations against his people. Both oracles are the first of a series of grave warnings, which at the beginning of the book continue until they terminate at 2:11 and give way to an oracle of promise, and at the end continue into ch. 7, in the course of which the tone changes with the commencement of the positive material bringing the book to a close. Chapters 1, 2 thus appear to parallel chs. 6, 7 in presenting a common pattern of a long block of negative oracles followed by a shorter

56. Cited by von Rad, *OT Theology,* vol. 2, p. 33, n. 1.

57. So many have held. Some, including Weiser, Bentzen, Pfeiffer, Fohrer, von Ungern-Sternberg, and Deissler, opt for a fourfold division of the book: chs. 1–3 (threat), 4–5 (hope), 6:1–7:6 or 7 (threat), 7:7 or 8–20 (hope), with alternation of threat-doom motifs. Others, including von Orelli, G. A. Smith, J. M. P. Smith, Wade, and Robinson, favor a threefold division, chs. 1–3, 4–5, 6–7. Cf. Willis, *ZAW* 81 (1969), pp. 191–214.

block hopeful in tone.[58] This demarcation suggests in turn that a second division occurs at ch. 3, which is favored by the appearance of the challenge *Hear* in 3:1, strikingly matching the opening word in 1:2 and 6:1. The imperative also occurs in 3:9; 6:9, where its appearance is of secondary structural importance, serving as an echo of the key word in 3:1; 6:1.

Chapters 4, 5 have been the object of three important investigations in recent times. E. Nielsen in 1954 viewed the chapters as a literary unit held together by a concentric structure: A. 4:1–4; B. 4:6–8; C. 4:9–5:6; B′. 5:7–9; A′. 5:10–15.[59] Part C is for him the nucleus, made up of (1) negative material, 4:9f., 11–13; 5:1, describing the distress of Jerusalem, and (2) positive material, 5:2–6, promising the birth of a Davidic king and deliverance from Assyria. This nucleus is surrounded by two layers. The first, 4:6–8; 5:7–9, revolves around the mention of the remnant in 5:3 and consists of promises to the remnant. The outer frame of the composition is made up of 4:1–4, promises of purified worship and peace, on the one side, and on the other 5:10–15, which predicts the removal of armaments and of objects associated with Canaanite worship. Nielsen's scheme is impressive; but it has drawbacks, especially in its failure to do justice to the obvious facts that (a) 4:9–5:1 contains a strong element of promise and (b) ch. 3, especially vv. 9–12, exhibits a close relationship of deliberate contrast with 4:1–4. Nielsen himself recognized and analyzed this contrast without drawing the conclusion that chs. 3 and 4 must be somehow related within a structural grouping.

Ten years later B. Renaud was inspired by Nielsen's analysis of chs. 4f. to produce a slightly different scheme, a chiastic one: A. 4:1–4; B. 4:6f. + 2:12f.; C. 4:8–5:1; C′. 5:2–6; B′. 5:7f.; A′. 5:9–15.[60] The basic differences from Nielsen's scheme are a fresh grouping of verses and the treatment of 5:2–6 as a foil to 4:8–5:1, corresponding impressively to the symmetry of the preceding and following material. However, J. T. Willis has subjected Renaud's thesis to a penetrating investigation and criticized it on structural and exegetical grounds.[61] First, it is extremely doubtful whether Renaud's division of the material into his various units, on which his general synthesis depends, is so natural as, say, that of Nielsen. Secondly, his interpretation of the units appears forced. For instance, unit A is treated as the salvation of subject nations and unit A′ as the chastisement of unsubdued nations. But in fact the end of ch. 5 is primarily concerned with the chastisement of Israel. Moreover, Renaud's work, even more than Nielsen's, suffers from his treatment of chs. 4f. in a vacuum and the ignoring of their relation to the preceding context.

Willis himself regards chs. 4f., or rather 3:9 (or 12)–5:15, as a

58. Willis, *loc. cit.* A few scholars before him had analyzed the book into chs. 1–2, 3–5, 6–7; cf. *loc. cit.*, p. 52, n. 34.
59. *Oral Tradition*. SBT 11 (1954), pp. 79–93.
60. *Op. cit.*
61. *Loc. cit.*

group of seven parallel units which are not sequential nor chiastic. All have a symmetrical structure in common, each consisting of two parts, a description of the present hopeless situation and an announcement of divine deliverance or vindication. Moreover, this contrast takes one of three forms in the various units: (a) a long section of doom can precede a short one of hope (4:9, 10a + 10b; 5:10–14 + 15); (b) a short section of doom can precede a long hope section (3:[9–]12 + 4:1–5; 4:11 + 12f.; 5:1 + 2–6); or (c) a passage of hope can contain allusions to the present hopeless situation (4:6–8; 5:7–9). All these units are concerned with the aims and results of the complete leadership of Yahweh in the coming age, and issue a challenge to his people to put their faith in him. To this end they all assume or state the impotence of Israel's leadership and/or the doom to befall Zion as a prelude to the rehabilitation of capital and people through Yahweh's power. Willis pays close attention to the verbal artistry that binds together the separate oracles into a well-arranged whole by the use of catchwords. With regard to 3:9–12 he evidently sees it as having a dual role. Chapter 3 is basically a short doom section preceding a long hope section, chs. 4f. The book has an overall A-B-A′ structure since chs. 1f. and 6f. both exhibit a pattern of a long doom section and a short hope section. Thus the oracle of 3:9–12 rounds off the shorter and negative half of the second main part of the book. But it also inaugurates the following series of seven units.

It will become clear to the informed reader of this commentary how heavily dependent the author is upon Willis' groundwork, in this as well as in other areas, especially with regard to his strophic analysis and his understanding of the artistic links between unit and unit. It is questionable, nonetheless, whether he has done justice to certain elements discerned by both Nielsen and Renaud. Moreover, 5:10–14 is more naturally viewed as a reference to God's future punishment of Israel than as a description of present distress. These questions and the impression he gives of the ambivalent role of 3:9–12 provoke an attempt at yet another analysis of chs. 3–5.

The parallelism of 4:6–8 and 5:7–9 is obvious both from their explicit mention of the remnant and their content of general hope mingled with allusions to present distress. This symmetry leads one to inquire whether it has a counterpart at the beginning and end of the overall composition which extends over chs. 3–5. 5:10–15 is in fact a section consisting of a long passage of future punishment and a short conclusion of promise. In this respect it bears a close relationship to 3:1–4:5, which although constituted on a larger scale has these same proportions. In the center remains Nielsen's nucleus of 4:9–5:6, which, divided into Willis's units of 4:9f., 11–13; 5:1–6, consists of three pieces, each beginning in the same way, with *now*. I. Willi-Plein has observed the crucial parallelism of these three units in which are thrice presented varying facets of Zion's present distress and her future hope. In fact these three pieces seem to move steadily toward a climactic conclusion. The first, 4:9f., is heavily weighted on the side of the crisis that confronts Jerusalem and is fated to worsen, and closes with a brief allusion to deliverance, yet only as the aftermath of exile. The second unit, 4:11–13, is more optimistic in tone, giving expression to the contemporary menace but devoting more space to the reversal Yahweh is to bring about. 5:1–6 marks a triumphant climax. The present distress of capital and king is dismissed in one line as the prelude to the coming royal glory, which is described at great length as spelling new hope for the nation.

The structure then is a concentric one, not unlike Nielsen's but covering more material and having a more complex nucleus than he acknowledged: A. 3:1–4:5; B. 4:6–8; C (1). 4:9f.; C (2). 4:11–13; C (3). 5:1–6; B′. 5:7–9; A′. 5:10–15. The whole presents a kaleidoscopic picture of the judgment and salvation of God's city and God's people. The focal point of the entire section is 5:1–6 with its promise of the establishment of the ideal theocracy under God's Davidic representative, for which Israel ever hoped. This is indeed the center and pinnacle of the whole book, for the function of chs. 1f. and 6f. is to play a supporting role for the central section. Within this section the structure of 3:1–4:5 and 5:10–15 forms a framework which echoes that of chs. 1f. and 6f. on a smaller scale. On the basis of this framework the twin remnant passages border the centerpiece.

<table>
<tr><td>I. 1:2–2:13</td><td colspan="3">1:2–2:11 long doom
2:12, 13 short hope</td></tr>
<tr><td rowspan="5">II. 3:1–5:15</td><td colspan="3">3:1–12 long doom
4:1–5 short hope</td></tr>
<tr><td colspan="3">4:6–8 (remnant) hope with distress allusions</td></tr>
<tr><td>4:9, 10
long distress and doom
+ short hope</td><td>4:11–13
short distress
+ long hope</td><td>5:1–6
short distress
+ longer hope</td></tr>
<tr><td colspan="3">5:7–9 (remnant) hope with distress allusions</td></tr>
<tr><td colspan="3">5:10–14 long doom
5:15 short hope</td></tr>
<tr><td>III. 6:1–7:20</td><td colspan="3">6:1–7:7 long doom
7:8–20 short hope</td></tr>
</table>

Heading (1:1)
I. Penalty and Promise (1:2–2:13)
   A. Punishment to come and the reason why (1:2–2:11)
      1. Samaria's disaster—Jerusalem's warning (1:2–9)
      2. Judah's disaster—Jerusalem's warning (1:10–16)
      3. Crime and punishment (2:1–5)
      4. Prophecy true and false (2:6–11)
   B. Promises of safety and liberation (2:12, 13)
II. Hope Beyond Affliction (3:1–5:15[14])
   A. Jerusalem's doom and destiny (3:1–4:5)
      1. Messages of punishment (3:1–12)
         a. Against the courts (3:1–4)
         b. Against the prophets (3:5–8)
         c. Against the establishment (3:9–12)
      2. Jerusalem's positive role (4:1–5)
   B. The future greatness of Israel and Jerusalem (4:6–8)
   C. Jerusalem's distress and eventual deliverance (4:9, 10)
   D. The menace of Jerusalem's enemies removed (4:11–13)
   E. Jerusalem's abject king and Israel's ideal king (5:1–6[4:14–5:5])
   F. The future roles of the remnant of Israel (5:7–9[6–8])
   G. God's punishment and deliverance of Israel (5:10–15[9–14])
III. Grace Triumphant over Sin (6:1–7:20)
   A. Messages of reproof and lament (6:1–7:7)
      1. God's case against Israel (6:1–8)
      2. Commercial trickery and its punishment (6:9–16)
      3. Lament over a decadent society (7:1–7)
   B. Confident hopes and prayers (7:8–20)

6. SELECT BIBLIOGRAPHY

A. Alt, "Micha 2, 1–5, *Gēs anadasmos* in Juda," *Interpretationes ad VT pertinentes Sigmundo Mowinckel septuagenario missae* (1955), pp. 13–23.
W. Beyerlin, *Die Kulttraditionen Israels in der Verkündigung des Propheten Micha*. FRLANT 72 (1959) (*KIVPM*).
K. Budde, "Das Rätsel von Micha 1," *ZAW* 37 (1917/18), pp. 77–108.
Idem, "Micha 2 und 3," *ZAW* 38 (1919/20), pp. 2–22.
K. J. Cathcart, "Notes on Micah 5, 4–5," *Biblica* 49 (1968), pp. 511–14.
T. K. Cheyne, *The Book of Micah*. CBSC (1895).
M. Collin, "Recherches sur l'histoire textuelle du prophète Michée," *VT* 21 (1971), pp. 281–297.
B. A. Copass and E. L. Carlson, *A Study of the Prophet Micah* (1950).
A. Deissler, "Micha vi, 1–8: Der Rechtsstreit Jahwes mit Israel um das rechte Bundesverhältnis," *TTZ* 68 (1959), pp. 229–234.
A. Deissler and M. Delcor, *Les petits prophètes. 2. Michée - Malachie*. La Sainte Bible 8:1 (1964).

B. Duhm, "Anmerkungen zu den Zwölf Propheten: iii. Buch Micha," *ZAW* 31 (1911), pp. 81–93.
O. Eissfeldt, "Ein Psalm aus Nord Israel. Micha 7, 7–20," *ZDMG* 112 (1962), pp. 259–268.
K. Elliger, "Die Heimat des Propheten Micha," *ZDPV* 57 (1934), pp. 81–152.
G. Fohrer, "Micha 1," *Das ferne und nahe Wort*. BZAW 105 (1967), pp. 65–80.
J. H. Gailey, *Micah to Malachi*. LBC (1963).
A. George, *Michée, Sophonie, Nahum*. La Bible de Jerusalem ([2]1958).
H. Gunkel, "The Close of Micah: A Prophetical Liturgy," *What Remains of the OT and Other Essays* (E.T. 1928), pp. 115–149.
E. Hammershaimb, "Some Leading Ideas in the Book of Micah," *Some Aspects of OT Prophecy from Isaiah to Malachi* (1966), pp. 11–34.
J. Harvey, *Le plaidoyer prophétique contre Israël après la rupture de l'alliance* (1967).
P. Haupt, "Micah's Capucinade," *JBL* 29 (1910), pp. 85–112.
Idem, "Critical Notes on Micah," *AJSL* 26 (1910), pp. 201–252.
Idem, "The Book of Micah," *AJSL* 27 (1911), pp. 1–63.
J. P. Hyatt, "On the Meaning and Origin of Micah 6:8," *Anglican Theological Review* 34 (1952), pp. 232–39.
A. S. Kapelrud, "Eschatology in the Book of Micah," *VT* 11 (1961), pp. 392–405.
T. Lescow, *Micha 6, 6–8. Studien zu Sprache, Form und Auslegung* (1966).
Idem, "Das Geburtsmotiv in den messianischen Weissagungen bei Jesaja und Micha," *ZAW* 79 (1967), pp. 172–207.
E. A. Leslie, "Micah the Prophet," *IDB*, vol. 3 (1962), pp. 369–372.
J. Lindblom, *Micha literarisch untersucht* (1929).
M. L. Margolis, *Micah* (1908).
J. Marsh, *Amos and Micah*. Torch Bible (1959).
H. M. McKeating, *The Books of Amos, Hosea and Micah*. Cambridge Bible Commentary (1971).
E. Nielsen, *Oral Tradition*. SBT 11 (1954).
G. von Rad, "The City on the Hill," *The Problem of the Hexateuch and Other Essays* (E.T. 1966), pp. 232–242.
B. Reicke, "Liturgical Traditions in Micah 7," *HTR* 60 (1967), pp. 349–367.
B. Renaud, *Structure et attaches littéraires de Michée iv–v* (1964).
S. J. Schwantes, *A Critical Study of the Text of Micah,* unpublished dissertation, Johns Hopkins University, 1962.
Idem, "A Note on Micah 5, 1 (Hebrew 4, 14)," *Andrews University Seminary Studies* 1 (1963), pp. 105–107.
Idem, "Critical Notes on Micah 1.10–16," *VT* 14 (1964), pp. 454–461.
J. M. P. Smith, *The Book of Micah*. ICC (1911).
L. P. Smith, "The Book of Micah," *Interpretation* 6 (1952), pp. 210–227.
N. H. Snaith, *Amos, Hosea and Micah*. Epworth Preachers' Commentaries (1956).
B. Stade, articles in *ZAW* 1 (1881), 3 (1883), 4 (1884), 6 (1886), 23 (1903).
J. Taylor, *The Massoretic Text and the Ancient Versions of the Book of Micah* (1890).
D. W. Thomas, "Micah," *Peake's Commentary on the Bible* (1962), pp. 630–34.
R. von Ungern-Sternberg, *Der Rechtsstreit Gottes mit seiner Gemeinde. Der Prophet Micha* (1958).
R. Vuilleumier and C.-A. Keller, *Michée, Nahoum, Habacuc, Sophonie*. Commentaire de l'AT, xi.b (1971).

H. Wildberger, "Die Völkerwallfahrt zum Zion, Jes. ii, 1–5," *VT* 7 (1957), pp. 62–81.

I. Willi-Plein, *Vorformen der Schriftexegese innerhalb des AT. Untersuchungen zum literarischen Werden der auf Amos, Hosea und Micha zurückgehenden Bücher im hebräischen Zwölfprophetenbuch.* BZAW 123 (1971).

J. T. Willis, *The Structure, Setting and Interrelationships of the Pericopes in the Book of Micah,* unpublished dissertation, Vanderbilt Divinity School, 1966.

Idem, "On the Text of Micah 2, 1a*a-b,*" *Biblica* 48 (1967), pp. 534–541.

Idem, "Some Suggestions on the Interpretation of Micah 1.2," *VT* 18 (1968), pp. 372–79.

Idem, "Micah 4.14–5.5–A Unit," *VT* 18 (1968), pp. 529–547.

Idem, "The Structure of Micah 3–5 and the Function of Micah 5.9–14 in the Book," *ZAW* 81 (1969), pp. 191–214.

Idem, "The Authenticity and Meaning of Micah 5.9–14," *ZAW* 81 (1969), pp. 353–368.

Idem, "The Structure of the Book of Micah," *SEA* 34 (1969), pp. 5–42.

Idem, "Fundamental Issues in Contemporary Micah Studies," *Restoration Quarterly* 13 (1970), pp. 77–90.

R. E. Wolfe, "The Book of Micah: Exegesis," *IB,* vol. 6 (1956), pp. 895–949.

A. S. van der Woude, "Micha 2.7a und der Bund Jahwes mit Israel," *VT* 18 (1968), pp. 388–391.

Idem, "Micah in Dispute with the Pseudo-prophets," *VT* 19 (1969), pp. 244–260.

TRANSLATION, EXPOSITION, AND NOTES

HEADING (1:1)

The message from Yahweh given to Micah of Moresheth during the reigns of the Judean kings Jotham, Ahaz, and Hezekiah, received by revelation concerning Samaria and Jerusalem.

An editorial introduction to the book briefly gives four fundamental pieces of information: the divine source of the following oracles, the identity of the prophet through whom they came, the period over which he ministered, and the scope of his oracles. The prophetic books generally have introductions of this type prefixed, although the amount of information supplied in them varies. This is in fact the fullest in range of all the prophetic headings. It bears closest similarity to the ones at the head of Hosea and Zephaniah.

Some of the other headings start with "The words of (the particular prophet)" or the like. This one stresses the supernatural origin of the prophetic oracles. Micah spoke not merely out of the depths of his own understanding of the spiritual relationship of his hearers to their God. His messages were grounded in the very mind and will of Yahweh. It is this fact that imparts to them importance for successive generations of God's people as well as for the generation or two among whom the prophet moved and ministered. This inspiration is the warrant for their preservation and their applicability to the situation of the contemporary heirs of the divine covenant.

The prophet is introduced by name and place of origin. The modern reader may clamor for biographical details concerning his parents, upbringing, etc., in order that he may better evaluate psychological and other influences on the prophet. Certainly these things are not unimportant: they are elements that go to make up his personality, and it is this whole personality that God prepared and used for the communication of truth. But we are supplied only with the results, the outpourings of a divinely guided mind. As Micah pointed beyond himself to God, so does his editor.

A person who was intimately associated with the area where he resided was generally called "X son of Y," obviously because not only he but his father before him were established members of the local community. But a newcomer was identified not with a patronymic but by the locality where he had originated and where the ancestral property of his clan was situated. Accordingly Micah, originally known as Micaiah, the longer form of his name,[1] was called by an adjective *Mōrashtî,* formed from his place of origin, evidently the Moresheth-Gath mentioned in 1:14. This was a country village or small town over on the western and lower side of Judah, halfway between Jerusalem and the Mediterranean coast. It has been identified with Tell ej-Judeideh (Tel Goded) and was thus a prominent landmark about 6 miles northeast of the important Judean city of Lachish.[2] Micah left his hometown and moved to Jerusalem, where apparently he delivered his oracles. There he was given the identifying label by which later generations also knew him.

The period of Micah's prophetic ministry is indicated by a chain of successive Judean kings. Jotham came to the throne c.740 B.C. and Hezekiah probably reigned till the early 680's.[3] Thus the period specified is roughly the second half of the eighth century B.C. Most of Micah's extant oracles appear to have been delivered during Hezekiah's reign. The evidence of Jer. 26:18f. that 3:12 was uttered in his reign is a valuable guide in this respect.[4] But certainly 1:2–9 must have been uttered in the reign of Ahaz. The editor's intention in including Jotham was probably to give a loose reference to the period after Uzziah, whose death marked a distinct turning point in Judean history.

An interesting verb is used to introduce the target of Micah's messages. Literally meaning "see," it is a technical term of prophecy which developed to refer not only to visions but to the wider perception of divine revelation. In Micah's case it was evidently of an auditory nature. Samaria and Jerusalem are said to be the concerns of his oracles. In fact Samaria comes under his attack only in 1:2–9, which explains the priority of order assigned to it in the heading.[5] It may be safely assumed that the rest of his messages were aimed at the capital of the Southern Kingdom.

Having set the scene and introduced the main characters, the editor steps aside and allows Micah to speak for himself. But let the modern reader not disregard the implicit warning he has issued, namely that the

1. Cf. Jer. 26:18.
2. And some 3 miles north of Mareshah mentioned in v. 15. S T equate the two places and have been followed by such scholars as Budde, Haupt, Wolfe, and Marsh. But most distinguish as separate places: no other place is referred to twice in the list of 1:10–15.
3. Some scholars place certain oracles in chs. 6f. in the reign of Hezekiah's successor, Manasseh.
4. From that statement the unwarranted assumption has sometimes been made that the whole of Micah's ministry must be assigned to Hezekiah's reign.
5. Some scholars have suggested that the unidentified city of 6:9 is Samaria.

words of Micah are grounded in the history of a particular epoch and particular places. The editor above all men had come to realize the value of reapplying the word of God to other times in the experience of God's people, but its timelessness can be fully appreciated only by the careful tracing of parallels (and differences) between Micah's own cultural environment and that of the later reader. Then the truths with which God confronted men of a now remote period may come alive as guidelines for believers in every age.

I. PENALTY AND PROMISE (1:2–2:13)

A. PUNISHMENT TO COME AND THE REASON WHY (1:2—2:11)

1. Samaria's Disaster—Jerusalem's Warning (1:2–9)

Hear, all you peoples,[6]
listen, world and your population, 3+3
and let the Lord, Yahweh,[7]
give evidence against you,
the Lord from his holy temple. 3+2+3
3 *For Yahweh is leaving his own place yonder;*
down he comes, to tread[8] *upon earth's heights.* 4+4
4 *Mountains melt beneath him*
and valleys crack open, 3+2
like wax too close[9] *to fire*
or water cascading down a slope.[10] 3+3
5 *Jacob's rebellion is the reason for all this,*
and the sin of the community of Israel. 3+3
What[11] *is Jacob's rebellion?*

6. These words recur in MT of 1 K. 22:28, prefaced by "and he said." They are missing in G and are generally taken as a later gloss falsely identifying Micaiah ben Imlah with our prophet.
7. G has only *kyrios*, "Lord," for both terms, and two Heb. mss. omit *the Lord*. Accordingly Duhm, Robinson, *BHK*, George, Schwantes, *BHS*, *et al.*, delete *the Lord* as an accidental anticipation of the next clause, noting that the line is metrically rather long. But repetition is a feature of Micah's poetry. Qp and Mur. 88 support MT. The line may be scanned as a tricolon. For this type of 3+2+3 line cf. Ps. 109:20 and M. Dahood, *Pss 3*, p. 105.
8. J. M. P. Smith and *BHK* omit *w^{e}ḏāraḵ*, "and treads," with G V Qp. But the omission has probably occurred by oversight in G (Ziegler, Willi-Plein) and in Qp (Collin, *VT* 21 (1971), p. 285). J. L. Crenshaw, *CBQ* 34 (1972), pp. 44f., argues that both verbs are original since (1) they are integral to theophanic descriptions and (2) Micah elsewhere uses double verbs in this fashion. The line is 4+4 (Willi-Plein).
9. Heb. *mipp^{e}nê*, lit. "from before," implies threat.
10. R. Köbert, *Biblica* 39 (1958), pp. 82f., understands Heb. *môrāḏ* as "drinking trough" like Arab. *maurid*. Then both comparisons are taken from human daily life, and the great and commonplace are impressively juxtaposed (cf. Ps. 8:3; Isa. 40:12, 15).
11. Heb. *mî*, "who?" can be used when persons are implied (GK 137a), here the leaders in the two capitals.

It can only be Samaria. 3+2
And what is Judah's sin?[12]
It can only be Jerusalem. 3+2

6 *"So I shall make Samaria*
a ruin in the countryside,[13]
plantations for the vines. 2+2+2
I shall hurl her stones down the valley
and expose her foundations. 3+2
7 *All her sculptured images will be smashed,*
all her proceeds of prostitution[14] *destroyed by fire;*
on all her idols shall I wreak havoc. 3+3+3
For from prostitutes' earnings she did amass them,[15]
and to prostitutes' earnings will they revert." 3+3
8 *This is why I must mourn and wail,*
go about barefoot and half-naked. 3+3
utter a cry of mourning as loud as jackals,
a lament as shrill as ostriches.[16] 3+3
9 *For she will never recover from her scourging–*[17]
and it will reach[18] *Judah, too.* 3+2
It will spread to my people's marketplace,[19]
right to Jerusalem. 3+2

The prophets frequently borrowed from the social life of the community in order to transmit their messages of God's attitude and

12. G S T imply *ḥaṭṭa't, sin* (G T add "house," but this is less likely to be original: T inserts it before every noun in v. 5 and G does before *Jacob*), which most scholars prefer for the sake of parallelism to *bāmôṯ,* "high places," in MT Qp V, doubtless originally a marginal comment on v. 6 inspired by the similar 3:12. The comment was misunderstood as an interpretation of *sin* in v. 5b and eventually displaced it. Cf. the similar variants in Jer. 15:13; 17:3, as explained by L. C. Allen, *JTS* 24 (1973), pp. 70f. The singular *sin* here suggests that in v. 5a the plural vowel letter of MT *ḥaṭṭô'ṯ,* "sins," should be omitted and *ḥaṭṭa'ṯ, sin,* read with G T mss., as the parallelism suggests.
13. Beyerlin, *KIVPM,* p. 36, n. 1, and Vuilleumier take *haśśāḏeh,* "the field," with the latter half of the line in the sense of "the city territory" (cf. Hitzig, Lindblom); but comparison with the use of *śāḏeh* in 3:12 does not favor this suggestion.
14. J. M. P. Smith, following Halper, and G. R. Driver in *Words and Meanings,* D. W. Thomas Festschrift (1968), p. 50, believe that here the word means "images" (=NEB).
15. Ewald, Wellhausen, J. M. P. Smith, Robinson, George, Schwantes, *et al.* read a plural passive *qubbᵉtsû* with S V T, but this is an easier and so secondary reading. A pronominal suffix is easily understood from the context. RSV, NEB rightly retain MT with G.
16. G. R. Driver, *PEQ* 87 (1955), pp. 12f., argues for the meaning "eagle-owl" (cf. KJV, NEB).
17. MT has a plural *makkôṯeyhā.* In view of the singular verbs the singular *makkāṯāh,* omitting the vowel letters, has been read by many since Wellhausen with G S V T. MT's interpretation of an original *mkth* has been influenced by the noun forms in v. 7: cf. its vocalization in Jer. 19:8 compared with 49:17; 50:13.
18. Here and in the next verb the Heb. uses "prophetic" perfects. There is no need to read *nāgᵉ'â* with Wellhausen, J. M. P. Smith, Schwantes, *et al.;* cf. G. R. Driver, *JRAS* (1948), pp. 164–176, for the well-attested lack of congruence.
19. Lit. "gate."

character. The lawcourt served as a favorite source of comparison. God is the great Judge and Plaintiff, while his people or other nations stand in the dock accused of grave crimes, awaiting his verdict. This poem preserves echoes of the summons to the defendant to stand trial, of the judge's coming to hear the case, of the call to recite the charges against the defendant, of the solemn verdict soon to be carried out, and of the gasp of horror from the spectators at its severity. Part of the allure of the prophets is the refreshing way they mix their motifs, juxtaposing a kaleidoscopic variety of cultural models. Inset in this lawsuit oracle is a motif drawn from the religious life of the community, which the prophet uses to communicate what is new from what is known. Micah quotes and adapts religious phraseology in v. 3. The dramatic language of theophany is taken up to evoke a sense of the majesty of the God who comes in victory—as a prelude to a surprising conclusion. In v. 8 the prophet draws upon the complex etiquette of mourning: he vows to engage in funeral rites in order to underline the note of crisis in his pronouncement. These borrowings illustrate the prophet's involvement in the culture, secular and religious, of his own times. They also demonstrate the need for the reader to immerse himself in that ancient environment through which God once spoke if he is to succeed in catching the tones and undertones of God's prophetic voice to him and his own generation.

The oracle obviously antedates the fall of Samaria to the Assyrians in 722 B.C.[20] Did Micah himself have the Assyrians in mind? The allusion to fire in v. 7 suggests military invasion,[21] as does the tenor of the latter part of the verse. From the 740's onward the ruthlessness of Assyrian imperialistic raids and reprisals was well known. But the accent is firmly on Yahweh as the prime mover behind history. Micah may well have expected danger for Judah as an immediate consequence of the fall of Samaria, but essentially he argues not politically but theologically. He sees disaster as a necessary eventual meeting-point between God and his people in the south as well as in the north. If Samaria was to pay for disobedience to God, as indeed she would, how could her guilty sister hope to get off scot-free?

This oracle of disaster for Samaria and Jerusalem falls into two eight-line stanzas, vv. 2–5 and 6–9, as a careful study of style and content indicates.[22] The first opens with the prophet heralding God's verdict of universal judgment (v. 2), while the second starts with God beginning to pronounce a verdict against Samaria (v. 6). The first closes by tracing a parallel between Samaria and Jerusalem (v. 5b), and so does the second (v.

20. See the Introduction.

21. Cf., e.g., 1 Sam. 30:1; Isa. 1:7.

22. G. Fohrer in *Das ferne und nahe Wort.* L. Rost Festschrift (1967), p. 71, discerns three stanzas, six lines of 3+3 meter (vv. 2–5a), another six of 3+2 (vv. 5b–7), and four of 3+3, except for 3+2 in v. 9b (vv. 8, 9). His main criterion is meter, but without arbitrary emendation the meter is too mixed to be a strophical guide.

9): in fact both end with the punch-word *Jerusalem*. Each stanza has the same hinge linking two parts: the backward looking *this* in vv. 5 and 8. In the former case it marks a development from a stylized description of God's catastrophic intervention to an analysis of the human cause that makes it inevitable; in the latter it is the pivot between the divine outworking of the catastrophe and the poignant reaction of the man of God who sees it as a harbinger of worse to come. The first stanza moves from a panoramic view of earth and heaven to gradual close-ups of Samaria and Jerusalem, and the second veers from the Samaria nearer home to Jerusalem. In both there is a narrowing sequence. The language of religious poetry in the first is used with dynamic realism in the second. The downrush of water in v. 4 turns into the downfall of stone buildings in v. 6, while the metaphorical fire flares into history as the incendiary warfare of v. 7. Both stanzas are marked by a double comparison to heighten the descriptions of the destructive effect of God's intervention in v. 4 and of the prophet's reaction of horror in v. 8.[23]

2 Many a prophetic oracle begins like this, calling for attention from those whom the oracle concerns. Here one might have expected Micah to name Samaria and even Jerusalem. Doubtless he delivered this message in Jerusalem; it is directed primarily against Samaria and ultimately against the southern capital. But the prophet sets his pronouncement against a vast backcloth of world judgment.[24] Micah's God is no provincial deity but the universal Overlord to whom all nations must render account. Is the prophet taking a leaf out of the book of his predecessor Amos? In his first recorded oracle Amos attacked a series of neighboring states before turning to threaten God's people. Undoubtedly his aim was to make a strong psychological impact upon his audience, winning their consent in depicting a God of might and right before making this accepted idea boomerang into their own guilty society. Micah is apparently adopting similar tactics. He begins by building up a nationalistically acceptable image of God as Judge of all the earth, thereby reminding his local audience of the greatness of their God.[25] Isaiah spoke in similar vein:

> *Yahweh stands ready to present his case,*
> *he stands to judge the peoples.*[26]

23. This final reaction is matched in the conclusion of the next oracle, v. 16, where again expressions of lament precede an explanation of its necessity.

24. There is little to be said for interpreting *peoples* with Ehrlich as Israel and Judah (still less as "tribes" with Hitzig) and "earth" as "land," i.e., Palestine. Nor is *against you* to be taken as a sudden change of addressee referring to Israel (Calvin, Keil, von Orelli, Wellhausen), since in v. 5 it is mentioned in the third person. For a thorough survey of this verse and an evaluation of its varied interpretations see Willis, *VT* 18 (1968), pp. 372–79.

25. The third person suffixes in *kullām,* "all of them," and *m*ᵉ*lōʾāh,* "its contents" (cf. GK 135r, 144p), may be intended as a hint that the address is a rhetorical device, the real target of the oracle being other than here specified.

26. Heb. *ʿammîm* is commonly emended to *ʿammô* with G S, but their reading looks

> *Yahweh is entering upon a lawsuit*
> *with the elders and leaders of his people.* (Isa. 3:13f.)

God appears as witness for the prosecution, with incriminating evidence to present against the peoples of the world. He is witness, plaintiff, and judge at one and the same time,[27] for he has the knowledge of wrongdoing, the right and concern to prosecute as the upholder of social welfare, and the wisdom and authority to judge with equity.

The divine Judge leaves his chambers to take his place in the courtroom. Micah knows Yahweh as "one who comes out of his sanctuary into the welter of events."[28] His God is no absentee landlord but at work in history, involved in the moral government of his world. Yet there is a careful balance between the immanence and transcendence of Israel's God: he issues *from his holy temple*. It is significant that *temple* and "palace" are one word in Hebrew: deity and kingship are intertwined.

> *Yahweh is in his holy temple,*
> *Yahweh, whose throne is in heaven;*
> *his eyes can see . . . men.* (Ps. 11:5[4])

In the prophet's mind, as in the psalmist's, is God's heavenly residence to which his earthly temple is a counterpart.[29] It is a mode of expression that denies any suggestion that Yahweh is limited to his terrestrial sanctuary. As in the psalm, it seems to supply a qualification for judgment: God is aware of all that goes on in the teeming world below. It speaks further of the awesomeness of God above.

> *Yahweh is in his holy temple:*
> *let all the earth keep silence before him.* (Hab. 2:20)

3, 4 The last phrase of v. 2 supplies Micah with a lead-in for a vivid description of the arrival of the Judge to the court of earth, where verdicts made in heaven are pronounced and carried out. At this point he deliberately borrows traditional religious language which was familiar to his audience from its use in their regular worship.[30] There is a tone of majestic whimsicality about this and similar passages in the OT and in other ancient Near Eastern literature, which writers such as C. S. Lewis and J. R. R. Tolkien have recaptured for our own age.

The OT motif of theophany contains two strands, the coming of Yahweh from his residence, terrestrial or as here celestial, and the reaction of nature, which cringes and crumples at his coming. Traditionally it had a ring of assurance about it: the great God has come or can be expected to come to aid his people against their foes.[31] A classic example is Judg. 5:4,

---

suspiciously like a naive harmonization with the next verse. For justification of MT see F. Hesse, *ZAW* 65 (1953), p. 48; J. Lindblom, *Prophecy in Ancient Israel* (1962), p. 366.

27. "Witness" is used of Yahweh in this wider sense also in Zeph. 3:8; Mal. 3:5.
28. R. B. Y. Scott, *The Relevance of the Prophets* ([2]1969), p. 166.
29. Cf. R. E. Clements, *God and Temple* (1965), pp. 68f.
30. Cf. Beyerlin, *KIVPM*, pp. 33–38.
31. Cf. Ps. 18:7–19 (8–20); Isa. 64:1–3 (63:19–64:2). For a form-critical study of the motif see Jörg Jeremias, *Theophanie. Die Geschichte einer alttestamentlichen Gattung*. WMANT

5, where the God of Sinai's deliverance of the Israelites from Jabin is celebrated:

> *"Yahweh, when you came out from Seir. . . ,*
> *the earth trembled. . . ,*
> *the mountains quaked before Yahweh."*

Amos had already associated an expression of this form with God's judgment of Israel (1:2).[32] Micah follows in his tracks, as the sequel to these verses shows, but doubtless to his audience only the judgment of foreign nations is as yet in mind.

The manifestation of the presence of God intervening in human affairs is anthropomorphically depicted as his descent from heaven to earth and his encountering first the tops of the mountains, upon which he treads to symbolize his dominion over them, like some Everest conqueror.[33] His powerful presence is next illustrated in traditional terms by describing its seismic effect upon the stable world of nature. So supernatural is his power that *mountains melt* at the intense heat of his wrath, and his heavy tread shatters into yawning chasms the *valleys* below.[34] Solid features of the landscape slither like melting *wax,* running away like fast-flowing *water*. Micah uses this terrifying poetry to build up an impression of God's irresistible power directed in catastrophe against his enemies.[35]

5 But who are the enemies and why this show of force? Up to now the oracle has been deliberately general. Micah's audience have had no reason to erect barriers against his words; their force has seeped into their minds and been fully accepted. Now comes a dramatic, typically prophetic turning upside down of conventional thinking. The Judge of all the earth is Judge of Israel; the great God who brooks no opposition from his foes is himself Israel's legal adversary. The sovereign Judge has had the world

10 (1965); C. Westermann, *The Praise of God in the Psalms* (E. T. 1965), pp. 93–101. For an important criticism of their work see A. Weiser, *The Psalms* (E. T. 1962), p. 38, n. 2; Crenshaw, *ZAW* 80 (1968), p. 206, n. 12.

32. Cf. Crenshaw, *loc. cit.*, p. 214: "Amos uses cultic materials deliberately to make contact with the people, then turns the sacred traditions against the hearers for non-cultic ends."

33. M. K. Wakeman, *JBL* 88 (1969), pp. 319f., sees a reference here to Yahweh's trampling the back of the underworld or primeval earth monster, citing Ugaritic mythological parallels. Although this traditional phrase probably did have such significance earlier in its history (cf. Job 9:8, RSV mg.), its use in the present context suggests that it has been reduced to a metaphorical expression of the victory of Yahweh. Cf. Crenshaw, *CBQ* 34 (1972), pp. 45, 52.

34. P. Reymond, *L'eau, sa vie, et sa signification dans l'AT*. SVT 6 (1958), pp. 83f., interestingly finds here reference to a storm, comparing Judg. 5:4f.; Ps. 97:3–5; Hab. 3:9: mountains are eroded, dissolving into a sea of mud, and the floodwater cuts the ground into deep channels. Earlier Cheyne had interpreted similarly. It is difficult to decide how many elements in the theophanic complex the prophet is alluding to. In Ps. 97 the imagery of melting wax seems to be related more closely to fire and lightning than to rain; cf. the way fire and wrath are linked in Ps. 18:7f. (8f.); Nah. 1:5f. Jeremias, *op. cit.*, p. 212, is more likely correct in not finding an allusion to storm here.

35. Cf. the same use of this wax simile to illustrate the defeat of God's foes in Ps. 68:1f. (2f.).

summoned to his tribunal. Who is to stand trial first? None other than his own people. The solemn accusation is levelled, for "the time has come for judgment to begin with the household of God" (1 Pet. 4:17). If any nation is due for a time of reckoning by reason of its misdemeanors, it is Israel.[36]

In this second half of the first stanza Micah becomes specific. But *Jacob* and *Israel* are deliberately ambiguous: they could refer to the Northern Kingdom, as for instance in Isa. 9:8, or to the whole people in both north and south, as in Isa. 2:6. The prophet's hearers probably assumed the former, and Micah does nothing yet to disabuse them. In fact he goes on in vivid question and answer to identify *Jacob* with the Northern Kingdom by mentioning its capital, only to attain a devastating climax by explicitly citing *Judah* and *Jerusalem* at the close. There is a break in the parallelism: *Jacob* is repeated but *Israel* becomes *Judah* to make the meaning starkly clear. In Micah's mind both *Jacob* and *Israel* in the first line stand for the whole nation, both parts of which are equally guilty before God.[37] He narrows the first term down to the northern element, which is his primary concern in this oracle, but by his sting in the tail he insists that Judah is not exempt.

The prophet has little to say about the content of the people's guilt beyond labelling it first as *rebellion,*[38] breaking free from obligations to an overlord, warrant enough for divine reprisals, and then as *sin,* strictly a falling short of the moral ideal, or failure to follow the right way. He does locate the source of this disaffection in the respective capitals. It is government circles that set the tone for the whole community: they are "the living embodiment of the corruption infecting the rest of the nation" (Wade). Samaria is the focal point of Israel's wrongdoing; Jerusalem lies at the center of her nation's sin. In each case the metropolis is "the heart whose pulses beat throughout the whole system" (Pusey). Micah lays upon the respective governments the responsibility for directing their nations amiss. If the punishment is to fit the crime, it is only just that in each case the seat of government, the royal capital, should suffer.

6, 7 So the time is ripe in history, and in Micah's oracle, for God's verdict upon Samaria to be made known. The second stanza begins with the prophet acting as mouthpiece for his God, passing on his message in direct speech, with grim effect.[39] Here is the continuation of and counterpart to the verdict declared as forthcoming at the opening of the first stanza. The cancer is to be cut out at the source. The magnificent city set upon a hill amid a green valley, to Isaiah's perceptive eye looking like an ephemeral garland on the head of a carouser (Isa. 28:1–4), is to become a ruined tell, a sad memorial to bygone splendor. Its slopes are to lose their

36. Cf. Isa. 1:24, 25; Amos 9:4, 7, 8, 10.
37. A. Kuenen, "Micha 1:5," *Études . . . dédiées à C. Leemans* (1885), p. 116; Cheyne; Willis, *SEA* 34 (1969), p. 21.
38. Cf. Isaiah's allusion to the rebellion of prodigal sons in Isa. 1:2.
39. Cf. 2:8.

urban character and be cultivated as vine terraces. Nothing less than the eradication of the capital is worthy punishment for its crimes against God. Micah proceeds to superimpose upon Samaria his earlier theophanic scene. Just as in imagination he had seen mountains dissolving beneath Yahweh's tread, so now he sees the superstructures built upon Mount Samaria collapsing before his eyes and tumbling into the *valley*. The cascade of water down the slopes turns into an avalanche of *stones* chasing one another to the foot of the hill, till all that is left are naked *foundations*.[40] Such is the poetic justice that Samaria deserves from the Judge of Israel. In fact history was kinder to Samaria, and her material destruction was only a shadow of this grim portrayal. Sargon did not demolish the city, but according to his annals actually improved it. It is an apt metaphor nonetheless for the political destruction of Samaria, whose citizens were deported to make way for foreign settlers in a new Assyrian province. Politically Samaria was crushed into nonexistence.[41]

Micah turns to stonework of a different kind, the stone *images* that evidently adorned the temple of Samaria.[42] The three short clauses that make up the one line begin similarly, to underline the completeness of the destruction. The active verb at the end makes clear that the two preceding passives, as is so often the case, are a device referring to the activity of God. The final phrase is a shocking play on words. The religious paraphernalia of Samaria (Heb. *shōmᵉrôn*) are fit to become only *shᵉmāmâ*, devastation. Once again the theophanic description comes live: the fire of v. 4 turns into martial *fire* lit by the torches of invaders behind whom stands Yahweh as general.[43]

The prophet now views Samaria's destruction as punishment for specifically religious sins, sounding like a second Hosea.[44] Hosea it was who had attacked the syncretism of the Northern Kingdom whereby Yahweh was worshipped as if he were Baal, with the accouterments and theology of the Canaanite fertility religion. All such borrowings were false

40. Heb. *muggārîm*, v. 4—*wᵉhiggartî*, v. 6.

41. Josephus (*Ant*. xiii. 10.3) by his allusive language apparently viewed the verse as a prophecy fulfilled in John Hyrcanus' total destruction of Samaria in 107 B.C.

42. Cf. Isa. 10:10f. On the question of the existence of a temple in Samaria see Robinson; M. Noth, *History of Israel* (E. T. 1960), p. 232.

43. It is frequently urged that the clause *all her proceeds . . . fire* is a later gloss, sometimes on the ground that Micah envisages Samaria's destruction by earthquake (e.g., Sellin, Lindblom, Robinson, Beyerlin, Vuilleumier), more often simply as overloading the line on the supposition that in the rest of the poem lines are made up of two members, not three. For the use of natural forces as a metaphor for enemy attack cf. Isa. 28:2, 17–22. *Fire* as an interlocking device between the first and second stanzas guarantees the authenticity of the clause in this tricolon, which is matched by vv. 2b, 6a.

44. The three cultic nouns occur frequently in Hosea. This is hardly a reason for considering vv. 6, 7 a misplaced utterance of Hosea (A. Jepsen, *ZAW* 56 [1938], pp. 96–99). Some scholars, including J. M. P. Smith, Sellin, and Wolfe, regard v. 7 as an exilic or postexilic expansion on the grounds that a polemic against idolatry fits better a later period and that v. 8 continues v. 6.

representations of Yahweh, for they degraded him into a fertility god, a personification of the cycle of nature, and dragged his worship down into a bartering system for man's selfish ends and into an orgy of religious prostitution. The destruction of its material representations is Yahweh's vindication of himself and his true character. Their end will fittingly repeat their origin, affirms Micah, making a rhetorical point about the fate of part of these fetishes. The reference is probably to the gold and silver plating on the images, melted down from the dirty money handed over for the use of religious brothels. Invading soldiers are to tear it off as loot and spend it as currency for further prostitution, as soldiers will.[45] Micah could hardly have voiced more strongly God's disavowal of Samaria's syncretistic cult as a despicable and impious thing.

8, 9 The last half of the second stanza is the prophet's frenzied reaction to the divine decree.[46] The form of this pair of verses is paralleled elsewhere as a conclusion to a prophetic oracle of doom.[47] Prompted by the declaration of coming disaster, Micah first indulges in a display of unrestrained grief which reinforces emotionally the severity of the catastrophe and gives a cue for the reaction he expects from his audience; then, far from dissolving into hysteria, he gives a supplementary rational explanation concerning the woe to come. The question is sometimes asked why Micah should grieve over the destruction of idols or even over the merited fall of Samaria. Undoubtedly it is the latter factor that is in his mind, as the first clause of the next verse makes clear. Amos, equally stern Judean prophet of doom for Samaria, had twice interceded with God for forgiveness and the averting of catastrophe (Amos 7:2, 5). Micah, too, was appalled at his message of woe and shrank in pain from his own words. He engages in the elaborate mourning rites of his age, going *barefoot* like David on the Mount of Olives (2 Sam. 15:30) and leaving off the conventional cloak, as David did with his turban.[48] For most of us mourning is traditionally a quiet affair symbolized by drawn curtains and the declining of invitations, but for the Israelite it was a matter of noisy expression of one's anguish. The more keenly felt the bereavement, the

45. Less likely, the point may be that idols whose craftsmen were paid by income from prostitution would be carried off as war trophies and dedicated to deities in the sanctuaries of the victorious aliens.

46. Fohrer, *loc. cit.*, p. 73, compares this lament with the motif of reaction to bad news analyzed by D. R. Hillers, *ZAW* 77 (1965), pp. 86–90; but it has nothing in common with the form of that stereotyped motif and is hardly to be divorced from the prophet's own feelings.

47. Cf. Jer. 4:8, drawing vv. 5–8 to a close: Heb. *'al zō't,* "therefore, this is why," refers to the destruction announced in v. 7b and introduces a call to mourning; then follows a causal clause introduced by *kî,* "because," giving a supplementary reason and expressing the theological meaning of the catastrophe. Cf. also Jer. 4:28; 2:12f.; and (without a *kî* clause) Amos 8:8. This is one good reason why here vv. 8, 9 should be attached to the earlier verses and not taken, as some suggest, with vv. 10–16. Another is that the reference to Samaria in v. 9 harks back to an explicit mention earlier. For yet another see n. 23 above.

48. It is sometimes claimed that like Isaiah in Isa. 20:2–4, Micah is acting out the symbolic part of a prisoner of war; but there is no hint of this in the context.

louder the shrieking. So Micah abandons himself to banshee cries, sounding like the plaintive howl of the jackal at night or the gruesome screech of the ostrich, so deep is his sympathy for the doomed nation. He goes on to spell out the hopelessness of Samaria's prospects and to affirm that the coming disaster is Yahweh's punishment, a fatal flogging for bad behavior.[49]

Thus far Micah has been grieving over the northern capital,[50] but he adds an extra reason for his sorrow, all the more shocking for being left till now. At the end of this second stanza he repeats the final theme of the first. Samaria's death knell tolls for *Jerusalem.* How can the flood tide of retribution be stayed at the frontier between Israel and Judah, since both live at the same low level? What right have the citizens of Jerusalem to claim exemption from Samaria's fate? From a countryman like Micah one might expect the big city to receive scant sympathy. But he feelingly calls it, literally, "the gate of my people." Jerusalem is to Judah what the gate is to the town. Just inside the gate of a Palestinian city was situated the *marketplace,* the hub of the community, where the people met. So the seer mourns for his nation and its pulsing heart. Micah the prophet was also a patriot, concerned for his estranged brothers in the northern territory, but concerned even more for his fellow Judeans with whom his birth and daily life aligned him. He is a man torn betwixt two, a servant of God and a citizen of Judah, and he feels keenly the claims of both tugging at his soul. He yearns for his nation and its capital as keenly as Paul did for his Jewish brothers in Rom. 9:1–3. As with every prophet, Micah's message of woe had the aim of prompting a change of heart and life, and saving his hearers from the brink. It is for this purpose that he ends the poem as he did the first stanza with the same somber drumbeat: *Jerusalem.* Samaria's southern twin deserves an identical fate.

This oracle contains profound truth about God, the covenant community, and the prophet. Yahweh is the universal Lord to whom all men must render humble account. He is the majestic Lord of history, intervening through human activity to work out his righteous will. He is the Lord of Israel, laying claims upon his people which they disregard at their peril. He is the exclusive Lord of his people, who for their part must therefore have no truck with other religions. Micah agrees with Amos that special privilege implies special responsibility:

> *"You only have I known of all the families of the earth,*
> *therefore I shall punish you for all your iniquities."*
>
> (Amos 3:2)

It fell to Micah's lot to stand over against the twin communities and courageously threaten them. Yet as mediator between God and man he

49. Isaiah used the same metaphor concerning Judah's suffering in 701 B.C. (1:5) and developed the metaphor to make Assyria the rod of Yahweh's anger (10:5).

50. *This is why* in v. 8 is a signpost back to the verdict on Samaria in vv. 6f., the first half of the stanza.

experienced the tension that came from standing with feet in both camps. He was filled with no vengeful, callous spirit but with heartbreak, concern, and empathy.

2. *Judah's Disaster—Jerusalem's Warning (1:10–16)*

"Tell[51] it not in Gath":
do not weep and sob. 2+2
In Beth-leaprah[52]
roll about[53] in the dust. 2+2
11 *Get moving,[54]*
population of Shaphir,
naked and humiliated. 2+2+2
The population of Zaanan
dare not come out. 2+2
Beth-haezel is in mourning:[55]
it withdraws its support from you.[56] 3+3
12 *Waiting anxiously[57] for good fortune[58]*
are Maroth's population. 2+2
Misfortune is sent down
by[59] Yahweh himself
to Jerusalem's gate. 2+2+2

13 *Harness[60] the chariot to the steeds,*
population of Lachish: 3+2

51. For MT *taggîḏû,* S presupposes *tāḡîlû,* "rejoice," and G Qp *taḡdîlû,* "boast," the latter evidently being a conflation of the two other readings (Schwantes). MT is satisfactory. S may have been influenced by the sense of 2 Sam. 1:20b.
52. "Beth-aphrah" (NEB) would be a more usual form of place name: S V T Theodotion so read. Is the *lameḏ* connected with the variant readings mentioned in the previous note, i.e., a misplaced marginal or interlinear note?
53. K *hitpallāshtî,* "I have rolled," has been influenced by the verbs in vv. 8, 9. It is necessary to read with G S V and most scholars a plural imperative *hitpallâshû*; cf. v. 10a and the feminine singular imperative in Q Mur. 88, *hitpallâshî,* influenced by the next verb. The textual corruption moved from *-û* to *-î* to *-tî*.
54. Heb. *lāḵem,* "for yourselves," is odd with a singular verb; probably the *mem* is to be taken as enclitic, with a feminine singular suffix (H.D. Hummel, *JBL* 76 [1957], pp. 99f.; Dahood, *Pss 2,* p. 147).
55. MT construct *mispaḏ* is to be pointed as an absolute *mispēḏ* and taken predicatively; cf. G. R. Driver, *JTS* 39 (1938), pp. 264f.; Thomas; NEB, who, however, all take it locatively, "place of mourning," which as Schwantes observes is a meaning not attested elsewhere.
56. This translation and the interpretation below are speculative. Heb. *'emdâ* apparently means "standing, power to stand." The basis of the wordplay is uncertain. Heb. *'ātsal* can mean "withdraw, withhold," which appropriately connects with the verb (Sellin).
57. Lit. "are in anguish," here of anxious longing (BDB).
58. R. Gordis, *JTS* 35 (1934), p. 187; G. R. Driver, *loc. cit.,* p. 265; and NEB take *leṭôḇ* as "greatly," a feasible rendering elsewhere but unlikely here since it ignores the play between good fortune and evil (Schwantes).
59. Heb. *mē'ēṯ,* an intensely personal form of preposition.
60. Heb. *reṯōm,* a *hapax legomenon* of uncertain etymology, yet its meaning is clear from the context. In view of the comparative scantiness of OT Heb. vocabulary and in view of the light

that[61] *is the main*[62] *sin*
of Lady Zion, 2+2
since in you may be found
Israel's rebel ways. 2+2
14 *So a dowry*[63] *must be bestowed*[64]
upon Moresheth-Gath. 3+2
Achzib's buildings prove a disappointment
to Israel's kings. 3+2
15 *A new successor will come*[65] *to you,*
population of Mareshah. 3+2
To Adullam will come
Israel's nobility.[66] 2+2

16 *Tonsure yourself and shave off your hair*
in mourning for the sons you dote on. 2+2
Give yourself as big a tonsure as the vulture's,
since their fate is deportation, leaving
you behind. 3+2

This second poem in Micah's collection, marked by extensive wordplay in the original, is a prediction of disaster concluding with a call to lamentation.[67] The prophet sees trouble ahead for the towns and villages of the Shephelah where he had been brought up. This "lowland" was a range of foothills, from 500 to 1500 feet high, between the plain of Philistia to the west and the mountain ridge of Judah to the east. It was dotted with

cast upon it by cognate languages especially in recent years, it is unwise to emend this verb out of existence. It is probable that the second masculine imperative should be repointed with J. M. P. Smith, *et al.*, to *rāṯōm,* an imperatival infinitive absolute.

61. Ehrlich, cf. Cheyne.

62. Willi-Plein with Wellhausen. Most interpret as "beginning."

63. Heb. *shillûḥîm,* evidently cognate with Ugar. *šlḥ,* "give (a present)," is here and in 1 K. 9:16 a marriage gift from a father to his daughter (A. S. van der Woude, *ZAW* 76 [1964], pp. 188–191).

64. MT *titt^enî,* "you (feminine singular) will give," is not expected in view of the metaphor; the subject is uncertain. To ease these difficulties probably the text should be slightly changed to *yitt^enû,* "they will give" (Robinson, *BHS*), or better to *yutt^enû,* "will be given" (Lindblom).

65. MT *'āḇî,* "I shall bring" (properly *'āḇî'*), as if Yahweh is speaking, but the prophet is evidently the speaker elsewhere in the oracle: cf. the third person reference in v. 12. The simplest change is to read *yāḇō',* assuming simple metathesis of *yb'* to *'by* with many since Ehrlich, including Robinson, Elliger, George, Fohrer, and Schwantes. Then the last couplet is bound together by repeated words like the couplet in v. 12 (see n. 80).

66. Lit. "glory": cf. Isa. 5:13 for this meaning.

67. K. Elliger, "Die Heimat des Propheten Micha," *ZDPV* 57 (1934), pp. 81–152 (cf. *BHS*), has persuaded many that vv. 8–16 constitute a lament concerning the loss of Judean towns to the Assyrians in 701 B.C. and that the restoration of the typical meter of lament, 3+2, is essential. To this end he holds that vv. 10–16 have suffered damage down the right edge of the sheet or column, which caused lacunae and other corruptions. Fohrer, *loc. cit.*, has rightly contested Elliger's views. He himself finds here, after much emendation, a regular 2+2 meter. There is certainly a preponderance of 2+2(+2), a jerky rhythm which here expresses emotional strain and shock.

communities that had long carried on their peaceful pursuits of agriculture and trade. But in his mind's eye Micah can see only disaster looming, as he thinks nostalgically of the hills and dales of his home region. The very names of the communities leap out at him with new and sinister significance. He makes a series of puns, which to the Semitic way of thinking were by no means weak jokes, but affirmations to be taken seriously. We have already noticed an isolated example of his wordplay in vv. 6f. Here Micah uses this technique extensively, apparently selecting those towns which most obviously lent themselves to this manipulation.[68] Names are treated as omens which, once observed, haunt the localities until they are fulfilled. They are revealed as clues to the curse that is to come upon the country. Isaiah produced a similar kind of composition in Isa. 10:27b–32, but there he was vividly describing the route of the enemy invader. Here there seems to be no such intention, since the place names are not mentioned in any obvious order. Micah reels off the names at random, glancing around in his imagination. Like the first oracle, this one appears to have been delivered in Jerusalem, to judge by v. 16, in which he addresses the unspecified city at the climax of the poem.

Structurally the oracle falls into three stanzas, two of seven lines each and a final short one of two.[69] The second is most easily discernible: vv. 13–15 fall into a threefold grouping of three, two, and two lines respectively, each ending with the key word *Israel*.[70] The third, v. 16, is a couplet characterized by a series of feminine singular imperatives and pronouns. The first stanza, vv. 10–12, consists of two, three, and then two lines depicting cameos of contrasting emotions, behavior, and fortunes. It is noticeable that the first stanza ends, and the second virtually begins, with reference to Jerusalem, which is addressed in the third. Micah keeps reverting to the significance of his tale of local woes for the capital. Moreover, the first stanza begins and the second ends with sinister allusions to David, the pioneer king of Jerusalem. The key word *Israel* in the second insists that the fate of the nation is at stake in Micah's message, which thus goes far beyond merely local import.

Doubtless the delivery of this oracle is to be linked historically with Sargon's campaigns against Philistia in 720 or 714–711 B.C.[71] Wars and rumors of wars in the adjacent area filled Micah with a presentiment of evil, and he feels moved by God to warn his own people of the peril that confronts them if they do not mend their ways. His foreboding came tragically true in 701 B.C., when the Assyrian troops of Sennacherib overran the area and Jerusalem all but fell.

68. Fohrer, *loc. cit.*, p. 79.

69. For this type of strophic structure cf. Fohrer, *loc. cit.*, pp. 70f., who, however, regards vv. 2–9 as falling into this pattern. Keil and von Ungern-Sternberg rightly divide vv. 10–15 into 10–12 and 13–15.

70. J. Muilenburg, "A Study in Hebrew Rhetoric: Repetition and Style," *Congress Volume, Copenhagen 1953*. SVT 1 (1953), pp. 97–111, esp. p. 106, refers to *Israel* as a frequent key word which often determines the structural pattern of a poem.

71. See the Introduction.

10–12 Micah sets the tone for the whole poem by quoting from the opening of David's elegy over Saul and Jonathan after Israelite defeat at the hands of the Philistines on Mount Gilboa (2 Sam. 1:20). David shrank from the humiliation of Philistine cheers and jeers when the news reached their cities. These words, shrouded in national disaster, are taken up by Micah as a fitting funereal overture to his oracle. They initiate the stylistic pattern of wordplay in which the prophet is to engage heavily.[72] Moreover, *Gath,* somewhere on the eastern edge of the Philistine plain, suits the topography of the poem as the nearest foreign city to the Judean Shephelah (see map on p. 238).[73] So greatly does the prophet shun the adverse publicity which the coming defeat is likely to evoke that he counsels refraining from open mourning. But his next words appear to have more sinister significance. Funeral rites celebrated under normal conditions had to be foregone in times of dire catastrophe.[74] Micah seems to imply the stunned condition of victims of war caused by the overwhelming shock of sudden invasion. The structure of ordinary life will be so shattered that the customary and comforting ritual will go unobserved.[75]

In the next line the prophet suddenly gives the opposite counsel. He glances from Gath in the west to *Beth-leaphrah,* probably over in the east of the Shephelah.[76] The name has an ominous ring for Micah; it suggests the Hebrew *'āp̱ār, dust.* Hearing the distressing news, the community on the other side of the Shephelah is fated to engage in the mourning rite of

72. Heb. *b*^{e}*g̱aṯ 'al-taggîḏû* repeats the palatal and dental letters (*g, t/d*).
73. The location of Gath has not yet been settled. Tell Sheikh Ahmed el-'Areini (Tel 'Erani), 4½ miles northwest of Lachish, the site favored by Albright, has yielded no confirmation to Israeli excavations, although H. E. Kassis, "Gath and the Structure of the 'Philistine' Society," *JBL* 84 (1965), pp. 259–271, has sought to explain the absence of Philistine artifacts there by the suggestion that Gath was ruled by a Canaanite king as vassal of Philistine overlords and that its culture was Canaanite. Tell eṣ-Ṣafi (Tel Ẕafit), 9½ miles north of Lachish, which some have preferred, is more probably to be identified with Libnah. Others have built upon the researches of B. Mazar, "Gath and Gittaim," *IEJ* 4 (1954), pp. 227–235, who has distinguished a northern Gath or Gittaim in the Shephelah from a more southerly Philistine Gath, thus doing justice to the implications of 1 Sam. 27. S. Bülow and R. A. Mitchell, "An Iron Age II Fortress on Tel Nagila," *IEJ* 11 (1961), pp. 101–110, suggested Tell en-Najileh (Tel Nagila), some 7 miles southwest of Lachish;but archeologists R. Amiran and A. Eitan have reported that the site was only sparsely inhabited during the Iron Age (*IEJ* 13 [1963], pp. 143–45, 333f.; *Archaeology* 18 [1965], pp. 115f.). G. E. Wright, "Fresh Evidence for the Philistine Story," *BA* 29 (1966), pp. 70–86 (cf. *HTR* 64 [1971], p. 446, n. 20), has argued for Tell esh-Shari'ah (Tel Sera'), 15 miles southwest of Lachish, on the edge of the Negeb. See K. A. Kitchen's discussion in *People of OT Times,* ed. D. J. Wiseman (1973), pp. 61f.
74. Cf. Job 27:15; Ps. 78:64; Ezek. 24:15–24.
75. In view of the exhortations to mourn in vv. 10b and 16, attempts are often made to get rid of the negative. Elliger, *loc. cit.,* p. 87, reads (in place of *bāḵô 'al-tiḇkû*) *b*^{e}*ḵû 'ap̱-tiḇkû,* "weep, certainly you should weep." Schwantes, followed by Fohrer, *loc. cit.,* p. 76, stays closer to the consonantal text by reading *biḇ*^{e}*ḵî l*^{e}*ṯiḇkû,* "with weeping you shall certainly weep," seeing here an emphatic *lameḏ*. Many have tried to get a place name out of *bāḵô* with G *en Akim,* but Elliger, *loc. cit.,* rightly raises the stylistic objection that elsewhere in the poem no more than one wordplay occurs per line.
76. Elliger, *loc. cit.,* pp. 125f., has plausibly identified it with eṭ-Ṭaiyibeh near Tarqumiya, viewing the Arab. name as a euphemism by association with the demon Aphrith.

throwing themselves on the ground and rolling in the dust to give vent to their emotions. The contrasting emotions match the different locations and reflect the confused reactions of distress into which the Judean foothills will be plunged.

Micah now employs wordplays of a different kind, playing on sense suggested rather than on sound. *Shaphir,* which is mentioned only here in the OT and has not been satisfactorily located, sounds like a word for "beautiful."[77] Moffatt accordingly renders "Fairtown" to bring out this allusion. But it is doomed not to live up to its name; instead its people will march away as prisoners of war, ignominiously stripped of their fine clothes.[78] As in v. 10 Micah had reversed his injunction, so now he proceeds to jerk his hearers to a different type of scene in order to express the chaos of the situation. He selects *Zaanan,* evidently not far from Lachish.[79] The name suggests the similar-sounding "go out" (Heb. *yātsā'*), but here again its ironic destiny is to betray its name. Its inhabitants do not come to fight but remain cooped up inside their walls, afraid to face the foe and to help their neighbors. A further non-ally of Shaphir is *Beth-haezel,* another place unknown to us. This town will be too engrossed in mourning for its own losses to come to the aid of its neighbors.

The lines of the last couplet in the first stanza are closely linked with each other both in form[80] and in contrasting subject matter of frustrated hopes and grim reality. *Maroth,* whose location is again unknown,[81] would have the sense of "bitter things" to the Hebrew ear. The place cannot evade the fate of its baneful name. It is destined to wait in vain for the change of fortune for which it yearns. On the contrary, ill fortune is to come not merely from the human enemy but as punishment from Yahweh above, threatening the very *gate* of the capital. There is an implicit play here between *Jerusalem* and Hebrew *shālôm,* "peace, welfare." Disaster would creep up to the very walls of the city whose name spelled blessing. It is striking that Sennacherib, who overran Judah some years later, speaks in his annals of Hezekiah "shut up like a caged bird" in his beleaguered city so that "any who went out of its city gate" was turned back.[82]

77. The verb *shāp̱ar* and related forms. Aramaic has an adjective *shappîr*.

78. The suggestion to delete *bōsheṯ,* "shame," with G as a gloss and then to reconstruct *'eryâ,* "nakedness," as *'îrāh,* "her city," or *mē'îrāh,* "from her city" (cf. G "her cities," repointing MT as *'āreyhā*), has the advantage of leaving the phrase "population of . . ." at the end of the line in accord with the pattern elsewhere in the poem, but it has the disadvantage of removing the wordplay, which is only arbitrarily restored by replacing the first two words with *hārî'û shôp̱ār* or the like with Duhm, Robinson, Fohrer, *et al.* The line is to be scanned as 2+2+2.

79. It is probably the same place as Zenan, Josh. 15:37, in the area of Lachish, v. 39.

80. Both lines begin with *kî,* used as an emphatic particle.

81. Its identification with Heb. *Ma'ᵃrāṯ,* Josh. 15:59, is doubtful in its assumption of a dropped *'ayin*.

82. *DOTT,* p. 67.

13–15 The second stanza opens with a cry to the important city of *Lachish*. In later years it was to fall to Sennacherib, who decorated the walls of his palace at Nineveh with reliefs depicting its capitulation. Excavations have identified it with Tell ed-Duweir (Tel Lakhish) on the edge of the Shephelah, 30 miles or so southwest of Jerusalem and 6 miles southwest of Micah's home town. Its doom lay in the distant future beyond anybody's ken, but Micah already has an uncanny awareness of disaster. For centuries it had been a military fortress. Rehoboam had strengthened it as part of his defense system to protect Judah from Egyptian or Philistine attack (2 Chr. 11:5–12). Doubtless Micah is thinking of the military equipment of this garrison when he makes a play on the name of this city and its chariot horses.[83] He cynically speaks of their use not in battle but in retreat.[84] Then he turns from cameo to commentary, expanding the hint of divine judgment given at the end of the last stanza. The note of sin and rebellion struck in the former oracle (v. 5) is sounded again. In another oracle Micah began a list of Judah's false mainstays with mention of horses and chariots (5:10[9]), and here likewise he condemns faith in the efficacy of the mobile chariot brigade as an offensive weapon. He like other prophets saw radical rivalry between pinning one's hopes on armaments and trusting in God. In a war-torn age this was the essence of secularism for the chosen nation. Thus it was that the prophet could point to Lachish as the stable of the nation's crimes before God.[85]

It is now the turn of Micah's home town to receive the ominous consequences of its name. Moresheth sounds very much like *mᵉ'ōreshet̠,* "betrothed." The prophet thinks of a girl leaving her family and coming under the new authority of her husband. *Moresheth-Gath* is promised to another. She is doomed to come under the jurisdiction of the enemy invader. Sennacherib's words spring to mind: "Forty-six of Hezekiah's strong-walled towns and innumerable smaller villages in their neighborhood I besieged and conquered."[86] To express the metaphorical allusion to marriage, Micah uses the illustration of a father's gift to his daughter when she married. In political terms it presumably speaks of an indemnity to be paid in addition to the loss of the town. Both are a penalty for the nation's sin.

In this couplet the prophet links with Moresheth-Gath the adjacent town of *Achzib*. The town list of Josh. 15 locates it in the Shephelah and catalogs it after Keilah and before Mareshah (v. 44). It seems to be the same place as Chezib in Gen. 38:5, which was evidently close to Adullam. The place has plausibly been identified with Tell el-Beda, 3 miles west of

83. Heb. *Lāḵîsh, lāreḵesh,* "to the steeds." It is apparently in order to achieve this play that Micah avoids the more usual construction "harness the steeds to the chariots."
84. For a similar prophetic reversal cf. Isa. 30:16.
85. The capital is cited as the place from which national policy is directed. It is personified as "daughter Zion" (cf. Isa. 1:8; Jer. 4:31; Lam. 1:6).
86. *DOTT,* p. 67.

Adullam and 5 miles northeast of Mareshah.[87] If so, it was only a few miles from Moresheth-Gath. Here again to Micah's ear, tuned to disaster, Achzib has a sinister ring. It sounds like *'akzāḇ,* "deceitful, disappointing," which is used in Jer. 15:18 of a wadi or flood stream to which thirsty travellers came hopefully, only to find a dry river bed.[88] The background to the reference is a mystery. A fascinating attempt to pierce the veil has been made with the aid of 1 Chr. 4:21–23, which evidently lists guilds in the employ of Judean kings.[89] The passage mentions potters who were "men of Cozeba," a place whose name may well be yet another form of Achzib, since the context refers to nearby Mareshah. Accordingly reference has been seen here to factories producing royal pottery, which presumably would close when the area was overrun and communications were cut off from Jerusalem, so that royal contracts could not be fulfilled.[90]

Micah glances south with his mind's eye to *Mareshah,* which has been certainly identified with Tell Sandaḥannah (Tel Maresha).[91] It was an important frontier town, another part of Rehoboam's defense system along with Lachish (2 Chr. 11:6–10). The bastion would be a rich prize eagerly sought by any invader, for it would open up the way into the interior of Judah. The prophet is well aware of this and makes this very point by relating the name to *yōrēsh,* "possessor, heir." Mareshah is to be taken over by a new heir. It is not insignificant that the word is often used of gains in war:[92] the right of inheritance is to be won by conquest.

The arrival of the conqueror at Mareshah is to be matched by an arrival of a different kind at *Adullam,* which has been identified with Tell esh-Sheik Madhkur, and so is some 7 miles to the northeast. Just as the first stanza began with ominous allusion to David, so now the second closes with a similar somber hint. To people doubtless fond of reliving in their imagination the glorious days of King David and wishing them back, the prophet can at the moment prophesy only a return to the gray days of that monarch. Here he harks back to the period when David was an outlaw in hiding to save his life from Saul, and became a magnet to a ragtag army of malcontents (1 Sam. 22:1f.). Micah draws a cynical picture of the aristocracy of the Shephelah retracing the tracks of those ancient dropouts to find safety behind Adullam's ramparts. Rehoboam had made it a

87. Elliger, *loc. cit.,* p. 124.

88. Cf. the poignant description of such an experience in Job 6:15–20.

89. A. Demsky, "The Houses of Achzib. A Critical Note on Micah 1:14b," *IEJ* 16 (1966), pp. 211–15.

90. It is hazardous in our present ignorance to emend with many *l^emal^eḵê,* "to the kings," to *l^emeleḵ,* "to the king," assuming dittography of *yoḏ* (cf. *BHS*). Is it a reference to co-regency? If Hezekiah was co-regent with Ahaz till 715 (cf. J. Gray, *I and II Kings* [²1970], pp. 74, 673), then this might suggest a pre-715 date for the oracle. Evidently *Israel* stands for the Southern Kingdom, as in v. 13 and 3:1.

91. The ancient name has been preserved in Khirbet Merash to the immediate west.

92. E.g., Josh. 12:1; Amos 2:10.

military bastion (2 Chr. 11:7), so that it was a suitable place of refuge from local catastrophe.

16 The last stanza is an address to personified Jerusalem, the city in which Micah stands.[93] He urges it to engage in full mourning rites. Behind the prophet's exhortation must have lain the impulse of his own aching heart. He has been speaking of places he knew better than most of his hearers, towns and villages springing from childhood memories. We recall his poignant reference to "my people" at the end of the former oracle: how much more would he be affected by the prospect of disaster overtaking his friends and acquaintances, his own kith and kin? So it is his personal sense of shock that inspires this appeal to Jerusalem to go into deep mourning. He alludes to the traditional custom of making a bald patch on the head.[94] Shaving one's hair, normally worn long by both sexes, was one of a number of external tokens of sorrow. So great would be the grief in this case that Micah calls for a larger area than usual to be shaved. To make his point vividly he cites the griffon *vulture,* whose white down-covered head looks like a bald pate.[95] The darling *sons* of whom the metropolis is to be bereaved are the population of the towns and villages who have been apostrophized earlier in the poem. But they are to be victims not only of death but of deportation. Micah dramatically uses a so-called prophetic perfect: "they have gone into exile from you." So certain is this fate that already they are as good as gone. Mass evacuation was a regular feature of Assyrian war policy if control through a satellite government proved unworkable. Sargon had inflicted it upon the Northern Kingdom a decade or so before, as Micah's audience would recall. This is the climax of his oracle, plainly spelling out his earlier hints of woe; hardly any other word could have caused a greater shudder. In fact Judah was fortunate to evade this fate for a time. It was left to Sargon's successor to put on record that from the Judean towns and villages which he had captured "I made to come out 200,150 people, young and old, male and female, . . . and counted them as the spoils of war."[96] Many a citizen of Jerusalem must have remembered Micah's words and pondered on their truth.

The impact of this powerful poem upon the modern reader is unfortunately marred by a cultural rift. Anyone who despises puns and prizes emotional restraint as a virtue has a long bridge to cross before he can enter into this particular section of the heritage God would have him make his own. Micah is not playing clever word games for the amusement of his listeners. Words for him and his audience are a web of associations for good or ill, a prey of mystic spells, which in the adverse sense are akin

93. The nonspecific address is paralleled in Joel 1:8.
94. Cf. Isa. 15:2; Jer. 16:6; Amos 8:10. It was discouraged by the legislation of Lev. 21:5; Deut. 14:1.
95. Heb. *nesher* can mean either "eagle" or *vulture*. Here it is obviously the latter.
96. *DOTT,* p. 67.

to the irrational superstition that surrounds the number thirteen for many today. The prophet is exploiting this cultural susceptibility, surrounding each place in turn with an aura of doom and evoking feelings of dread and despair. In the middle of this rhetorical *tour de force* he reveals to wide-eyed hearers, aghast and ready to hear the worst, that behind the grim future stands the person of Yahweh, no longer a safe stronghold but his people's enemy. He is forced to stand against them because they have left his side and taken refuge in secular alternatives which are no alternatives at all. Micah whips up his hearers' emotions and pushes them into inconsolable grief in order to dispel their complacency and arouse in them a sense of their own sin and liability to punishment.

The first two oracles of the book have been set side by side despite their origin in different periods of time. The juxtaposition is a masterpiece of matching, for the second is a louder echo of the first. Both speak of Yahweh as the one who punishes his people's sin and rebellion. Both culminate in a call to lamentation as response to the expected doom. But whereas in the former Samaria's end is made the prototype of doom for Jerusalem, in the latter the harbinger comes disturbingly closer. The downfall of the Shephelah communities brings disaster to Jerusalem's doorstep. In both poems the prophet keeps coming back to the southern capital as the eventual target of his messages.[97] Micah intends his audience in Jerusalem to ask themselves, in words Isaiah put on others' lips about the very time the second oracle was delivered: "And we, how shall we escape?" (Isa. 20:6).

3. *Crime and Punishment (2:1–5)*

Alas for those who think up wrong
and lie in bed working out[1] *evil,* 3+3
then at break of day put it into operation,
using the power that lies in their hands. 3+3
2 *They want land—and grab it;*
houses—and just take them. 3+2
They do violence to a man and his home,
to individuals and what is theirs by ancestral right. 3+2

97. "The gate of Jerusalem," v. 12, corresponds finely and, for the editor, intentionally to "the gate of my people, Jerusalem," v. 9. For this reason the plural "gates" of G S T, followed by many scholars, is to be rejected.

1. G. A. Smith, cf. Margolis, Wade. The verb generally means "practice," obviously unsuitable here. Ps. 58:2(3), where the present sense is often claimed, is a difficult passage. But Ehrlich cited as a good parallel the use of *'āśâ,* "do," in Isa. 37:26 in the sense "plan." Thus there is no need to repoint to *ûpo'ᵒlê rā',* "and evil deeds" (Robinson, following Halévy, cf. NEB). Nor is it warranted to omit the phrase as a gloss (Wellhausen, J. M. P. Smith, Lindblom, Willi-Plein): *rā'* is required to balance *rā'â* in v. 3 (Willis, *Biblica* 48 [1967], p. 535).

3 *So this is the message of Yahweh:*[2]
"Now it is my turn to think up
against this crowd[3] 2+2
evil[4] *from which you will not*
free your necks 3+2
nor will you be able to walk erect,
a time of such evil will it be." 3+3
4 *On that day folk will raise on your behalf*
a taunt-song, groaning, moaning and bemoaning,[5] 4+4
"Ruined! We are ruined![6]
He cancels my people's right to the land. 2+3
How terrible he should remove it from me!
He assigns to a renegade the right to our fields." 2+3
5 *So you*[7] *will have no one*
to put in place the measuring line
by lot among the congregation of Yahweh. 3+2+3

The oracles of the prophets are time and again put in a traditional pattern of a reasoned condemnation. First an outline is given of the situation and of the persons who have offended God, like a police "wanted" notice which describes the criminal and his offense. Upon this logical basis is constructed a forecast of the retribution that will befall the offender. This formal two-part scheme may be observed in Nathan's denunciation of King David in 2 Sam. 12:7–12 or more simply in Ahijah's condemnation of King Jeroboam in 1 K. 14:7–11. The pattern could be varied in a number of different ways. One variation appears in the oracles of Amos, Isaiah, and Jeremiah, and in this one of Micah's. An exclamation of foreboding shock prefaces a lengthy description consisting of a series of statements cataloging the offenses and their perpetrators. Then a connecting "therefore" turns it into a cause for dire consequences. Here is one example:

"Alas for those at ease in Zion

2. The clause is in anacrusis.
3. Haupt "clique," NEB "brood," JB "breed."
4. Heb. *rā'â* rhythmically belongs to the next line (G. R. Driver, *JTS* 39]1938], p. 266).
5. The Heb. uses three cognate words, a verb and two nouns. MT adds *'āmar,* "he said," which is uncoordinated with the preceding. *W^e'āmar,* the reading of some Heb. mss. and of S, read by many since Ehrlich, including *BHS,* would be syntactically easier, but it may well be a scribal note calling attention to direct speech, as sometimes elsewhere; cf. T. H. Robinson, BZAW 66 (1936), p. 39.
6. Very many scholars have followed Stade in transposing clauses to obtain a *qinah* meter of 3+2, but MT's order makes a powerful beginning, as in Jer. 9:19(18), where indeed the 3+2 rhythm is not used. 2+3 appears to be a legitimate variation; cf. G. B. Gray, *The Forms of Hebrew Poetry* (1915), pp. 176–181; T. J. Meek, "Lamentations," *IB,* vol. 6 (1956), p. 4.
7. For *l^ekā,* singular, it is contextually better (cf. v. 4) to read *lākem,* plural, with Ehrlich and others, assuming haplography of *mem.* Vuilleumier, following Procksch and H. Schmidt, takes the verse as the landowners' reply to Micah.

and for those who are secure on Mount Samaria,
the elite of the first of the nations. . . .
Therefore they will soon be the first in the journey to exile.''
(Amos 6:1–7)[8]

Micah's oracle falls into several parts: first the introductory exclamation and basic accusation (v. 1), which is developed in v. 2; then after the hinge linking cause and effect comes the authoritative ''Thus has Yahweh said,'' the messenger formula often adopted by the prophets as a preface to a divine statement of coming intervention (v. 3); next, the result of this intervention, which incorporates a taunt-song (v. 4); and finally a supplement marking a logical conclusion (v. 5).[9]

The traditional rendering of the introductory cry as ''woe'' gives the misleading impression of a curse like ''woe betide.'' In fact the original setting of the emotional cry *alas* appears to have been a funeral. In 1 K. 13:30 the cry ''Alas for my brother!'' is raised at the tomb. It was a normal expression of shocked sorrow at somebody's death. Jeremiah threatened that there would be no proper funeral and no regrets when King Jehoiakim died; no one would say, ''Alas for my brother!'' or ''Alas for His Majesty!'' (Jer. 22:18). On the other hand, King Zedekiah would be honored with a state funeral and people would say, ''Alas for His Majesty!'' (Jer. 34:5). The prophets took up this ordinary funeral lament and turned it into a heavily ironical expression of regret.[10] It was made the signal of a tragic situation, the seer's reaction to the fate that God had told him was to befall a certain group of people, and which he was about to announce. An obituary-like description of their characteristics paves the way for this announcement.

At the beginning of the divine pronouncement of disaster in v. 3 stands an element often found at this juncture.[11] It is difficult to render in modern English. Traditionally rendered ''behold,'' it is strictly demonstrative and serves to herald dramatically the sudden intervention of God: ''Here I am about to. . . .'' By it God presents himself and his proposed action as the answer to the critical situation. He it is who takes up the key word uttered early in the preparatory passage and hurls it back at its perpetrators: God has his counterplan. Further correspondence appears in the matching of *evil* with *evil,* in the eventual powerlessness of those who have abused their power, and in the removal of land from those who have

8. Cf. Isa. 5:8–10; 30:3–5; Jer. 22:13–19.

9. C. Westermann, *Basic Forms of Prophetic Speech* (E. T. 1967), p. 175; E. Gerstenberger, *JBL* 81 (1962), p. 250.

10. Cf. R. J. Clifford, ''The Use of *Hôy* in the Prophets,'' *CBQ* 28 (1966), pp. 458–464; W. Janzen, *Mourning Cry and Woe Oracle*. BZAW 125 (1972), *passim*. Here ''the prophet exclaims 'hôy!' because the time will come when mocking mourners will sing their lamentation'' (*ibid.*, p. 64, n. 83).

11. Cf. K. Koch, *The Growth of the Biblical Tradition* (E. T. 1969), pp. 205f., 211.

rendered others landless.[12] Such correspondence between accusation and verdict is a well-attested prophetic feature. For instance, in 2 Sam. 12 Nathan accuses David of stealing Uriah's wife and killing Uriah with the sword; in turn he is to be robbed of his wives and the sword will never depart from his house (vv. 7–12). Rather like Micah, Ahijah in 1 K. 14:9f. announces to Jeroboam that God will bring evil upon him because he has done evil.

The two parts of the oracle are closely interlocked in order to express how inexorably the villains are to be paid back in their own coin. The structure is based on the counterbalance of ideas and words rather than on strophe and meter. The whole unit is tied together by a remarkable chain of assonance. The consonantal combination *m-š* occurs seven times in this poem. With his keen ear for sound Micah forcefully spells out the fate that is inevitably to fall upon this *crowd* (Heb. *mishpāḥâ*) who use their beds (*mishkᵉḇôṯām*) amiss, by taking up the sound in succeeding lines.[13] Metrically the poem is mixed; there is a tendency to group together lines in couplets by employing the same meter.

1, 2 Micah uses the inauspicious word *alas* as a means of describing and identifying the people for whom God has a lamentable fate in store. They are no victims of sudden temptation but deliberate wrongdoers of long standing. The prophet describes the careful planning that lies behind their malpractices. Here, as in the Psalms,[14] one's *bed* is the place in which to indulge in private thoughts and aspirations for which the bustle of daily life leaves little opportunity. These men must spend sleepless hours of wicked scheming, to judge by the crafty policy of evil they pursue in the daytime. They can hardly wait for the crack of dawn before they put their plans into practice. No sluggards these, lying abed, for there is work to be done. They rise with alacrity and do their daily work with a diligence that would be commendable were it not misapplied. Their success is guaranteed, for they possess power which they may exploit to achieve their selfish ends. Micah draws with ironic strokes a scathing word-sketch of dedicated and unscrupulous villains.

So far the prophet has tantalizingly divulged to his audience a glimpse of ugly endeavor and industry. Now he proceeds to speak more plainly and specifies the nature of this misconduct. His protest is directed against the same type of offense as his contemporary Isaiah once attacked in the same rhetorical vein:

Alas for those who add house to house
and attach field to field

12. Cf. too *tāmîshû*, "free," v. 3—*yāmîsh*, "remove," v. 4.
13. Heb. *tāmîshû mishshām*, "free from," *māshāl*, "taunt-song," *yāmîshû*, "remove," *mashlîḵ*, "put in place."
14. Ps. 4:4(5); 36:4(5); 63:6(7).

until there is no more space
and you are left to live alone
in the middle of the land. (Isa. 5:8)

These are land barons, who buy up farm after farm until vast tracts of country are theirs and they are monarchs of all they survey from horizon to horizon. They accumulate acres like the landlords of the great Italian *latifundia* in the Roman period. The eighth century B.C. was a period that saw great change. There had been an influx of new wealth into the country under King Uzziah, which had evidently benefitted some more than others. The exploitation of new capital and economic opportunities was resulting in the squeezing out of the small man from the agricultural scene, just as today there is pressure in many Western countries upon the small shopkeeper and businessman. Micah, country cousin to the urban Isaiah, must have known at close hand the tragedy and heartbreak that the landgrabbers caused. He protests more ardently than Isaiah at their cruel selfishness and callous greed. He deplores the unscrupulous way in which they acquire new property. They are heedless of the suffering they cause, unbothered by scruples about the shady tricks they play to get more and more land.

It is significant that he uses a word that occurs in the Decalog, usually rendered "covet": "You must not covet your neighbor's house. . . ."[15] Such craving is particularly repugnant to the profession of a faith in the moral God of the Bible. Paul with insight could call covetousness "idolatry" (Col. 3:6). "There is a sort of religious purpose, a devotion of the soul to greed, which makes the sin of the miser so hateful."[16] It ever sets up a golden calf whose worship is incompatible with that of the God of Paul and Micah. The prophet's terms *grab* and *do violence* are a pair often repeated in the OT.[17] Significantly it is prohibited to treat a neighbor thus in the ancient stipulation of Lev. 19:13. One gets the impression that it is not only the humanity but also the piety of the prophet that is affronted by these outrages.[18] This impression is reinforced when one recalls the peculiar importance attached to the occupation of land in Israel. At the forefront of Israelite economic theory stood the principle that the land was Yahweh's[19] and that the people received it from him as a sacred trust which

15. Heb. *ḥāmaḏ*, Exod. 20:17; Deut. 5:18. In recent times the verb has been understood to refer not only to mental desire but to the practical intrigues that lead to taking possession of the thing desired; cf. the review and discussion in J. J. Stamm and M. E. Andrew, *The Ten Commandments in Recent Research*. SBT 2:2 (^{2}1962), pp. 101–107. H.-J. Stoebe, *Wort und Dienst* N.F. 3 (1952), p. 110, has observed that this new understanding is hardly supported in this present passage, in which in the light of v. 1 desire becomes an actuality not by a logic inherent in the verb but by unscrupulous rapidity.

16. J. B. Lightfoot, *Saint Paul's Epistles to the Colossians and to Philemon* (1892), *in loc*.

17. Cf. Ps. 62:10(11); Jer. 21:12; 22:3; Ezek. 18:18; 22:29.

18. Cf. Beyerlin, *KIPVM*, p. 57.

19. Lev. 25:23: "The land is mine: you are only aliens and guests staying with me." Cf. Num. 36:2, 7.

was handed down from generation to generation, from heir to heir.[20] It is this presupposition that underlies the protest of Elijah against King Ahab's takeover of Naboth's vineyard in 1 K. 21. That whole chapter is a good commentary on this present passage although it took place over a century before in the Northern Kingdom. "Yahweh forbid that I should sell you my ancestral heritage" (1 K. 21:3) was Naboth's indignant refusal, which many of Micah's contemporaries must have echoed.[21] It was Yahweh who protected the rights of his tenants to their holdings, and ideally it was the duty of those in authority in theocratic Israel to keep vigil on his behalf. But in permissive days it fell to the prophets to raise lonely voices on behalf of the victims of loss of land.

3 So it is that Micah performs explicitly as Yahweh's spokesman. The authority for his words lies not just in his own conscience but in the divine will. The prophet stresses the weight attaching to the words that follow. It is no less than the decree of Israel's God that he must utter.[22] He transmits the grimly ironic message that Yahweh is to intervene by treating the land barons as they have treated others. Their evil scheming will find a sure counterpart in the scheming of God to make them suffer an evil fate. Micah here takes advantage of the fact that the one Hebrew word *rāʿâ* has the dual sense of moral evil and amoral misfortune. Our prophet is especially fond of this principle of "an eye for an eye." He has a keen sense of fair play and a passion for poetic justice.[23] This penchant, which finds frequent expression throughout the OT, has been inherited in the New in the form of such sentiments as reaping what one sows.[24] "It is the peculiar

20. Cf. K. A. Henrey, "Land Tenure in the OT," *PEQ* 86 (1954), pp. 5–15; G. von Rad, "The Promised Land and Yahweh's Land in the Hexateuch," *The Problem of the Hexateuch and Other Essays* (E. T. 1966), pp. 79–83. This entailing of land was a West Semitic pattern, attested at Mari and Ugarit, but in Israel it was completely undergirded with theological sanctions (A. Malamat, "Mari and the Bible: Some Patterns of Tribal Organization and Institutions," *JAOS* 82 (1962), pp. 143–150; F. I. Andersen, "The Socio-Juridical Background of the Naboth Incident," *JBL* 85 (1966), pp. 46–57.

21. 1 K. 21 also illustrates the lengths to which the land-hungry were prepared to go in order to sate their greed. Effective measures doubtless often taken were loans at extortionate interest rates, foreclosure of mortgages, and bribery of witnesses and judges. There are no grounds for the supposition of H. M. Weil, "Le chapitre ii de Michée expliquée par Le Premier Livre de Rois, chapitres xx-xxii," *RHR* 121 (1940), pp. 146–161, that the actual historical setting of Mic. 2 was in the events of 1 K. 20–22.

22. But there is little justification for drawing a sharp distinction in essence between man's words and God's words in cases such as these where the messenger formula occurs after the prophetic motivation and before the prediction of disaster. R. Rendtorff, "Botenformel und Botenspruch," *ZAW* 74 (1962), p. 175, n. 30, has criticized in this respect the view of Westermann, *op. cit.*, p. 179, and von Rad, *OT Theology,* vol. 2 (E. T. 1965), pp. 71f. He observes that there is no reason to take as formally original and fundamental the positioning of the messenger formula between the two parts, since in practice sometimes the formula occurs before the motivation (e.g., 1 K. 20:28, 42) and occasionally the motivation occurs after the prediction of disaster so that the formula prefaces the whole oracle (e.g., 1 K. 11:31–33).

23. Cf. Willis, "On the Text of Micah 2, 1a*a-b*," *Biblica* 48 (1967), pp. 539–541. Janzen, *op. cit.*, pp. 35–39, 63, 82, shows that such reversal is typical of the woe-oracle.

24. Cf. Matt. 7:1; 2 Cor. 5:10; Gal. 6:7, 8.

office of God . . . to render to each the measure of evil they have brought on others'' (Calvin). So it will be for the folk the prophet disparagingly calls *this crowd,* these kindred spirits in crime, these cronies in selfish aggrandizement. Does he promise them a literal subjugation such as the Assyrians cruelly imposed on their prisoners of war?[25] Is he speaking metaphorically of the crushing and inescapable yoke of disaster which will bring low the high and mighty property tycoons? Perhaps Micah knew hardly more than vague presentiment, but more likely he had the sinister prospect of Assyrian domination at the back of his mind as God's means of humbling these magnates who placed themselves above the laws of Israel.[26] He reinforces the certainty and seriousness of the retribution of evil for evil by echoing it at the close, a repeated thunderclap heralding the storm.[27]

4 With the link *on that day* the prophet goes on to explain the consequences of divine intervention.[28] He announces the grim downfall of the land profiteers through the mouths of those who are to witness it. The term rendered *taunt-song* primarily means ''example, object lesson.'' The fallen are made to serve as an example to be shunned, a lesson to others not to travel the path that leads to this disastrous end.[29] It may indeed be an ironic echo of the dirge of the yeomen evicted earlier, soon to be repeated in bitter derision when the tables are turned against their oppressors.

A cry of utter desolation forms a powerful beginning: ''Lost, everything is lost.'' The realism of this pseudo-lament comes out in its excited jerkiness as it oscillates between *I* and *we*. Another realistic feature is its deliberately nonspecific allusions to God, probably a superstitious avoidance lest direct mention of his name bring down further calamity.[30] A legal term is employed in the phrase *cancels* the *right*.[31] God was transferring the land from its present owners by a dire act of conveyance. A plaint of astonished indignation on the lips of the now landless landowners is parodied: How could God do such a thing—take away my land?[32] God

25. Cf. 2 K. 19:28; Amos 4:2.
26. Cf. the use of the figure of a yoke to express foreign subjugation in Deut. 28:48; Isa. 9:4; Jer. 27:8.
27. The repetition of a term or motif at the beginning and end of a passage, technically inclusion, is a frequent poetic device in Heb. literature.
28. Cf. A. Lefèvre, ''L'expression 'en ce jour-là' dans le livre d'Isaie,'' *Mélanges bibliques . . . André Robert* (1957), p. 179; the phrase is used normally to introduce the result, the conclusion in which the sense of an event is revealed, and it always concerns the manifestation of the power of Yahweh (e.g., Isa. 3:7; 7:18; 10:27).
29. A. R. Johnson, ''Māshāl,'' *Wisdom in Israel and in the Ancient Near East*. SVT 3 (1960), p. 166. Other examples are in Isa. 14:4; Hab. 2:6.
30. Cf. Amos 6:10.
31. Heb. *yāmîr*; cf. *t^e^mûrâ,* Ruth 4:7, which confirms the present text (Weil, *loc. cit.*, p. 148); cf. NEB ''changes hands.'' Since Ewald many, e.g., JB, *BHS,* have adopted G's underlying *yimmaḏ,* ''is measured'' (an *r/d* error as with the same verb in G at Ezek. 48:14).
32. Wolfe. The text has often been questioned. Many emend with Stade to *'ên mēshîḇ (lô)* on the basis of G, which Janzen, however, noting the appropriateness of *'êḵ,* ''how,'' in a taunt-song (cf. Isa. 14:4, 12), calls ''a form-critically insensitive facilitating reading'' (*op.*

was reallocating their estates, as indeed was his right; but to their shock and annoyance the new tenants were from the lower classes and had none of their own meritorious piety. The situation envisaged seems to be the forced evacuation of the landed elite, who are marched away by the foreign invader while their estates are left to their erstwhile serfs, who are contemptuously spoken of as religious renegades.[33] In similar vein Jeremiah could exclaim:

> *"These are only the poor . . . ,*
> *they do not know the way of Yahweh."* (Jer. 5:4)

5 Micah draws a conclusion supplementary to that of v. 3. In content it follows on directly from the taunt-song. The squires will not only lose their land, they will also lose the right to participate in the sacred redistribution of territory. There will be no hope of rehabilitation for them, but full and final excommunication.[34] The reference is apparently to territory in the category of communal land owned by a tribe or clan, which would be reallocated periodically to the constituent families at a religious ceremony attended by all the group or at least the representatives of each family.[35] But Micah's curse is that certain families will have no representative left to stake their claim. Evidently a solemn lottery took place, and according as the marked stones were drawn so it was determined where the measuring line demarcating one family's allotment from another's should be placed.[36] It is this ceremony that underlies the metaphor of Ps. 16:6:

> *The lines have been allotted to me in a lovely position;*
> *yes, a fine property has come to me.*

In the OT, as indeed in Acts 1:26, such lot-casting, attended by the people in communal dependence upon God, was regarded as a sure means of ascertaining the divine will. The teacher of wisdom was certain that when lots were thrown "the result comes wholly from Yahweh" (Prov. 16:33).

The oracle is a powerful display of moral indignation. Micah takes an uncompromising stand as a champion of civil rights. Uncowed by those who now hold the whip hand, he declares the word of God against injustice and oppression in the community. Yet it is no role of his to be an active revolutionary. He confidently looks ahead to a great reversal of circumstances to be set in motion by God himself. His conviction that history is the moral workshop of Yahweh comes to the fore again. Christianity with its center of gravity pushed forward into a posthistorical day of

---

cit., p. 63, n. 81). Willi-Plein reads the consonantal text as *yimshôl,* taking the following *l^eshôḇēḇ* as a verb with G: "How is it possible to annul?" (cf. NEB).

33. Cf. 2 K. 25:11, 12. A frequent emendation of *leshôḇēḇ* since Stade is *leshôḇênû,* "to our captors" (e.g., RSV, *BHS*). The old interpretation of MT as a reference to the Assyrians (e.g., Keil) does not suit the term, which must refer to deserting one's national faith.

34. Contrast the thought of Isa. 34:17.

35. Cf. A. Alt, "Micha 2,1–5. *Gēs anadesmos* in Juda" (see Bibliography), pp. 19f.

36. J. Lindblom, "Lot-Casting in the OT," *VT* 12 (1962), pp. 164–178; von Rad, "The Promised Land. . . ," p. 86 and n. 14.

reckoning has tended to pay less attention to this belief. But common to the faith of both Micah and the Christian is the confidence that justice will eventually be seen to be done. "God is not mocked: for whatever a man sows he will also reap" (Gal. 6:7).

The prophet's sense of sacred privilege in the holding of land finds to some extent a parallel in the NT doctrine of stewardship. As a family was entrusted with God's property to cultivate and cherish and to pass on to the next generation, so the local church and the individual Christian have the task of guarding what has been entrusted to their faithful care.[37]

4. *Prophecy True and False (2:6–11)*

"Stop your preaching," they preach.
They[38] should stop preaching in this vein:[39] 2+2
"Humiliation won't overwhelm us:[40]
7 *the community of Jacob is party to the covenant.[41]* 3+2
Has Yahweh lost his temper?[42]
Is this the way he acts? 3+2
Do not his promises[43] spell good fortune?
Do we not keep company[44] with one who keeps his word?"[45] 3+2
8 *But you like an enemy*
attack my people.[46] 2+2

37. 1 Tim. 6:20; cf. 1:5, 6; 1 Cor. 4:1, 2.
38. The subject is naturally to be taken as the same as that of the immediately preceding verb (H. Donat, *BZ* 9 [1911], pp. 356–58, following Knabenbauer).
39. Heb. *lāʾēlleh.* The preposition introduces the theme, as in v. 11.
40. Heb. *yissag,* "depart," is best taken with most scholars as originating in an orthographical variant for *yaśśīg,* "overtake." The object may be easily understood from the context. For the thought cf. 3:11b.
41. Heb. *heʾāmûr,* apparently "is it said?" Micah is most probably quoting his rivals here. The text has been frequently emended to *heʾārûr,* "is . . . cursed?" since Klostermann, in which case v. 7 is regarded as a continuation of the quotation (cf. JB). G. R. Driver, *JTS* 39 (1938), p. 266, followed by Schwantes, stays closer to the consonantal text by reading *haʾmûʾār* with the same meaning. The simplest change of all is to revocalize the existing consonants as *heʾemîr* (A. S. van der Woude). Cf. the exposition below and n. 59.
42. Cf. for this phrase Job 21:4; Eccl. 7:8.
43. Most read with G *debārāyw* for MT *debāray,* "my words" (as if Yahweh were speaking). The meter suggests that this verse closes the citation of the prophets' words. *Waw* evidently fell out by pseudo-haplography between *yoḏ*'s.
44. Lit. "walk" (cf. 6:8). Strictly *the community of Jacob* is the subject. Perhaps the verb should be vocalized as an infinitive absolute *hālôḵ.* The first line is commonly rendered "with him who walks uprightly." But (1) this is an extremely unnatural rendering of the Heb.; (2) comparison with the previous line suggests a separate clause here; (3) to stress the moral demands of God upon his people is contrary to the context. The initial *halōʾ* extends over both clauses. The frequent emendation to *ʿim ʿammōh yiśrāʾēl,* "with his people Israel," is too radical to be likely.
45. Lit. "the upright one." Cf. the combination of "good" and "upright" in 7:4 and concerning Yahweh in Ps. 25:8.
46. Reading the consonantal text as *weʾattem leʿammî . . . qāmīm* with Ehrlich and many (cf. *BHS*) for MT *weʾeṯmûl ʿammî . . . yeqômēm,* "But formerly my people were rising." The slight

You strip cloaks[47]
off the peaceful,[48] 2+2
from innocent passers-by
with no warlike intent.[49] 2+2
9 *Womenfolk among my people you evict*
from their[50] *cosy homes.* 3+2
From their[50] *babes you take away forever*
the glorious heritage I gave them.[51] 3+2
10 *On your feet! Get going!*
You're not staying here. 2+2
Because of your moral filth
you will be broken,[52] *painfully broken.* 3+2
11 *If anybody who deals*
in mere wind and deceit[53] 2+2
were to lie,[54] *"I shall preach to you*
about wine and spirits," 2+2
he would be the preacher
for this people. 2+2

This next oracle follows in part the normal pattern of indictment and verdict. It is directed once more against the landowners whom Micah had attacked in vv. 1–5. The core of the message, vv. 8f., makes this clear: first, in God's name accusations are levelled and then punishment is

---

change is necessary because (1) in v. 9 *my people* are the objects of oppression and (2) the later verbs have a second plural subject. The extra *yoḏ* in MT was doubtless added when *'ammî* was wrongly taken as subject.

47. Heb. *'eḏer*. Elsewhere the form is *'ᵃḏereṯ,* which many read, assuming haplography of *taw,* but this may be a rare masculine form.

48. Heb. *śalmâ,* another and more common word for "cloak." It may well be a gloss on the rare term, replacing a similar word *shālēm,* "peaceful," which fits the context (cf. Schwantes, following *BHK*). For this text-critical phenomenon cf. L. C. Allen, *JTS* 22 (1971), pp. 143–150; 24 (1973), pp. 69–73. The consonantal *śmlh 'dr* may have been wrongly divided from *šlm h'dr* (". . . the cloak") (*BHK*). The preceding preposition *mimmûl,* lit. "from the front of," has been commonly emended to *mē'al* since Wellhausen, but it can possibly stand as a strong expression "right away from" (Keil).

49. P. Wernberg-Møller, *ZAW* 71 (1959), p. 59, points Heb. *shûḇê* as *shûḇî,* regarding it as a variant spelling for *shᵉḇî,* "prisoners." Many read *shᵉḇî* with Wellhausen. Some, including J. M. P. Smith, take *shᵉḇî* as "spoil" and a second object of the verb *strip,* but evidence for this rendering is doubtful.

50. Heb. "her . . . her." G S V T "their" probably presupposes *-hem,* corrupted by haplography of *mem* in the first case (Willi-Plein) and then adapted in the second. *-hen,* often read, is unnecessary, since the third masculine plural suffix can be used for the feminine.

51. Heb. *hᵃḏārî*, lit. "my glory."

52. Heb. *tᵉḥabbēl wᵉḥeḇel,* apparently "(which) destroys and destruction." The second plural verbs of v. 10a favor G's redivision as *tᵉḥubbᵉlû ḥeḇel*. Ehrlich was the first of a number who interpret the Heb. in terms of a homonymous verb and noun "pledge" (cf. JB), but this involves not only a more radical treatment of the consonantal text but also a less likely interpretation of the verse. See further n. 77 below.

53. Adverbial accusatives: cf. Prov. 6:12.

54. This verb is probably to be taken with the next line for the sake of meter (Willi-Plein).

announced. But this nucleus is set within a larger framework. Verses 6f. are concerned with a group of rival prophets whose benign point of view Micah sets out at length as a dramatic prelude to his own savage pronouncements. This first section of the oracle is a report, and in part a continuation, of a heated controversy already raging between Micah and his prophetic opponents. To this disputation he explicitly returns in v. 11.

The most obvious stylistic feature is the way the oracle comes back full circle to its starting point. Reference to prophetic preaching begins and ends the oracle, and thus marks out its boundaries. The last verse corresponds to the first two in disparaging allusion to the other prophets and their bland ministry. The accusation and command of punishment in vv. 8–10 are interlocked by the repetition of a key word: those who rise against God's people are to rise and leave God's land.[55] As in vv. 1–5, there is verbal correspondence between crime and punishment, though not so developed. Metrically there is a preponderance of the 2+2 rhythm, used especially when the prophet is countering his rivals, to express excited vehemence. His quotation of their preaching is distinguished by a different meter.

6, 7 It was predictable that there would be an adverse reaction to Micah's condemnatory *preaching,* of which we have notable examples in vv. 1–5 and in the following chapter. Isaiah ironically complained of the disregard of prophetic truth by his contemporaries,

> *who say to the seers, "Do not see,"*
> *and to the prophets, "Don't prophesy the truth.*
> *Speak to us smooth words,*
> *prophesy fantasies."* (Isa. 30:10)

Some years earlier in the Northern Kingdom Amos had had the more distressing experience of being opposed in God's name by the chief priest of the Bethel sanctuary, who was financially dependent on the king since his post was in the royal living (Amos 7:10–13). This conflict between prophetic faith and established religion with its vested interests at stake is reproduced here, except that both parties now bear the name of prophet—surely the most poignant situation of all.[56] The protest of Micah's opponents is reported in the same breath as his attacks on the landowners; this grouping seems to imply that the two parties were hand in glove. He brackets together prophet and profiteer, the former as the henchman of the latter.

This is why the prophetic conflict is relevant to Micah's denunciation of the land barons. He fights two sets of enemies, but both are allied. He begins this phase of the struggle by reporting the ban laid upon his preaching[57] by his rivals. Apparently Micah stands among a group of

55. The Heb. root *qûm* occurs in vv. 8 and 10.

56. Cf. 3:5. For a survey of scholarly work on the false prophets see J. L. Crenshaw, *Prophetic Conflict: Its Effect Upon Israelite Religion*. BZAW 124 (1971), pp. 5–22.

57. Heb. *taṭṭîpû* is not used in any derogatory way *contra* Cheyne, "prattle," G. A. Smith

like-minded prophets, since the imperative is plural. It is good to know that he did not stand alone. His comment on the ban is simply to throw it back. If any prophets were to be silenced, then his own group had a better right to speak than theirs. He criticizes his critics and counters their "no" with his own stronger "no."[58] So far only stalemate, but Micah follows up his counterprotest by citing the gist of his opponents' point of view in order to show how ill it accords with reality. The preaching he disdainfully quotes is optimistic in tone. It is a deliberate denial of the pessimism of Micah and his ilk, as the next line makes clear. It is a contradiction in terms, runs the argument, to prophesy that Yahweh will visit his own people with disaster. Appeal is apparently made to the covenant between Israel and Yahweh, as a source of eternal assurance for the former. The verb used is most probably the same one that occurs in Deut. 26:17f. concerning the solemn declaration of assent to the covenant:

> *"You have this day declared Yahweh to be your God . . . ; and Yahweh has this day declared you to be his very own people."*[59]

A solemn seal had been set upon the relationship between Yahweh and Israel, that is, his people in Judah.[60] Since God is the more powerful partner, he can be expected to protect his people from their enemies. Israel is the object of his special care, and it is hardly likely that he would change sides and support uncircumcised foreigners against his own people. It is true that individuals may from time to time commit misdemeanors, but Yahweh is the great forgiver. Let no aspersions be cast on the compassionate character of God, traditionally long-suffering,[61] or on his mighty deeds, which prove how able he is to save and to keep.[62] Israel's covenant partner is Yahweh, who is "the Upright One," thoroughly straight and reliable.[63] He can be trusted to keep his *promises* of blessing.

Such was the case of the optimistic prophets, so plausible in its half-truths,[64] so convincing to those who longed to believe it. Who could be so foolish as to want to demolish such comfortable doctrine? Playing Mr. Micawber to Micah's Scrooge, they feel a not unnatural resentment

---

"rave," JB "harp," NEB "rant": cf. the parallelism of "prophesy" and "preach" in Amos 7:16; Ezek. 20:46 (21:2); 21:2(7).

58. The second negative, *lō'*, is stronger than the first, *'al*.

59. A. S. van der Woude, "Micha ii.7a und der Bund Jahwes mit Israel," *VT* 18 (1968), pp. 388–391, citing Th. C. Vriezen. Van der Woude leaves open whether Yahweh or the community of Jacob is subject here. The latter is more probable since Yahweh is the explicit subject of the next clause and so apparently not of this one.

60. Cf. the use of "house of Jacob" to refer to the Southern Kingdom in Isa. 2:5; 8:17.

61. Cf. Exod. 34:6.

62. Beyerlin, *KIPVM*, p. 73, usefully refers to the divine "deeds" (Heb. *ma'ᵃlālîm* as here) of Ps. 77:11f.(12f.); 78:7.

63. For this use of *yāshār* cf. Ps. 33:4, where it is parallel with the idea of faithfulness. It can signify one who lives up to the claims of a personal relationship, one who is "always to be relied upon" (W. O. E. Oesterley, *The Psalms*, vol. 2 [1939], p. 413 *ad* Ps. 92:15[16]).

64. "False theology did not so much pervert the truth of God as reduce and restrict the truth to an ideology, to a static quality" (van der Woude, *Vox Theologica* 44 [1970], p. 70).

toward this cheerless iconoclast. Why was there such a gulf between the two prophetic groups? Because these merchants of blessing misapplied truth, like Job's comforters. Theirs was a word for the wrong people at the wrong time.[65] They believed with fervor, but their faith was lopsided in its content. Subconsciously picking and choosing among God's revealed truths, they glossed over aspects of his character that were more relevant to the present state of his people. Their very complacency was a symptom of a widespread disregard of God's moral demands upon his people.

8, 9 Micah has quoted at length the religious ideology of his rivals as a prelude to his presentation of God's real word for the hour. He startlingly contrasts true preaching with false. From citing the prophets he now turns to face their patrons. He does not pause to correct the prophets' theorizing but exposes its practical results. With grave accusation he proceeds to show that they are unfit to qualify for God's blessing. Laid upon the covenant people, he implies, are serious responsibilities which they disregard at their peril. The proof of the validity of his own prophetic approach he finds in the misconduct of his rivals' clients. His attack is at once an indictment of the prophets and of the men of power to whom they blithely minister.

In God's name Micah points to the tragic rift within the nation whereby the powerless are the prey of the powerful. He boldly characterizes the rift as the difference between the people of God, to whom implicit reference has been made in the covenant affirmation of v. 6, and their enemies. The oppressors have by their oppression placed themselves outside the category of the chosen people! They have transferred themselves to the camp of Israel's foes.[66] One is reminded of the symbolic name of Hosea's second son Lo-ammi, "Not-my-people." But here there is a distinction drawn between genuine Israel and nominal Israel within the community. Micah is close to Paul, his spiritual heir: "Not all who are descended from Israel are Israel nor because they are Abraham's posterity are they all his children."[67] For Micah, character expressed in social conduct is a better guide than creed or race to identifying God's true people. This badge of character was missing from the lives of the victimizers, and so the logical conclusion is ruthlessly drawn. The title that they assume is theirs can belong only to those whom they despise. They have disqualified themselves from holding it.

Just as the previous oracle moved from the general to the particular in vv. 1f., this one passes to more specific charges after the shattering implication of excommunication contained at the beginning of the divine accusation. Unfortunately it is not at all clear what the precise nature of the

65. "The true prophet . . . is . . . one who views the total historical situation before formulating a message" (Crenshaw, *op. cit.*, p. 17, citing M. Buber).

66. Cf. Isa. 1:21–26, esp. 24.

67. Rom. 9:6f. Cf. John 8:39, "If you were Abraham's children, you would do Abraham's deeds."

charge is in the rest of v. 8. Are gangs of thugs hired by the wealthy to roam the streets and rob people of their cloaks? Or are these bailiffs sent by creditors to collect debts, who without warning roughly seize the debtors' cloaks as pledges? If the former is the case, then the offense is stealing.[68] If the latter, which better fits the economic context of this and the former oracles, then the implication is that the cloaks are retained in violation of the ancient stipulation:

> *"If you take in pledge your neighbor's cloak, you should return it to him before sunset because it is his only covering, it is his cloak for his body. What else has he to sleep in?"* (Exod. 22:26f.)

It is significant that *warlike* picks up the previous key word *enemy* and underlines it. Those who thus wage war on God's people place themselves in the ranks of their enemies.

The next lines provide firmer ground for the expositor. Women, presumably widows, are turned out of their *cosy* hearths and homes. Micah uses the same word as for "darling" in 1:16. Unashamedly sentimental, it speaks of tender attachment and delight. It conjures up by contrast an eloquent accusation of heartlessness. Jesus, too, with the same criticism of hypocrisy attacked "those who devour widows' houses and then pray long prayers for show" (Mark 12:40). There may be a *double entendre* here. The word for *evict* can have a military connotation. It is used of hostilities on the part of Israel's enemies: Balak tried to "drive out" Israel from Moab (Num. 22:6, 11).[69] Is the theme of the preceding lines continued here? It is noteworthy that *my people* is indignantly repeated. The landlords' callous actions are tantamount to an act of war against Israel. How then can they glibly claim to be recipients of his covenanted mercies?

Not only widows but their fatherless children suffer at the hands of these brutes. They too are evicted from their rightful property, the holdings their fathers had farmed, which by rights should pass to them. Micah uses the word "glory," which is to be compared with a similar word used of the God-given land of Palestine in Jer. 3:19: "a heritage more glorious than any other nation's."[70] These children were cruelly denied their share in God's beautiful heritage and any prospect of ever enjoying it. The prophet is here echoing a theme which must have been dear to the heart of every Israelite, the high value set upon his native soil as a prized possession given to his nation by God himself. Micah had spoken in a similar vein in the earlier oracle (v. 2), but here he raises the emotional temperature by his reference to defenseless women and children. Moreover he is undoubtedly claiming the contravention of sacral law. The Book of the Covenant specifically includes among its statutes: "You must not illtreat any widow

68. Cf. Exod. 20:15; 22:8(7).
69. Heb. *gērash,* as here; cf. 1 Sam. 26:19; 2 Chr. 20:11.
70. Cf. Ezek. 20:6, 15; Dan. 11:16, 41. Cf. too 2 Sam. 14:16, where the woman of Tekoa speaks of herself and her son being destroyed from God's heritage.

or orphan'' (Exod. 22:22[21]).[71] These who boast of covenant grace can make no such vaunt of covenant law. Micah has presented a damning case against the land barons. Its stern vigor is enhanced by contrast with the wishful thinking of his prophetic colleagues.

10 He moves from accusation to verdict. What other penalty can there be but that they in turn should be evicted and have the right to their land withdrawn?[72] They are given their marching orders, perhaps in grim parody of the orders their own bailiffs had served on many a poor fellow to quit his homestead. Once again the punishment aptly fits the crime. Is there another *double entendre* here? The causal clause means primarily that this is no place for the oppressors to stay in. But the same word *mᵉnûḥâ*, ''resting place,'' has special associations. It is used of the promised land in Deut. 12:9; Ps. 95:11.[73] Perhaps here likewise the sense is that there can be no resting place in Canaan for those who have violated the terms of the covenant.[74] Once more Micah appears to envisage deportation as the divinely ordained destiny of these sinners against the covenant.

The prophet goes on to echo another of the land traditions apparently current in his time. Lev. 18:24–28 speaks of the Canaanites being expelled from their land because they had defiled it by their impure religious practices, and individual Israelites are warned against incurring a similar fate. Micah seems to acuse his victims of failing to observe such an injunction. Their dirty conduct in illtreating their needy neighbors[75] has rendered them unfit to tread Canaan's soil any longer.[76] So they are doomed to suffer agonizing ruin, involving loss of land, livelihood, and liberty.[77]

11 The oracle is rounded off with a derisive reference to Micah's rivals and the gullibility of their hearers. He speaks in general and hypothetical terms, but his implication is clear. The prophets who accuse him of error are guilty of a gross materialism which is scarcely less than his

71. Cf. Beyerlin, *KIPVM*, p. 60. The protection of widows and orphans, a policy counselled in the common law of the ancient Near East, was inherited by Israel from their forebears and incorporated into the highly ethical religion of Yahweh (cf. F. C. Fensham, ''Widow, Orphan and the Poor in Ancient Near Eastern Legal and Wisdom Literature,'' *JNES* 21 [1962], pp. 129–139). G. Fohrer, *JBL* 80 (1961), pp. 315f., considers that the uniquely novel factor in Israel was the extension of oriental royal duty to every individual Israelite.
72. Cf. Amos 7:16f.
73. Cf. von Rad, ''The Promised Land and Yahweh's Land in the Hexateuch'' and ''There Remains Still a Rest for the People of God: An Investigation of a Biblical Conception,'' *The Problem of the Hexateuch and Other Essays*, pp. 79–93, esp. 92, 94–102.
74. Vuilleumier finds here ''la negation de la formule d'alliance.''
75. Cf. Isa. 1:16f. and also the ethical use of Heb. *ṭāmēʾ*, ''unclean,'' in Isa. 6:5.
76. Micah would have agreed with James that ''religion which is pure and *undefiled* before God . . . is to visit orphans and widows in their affliction'' (James 1:27).
77. Does the last clause mean ''you shall be tied with a strong rope''? Cf. P. Haupt, *JBL* 29 (1910), p. 101, n. 55: ''ye will be ensnared with a deadly snare.'' The verb means ''tie'' in Zech. 11:7, 14; for the rendering ''strong'' cf. N. S. Doniach, *JTS* 31 (1930), p. 291. Then there is a reference to the way prisoners of war were roped together; cf. v. 3 and 1 K. 20:31f.

imaginary case. He is lampooning them, but he chooses his words with care. What is their message but airy-fairy nonsense?[78] There is no substance in their fantasies. Their prophesying is a tissue of lies, a travesty of the truth.

Micah gives an ironic caricature of the sensual nature of his rivals' messages.[79] They are tantamount to promises of alcohol galore. Hardly anything more elevating have they to say than that. They pander to the base desires of their hearers in a despicable manner. No wonder Micah's message sounds so unpalatable. There may be an allusion here to such sterotyped formulas of blessing as that preserved in Amos 9:13:

> *"The mountains will drip sweet wine*
> *and all the hills will run with it."*[80]

His rivals were ready enough to repeat such liturgical promises of material blessing meant for the faithful, but neglected to add the underlying conditions or to relate them to spiritual values. And how eager their hearers were to swallow such lies as gospel truth! But what could one expect of *this people*? The phrase has a contemptuous ring and implies that Micah and they were poles apart in spiritual understanding.[81]

This dramatic contrast between creed and conduct exposes the weakness of the concept of the covenant held by Micah's rivals. They had fallen into the trap of stressing part of the truth, like most heretics, instead of declaring what Paul called "the whole counsel of God" (Acts 20:27). They had raised divine promise to an absolute level and cut away the attached strings of condition and conscience that linked it to divine reality. For all their glib talk of "walking with the Upright One" they had forgotten what it meant for Israel to be God's covenant partner. Such language signified for them that the onus rested completely on God and hardly at all on themselves. Their easygoing idea of religion was to chain God to their service and yet themselves be free of solemn responsibility. Micah is one of many in the Bible who were called to expose this attitude as a perversion of true religion. Before much more than a century had passed Jeremiah was to receive the mantle of Micah, denouncing the descendants of Micah's prophetic opponents and forecasting destruction as the end of this broad and easy path (Jer. 23:36, 39f.). Paul indeed was accused of antinomianism as the corollary of his doctrine of grace (Rom. 3:8), but none stressed more than he the claims of God on the moral and social lives of his people. John, who knew of false prophets in his own Christian community, emphasized that brotherly love in action was the necessary criterion of fellowship with God (1 John 1:6; 2:10; 3:16–18). In

78. Heb. *rûaḥ,* "wind." There may be a wordplay here since it also means "spirit": *'îsh hārûaḥ,* "the man of spirit," is a term for prophet in Hos. 9:7. Cf. Jer. 5:13. What should have been inspiration was nothing more than wind.
79. Heb. *lᵉḵā,* "you," is singular, perhaps indicating that private oracles were in view; cf. 3:5.
80. Keil. Cf. Lev. 26:5; Joel 3(4):18.
81. Cf. Isa. 8:6, 11f.; 29:13f.

this he echoed the high value his Master had set upon the command to love one's neighbor as oneself (Mark 12:31). Promise-box religion is a snare in every age. The challenge to proceed from spiritual lethargy to ethical and social concern that echoes the love of God is a less popular choice, except that there is no real choice. ''You can tell them by their fruit'' (Matt. 7:16) is the Lord's test for every believer to apply to himself. Which sort of preacher do you, Micah's modern reader, prefer?

B. PROMISES OF SAFETY AND LIBERATION (2:12, 13)

I promise to gather
    you all, Jacob, 2+2
I promise to collect up
    the remnant of Israel. 2+2
I shall bring them together
    like sheep to the fold,[82] 2+2
like a flock in the meadow,[83]
    bleating in fear of men.[84] 3+2
13 *One who breaks out will lead the campaign.*[85]
    They will break out, pass[86] *through the gate and go out by it.* 3+4
Their King[87] *will lead the procession,*
    Yahweh will be at their head. 3+2

The first section of the book is rounded off with a message of hope. This oracle has a completely different tone from all the preceding four,[88] so much so that inevitably many questions are raised in the reader's mind. This about-face sounds so extreme that it would be much easier to credit it to a prophet other than Micah. Is this another quotation from Micah's

82. MT ''Bozrah.'' Some infer that the area was famed for its sheep. It makes better sense to repoint the Heb. with most as *batstsīrâ* (V T); cf. Arab. *tsîra,* ''fold,'' Heb. *tîrâ,* ''encampment,'' Syr. *t*^{e}*yārâ,* ''fold.''

83. Heb. *haddoḇrô,* unusually combining article and pronominal suffix: ''the/its meadow.'' There are parallels (cf. GK 127i; C. H. Gordon, *JNES* 8 [1949], p. 112), but the following feminine plural verb renders this unlikely; it is simple to redivide the letters, taking the final *waw* with the verb and reading *haddōḇer w*^{e}*ṯ-* with many since Roorda.

84. Cf. NEB ''which stampedes at the sight of a man.'' Heb. *min* refers here to the cause of fear (cf. BDB, p. 580a). The verb is feminine plural, as frequently with the collective *tsō'n,* ''flock of sheep''; cf. GK 145c. Many emend the text to a form derived from the more usual root *hāmâ* instead of *hûm,* but the verb in Ps. 55:2(3) and the noun *t*^{e}*hûmâ* permit MT to stand.

85. Heb. *'ālâ,* ''go up,'' is a military idiom: cf., e.g., 1 Sam. 29:9.

86. *Waw* consecutive and the imperfect is used in continuance of the prophetic perfect: cf. GK 111w.

87. The parallelism suggests that God is meant.

88. ''I see not how the prophet could pass so suddenly into a different strain,'' observed Calvin. With Kimchi he found here a gathering to destruction and exile. But v. 13b implies triumph.

rivals?[89] Or is it an editorial addition from another, much later source to supply a happy ending to the former oracles of woe?[90]

The oracle is a promise of salvation. In form and content it falls into two halves. First Yahweh pledges his intention to protect Israel, then the prophet takes up the strain, describing how Yahweh's subsequent deliverance is to be effected. In both parts there is stress upon the initiative and leadership of Yahweh. Comparison with the strikingly similar oracle credited to Isaiah in 2 K. 19:31 suggests that in fact this one had its origin in the situation of 701 B.C. and may be regarded as Mican.[91] It is obviously not to be viewed as a direct continuation of his oral ministry reproduced in his preceding oracles, since it presupposes a different stage both of historical period and of development in the prophet's thinking. The present placing is a feature of the literary composition of the book. But why should this particular oracle have been placed at this point? Has it any special relevance to the foregoing messages? Indeed it has. For the editor, *gate* in v. 13 harks back to the mention of "the gate of Jerusalem" in 1:12; compare the description of Jerusalem in 1:9 as "the gate of my people." Recurrence of this key word here binds together the oracle with the earlier material as an intentional collocation. Moreover, it strongly suggests that the editor who pieced together the oracles in this particular order understood that Jerusalem was in view. Disaster had not been God's last word for his people and their capital. There was a silver lining to the lowering stormcloud. Catastrophe had loomed at the very gate of Jerusalem, only to be vanquished on the eve of its triumph.

This oracle of salvation provides too a reassuring commentary on the fate of the citizens of the Judean towns cataloged in 1:10–15. Although 1:16 had spoken of exile as their lot, yet in fact God graciously provided a means of escape for many, namely, Jerusalem as a city of refuge. In light of 2:6–10, the reader is meant to understand that the oppressors were certain to be deported but God's own people would be kept safe from the danger. Moreover, the oracle casts light on the prediction of 2:1–5. The adversity of vv. 3f. was to befall the irresponsible men of wealth, but before the reallocation of the land mentioned in v. 5 could take place there had to occur the saving events of vv. 12f. Thus the oracle dovetails neatly into those which precede, answering questions they raise and developing hints they drop.[92]

89. So, e.g., Ibn Ezra, Michaelis, Ewald, von Orelli, *BHK*, and most recently van der Woude, *VT* 19 (1969), p. 257.

90. So many since Stade, *ZAW* 1 (1881), pp. 163f., regarding it as exilic or postexilic, chiefly on the ground of parallels in Isa. 40:11; 52:12; Jer. 23:3; Ezek. 34:12, which refer to release from exile. But the motifs of shepherd and king were not newly minted then, and their application to the Exile does not preclude their applicability to another period if the circumstances were equally fitting.

91. See the Introduction.

92. Accordingly the theory of misplacement from a position after 4:7 (A. Condamin, *RB* 11 [1902], pp. 383–86; Renaud, *Structure et attaches littéraires* [1964], pp. 20–25) or the like is an unnecessary expedient.

12 God's solemn promise is a direct answer to the crisis envisaged at the beginning and end of the verse. His people are so reduced that their entirety may be described as a *remnant*. But all is not lost. The imagery of sheep and shepherd reassuringly brings the chaos in which Judah finds itself into the orbit of God's traditional role in relation to his people. They are like a flock of frightened sheep. *Men,* evidently not their shepherds but strangers, have sent them bleating and scurrying away; they pose a threat to the flock. This reference to turmoil echoes a term characteristic of OT laments.[93] The prophet as God's mouthpiece assures the people that their cries of terror, their sheeplike bleatings, are not overlooked by the divine Shepherd. He takes up a typical lament in a soothing promise of help which answers the heartfelt need of the community. The imagery of God as Shepherd of his people was a religious metaphor traditionally associated with the Exodus:

> *He led his people like sheep*
> *and guided them in the wilderness like a flock.*
> *He led them safely so that they were not afraid,*
> *while the sea covered their enemies.* (Ps. 78:52f.)

A psalm probably from the Northern Kingdom addresses God thus:

> *Give ear, Shepherd of Israel,*
> *you who lead Joseph like a flock.* (Ps. 80:1[2])[94]

God who had led Israel of old out of their oppressors' reach was leading his people still. The true people of God in Judah[95] would be brought to a place of security. Those who escaped the sword or rope of the invader would be gathered safely into the fold.

The city, which in 1:9 had been described as the gate, the marketplace of God's people, is here by implication likewise designated as the focal point of the nation, now with a pastoral reference. As in peacetime Jerusalem was the center to which the nation looked and upon which it periodically converged, so it now provided a natural rallying point, especially in flight from attackers in the west of Judah.

13 But even as the refugees gather from the various towns and villages of Judah in this final bastion of hope, they look behind them apprehensively at the pursuing foe. Are they safe? Will not Jerusalem fall like many another fortified city in Judah? As the last Judean villagers get through before the capital is blockaded by the Assyrian army, the prophet issues this oracle which not only assures that God is driving his people into this fold of safety, but looks confidently to the future with the forecast that the God who has led his people in will eventually lead them out in peace. Sennacherib was later to boast how he had "shut up Hezekiah inside Jerusalem his royal city like a bird in a cage," blockading the capital and turning back "any who went out of its city gate." Significantly he makes

93. For Heb. *hāmâ* and *hûm* in psalms of lament see Ps. 42:5, 11(6, 12); 43:5; 55:2(3); 77:4.
94. In Ps. 23 the metaphor is beautifully transferred from the nation to the individual.
95. As in v. 7, *Jacob* stands for the Southern Kingdom.

no mention of the overthrow of the city, for the day came when orders for withdrawal were given and the Assyrian army marched off Judean soil. The prophet portrays Jerusalem's survival as due to Yahweh's control of the situation. He it is who will break the siege.[96] The barricade of men and armaments will be swept away with irresistible might. The refugees will be able to sally forth with heads high *through the* city *gate*. Yahweh it is who will liberate his people and lead them in triumph. Once again an old motif is echoed. Had not God gone before his people by day in a pillar of cloud and by night in a pillar of fire (Exod. 13:21)? They would soon meet Yahweh, the God of the Exodus, as the same God of power at the head of his people. The themes of Yahweh's breaking through his enemies and of his going before his people both occur in 2 Sam. 5:20, 24 in connection with David's victories over the Philistines. Micah culls his vocabulary from the rich heritage of divine dealings with Israel. This is especially true of his designation of God as king, another motif resonant with tradition, which spoke of the defeat of Israel's foes and the victory of Israel's God.[97] Divine kingship was celebrated in the Jerusalem temple, as psalm after psalm bears witness. There the sovereignty of Yahweh was acknowledged and proclaimed, and the worshipping people looked forward to its consummation. Isaiah in his inaugural vision of God's mighty holiness had exclaimed in the temple:

> *"My eyes have seen the king, Yahweh of hosts."* (Isa. 6:5)

Jerusalem was supremely "the city of the great king" (Ps. 48:2[3]). Micah applies to the religious crisis into which Jerusalem was plunged these religious truths celebrated within and concerning the capital. There was to be a worthy manifestation of divine kingship in the very city where generations of God's people had proclaimed it.

Micah had seen Judah invaded and overwhelmed, town after town falling before the merciless enemy until Jerusalem was isolated, "like a hut in a cucumber field," as Isaiah quaintly put it (Isa. 1:8). He did not believe in the grandfatherly God of his prophetic rivals, and in this he was proved right, for had he not now seen, as formerly he had foreseen, God's chastisement of his people? "The true prophet must be able to distinguish whether an historical hour stands under the wrath or the love of God."[98] Evidently God had not finished with Israel, for the prophet received this conviction of eventual victory. In this blackest hour he looked forward with confidence to a fresh revelation of the God whom Israel had found to be their help in ages past.

96. The interpretation of Heb. *happōrēṣ* as bellwether, leading ram (e.g., J. M. P. Smith, Robinson, Lindblom), is unlikely. In light of what follows, Yahweh is meant. Just as the motif of shepherd was associated with kingship, so the piece passes naturally from one aspect of God's leadership of his people to the other. S. R. Driver, *Expositor,* 3rd series, 5 (1887), pp. 266–69, examined the claim of Pococke, Pusey, *et al.,* that the term was interpreted messianically by Jewish expositors and showed that it was understood to refer to Elijah, while *their King* was certainly taken as the Messiah.

97. Cf., e.g., Ps. 44:4f.(5f.).

98. E. Osswald, cited by Crenshaw, *op. cit.,* p. 54, n. 45.

II. HOPE BEYOND AFFLICTION (3:1–5:15[14])

A. JERUSALEM'S DOOM AND DESTINY (3:1–4:5)

1. Messages of Punishment (3:1–12)

Three oracles here form a literary unit of three stanzas. *Justice* is the key word linking all three (vv. 1, 8, 9). The similar form of the first and third provides a neat and impressive structure. With increasing severity Micah inveighs against the leaders of Jerusalem and pronounces their doom. The final oracle amplifies and sums up the previous two, and brings them to a devastating climax.

a. Against the courts (3:1–4)

Then I said:
Listen, you heads of Jacob,
leaders of Israel's community. 3+3
You ought to know
what justice means, 2+2
2 *yet you hate good*
and love evil. 2+2
You tear off their skin,
the flesh off their bones. 3+3
3 *You are eating*
my people's flesh, 2+2
stripping off their skin,
chopping up their bones 3+3
and cutting them up like meat[1] *into a cauldron,*[2]
like meat into a stewpot.[3] 3+3
4 *Then*[4] *they will cry out to Yahweh,*
but he will give them no answer. 3+3
He will hide his face from them
at that time
in fitting return for their evil behavior. 3+2+3

The three oracles in this chapter are clearly marked out by their separate introductions. They are in form all fairly typical two-part prophetic pronouncements. This first one, like the third, is heavily

1. Heb. *ka'ᵃsher,* "as." In accord with the expected parallelism *kishᵉ'ēr* is generally read with G. For an explanation of the error in MT see L. C. Allen, *JTS* 24 (1973), p. 71.
2. Heb. *sîr,* a large, two-handled, round-based, open-mouthed cooking pot (A. M. Honeyman, *PEQ* [1939], p. 85).
3. Heb. *qallaḥaṯ* occurs only here and in 1 Sam. 2:14. Its size and shape are unknown.
4. Dahood, *Pss* 2, p. 47, assigns to Heb. *'āz,* "then," the sense "when" in Ps. 56:9(10) in accord with Ugar. *id* and Arab. *'idā*. This line could then mean, "When they cry . . . , he will give. . . ."

weighted on the side of accusation.[5] Micah is denouncing the judicial leaders of the community for their lack of responsibility. The introduction (v. 1a) consists of a call for attention[6] and a specification of the national leaders as those to whom the oracle is addressed. Then the prophet launches into a basic accusation consisting of an indignant question in the Hebrew[7] and a general charge (vv. 1b–2a), which is then developed at length in a gruesome extended metaphor in vv. 2b–3. In v. 4 occurs first an oblique announcement of the punishment that is to befall the targets of his attack. Finally the oracle is rounded off by harking back to the reason for this punishment.

Metrically the deliberate 3+3 rhythm predominates in this nine-line poem. It is significantly varied in the more emotional 2+2 meter of the basic accusation. The oracle is bound together by the link-words *evil* and *evil behavior* toward the beginning and at the end,[8] and throughout the piece are scattered punning links,[9] a characteristic trait of Micah.[10]

A problem is posed by the initial *Then I said,* prefacing the oracle in v. 1.[11] Perhaps the best solution is to take it with many[12] as the relic of an autobiographical narrative, such as is preserved in Hos. 3:1–5 and Isa. 6. There is possibly a hint that the oracle belonged to a larger composition in the enigmatic allusiveness of v. 4. *Then* and *at that time* are heavily stressed expressions of time; yet the occasion of the outcry in which they will engage, presumably the intervention of God in sending disaster into their lives, has to be inferred from the context. The verse suggests that the oracle is a reply to, or at least a continuation of, what once went before, to which the prophet need make only passing allusion to recall it to his hearers' minds. Divinely caused catastrophe on the general lines of 2:3 had evidently already received mention in a portion the editor did not see fit to include.[13]

1–2a Micah singles out the government of his day as the object of

5. Cf. the analytical table in C. Westermann, *Basic Forms of Prophetic Speech* (E.T. 1967), p. 175.
6. Cf. 1:2 and comment.
7. "The use of the interrogative . . . serves merely to express the conviction that the contents of the statement are well known to the hearer and are unconditionally admitted by him" (GK 150e).
8. Heb. *rāʿâ,* v. 1—*hērēʿû,* v. 4: an example of inclusion (see the note on 2:3).
9. Heb. *mishpāṭ, justice,* v. 1—*hip̱shîtû,* "chopped," v. 3; *mēʿalêhem,* "off them," vv. 2, 3—*maʿalelêhem, their behavior,* v. 4.
10. For other examples of wordplay cf. 1:6f., 10–15 and the recurring *m-sh* sound in 2:1–5.
11. For a survey of the solutions offered see Willis, "A Note on *w'mr* in Micah 3:1," *ZAW* 80 (1968), pp. 50–54.
12. Including Budde, *ZAW* 39 (1921), pp. 222f.; Sellin; Weiser. Lindblom observes that elsewhere in prophetic literature it always occurs in dialogue. M. Buber, *The Prophetic Faith* (1949), p. 155, speculated that the chapter represents fragments of an account in which Micah described how he was brought to trial and counteraccused his judges.
13. Cheyne supposed that between vv. 3 and 4 there was originally a description of the day of Yahweh. It is preferable to relate the twin problems of vv. 1, 4 and to regard them as double evidence of extra material preceding the oracle.

his denunciations, especially in its role as the guardian of justice. The terms *Israel* and *Jacob* are used of the Southern Kingdom, as in 1:13f.; 2:12. Only Judah was left to represent the covenant people of God, now that the north had been wiped out by Assyria.[14] It is likely that there is also to be seen here a survival of the religious usage of the terms in Jerusalem since before the secession of Jeroboam I.[15] Now religious tradition and political reality had strangely met up again. Jerusalem was once more in sole control of the theocracy, and upon its officials rested the full weight of responsibility for guiding God's people aright.

It is against the judicial side of the administration that Micah levels criticism. He refers first to *heads,* officers in the national courts.[16] Strictly it is a sociological term, referring traditionally to the heads of "fathers' houses" or extended families, who had the authority and responsibility for keeping their houses in order. Representatives of this group evidently formed an ancient court. Exod. 18 relates a tradition of its establishment by Moses as a body empowered to act in straightforward cases with judicial authority delegated from him. This people's court was apparently still in existence in Micah's time. It was under royal control, nominally at least, with regard to appointment and policy.[17] Micah also uses the more general term *leaders* to describe these judges and to stress the position of responsibility they hold.[18] Such key figures in society the prophet calls before the bar of a higher court as guilty of corruption. In terse, shocked contrast he pits the ideals of their office against their failure to attain them. To their hands was entrusted the administration of justice, and Micah indignantly reminds them of their obligations. They of all people ought to maintain the standards of right and wrong contained in the legal traditions handed down to them. In Israel these were given the force not merely of civil law backed by the authority of the state, but also of religious sanction. Yahweh was the archetypal lawgiver: it was the terms of his covenant that the custodians of law and order were meant to enforce.[19] So it is by no means inappropriate that Micah comes forward, for as the prophet of God he represents the source of justice (cf. v. 8).

He accuses the judicature of abandoning time-honored and God-honoring standards and putting in their place an immoral set of legal expedients. They had ceased to make what was *good* the criterion of their

14. For the date of this oracle see the Introduction.
15. Cf. Beyerlin, *KIPVM,* pp. 25–28.
16. Cf. v. 11. See R. Knierim, *ZAW* 73 (1961), pp. 158f.; J. R. Bartlett, *VT* 19 (1969), p. 4.
17. 2 Chr. 19:5–11 implies that it had lapsed by the ninth century and was revived by Jehoshaphat.
18. Etymologically Heb. *qātsîn* has to do with a judicial decision, in light of the use in Arabic, from which the word "cadi" is derived. But the Heb. word is used generally; cf. Judg. 11:11; Isa. 1:10; 3:6f.
19. Heb. *mishpāt, justice,* is closely linked with the covenant stipulations: cf. Exod. 21:1. It is "the sum of all the obligations which were incumbent upon the people by virtue of the covenant" (Lindblom, *Prophecy in Ancient Israel* [1962], p. 348).

verdicts; instead they deliberately cherished *evil*. Micah's charge is reminiscent of Amos' appeal to the courts of the Northern Kingdom:

Hate evil and love good,
maintain justice in the gate. (Amos 5:15)

Isaiah too had preached in similar terms, helpfully filling in the defects of the contemporary courts behind Micah's general indictment:

"Stop doing evil, learn to do good:
aim at justice, correct oppression,
defend the orphan, take the widow's side." (Isa. 1:16f.)

Micah himself attacks such implied malpractices in the two denunciatory oracles preserved in ch. 2. Here he lays the blame at the doors of the courts for failing to check them. Those who should have been the watchdogs of public welfare and guardians of the old morality have betrayed their trust. They comprise instead a power for evil, aiding and abetting criminals against society.

2b–3 The prophet now launches into a lengthy metaphor of savagery with which to develop his accusation. He starts deliberately with a term that acts as a connecting bridge between the indictment and its illustration. In 2:2 Micah used a verb rendered "grab," which, it was noted, belongs to the OT vocabulary for social oppression.[20] This same term he now employs in the sense of "tear," but it retains its overtones of illegality. His metaphor thus grows quite naturally from the grim reality of the situation. By selecting and setting first a key word of antisocial behavior he makes clear the nature of the crimes with which he associates the judges.

Those who suffer at their hands are members of the covenant community. It is *Jacob* and *Israel's community* to whom the prophet refers back in speaking of *their skin*. The reference is made explicit by the mention of *my people* in the next line. The courts were run by officials no better than butchers who skin and bone carcasses—so impoverished of property and deprived of legal rights were those who sought redress at their tribunals. Micah's words give the impression of a wicked conspiracy at work. The judges were hand in glove with the criminal elite who made it worth their while or were even included in their ranks. The defenseless were skinned of property and money to swell the fortunes of those who should have been their protectors.

The prophet proceeds with a more conventional figure. "Eating" people or "eating their flesh" was a common expression for oppression.[21] Victims of aggrandizement were thrown into court, fodder for their tyrants' greed. A century later Zephaniah spoke of Jerusalem's courts in similar vein:

20. In addition to the texts cited there, Isa. 61:8 and Eccl. 5:8(7) are significant for their explicit contrast of this term with justice.
21. Cf., e.g., Ps. 14:4; 27:2; Prov. 30:14.

Her officials within her are roaring lions,
her judges evening wolves
that leave nothing for the morning. (Zeph. 3:3)

Micah's indignation is born of passionate sympathy, for it is none other than *my people,* says he, who are suffering. Once again the deep note of 1:9 is sounded. These are his kith and kin, folk he knows and others like them. How dare these brutes so illtreat his brothers and sisters under God! Micah feels the same spirit of loyal fellowship that Paul later coveted for the Church. The apostle viewed God's ordering of the body as a parable:

There should be no discord in the body but each part should show equal concern for all the others. If one part of the body suffers, they all suffer with it. (1 Cor. 12:25f.)

As in 2:8f., there is here the hint which rises to the surface in the next verse that those who set themselves against God's people in neglect of covenant responsibility will find themselves bereft of covenant privilege and protection. It is Micah's outraged sense of solidarity that drives him to pile clause upon clause to describe the ruthless savagery he had doubtless witnessed time and time again. To the uninvolved modern reader the description sounds labored. Micah had to witness the brutal lawlessness he depicts, powerless save for the weapon of his scathing rhetoric. With that he lays about him wildly.[22] He deplores the heartless cruelty he has seen at the courts of injustice. They butcher and batten on their victims like cannibals, unconcerned for the heartbreak they cause and heedless of the lives they mangle.

4 This state of affairs could not be allowed to go on. The time must surely come when their misdeeds would catch up with them. Micah turns to consider the disaster that will overwhelm these notorious judges. He delivers a prediction of punishment to come, not speaking in God's name, as in 1:6; 2:3, 8, but in his own; for throughout this oracle it is the prophet who speaks. He makes sinister and repeated allusion to this day of reckoning that the God of justice would cause to dawn. It would bring *fitting return*[23] for their wickedness, an exquisite correspondence of punishment to crime. It is not difficult to read Micah's meaning between the lines of his forecast. These judges who had turned deaf ears to the plea of orphan or widow would find God equally unresponsive to their own cries for help. The term *cry out* is a technical one for appeal to a judge for help against victimization. The woman of Shunem exercised this legal right of protest when she returned home after seven years in Philistia and found her farm taken over by others: she appealed to the king, who saw to it that justice was done (2 K. 8:1–6). No such equity had these judges shown. In return they would find their own appeals to God unavailing in their hour

22. "The turbulent redundance of Mic. 3:2–3 is understandable; the lines were forged in the white heat of indignation" (M. B. Crook, *JBL* 73 [1954], p. 149, n. 26).
23. Heb. *ka'ᵃsher,* "according as."

of need. They did not qualify for the promise given to the righteous that Yahweh's "ears are inclined to their cry for help" (Ps. 34:15[16]).

> *"The man who shuts his ears to the cry of the poor will get no answer when he cries out himself."* (Prov. 21:13)

For God to *hide his face* was a dire threat in the OT. It had associations much more ominous than the Christian conviction that "behind a frowning providence" God "hides a shining face." It had its origin in the spiritual experience of God in worship whereby he "made his face shine" upon the believer with the radiance of grace and blessing.[24] In contrast to this saving glory of God's face was a dread alternative, which was used with a number of different nuances.[25] Here it has the connotation of unavailability and refusal to help. Both these links are a reversal of such prayers in the Psalms as,

> *Hear, Yahweh, when I cry aloud,*
> *be gracious to me and answer me. . . .*
> *"Your face, Yahweh, I seek."*
> *Do not hide your face from me.* (Ps. 27:7–9)

Micah takes up this familiar devotional language to drive home the truth that God will abandon them to their fate. They have no claims on God, for they have repudiated those by their irresponsibility to covenant obligations.

His oracle is a cry from the heart. Through his quivering emotions is expressed God's own disgust at corruption in the lawcourts. With rhetorical fervor the prophet attacks ethical and social defects in the handling of legal cases. He focuses attention not so much on the civil rights of the oppressed as on the moral rottenness of the judges, their cold inhumanity, and the collapse of communal solidarity. Against the perpetrators of such ills he threatens a God-forsaken end. In Micah's words the Christian can hear echoes of his Master's voice:

> *"Many will say to me on that day, 'Lord, Lord! . . .' Then shall I tell them plainly, 'I never knew you. Get away from me, you evildoers.' "* (Matt. 7:22f.)
>
> *" 'I was hungry but you gave me no food . . . , naked but you did not clothe me.' . . . 'I assure you, insofar as you failed to do it to one of the least of these, you failed to do it to me.' "* (Matt. 25:42–45)

b. Against the prophets (3:5–8)

This is Yahweh's message for the prophets
who lead my people astray, 3+2
who proclaim peace and plenty

24. Cf. Num. 6:25 and the refrain in Ps. 80.
25. S. H. Blank, *Prophetic Faith in Israel* [1958], pp. 189f., analyzes the phrase into seven shades of meaning.

when they are given a bite to eat, 2+2
but launch a crusade against the man
who puts no food in their mouths! 3+3
6 *"As a result you face night unillumined by*[26] *visions,*
darkness[27] *unrelieved by divining.* 4+3
The sun will set on the prophets,
the day will darken about them. 3+3
7 *Visionaries will be shamed,*
diviners confounded. 2+2
They will all clap hand to mouth
because no divine answer[28] *comes."* 3+3
8 *Not so I,*
full of power, 2+2
aided by Yahweh's spirit,
full of justice and valor, 2+2
ready to charge Jacob with his rebellion,
Israel with his sin. 3+2

Micah turns to confront another influential element in society, colleagues of his who betrayed their calling. He starts with the prophetic messenger formula, which enables him to specify the intended recipients and the repugnant situation that has occasioned the message (v. 5). On the basis of these accusations is erected the message itself, pronouncing doom for the guilty (vv. 6, 7). Finally, over against the prophets whom God thus discredits, Micah states his own authority (v. 8). This ten-line oracle, metrically quite mixed, falls into a two-part pattern of charge and verdict, like most condemnatory oracles. Instead of rounding off the piece with a final motivation for punishment referring back to the preliminary accusation, as the prophets often do, this time Micah underlines the inadequacy of his rivals by contrast with his own principles. His affirmation has the structural function of knitting the oracle together at beginning and end as an integral unit.

5 The oracle preserves another fragment of the campaign Micah waged against colleagues who embarrassed him—as he embarrassed them—by voicing quite different sentiments in their prophecies. 2:6–11 recorded the blows he rained upon them for giving religious support to the unscrupulous upper class. There he had assailed both prophet and patron; in this fresh attack he singles out the prophets. He makes it plain that his motivation is not personal animosity nor a difference of opinion on the human level. He stresses that the source of his authority lies beyond himself. He claims to be the true representative of the divine purpose and the mouthpiece of God himself, merely transmitting the message he has

26. Heb. *min,* here "without": cf. GK 119w.
27. Heb. *w*^{e}*ḥāsh*^{e}*ḵâ,* "and it will become dark." The consonantal text is generally repointed *waḥ*^{a}*shēḵâ* with G V, as the parallelism suggests.
28. Lit. "answer of God," apparently used here as a stereotyped expression in this *Jahwerede* (Sellin).

received. Micah turns this prophetic weapon against those acknowledged to be *prophets* themselves. What an indictment that practitioners of God's will must be designated as opposed to God's true intent! He continues in the same vein: far from declaring the truth about God and their society, as prophets should, they mislead the people and misrepresent God's real messages for them. The people are left no nearer God than before they inquired of his word. Lam. 2:14 provides a good commentary on what Micah means:

> *Your prophets have revealed to you false and unseemly visions. They have not exposed your iniquity to change your fortunes, but have revealed to you false and misleading oracles.*

It is this failure to take an uncompromising stand against a corrupt society that is in the prophet's mind, as the content of v. 8 makes clear. But as yet he speaks only in general terms. Again comes the key phrase *my people*. He loved the sheep that these bad shepherds led astray, and longed to bring them back to the paths of righteousness and the pastures of God's truth. Micah always uses his favorite phrase with a feeling of outrage. How dare they misdirect them! The people for whom he feels so responsible deserve better prophets than these, yet their presence makes his own task harder.

He proceeds to back up his claim and general charge with a specific indictment. His rivals, too, doubtless used the messenger formula to bolster up their own pronouncements,[29] and would throw back in his face his charge of misdirection. To add weight to his case Micah tosses an objective test into the balances. He accuses them of lack of principle in the matter of fees. It was an ancient and respectable practice for a prophet to accept payment for services rendered to his clients.[30] After all, as Jesus affirmed, "the worker is entitled to his wages" (Luke 10:7). But with so apparently subjective a craft as prophecy there was ever a temptation. Why not make the message match the customer's pocket? No doubt the client hoped that by crossing the prophet's palm with extra silver he could improve on his future prospects. Unfortunately these prophets complied with this wish. Selfish expediency had become their criterion for the content of their oracles, on the principle that he who pays the piper calls the tune. Eventually they were in the prophecy business for what they could get out of it. Corrupted by cupidity, they turned into religious charlatans, dressing with the right prophetic trimmings their bogus oracles. Micah finds the evidence for this debasement in the suspicious circumstance that favorable messages were given only to the wealthy. *Shālôm* was always the happy word for them: "Everything will be all right. God's best is coming your way."[31] Did these oracle-mongers console themselves with the

29. Cf. 1 K. 22:11; Jer. 28:12.

30. Cf. 1 Sam. 9:8; 1 K. 14:3; 2 K. 4:42; 8:8f.

31. Heb. *shālôm* primarily indicates wholeness; it is attained by God's blessing. It is "a comprehensive kind of fulfilment or completion, indeed of a perfection of life and spirit which

thought that they were doing much good with their prophetic placebos, releasing psychological tension and enabling high-placed men to work more efficiently? Jeremiah was inspired to agree with Micah:

> *"They have healed the wound of my people lightly,*
> *saying 'Peace, peace,' when there is no peace."* (Jer. 6:14)

Micah is speaking of individual oracles given to rich clients. To poor folk who consulted them the prophets never had a good word to say. If one could not afford the fee expected, it was a foregone conclusion that the prophet would retaliate spitefully by giving an unfavorable oracle. To "preach holy war" or "wage a religious campaign" refers to the sacred preparations made in ancient Israel before undertaking a war against God's enemies, *a crusade* against infidels.[32] In this high-sounding phrase Micah echoes the pretentious claims of racketeering prophets to proclaim the vengeance of God against those who could not or would not give them a penny.

6, 7 Upon this prostitution of the prophetic office must fall the judgment of God, as Micah proceeds to declare with rhetorical amplification. He prefaces the verdict with "therefore," which attests its logic and justice. These who have abused their prophetic gifts are doomed to be deprived of them. Their spiritual illumination will cease.[33] Their insight into the future will fade into black blindness. The sinister figure of night is a multiple metaphor which alludes to calamity afflicted by God[34] as well as to the loss of prophetic enlightenment. Shades will gather and smother in their gloom that good light which has been put to evil ends. The prophet apparently does not deny that his opponents are endowed with God-given talents;[35] his stress is that those psychic gifts will be taken away because they have been used improperly. The seers will lose their clairvoyant powers. The revelation that they have suppressed or transmitted in part or overlaid with their own imaginings will finally desert them. They will soon have had their misspent *day*. Those equipped to read signs of the future from various material means[36] will find only a blank before them because they have used their gifts for base gain. Those who have made glib merchandise of their various gifts will to their horror find themselves struck strangely dumb. Previously satisfied clients will disown them in disgust at the sudden suspension of their communication with the

quite transcends any success which man alone, even under the best of circumstances, is able to attain, . . . man's realization, under the blessing of God, of the plan which God has for him and the potential with which God has endowed him" (J. I. Durham, "*Shālôm* and the Presence of God," *Proclamation and Presence*. G. Henton Davies Festschrift [1970], p. 280).

32. Cf. Josh. 3:5; 1 Sam. 13:8–12; Joel 3(4):9.
33. Cf. Ps. 74:9; Lam. 2:9.
34. Cf. 1 Sam. 2:9; Isa. 8:22; Amos 5:18.
35. A. R. Johnson, *The Cultic Prophet in Ancient Israel* (^{2}1962), p. 31, n. 1, rightly cautions against easy generalizations with regard to "false" and "true" prophets.
36. Cf. the analysis of these means given by Johnson, *ibid.*, pp. 32–34.

infinite. They will have to acknowledge that their mysterious powers will not work for them any more. Micah dramatically refers to a common gesture of grief to which his opponents will resort in their shocked dispair, that of covering the upper lip.[37] Ironically it will also be a fitting sign that they have nothing to say; dumbfoundedness will be an apt reaction to their being silenced.

A surprising feature of this pair of verses is that Micah credits his opponents with genuine gifts. *Diviners* especially were regarded with grave suspicion in many quarters of Israel as a foreign import.[38] But it speaks well for Micah's objectivity and fairmindedness that he concentrates his attack not on methods but on motives as evidenced by the facts. He is prepared to recognize his rivals as basically his equals, and to judge them solely on the ground of the results. It is for this reason that he does not trust them. To him it is a tragedy that men have, by self-seeking, debased gifts that they should have used for higher ends. More, it is a crime against God that cannot go unpunished; he will silence them for good and all.

8 Enough of these despicable renegades grovelling in the dirt for dishonest pennies! Micah has written off their popularity and prosperity as the mere prelude to inevitable powerlessness. He turns in contrast to present his own credentials as a spokesman for God. He does so in no mood of self-congratulation. He speaks not to bolster his own ego but to convince his contemporaries of the truth. His thought is that of the apostle Paul:

> *The gift of God's grace . . . was given me through the working of his power. To me, less than the least of all the saints, was given this grace to preach.* (Eph. 3:7f.)

Micah is filled with a *power* not his own, for which he can claim no credit. This power of which Micah is conscious is a contrast not only to the weakness that will be his rivals' doom, but also to their vacillating oracles, which vary according to the client's purse. Micah is bent by no such human considerations. He is conscious of a power compelling him to speak. Jeremiah, no stranger to this irresistible power, described it thus:

> *There is in my heart what feels like a burning fire,*
> *locked up inside my bones.*
> *I am weary with holding it in*
> *and I cannot.* (Jer. 20:9)[39]

This is the first of Micah's credentials, and the evidence that assured him that his prophecy was genuine. To be sure, it is subjective and by its very nature cannot be proved, but at least the fairminded can assess for themselves this sincere testimony.

37. Cf. Ezek. 24:17, 22.
38. Cf. Deut. 18:10–14; 1 Sam. 15:23; 2 K. 17:17.
39. Lindblom observes that Jer. 1 is a good commentary on this whole prophetic confession.

He continues with an affirmation of his inspiration.[40] One could never be sure whether his rivals were tampering with a particular communication, and replacing it or toning it down with words drawn from a source no higher than themselves. But Micah claims that his words consistently come from a divine source, from that "indefinable extension of [God's] personality which enables him to exercise a mysterious influence upon mankind."[41] *Yahweh's spirit* was the medium by which his will was communicated to the prophets.[42] In Isa. 30:1 the Judean officials whose pursuit of a pro-Egyptian policy was "not of my spirit," said Yahweh, were guilty of not consulting the prophetic oracle to check whether God approved. It was the spirit that kept the prophet in personal touch with his God and gave impulse, direction, and authority to his oracles. This spirit Micah claims to possess, or to be possessed by, as the motivating force behind his words.

Justice is another criterion that stamps Micah as a true prophet. This test is more objective, for it appeals to the moral conscience of his hearers. He asserts that his message is based on a true sense of right. He gets no material advantage out of preaching as he does. His rivals have joined society's moneymaking entourage, but Micah is disinterested. His sole motive is to encourage right and discourage wrong. His last claim is to *valor*. Uninfluenced by fear or favor, he is filled with courage to speak unflinchingly in God's name, unpopular though his message may be. It is one thing to possess a knowledge of what is right, but to be effective also requires the fortitude to pass on that knowledge. This was the quality that regularly marked out the true prophet who challenged society in OT times.[43] "Let them not yield," said Calvin of would-be prophets of Micah's stamp, "to any gales that may blow nor be overcome by threats and terrors. Let them not bend here and there to please the world." Once again Paul spoke with Micah's voice when he reminded the Thessalonians of his "boldness in our God to tell you the gospel of God in spite of much opposition," unprompted by guile, flattery, greed, or desire for honor (1 Thess. 2:2–6). The prophet had come to know this enabling. How else could he face the opposition of society, unless he had been filled with holy

40. Heb. *'eṯ-rûaḥ yhwh* has generally been deleted since Wellhausen as syntactically and metrically superfluous. It is to be retained with Lindblom, *Prophecy in Ancient Israel,* p. 175, n. 109, who takes the meter as 2+2, 2+2; *'eṯ-* is not the object sign but a preposition "with (the help of)."

41. Johnson, *The One and the Many in the Israelite Conception of God* (^{2}1961), p. 16. It is noteworthy that he warns against regarding the spirit as merely an impersonal force.

42. Cf. Num. 11:29; 1 K. 22:24; Hos. 9:7; Joel 2:28 (3:1). S. Mowinckel, " 'The Spirit' and 'the Word' in the Pre-exilic Reforming Prophets," *JBL* 53 (1934), pp. 199–227, attempted to show that they "never express a consciousness that their prophetic endowment and powers are due to possession by or any action of the spirit of Yahweh." His position has been criticized as out of accord with the evidence by Lindblom, *op. cit.*, p. 177, n. 112; Crenshaw, *Prophetic Conflict* (1971), pp. 16, 55.

43. Cf. 1 K. 22:24–28; Jer. 38:4–6; Amos 7:10–15.

boldness? When in a later century the Jerusalem authorities saw Peter and John's boldness, "they were amazed" (Acts 4:13).[44] Micah's hope was doubtless that his earnestness in preaching undeterred messages of condemnation in the capital would impress men and set them thinking about their truth.

His messages were indeed condemnatory. God's present word through him was no happy one. It was his task to expose the community's *sin* and *rebellion* against God. The terms the prophet uses are regular ones of his.[45] This for Micah is the final proof of his divine mission. Why should he run the gauntlet of society's hostility? And why did Amos court banishment, Jeremiah imprisonment, and Uriah ben Shemaiah death unless they prophesied at God's behest? How much easier it would be for Micah to curry popularity and line his pockets in the process. But it is not for him to choose his message. God's mind at the moment is set against his people's sin, and this man of God can only follow suit. His steadfastness rings out, like Martin Luther's: "Here I stand. I can do no other."

This scathing oracle of denunciation stands out for its vigor. It needed to, because its content was crucial. Were the people bewildered, uncertain which of the two prophetic voices to heed and naturally inclined to accept the easy option of Micah's rivals? How necessary it was to endeavor to get across the truth of the matter. Otherwise he would be dismissed as a puritanical crank instead of being acclaimed as the herald of God. Herein lies the importance of this oracle. It is a stirring call to reason, to morality and to reality. With its ring of sincerity and passion for truth, it sets up standards that the servant of God in every generation must covet, and warns of temptations that he must pray for power to shun. In an age when "the car or the cake mix or the toothpaste is presented as the hope of social security or health or attractiveness or the envy of neighbours or friendship or confidence," Christians can see around them many "a prophet of materialism, a seller of dreams that perish."[46] Upon them falls the mantle of Micah to see through the flimsy webs of a materialistic society and valiantly to help their neighbors toward divine reality.

c. *Against the establishment (3:9–12)*

Listen to this,
you heads of Jacob's community,
leaders of Israel's community, 2+2+2
who loathe justice
and bend all its inflexible rules, 2+3

44. "Boldness" is a key word of Acts. For a study of this fundamental NT term see W. C. van Unnik, "The Christian's Freedom of Speech in the NT," *BJRL* 44 (1961/62), pp. 466–488.
45. Cf. 1:5, 13; 6:7.
46. E. Rogers, "Important Moral Issues: X. Advertising," *ET* 77(1965), p. 46.

10 *who build*[47] *Zion with blood,*
Jerusalem with wrongdoing. 3+2
11 *The city's heads may be bribed to give a verdict,*
its priests suborned to give instruction. 3+3
while its prophets divine for money.
Yet they lean on Yahweh with the words, 3+3
"Yahweh is among us, isn't he?
Disaster cannot overwhelm us." 3+3
12 *So it will be your fault*
when Zion is plowed into a field, 2+3
when Jerusalem is turned to rubble,
and the temple mount into a scrub-covered hill.[48] 3+3

This third oracle is very similar in form to the first (vv. 1–4). Again its two traditional parts are lopsided: the bulk of the oracle is given over to grounds of complaint, and only the last pair of lines is devoted to a disclosure of retribution. The earlier part begins with a summons to hear the prophetic word and designates the sector of society that must pay heed (v. 9a). This designation leads on to the basic accusation of the general crime of which they were guilty (v. 9b), which in turn is developed into a series of specific charges, culminating in a citation of optimistic confidence (vv. 10, 11). Finally this confidence is shattered dramatically with the announcement of future destruction as the result of God's intervention (v. 12). This announcement is prefaced with a hinge connecting fault with fate: "therefore because of you."[49] The oracle is presented as a word of the prophet rather than of Yahweh. Interestingly in Jer. 26:18, where the final verse is quoted, it is introduced by "Thus has Yahweh of hosts said." This difference provides a warning against distinguishing pedantically between the respective authority of *Jahwerede* and *Prophetenrede*.[50]

Apart from the hinge between denunciation and the declaration of destruction at the head of v. 12, there are other interlocking devices in the oracle. Zion and Jerusalem feature in both parts, and its new buildings rise only to be blitzed (vv. 10, 12). Metrically this eight-line oracle is mixed, exhibiting regularity only in the three 3+3 lines of specific indictment in v. 11.

9 Micah reissues the challenge he delivered at the start of the first

47. Heb. *bōneh* is singular. G S V T presuppose a plural, probably construct *bōnê,* which is generally read since it fits the preceding plurals. MT has doubtless been influenced by Hab. 2:12.
48. Heb. *l^{e}ḇāmôṯ,* "to high places," is better vocalized as a singular *l^{e}ḇāmaṯ* with Symmachus and Theodotion (cf. G). The parallelism suggests that the word is used in a physical rather than in a cultic sense; cf. 1:6.
49. Cf. the analysis in Westermann, *op. cit.*, p. 175.
50. Cf. the comment and note on 2:3. Westermann, *op. cit.*, p. 179, finds in the fact that only the announcement of disaster is cited a presupposition that the real word of God is the announcement; but the abbreviation of the whole oracle to its climax is a not unnatural phenomenon, since only the climax was relevant in the circumstances.

oracle recorded in this chapter. But the sequel makes it clear that the area of his attack is wider than before. There he had the courts in mind. Here he includes them, as v. 11 shows, but only as part of a wider indictment. So in this initial summons *heads* refers to judges, but *leaders* must be taken to signify other authorities in Jerusalem. Isaiah gives an informative list of men of influence in the capital and country:

> *. . . general and professional soldier, judge, prophet, diviner and elder, army captain and aristocrat, counsellor, sorcerer and soothsayer.* (Isa. 3:2f.)

The list is incomplete as a sociological analysis: for instance, it omits the priest, who figures in Micah's smaller list (v. 11). But it provides a valuable contemporary commentary on *leaders,* the authoritative members of the Judean establishment who held in their hands the reins of society.

Micah finds fault with their control of the community on moral grounds. They do not share his passionate concern for justice. In fact, to them it must be a loathsome, abominable thing. Such is the only conclusion to be drawn from the unjust verdicts for which the courts were evidently notorious. The leaders of society were marked by moral perversity. They permitted and practiced crookedness instead of equity. The prophet is speaking in terms similar to those of v. 1 and also to the invective of Isaiah:

> *Alas for those who call evil good and good evil,*
> *who put darkness for light and light for darkness,*
> *who put bitter for sweet and sweet for bitter!* (Isa. 5:20)

Known morality was openly defied in the name of the state. Social concern laid down in covenant law was absent from the list of government priorities. Corruption was rife among the men at the top. Those who should have been upholders of law and moral order participated in a tyranny of evil.

10, 11 Micah proceeds to elaborate this shocking basic charge. He looks with distaste at the new buildings that had evidently mushroomed throughout Jerusalem. Vast sums had been spent by the pacesetters of society. But the prophet wastes no time admiring the architectural splendor of these new properties. Instead he criticizes the immoral means by which they were built. Jeremiah's attack on King Jehoiakim a century or so later fills in details that may well have been relevant in Micah's day:

> *"He makes his neighbor work for nothing*
> *and gives him no wages.*
> *He says, 'I shall build myself a large house*
> *with spacious rooms upstairs,'*
> *and cuts out windows for it,*
> *panels it with cedar*
> *and paints it with vermilion."* (Jer. 22:13, 14)

Jeremiah went on to accuse the king of "shedding innocent blood and practicing oppression and violence" (22:17). An eviction order here, a whisper there to arrange compulsory purchase, drafting "volunteers" into forced labor squads—in these and doubtless other more murderous ways[51] the men with the whip hands held cheap the God-given rights of property, liberty, and life.

Next comes a survey of the services available in the capital. A legal problem? Take it to the judge. A religious problem? Take it to the priest. A personal problem? Take it to the prophet. A satisfactory answer was guaranteed if money passed from hand to outstretched hand. In court one could get away with anything if one brought enough cash in the breastfold of one's cloak (Prov. 17:23). A judge would gladly "acquit the guilty for a bribe and deprive the innocent of justice" (Isa. 5:23). In fact, cases brought by poorer members of the community had a habit of getting squeezed out of the busy court schedule (Isa. 1:23). The OT prophets refused to shrug their shoulders at this judicial corruption, but exposed it as abhorrent to the God of the covenant. They doubtless knew of covenant traditions expressly banning venality in the lawcourts. It is no accident that one can read such a prohibition imbedded in the Book of the Covenant (Exod. 23:8) and in the ancient curse list of Deut. 27 (v. 25).[52]

The priests were available as the fount of religious knowledge.[53] It was their responsibility to enforce the maintenance of moral standards as proper qualification for admission into the sanctuary and to this end to instruct in the ethical traditions of the covenant.[54] Such was the type of instruction the public might seek at the hands of these guardians of Israel's religion,[55] only to find themselves victims of a moneymaking racket. Evidently the service was commercialized, and for a consideration the priest would wink at the inquirer's shortcomings.

Micah concludes this survey of the shaky pillars of society by mentioning the prophets. If one wanted guidance over a perplexing personal problem such as the advisability of some course of action, one went to the prophet to find out God's will in the matter.[56] Unfortunately, Micah complains, adequate help was not necessarily forthcoming unless an extortionate fee was paid by the anxious inquirer. His words in v. 5 provide his own commentary on his meaning here.

The prophet has outlined the corruption with which the establishment was riddled. He has accused the men who matter of irresponsibility

51. Calvin was possibly right in considering that Micah was using hyperbole (cf. Sir. 34:21f.), but the actions of Ahab (1 K. 21) and Jehoiakim (Jer. 22:17) support a literal interpretation of premature death caused directly or indirectly.

52. Beyerlin, *KIPVM,* p. 56.

53. See von Rad, *OT Theology,* vol. 1 (E.T. 1962), pp. 244f.; A. Cody, *A History of OT Priesthood.* Analecta Biblica 35 (1969), p. 116.

54. Ps. 15; Hos. 4:6; Mal. 2:7; cf. 2 K. 12:2(3).

55. Some interpret the text in a forensic sense. G. Östborn, *Torah in the OT: A Semantic Study* (1945), p. 89, n. 2, finds here reference to fraudulent procedure when reading oracles during assessment of legal disputes (cf. J. M. P. Smith). J. Weingreen, *JSS* 6(1961), pp. 170f., renders "give judicial directives for a bribe" and compares Deut. 17:8–11.

56. Cf. 1 Sam. 9:6; 28:6; 1 K. 22:5f.; 2 K. 8:8; 22:12.

with regard to the covenant. The climax of his indictment is that they all nevertheless cling to the security of Yahweh's covenant relationship with Israel.[57] How tragic that they could see no inconsistency between selfishly exploiting their wards and sanctimoniously expressing faith in the protective presence of their God! But such promises cannot survive in a moral vacuum, as Amos had warned his northern audience:

Seek good and not evil
so that you may live
and thus Yahweh, the God of hosts, may be with you,
as you have said. (Amos 5:14)

The claim was a cultic one. Amos, probably speaking at the Bethel sanctuary, was pointing its worshippers to the true way of blessing. It is significant that Micah is standing in the religious as well as secular capital of the nation. Was not Jerusalem "the city of God, the holy dwelling of the Most High"? Then it followed that "God is in her midst; she will never be overthrown" (Ps. 46:4f.[5f.]). Within the temple stood the ark, sure token of God's presence with his people. At its services God regularly manifested himself in blessing. Jerusalem was safe, surrounded by the aura of hallowed power that emanated from the shrine. Jeremiah informs us of the hypnotic spell that lulled Israel's conscience to sleep: "This is Yahweh's temple, Yahweh's temple, Yahweh's temple" (Jer. 7:4). The watchword of piety in a purer age turned into gibberish in the mouths of the complacent. The guarantee of protection vouchsafed to the loyal lost its relevance on the lips of the arrogant. To *lean* upon God is an expression that sometimes belongs to the OT vocabulary of faith.[58] Here it betokens false security, unconsciously making a convenience and a cushion out of God. This was the very charge that Paul was to bring much later against the Jews of his day who "rely upon the law,"[59] not realizing that it was "a heap of cinders marking a fiery miracle which has taken place, a burnt out crater disclosing the place where God has spoken, a dry canal which in a past generation and under different conditions had been filled with the living water of faith and of clear perception."[60]

12 The leaders of Jerusalem would soon be awakened rudely from their superstitious fantasies. Micah drowns the "no" of the accused to hint of doom with a defiant "yes." In an announcement of the penalty for their wrongdoing he shockingly throws back into their faces a reversal of their belief in immunity for them and their city. It is ironic that their own

57. The reference here is more probably to popular opinion shared by the various leaders than to a solely prophetic pronouncement. The difference of subject in the two halves of the previous line shows that the second half of this one does not necessarily have the prophets as the exclusive subject. Cf. NEB "and yet men. . . ." For a valuable study of the *vox populi* see Crenshaw, *op. cit.*, pp. 24–36.
58. Cf. Isa. 10:20; 50:10.
59. Rom. 2:17, Gk. *epanapauē,* the very verb used in G here.
60. K. Barth, *The Epistle to the Romans* (E.T. 1933), p. 65.

injustice would be the lever to set destructive forces in motion. They have only themselves to blame. The irresponsible actions that belie their religious claims are the prelude to proof of the baselessness of those claims. He harks back to the building program undertaken in the capital, which provided monuments to covenant infidelity (v. 10). The fine residences of those who had built *Zion with blood* would have to come down. "If Yahweh does not build the house," do not "they labor in vain who build it" (Ps. 127:1)? God's demolition team would be set to work until the site was cleared: *Zion* would be *plowed into a field.* The passive verb makes silent, sinister allusion to the agency of God,[61] present indeed, but only to punish. Again, had not these magnates built *Jerusalem with wrongdoing*? Then there was no alternative: *Jerusalem* would have to be reduced to piles of *rubble.*[62] With dreadful clarity Micah spells out step by step the logical fate of the capital. Expressed in this destruction will be the divine sense of outrage, till now concealed, that the skyline of the sacred city should be broken by buildings erected on morally weak foundations. But he has not finished. Was not the antidote to harm, cited in v. 11, a drug distilled from the holy water of the temple? Then, lest the temple stand between Israel and their God as a barrier, that too must go. On that hill where the temple now stood in awesome splendor would spread a wilderness of bushes and brambles.

Micah's pronouncement is strikingly similar in tone and motivation to the one he had made in earlier years concerning Samaria (1:5, 6). The northern capital had been the embodiment of the nation's sin: within the shelter of its walls had worked those who set political, social, and religious trends for the nation. It was therefore appropriate that their den should be wiped out. In that oracle he had hinted that Jerusalem too needed to take warning from his prediction. Now he has come to the point of spelling out Samaria's doom for Jerusalem also. The only way to get rid of these leaders who abused their leadership was to root them out, capital and all.

The prophet's words fell like a bomb on an astounded audience. "It was as though God had thrown heaven and earth into confusion, inasmuch as he himself was the founder of the temple" (Calvin). Micah had denied all they held dear and contradicted all they had been conditioned to believe. The bombshell of the seeming blasphemy set up shock waves whose reverberations were still felt a century later. It is not often that we are privileged to know contemporary reactions to the divine word. Much of the

61. Cf. the comment on 1:7.

62. Is there reference in this verse to a tripartite topographical division of the city? J. Simons, *Jerusalem in the OT* (1952), pp. 235f., takes *Zion* to be the area of the old Jebusite city, the southeast hill, the *temple mount* the area north of Zion, and *Jerusalem* the southwest hill where he claims was then the largest conglomeration of private dwellings. Cf. R. Hentschke, *Die Stellung der vorexilischen Schriftpropheten zum Kultus*. BZAW 75 (1956), p. 30. But essentially Micah is taking up the terms, explicit and implicit, of his accusation, and in v. 10 *Zion* and *Jerusalem* appear to be used as poetic synonyms (cf. Hab. 2:12).

Bible reads like a one-sided set of correspondence, the replies to which have not been preserved. But the advent of Jeremiah with a message similar to Micah's jabbed people's memories. When Jeremiah was threatened with death, they remembered the precedent of Micah's survival. "Did King Hezekiah of Judah and all Judah put him to death? Did he not, fearing Yahweh, entreat Yahweh's favor, and did not Yahweh relent of the disaster with which he had threatened them?" (Jer. 26:19). It is significant that it was Micah's prophecy that was remembered; Isaiah had not spoken in such vehement and direct terms of Jerusalem's fate.[63] One is glad to learn that for a time at least Micah's oracles left their mark in prayers of repentance, and presumably attempts to get rid of the faults he had exposed. May we conclude that, as the newly found scroll spurred on Josiah's reforming endeavors, so the oral messages of Micah were a contributory factor in Hezekiah's religious and, one hopes, social reformation?[64] In the divine reprieve of Jerusalem, inferred from the nonfulfilment of the oracle, we are invited to see the sequel to the true fulfilment of God's word. Yahweh's purpose in prophecy of disaster was ever to erect a warning notice lest the people, walking their present path, fall to their doom. Isaiah's great "either-or" (Isa. 1:19, 20) is implicit in every threat. Alas, the reprieve proved only a postponement.[65] It fell to Jeremiah to reissue Micah's message, but the king to whom he brought God's warnings was of more stubborn stock. The day came when the psalmist could say, probably of the Babylonian foe: "They have turned Jerusalem to rubble" (Ps. 79:1).

Micah's words, remembered for their shocking severity a hundred years later, deserve to be taken to heart by each generation of God's people. They challenge every attempt to misuse the service of God for one's own glory and profit. They are a dire warning against the complacency that can take God's love and reject his lordship. They are a passionate plea for consistency between creed and conduct. The Lord is content with nothing less.

2. *Jerusalem's Positive Role (4:1–5)*

When present days are past,
Yahweh's temple mount will stand 3+3
supreme above the mountains,
higher than the hills. 3+3
Peoples will stream over it,
2 *many nations will come.* 3+3

63. But cf. Isa. 1:21–26; 5:14; 32:14.
64. Cf. M. Buber, *op. cit.*, p. 155. The eulogies of 2 K. 18:5f. and 2 Chr. 31:20f. point beyond the cultic sphere.
65. Cf. 2 K. 20:16–19.

They will say,
"Come, let us go up to Yahweh's mountain,
to the temple of Jacob's God. 3+3
We want him to instruct us in his way of life,
we want to travel his road." 2+2

From Zion will issue instruction,
Yahweh's revelation from Jerusalem. 3+3
3 *He will judge many nations' claims,*
arbitrate for foreign powers far away. 4+4
They will hammer their swords into hoes,
their spears into pruning tools. 3+3
No nation against nation will draw sword,
no longer will they do military training. 4+4
4 *Every man will sit under his own vine,*
beneath his own fig tree, free from fear. 4+4
So declares the mouth of Yahweh omnipotent. 4

5 *Though*[1] *all other nations devote their lives*
to their various gods, 3+3
for our part we shall devote
our lives to our God Yahweh,
for ever and ever. 2+2+2

The long passage denouncing Jerusalem's leaders and announcing Jerusalem's destruction is counterbalanced by a short one of glorious hope for the capital under Yahweh's leadership. God's last word is not judgment: that is but a necessary phase in his people's history, which is to culminate in salvation. There is a deeper message to be drawn from the juxtaposition. The accusations of ch. 3 indicate an ignoring of Yahweh by setting aside his demands for justice. The human leaders of Jerusalem were no true representatives of Yahweh's theocratic rule; they only led astray (3:5). God's answer to their failure is not merely negative, setting aside the leaders and destroying their lair. This oracle presents a positive reply. In the place where he was allowed to rule only in name (3:11), he is to be honored and obeyed, and not merely by Israel but by the other nations of the world. He whose word and will had been suppressed by prophet and priest, by politician and judge, was to receive universal submission.[2] Jerusalem, which had sunk in men's estimation to a haunt of violence and corruption, was to be exalted to the position of a fitting throne for the universal Overlord. Yahweh and his earthly residence would together be

1. For the concessive use of Heb. *kî* see the note on 7:8.
2. It is no accident that in Isa. 2 this poem is followed by an oracle forecasting the time when "Yahweh alone will be exalted" (Isa. 2:11, 17). As in Ps. 46:10(11), "the ultimate goal . . . is not the fulfilment of human desires but the revelation and self-glorification of God. . . , that *his* will be done" (A. Weiser, *The Psalms* [E.T. 1962], p. 373).

vindicated in men's eyes. Such a God, who was to receive universal acclaim, was worthy of Israel's loyal trust and service.

Probably Micah here takes over an existing composition, which his editor has strikingly and deliberately placed alongside oracles of disaster.[3] It is closely connected with the cultic traditions attested in the temple hymnbook. The Songs of Zion celebrate Jerusalem's dramatic escape from the nations' clutches and the defeat of her foes.[4] An obvious place for the positive role for the nations which is described in this poem is after their defeat. Does this piece take up the story after the demonstration of Yahweh's exaltation among the nations by breaking the bow, snapping the spear, and burning the chariot (Ps. 46:9f.[10f.])?[5] The theme of the poem can indeed be regarded as one aspect by which was celebrated the blessing of all nations promised of old.[6] God was not to leave his enemies in the dust but would transmute their lust for war and guide their misguided energies to better ends. From another point of view the poem may be regarded as a photographic enlargement of a familiar scene. Year by year bands of pilgrims would make their way to Jerusalem to engage in festive worship, in the course of which they would receive instruction in the moral traditions of the covenant.[7] This Israelite pilgrimage is here magnified to universal dimensions. Not merely Israel, but their pagan neighbors from all around would one day wend their way to Yahweh's earthly residence, and there learn lessons which they would put into practice back in their own communities.

The poem contains two stanzas of five lines each. The first, vv. 1–2a, celebrates Jerusalem as the center on which the nations converge. The second, vv. 2b–4, describes how truth learned at Jerusalem radiates out and transforms the international scene.[8] The poem closes with a short line of attestation, v. 4b,[9] but attached to it is an appendix of Israelite affirmation in response to the implicit challenge of the foregoing (v. 5). The rhythm is mixed, but a 3+3 meter predominates.

The piece is tightly bound together. *Nations* and *peoples* figure in both stanzas; the verb of instruction at the end of the first is resumed in the noun at the start of the second; the appendix echoes a number of themes already employed.[10] More significant still is the impression of careful dovetailing into the previous cries of disaster. Most obviously, it begins at

3. See the Introduction.
4. See the Introduction.
5. G. Wanke, *Die Zionstheologie der Korachiten in ihrem traditionsgeschichtlichen Zusammenhang*. BZAW 97 [1966], pp. 99, 116.
6. Gen. 12:3; cf. Ps. 87. Cf. H. Gross, *Die Idee des ewigen und allgemeinen Weltfriedens im Alten Orient und im AT*. Trierer Theologische Studien 7 (1956), pp. 112f.
7. Von Rad, "The City on the Hill," *The Problem of the Hexateuch and Other Essays* (E.T. 1966), pp. 232–242; H.-J. Kraus, *Worship in Israel* (E.T. 1966), p. 189.
8. It begins and ends with a line of chiastic order, vv. 2b and 4a.
9. Cf. G. Fohrer, "Über den Kurzvers," *ZAW* 66 (1954), pp. 199–236.
10. "Peoples," "each," "come," *Yahweh, God*.

the point where they left off, *the temple mount*. Yahweh's judging the nations aright in v. 3 stands in stark contrast to the former injustice of 3:1, 9, 11 and takes up in grander style the prophetic justice of 3:8. The desire for divine instruction in v. 2 reverses the disappointment at priestly instruction in 3:11. *Zion* and *Jerusalem* of 3:10 are given a more worthy role in v. 2. The *heads* of 3:1, 9, 11 give way to a new headship in v. 1. The people of *Jacob* (3:1, 9) receive fleeting mention in v. 2. The mock "war" of 3:5 is echoed in the abolition of real warfare in v. 3, while the spurious "peace" described in 3:5 comes true at last in the representations of vv. 3b–4a. All this amazing interlocking demonstrates that we are meant to see a literary unit extending from 3:1 to 4:5.[11]

1–2a The time for the fulfilment of this majestic ideal is stated to be simply the future. The term used is one of chronological sequence; it refers not to the end of time but to an important turning point within history when Yahweh will bring about his will among men as never before.[12] The future was bright with hope for the world. In that hope God's city was to play a vital part. Jerusalem was to be the focal point of humanity, and its supremacy was to be acknowledged by all. Yahweh it was who would bring about this transformation; as before, passive verbs are a paraphrase for divine activity.[13] A Song of Zion celebrates Jerusalem as the place "God establishes for ever":[14] here this establishment is echoed and carried forward to Jerusalem's glorious destiny. There were many holy mountains in the ancient world. The psalmist describes how Mount Hermon for all its grandeur must yield to Zion:

O divine mountain, mountain of Bashan,
O many-peaked mountain, mountain of Bashan,
why do you look with envy, many-peaked mountain,
at the mount God has chosen for his home,
where Yahweh is to live for ever? (Ps. 68:15f.[16f.]).

Indeed, Zion claimed the title of Zaphon, the home of the gods in Canaanite myth: here, not there, was the true seat of deity.[15] Now the claims of Zion to be God's abode were to be fully substantiated. Whether we are to think of literal, miraculous elevation of the low mountain of Jerusalem, which stands a mere 2400 feet above sea level,[16] or see here

11. P. R. Ackroyd, "A Note on Isaiah 2:1," *ZAW* 75 (1963), pp. 320f., likewise finds in Isa. 1:2–2:4/5 a "kerygmatic unit of material." He traces links between this poem and Isa. 1, and makes the interesting suggestion that Isa. 2:1 was intended as a later affirmation of the Isaianic authorship of the following oracle.
12. Cf. G. W. Buchanan, "Eschatology and the 'End of Days,' " *JNES* 20(1961), pp. 188–193; H. Kosmala, "At the End of the Days," *ASTI* 2 (1963), pp. 27–37. In its original setting the poem may have followed an account of Yahweh's victory over the nations (cf. vv. 11–13); in its present literary setting it forms the sequel to Jerusalem's destruction.
13. Cf. 1:7; 3:12.
14. Ps. 48:8(9) *yᵉḵônᵉnehā*: here *nāḵôn*.
15. Ps. 48:2(3). Cf. Wanke, *op. cit.*, pp. 64–66; Clements, *God and Temple* (1965), p. 82.
16. Cf. Ezek. 40:2; Zech. 14:10.

simply the language of poetic imagery and symbolic hyperbole, cannot be determined. Men are to look up to Jerusalem as superior to all other mountains, the sole place on earth where God reveals himself, the center of the world.[17]

The constant stream of nations is reminiscent of the river celebrated in one of the Songs of Zion as bringing joy to God's city.[18] It reads like a play upon that sacred theme: the river comes alive in the form of foreign pilgrims. Zion's role was to be the Mecca of the future world. The poet cites an invitation to pilgrimage such as: "Come, let us go to Gilgal."[19] But this is a pilgrimage on a colossal scale in which nations participate, no longer merely Israelite tribes. All roads lead to Jerusalem. With eagerness the foreign folk urge one another to visit the sanctuary of *Jacob's God*. This divine appellation is a favorite in many psalms connected with Zion, occurring in the pilgrims' song, Ps. 84.[20] We overhear their excited tones as they look forward to receiving the regular instruction available in the temple concerning the way Yahweh wanted men to live.[21] In Micah's own time the priests were dealing amiss with those who sought them out for instruction, but in this vision of a purified and exalted Zion men were to learn truth and to receive it freely. Glad day when men want to know God's will! Gladder day when their search is unhindered by man-made barriers!

2b–4 The poem swings around from a centripetal to a centrifugal orientation.[22] Zion has been the focus of humanity, the rainbow's end in man's quest for truth. Now the poet looks out from Zion and surveys the outreach of God's word in far-reaching effect. Is he thinking again of that sacred river which in ancient lore flows from the sanctuary and brings life and healing where it flows?[23] Jerusalem was to become the international court whose findings would be accepted without quibble. Disputes would be settled amicably, for such would be Yahweh's prestige that even great nations in far-flung corners of the world[24] would acknowledge his equity.

17. Cf. A. J. Wensinck, *The Ideas of the Western Semites Concerning the Navel of the Earth* (1916), pp. 13f., 22.
18. Ps. 46:4(5) *nāhār*: the word here is a verb *nāhᵃrû*.
19. 1 Sam. 11:14; cf. 9:9; Ps. 122:1. *Go up* is a technical term for pilgrimage.
20. Verse 8(9); cf. Ps. 20:2; 46:7, 11 (8, 12).
21. Cf. Ps. 25:4.
22. Cf. Kosmala, *VT* 14(1964), p. 441.
23. Cf. Joel 3(4):18, "a fountain shall issue from Yahweh's house"; also Ezek. 47:1f., 8–12; Zech. 14:8.
24. It has often been urged since Duhm that *far away,* which is lacking in the parallel in Isa. 2, should be deleted on metrical grounds and because it contradicts the peoples' coming to Zion. The second ground ignores the difference of aspect in the second part of the poem. As to meter the phrase simply implies a different metrical scheme, as does the presence of *hû'* in v. 1, which again is missing in Isa. 2. These are recensional differences whose fittingness we may discuss but with whose presence we may not tamper. The reference to "far countries" in Isa. 8:9f. (cf. 10:3; 13:5), which has affinities with the theme in the Psalms of the nations' attack upon Jerusalem, justifies the present phrase in this development and reversal of that theme.

How fitting that Jerusalem should become renowned for justice after the travesty that Micah had known within the contemporary courts! No more bribery, no more fixed verdicts; men could be sure of finding justice.

The wonderful result of this arbitration would be that armaments and training camps would be rendered obsolete. The Sandhursts and West Points of this world would be relegated to quaint museums. Suspicion and desire for *Lebensraum* could be checked without recourse to aggression or need for military deterrents. A Song of Zion speaks of a war to end all wars and of general disarmament,[25] but this piece goes further and spells out the positive aftermath. Valuable metal wasted in military attack and defense could be turned to constructive instead of destructive use, for now pursuits of peace would replace men's martial exploits. The blacksmith's forge would be busy, refashioning the swordblade into the heavy hoe[26] and the spearhead into the pruning knife.

The idyllic theme that brings the oracle to a fitting close is a proverbial expression treasured by God's people: they looked back to its fulfilment under King Solomon and forward to its coming true again.[27] No doubt many an Israelite sighed for its realization in the war-torn Palestine of the eighth century B.C. But here it is copied onto a larger canvas. Just as Israelite pilgrimage was enlarged to worldwide dimensions, so the Palestinian longing is promised a consummation on a universal scale, since the subject in this verse evidently remains the same as before.[28] It is an ideal that spells freedom: freedom from hunger and oppression, the free right to one's own property, to be one's own master. The sturdy peasant, relaxing at noon under the cool shade of his fruit trees and quietly surveying his own small holding maintained by honest toil, epitomizes a beautiful ideal of human fulfilment so often lacked and longed for. The reinforcing phrase "with none to make afraid" expresses what is already implied, namely, the freedom from fear which cramps the development of life and personality.

Could such hopes as these ever come true? the hearers of the poem must have mused. They were assured that these were no idle dreams by the concluding statement, which seals the oracle with the stamp of divine origin. This was not merely the wistful aspiration of human hearts but a promise made by the God of power,[29] certain to be kept.

The divine manifesto outlined in the second stanza strikes a

25. Ps. 46:9(10); cf. 76:3(4); Isa. 9:5; Hos. 2:18.

26. Cf. S. T. Byington, "Plow and Pick," *JBL* 68 (1949), pp. 49–54. Heb. *'ittîm* is often rendered "plowshares," but its occurrence in 1 Sam. 13:20f. (in the forms *'ēṯîm, 'ēṯô*) alongside *maḥ^arēshâ* as iron agricultural implements which required sharpening suggests otherwise, since the latter by etymology and later usage has better claim to that meaning. Symmachus there rendered *skapheion,* "hoe."

27. 1 K. 4:25 (5:5); Zech. 3:10. Cf. the subtle appeal in the propaganda of 2 K. 18:31.

28. The Heb. verb is plural.

29. For a survey of the usage and suggested meanings of "Yahweh of hosts" see Wanke, *op. cit.*, pp. 40–46; Crenshaw, *ZAW* 81(1969), pp. 167f. Its use in a Song of Zion, Ps. 46:7, 11(8, 12) (cf. Ps. 84 *passim*), is significant.

responsive chord in every human heart, but its fulfilment essentially depends on the prior condition of the first stanza: submission to the God of Israel. One should not read into the passage clarifications that one would like to see. There is no mention of conversion in the sense of abandonment of national religions; sacrifice plays no explicit part. The nations retain autonomy and self-government, but form a loose federation under Israel's God. Strangely perhaps, to judge from other parts of the OT, there is no thought of an empire managed by Israel for God; Israel receives scant mention solely in a label by which to identify Yahweh.

In light of such NT passages as John 4:21–24, the Christian will set little value on the geography of the piece and regard it as a cultural adornment to a deeper and universal truth. Today's world, no less than yesterday's, would dearly like to know how war is to be unlearned. This is no man-sized task. A pre-Hitler commentator could glibly write in hopeful terms which subsequent history belied: "We seem to discern in this oracle an adumbration of the order of ideas which has taken form in our days in the League of Nations and proposals for general disarmament."[30] Bitter experience has shown the need in all quarters for a missing "resolute endeavour to change an old way of life for a new one, persisted in even when the pull to the old from time to time overcomes us. That was where the League of Nations failed. . . . These adventures towards the light are possible only when the impulse springs from the heart and remains in the heart and grows there to fruition."[31] As to how the necessary transformation was to be initiated this oracle does not enlighten us: it presents only the vision of a world centered in biblical religion, craving instruction in God's ethical ways. Until man's religious instinct is truly satisfied on the basis of the revelation given through Israel, this oracle presents no hope of a lasting repeal of the law of the jungle. The brotherhood of man remains a dead phrase until it comes alive in a feeling after the fatherhood of God.

5 But what of the present? Should one wait with folded or even praying hands until man's dream and God's decree come true? No, this vision of what Yahweh was to be and do should become a spur to present endeavor. The future greatness of God was to prompt worship here and now. At the moment there was certainly no sign of any turning of *the nations* to Israel's God. Regardless, Israel's witness should shine all the brighter amid the darkness. The community was to live in the light of the future. A NT note is struck in anticipation: "What sort of persons ought you to be in holy and godly living as you wait for the day of God to come?" "Every one who has this hope in him keeps himself pure" (2 Pet. 3:11f.; 1 John 3:3). This supplement to the oracle presents an affirmation put upon the lips of the community, a determination to walk under God's

30. W. W. Cannon, "The Disarmament Passage in Isaiah II and Micah IV," *Theology* 24 (1932), pp. 2–8, esp. p. 8.
31. H. Spring, *In the Meantime* (1942), p. 59.

banner. It corresponds to the resolve of the nations expressed earlier: "Let us walk in his paths." In solemn pledge the call is taken up by Israel at least. Here is one nation that steps forward, the first to obey the invitation to a life of pilgrimage.[32] They vow to "walk in Yahweh's name," acknowledging his claim upon their lives and their desire to obey his will. He is *our God*—no proud and selfish vaunt, but a humble recognition of the responsibility of the covenant. No less than lifelong devotion and wholehearted service was worthy response from the community of Israel to the divine proclamation.

B. THE FUTURE GREATNESS OF ISRAEL AND JERUSALEM (4:6–8)

That will be the time, runs Yahweh's oracle, when
"I gather the limping flock,
bringing the strays together
and those whom I have injured. 2+2+2
7 *I shall make the limping flock into a remmant,*
the stragglers[33] *into a national power."* 3+3
Yahweh will reign over them
in Mount Zion
from then on and for ever. 3+2+3
8 *As for you, watchtower of that flock,*
citadel of Lady Zion, 3+2
to you will come
your sovereignty of old, 2+2
will come[34] *the royal rule*[35]
that belonged to Lady Jerusalem. 2+2

32. "It is for Israel to begin this going that the nations may be able to follow" (Buber, *The Prophetic Faith* [1949], p. 150).
33. Heb. *hannahᵃlā'â,* Niphal participle of a denominative verb from *hālᵉ'â,* "yonder." So G T (cf. S) evidently took it, and it corresponds well in external parallelism with *hanniddāḥâ,* "the straying (sheep)," in v. 6b. Dahood, *Pss 2,* p. 48, finds in Ps. 56:13(14) a Piel infinitive absolute of the same root. V implies *hannil'â,* "the weary," which many prefer. Wellhausen and others emend to *hannaḥᵃlâ,* "the diseased." Haupt suggested that MT is a mixed reading, combining *hannil'â* and *hannaḥᵃlâ* with a *ḥ/h* confusion.
34. In MT this second verb precedes *sovereignty,* which leaves the last phrase without a verb and creates metrical difficulty. Probably it belongs later (J. M. P. Smith, following Roorda, Wade, Schwantes, *et al.*), having slipped to its present position because of the similarity of Heb. *hmmšlh* and *mmlkt*.
35. Heb. *mamleḵeṯ* is construct form before a preposition; cf. GK 130a. *BHS* suggests repointing to *mamlāḵûṯ,* an absolute. G adds "from Babylon," probably displaced from v. 10: an underlying Heb. gloss intended to qualify "from the hand of your enemies" strayed from a point between *wb't* and *w'th* to a position between *wb'h* and *'th*. Originally it was meant to identify Jerusalem's enemies as Babylonian.

This next unit is a message of encouragement in dark days. Sympathetic allusion is made in the course of the message to present distress. In place of weakness is promised new strength, with the restoration of past glory. The unit, which is metrically irregular, falls into two sections of three lines each, linked by the themes of sheep imagery, kingship, and Jerusalem. The end of the first section is marked by the final thought of everlastingness. Possibly the second was originally a separate oracle or fragment of an oracle, added to form a new literary unit.[36] The transition in the first section from Yahweh's direct speech to a third person reference is matched in the second by a similar switch from direct address of Zion to a statement about the capital.[37] The piece has obviously been selected carefully so as to link up with the previous oracle. There is a recurrence of the related group of terms Jerusalem–mountain–Zion. "Strong nations" (v. 3) becomes singular, with reference to Israel. Yahweh's imperial kingship echoes and develops his supremacy over the nations, celebrated in the earlier song. The permanency of his rule over Israel is made a confirmatory response to his people's vow of permanent vassalage in v. 5.[38] Now the main stress is not the relation between Jerusalem and the nations but that between Jerusalem and Israel, yet the hint is dropped that Jerusalem's control of surrounding nations would be restored. Although quite different in tone from the preceding oracle, it shares the theme of Jerusalem's coming importance under God. Yahweh is to bring about a glorious turn for the better. The unit is a summons to faith in the God who is able to transform the powerlessness of his people into power and glory.

6, 7 The oracle proper is prefaced with a prose introduction, which has a twofold function. Its first aim is to provide a link with the preceding oracle, harking back to the future reference in 4:1. That oracle spoke of future exaltation for Jerusalem, the seat of the God of Jacob. But how was this to be attained? It remained only a dream while the people and territory of this God languished in the doldrums of disaster. This present message provides a necessary intermediate link between a present state of despair and the attainment of future expectation. The second function of the introduction is to certify that what follows is indeed of divine origin.[39]

It is a characteristic of many OT oracles of promise that they do not merely record hope for the future, but lay a realistic trail from the hopelessness of the present to prospects of coming glory. The prophet brings the divine message to the people where they are. With such psychological preparation there is even more likelihood that the word of

36. C. Westermann, cited by T. Lescow, *ZAW* 79 (1967), pp. 195f., has found in 4:8 and 5:2(1) a traditional form of promise in which a locality is emphasized.
37. The parallel is not exact since strictly in v. 8a only part of Zion is addressed.
38. Cf. too the link between *bᵉrō'sh,* "at the head," v. 1, and *hārī'shōnâ,* "former," v. 8.
39. Cf. F. Baumgärtel, "Die Formel *ne'um jahwe,*" *ZAW* 73 (1961), pp. 277–290.

promise will take root in weary hearts and engender a positive, vigorous attitude to life's ills. So the seer proclaims that God is not overlooking the people's present woes. Their depression cannot be lightly waved away, for it is sufficiently grounded in reason. His hearers present a pitiable spectacle: they are like limping sheep which have strayed from the flock. The community has disintegrated, and they have lost that sense of solidarity and security which is the foundation of normal living. Centuries later the Evangelist was to record that Jesus, "seeing the crowds, had compassion on them because they were harassed and dejected, like sheep without a shepherd" (Matt. 9:36). The same spirit of compassion throbs through this oracle. God knows full well, claims the prophet, the sorry state of his people, and himself enters into their distress. But this expression of sympathy is marked by a note of sinister realism rather than of sentimentality. The people have suffered at God's own hands. The unspoken implication is a sinful past, such as the earlier portions of the book have exposed. The injuries inflicted by God are just retribution, tokens that the people must themselves own responsibility for their present state. But the God who has demonstrated his power to break and mar has also the power to mend and make anew. In fact the sorry imagery of sheep has the hopeful corollary of a Shepherd who cares for his flock. Divine intervention is promised which will radically alter the present situation of despair. Now that God's people have been so reduced, they qualify for the cluster of prophetic promises that surround like sentinels the idea of the remnant and wrest new life from the jaws of death. The depleted nation is eventually to constitute a dynamic nucleus, a sturdy stock from which to breed and develop with new strength.[40] Israel will enjoy the status and stability of nationhood, taking a bold place among the nations as a power to be reckoned with instead of a victim of powerful aggression.[41]

The appellation "shepherd" was in the ancient world inextricably associated with kingship, and so the oracle moves smoothly into its next phase, specifying Jerusalem as the royal capital of a realm that would never be eroded.[42] Constantly underlying the concept of Israelite kingship was the tenet that the human king was no autocrat to impose his whims upon a servile people. Rather, he was but a viceroy, accountable to his divine superior who ruled through him. Beside the royal palace stood the temple as a perpetual reminder of theocracy, for hidden within its walls lay the ark, symbol of the presence of God "enthroned between the cherubim."

40. "The restless shoot that must blossom and bear fruit" (Snaith, *ad* 2:12). See the Introduction.
41. Cf. E. A. Speiser, " 'People' and 'Nation' of Israel," *JBL* 79 (1960), pp. 157–163; A. Cody, "When is the Chosen People Called a *gôy*?" *VT* 14 (1964), pp. 1–6.
42. Cf. Exod. 15:17f. The change to third person here is surprising: apparently the prophet suddenly speaks. Verse 8 reads like a *Jahwerede*, like 5:2. A conjectural emendation *ûmālaḵtî*, "and I shall reign," has often been proposed, assuming confusion of a final *yoḏ* with an abbreviation of the divine name.

8 The shepherd motif is skillfully woven into the thought of Jerusalem as the seat of royalty by referring to it as a watchtower overlooking the fold in which the sheep were gathered, from which the shepherd could look out upon the surrounding countryside for wild animals and sheepstealers. It may have more sinister overtones of a landmark rising stark from a lonely landscape,[43] which would reflect the devastation suffered by the country of God's people. If so, it fittingly summons from the hopeless present to a happier prospect. Here the term "sheep-tower" is applied to the south end of the temple hill, designated the *citadel* or "acropolis."[44] It was in this general area, where the old Jebusite fortress had stood, that the temple and palace were erected as joint tokens of divine rule mediated through an earthly king.[45] Appropriately it is this crucial area of the city that is singled out to be bearer of a promise that past splendor would be restored. Jerusalem had once known days of glory, but now it existed as a shadow of its former self. Its citizens must have sighed wistfully for days of yore when David's sword had carved out a mighty empire from neighboring territories, when Solomon's peace had developed its rich potential, and the temple had been erected as a monument to realized theocracy. Once again Jerusalem was to stand in noble dignity as proud capital of a realm fit for the King of kings. With so stirring a promise God's people were to be sustained. They were encouraged to endure present trials with eyes of faith set upon the God of the glorious past, who would not fail to manifest his power afresh in future splendor.

This and similar promises stayed in men's hearts for many a century. God's people and city did see happier days, which often appeared to be the prelude to fulfilment of God's great words. But they passed unfulfilled into the heritage of the Church, living still in a Christian seer's vision of a "new Jerusalem" wherein is to be placed "the throne of God and of the Lamb" whose servants "will reign for ever and ever" (Rev. 21:2; 22:35).

C. JERUSALEM'S DISTRESS AND EVENTUAL DELIVERANCE (4:9, 10)

Why are you now
shouting so loudly? 2+2
Have you no king among you?
Is your counsellor dead? 2+2
Why else does agony grip you
like a woman in labor? 2+2

43. Cf. 2 Chr. 26:10.
44. Cf. 2 Chr. 27:3; Neh. 3:26; Isa. 32:14.
45. There is no antithesis between the rule of God and the ideal rule of his earthly counterpart.

10 *Writhe in agony and shriek,*[46]
Lady Zion, like a woman in labor. 2+2
For shortly you must leave the city
and camp out in the country. 3+2
You must go to Babylon,
there to be rescued. 2+2
There will Yahweh claim you back
from the clutches of your foes. 3+2

This oracle is the first of three that present the crisis of Jerusalem threatened by enemy attack and give three different solutions. Each begins with *now* (the second with "and now") and describes in its own way the present distress before contrasting it with future prospects. The first one, spoken by the prophet, reflects the emotional tension and excitement gripping the people of the city, in the 2+2 meter that predominates in its seven lines. It falls into two sections of three and four lines respectively. The end of the first half is taken up artistically in the beginning of the second.[47] Steeped in satire, the piece consists of (1) a series of reproachful questions concerning the distress of the people of Jerusalem and (2) an exhortation to indulge in further demonstrations of distress, which is explained by a causal clause stating that much worse is to befall them; finally (3) a promise is given that Yahweh will deliver them—eventually. Thus most of the oracle is taken up with an implicit description of present distress and forecast of more woe. It concludes on a hopeful note which would have brought little comfort to the hearers. The overall impression is of accusation of loss of faith in Yahweh, their true leader, together with an assurance that he would intervene to save them, but much later than they hoped. The addressee of the oracle is identified only in the second part, a phenomenon that is to be paralleled in the next oracle. The piece is linked with the preceding one by a common reference to "daughter Zion" and by a contrast between the victory of the divine king (v. 7) and the failure of the human king (v. 9).[48]

9 This first part of the oracle comments on the wails of distress to be heard throughout the city. Evidently catastrophe had overwhelmed Jerusalem; in view of the way the piece continues, the catastrophe must be construed as the proximity of enemy forces. The prophet affects surprise. Surely there was no cause for despair. After all, they had their king to

46. The precise meaning of Heb. *gōḥî* is uncertain. Its basic meaning appears to be "strain" (G. R. Driver, *JTS* 41 [1940], p. 172). Here a sense of straining one's voice would suit both the reference to shouting in v. 9 and the vocal allusion in the convention of the "reaction to bad news" (cf. n. 50 below); cf. Ezek. 21:12 "sigh." G, not knowing the word, rendered as if it were *gᵉʿî*, varying the guttural.
47. And *ʿattâ* occurs in both sections (*now, shortly*).
48. Notice too the homophonic link between *hᵃrēʿōṯî*, v. 6, and *tārîʿî rēaʿ*, v. 9. For the setting and date of the oracle see the Introduction.

direct operations and counsel them with his royal wisdom.[49] What better guide could they have? They had trusted him and applauded his policies so long that it was inconsistent now to refuse to back him to the bitter end. So Micah satirizes the failure of human leadership and implicitly accuses his hearers of lack of faith in God. Both the situation and the sentiment are akin to those of Isaiah, who accused Judah's leaders of carrying out plans that had not come from Yahweh, and of not consulting him but instead looking to Egyptian armaments as the way out of their difficulties (Isa. 30:1; 31:1). Micah is speaking at a time when the futility of such counsels has become clear to all. The last part of the verse draws upon conventional language representing a characteristic reaction to bad news.[50] There are a number of features that belong to the convention in its full form; here the prophet selects one referring to psychosomatic pains as severe as the pains of childbearing.[51] By using this conventional expression he means to categorize the situation as one of crisis, warranting dismay and alarm.

10 Micah can promise his audience no immediate alleviation of their distress. He moves from question and description to exhortation, but a constant factor is the reiteration of the reaction to bad news. There is cause indeed for them to continue in their despair. The repetition of vocabulary underlines strikingly the inexorable gravity of the situation. The people's reaction is more justified than they realize, for the prophet has worse news to announce. The city is to fall and be evacuated. The people are to surrender and lose the comfort and security of city life; they will have to adjust to a different way of life, camping out in the countryside in between trudging the weary road of deportation to Babylon. Their hopes of victory are doomed to come to nothing. The prophet finally tosses an ironic crumb of comfort. At the end of a long, dark tunnel he can glimpse a gleam of light. The destiny of Jerusalem's citizens is to tread an arduous path before Yahweh intervenes as they desire. There seems to be deliberate stress in Micah's repeated *there*.[52] The venue of deliverance will not be here in Jerusalem, as his hearers fondly hope. They are not entitled to this hope to which they are clinging. To huddle under promises concerning the holy

49. Many of those who regard the oracle as of an early sixth-century origin find here a reference to Zedekiah's flight from Jerusalem (2 K. 25:4). But the question rather suggests that the king was present but held of no account. This is rightly recognized in the interpretation that takes *king* as a reference to Yahweh (cf. Jer. 8:19). But Heb. *'āḇaḏ*, "perished," better suits a human reference.

50. Cf. D. R. Hillers, "A Convention in Hebrew Literature: the Reaction to Bad News," *ZAW* 77 (1965), pp. 86–90. He does not mention this passage, but it is obviously to be included among such examples as Exod. 15:14–16; Ps. 48:5f.(6f.); Isa. 13:7f.; Jer. 6:24; Ezek. 21:11f. The widespread range of this convention in Ugar. and Heb. literature does not favor the claim of Robinson and Willi-Plein that the oracle's use of language employed by Jeremiah indicates a date later than Micah.

51. The others commonly found are limp hands and melting heart.

52. For such pointed repetition cf. "my people" in 2:8f.

city is useless. Yahweh will indeed be gracious, and will certainly redeem his people; but they can lay no claim to instant deliverance as the automatic right of God's covenant people. It is hardly accidental that the prophet uses vocabulary associated with the Exodus. A people in whose worship God's mighty acts of old were regularly celebrated might well have claimed that he would work again with comparable proof of covenant love.[53] Yahweh had indeed snatched Israel from their Egyptian foes in days gone by and laid claim to his people, recovering them from alien hands.[54] But the ironic point is made that to qualify for a fresh display of God's Exodus power they have yet to sojourn again in enemy territory! Micah here seems to be taking up deliberately the motifs of popular religion, voiced perhaps by his prophetic rivals, and sardonically claims their validity only if certain obviously unacceptable conditions are met.[55]

Micah must have made himself thoroughly unpopular by delivering this oracle. Evidently his basic thought is that reliance upon human leaders whose policies are incompatible with Yahweh's kingship is the start of a road that leads away from blessing and toward failure, which cannot be averted by glib recourse to God's obligations to his covenant people. As to its nonfulfilment, are we to think along the same lines as in 3:12, of repentance which saved Jerusalem at the very brink of disaster?[56] Obviously such an oracle as this would scare Micah's hearers, as was intended, and his hope was to make them think again before it was too late.

D. THE MENACE OF JERUSALEM'S ENEMIES REMOVED (4:11–13)

Now are massed against you
many nations, 3+2
who say, "Let her be desecrated,
let us gloat over Zion." 2+3
12 *But they are ignorant*
of Yahweh's designs, 3+2
they have not realized his intent
to gather them like sheaves to the threshing floor. 3+3
13 *"Get threshing, Lady Zion.*
Your horn I shall turn to iron, 3+3

53. Cf. 2:7; 6:4f.
54. Heb. *nṣl,* "rescue," is used of the Exodus, e.g., in Exod. 5:23; 12:27; and *g'l,* "claim back," is so used, e.g., Exod. 6:6; 15:13; Ps. 74:2.
55. Van der Woude, *VT* 19 (1969), 249–252, regards v. 10 as Micah's reply to words of his prophetic opponents cited in v. 9, which is taken as a pastoral reassurance that Yahweh dwells in Zion (cf. 3:11b). He does not mention an element of satire in v. 10; he leaves open the question of the authenticity of the reference to Babylon, but adduces arguments for retaining it, including his view that the meter is against deletion.
56. Cf. 2 K. 19:3; Isa. 22:12.

your hooves I shall turn to bronze,
and you will crush many peoples.'' 3+3
You will devote[57] *their looted property to Yahweh,*
their wealth to the Master of all the world. 3+3

This is the second oracle in the nucleus of three devoted to Jerusalem's danger. Like the first it presents a *now* and ''then'' contrast of present distress and future deliverance, but this time the weight of the oracle is tilted on the side of hope. Its basic structure is rather similar to the previous piece. Another seven-line oracle, it again falls into two short sections, this time of four and three lines respectively. The boundaries of the first are marked by an echo of the opening verb in the synonymous verb at its close. Mention of the threshing floor at the end of the first section glides artistically into the call to thresh at the start of the second. The whole oracle is tied together by the reminiscence of *many nations* (v. 11) in *many peoples* and *all the world* at the end. Metrically the piece settles into a stately 3+3 rhythm in the second section. The first section, in which the prophet describes the threat confronting Jerusalem, is the prelude to the second, in which appears first a divine exhortation specifying the addressee, ''daughter Zion,'' and then a prophetic explanatory clause which develops the promises of victory. Despite similarities to the previous oracle, this structural skeleton is clothed in quite a different manner. The description at the head of the first part, which takes up the traditional theme of the nations' gathering for battle against Jerusalem,[58] passes into a vivid citation of the claims of Zion's foes, only to counter them with a statement of God's own strategy. In the second part this strategy is unfolded in the tactical orders issued to Zion by Yahweh, which culminate in his final glorification. This latter half of the oracle follows the well-authenticated form of a battle summons.[59] If the previous oracle was suffused with prophetic satire, this one is marked by divine irony in a manner that recalls 2:1–5.

The piece is obviously connected with the previous one by its addressing ''daughter Zion'' and contrasting the present (*now*) with the future. The lack of confidence in the royal *counsellor* of v. 9 is here capped by an implicit call to faith in the success of divine ''counsel'' in v. 12. There are also echoes of the earlier oracles of the chapter. The verbs of the divine gathering of Israel in v. 6[60] are here taken up to describe another gathering, that of the nations, which is at first sinister but is then shown to

57. Heb. *wᵉhaḥᵃramtî* is an archaic form of the second feminine singular (so G S V T): cf. GK 44h. Theoretically it could be first person but it is awkward to think of Yahweh devoting spoils to himself.
58. Cf. H.-M. Lutz, *Jahwe, Jerusalem und die Völker*. WMANT 27 (1968), pp. 91–97.
59. Cf. Joel 3(4):9–13; Obad. 1f. The form has been analyzed by R. Bach, *Die Aufforderungen zur Flucht und zum Kampf im alttestamentlichen Prophetenspruch*. WMANT 9 (1962), pp. 51–91.
60. Heb. *'āsap̱, qibbēts*.

be under the control of the same God of Israel as in v. 6. Most striking of all is the peculiar relationship of this oracle to 4:1–5; there and here *many nations* and *many peoples* feature, but in quite a different context. The beneficent influence of Zion upon the world meets a shocking reversal in her violent subjugation of the nations who come now not for instruction but for destruction. The paradox is to be posed even more sharply in 5:7–9 (6–8).

11, 12 Jerusalem is menaced by a cosmopolitan army. Ancient imperial treaties included clauses calling upon vassal states if the empire was attacked by external assault or insurrection. Accordingly detachments of national troops were forced to rally to Assyria's aid, led by their local princes: Isaiah mentions Elam and Kir as represented in the Assyrian army (Isa. 22:6). The presence of different *nations,* probably standing out with their different uniforms and standards, increases Jerusalem's sense of isolation and panic. The prophet imaginatively portrays the malicious gloating of Zion's enemies over her imminent downfall. He puts into their mouths a statement reflecting the standpoint of their victims.[61] Their intent is nothing less than to *desecrate* Zion. This impious claim runs blatantly counter to the traditional aura of sanctity that surrounds Jerusalem as the holy city of God.[62] It contains within it the seeds of hubris, which are destined to develop into a harvest of destruction. But this is only on further reflection; at first hearing it merely arouses a sense of frustrated outrage. Yet the hearer has not long to wait before he is assured that God too has taken note of these sacrilegious thoughts[63] and has designs of his own of which the enemies are as yet unaware.[64] This development in the oracle is reminiscent of 2:1–3, where God's counterplan is his reaction to the planning of evildoers. At this time when God seems absent from his people, on the very eve of their enemies' victory, the prophet can reveal that he is firmly in control despite all appearances. He lets his audience into the divine secret. Their foes have reckoned without Yahweh in their assessment of the situation. In fact their campaign has been masterminded by a strategist greater than their generals. The prophet savors the delicious irony of the whole affair. They had marched to their annihilation. The magnet that drew them to Jerusalem was not merely their warlust but God's providential will. Their martial greed had been the means of leading them into an unsuspected trap and luring them to their doom. The cup of victory would be snatched from their expectant lips and handed to Jerusalem. The

61. Cf. Isa. 30:10f. for a similar prophetic slanting to bring out the import of an attitude (cf. H. W. Wolff, "Das Zitat im Prophetenspruch," *Gesammelte Studien zum AT* [1964], pp. 36–129, esp. pp. 83–85).

62. Cf. Ps. 2:6; 46:4(5); 48:1(2).

63. "Saying" often has the connotation of thinking; cf. Ps. 14:1.

64. Wisdom terms are echoed and developed in this prophetic "view of the political scene from the standpoint of faith in Yahweh as the only effective policy maker and executive" (W. McKane, *Prophets and Wise Men.* SBT 44 [1965], pp. 87f.).

surprising content of the divine plan[65] is spelled out in metaphorical terms whose import Isaiah explains:

"*. . . to break the Assyrian in my country*
and to trample him upon my mountains." (Isa. 14:25)

Micah uses an agricultural simile, all the more sinister because it had long been associated with ruthless warfare.[66] Amos had accused Damascus of "threshing Gilead with iron threshing-sledges."[67] The allusion is to the threshing machine studded underneath with iron spikes, which the ox dragged over the stalk-strewn *threshing floor* to chop the straw and loosen the grain, thereby preparing it for the next stage of winnowing. Micah uses this metaphor of the terrible fate that awaits the invaders. Those who have taken up the cruel sword are doomed to perish by it.

13 The divine exhortation rings out to Zion as she cowers in fear and hopelessness. Yahweh intervenes through his prophet to transform human despair into assurance of victory—a victory not of man's doing but of God's. The repeated verb *I shall turn* stresses divine agency and empowering, using "what is weak in the world's eyes to confound the strong" (1 Cor. 1:27). Micah plays the part of an old prophet of holy war whose task it was to stir up the Israelite troops and urge them to fight with the confidence that Yahweh was on their side.[68] The imagery veers in verbal midstream from the threshing ox to the bull as a fighting figure of unconquerable might. The prophet is drawing upon ancient tradition here. One of Ahab's prophetic yes-men had made iron horns and, one can imagine, pranced about with them held to his head as he predicted, "With these you will gore the Arameans until they are destroyed."[69] This symbol of conquest is paralleled by a similar one concerning strong hooves with which to kick, maim, and *crush*. Against the strong armor with which God can equip his beleaguered people their foes will find no defense.[70] So the giant biter will be bit, afflicted with the very slaughter he meant to inflict upon his tiny foe.

In the last line the prophet takes up the divine exhortation with encouragement of his own.[71] In this situation of despair he can already speak of the disposal of the spoils of victory, so keen is his faith which he would have his audience share. To *devote* is again a technical term of holy war, referring to the ritual destruction of enemy property and the dedication

65. For divine planning in the OT see B. Albrektson, *History and the Gods*. Coniectanea biblica, OT series 1 (1947), pp. 68–97.

66. It is hardly necessary to conclude with Wolfe that the verse depends on Isa. 41:11–16.

67. Amos 1:3; cf. 1 K. 13:7.

68. Cf. Bach, *op. cit.*, pp. 101f. The initial imperative *qûm*, "arise," is typical of the battle summons: cf. Isa. 21:5; Jer. 49:14, 28, 31.

69. 1 K. 22:11; Num. 23:22; Deut. 33:17.

70. There were two types of holy war, one in which Israel stood aside to let God act and a second, echoed here, in which Israel fought with divine aid. Isaiah followed the former type.

71. Cf. Bach, *op. cit.*, p. 71; Lutz, *op. cit.*, p. 94.

of metal objects to the sanctuary.[72] Jerusalem's foes would not enjoy for long their ill-gotten gains of war. The loot they had recently seized would be confiscated and ceremonially burned or transferred to the sacred treasury in token that the victory was Yahweh's. The power was his, and his too must be the glory. Sennacherib called himself "king of the world,"[73] but the prophet claims the title for his God by echoing what seems to have been an established cultic title.[74] The vocabulary of Israel's hymns was to find fulfilment in the arena of history. Their God would by this conquest of the nation be vindicated as superior to their gods. He would stand supreme in solitary splendor, worshipped and adored by the grateful people he had delivered from the jaws of death.

So fainting hearts were infused with fresh hope. Micah took over ancient motifs in order to infect with their primitive enthusiasm a people obsessed with sophisticated, earthly realism. Against their skeptical despair he pits a greater reality, the overruling providence of a God to whom the princes of this world are but pawns in a supernatural game. He reminds them of their weakness only that it may serve as an inducement to turn to a mighty God. The NT took up the motif of holy war and transposed it to a spiritual, cosmic key:

> *Be strong in the Lord and in the strength of his might. . . . For we are fighting . . . against the spiritual forces of evil in the heavenly regions.* (Eph. 6:10, 12)

Micah's enthusiasm in the face of overwhelming odds shines out again in these stirring exhortations of Paul, just as they do in his convictions of Rom. 8:35–38.

> *Soldiers of Christ, arise*
> *and put your armour on,*
> *strong in the strength which God supplies*
> *through his eternal Son. . . .*
> *Who in the strength of Jesus trusts*
> *is more than conqueror.* (Charles Wesley)

72. Cf. Josh. 6:17, 19, 24. This verb *heḥᵉrîm* appears in a battle summons also at Jer. 50:21, 26; 51:3.
73. *ANET*, p. 288.
74. It occurs in Ps. 97:5 amid a number of traditional elements in a description of theophany for the purpose of world judgment. Dahood, *Pss 2*, p. 361, compares a phrase in an unpublished Ugar. text *adn ilm rbm*, "master of the great gods." Its use in Zech. 4:14; 6:5 does not necessarily indicate a late origin. In Josh. 3:11, 13 the phrase is often regarded as a liturgical amplification of the text in view of its lack of coordination in v. 11; but J. A. Soggin, *Joshua* (E.T. 1970), p. 59, emending the text with S, retains it. Lutz, *op. cit.*, p. 94, follows Kraus in regarding the phrase as taken over from the cultic traditions of pre-Israelite Jerusalem.

E. JERUSALEM'S ABJECT KING AND ISRAEL'S IDEAL KING (5:1–6[4:14–5:5])

Now you are gashing yourself, Lady under attack.
Siege is laid[1] *against us;* 3+3
with their stick they are striking
on the cheek Israel's judge. 3+2
2 *"But from you, Bethlehem Ephrathah,*
home of one of Judah's smaller clans,[2] 4+4
from you will emerge for me
one who is to be sovereign over Israel, 3+3
one whose origins stretch far back
to days of yore." 3+2
3 *So he will surrender them only until the time*
when she with child gives birth. 3+2
Then the rest of his brothers will be restored
to Israel's people. 3+2
4 *He will be installed to shepherd his flock by Yahweh's enabling,*
with the majestic authority of Yahweh his God. 4+4
They will remain undisturbed because he will then be held in great honor
at earth's farthest bounds. 3+2
5 *This is the one who will bring peace*
"if[3] *Assyria invades our country,*
if they set foot in these mansions of ours. 3+3+3
We shall appoint against them seven shepherds,
eight men as generals. 4+3
6 *They will crop Assyria's country with the sword,*
Nimrod's country[4] *with the naked blade."*[5] 4+3
He will save us[6] *from "Assyria if they invade our country,*
if they set foot on this territory of ours." 4+3

This oracle brings to a climax the group of three that are marked by a contrast between present trouble and future greatness.[7] Like the previous

1. MT *śām,* apparently an indefinite singular, "one has laid." Very many emend to a plural *śāmû* with S V T in parallelism with the following verb, but this smacks of an easier and so inferior reading. G supports MT; if change is deemed necessary, it is better to repoint as a Qal passive *śīm*: cf. Symmachus, and Dahood, *Pss 1,* p. 310.
2. Lit. "small in respect of being among Judah's clans" (T. Lescow, *ZAW* 79 [1967], pp. 172–207, esp. p. 195). But there is no need to delete with him *lihyôṯ* in the next line; for repetition in adjacent lines cf. 1:12, 15; 2:13; 3:2b–3.
3. Heb. *kî,* "in the case that, if" (BDB, p. 473a).
4. Cf. Gen. 10:8–12, where Nimrod is associated with Assyria.
5. MT *bip̄eṯāḥeyhā,* "in its entrances," has evidently been transposed from *bappeṯîḥâ* in light of the first-century A.D. Jewish recension of G (D. Barthélemy, *Les devanciers d'Aquila.* SVT 10 [1963], pp. 228f.); cf. Quinta, Aquila, V, and Ps. 55:21(22).
6. "Us" is easily supplied (K. J. Cathcart, *Biblica* 49 [1968], pp. 511–14, esp. p. 514). There is no need to read *wehitstsîlānû* (or *-ûnû*) with Wellhausen and Robinson.
7. 4:13 "seems to form a natural conclusion to the preceding oracle," and 5:1(4:14) brings "a renewed summons to lamentation. It is therefore probable" that 5:1 "is actually the

one, it is composed of a short sinister section and a long happy one, while the first of the three (4:9, 10) had reversed the proportions. The climactic progression is demonstrated by a marked increase in length in the promise of future blessing, compared with the previous oracle. A call to faith in Yahweh rather than in military means to meet the current crisis is based on an extended description of coming weal. The thirteen-line oracle falls into three unequal parts: (1) two lines describing in terms of lament the calamity that has overtaken both capital and king; (2) seven lines of promise of salvation via a new king who is to be heir of an ancient heritage, herald of national blessing, and divinely empowered head of a universal realm; and (3) four lines emphasizing that he is to be the only answer to the menace of Assyria. The prophet speaks throughout apart from v. 2, which Yahweh proclaims. The meter is irregular, but there is a preponderance of the 3+2 rhythm in the second and of 4+3 in the third. The last part, which in its present form could hardly stand by itself,[8] appears most clearly as a subunit. Basically a popular song with a refrain at beginning and end,[9] it has been skillfully adapted with a new parallel start and finish. Its purpose is to define and illustrate the success of the coming king which was outlined or implied in the previous section, especially vv. 3f., and to stress that Israel's salvation from their giant enemy lies in none other.[10] The first section is closely linked with the second by the threefold occurrence of *Israel* at the end of lines (vv. 1b, 2a, 3), a phenomenon previously observed in 1:13–15.[11] The first and third are interlocked by the common theme of the enemy invader, specified as Assyria in the third, and by the reference to the people with first plural pronouns in both. The piece begins and ends with the Assyrian invasion as seen through the people's eyes, first in the form of a descriptive lament and finally in the form of sanguine hopes of victory. The tables are neatly turned by the reversal of enemy attack *against us* to victory *against them*. All three sections are shot through with variegated hues of Davidic kingship. The whole unit is marked by close integration and clear progression of thought.

This royal oracle is obviously intended to be the central peak of the

---

introduction to the next passage'' (A. S. Kapelrud, *VT* 11 [1961], p. 397). The coherence of 5:1–6 has been well argued by Willis, *VT* 18(1968), pp. 529–547. His positive arguments are: (1) the logical progression from present disaster to future deliverance in a pattern similar to adjacent units; (2) a uniform historical background; (3) emphasis on Davidic traditions; and (4) the presence of interlocking devices.

8. Yet a number of scholars, including J. M. P. Smith, Wolfe, Thomas, and Renaud, take this part as independent.

9. Cf. Renaud, *Structure et attaches littéraires* (1964), pp. 19f. Van der Woude, *VT* 19 (1969), p. 255, following Vriezen, ascribes vv. 5b–6(4b–5) to false prophets.

10. Heb. *w^{e}rā'â,* ''and he will shepherd,'' is a correction of *rō'îm,* ''shepherds,'' v. 5(4), and of *w^{e}rā'û,* ''and they will shepherd,'' v. 6(5).

11. The second part is bound together not only by the repetition of *Israel* but by the echo of the sound of *y^{e}shûḇûn,* ''they will return,'' v. 3(2), in *w^{e}yāshāḇû,* ''and they will dwell secure,'' v. 4(3).

range of oracles in chs. 4 and 5. It presents a longer hope section than any other unit, and points to the fulfilment of royal promise as the key to the greatness of Jerusalem and Israel heralded in the surrounding pieces. The first section is reminiscent of 4:11, but there is a closer parallel with 4:9 in that a description of lament is linked with mention of the king.[12] The term "daughter of attack" takes up the preceding "daughter Zion" in ominous fashion, while the direct address to *Bethlehem* echoes that to the flock-tower in 4:8.[13]

1 Jerusalem is addressed in this description of woe. The scene is concisely set by the new title *Lady under attack*[14] in place of Lady Zion. By a play on similar-sounding words[15] the point is made that her activity befits her condition, a practice associated with funeral rites.[16] Lacerating one's body was one of the means employed by a society more extroverted than our own to give vent to its grief over death or similar misfortune. Here is reason enough for mourning, as the prophet proceeds to explain. He aligns himself sympathetically with the beleaguered people of the capital; he is fully at one with them in their distress, weeping with them as they weep. He has a message of good news to impart, which, however, cannot be appreciated until they realize to the full the gravity of their situation and their hopelessness apart from God. The siege referred to is apparently the result of Sennacherib's invasion. The narratives in 2 K. 18f. are evidently selective, but the Assyrian record suggests that a siege did take place in 701.[17]

What a humiliation for the Judean king! The prophet spells out the dire significance of this event for Hezekiah. His reputation gone along with his realm, it was a slap in the face for this shadow of a king.[18] Micah uses this description of degrading treatment to express the sorry state to which

12. Note too how *kî'attâ,* "for now/soon," 4:10, is matched in 5:4(3).
13. Both begin with *w^e'attâ,* "and/but you," while the "rule," *memshālâ,* of that verse is echoed in the "ruler," *môshēl,* of 5:2(1).
14. Heb. *baṯ g^eḏûḏ,* lit. "daughter of a raid"; cf. Symmachus "confined (or besieged) daughter."
15. Heb. *titgōḏ^eḏî—g^eḏûḏ.* Wellhausen's conjectural emendation *hitgôḏēḏ,* an infinitive absolute, "severely," for *baṯ-g^eḏûḏ,* followed by Duhm, J. M. P. Smith, Lindblom, *et al.*, kills the poetic artistry. S V T̄ take the verb as denominative of *g^eḏûḏ,* "mobilize oneself." Comparison with 4:9 suggests rather that the prophet is describing popular reaction to the city's crisis. The descriptive nature of the parallel 4:9, 11 renders unlikely the interpretation preferred by so many commentators and translators, whereby the verb is taken as second person jussive and rendered as an imperative. G in both cases presupposes a root *gdr,* which provides a good parallel to the following mention of siege and doubtless for that reason is followed by Robinson, George, *et al.* (cf. RSV, JB, NEB); but synonymous parallelism is not necessary. The two half-lines are linked as effect and cause (cf. 2:1, 3; 3:4; 4:12).
16. Cf. Deut. 14:1; Jer. 16:6.
17. *ANET,* p. 288. J. B. Geyer, *VT* 21 (1971), pp. 604–606, finds in the expressions "I shut him up like a bird in a cage" and "I surrounded him with an earthwork" the connotation of siege, comparing usage in other Assyrian annals.
18. To be struck on the cheek was a gross insult (Job 16:10; Lam. 3:30).

the king had sunk. But he appears to be operating subtly on several levels of meaning. It was the task of the Hebrew king to wield justice in his domain. He was the heir of the old office of judge which existed in the days of the tribal federation, the bona fide *judge of Israel*.[19] In the royal psalm, Ps. 72, pride of place is given to a prayer that the king may be endowed with a divine aptitude for justice (vv. 1, 2). In Isa. 11, where we are meant to see a projection forward of a perpetual royal ideal, this standard of justice is described as "striking . . . with the rod of his mouth" (v. 4). This expression is probably borrowed from the style of Judean royal psalms, to judge by its use in Ps. 2, where rebellion is quelled by breaking "with a rod of iron." Micah's hearers would have known from coronation hymns and the like that it was the task of the king as judge to *strike* with his scepter, as it were, the wrongdoer, be he native or foreigner. But what a reversal has taken place here! No solemn exercise of the high dignity of jurisdiction: the king is cooped up in his capital, cringing beneath insulting blows like a criminal. Nor is the multidimensional nature of Micah's meaning yet fully revealed.[20] Isaiah refers to Assyria's attack on Judah as striking with a rod, thinking perhaps of the club a soldier might carry.[21] Whether this was Isaiah's own coinage or a popular expression, Micah seems to take it up: here too was the Assyrian hitting with his club. References to Assyrian hostility, common insult, and royal responsibility are cleverly run together to expose the low level to which the fortunes of the Judean monarchy have sunk. The prophet points out the grim incongruity of this happening with another wordplay, *shēḇeṭ,* "rod" and *shōp̄ēṭ,* "judge." The venerable judge has become but a whipping boy.

2–4 It is within this drab frame of royal misfortune that Micah sets a glorious picture of royal majesty. The figure of failure of v. 1 stands as a foil to his radiant counterpart here. The prophet first delivers a divine apostrophe to *Bethlehem Ephrathah,* the birthplace of the Davidic dynasty.[22] The very names "house of bread, fruitfulness" conjure up visions far different from the present spectacle. Surely the omens of prosperity that clustered round such names were not destined to die out in the squalid nadir of Assyrian occupation. No, for God promises that new splendor is to radiate from this fount of kingship. Can new vitality spring out of the

19. Cf. Beyerlin, *KIPVM,* pp. 19–21; H.-J. Kraus, *Worship in Israel* (E.T. 1966), p. 188; D. A. McKenzie, "The Judge of Israel," *VT* 17 (1967), pp. 118–121.

20. Kapelrud, *loc. cit.*, p. 400, and McKeating also find in the phrase a reference to the ritual of the New Year Festival, since striking the king with a rod featured in the Akkadian Akitu ritual (*ANET,* p. 334).

21. Isa. 10:24; 14:29; cf. 30:31.

22. David's father is described in 1 Sam. 17:12 as "an Ephrathite from Bethlehem in Judah." Ephrathah appears to have been the district in which Bethlehem lay; the places are identified in Gen. 35:19; 48:7; Ruth 4:11. G reads "Bethlehem house of Ephrathah," which scholars have often interpreted as an indication that in MT *Bethlehem* is a marginal gloss which displaced *bêṯ,* "house." Recent scholarship favors the retention of MT (Schwantes; Lescow, *loc. cit.*, pp. 193f.; *BHS*).

moribund state of the Judean monarchy? In reassurance God points to the "little town of Bethlehem" as a parable for present times.[23] Who could have dreamed that so unimportant a place would breed a David? Of all the clans[24] of the tribe of Judah, the Ephrathite clan around Bethlehem would hardly supply a respectable army unit at times of tribal levy. How strange that God summoned the man of his choice from so insignificant a source![25] He can take acorns and turn them into mighty oaks; Jerusalem and her king are reassured that, low though they have sunk in the eyes of the world and shrunken though the royal power is, yet God can restore and grant new greatness.[26] Yahweh has not cast aside the Davidic covenant. As once he had told Samuel to visit Jesse because "I have provided for myself a king from among his sons" (1 Sam. 16:1), so now he declares that from that ancient line will issue again a king *for me,* one who would fulfil God's own purposes and be devoted to his will, like David of old.[27] It is significant that the new monarch is not given the title "king," but called merely "ruler" or *sovereign.* There is a vital distinction: he is to be no rival to the divine King, but is to rule with due subordination. From a dynasty now diminished in a way reminiscent of its beginnings in Bethlehem's tiny clan, there will issue a national leader under God, to rule over a people who are heirs of the ancient tribal federation. This royal promise secures with it the destiny of God's people.

The word for the future is backed by the heritage of the past. The appearing of this ruler is to be validated by hereditary right; the same root is deliberately taken up and used again.[28] He is to come not of common stock but of kingly lineage, and this constitutes the guarantee of his coming. The phrase used in the first half of the last line in v. 2 is ambiguous, but OT usage of the parallel phrase rendered *days of yore* makes it clear that allusion is being made to a time in finite history, i.e., the distant past.[29]

23. Reference is made to Bethlehem first as an assurance that there would arise an ideal king of the Davidic dynasty, which had its origin in Bethlehem (J. Klausner, *The Messianic Ideal in Israel* [E.T. 1956], p. 77; J. L. McKenzie, *CBQ* 19[1957], pp. 43f.), and secondly as a cipher for the Judean monarchy in its present low state (Lescow, *loc. cit.*, pp. 197f.). Alt's view that Micah saw no future at all for Jerusalem, and so envisaged Bethlehem as the source of the new ruler (*loc. cit.* in n. 35 on 2:5), is a hazardous reconstruction of a prophetic program. It depends on too narrow a conception of the authenticity of oracles ascribed to Micah. Moreover, the ideology of Davidic kingship was centered upon Jerusalem, and there is nothing in this passage that suggests a break with so firm a part of the tradition.
24. Heb. *'al^e^p̱ê,* units of fighting men supplied by *mishpāḥôṯ* or phratries, tribal subgroups. Cf. Judg. 6:15; 1 Sam. 10:19; 23:23.
25. Cf. this motif in the traditions of Gideon and Saul (Judg. 6:15; 1 Sam. 9:21).
26. Cf. v. 4b(3b).
27. Pusey; Keil; Lescow, *loc. cit.*, p. 197.
28. Heb. *yētsē'*, "he will go out"—*môtsā'ōṯāyw,* "his outgoings."
29. Heb. *y^e^mê 'ôlām* is always set within a historical framework (Isa. 63:9, 11; Amos 9:11; Mic. 7:14; Mal. 3:4). This time can only be the days of David, to which the earlier parts of the verse have been harking, as in Amos 9:11 (cf. Neh. 12:46, where *miqqeḏem,* which occurs in the first half of this line, is used of David's age). Amos 9:11 has frequently in the past been

The king whose coming is foretold is to be a son of David, with truly royal blood flowing in his veins. This is far more than appeal to snobbery or patriotic sentiment. People looked back to David's reign not only to observe an example of a particular political institution working at its best. For them the monarchical dynasty founded so gloriously by David had deep and permanent religious significance. Men remembered with awe the covenant Yahweh had made with David of a perpetual royal line, and the evident signs that God was indeed his covenant partner. The tradition of election recorded in 2 Sam. 7 and commemorated in Ps. 89 became the lodestar of Hebrew hopes for evermore:

> *"Once for all I have sworn by my holiness,*
> *I shall not lie to David:*
> *his dynasty will endure for ever,*
> *his throne as long as the sun before me."* (Ps. 89:35f.[36f.])

In these days of royal weakness Yahweh reaffirms through Micah that his will is not to sweep aside a worn-out, dying institution. It will flourish again in all its pristine beauty. The sacred promise of old will come true in a new demonstration of divine blessing.

The prophet proceeds to apply God's message to the people in their present weakness. He spells out the significance of the divine oracle.[30] God has slackened the reins of Israel's foes, but his abandonment of Israel[31] can be only a temporary phenomenon, for in the promise of a king corresponding to the Davidic ideal is included national blessing. Fortunes of king and people are closely intertwined, for is he not to be *sovereign*

---

ascribed to a period later than Amos, but its authenticity has been defended in more recent study. Accordingly even in the eighth century B.C. the period of David was regarded as antiquity. A longer form of *miqqeḏem,* which is rendered in KJV, RV, "from everlasting," is translated "from days of old" in 7:20. Keil and older commentators interpreted in terms of the past eternity of Christ. Similarly Weiser, following Bentzen and Mowinckel, finds here reference to a mythological primeval man ("Urmensch").

30. Heb. *lāḵēn,* "therefore," is here used in association with a promise of salvation to indicate transition not from present situation to future promise, as in Jer. 35:19, but from divine promise to prophetic application: note the change from first person to third in referring to Yahweh, as in v. 4(3). Verse 3(2) has been viewed by many as a later addition, partly because exposition of an earlier prophetic promise is regarded as a postexilic phenomenon and partly because v. 4(3) is a natural continuation of v. 2(1). But Micah is echoing and endorsing popular expectation, admittedly based on prophetic promise, rather than directly citing Isa. 7. Verse 3(2) relates the promise of v. 2 to the catastrophe of v. 1 and expounds the significance of the promise for *Israel* of vv. 1f.: *Israel* occurs again at the end of v. 3, locking together vv. 1–3. The reference to birth may be bringing out an implication of *yētsē',* "will come forth," which can connote childbirth (cf. Renaud, *op. cit.,* p. 52). The change of subject to Yahweh in v. 3 accords with the overall focus on the purposes and power of God in vv. 2–4: it is grammatically but not logically abrupt. The theme of the people in v. 3 is continued in v. 4b. Throughout the passage king and people are the prophet's common concern. It has sometimes been claimed that v. 3 is written in prose, but it may easily be taken as two lines of 3+2 with *BHS*. Sellin, Weiser, von Ungern-Sternberg, Willis, and Vuilleumier are among those who maintain the integrity of the verse.

31. *Israel* is the antecedent of *them*; cf. 3:2.

over Israel? The king's coming will be the signal for the nation to be freed from their enemies. All their hopes hang on the birth of the royal prince. The brief reference to the confinement of the woman *with child,* obviously the mother of the promised king,[32] evidently alludes to a popular expectation too well known to require amplification. This expectation is doubtless to be related to Isaiah's mysterious promise of Immanuel's birth (Isa. 7:14) pronounced over thirty years earlier.[33]

The problem confronting the people of God is not only the presence of their enemies. It is also the absence of so many of their fellows. Enemy occupation of Judah and the siege of Jerusalem were but the culmination of a process of shrinking which had begun two centuries before in the breakaway of the northern tribes from Davidic rule to form a separate state,[34] and had continued in the deportation of the people of the Northern Kingdom some twenty years earlier. Judeans in an occupied country and a besieged city were now the only representatives of that federation of tribes which had been proud bearers of the covenant. In war-torn Judah lay the sole vestiges of sacred nationhood, "the sons of Israel."[35] How could the nation be complete without their separated and exiled brothers—brothers, indeed, of the promised king? Therein lies their promise of restoration and return. In the chosen brother resides hope for all the family, including the missing "remainder."[36] We may again see in *his brothers* a Davidic allusion: had not the northern tribes referred to David as their own flesh and blood?[37] In 4:8 the united kingdom of David and Solomon was likewise held up as an ideal to be reattained. Prophet after prophet in the OT reflects wistfully the popular craving for the reunion of the northern and southern tribes, to which the restoration of the former is seen as a necessary

32. Calvin, von Orelli, Wolfe, Marsh, and Renaud (*op. cit.*, pp. 71f.) interpret of Israel. Lescow, *loc. cit.*, pp. 199–204, takes proverbially as a reference to the end of crisis, but comparison with such passages as 4:9 is hardly relevant since they represent a stereotyped and easily recognizable motif which is absent here.

33. Cf. Heb. *yōleḏeṯ,* "about to give birth," there with *yôlēḏâ yālāḏâ* here. "The Immanuel prophecy is well known for its difficulties of interpretation, but most probably the prophet is here foretelling the birth of a royal heir through whom the promises to the Davidic dynasty would find fulfilment" (Clements, *Prophecy and Covenant* [1965], p. 51, n. 1, referring for support to Mowinckel, E. Hammershaimb, and C. R. North).

34. The sense of shock still felt in eighth-century Judah is interestingly reflected in Isa. 7:17.

35. The term is used of the people of Judah as heirs to the traditions of the tribal federation. It had been used cultically in Jerusalem before the political break-up under Rehoboam, and was retained during the period of the divided kingdom as a reference to the total community of the twelve tribes represented in the partial form of the Southern Kingdom. Since the downfall of the Northern Kingdom Judah's claim to the name had received new and tragic justification. Cf. Beyerlin, *KIPVM,* pp. 21–23.

36. Heb. *yeṯer* here means "that additional portion of a given entity not included in the portion referred to" (W. Harrelson in *Israel's Prophetic Heritage*. J. Muilenburg Festschrift [1962], p. 518). An allusion to Isa. 7:2 "Shearjashub," "a remnant will return," seen here by many since Wellhausen, is not likely. In Isaianic terms Judah would have been termed the remnant.

37. 2 Sam. 5:1. The Heb. idiom is "flesh and bone," as in Chinese.

prelude.[38] This cry for completeness is a noble hope which is most fitting here as a promise of the replenishing of the nation to its former glory as a sacred federation, *Israel* of old.

The royal brother, key to the destiny of brethren both present in Judah and absent in foreign parts, is to *be installed* as ruler of his people. There is probably an allusion in the first verb of v. 4, literally "stand," to the traditional coronation ceremony in which the royal prince stood beside a pillar in the temple to be anointed in God's presence and acclaimed as king by the people.[39] His role is to be that of a shepherd tending his flock. The figure is one that embodies an ideal of Israelite kingship.[40] Although it was a royal metaphor prevalent throughout the ancient Near East, in Israel it recalls Davidic tradition, for David was taken from his sheep to care for a greater flock, the people of God.[41] The coming king is once more portrayed in the dress of the founder of the dynasty. There is no contradiction with the concept of Yahweh as shepherd, of which 2:12 and 4:6–8 had spoken so eloquently, just as there is none between the kingship of Yahweh and human kingship as it is here presented. Ideally the human king rules theocratically as representative of the divine King and is responsible to him. Accordingly he is appointed as undershepherd of the flock, carrying out Yahweh's will concerning it, a task that calls for "upright heart" and "skillful hand."[42] This new shepherd will be faithful to his task, and will tend his charges well.

He will not be prey to human weakness, such as many a nominal heir of David had proved to be, for he will be endowed with "Yahweh's strength." There is a royal psalm, perhaps a coronation ode, which celebrates the divine enabling of the king by which alone his reign is a success.[43] The claims and aspirations of Judean kingship, belied so often in experience, are here promised true fulfilment. There will reign a king worthy of the throne of David, the secret of whose success the religious historian declared to be that "Yahweh was with him" (2 Sam. 5:10). He would rule not in his own might and right but in the power of Yahweh and with *majestic authority* derived from him. *Authority* is literally "name": just as God's name stood in 4:5 for authority accepted, so here it stands for authority delegated. Between Yahweh and the king was to be a close relationship so that the former was in a special sense *his God*. This relationship echoes that granted in the divine covenant with David and his successors; it is often celebrated in the books of Samuel and Kings.[44] It is

38. Cf. Hos. 1:10f. (2:1f.); 3:5; Isa. 11:12f.; Jer. 30:10f.; 31:2–6, 15–20; Ezek. 37.
39. 2 K. 11:14; cf. 23:3. Schwantes refers to the use of the verb in Dan. 8:23; 11:2f.
40. Cf. H. Gottlieb, *VT* 17 (1967), pp. 190–200.
41. 2 Sam. 7:7f.; Ps. 78:70–72; cf. 2 Sam. 5:2.
42. Ps. 78:72; cf. Ezek. 34:12, 23f.
43. Ps. 21:1, 5; cf. 1 Sam. 2:10.
44. E.g., 1 Sam. 30:6; 1 K. 5:17; 15:4 (of David); 1 K. 11:4 (of Solomon); 2 K. 16:2 (of Ahaz).

stressed again that here was to be manifested an heir to the Davidic covenant. Micah gathered up all the nostalgia that in people's minds lingered around the throne and bade them look not back but forward to a mighty fulfilment of the best and greatest of their wistful dreams.

In the God-given power of this coming king is grounded the security of his people: once more the solidarity of king and people comes to the fore. It is probably not insignificant that the traditional form of Nathan's oracle to David promises Israel that, as a consequence of his rule, God "will plant them and they will remain where they are, never to be disturbed again."[45] This ideal, sadly frustrated up to now, would be realized in the powerful reign of the coming one, whose renown was to spread throughout the world. Indeed the usage of the phrase "the ends of the earth" in the Judean royal ideology implies a universal empire. A motif of ancient Near Eastern royal claims, it is employed in the royal psalms to indicate high hopes for the Davidic king.[46] The aspirations of court poet and prophet for each new king would at last find fulfilment. Their rhetorical cravings are used as a model for future realization in David's coming son.

5, 6 The last section of the oracle has a strangely composite ring. Conquest of Assyria is promised paradoxically through different agencies: the king on the one hand and generals appointed by the people on the other. Obviously the section consists of an integral core supplemented at beginning and end with expressions of royal victory. In origin it is evidently a national war-song, yet not a song of victory but one expressing confident hope of victory such as has fired every generation at war. Like other Hebrew popular war-songs it is marked by a rhyming jingle of first person plural pronouns.[47] With nationalistic fervor the claim is made that *if* the enemy sets *foot on* Judean *territory,* he will find himself driven back by so vigorous a counterattack that his own country will be invaded. Judah will have no lack of leaders[48] (Judean or from an anti-Assyrian coalition of western states?) to shepherd a flock of troops into pastures new and green—Assyria, where *the sword* will cut a cruel *crop* of swathes. We can imagine the rousing shouts and cheers: "Let them dare attack us—we'll show 'em." Particularly fitting in its context is the term *mansions*. These were the tall, grand buildings of the wealthy. Often fortified, they stood out from older structures and symbolized the affluence and self-sufficiency of urban culture like the skyscrapers that have mushroomed in every modern city. In the Northern Kingdom half a century before, Amos had declared Yahweh's loathing of Jacob's nationalistic pride and their mansions, its

45. 2 Sam. 7:10. Cf. Beyerlin, *KIPVM,* p. 84.
46. Ps. 2:8; 71:8 (Beyerlin, *KIPVM,* p. 83).
47. Judg. 16:23f.; Jer. 21:13.
48. The numerical gradation 7/8, a literary device to suggest multiplicity, is found besides in Ugaritic literature, a Phoenician inscription, and Eccl. 11:2 (Cathcart, *loc. cit.,* p. 512).

visible expression (Amos 6:8). The term has jingoistic tones exactly in keeping with the original setting.[49]

Bawled out with conviction at first, then in order to bolster sinking hopes, the song must have died away as the war news worsened, never to be heard again until Micah ironically revived it. To the chagrin of his audience he chanted the familiar words in a new setting. He took up this enthusiastic expression of Judean confidence, and skillfully wove it into his oracle of the coming king in order to direct his hearers to a sounder source of confidence. It was not their own armaments nor wealth of military leadership that would win the war. Instead the person raised up by God would be the agent of victory and peace. Micah makes this clear by his adaptation of the song, inserting at key points *This is the one who will bring peace*[50] and *He will save,* and so pointing back to the subject of the preceding promises. His first insertion refers to a familiar element in Zion's royal ideology preserved in Ps. 72, which includes prayers for peace during the king's reign.[51] One is reminded of the title "prince of peace" in Isaiah's great counterpart to this present oracle (Isa. 9:5). The theme of victory over foreign foes has a constant place in royal psalms.[52] It is implied here that the generals would be subordinate to God's man: their "shepherding," v. 6, corresponds to his own in v. 4 as merely the outworking of royal policy. Micah's additions stress that not they but he would be the key to victory, the focus being shifted to him. The enthusiasm of the discarded patriotic song sounds out again, but it is directed into a new channel by being linked with the royal representative of God. Popular fervor is harnessed to the cause of the savior-king.

National and royal humiliation proved to be the matrix of promises of royal and national exaltation. From darkest depths shoots a star of hope to its radiant zenith: God has reserved his best for release on the grimmest

49. It is often suggested that *bᵉ'aḏᵉmāṯēnû,* "in our land," should be read with G S for MT *bᵉ'armᵉnōtênû* in order to secure parallelism, internally with "in our country" and externally with "in our territory" in the refrain of v. 6. Such exact parallelism is not required, and the change bears the hallmark of an easier and so inferior reading. Evidently the Gk. translator of the Minor Prophets did not know what the Heb. word meant: he rendered *chōra,* "land," here and in Amos 3:9–11; 6:8, construing the Heb. as a similar-looking word. *BHS* and NEB ("castles") wisely keep MT. Cathcart, *loc. cit.,* p. 513, takes the previous *'artsēnû* as "our city" and *gᵉḇûlēnû* as "our city boundary" (cf. Num. 35:27; Ps. 147:14), seeing a reference to Jerusalem rather than to Judah; but the contrast with the country of Assyria does not favor this interpretation.

50. Lit. "be peace," a typically Heb. predicative use of a noun (cf. GK 141c): so, e.g., Duhm, J. M. P. Smith, Thomas, Willis (*VT* 18 [1968], p. 544). Note should be taken of a rendering "and he will be the one of peace" (J. M. Allegro, *VT* 5 [1955], p. 311; Beyerlin, *KIPVM,* pp. 79, 84; Cathcart, *loc. cit.,* pp. 511f.; Dahood, *Pss 3,* p. 44) by comparison with the titles *zeh sînay,* "the One of Sinai," in Judg. 5:5 (cf. the similar usage of cognate elements in Akkadian, Ugaritic, and Arabic) and "prince of peace" in Isa. 9:5.

51. Verses 3, 7 (Beyerlin, *KIPVM,* p. 84). Verse 12 uses *hitstsîl,* "save," of deliverance from oppression in the state.

52. E.g., Ps. 45:5(6); 72:9; 89:23(24); cf. 2 Sam. 7:9, 11.

day. It is a promise that takes up ancient themes dear to Israel's heart. The prophet is herald to a king who will be a true son of David, heir to the Davidic covenant in a way no previous successor to David's throne had been. Through him will be accomplished the purposes of God as a man after God's own heart. The looked-for king is also characterized as the fulfilment of post-Davidic royal hopes in Judah. The royal psalms preserved and extended the Davidic traditions. They celebrated in the extravagant language of the Orient the coronation and subsequent career of each new king. These pious hopes are shown to fit like a glove the fortunes of the coming ruler. No longer will there occur that disappointing hiatus between royal aspiration and royal achievement.[53] Here at last will be one who lives up to the ideals of the royal manifesto. The logical conclusion of the king's being the nominal vicegerent of Yahweh will be realized. He will reflect the universal power of Yahweh in the effectiveness of his rule and in the extent of his realm.

It is evident that Micah placed the fulfilment of these promises in an eighth-century B.C. setting of threat of Assyrian invasion. The coming of this royal hero is presented as the eventual antidote to the threat and fact of Assyrian invasion. Eventual, because his birth lies still in the future and so his saving activity is to be later still. There will be no immediate end to Assyrian domination.[54] The attacking imperialist will be allowed his fling for a time, but is doomed to meet his match in the person of the victorious king of Israel. In this respect Micah agrees with his greater contemporary Isaiah, who also depicted this promised king as the answer to the menace of Assyria. There are other links in their representations: in both cases he is portrayed as heir of the Davidic covenant, as one whose birth is to be the signal for God's special intervention, and as the embodiment of divine might and authority.[55]

Particularly prominent in Micah's delineation is the theme that the people of God will attain their true destiny with the coming of the expected king. This theme is akin to that of the sacred historian who related that "David realized that Yahweh . . . had made his reign so outstanding for the sake of his people Israel" (2 Sam. 5:12). Indeed it is a general motif of Israelite kingship that people and king are bound together in solidarity. So it is by no means unexpected that a promise of restoration and unification plays a part in this royal oracle. The folk of the north were to come home, not to their old separated existence but to share in the common life of their

53. "It can be said of the history of the kingdom in Israel that it was a history of failure" (C. Westermann, *The OT and Jesus Christ* [E.T 1968], p. 49).

54. Cf. Jeremiah's emphasis that the exile would not end quickly.

55. Cf. Isa. 7:14–17; 9:2–7(1–6); 11:1–5. Isaiah goes further than Micah in a number of respects, notably in his development of the theocratic relationship of the king to Yahweh to the point of a mirror-image reflection of divine kingship in the human counterpart (Isa. 9:6[5]).

fellow heirs of the old national traditions. In the empire won by the new ruler they were all to find their security and guarantee of continuity.

It is not surprising that the NT takes up this royal promise and finds it fulfilled in the person of Jesus Christ. The loose citation in Matt. 2:6[56] and the allusion in John 7:42 reveal that in the first century A.D. the hope of Mic. 5:2 was cherished as part of Jewish messianic expectation, and Bethlehem was famed as the future Messiah's birthplace. Matthew gladly reproduces it as one of his proof-texts for the authenticity of Jesus as the true Messiah, eager to communicate his glory in terms accepted by his Jewish contemporaries. Paul apparently took over the messianic interpretation of the passage as part of his Jewish heritage, and he too saw its fulfilment in Christ, albeit in a more sophisticated way. In Eph. 2:14 he gives what must be regarded as a rendering of v. 5a: "he is our peace." He relates it to its context of vv. 3, 4, and blends the motifs of the unification and completion of the people of God on the one hand and the universal sway of the Messiah on the other. The apostle finds the achievement of Christ to be that Gentile and Jew are brought together in the commonwealth of Israel. The traditions of a united Israel and the hope of world dominion associated with the Davidic king come true in a new synthesis in Paul's theology of Christ and the Church.

The Christian claims to see his Lord as the goal of hopes clothed in the cruder garb of eighth-century B.C. Judean expectation. This claim is consonant with the witness of the NT, whose inspiration he accepts. But it is obvious that Micah himself would be rather surprised at the transmutation of the plain words of his period piece. What logical bridge can span the gulf of divine statement and divine intent? Religious truth can never be communicated in a vacuum. It must be given a firm place within the religious frame of reference held by its hearers, conforming to their own general beliefs and tailored to their mental attitudes. Otherwise it would be a meaningless conundrum. "The future is presented as an evolution from the historically existing":[57] it is grounded in the demands of the present situation and builds upon the current stage of development in the awareness God's people have of his will for the future. The hitching of the kingly star to the eighth century B.C. is a feature that belongs to many an OT hope. Is such prophetic foreshortening far different from the NT summons to its first-century A.D. readers to get ready for the Second Coming, and from Augustine's axiom that the last day is hidden that every day may be so regarded, with the intent that every generation in turn may be prepared for Christ's appearing? The revelation, repeated by a host of prophets, that the northern exiles were to return to one king and country was doomed to a literal nonfulfilment. But its underlying passion for completeness was to

56. For the textual relation of the quotation to Mic. 5:2 see K. Stendahl, *The School of St. Matthew* (1954), pp. 99–101; R. H. Gundry, *The Use of the OT in St. Matthew's Gospel*. SNT 18 (1967), pp. 91–93.

57. J. Orr, *The Problem of the OT* (1906), p. 461.

reach a higher goal in a unity of Jew and Gentile. Paul is heir to Micah in Rom. 11, where in similar vein he views a mainly Gentile Church as a lopsided thing and looks forward to the time when Jewish believers would be added in appropriately large numbers. Eventually the prophetic trappings fell away, their purpose served, when the reality appeared in the person of Christ, "great David's greater Son," the glory of whose reign and realm has yet to be revealed.[58]

It is via Mic. 5 that the royal road runs that leads to the concept of Christ as Shepherd of his people.[59] The linking of Mic. 5:2 in the Matthean citation with 2 Sam. 5:2 in the final part, "a leader who will shepherd my people Israel," merely adapts an expression of pastoral imagery which already exists in Mic. 5:4. Here is an important forward-looking manifestation of the royal complex of ideas upon which NT literature builds so much. It is "our Lord Jesus" who is "the great shepherd of the sheep," "the shepherd and guardian of our souls," "the chief shepherd" of the human flock served by its leaders as undershepherds, "their shepherd" who "will lead them to springs of living water"—a striking application of the divine imagery of Ps. 23:1, 2 and Isa. 49:10 to Christ—and above all "the good shepherd" who "lays down his life for the sheep," who must fetch "other sheep that are not of this [Jewish] fold."[60]

F. THE FUTURE ROLES OF THE REMNANT OF ISRAEL (5:7–9[6–8])

The remnant of Jacob,
surrounded by many peoples, 3+3
will become like dew sent from Yahweh
or heavy showers on grass, 3+3
which do not await man's bidding
nor tarry at men's behest. 3+4
8 *The remnant of Jacob among the nations,*
surrounded by many peoples, 4+3
will become like a lion among forest beasts
or a lion[61] *among a flock of sheep,* 3+3
which tramples as it prowls,
and mauls its helpless victims. 3+3
9 *Raise your hand high above your foes*
and let all your enemies be wiped out. 3+3

58. Cf. R. E. Murphy, "Notes on OT Messianism and Apologetics," *CBQ* 19(1957), pp. 5–15.
59. Cf. R. T. France, *Jesus and the OT* (1971), p. 208. The NT imagery most obviously joins the road at the point of Zech. 13:7, which is quoted in Mark 14:27.
60. Heb. 13:20; 1 Pet. 2:25; 5:4; Rev. 7:17; John 10:11, 16.
61. Hebrew has a number of words for "lion." Whether *k*ᵉ*p̱îr* here is a "young lion" or simply a synonym for the earlier term is uncertain; cf. L. Koehler, *ZDPV* 62 (1939), p. 121.

This piece is a pair of national promises, followed by an exhortation pertaining to the second. The most obvious thing about this oracle, which is spoken by the prophet throughout, is its fine symmetrical structure. Apart from the concluding exhortation there are two stanzas exquisitely matched. Each begins with a practically identical description of Israel's weakness, continues with a double simile, and closes with a development of the simile in a relative clause. Apart from the last line of the first stanza and the first of the second, the meter of this seven-line oracle is consistently 3+3. In the second stanza the external parallelism with the opening of the first has been varied stylistically by an extra word; this is a typical example of Hebrew "symmetriphobia," a word coined by G. A. Smith to describe the avoidance of carbon-copy monotony.[62] But the resultant 4+3 rhythm has been cleverly matched by a corresponding 3+4 line immediately before, which cements the two stanzas together in chiastic fashion.

If the stanzas are structurally symmetrical, they are all the more strikingly diverse in content. The antithetic nature of their parallelism is shown in the use of contrasting imagery: the gentle, refreshing *dew* and the savage, destructive *lion*. In paradoxical fashion the two different roles of the remnant are spelled out: to be channel of divine blessing and agent of divine judgment. The piece thus presents in miniature form the violent contrast evident throughout chs. 4 and 5, and belies the hasty presumption of necessarily separate origins for these ambivalent attitudes.[63] It is a message for difficult days, and embedded in the first lines of both stanzas and in the final exhortation are allusions to the weakness and trials of the community. It is reduced, and feels the heavy pressure of surrounding nations who threaten or attack. The prophet issues a call to faith in God's purposes for Israel and his ability to deliver.

As to the relation of the oracle to its present literary context, it stands alongside the central feature of chs. 3–5, namely 4:9–5:6. Labelled "remnant," it is obviously intended to match 4:6–8. The two passages are supporting buttresses flanking the central structure. There are several links joining it to other parts of this literary monument. The repeated *many peoples* is a catch-phrase that takes up the wording of 4:3, 13 and brings together the different themes of their contexts into a single unit. *Your enemies* in v. 9 echoes the expression in 4:10. The helplessness of Israel's foes in v. 8 serves to reinforce the royal promise of Israel's deliverance in v. 6.[64] The brute force in this verse is reminiscent of that of 4:13, with change of animal from bull to lion.

62. *The Early Poetry of Israel in its Physical and Social Origins*. Schweich Lectures 1910 (1912), pp. 17f. G S and one Heb. ms. add "among the nations" in v. 7(6), exhibiting the consistency of small-minded copyists.

63. Cf. the fascinating study of this phenomenon in individual English poets by W. Empson, *Seven Types of Ambiguity* ([3]1961), ch. 7. It appears in Heb. wisdom literature (Prov. 17:27f.; 26:4f.); cf. von Rad, *OT Theology*, vol. 1 (E.T. 1962), p. 422.

64. Heb. *w*[e]*hitstsîl*, v. 6(5)—*matstsîl*, v. 8(7).

7 The plight of the nation is portrayed sympathetically as the prelude to a promise of better things to come. The community, here labelled *Jacob* as frequently in the book, is drastically reduced in numbers and feels cramped and confined by the presence of surrounding nations. The harsh reality of the present situation of bombardment is tempered by a reminder of Israel's role of blessing, which, one day, there will be a renewed opportunity to exercise. Men's heavy hearts must have been lightened by the very mention of the dew and rain falling on thirsty grass. The dew means more to the Palestinian than it does to those who live in areas where rainfall is spread more evenly over the year. Micah's geophysical environment was one where rain is almost totally lacking from June to September. In such an area the dews, which could be very heavy (cf. Judg. 6:38), were of great importance to vegetation. On clear nights the air laden with moisture from the Mediterranean was cooled by radiation, and the moisture condensed on the ground. In the delightfully direct thinking of Israel, dew was a literal godsend. While we, in the maze of processes by which God's gift reaches us, can lose sight of the Giver, they with minds uncluttered by scientific thinking ever regarded nature as the busy workshop of its Creator. In their predominantly agricultural economy they were especially alert to God's "bountiful care," which

sweetly distils
in the dew and the rain. (Robert Grant)

As in the hymn, mention of dew leads on to the spring *showers* needed for the development of the young cereal crops. The amplification of the similes in the relative clause of the next line expands the theme of the divine initiative behind the dew and rainfall. Man is singularly impotent over water supplies. He can store rainwater and tap underground springs, but his native helplessness before the cruel sun comes to the fore in times of prolonged drought. Ultimately man can neither help nor hinder the supply of so basic a commodity. Human lack of control made a deep impression on the prophet, who stresses man's dependence on God's providential mercies.

The first stanza comes to a close evidently with its point adequately made. But the modern reader is left at a loss as to the precise point Micah is making. Is he referring to the multiplicity of the raindrops and beads of dew, and promising that Israel, now so few, will become an innumerable host?[65] Such a promise would accord with OT expressions of Israelite fecundity like stars, dust, and sand. But the symmetry of the two stanzas suggests rather that the prophet's intention is to describe the *effect* of dew and rain, as later the effect of the lion on lesser beasts. What is the frame of reference of this type of simile in the OT? In Deut. 32:2 and Ps. 72:6 it is used in two quite different contexts, of religious instruction and of

65. E.g., von Orelli, Wade, Thomas, Willis. Cf. McKeating's view, with reference to 2 Sam. 17:12, of a "silent, irresistible and thorough" force.

royal government,[66] but in both cases it refers to good effects upon others. So is there here the thought of God's blessing of Israel, as many have held?[67] The advantage of this view is that it makes a logical complement for the next stanza: the nation is first increased and then it can turn its God-given might against hostile peoples. Its difficulty is that it, too, violates the deliberate symmetry of the piece. *Grass* is taken to be the antecedent of the relative clause; but in the next stanza it is the *lion* of the double simile which is the subject of the relative clause, and accordingly the *dew* and rain should be the subject here.[68] So the point appears to be the beneficent effect of Israel on the *nations,* bringing life and renewal.[69] This sacred obligation to be the channel of God's grace, although often obscured in the vicissitudes of the nation's history, is a basic ingredient of Israel's self-understanding. Its role as a mediator of divine blessing is not only stressed at the outset of the Abraham narratives but taken over by the ideology of Davidic kingship.[70]

8 This second of a set of rhetorical twins follows the pattern already laid down apart from the minor variation in the length of the first line. But now the role is far different. Gone is the gentle rain from heaven. Israel is metamorphosed into a raging *lion,* king of the forest and terror of the flock. The vehemence of the language is attributable to the present humiliation of God's people. By contrast of prospect with present, the truth is taught that the tables are to be turned and the victims of aggression are to become victors. The imagery of Israel as a lion is an ancient one,[71] which stands for irresistible conquest of all opposition. The prophet is recalling a traditional role associated with holy war. There is no mention of God in this stanza, but the prophet's theme is highly theological. The final phrase "and none will be able to deliver" is used frequently in connection with Yahweh's punishment of his enemies.[72] Here there is a shift of application to Israel as the earthly representative of the divine Victor. God's cause, with which Israel is identified, must triumph.

There is a contrast here not only between the present and the consolation of a far different future, but much more obviously between the twin roles of Israel. It exposes with the intensity of a check pattern the fundamental contradiction between the traditional ideals of Israel. The prophet boldly embraces both of them as crucial for the nation's destiny. By this association of opposites he gathers up the heritage of past thinking concerning the significance of the people of God for the life and death of

66. In Prov. 19:12 the similes of both lion and dew are interestingly applied to the king.
67. E.g., Calvin, J. M. P. Smith, Lindblom, Snaith, George.
68. Renaud, *op. cit.,* p. 16.
69. Keil, Horton, Robinson, Weiser, Renaud, Vuilleumier; also Wolfe and Marsh, who, however, separate vv. 8f.(7f.) from v. 7(6), ascribing them to different origins.
70. Gen. 12:3; Ps. 72:17.
71. Cf. Num. 23:24; 24:9. In Gen. 49:9 the tribe of Judah is so depicted.
72. Deut. 32:39; Job 10:7; Ps. 50:22; Hos. 5:14.

the world. He flings this ideological package at his hearers to ponder and so to enrich their understanding.

9 The supplement to the piece does a little to resolve the preceding tension. It takes up the second of Israel's roles in an exhortation to aggression.[73] Their hands hang limp, according to a Hebrew metaphor for ineffectiveness and lack of morale,[74] but they are stirred to courageous activity. Following on from the solemn pronouncement of Israel's victory, the exhortation is invested with a note of confident certainty reminiscent of 4:13. Israel is not to rest idle in the promise of triumph but to engage in the struggle, cooperating with God to make his promise come true. The nation's more immediate task is to ward off their enemies before they can commence the more positive work that is theirs. First a war must be won before the role that belongs to peace can be played. Judgment of the oppressors and vindication of the oppressed must come before the peaceable fruit of salvation can be borne. The paradox thus appears to be given a chronological resolution of immediate and subsequent relevance.

The Christian has received the paradox in turn as part of his OT heritage given with Christ, but for him the element of contradiction has been removed by transference of the second motif to a spiritual realm. This is illustrated strikingly by Paul's reference to "readiness for the gospel of peace" as the boots the soldier of Christ must wear (Eph. 6:15). The divine plan for the Church is at once to fight the forces of evil and also to offer to men who are God's enemies the benefits of life and salvation. God's purpose is our imperative. To a twentieth-century Church that often feels powerless in a pagan environment, a dwindling minority attacked by hostile forces on every hand, is given this prophetic word of encouragement and stimulus.

G. GOD'S PUNISHMENT AND DELIVERANCE OF ISRAEL (5:10–15[9–14])

That will be the time,
runs Yahweh's oracle, 3+2
when I wipe out your horses from your society
and destroy your chariots. 3+2
11 *I shall wipe out the cities of your country*
and overthrow all your fortresses. 3+2

73. As J. M. P. Smith observed, biblical usage of lifting one's hand suits either a prayer or an exhortation. It is less likely that this is a prayer. God has not been mentioned in v. 8(7). Moreover "your enemies" in the sense of Israel's enemies echoes the phrase in 4:10, which suggests that the editor at least took it in the same way, an interpretation there is little reason to doubt.
74. Cf. Job 4:3f.; Isa. 35:3f.; Heb. 12:12.

12 *I shall wipe out the magical apparatus you hold in your hands,*
and you will lose your sorcerers. 3+2
13 *I shall wipe out your images*
and your sacred pillars from your society. 2+2
No longer will you bow down
to what your hands have made. 3+2
14 *I shall root out from your society your Asherim*
and destroy your idols. 3+2
15 *Then shall I wreak vengeance in anger and fury*
upon the nations who refused to obey. 4+4

Most of this oracle, vv. 10–14, is an implicit indictment of God's people. They have pinned their faith to various secular and religious substitutes for God, which must be destroyed; and destroyed they would be. In the name of Yahweh the prophet announces to the nation God's intention to intervene and strike away these artificial supports. Alongside this announcement of punishment is placed in v. 15 a short statement of God's future destruction of the foreign nations, which represents an implicit promise of divine deliverance.[75] The eight-line oracle, which is spoken by Yahweh throughout with an almost unbroken series of first singular verbs, thus falls into two unequal parts of six lines and one, after an introductory line. The division is marked by a change in rhythm: vv. 10–14 are almost completely in 3+2 meter, while v. 15 changes to a solemn 4+4. A striking feature of the first and longer part is its use of repetition and rhyme. Four consecutive lines begin with the same word *wᵉhiḵrattî,* (and) *I shall wipe out*. The first line of the oracle proper, v. 10b, and the last one of the announcement of punishment, v. 14, match with their repetition of "from your midst."[76] The conclusion of every half-line save one is made to rhyme with a second masculine singular pronoun. Yahweh's destructive enounter with his people is stressed throughout. Military and religious objects of faith are to be struck from Israel's grasp. God's implied purpose is that the people should be brought to faith in him alone. Then, and then only, will they be given the victory they crave, which they have sought by improper means.[77]

What part does the piece play in the overall structure of chs. 3–5? Just as 5:7–9 was designed to match 4:6–8, so the architectural function of this final oracle is to serve as a counterpart to the first unit, 3:1–4:5. Both are marked by the sequence of a long denunciation and a short word of promise, although this last piece is constructed on a smaller scale. Both in their long initial passages of condemnation expose sins of the community or its leaders before turning to statements concerning the nations which

75. Willis, *ZAW* 81(1969), p. 356, notes the parallelism in structure and thought to 4:9f.: Yahweh will "remove these false objects of faith and will then give victory to Israel."
76. It also occurs at the end of the fourth line.
77. "The salvation of God could not otherwise come to them than by stripping them of all vain and false confidence" (Calvin).

imply or express hope for God's people or their capital. Both in their second and shorter parts hail Yahweh as Suzerain of the nations, who are obliged to accord him vassalage. The passage has been carefully selected to function not only as the artistic counterpart to the first unit of the second section of the book but also as a sequel to the foregoing oracle. Verse 10 is attached to v. 9 by a hook-and-eye device of repeating the verb *wipe out*. *Your hand(s)* in vv. 12f. strikingly repeats the phrase of v. 9, as if to warn that the hands of God's people must be emptied of all that smacks of help not derived from God if he is to give victory to their hands when they strike in battle.

10–14 Before the oracle proper is placed a preparatory line containing a temporal link looking to the future and a statement of the divine origin of the piece that follows, both features found also in 4:6 and discussed in earlier comments. The first two lines of the actual oracle are concerned with military security. Hezekiah had evidently built up a strong corps of light horse-drawn war chariots supplied by Egypt in anticipation of a rising against Assyria.[78] The presence of this foreign aid was obnoxious to both Isaiah and Micah. The former bluntly accused the government of failing to consult the Holy One of Israel. There is no evidence that Micah echoed Isaiah's isolationist policy, but their teaching does overlap. The war-song embedded in vv. 5f. probably preserves the mentality against which Micah is inveighing here. It is a truism that politics and religion went hand in hand in the ancient Near East, but Micah could see little true religious faith in the nationalistic and militaristic fervor that buoyed up Judean spirits and brightened their eyes. His implicit desire is to bring the nation to the maturity of the psalmist's affirmation:

> *Some talk confidently of chariots, some of horses,*
> *but we of the name of Yahweh our God.* (Ps. 20:7[8])

The prophet looks with disgust at the fortifications with which Judah bristled. He is thinking of the fortified *cities*,[79] cities surrounded by strong walls and gates which would present a stubborn obstacle to an enemy invader. But what if the enemy were Yahweh? Isaiah had seen a day coming when Yahweh would intervene in judgment "against every high tower and against every fortified wall" (Isa. 2:15). The time was destined to come when Assyria, the rod of God's anger (Isa. 10:5), would boast of the capture of forty-six walled cities. God could cut off at a stroke Judah's military build-up, and the year 701 B.C. was to see a tragic fulfilment of Micah's words.

But armaments and fortifications were not the only ways along which the people went wandering from their God. There is ever a temptation for man to veer from true religion to the occult. A certain area

78. 2 K. 18:24; Isa. 31:1.
79. *Cities . . . fortresses* is simply a stylistic device of Heb. poetry to secure parallel terms; prose would use a compound term "fortified cities," which is the standard OT phrase (E. Z. Melamed, *Scripta Hierosolymitana* 7 [1961], p. 135).

of the supernatural had early been marked off as forbidden territory for God's people. Both the Book of the Covenant and the Holiness Code make it plain that witchcraft and sorcery are not included in the divine will for Israel.[80] That such practices were prevalent in eighth-century B.C. Judah is evidenced in Isa. 2:6, where Isaiah condemns them as a foreign import and no part of the tradition of faith in Yahweh. Here the paraphernalia of occultism and the presence of its practitioners are denounced as abhorrent to God. He will clear away these intrusions into the life of his people.

Equally sinister a phenomenon was the growing use of material representations of deity in the religion of Judah: "their country is filled with idols" (Isa. 2:8). Here again it was the prophets' task to call the people back to an earlier pattern. There is an extremely strong tradition which pervades the lawcodes to the effect that the worship of Yahweh was originally and essentially aniconic, so that the introduction of *images* was an incongruous perversion.[81] Israel's neighbors made full use of images in their religion, and there was constant pressure to conform to these norms in their religious environment. The high rating given to the prohibition of image-based religion in the structure of the Decalog reflects the great need to counteract the fascination of Canaanite forms of worship. Micah had already described the downfall of Samaria as retribution for sins which included idolatry: "her sculptured images" were to be "smashed" (1:7). He employs the same term here for Judah's icons, and doubtless the same ominous implication of enemy agents of Yahweh's destruction belongs to the verb.

Objection is also raised against *sacred pillars,* a technical term for stones set up on end in a sanctuary. The *matstsēḇâ* was a feature of Canaanite religion so closely associated with the male deity that it was venerated as a material representation. It was part of the standard equipment of the Canaanite "high place" or local sanctuary, which was often taken over or copied by the Israelites. According to 2 K. 18:4 the demolition of sacred pillars was included in Hezekiah's reformation. Evidently they had crept into the religion of Judah and were syncretistically regarded as representations of Yahweh. They are mentioned here as not unnatural concomitants of *images,* both grotesque objects of God's ire. Hezekiah heeded Micah's strictures. Just as 3:12 apparently impelled him to government reforms, so this oracle served as a stimulus to an iconoclastic religious overhaul.

The prophet now breaks the structure of the first part of the poem with a line that accordingly stands out in an even greater emphasis. With bitter irony he points disparagingly to the worship of objects that have

80. Exod. 22:18(17) uses the root *kšp* as here in v. 12a(11a); Lev. 19:26 uses the root *'nn,* as in v. 12b(11b). Cf. Beyerlin, *KIPVM,* p. 63.
81. Exod. 20:4, 23; 34:17; Lev. 19:4; 26:1; Deut. 27:15. Cf. Beyerlin, *ibid.*

issued from a source no higher than their worshippers. Isaiah described his contemporaries similarly:

> *They bow down to the work of their hands,*
> *to things their fingers have made.* (Isa. 2:8)

Hosea had shown similar amazement at the paradox of the veneration of man-made images (Hos. 8:5), which "reduced the transcendent majesty of God to measurable certainty and manageable size."[82] God was contracted to a span, incomprehensibly man-made! Such a notion is repudiated as a perilous corruption of true deity. Isaiah observed how irreconcilable with true faith in Yahweh was such syncretism, in his description of a future transformation:

> *On that day men will look to their Maker, and their eyes will focus upon the Holy One of Israel. They will not look to . . . what their fingers have made, Asherim or incense-altars.* (Isa. 17:7f.)[83]

Finally in this religious indictment, sentence is passed on other cultic objects which misrepresented Yahwism and dragged it down to the level of pagan religions. The *Asherim* were symbols of the mother-goddess Asherah, the wife of El, who was head of the Canaanite pantheon. Over a century earlier Elijah had eradicated her cult in the Northern Kingdom along with that of the Tyrian Baal, both propagated with missionary zeal by the Phoenician Jezebel, daughter of the priest-king of Tyre (1 K. 18:19). Driven out as a separate religion, the cult of Asherah crept back insidiously to become a syncretistic part of Israel's own religion and presumably to provide Yahweh with a consort on the pattern of Canaanite fertility religion. Whether her representation took the form of a sacred tree, real or stylized as a pole, or an image in more human likeness is not clear. But it was made of wood and fixed in the ground; hence the reference to rooting out or uprooting is appropriate.[84] Hezekiah chopped down an Asherah according to 2 K. 18:4, presumably one he found in the Jerusalem temple.

The last reference, here rendered *idols,* is a more general word. Its form is the same as that of *cities* in v. 11,[85] and it has sometimes been supposed that the whole line is a summary of the foregoing indictment of military resources and religious makeshifts. However, the use of a new and specific term in the first half of v. 14 suggests rather that the prophet is not summarizing but continuing the religious aspect of his indictment. Then the last noun is to be taken not as *cities,* which would be out of place at this point, but as a cultic term parallel to *Asherim*. Recourse is often had to

82. J. M. Ward, *Hosea: A Theological Commentary* (1966), p. 147.
83. S. Erlandsson, *The Burden of Babylon: A Study of Isaiah 13:2–14:23*. Coniectanea biblica, OT series 4 (1970), p. 74, has presented a reasonable case for the authenticity of this passage.
84. Cf. Exod. 34:13; Deut. 16:21.
85. Heb. *'ārê,* v. 11(10)—*'āreyḵā,* v. 14(13).

emendation,[86] but it is probable that the Hebrew language possessed a homonym of its word for "city" with a meaning like "idol."[87]

15 When Yahweh has cleared away these barriers to communion between himself and his people, he promises to deal with the hostile *nations*. Judah had built up their own means of security: military equipment and installations, use of the occult to gain magical power for themselves, and a religious fervor doubtless governed by the theory as well as the practice of Canaanite religion, to attract divine might to their side. This whole approach is condemned as out of harmony with the nature of Yahweh and his covenant relationship with Israel. Micah proceeds to use language associated with the concept of holy war. His underlying demand in the earlier section has been for genuine faith in God alone, a firm part of the holy war traditions. Isaiah, who revived from this ancient source a stress upon faith,[88] dramatically reversed the doctrine of a warrior God and turned it against the people of Yahweh:

> *"Ah, I shall relieve my emotions on my enemies. . . .*
> *I shall turn my hand against you."* (Isa. 1:24f.)

This attack was to be the paradoxical prerequisite of ultimate victory wrought by God (Isa. 10:12; 29:1–8). Micah implies the same twofold manifestation of martial force. His various verbs of destruction recall ancient accounts of Israel's annihilation of their enemies with Yahweh at their head. God must first do a destructive work within Israel's borders. Only then can he turn to deal with Israel's foes. In describing the second stage of God's two-part plan for Israel, Micah can return to an orthodox use of the idea of holy war on the lines of Ps. 18:47f. (48f.):

> *The God who gave me vengeance*
> *and subdued peoples under me,*
> *who rescued me from my enemies. . . .*

It is a people who have first felt the burning heat of divine fury upon their own community and culture who are to witness its operation upon their enemies. Not to Israel as they are, but to an Israel cauterized of their faithlessness will God show himself as their strength and shield. He will act in *vengeance,* a legal term for the action of a royal suzerain against rebels who will not acknowledge his sovereignty.[89] *The nations* are described as

86. E.g., *BHS* suggests that either *'atsabbeyḵā* or *tsīreyḵā* be read. G S V T support MT.

87. T. H. Gaster, *JTS* 38 (1937), pp. 163f., refers to an Ugar. text where *ǵr* occurs in parallelism with *psl,* which is the first term in v. 13(12). G. R. Driver, *Canaanite Myths and Legends* (1956), p. 142, n. 26, renders the Ugar. term "blood-daubed stone" in light of an Arab. cognate word. Dahood, *Pss 1,* pp. 55f., renders the Heb. word "your gods," relating it to an Ugar. and Heb. root *'îr,* "protect." Cf. T "enemies," interpreting the Heb. as an Aram. homonym which occurs in Dan. 4:16 (cf. 1 Sam. 28:16; Ps. 139:20), doubtless judging a repetition of "cities" unsuitable.

88. Von Rad, *OT Theology,* vol. 2, pp. 159f.

89. Cf. G. E. Wright in *Israel's Prophetic Heritage* (1962), p. 31, n. 19, p. 57, with reference to Deut. 32:35, appealing to an unpublished work of G. E. Mendenhall. See now Mendenhall, *The Tenth Generation. The Origins of the Biblical Tradition* (1973), ch. 3.

hostile to God's will: they have "defied" him (Knox), they "would not obey" (JB).[90] As in the teaching of Amos and Isaiah, Yahweh is portrayed as the great Overlord of the nations with right of jurisdiction over his vassal states. Micah's reference to disobedience suggests a link with Isaiah's accusation that Assyria had gone beyond the limits of God's mandate.[91] Yahweh would vindicate his own people by punishing their wilful oppressors. His anger is that of "a guardian whose helpless wards have been maltreated."[92]

Paul made striking use of the complex of ideas expressed by this line in his delineation of the Last Judgment. Upon those who "do not obey the truth but obey wickedness" would come "anger and fury" (Rom. 2:8). "Vengeance" would be inflicted "upon those . . . who do not obey the gospel of our Lord Jesus" (2 Thess. 1:8). The context of the latter passage is especially close to the present one in that there God is "justly to recompense with affliction those who afflict you and with relief you who are being afflicted" (2 Thess. 1:6f.). Both are based on God's compassion for his oppressed people and the necessity inherent in his revealed nature for full justice to be done.

Micah issues a clarion call to Israel for true faith in their God, a faith that transcends nationalism and addiction to religion and to the metaphysical, a faith that is grounded in the revelation of God's character and will. His call comes echoing down the centuries to our own day. Wherein does our supposed security lie? In the safety of Mother Church? In a form of faith that is molded by expediency and compromise? In a God made in the image of twentieth-century man? The prophet bids us beware lest our vaunted faith be a cover for self-sufficiency or self-advancement. He challenges us to study the impact of secular and pagan culture, past or present, on our religious thinking and forms of worship, lest the essence of Christianity be obscured by its subsequent trappings.

> *It is as much idolatry to worship God according to a false mental image as by means of a false metal image. The mental image misrepresents God and has the same disastrous effects on character. If your conception of faith is radically false, then the more devout you are the worse it will be for you. You are opening your souls to be moulded by something base. You had much better be an atheist.*[93]

90. The interpretation of Calvin and KJV "such as they have not heard," taking *vengeance* as the antecedent, is followed by Moffatt ("unheard of punishment") and Wolfe. It is syntactically possible but contextually less apposite.
91. 2 K. 19:22–28; Isa. 10:6–11.
92. R. B. Y. Scott, *The Relevance of the Prophets* (^{2}1969), p. 119.
93. W. Temple, *Christian Faith and Life* (1931), p. 24.

III. GRACE TRIUMPHANT OVER SIN (6:1–7:20)

A. MESSAGES OF REPROOF AND LAMENT (6:1–7:7)

1. God's Case Against Israel (6:1–8)

Listen to what Yahweh is saying.[1]
"Stand up, present the case before[2] *the mountains,*
let the hills hear your voice." 3+3
2 *Mountains, hear Yahweh's case,*
you enduring ones, earth's foundations. 3+3
For Yahweh has a case to bring against his people,
a dispute to settle with Israel. 3+3
3 *"My people, what have I done to you?*
How have I made you tired of me? Give evidence against me.[3] 3+3
4 *Indeed it was I who brought you up from Egypt,*
I released you from your slave-quarters. 3+3
I sent to go before you Moses,
Aaron, and Miriam. 3+2
5 *My people, remember what plot was laid*
by King Balak of Moab 3+3
and what answer he received
from Beor's son Balaam. 3+2
From Shittim to Gilgal–
try to[4] *appreciate*
Yahweh's saving acts." 2+2+2

6 *"What should I bring into Yahweh's presence,*
when I bow low to God on high? 3+3
Should I bring burnt offerings into his presence
or yearling calves? 3+3
7 *Would Yahweh be pleased to get rams by the thousand*
or rivers of oil by the ten thousand? 4+3
Should I give my eldest son to atone for my rebellion,
my own child[5] *for my personal sin?"* 3+3
8 *Man, you have been told*[6] *what is good.*

1. G's longer text "the word of the Lord, the Lord said" probably represents an original paraphrase supplemented with a later literal revision.
2. Heb. *'ēṯ* must have this meaning in the context, though it would more naturally be rendered "with." Cf. Gen. 20:16; Isa. 30:8 for the present meaning.
3. As often, *'ānâ b^e* is forensic; it paves the way for vv. 6f. (J. Harvey, *Le plaidoyer prophétique contre Israël après la rupture de l'alliance* [1967], p. 43).
4. Lit. "in order to."
5. Lit. "the fruit of my body."
6. Heb. *higgîḏ*, lit. "he has told," either with Yahweh as subject (but the next clause implies that Yahweh is introduced there as a new subject) or indefinite "one has told" (Keil; A. Deissler, *TTZ* 68 [1959], p. 230). Perhaps the verb should be revocalized as passive *huggaḏ*, "it has been told," with G and Theodotion, yet this may be a natural paraphrase of an active indefinite. The reference is to the priestly transmission of the covenant stipulations.

What does Yahweh require of you 3+3
other than to practice justice,
love loyalty,
and walk carefully[7] *with your God?* 3+2+3

Whereas most messages of accusation in the prophetic literature culminate in an announcement of disaster, there are some that end by issuing a warning and providing an explicit opportunity for the miscreants to mend their ways. This is a notable example of the latter. It is composed of two formal elements. The first is an elaborate representation of a legal case "Yahweh *v.* Israel," in which God brings a grievance against his people. The second is molded on a cultic "entrance liturgy," an individual's inquiry as to the conditions of admittance to the sanctuary and an official answer. These quite diverse genres have been constructed into an impressive unity built around the theme of the divine covenant and its outworking in human society.[8] Viewed as a unit, it represents an adaptation of a traditional type of speech, the covenantal formulation, extant in miniature in Exod. 19:3–6 and in fuller form in Josh. 24 and 1 Sam. 12.[9] These covenantal formulations consist of two essential parts, a recital of Yahweh's saving deeds and a call to obedience. It is these two motifs that are here dressed in garb borrowed from the lawcourt and the sanctuary. The resultant composition bears close comparison in its structure with yet another distinctive speech-form, often called a covenant lawsuit, examples of which may be found in Deut. 32 and Ps. 50.[10] It falls

7. Heb. *hatsnēa'*. Cf. D. W. Thomas, "The Root צנע in Hebrew. . . ," *JJS* 1 (1949), pp. 182–88; J. P. Hyatt, *Anglican Theological Review* 34 (1952), pp. 232–39; H.-J. Stoebe, "Und demütig sein vor deinem Gott. Micha 6, 8," *Wort und Dienst* N.F. 6 (1959), pp. 180–194. The term refers in Prov. 11:2 to pride, but this appears to be a secondary meaning. There is impressive evidence that the root *ṣn'* had a more primary significance "be careful." Its basic meaning appears to be "guard, hold back," as in Aramaic, and it then developed to mean "be careful." This is clearly its meaning in Sir. 16:25; 31(34):22; 32(35):3; 42:8, and this is how G interprets in the first and third cases. Here Theodotion, Quinta, and V render "take care," and so does Symmachus in Prov. 11:2. The Heb. term evidently had its home in wisdom circles and is one of many instances of prophetic borrowing from this source. Stoebe defines the present phrase as "walking with God with full insight into what he has done for his people."

8. The use of different *Gattungen* in vv. 1–5 and 6–8 does not warrant a denial of unity, as urged by some, e.g., Robinson and T. Lescow, *Micha 6, 6–8: Studien zu Sprache, Form und Auslegung* (1966), pp. 46f.

9. Cf. Beyerlin, *KIPVM,* pp. 69f.; J. Muilenburg, "The Form and Structure of the Covenantal Formulations," *VT* 9(1959), pp. 347–365.

10. G. E. Wright, "The Lawsuit of God: A Form-Critical Study of Deuteronomy 32," *Israel's Prophetic Heritage.* J. Muilenburg Festschrift (1962), pp. 26–67, following Würthwein, claims that the cult contained a regular lawsuit conducted against covenant-breakers. H. B. Huffmon, "The Covenant Lawsuit in the Prophets," *JBL* 78 (1959), pp. 285–295; J. Harvey, "Le 'rîb-pattern', réquisitoire prophétique sur la rupture de l'alliance," *Biblica* 43 (1962), pp. 172–196; and J. Limburg, "The Root *Rîb* and the Prophetic Lawsuit Speeches," *JBL* 88 (1969), pp. 291–304, all find a pattern based on Near Eastern vassal treaties. Others, such as C. Westermann, *Basic Forms of Prophetic Speech* (E.T. 1967), p.

into five constituent parts:[11] (1) an introduction summoning heaven and earth as witnesses (cf. Deut. 32:1, 2; Ps. 50:1–6); (2) a basic statement of the case by Yahweh's counsel, including interrogation of the guilty party (Deut. 32:4–6; Ps. 50:16f.); (3) an accusation of Israel's ingratitude, including a recital of the benefits they have received from Yahweh (Deut. 32:7–15; Ps. 50:7–13, 18–21); (4) rejection of recourse to sacrifice to Yahweh or other gods (Deut. 32:16–18; Ps. 50:8–13); (5) either a verdict of punishment (Deut. 32:19–25) or a caution urging a change of conduct (Ps. 50:14f., 22f.). The first four parts obviously correspond to vv. 1f., 3, 4f., 6f. of this passage. Verse 8, representing the last part, parallels Ps. 50 rather than Deut. 32.

The piece consists of fifteen lines of verse prefaced by an introductory prose statement. Metrically there is a preponderance of the 3+3 rhythm, ten lines being so formed. Many have succumbed to the temptation of using this major meter as a means of bringing the rest into conformity, but the conjectural results[12] reflect little more than an exercise in versification. The poem falls into three sections. In the first the prophet states Yahweh's case against Israel (vv. 1b–5); in the second the defendant poses self-justifying questions (vv. 6, 7); while in the third the prophet answers, elaborating Yahweh's requirements of his covenant people (v. 8). The passage is held together as a unit not only by the overall covenant theme but also by the interlocking effects of repeated or complementary terms and ideas. The interrogative pronouns *mah-*. . . *ûmâ,* literally "what . . . and what?" occur twice in the first section (vv. 3, 5) and once in the third (v. 8), and correspond to the series of questions throughout the second section, the first of which uses *mâ*. The catalog of benefits in the first stanza is answered by a catalog of suggested sacrifices in the second. The verb of doing in v. 3 with Yahweh as subject as one who, it is implied, has done only good, matches the same verb in the infinitive in v. 8, in a summons to Israel to do good. The repeated *my people* in the first section (vv. 3, 5) corresponds to the repeated *Yahweh* in the second (vv. 6, 7), while the prophet's repetition of the divine name early in the oracle (v. 2) finds a parallel in his mention of *Yahweh* and *your God* at the end (v. 8).

1–5 The piece opens with the prophet's appeal to the people to hear Yahweh's revelation to them. He repeats the personal divine order to act as counsel for Yahweh and to initiate legal proceedings.[13] Who the

---

89, following Wolff, and F. C. Fensham, *ZAW* 74(1962), p. 8, are probably correct in considering the prophetic form to have been derived from the civil processes of Israelite law: cf. Clements, *Prophecy and Covenant* (1965), pp. 78f. Other examples of this speech-form in the prophets are Isa. 1:2–20; Jer. 2:5–37, but these are rather literary creations out of separate, shorter oracles.

11. Cf. Wright, *loc. cit.*, p. 53; Harvey, *op. cit.*, p. 44.

12. Cf. Lindblom and the proposals listed in the critical apparatus of *BHS*.

13. The initial prose statement may be an editorial addition partly to provide a catchword linking this section of the book with the preceding one (Heb. *shāmēʿû,* "they heard"—*shimeʿû,* "hear").

defendants are to be is intriguingly concealed from Micah's hearers. A rhetorical impression of grandeur is created by the mention of his first task. It is to call witnesses, none less than the majestic *mountains* and *hills*.[14] They are to be summoned to concur in the divine judgment, with their knowledge of generations of men's misdeeds upon which they have gazed as silent observers since time immemorial. Impressiveness is increased as Micah piles up terms to describe the might and dignity of the inanimate witnesses. They are *mountains,* "established ones,"[15] *earth's foundations*.[16] Calling such important witnesses stresses the seriousness of the case and its epoch-making quality. Who can be the guilty party at so awesome a court hearing? Micah finally satisfies the deliberately aroused curiosity of his audience with the shocking news that the one to stand trial is Yahweh's *people, Israel,* the Southern Kingdom by its covenant name. One partner is to confront the other, with the charge of breach of contract.

With passionate directness Yahweh speaks through the prophet in the first person. His opening word is one of pleading, loaded with pathos: *my people*. Pusey was right: "This one tender word contains a whole volume of reproof." God satirically claims to search his own heart and actions. Can it be his own fault that they have cooled in their affections toward him? He is quite ready to hear *evidence against* himself, if such can be procured. Is there something he has done to drive Israel from him, to encourage apathy and neglect? Has he let them down, or somehow failed to do his part? The questions are broached only to prompt obvious negative replies in the minds of all who hear. Clearly the only disappointment has been on Yahweh's side; Israel has no excuse. The words of defense have the force of an implicit accusation. In the terms of Isaiah's parable:

> *What else could I have done for my vineyard*
> *that I did not do in it?* (Isa. 5:4)

The evidence is all in support of Yahweh, and he proceeds to set it out. The history of Israel is a history of covenant grace. The benefits that form the first half of the covenant formulations are recited afresh, not now simply as inducements to Israel to yield the willing obedience that springs from a

14. The appeal to *mountains* and *hills* may preserve an ancient ingredient of traditional covenant phraseology going back to pre-Israelite usage. The old Hittite vassal treaties invoke deified mountains and other natural elements as witnesses. Cf. the appeals to heaven and earth in Deut. 32:1; Ps. 50:4.

15. Many have followed Wellhausen in emending to *w^{e}ha'^{a}zînû,* "and hearken" (e.g., *BHS*), as a synonymous parallel to the first verb in the line. It is extremely difficult to understand how such a straightforward term could ever have been corrupted into MT's striking reading. This difficulty has inspired conjectural emendations closer to the consonantal text. G. R. Driver proposed an Aramaism *w^{e}hiṯ'amm^{e}nû,* "and pay firm attention" (*JTS* 41[1940], p. 172), while Dahood has suggested *w^{e}hē'āṯûnîm,* "and come before me," a Niphal (not otherwise found) with a dative suffix and an enclitic *mem* (*Pss* 2, p. 127). MT is quite explicable: for the syntax Isa. 23:12 provides a perfect parallel and for the meaning Job 12:19 a close approximation.

16. Apparently another term for mountains, viewing them as having deep roots which serve to support the earth (cf. Jon. 2:6[7]).

grateful heart, but as goads to stir a sluggish conscience to a sense of sin. God's basic act of grace on behalf of his covenant people was the Exodus, which in the OT was an event invested with much of the significance that the Cross and Resurrection bear in the NT. To it many a psalmist and prophet look back as proof and pledge of God's election love and saving power. It was the fountainhead of covenant grace, which took theological as well as chronological pride of place in the recital of the events of salvation history celebrated by Israel in their regular worship. This particular way of referring to the Exodus stresses that it was the first of a chain of blessings. God did not only bring Israel out but *up*: the implication is that it was a prelude to bringing them safe and sound to the promised land.[17] It was the first gift carrying with it a promise of other gifts to come. A brushstroke evincing Micah's artistry can be glimpsed in a soundplay that binds the beginning of the recital of benefits to the previous entreaty: *hel'ēṯîḵā, I made you tired,* and *he'ᵉlīṯîḵā, I brought you up*. Sensitive to the subtle power of sound upon his Judean audience, the prophet contrasts supposition with substance, wild theory with sober fact, as if to say, "I have not let you down—on the contrary, I brought you up."

A significant and recurring feature of such credal formulations as this is the close link between the past history of the nation and the present generation. *I . . . brought you up from Egypt:* this was no ancient history in the disparaging sense of bygone irrelevance. The chronological chasm between the remote past and the time then present was bridged by a community whose cultural heritage was continually kept alive. Each succeeding generation of worshippers received it, treasured it, and passed it on. Those of God's people living at any one time were but representatives of a larger entity. So dynamic was their sense of sharing in the community of their forebears, dead and gone for hundreds of years, that it could be said that they had a share in the Exodus event. Every generation could say in turn, "We were there when Yahweh brought Israel out of Egypt." It is this awareness of involvement that is exploited here. Focal point of every worshipper, the Exodus symbolizes not only the covenant love of God but also his claim upon the covenant loyalty of his people. His liberation of Israelite slaves from Egyptian servitude[18] was intended to create a permanent bond of allegiance between him and their descendants.

17. Cf. J. Wijngaards, "הוציא and העלה, a Twofold Approach to the Exodus," *VT* 15(1965), pp. 98–101.

18. Heb. *pᵉḏîṯîḵā,* lit. "I ransomed you," has here the general sense of release with no thought of payment to the Egyptians. L. Morris, *The Apostolic Preaching of the Cross* (1955), pp. 16f., deduces an implication of the cost to God from the effort and display of power involved in the use of this verb in many OT passages. The second clause in v. 4 uses terminology closely associated with Deut. (e.g., 7:8; 13:5). If that book represents traditions treasured in the north and only made public in Judah in Josiah's reign, its use by Micah a century or so before constitutes a problem. Beyerlin, *KIPVM,* pp. 67f., finds here language of the eighth-century cult which was taken over into Deuteronomy. N. Lohfink, *Das Hauptgebot.*

My chains fell off, my heart was free.
I rose, went forth and followed thee.
(Charles Wesley)

The covenant formulations insisted on this relationship between divine initiative and Israelite response; this prophetic lawsuit refashions their challenge into an accusation of disloyalty.

God's grace shone not only in the personal deliverance of Israel but in the provision of human leaders. Here there is a striking point of contact with the covenant formulations of Josh. 24 and 1 Sam. 12. Both link a reference to the Exodus with mention of Moses and Aaron as "sent" by Yahweh.[19] This apparently fixed motif is echoed here with the addition of Miriam, who was associated with a poem of the Exodus tradition in Exod. 15 as a singer and "prophetess, sister of Aaron."[20] This lawsuit, which leans heavily on covenant traditions and forms, stands close to Josh. 24 with its *I–you* style. Another link with Josh. 24 is supplied by a common reference to the Balaam traditions known to us from Num. 22–24. In both, Balaam is given his patronymic and Balak his royal title.[21] The recital has now moved on to an incident drawn from the end of the period of wandering before the crossing of the Jordan. To mark the new phase in the recital the poignant appeal of v. 3 is made once again: *my people*.

Israel are summoned to *remember* an episode in their salvation history. Their remembering is not at all the type of memory work necessary in studying for a history examination. It marks rather the impact of God's past work for Israel on the life of the present generation. Although the language is anthropocentric, there is an underlying implication of the outworking of divine providence, which is made explicit in Josh. 24 by a theological interpretation: "I delivered you out of his [Balak's] hand" (v. 10). God's people need to seek their Lord in the challenge of their history, to be brought face to face with the living God, who on Israel's behalf foiled the fell purposes of knavish kings. What response is appropriate to this covenant God of their fathers? Memories such as these should impel toward a commitment to God that shows itself in a radically different way

---

Analecta Biblica 20 (1963), pp. 100f., notes the occurrence of "house of slaves" in Exod. 20:2 and calls the phrase "Dekalogsprache." Cf. its use in the people's response to Joshua's challenge in Josh. 24:17, although its absence from G may be significant.

19. Josh. 24:5; 1 Sam. 12:6. The Josh. reference, missing from G, is often deleted; but J. L'Hour, *RB* 69(1962), p. 24, n. 101, finds its recurrence in Mic. a pointer to its traditional nature.

20. It is sometimes claimed, e.g., by G. Widengren, "What Do We Know About Moses?" *Proclamation and Presence*. G. Henton Davies Festschrift (1970), p. 23, that the Exodus traditions known in eighth-century Judah could not have included references to Aaron and Miriam. This assessment ignores the evidence of the pattern exhibited in the two covenant formulations.

21. The conjectural proposals to delete these appositional phrases and also to emend *'ammî, my people, to 'immô,* "with him," taking it with v. 4, are inspired mainly by a desire for metrical uniformity. *My people* is stylistically appropriate at this point.

of life.[22] What less should they give than total obedience to his claims in every area of life?

The significance of Balak's plotting against old Israel was that they were in danger of failing to reach the promised land even as they drew near to its threshold. According to the Numbers account, the king of Moab and the elders of Midian put their heads together in a desperate attempt to resist the invaders. They thought to aid the fair means of fighting with a foul one, namely, that of putting an evil spell on the Israelites. However, Balaam, who had been enlisted to do this cursing, was strangely reluctant, despite promise of reward; eventually at the behest of Israel's God he issued a powerful threefold blessing instead. Thus not only did God set his people on their travels by releasing them from Egypt, but near their journey's end he saved them from uncanny perils. All these were benefits indeed for the chosen nation, which they should bear in mind and make the basis for their lives, standing as they do on redemption ground.

The next phrase, *from Shittim to Gilgal,* poses a syntactical problem, but exegetically its intent is clear. It is possible that a phrase like "your crossing" has fallen out, although there is no ancient evidence for this.[23] If the present text is correct as it stands, it must be viewed as an example of a broken construction, implying an impatient "How many more examples do I have to give?"[24] The crossing of the Jordan is obviously meant.[25] *Shittim* was the last stopping point before crossing and *Gilgal* the site of the first encampment on the west side (Josh. 3:1; 4:19). In between lay the Jordan, frontier of the land of promise and traditional scene of a miraculous event commemorated in future years at Gilgal (Josh. 4:19–24). Thanks to a manifestation of Yahweh's goodness and power they arrived at their destination. There is another link here with Josh. 24, which explicitly mentions the Jordan crossing.

The recital of the saga has ended, but it has left untold further chapters, which Josh. 24 and 1 Sam. 12 do not hesitate to recite. We may imagine that the prophet breaks off impatiently under the influence of strong emotion, already evinced in the pathos of the repeated *my people.* He comes back to the point of the recital, that Israel may remember and *appreciate* what God has done on their behalf and order their lives

22. "When man remembers God, he lets his being and his actions be determined by him" (J. Pedersen, *Israel. Its Life and Culture,* vols. 1–2 [1926], p. 106). Cf. B. S. Childs, *Memory and Tradition in Israel.* SBT 37 (1962), p. 57; W. Schottroff, *"Gedenken" im Alten Orient und im AT. Die Wurzel zākar im semitischen Sprachkreis.* WMANT 15 (1964), p. 134.
23. Heb. *'oḇreḵā,* "your crossing," dependent on the earlier imperative "remember," or *be'oḇreḵā,* "when you crossed," is frequently supplied on the ground either of pseudo-haplography after *ben-be'ôr* or of corruption of the one into the other. Some, e.g., Ewald, G. A. Smith, Thomas, regard the phrase as a latter gloss.
24. For aposiopesis in the OT see GK 167a.
25. Ehrlich's suggestion that Shittim is cited as the place where Baal-Peor was worshipped (Num. 25:1), and Gilgal as a pagan cultic center (Hos. 4:15; Amos 4:4), with the implication "Remember how you served other gods," is irrelevant to a recital of Yahweh's benefits.

accordingly. The history of their salvation is summarized as Yahweh's *tsiḏ^eqôṯ,*[26] "righteous acts" or better "acts of vindication." It is a traditional term, which occurs not only in Judg. 5:11 but also in the formulation of 1 Sam. 12 at v. 7, where it is used as here in the general context of an appeal to Israel to remember their obligations to Yahweh. It speaks of what God has done on his people's behalf, whereby he singled out Israel as his chosen nation and revealed his intent to be their God. The word "righteous" and its derivatives in the OT have their home in the lawcourt, referring to a legal party as "in the clear, in the right." The duty of a judge in Israelite lawsuits was to champion the oppressed against their oppressors, to protect and vindicate against wrong treatment. Here the forensic flavor lingers in that Israel, languishing under Egyptian oppression, found a champion in Yahweh, who delivered them and put them on the high road of blessing as his own people.[27] Such benefits as these constitute a claim upon Israel; they create an open-ended situation, inviting from Yahweh's covenant partner a due response of obedience and gratitude, a "walk worthy of the gospel."

6, 7 In the prophet's poem Israel, formerly addressed, now take up in querulous tones the challenge to give evidence on their own behalf.[28] Another speech-form is skillfully woven into the composition at this point. Micah borrows from the entrance liturgy, of which examples survive in Pss. 15 and 24 and in another prophetic borrowing at Isa. 33:14–16. It is characterized by question and answer, and sets out the requirements for would-be worshippers which they must meet before they can enter the sanctuary. Here the questioner is inquiring what sacrifices he should bring with him as he comes to worship. He is quite prepared to give whatever is required of him. He seeks only to know the particular demands of Yahweh, ready in his devotion to satisfy any whim or craving the Deity may have. Micah cites satirically a supposed cultic inquiry such as was the priests' responsibility to answer. In the prophetic representation Israel is made out to be entirely obedient and dutiful at first sight. Due recognition of the transcendence of God is expressed in a fine contrast. He is so exalted that theirs it is to bow in deep reverence and lowly submission.[29] This is only right, Israel admits, and this they are prepared to do. Tell us, they say, what gifts we are to bring to so great a God, and we shall bring them. They knew that they should not appear before him empty-handed.[30] Should they

26. A first person pronoun "my" is expected in this *Jahwerede*. Either the passage slips into a *Prophetenrede,* or more likely the phrase is used as a stereotyped one (cf. the note on 3:7).
27. Cf. Ps. 103:6f.
28. Cf. R. Hentschke, *Die Stellung der vorexilischen Schriftpropheten zum Kultus*. BZAW 75 (1956), p. 105; Huffmon, *loc. cit.*, p. 287. "You point out our various failures, but you should also take note of the services we have rendered to God" (Calvin, *apud SJT* 23 [1970], p. 168).
29. For the unique expression *'^elōhê mārôm* cf. Ps. 92:8(9).
30. Exod. 23:15; 34:20.

bring *burnt offerings*? This form of sacrifice was a demanding one in that the whole animal was offered, unlike another type in which part of the victim was eaten by the worshipper at a cultic meal. Nevertheless, the worshipper was prepared to opt for this form, if need be. He would gladly give *yearling calves* as his sacrifice. Calves were eligible for sacrifice from the age of seven days, but yearlings were regarded as the best.[31] Obviously the older the beast the more had been spent on its upkeep and the greater the economic loss to the worshipper. But he is prepared to keep his steers till their prime to provide a valuable offering. Only the best was good enough for God.

Just what is acceptable to Yahweh?[32] The worshipper is so eager to do his will, but he thinks he does not yet know it. He turns from quality of offering to quantity. Can it be that God requires hecatombs from Israel? These were mammoth offerings such as Solomon and other kings sometimes made, doubtless at state expense.[33] Or would God like libations of gallons and gallons of *oil*? Oil was the ceremonial accompaniment of a number of offerings, obviously in relatively small quantities, but here its amount is rhetorically exaggerated.[34] The series of hypothetical questions rises to a hysterical and ghastly crescendo in the ultimate offer of child sacrifice. Neighboring nations practiced the sacrifice of the firstborn, but in Israel an animal victim was substituted as a means of redemption. However, the pagan practice did creep in along with the worship of other gods. A god especially associated with child sacrifice was Molech, who was given a sanctuary called Topheth, "burning place," somewhere on the southern side of Jerusalem, where the grisly rite was performed.[35] Undoubtedly it was to this god that both Ahaz and Manasseh sacrificed their sons.[36] It is hardly warranted to conclude that the practice was widespread at the time of the present composition, any more than that of offering *rivers of oil by the ten thousand*. Rather, as Wellhausen perceived, it is cited hypothetically as the logical climax of sacrifice, the acme of religious zeal, to be prepared to give one's dearest possession to God. Here the purpose of this sacrifice is explicitly stated to be for *sin* and *rebellion*.[37]

31. Cf. Lev. 9:3; 22:27.
32. Heb. *rāṣâ* is a technical term for the acceptance of sacrifice (cf. Lev. 1:4; 22:25; etc., and von Rad, *OT Theology,* vol. 1, pp. 261f.).
33. 1 K. 3:4 "1000 burnt offerings"; 8:63 "22,000 oxen and 120,000 sheep"; 2 Chr. 30:24; 35:7.
34. For the figure cf. Job 20:17; 29:6.
35. 2 K. 23:10; Jer. 32:35.
36. 2 K. 16:3; 21:7.
37. Grammatically the nouns are more likely causal accusatives than appositional terms "transgression offering, sin offering," *contra,* e.g., BDB; Sellin; Fohrer in *Words and Meanings*. D. W. Thomas Festschrift (1968), p. 100. *Ḥaṭṭā'ṯ* may mean "sin offering," but *pesha'* has this developed sense nowhere else, and its position before *ḥaṭṭā'ṯ* suggests that both are used in an undeveloped sense.

If the worshipper has offended, he knows that atonement must be made for his sin;[38] but how weighty are God's demands? He yearns to find out.

This part of the poem is obviously an extreme representation of an attitude prevalent in the prophet's day, since the same enthusiasm for sacrifice is attested in Isaiah's criticisms in Isa. 1:10–17. Its function in the poem is to counter the lengths to which Yahweh has gone for his people with the extent to which the people are prepared to go for him. They are ready to shower him with gifts so as to ensure that he receives the honor due his great name. They are willing to give their all to restore the relationship whenever it is broken by their sin. How else can they show their religious devotion and appreciation of covenant grace?[39] The purpose of the alleged citation is to register a protest against the denunciation of the earlier section. The accusation that Israel was sick and tired of Yahweh was a patent untruth which must be repudiated. How dare God level against them the implicit charge that they have failed to remember or appreciate all he has done for them? They do not deny that they have been delinquent on occasion, but they have been quick to repair the fault. In fact both parties to the covenant are well-nigh matched in their mutual displays of devotion, as they imply by their nervous, excited questions. The passionate pathos of the first stanza has evoked the emotional agitation of this part of the composition. The people are represented as offended by the divine attack, which in their eyes is quite unwarranted.

8 The tension is now resolved. This concluding section follows on in form from the preceding one, providing an authoritative answer to the barrage of questions. Posing as a priest, the prophet in measured tones replies to the people's basic question about the response God wants from his people. As the individual worshipper of vv. 6, 7 was a personification of Israel, so he is here as the *man* now addressed. This is more obvious in the original: *'āḏām* is more often used collectively than of a single person. It takes up the thought of the distance between Yahweh and Israel expressed at the head of the previous section. *Man* is frequently used in the OT as a contrast to divine power and glory, stressing what is creaturely in the human constitution.[40] Here it is intended to remind the people of their subordination to God and to cut them down to size after their presumptuous retort.[41] In the role of priestly teacher Micah passes on a traditional answer. He has nothing new to say with regard to the divine will. Israel has

38. "This extremely important aspect is often overlooked in explanations of the *minḥâ* [cereal offering] and *'ôlâ* [burnt offering]. It was J. Pedersen's great achievement that he emphatically pointed out that every sacrifice contains the germ of 'the idea of the atonement' [*Israel. Its Life and Culture,* vols. 3–4 (1940), p. 359]" (H.-J. Kraus, *Worship in Israel* [E.T. 1966], p. 116).

39. The sacrifices "were not 'man's expedient for his own redemption', as Köhler suggests, but were 'the fruit of grace, not its root' (A. C. Knudson)" (R. J. Thompson, *NBD,* p. 1121).

40. Cf. Ps. 144:3f. (of Israel); Isa. 31:3.

41. Cf. Hentschke, *op. cit.,* pp. 106f. He compares Isa. 2:9, 11.

already been given the message long ago and reminded of it regularly by cultic proclamation.[42] The prophet is appealing to the other side of the covenant formulations, the summons to Israel to obey. This second side is now stressed in a manner akin to 1 Sam. 12, where the summons is linked with Samuel's instruction of the people "in the good and right way" (v. 24). In view of the covenantal framework the reference must be to the stipulations of the divine covenant. This use of *good*, which makes a comprehensive appeal to previously accepted covenantal standards of manifold type, occurs explicitly in Hos. 8:1–3,[43] where the people of the Northern Kingdom are described thus:

They have infringed my covenant
and rebelled against my law.
To me they cry, "My God,
we, Israel, know you."
Israel has rejected the good.

The last statement is a paraphrase of the earlier pair.[44] The northerners had in their conduct repudiated Yahweh's covenant claims while in their worship they were claiming their covenant relationship with him. Micah's message is a similar one.

A characteristic of the entrance liturgy was to give a short, catechetical answer to the questions of the one who sought advice.[45] So, following his model, the prophet gives a summary of the requirements Yahweh has laid upon Israel. His words are a classic definition of the people's duty toward each other and toward their God. It is comparable with Jesus' epitome of the manward side of OT piety: "Treat people in the way you would like them to treat you: this is the intent of the law and prophets" (Matt. 7:12). It bears more precise comparison with his selection of the two commandments, to love God and one's neighbor, as a terse description of the essence of Israel's double duty (Mark 12:29–31). Micah's summary is in form and content strongly reminiscent of Hosea's injunction at the end of a similar call to trial:

"Maintain loyalty and justice
and always wait trustingly for your God." (Hos. 12:6[7])

The first of Yahweh's requirements is oriented toward the human

42. Ps. 147:19 (cf. Deut. 4:13) is an example of this cultic use of the verb *higgîḏ*, "declare" (cf. Beyerlin, *KIPVM*, pp. 50f.).
43. Cf. Amos 5:14f.; Isa. 1:17.
44. Cf. Jer. 6:16. "The Hebrew [ethic is concerned] with the relation of the individual and the community to the will of a personal God. . . . The governing factor is the relation of human persons to a divine Person; and that means that the good is not so much the object of philosophical enquiry as the content of divine revelation" (T. W. Manson, *Ethics and the Gospel* [1960], p. 18). Goodness in the OT is "the total response of man's moral nature, in the human and social context of his conscious life, to a God who is God because his power and his purpose are good" (R. B. Y. Scott, *The Relevance of the Prophets* [^{2}1969], p. 212).
45. Cf. Ps. 24:4; Isa. 33:15; a longer answer is provided in Ps. 15:2–5a. These passages are virtual commentaries on the present one.

community. The OT believer stood within a circle of other faithful men, all bound together by common membership of a covenant relationship with Yahweh. Social and moral standards were laid down for the individual to practice in his relations with his companions in the faith. Commitment to Yahweh included commitment to the covenant community. *Justice* is the key word so often used by the prophets to sum up this social obligation. It covers and transcends a host of negative precepts, such as prohibition of oppression, perjury, and bribery. It calls for a sense of responsibility toward weaker members of society lest they go to the wall. It insists on the rights of others; it demands an instinct for *social* preservation.

The second part of the summary likewise stresses communal obligations. *Ḥeseḏ,* rendered *loyalty,* is a term that Hosea especially made his own as a definition of the panorama of Israel's theology and ethics. It is a word of relationship, expressing an attitude of covenant obligation.[46] Fundamentally it describes the divine "love that will not let me go," the firm and faithful loyalty of Yahweh toward Israel, his quality of constancy toward his own.[47] In grace God had tied himself in covenant bond and voluntarily taken upon himself obligations he was honor-bound to fulfil. The resultant attitude of heart was *ḥeseḏ*. As a word of partnership it betokens mutual loyalty, not only the faithfulness of God to man but man's faithfulness to God. Through Hosea Yahweh had complained in bitter, disappointed tones how fickle and fleeting was Israel's *ḥeseḏ,*

like a morning cloud,
like the dew that disappears so early. (Hos. 6:4)

Nor was the content of the term yet exhausted. It was used to describe not only the response of man to God but also the manifestation toward one another of this same loyal spirit. Like the injunction to love in the NT, it took its cue from the revelation of God's own heart. It represented the high ideal of a national solidarity enriched and empowered by the solidarity of divine commitment to Israel. Alas, it fell to Hosea again to deliver to the Northern Kingdom Yahweh's indictment:

There is no faithfulness or ḥeseḏ
and no knowledge of God in the country.
There is cursing, perjury, murder;
robbery and adultery abound
and bloodshed follows bloodshed. (Hos. 4:1, 2)

In striking alignment with such covenant traditions as the Decalog and Lev. 19:11–18 in the Holiness Code, Hosea exposed the disparity between the community spirit enjoined upon Israel and the wretched reality. Micah calls the Southern Kingdom to a higher ethic than their northern neighbors

46. "It expresses the moral bondage of love, the loving discharge of an admitted obligation, the voluntary acceptance of a responsibility" (H. W. Robinson, *Two Hebrew Prophets* [1948], p. 47).
47. J. P. Hyatt, *loc. cit.,* takes *'ahᵃḇaṯ ḥeseḏ* together as "faithful love," as evidently the Qumran community did; but for "love" as a verb cf. Ps. 37:28; Amos 5:15.

managed to attain. At the divine behest he summons them to reflect in every corner of their society God's own concern for them. If *ḥesed* modelled upon their Lord's is cherished among them, then will the covenant purpose of God have reached its goal in the establishment of a society where theology and ethics are one.

If the first two requirements of this formula for fulfilment of the covenant are oriented toward a human ethic, they are nonetheless grounded in the revelation of God's character and will. This latent motivation is expressed in the third requirement, a careful walk with God. Paul was doubtless echoing it when he urged the churches of Asia Minor to "look carefully how you walk, like sensible not senseless people. . . . Do not be thoughtless, but discern what the Lord's will is" (Eph. 5:15, 17). Over against a natural tendency to self-centeredness and turning every one to his own way, Micah counsels a life of fellowship with the God of the covenant. *Your God* is one half of the traditional description of the covenant, a counterpart to *my people*.[48] It thus forms a fitting conclusion to a passage that had earlier referred to *my people*. Israel's life in partnership with God is described as walking with him. By virtue of Yahweh's special relationship with Israel they were offered communion which it was possible for them either to respond to or to reject. The response God sought was a comprehensive one of constant consideration of his grace in the past and of his will for the present, and a readiness to be guided by him in all life's ventures. There were many in Micah's day to whom fellowship with God was a comfort: to "walk with the Upright One" (2:7) was the privilege of being kept by a faithful God. The prophet urges that it should mean a continual challenge and involvement with God in dedicated living.

Micah's prescription of covenant responsibility to man and God represents a considerable broadening of the scope of the response Judah evidently expected to give. The purely religious dimension of vv. 6, 7 is judged inadequate. It would be unfair to conclude that Micah replaces the forms of religion with social ethics, for God's covenant with Israel traditionally included a strong cultic emphasis as an integral part. So a careful walk with God would find *partial* fulfilment in the observance of ritual laws.[49] The message of the Master is here foreshadowed: "First be reconciled to your brother, and then come and offer your gift" (Matt. 5:24). To a generation preoccupied with things ceremonial to the neglect of weightier matters of the law, Micah needs to bring a counterstress on the impact of the covenant upon all of life's concerns. "The prophets did not believe that a change in the ritual was essential: they merely shifted the emphasis from form to substance, from the acts of worship to the life of the

48. Cf., e.g., Lev. 26:12; Ps. 50:7; Hos. 2:23(25); 4:12; Jer. 11:4.

49. "Le sacrifice n'est pas nécessairement condamné, mais il prend un sens nouveau. Il peut être une expression légitime de la foi, un geste de reconnaissance, de soumission, de repentance, de communion" (Vuilleumier).

worshipper, from rites to character."[50] To keep Yahweh confined in a gilded cultic cage was a travesty of faith in a moral God who on Israel's behalf had proved himself Lord of history.

> *"Does Yahweh appreciate burnt offerings or sacrifices*
> *as much as obeying Yahweh's voice?*
> *No, better is obedience than sacrifice*
> *and submissiveness than rams' fat."* (1 Sam. 15:22)

Participation in a divine covenant was basic to Israel's self-understanding. But surrounded as they were by religion of a different type, they were ever prone to a misunderstanding of the nature and purpose of the covenant. They succumbed to the heresy of straining a partial truth beyond its proper limits. The specifically religious side of Israelite faith was stressed in such a way that it was conveniently forgotten that Yahweh's sovereignty extended over the whole of life. Ceremonies discharged with emotional feeling and material extravagance became the sum total of spiritual commitment. "They would offer everything excepting what alone he asked for, their heart, its love and its obedience" (Pusey). Nor did such distortion die in the eighth century B.C. The letters of John and James are eloquent pleas for a balanced and consistent faith permeating life in its entirety and leaving no corner unillumined by God's glory. The "living sacrifice" and "figurative worship" of Rom. 12:1 are the response demanded by God's "mercies" revealed in the events of Christmas, Easter, and Pentecost.

2. *Commercial Trickery and its Punishment (6:9–16)*

Hark, Yahweh is calling to the city,
[It is good sense to fear[51] your name]
listen, tribe and assembled citizens.[52] 4+4
10 *Can I overlook[53] the wrong measure[54]*

50. R. H. Pfeiffer, *Religion in the OT* (1961), p. 134. "As it is vain for a man to bestow all his goods to feed the poor and to give his body to be burned, if he has not *agape,* so for the Israelite it is vain to offer thousands of rams. . . , if he love not *ḥesedh*" (G. W. Anderson, *SJT* 4[1951], p. 195).

51. MT *yir'eh,* "he will see, (that) one should see," is generally repointed *yir'â,* "to fear." Cf. G S V "fearers," which accords with *yir'ê* read by some Heb. mss. For the phrase "fear your name" cf. Ps. 86:11.

52. MT "(the) rod. And who appointed it? Still," apparently a reference to punishment and its divine agent. Heb. *maṭṭeh,* "rod, tribe," is more probably to be taken in the latter sense and as a vocative with G. Heb. *'ôḏ,* "still," is also to be restored with G to *'îr,* "city," assuming a common *r/d* error in MT: this suits the earlier reference to the city. Then with most since Wellhausen *ûmî yᵉ'āḏāh ('îr)* is to be redivided into *ûmô'ēḏ hā'îr,* "and assembly of the city."

53. MT *ha'ish,* apparently "is there?" (cf. 2 Sam. 14:19), is generally regarded as a product of a form defectively written either for *ha'eśśā',* "can I bear" (Duhm), or for *ha'eshsheh,* "can I forget" (Wellhausen), which thus secures an expected external parallelism with the next line.

54. MT *bêṯ rāshā',* "house of (the) wicked," is to be repointed with Duhm *baṯ resha',* "*bath*

and the accursed skimped bushel? 3+3
11 *Can I condone*[55] *the wrongly set scales*
or the bag of false weights? 3+3
12 *Her*[56] *men of wealth are addicted to violence,*
her citizens speak lies,
the tongues in their mouths are utterly deceitful.[57] 3+3+3
13 *For my part, I shall deal you a crippling blow,*[58]
devastating you for your sins. 3+3
14 *You will eat,*
but not feel full. 2+2
Your child[59] *in your womb you will strive to produce,*[60]
but be unable to bear.[61] 3+2
What you manage to bear[62]
I shall consign to the sword. 2+2
15 *You will sow,*
but never reap. 2+2
You will tread olives,
but never rub on their oil, 3+3
grapes, but never
drink their wine. 2+2
16 *Omri's rulings have been followed,*[63]

---

of wickedness,'' in the light of the context. MT adds ''treasures of wickedness,'' which appears to be a later comment on the earlier phrase after *baṯ* had been misconstrued (T. H. Gaster, *JTS* 38[1937], p. 164). This line and the next are then exactly parallel.

55. The construction is difficult: lit. ''shall I be pure with (= in tolerating?).'' Possibly the verb should be repointed as a Piel *ha'ᵃzakkeh,* ''can I regard as pure'' (cf. V), but the preposition *bᵉ* is not used elsewhere with this verb to introduce the object. Some understand an object ''can I regard as pure (the man) with.''

56. MT ''whose'' lacks an antecedent: ''city' lies outside the oracle proper in the prophetic introduction. Accordingly many follow Marti and J. M. P. Smith in placing v. 12 next to v. 9, but its indicting contents fit better here; cf. v. 16 for another implicit reference to the city. Probably the relative *'ᵃsher* should be deleted with Lindblom, *BHK,* and Schwantes as a corrupt dittograph of the following *'ᵃshîreyhā.*

57. Lit. ''are deceit,'' a predicative noun indicating emphasis.

58. A prophetic perfect. Many revocalize MT *heḥᵉlêṯî* as *haḥillôṯî,* ''I have begun (to strike you),'' with G S V Aquila and Theodotion. But the idiomatic juxtaposition of the two roots for ''be sick'' and ''strike'' in Jer. 10:19; 14:17; 30:12; Nah. 3:19 justifies the retention of MT with Symmachus and T (so NEB). For the construction cf. GK 114n.

59. Heb. *yeshḥᵃḵā* is a *hapax legomenon* whose meaning can only be conjectured from the context. G related to *ḥšk,* ''be dark,'' V to *šḥḥ,* ''humiliation,'' and Symmachus to *šḥt,* ''destroy''; S rendered ''dysentery'' and T ''sickness.'' The translation follows the suggestion of H. Torczyner, *ZDMG* 70(1916), p. 558, who interprets as ''embryo.''

60. MT *wᵉtassēg* appears to be an orthographical variant for *wᵉtaśśēg* (cf. 2:6), ''make to reach,'' as V T and Aquila took it; sc. ''the mouth of the womb'' (G. R. Driver, *JTS* 39[1938], pp. 267f.). The medieval Jewish commentators Ibn Janach, Ibn Ezra, and Kimchi interpreted thus.

61. Heb. *taplîṭ* is evidently used of birth, as in Job 21:10 (cf. *mlṭ,* Isa. 34:15; 66:7).

62. Heb. *tᵉpallēṭ,* a Piel after a Hiphil earlier. Many repoint, but J. M. P. Smith rightly compares *millēṭ* and *himlîṭ* in the same sense of ''deliver.'' For other examples of stylistic variation by using different conjugations of the same verb see Dahood, *Pss 2,* p. 229.

63. Heb. *wᵉyishtammēr* is used as the passive of a Piel ''carefully regard'' (Jon. 2:8[9]) (G.

and all the practices of Ahab's royal house;
you have pursued their policies. 3+3+3
I must make you[64] *an object of horror*
and her citizens a source of shock;
you will have to endure the peoples'[65] *jibes.* 3+2+3

Basically this oracle falls into the familiar two-part pattern of exposing wrongs and announcing the penalties God must inflict upon their perpetrators. The first line is an introductory one in which the prophet calls for attention to Yahweh's message. It has been interestingly annotated with a liturgical parenthesis.[66] Then follows the oracle proper, in which Yahweh speaks throughout. It falls into three sections, discernible only by subject matter: (1) a catalog of commercial and social vices (three lines, vv. 10–12); (2) a list of various penalties that God is to deal out (seven lines, vv. 13–15); (3) a summary statement of sin and punishment (two lines, v. 16). Metrically the thirteen-line piece is quite varied, although a 2+2 rhythm predominates in the second section.[67]

A link with the preceding covenant-oriented oracle of vv. 1–8 is provided in the second section: the penalties prescribed take the form of curses associated with breaking the covenant. The two oracles are akin in their accusing tone, but whereas the first develops into a warning exhortation, this one more conventionally culminates in dire threats.

9 The prophet acts as herald for Yahweh's message of charge and verdict. He prefaces the delivery of the message with a call to its intended recipients to pay heed. It is directed first to *the city,* most probably Jerusalem, the usual venue of Micah's oracles.[68] If the textual evidence has been evaluated aright, he goes on to specify a wider audience, the *tribe,* evidently Judah. Presumably he is speaking on some communal occasion when tribal representatives are gathered in the city, either for a political meeting or a religious one, or simply on a market day, with which the subsequent references to trading would accord. If the last supposition is correct, one can imagine Judeans flocking into the capital to sell or barter their wares. Then the "assembly of the city" is the concourse of citizens of Jerusalem who turned out in force to trade and make a dishonest penny at the expense of their country cousins. The prophet interrupts this unholy

---

R. Driver, *JTS* 35[1934], p. 385, referring to GK 145o for the syntax; Schwantes). There is no need to change to *wattishmōr,* "and you kept," with most since Wellhausen, following S V T and Theodotion. For G's reading, which indirectly supports MT, see L. C. Allen, *JTS* 24(1973), pp. 72f.

64. For the variation in this verse between singular and plural second person references Willi-Plein compares the feature in Deuteronomy.

65. MT *'ammî,* "my people," is contextually inappropriate. It is generally corrected to *'ammîm* with G. MT's form may be a mistaken abbreviation.

66. See the Introduction.

67. Lindblom makes a ruthless attempt to secure metrical harmony: five lines of 3+3, five or six of 2+2, and two of 3+3.

68. See the Introduction.

commerce and begs silence for Yahweh to speak. To a city teeming with both countryman and town dweller he brings God's word of rebuke.

10–12 The first two lines are parallel in form and content. They express divine disapproval of exploiting customers by giving short measure and weight. Amos had found similar dishonest practices in the markets of the Northern Kingdom.[69] He cited commercial cupidity,

> *"that we may make the ephah small and the shekel large and cheat with false scales."* (Amos 8:5)

Jerusalem's market was no better. Two measures are mentioned, the "bath" and "ephah." These are respectively liquid and dry measures of the same capacity, about five gallons. The *bushel* is the nearest modern equivalent of the latter. In the absence of a weights and measures inspector, the customer was dependent on the vendor's honesty. He could do little to check the amounts he was given. There were indeed sanctions written into the ancient lawcodes: Lev. 19:35, 36 and Deut. 25:13–16 use strong language to demand among other commercial standards a full and fair ephah.[70] But apparently cheating was rife, and tricks of the trade were practiced with impunity. Another trick was to tamper with scales so that the buyer received less than he paid for. A variation of this kind of deception was to use stone weights heavier than the standard, like the shekel mentioned by Amos. *Caveat emptor*! But what could a customer do against the wiles of contemporary commerce if the authorities turned a blind eye? The divine Guardian of the downtrodden intervenes to register his protest. He who had laid down the ancient requirements of commercial equity for his covenant people speaks again in a manner that assumes prior knowledge of them. He will not let the offenders cheat with impunity in trading transactions. The rhetorical questions express powerfully how intolerable, how abhorrent to God this situation is. They are designed to stir Israel's lazy conscience. Their God is no Olympian, remote from everyday living. He is the Lord of the shopping center, whose claims over his people extend to the most mundane of life's duties.

The get-rich-quick merchants who lived in the capital are now condemned for depriving social inferiors of their legal rights. *Violence* is a term for lawlessness, the breach of law and order in Israelite society.[71] The reader has already encountered in Micah's previous oracles examples of this arbitrary attitude in the seizure of property and in the refusal to prosecute social vampires.[72] It may well be that we are to think here specifically of corruption in the lawcourts.[73] In that case the collapse of integrity among Jerusalem's inhabitants would refer to the way they aided

69. Cf. Hos. 12:7f.(8f.).
70. Cf. Beyerlin, *KIVPM*, p. 61.
71. Cf. E. A. Speiser, *Genesis*. Anchor Bible (1964), p. 51.
72. Mic. 2:2, 8f.; 3:2f., 11.
73. M. A. Klopfenstein, *Die Lüge nach dem AT* (1964), pp. 157f., notes that Heb. *ḥāmās*, "violence," and *sheqer*, "lies," occur together in Ps. 27:12 in a forensic setting.

and abetted their wealthy patrons, swearing falsely in their favor, perhaps to the detriment of a defrauded man from the country.[74] Their *tongues* did nothing but deceive; they could not be trusted to tell the truth.[75] By their *deceitful* cunning they bolstered up the claims of the wealthy against those economically weaker. Heedless of the suffering caused to their unfortunate neighbors, they supported the unscrupulous elite in their aggressive greed.

13–15 Yahweh cannot stand aside from the scene, so infested was the capital with swindling and corruption. Doubtless the blame was to be apportioned between sellers from both city and country, each vying to outdo the other in underhand dealing. He now addresses directly the people of Judah and Jerusalem in a collective reference to them as his covenant partner. They have amassed such liability that he can only intervene in terrible judgment. In no less a way can the slate be cleaned of their debt of guilt. The threat is a sinister one, which hints at enemy invasion. After the 701 B.C. crisis, Isaiah spoke of the desolation that the Assyrian invaders left behind them in terms of a grossly disobedient son or slave receiving corporal punishment until he was seriously ill with his wounds (Isa. 1:5–7). Such imagery is intended not to portray divine vindictiveness, but to reflect the enormity of the sin, which a moral God cannot leave unpunished.

The success story of these trespassers who have been taking shortcuts to prosperity will be abruptly concluded. Their path through life, made easy by using others as stepping stones, will deteriorate into a morass of frustration. These next six lines are couched in the form of "futility curses."[76] The popular origin of such solemn imprecations as are pronounced here may be seen in Job's powerful speech of moral self-scrutiny in Job 31, for instance in v. 8:

> *"Let me sow and another eat,*
> *and let my crop be uprooted."*

The futility curse was traditionally used in association with the covenant as a warning against its infringement.[77] The secular background of the covenantal use of this and other types of curse is the international suzerainty treaty.[78] Within the regular cultic proclamation of the covenant in Israel were evidently included promises for the obedient and threats for the disobedient.[79] There can be little doubt that Micah was aware of this covenantal

74. Heb. *sheqer* is frequently used of perjury, e.g., in Exod. 20:16; Prov. 6:19.
75. Sellin, J. M. P. Smith, Weiser, George, *et al.*, delete the last clause of v. 12 as a later gloss drawn from Ps. 120:2f. and as metrically superfluous. Klopfenstein, *op. cit.*, p. 408, n. 676, argues for its authenticity. The occurrence of the phrase "lying tongue" in both places is hardly a sure sign of borrowing. The reluctance to admit tricola as legitimate lines alongside bicola is a critical attitude frequently belied by the phenomena of Heb. poetry.
76. Cf. D. R. Hillers, *Treaty Curses and the OT Prophets*. Biblica et Orientalia 16 (1964), pp. 28f.
77. Lev. 26:14–26; Deut. 27:11–26; 28:15–68; Josh. 8:34.
78. Cf. F. C. Fensham, *ZAW* 75(1963), pp. 155–175; K. Baltzer, *The Covenant Formulary* (E.T. 1970), pp. 10, 14f.
79. Cf. A. Weiser, *The Psalms* (E.T. 1962), pp. 32f.; R. E. Clements, *Prophecy and Covenant*. SBT 43 (1965), pp. 40f.

setting of the futility curse and deliberately echoed it. The unneighborliness of Hebrew to Hebrew in commerce and court of law constituted a breach of the covenant, and called for the application of the curse sanctions written into it.

It is striking that the first curse occurs also in the catalog of curses in Lev. 26 at v. 26 in connection with famine.[80] Here enemy invasion is evidently envisaged, in which food supplies are cut off and besieged townsfolk reduced to extremity.[81] The next two lines are impossible to interpret with certainty; the most probable meaning, which is backed by a Jewish exegetical tradition, is a reference to difficulty in childbirth, resulting in a decreasing birthrate, and the death by enemy action of those who are born. The Israelite view of children as a gift from God[82] is here invoked in dread reversal, as in Hos. 9:11f., 16.[83] Either the promise of conception will not come true in childbirth or else the promise latent in childhood will not receive the fulfilment of adult life. In both cases not only would temporary distress be caused, but the outlook for the community would be bleak without the assurance of a new generation in adequate numbers.

The disappointment of losing a crop one has painstakingly sown is also one that appears in the comprehensive series of curses in Lev. 26: "You will sow your seed in vain—your enemies will eat it" (v. 16). Similarly Deut. 28:33 speaks of foreign foes eating up the fruit of one's ground and labors, while v. 38 mentions carrying a lot of seed into the field but harvesting little because locusts have been there first. In a predominantly agricultural economy, life depended on the unbroken cycle of seedtime and harvest. Disruption that had been occasioned by pestilence or enemy incursion, as evidently here, posed a threat to the very existence of the community. The complex of traditions Micah is following is akin to that of Deut. 28, since in both cases the references to the vintage and the olive crop follow mention of a poor cereal harvest, albeit in reverse order in Deut. 28:39, 40.[84] But whereas Deut. 28 explains the crop failures in terms of natural causes, here there is no explanation; yet in the light of the context and the frequent implication of enemy invasion in Micah's oracles, the anticipated background is the ravaging of the land and the pillaging of stores of oil and wine.

Olives were usually pulped in a mill by a revolving millstone or in an oilpress by a weighted beam. Evidently these methods could be supplemented or replaced by a more primitive one of treading in a vat.[85]

80. Hos. 4:10 also employs it.
81. Cf. 2 K. 6:25, 28; 18:27; Jer. 52:6.
82. Cf. Gen. 33:5; Ps. 127:3–5; 128:3.
83. Cf. Deut. 28:18.
84. Micah's order is less logical, since the olive harvest in October–November followed the gathering of grapes in September.
85. Another reference to this method occurs in Deut. 33:24.

The mention of not enjoying the use of the *oil* coincides exactly with the wording of Deut. 28:40. Treading out oil was a laborious business, and it would be particularly galling to see no reward for such toil. Oil was widely used for rubbing on after a bath to condition the skin in a hot climate.[86]

The last of the curses is reminiscent not only of Deut. 28:39 but of Amos 5:11 too, which follows a tradition similar to that known to Micah:

You have planted pleasant vineyards,
but you will not drink their wine.

The common echo in the prophets is interesting: both apparently assume enemy attack to be God's imminent means of fulfilling the traditional curse.[87] Micah's standpoint is unique in his reference to treading as the basic activity that is to go unrewarded. The treading of *grapes* in the winevat was an occasion of great festivity, enhanced by the prospect of enjoying *wine* in abundance during the coming year. This imagined cup is dashed from their lips by the prophet's demoralizing curse.

The economy was to grind to a halt. The fresh food displayed so lavishly on the market stalls among which Micah prophesied would soon be a mocking memory. Cornfields that yesterday had yielded the golden grain on sale today would tomorrow be spoiled and trampled by enemy boots, while casks of oil and wine like those heaped here and there would fall into enemy hands. Such was the doom that the vendors' deceitfulness was to unleash.

16 The momentum of the oracle is broken as the prophet pauses to formulate a final damning accusation as warrant for the nation's punishment. Just as in the opening oracle of the book Micah makes the imminent downfall of Samaria the basis of a warning for Jerusalem, so here ominous allusion is made to a cause of the Northern Kingdom's fate. Judah and its capital are guilty of practices associated with the infamous ninth-century northern kings *Omri* and *Ahab*. The official Judean history has little to say about the former beyond his having made Samaria his capital. He evidently consolidated the nation during his twelve-year reign, retrieving it from political unrest and eventually handing on to his son a peaceful and prosperous realm. His alliance with the great trading city of Tyre, cemented by the marriage of his son to Jezebel, a Tyrian princess, and his subjugation of the wealthy state of Moab,[88] are strong indications that he built up a flourishing economy. In the context it is likely that the reference is to economic and commercial practices associated with those kings rather than to Jezebel's importation of the Phoenician Baal cult against which Elijah fought.[89] Ahab is renowned for the Naboth incident related in 1 K.

86. 2 Sam. 12:20; 14:2.
87. Wolfe's view that Micah is here indebted in imagery and phraseology to Amos is not likely.
88. Attested on the Moabite Stone.
89. "A law-code of . . . individualistic commercialism" (R. B. Y. Scott, *The Relevance of the Prophets*, p. 37, cf. p. 178).

21, which illustrates the ruthless overriding of personal and traditional values rampant in the new regime. The presence in the south of a similar emphasis on commercial profiteering augured ill for its future. If the wages of such sin was destruction in the case of one, what alternative faced the other? The original wording contains a note of inevitability: these malpractices were committed "in order that I might . . . ," which here means, "so that I am forced to. . . ."[90] A God who upholds moral standards has no option but to make a terrible example of the southerners. The nation is to encounter a fate that will dumbfound its spectators. The citizens of Jerusalem will undergo ghastly experiences.[91] Furthermore they will all have to face the taunts of neighboring nations. The reference here is not only to the world's way of kicking a man when he is down. In a culture where calamity and culpability were held to be synonymous, the natural assumption, with which the book of Job joined battle, was that the sufferer must have been guilty of wrongdoing commensurate with his suffering. Hence Judah and Jerusalem are to undergo an experience so bad that they will face the humiliation of hearing from other nations the jibe, "serves them right." Loss of reputation is ever the final indignity which rubs salt into the wounds of suffering.

Such callous-sounding threats as these are not for the squeamish to read and reflect on, but neither are the injustices that occasioned them. God's way was often to shock his people to their senses. We know that his emissary Micah succeeded, temporarily at least, in this respect in the even more outspoken oracle of 3:9–12. Indeed there is an overall similarity between the two oracles. This one is narrower in its charges, which are mainly commercial, and wider in its range of culpability, since the tribe of Judah appears to be as much to blame as the people of the capital. But there is the same categorical stress on the accountability of those who are bound to Yahweh in a special way. Those who throng great Jerusalem, the "gate" or "marketplace" of his people (1:9), can claim no exemption from the ethical stipulations of the covenant. "God is not mocked" with impunity (Gal. 6:7). The Christian too must heed the challenge of this passage if he is a working member of a capitalistic society based on commerce. "The prophet would condemn all exploitation of the public, all restrictive practices, whether by employer or employee, all price rings and every person whoever he be who seeks to take out more than he puts in" (Snaith).

90. Heb. *l^ema'an* is used of inevitable consequence rather than designed purpose: "the purpose seems to animate the action rather than the agent" (S. R. Driver, *Hebrew Syntax* [³1906], p. 200).
91. Heb. *sh^erēqâ*, "object of hissing," refers to a feeling of horror expressed in a hissing expulsion of breath. This type of curse was common in ancient treaties (Hillers, *op. cit.*, pp. 76f.).

3. *Lament over a Decadent Society (7:1–7)*

What a sorry plight I'm in,
    like being in an orchard after the fruit is gathered,
    in a vineyard when the grapes have been gleaned.[1] 2+2+2
No bunch of grapes to eat,
    none of the early figs I love so much. 3+3
2 *Dead and gone from the country is the devout man,*
    society no longer includes an honest member. 3+3
They all lie in ambush with murderous intent;
    kinsmen hunt each other down, net in hand. 3+4
3 *With both hands they are so good at grasping after wrong.*[2]
    Royal official asks, along with judge, for a bribe. 3+4
As for the bigwig, he[3] *has only*
    to say what he wants
    and they wangle it. 2+2+2
4 *The best of them is like a briar,*
    the straightest worse than a hedge.[4] 2+2
The time your watchmen predicted, your punishment, is coming;[5]
    havoc they proclaimed will soon be here. 3+3

5 *Don't trust a companion,*
    don't[6] *confide in your best friend.* 2+2
From the woman who lies in your arms
    keep your lips sealed tight. 2+3
6 *Son despises father,*
    daughter defies mother, 3+3
daughter-in-law her husband's mother.
    A man's worst enemies are those who live in his own home. 2+3
7 *For my part, I am watching for Yahweh,*
    I am waiting for my Savior-God;[7]
    my God will listen to me. 3+3+2

1. Evidently the preposition *k*^{e} is used in a compressed way, as frequently (GK 118s-w). In the context its significance must be "as after" (Lindblom).
2. Lit. "upon evil (are) both hands to do (it) well." Many read *kappêhem,* "their hands," for MT *kappayim,* claiming the support of G S V T; but J. Ziegler, *ZAW* 60 (1944), p. 118, is most probably correct in seeing in G's pronoun an exegetical addition, which may well be the case with regard to the other translations.
3. Heb. *hû',* "he," is used idiomatically as a resumptive pronoun (S. R. Driver, *Hebrew Syntax* [^{3}1906], pp. 149f.).
4. Heb. *yāshār mimm*^{e}*sûḵâ* is frequently emended to *y*^{e}*shārām kim*^{e}*sûḵâ,* "the most upright of them like a hedge." But MT can stand: the pronominal suffix on the previous adjective can carry over (Keil; cf. note on v. 19), and *min* is used comparatively; cf. Isa. 10:10.
5. Heb. *bā'â* is accented in MT as a prophetic perfect, but it is better taken as a participle.
6. *W*^{e}*'al,* "and don't," read by Mur. 88 and many other mss. and presupposed by G, is preferred by Collin, but the staccato tones of vv. 4a and 6 favor MT.
7. The suffix on "salvation" governs the whole phrase (J. Weingreen, *VT* 4 [1954], p. 53).

This next oracle falls into the category of a lament in the sense not of a funeral dirge but of a type of composition of which so many examples are to be found in the Psalms. In fact nearly a third of all the Psalms may be assigned to this class.[8] There are two groups of lament, the community lament and the individual lament; this oracle belongs to the latter type, a grief-laden description of catastrophe in which one is involved, which one brings to God in prayer and to his people to share at their worship. Other examples are Pss. 5, 13, 22, 31, 55, and 71. Micah uses this form to express how heavy upon his shoulders he feels the burden of the state of contemporary society. The prophet stood as mediator between God and Israel, not only to pass his word on to them but to pray concerning them.[9] This lament fulfils both functions, relieving before God his feelings of despair and trust and also making plain to the people the divine view of their corruption, a view the prophet fully shares as God's representative. Adopting this speech-form as a means of communicating divine truth in a manner familiar and acceptable to the people, he uses it to convey the normal prophetic message of accusation and punishment. By its very nature it may be assumed that it was delivered in the temple.

The lament begins as a meditation, describing with sorrow the moral degeneration of contemporary society (vv. 1–4a). Then it expresses to God the prophet's confidence that this state of affairs cannot go unpunished (v. 4b). Next, turning to his audience, the prophet describes further the degeneration around him (vv. 5, 6). The piece concludes with a personal affirmation of faith in God (v. 7). Such oscillation of address to God and to people,[10] and the repetition of descriptive laments[11] together with avowals of confidence and faith,[12] are all features that find parallels in the psalms of lament; Ps. 55 especially is a lament that will repay close comparison.

The thirteen-line oracle shows little metrical consistency. It falls into two stanzas, each consisting of a long description of social degeneration and concluding with a short affirmation of faith (vv. 1–4, 5–7).[13] Both

8. A. Weiser, *The Psalms* (E.T. 1962), p. 66.
9. Cf. Amos 7:2, 5; Jer. 11:14.
10. Cf. Ps. 31:19–24(20–25).
11. Cf. Ps. 35:7, 11–16, 20f.; 102:3–11(4–12), 23f.(24f.).
12. Cf. Ps. 31:3–5(4–6), 14f.(15f.).
13. They begin with similar sounds, *'alelay,* v. 1, and *'al,* v. 5. The repeated *'ên, 'āyin,* "there is not," of vv. 1, 2 is matched by the repeated negative *'al* in v. 5; *'îsh* occurs in vv. 2, 6; *metsappeyḵā, your watchmen,* v. 4, corresponds to *'atsappeh, I am watching,* v. 7. George rightly notes that v. 4 marks a conclusion, but, following Sellin, he transfers it after vv. 5, 6, ignoring the strophical structure of the poem. Commentators have been divided as to whether v. 7 belongs with what precedes or what follows. In form and content it can be shown to be a good conclusion: especially significant is *wa'anî,* "and I," which begins the verse, suggesting a continuation (cf. Josh. 24:15; Ps. 13:5[6]; Mic. 3:8). As Lindblom observes, the detachment of v. 7 would leave the preceding without an ending. Countering Gunkel's citation of psalms that begin with an expression of trust, he quotes others that begin like v. 8 by mentioning the enemy: Pss. 3, 35, 59, and 79.

are marked by analysis and generalization; the first scans society at large, while the second focuses on the narrower grouping of family and friends.

1–4a The prophet begins with a cry of distress, an exclamation to indicate his personal plight. He explains himself with a double metaphor of frustration. His emotions he compares to those of a man who craves some fruit but arrives at the orchard or vineyard too late: the trees or vines are bare. The hungry man turns away deeply disappointed, with his craving for a cluster of *grapes* or an early fig unsatisfied.[14] The sentiment and imagery are reminiscent of Isaiah's parable of the vineyard, where God's expectation of a harvest of fine grapes was unfulfilled; or in plainer speech:

> *He looked for justice but found bloodshed,*
> *for righteousness but found a plaintive cry.* (Isa. 5:7)

Here Micah speaks for God and expresses the divine viewpoint similarly. Like his God, the prophet yearned to see among his people what Amos had called and Paul in turn was to call "the fruit of righteousness."[15] The metaphor is carried over elsewhere in the NT; it reappears especially in the Johannine allegory of the fruit-bearing branches of the vine (John 15:1–8) and in the ethical "fruit of the Spirit" of Gal. 5:22f. The God of the Bible is consistent in his expectations of moral and social faithfulness from his people, be they Israel or the Church. When Jesus came from Bethany to Jerusalem early in Holy Week and tried to find figs on the fig tree to satisfy his hunger, it is probable that he was acting out a reference to this very verse, and symbolically expressing both his desire to find a response to his ministry and his disappointment at the fruitlessness represented by mounting opposition from the leaders of the nation.[16]

Micah moves from metaphor to plain meaning. The fruit missing from Israel's trees is a moral and social concern motivated by piety. In the prophet's first term sounds an echo of his demand for *ḥeseḏ* in 6:8; here the corresponding adjective *ḥāsîḏ* is used, a term that like the noun speaks of a twin responsibility to God and to his people, and a commitment to both which shows in one's way of life. It is a devotion from which the most pious of hermits would be barred, since it has a distinctly social emphasis. When Hosea condemned the people of the north for the prevalence of murder, robbery, adultery, and the like, he summed up the situation thus: "There is no . . . *ḥeseḏ* in the country" (Hos. 4:1, 2). Micah's complaint is similar as he surveys the Southern Kingdom.

Nor is honesty to be found, the quality of the "upright" man who maintains high moral standards and deals fairly with his neighbor. These ideas, old-fashioned in any age, are here stated to be obsolete. Wherever

14. The early fig ripened in June, while the general crop was not gathered till August. Early figs had the appeal the first strawberries of the season have for an Englishman.

15. Amos 6:12; Phil. 1:11.

16. J. N. Birdsall, "The Withering of the Fig-tree (Mark xi.12–14, 20–22)," *ET* 73 (1962), p. 191; cf. A. de Q. Robin, "The Cursing of the Fig Tree in Mark xi. A Hypothesis," *NTS* 8 (1961/62), pp. 276–281. Cf. Luke 13:6–9, 34f.

the prophet looks he can see only the lamentable spectacle of hostility and internecine strife among a people who should have been bound together by strong ties of religion and race. He makes use of two traditional pictures that often appear in psalms of lament concerning the treatment of the suffering psalmist, pictures derived from war, brigandage, and hunting. For example, in Ps. 10:8f. the wicked man is represented thus:

He sits in ambush in the villages,
in hiding places he kills the innocent. . . .
He catches the poor man, dragging him off in his net.

In fact this quotation has affinity with Micah's accusations of the leaders of this nation in 2:2, 8f.; 3:9–11. But here it is a case of "like leader like people." There was a general prevalence of self-centered ruthlessness and riding roughshod over the lives of fellow Judeans. People were going to any lengths to get the better of their neighbors. If the grapes and figs of v. 1 have their counterpart in the "fruit of the Spirit," this second verse is a mirror image of the "works of the flesh" of Gal. 5:19f., especially enmity, strife, and dissension. Micah employs the term "brother," clearly more than a cliché. It accentuates the heinousness of the situation: brother hunts down brother. Those who should have been united in the national solidarity of a common faith in Yahweh are torn asunder. Members of the covenant community of Israel treat one another like warring enemies and wild animals. Gone is the fellowship that was based on traditional ties and upheld conservative values. Society has disintegrated into a struggling mass of hostile individualists.

Micah observes ironically that the one thing the people are good at is a dexterity for evil. They are ready and eager to meddle in the lives of others for their own evil ends. The prophet proceeds to give examples of the self-interest of the establishment in terms strongly reminiscent of his earlier oracles in the book. He examines the judiciary, whose office calls supremely for impartiality and objectivity. He sees bribery to be rife, and a consequent reversal of justice. It was the task of the king as head of the judicial system to take responsibility for the maintenance of equity, law, and order. To this end he appointed officials throughout Judah with delegated authority to administer justice.[17] But in reality Isaiah's complaint was justified:

Your court officials are rebels,
accomplices of thieves.
Every one of them loves a bribe
and chases after presents.
They do not defend the orphan
and never hear the widow's case. (Isa. 1:23)

What was true of the government applied generally to men in authority.

17. R. Knierim, *ZAW* 73 (1961), pp. 159f., 170. He notes that *śārîm,* here used in the singular, are mentioned in Hos. 3:4, etc., next to the king; cf. Isa. 32:1.

Power was perverted into a weapon for achieving personal aims. A word from the man in charge, and his minions hastened to fulfil his whim by fair means or foul. *Wangle* is literally "twist, weave," a sinister reference to intricate manipulations of time, place, and persons necessary to secure the selfish end desired by the man at the top.

Micah makes a sardonic reference in v. 4a to the lowering of moral standards. He may be alluding to people in authority, but it is more likely that he refers to society generally, as in v. 2, and that the authorities have just been cited as blatant examples of the degeneration evident throughout society.[18] The "good" man is by definition one who is benevolent and helpful; the "upright" man is literally straight, honest, and honorable in dealings with his fellows. Both are terms with an interpersonal connotation. The highest examples of honor and helpfulness are but hindrances to the welfare of society, so abysmally low is the level of moral responsibility. They are grit interfering with the smooth running of the social machine, or in the traditional metaphor employed by Micah, they are thorns in the neighbors' sides, pricking and hurting where they should help and love.[19] In their failure to honor obligations they constitute thorny barriers impeding their fellows, instead of constituting smooth and level paths.[20] These are the levels of individualist anarchy to which the nation has gone in its departure from expressions of communal solidarity.

4b Thorns and briars have another connotation: they are a quick-burning fuel.[21] It may be this association that makes Micah turn from diagnosis to prognosis. He binds the transition with a play on words, *m^e^sûḵâ, hedge,* and *m^e^ḇûḵâ, havoc,* to show the inevitable relation between state and fate. The second person references at this point have baffled many a commentator, textual critic, and translator; but consideration of the form of the oracle elucidates their function. A common feature of the psalm of lament is a movement from description to an invocation of God to intervene in salvation, or to a confident affirmation that he will. It is this feature that appears here, as in Ps. 55:23:

But you, God, will throw them down
into the lowest pit.[22]

Micah addresses God in a prayer of confidence that the stand he has taken will be vindicated.[23] In the prophet's use of the lament the affirmation of confidence here takes on the function of the usual announcement of punishment in the prophetic oracle. God will bring about a catastrophic

18. The pronouns refer to the subject of the verbs in v. 2b.
19. Cf. Num. 33:55; Josh. 23:13; Ezek. 28:24; 2 Cor. 12:7. H. N. and A. L. Moldenke, *Plants of the Bible* (1952), pp. 221f., identify the *briar* with the Palestinian nightshade, *Solanum incanum,* noting that its Arab. names are similar to the Hebrew.
20. Cf. Prov. 15:19; Hos. 2:6.
21. Ps. 58:9(10); Isa. 9:18; Eccl. 7:6.
22. Cf. Ps. 22:11(12); 25:20f.; 142:5(6). Weiser, *op. cit.,* p. 76, gives a full list.
23. B. Reicke, *HTR* 60(1967), p. 357; Willi-Plein.

harvest of destruction of which present social dissolution is the seed. Nor has this fate gone unheralded. Warning after warning was given to the people in the messages of the prophets. They had been "sentinels" appointed by God to herald the approach of disaster.[24] But the implication is that their cries of danger had gone unheeded. Isaiah, too, like Amos before him,[25] had noted the people's folly in refusing to listen to God's messengers:

They say to the seers, "Do not see,"
to the prophets, "Do not prophesy the truth to us."
(Isa. 30:10)

Soon God will vindicate the warnings given by the guardians of his people.

5, 6 Micah renews his lament, launching upon a description of the deplorable situation he saw around him. The description is parallel to that of vv. 2–4a. This time he focuses attention on a narrower portion of society, the circle of personal relationships with friend and family relative. Exhortation of the congregation after the style of wisdom teachers does occur from time to time in various types of psalm,[26] but here the prophet uses it as a vehicle for further lament. His cautions are a rhetorical means of communicating the breakdown of trustworthiness, in a manner similar to that of Jeremiah in Jer. 9:4(3). The maintenance of any social structure depends on mutual trust, loyalty, and respect. Man is so made that he finds security in a small group among whom he is accepted and receives support. At the heart of the concentric circles of people known to him there must ever be a stable core of friends, and usually family, if his psychological equilibrium is to be maintained. The prophet gradually penetrates to the center of these inner circles of familiarity: friend—best friend—wife. A man is now forced to go against his nature, retiring within himself and keeping his own counsel, if he is not to face betrayal. His nearest and dearest cannot be relied on to keep faith with the secrets of his heart. Intimacy is no guarantee of fidelity.

The extended family was an important stabilizing and integrating structure within Israelite society. Its cohesiveness depended on the absolute authority of the paterfamilias and the respect of his children, whether grown or young, for him and his partner(s). Included in the family was the daughter-in-law, who upon marriage left her own family and became attached to that of her husband, who remained subject to his father although he might live apart. The Fifth Commandment illustrates the emphasis laid upon family solidarity in Israelite culture. It is difficult for modern Western individualists to appreciate this background to Micah's words or the sense of shock with which they are invested. We almost take it for granted that generations are walled off from each other and have little mutual understanding or respect. In Israel one factor that eroded the family

24. Cf. 2 Sam. 18:24; Jer. 6:17; Ezek. 3:17; Hos. 9:8; Hab. 2:1.
25. Amos 2:12; cf. Hos. 9:7, 8.
26. Cf. esp. Ps. 32:9; 62:10(11); 146:3, and the list of passages in Weiser, *op. cit.*, p. 86.

spirit, as it has our own, was the growth of urban life and the movement of people away from ancestral homes and from a predominantly agrarian economy. It was a process that had been going on since the institution of the monarchy, but the eighth century especially was a period of change and so of tension and distress. It is this situation that is reflected in tones of horror. How terrible that a son should call his father a fool! So the original may be literally rendered. It must be remembered that the Hebrew word "fool" has the connotation of "moral depravity, spiritual irresponsibility and social insensitivity."[27] Rebellious defiance of the mother by daughters of birth and marriage is another example of the unnatural breakdown of cohesion in the home, the microcosm of society. This breakdown is finally summarized in a comprehensive statement. Enmity between members of the family is the climactic counterpart to the hostility shown by one brother Judean to another (v. 2).

Verse 6 is a classic definition of dissolution of family ties, which was taken up by later generations and applied to a context far different from its present one. Various circles within Judaism interested in apocalyptic applied the theme to the time of distress preceding the messianic kingdom.[28] It is in the light of this new eschatological perspective bestowed on the verse that we must understand the way in which Jesus echoed it according to Matt. 10:35f., its parallel Luke 12:53, and also Mark 13:12.[29] By this citation of a text which had now become tinged with apocalyptic coloring he was laying claim to be the fulfiller of messianic hopes and inaugurator of the messianic community. He was also promising persecution to his followers, such as not only the early Church experienced but also the modern Church in such countries as Germany and Russia, Kenya and the Congo.

7 The tone of the lament changes from general pessimism to personal optimism. The change is typical of the lament form. For instance, in Ps. 31:14(15) the psalmist breaks out of the foul atmosphere of enemy plots into the fresh air of an avowal of faith:

But I put my trust in you, Yahweh,
I say, "You are my God."

Even closer with its oblique reference to God is the form of the affirmation in Ps. 55:16f.(17f.):

I have been appealing to God,
and Yahweh will save me. . . .
He will hear my voice.[30]

27. D. A. Hubbard, *NBD*, p. 433.

28. Cf. 1 Enoch 56:7; 100:2; Jub. 23:19; 4 Ezra 6:24.

29. Cf. L. Hartman, *Prophecy Interpreted*. Coniectanea biblica, NT series 1 (1966), pp. 168f.; E. E. Ellis, *The Gospel of Luke*. New Century Bible (1966), p. 182.

30. Cf. too the close of the psalm and the references given in n. 22 above. Lindblom observes that many laments end with an expression of hope and restoration, including Pss. 5, 10, 13, 17, and 28.

The Hebrew language has a rich vocabulary of faith, to which belong watching and waiting. The first recurs in Ps. 5:4, while the other is found over a dozen times on the pages of the Psalter.[31] Here the faith is essentially prophetic: Micah looks forward to the fulfilment of divine prophecies. Isaiah used two other expressions of faith in a similar way in Isa. 8:17. Micah looks to God to vindicate the stand he has taken and so to *save* him. There was much in his environment that said "no" to all he believed and represented, but his cry of affirmation rings out, drowning the denials. This prophet is a man of faith, and he echoes with sincerity the language of devout psalmody. God is his God and his *Savior-God,* both expressions occurring in the Psalter.[32] For a prophet the phrase *my God* was doubly true, for Yahweh was linked with him in a special way[33] which transcended the divine relationship with a devout worshipper. The prophet, like any other saint not immune to attacks of doubt, here strengthens himself in his God and bears bold witness to divine reality beyond the dark clouds of human discord.

So timeless a passage has an especially modern ring in an age when authority is repudiated and talk of anarchy is rife. Riots and demonstrations, the expression of inner conflict and frustration, are but one indication of a general malaise of society and of individuals, such as Micah diagnosed so long ago and far away. His pessimism did not drive him to despair, but into the arms of the God to whom he was personally related. His faith thereby grew and shone out all the brighter. The Christian is called "among a crooked and perverse generation" to "shine like lights in the world, offering them the word of life" (Phil. 2:15f.). His message may well, like Micah's, include a note of fatality which is the inevitable consequence of mortal sickness in society, but it also contains the glad news of judgment borne and healing available through him who was "bruised for our iniquities." Like Micah elsewhere, he can look forward to a better day and to renewal under God. These in fact are the themes developed in the next composition.

B. CONFIDENT HOPES AND PRAYERS (7:8–20)

Do not laugh at me, my enemies:
though[34] I have fallen down, I shall get up. 3+2
Though I sit in the dark,
Yahweh will give me light. 2+2

31. E.g., Ps. 38:15(16); 43:5.
32. For the latter see Ps. 18:47; 25:5; 27:9; Hab. 3:18.
33. Cf. Isa. 7:13; Hos. 9:17.
34. Heb. *kî* here has a concessive sense (Th. C. Vriezen in *Von Ugarit nach Qumran.* O. Eissfeldt Festschrift. BZAW 77 [1958], pp. 267f.; J. Montgomery, *HUCA* 32 [1961], p. 147).

9 *I must bear the burden of Yahweh's wrath*
because I have sinned against him– 3+2
until he takes up my cause
and wins my case. 3+2
He will bring me out into the light,
I shall see right done by him. 2+2
10 *My enemies will see it too,*
and be covered with chagrin. 2+2
Those who said to me,
"Where is your God Yahweh?"
I shall gloat over. 2+3+2
Then they will be troden down
like mud in the streets. 3+2

11 *It is time for your walls to be rebuilt.*
It is[35] *time for your frontier*[36] *to be extended far.* 3+3
12 *It is time for it to come into your possession,*[37]
stretching from Assyria to[38] *Egypt,*[39] 4+4
from Egypt to the River,
from sea to sea and mountain to mountain,[40] 4+4
13 *while the outside world will be devastated*
on account of[41] *its population, as the result of their deeds.* 3+3

14 *Shepherd your people with your crook,*
the flock that is your property, 3+2
that lives[42] *alone in scrubland*
while pastures lie around. 3+2
May they feed in Bashan and Gilead,
as they did in days of yore. 3+2

35. In light of *yôm hû'* in v. 12 the anomalous *yôm hahû'* should most probably be corrected accordingly.
36. The suffix in *gᵉḏērāyiḵ* earlier carries over to *ḥōq*; cf. the note on v. 19. In view of the parallelism *ḥōq,* primarily something inscribed or marked out, must mean *frontier*; cf. the meaning "limit" with reference to the sea in Jer. 5:22, etc. For the use of the verb cf. Isa. 26:15.
37. Heb. *wᵉ'āḏeyḵā* has a masculine suffix; it is generally repointed with a feminine form, *wᵉ'āḏayiḵ*.
38. MT *wᵉ'ārê,* "and cities of," is generally emended to *wa'ᵃḏê* in light of the next phrase; cf. the doublet in V "and to the cities." For the error cf. G's misreading of *w'dyk* earlier as *w'ryk*.
39. Heb. *māṯsôr* is apparently another form of *mitsrayim*; cf. 2 K. 19:24 = Isa. 37:25; Isa. 19:6. Some scholars dispute this identification (e.g., P. J. Calderone, *Biblica* 42 [1961], pp. 423–432).
40. The necessary meaning but not the syntax of MT is clear: lit. "and sea from sea and mountain (of) the mountain." Conceivably the force of "to" can carry over, but at least it seems obligatory to read with most *mēhār,* "from mountain," for *hāhār* (cf. V).
41. G's interpretation "along with" is also possible.
42. MT *shōḵᵉnî,* a masculine singular form, is strange since *flock* is feminine; possibly its gender is due to *people*. But G S V T presuppose a pointing as a plural *shōḵᵉnê,* probably correctly; it accords with the later plural verb.

15 *As when you came out*
of the country of Egypt,
let us see[43] *wonders.* 2+2+2
16 *May the nations see them and feel let down*
by all their power[44] 3+2
May they clap hand to mouth,
may their ears be deaf. 3+2
17 *May they lick the dust like snakes,*
like serpents on the ground. 3+2
May they come quaking out of their strongholds
to Yahweh our God.[45] 3+2
May they be in dread and afraid of you.[46] 3

18 *What God is there like you,*
who forgives wrong 2+2
and overlooks the rebellion
of his own people's remnant, 2+2
who does not retain his anger for ever
but delights in constant love? 3+2
19 *He will show us his affection anew,*
he will vanquish[47] *our wrongdoing.* 2+2
You will hurl into the depths of the sea
all our sins.[48] 3+2
20 *You will keep faith with Jacob*
and prove to Abraham your constant love, 3+2
as you promised on oath to our forefathers
in olden times. 3+2

It is to better times ahead that this last part of the book looks with assurance. It takes the form of a psalm in which more than one voice is

43. MT construes the verb as "I shall cause him to see," as if this is a divine answer to the prayer of v. 14. But the end of v. 17 indicates that the prayer continues. It is necessary to repoint as *'ar'ēnû,* the imperative of an Aramaic-type Aphel conjugation (Ewald, cf. Dahood, *Pss 2,* p. 31).
44. I.e., it will not help them; cf. *bôsh min* in Isa. 20:5, etc. (P. Haupt, *AJSL* 26[1910], pp. 228–230).
45. MT takes this phrase with what follows, but the meter suggests otherwise. For the construction cf. Gen. 42:28; 1 Sam. 21:1(2). Dahood, *Pss 1,* pp. 117f., divides the clauses thus, although he renders differently. The third person reference to Yahweh is derived from court style: cf. Dahood, *Pss 2,* pp. 368f. *ad* Ps. 99:1, 3.
46. A short line; cf. 4:4 and note.
47. Some scholars, e.g., Haupt, J. M. P. Smith, G. R. Driver (*JTS* 39[1938], p. 269, n. 7), repoint MT *yiḵbōsh* as *y^{e}ḵabbēś* or read *y^{e}ḵabbēs,* "wash away" (cf. Ps. 51:2, 7[4, 9]).
48. This is obviously the required meaning, and so G S V render. It is a moot point whether MT *ḥaṭṭ'ôṯām,* "their sins," should be emended to *ḥaṭṭ'ôṯēnû, our sins,* with four Heb. mss. (so most scholars; cf. *BHS*; R. Weiss, *JBL* 82(1963), p. 162). It is possible to regard the *mem* as enclitic and the preceding first plural suffix as doing double duty (H. D. Hummel, *JBL* 76[1957], p. 95; Dahood, *CBQ* 20(1958), pp. 45f., with reference to G. R. Driver, *JRAS* [1948], pp. 164f.).

heard, and so technically it is a liturgy.[49] It is a comprehensive unit made up of four parts. The first is a psalm of confidence spoken by Zion (vv. 8–10), comparable to Ps. 27:1–6 and Pss. 62, 90. The second is an oracle of salvation, which puts a divine seal on Zion's hopes and shows them to be grounded in God's own purposes for the land of his people (vv. 11–13). Such oracles are a feature of a number of psalms: compare Pss. 12, 50, 75, 81, 82, and 95. The third section is a prayer of supplication (vv. 14–17) on the lines of Pss. 44, 77, and 80, virtually asking that the preceding oracle may be fulfilled. The last part has the form of another psalm of confidence (vv. 18–20) and begins in the style of a hymn of praise to God (v. 18). The first, third, and fourth elements of the composition have stylistic associations with the lament: compare Ps. 90, a lament dominated by notes of faith and praise. An oracle is a typical sequel to a lament in the OT, although evidence in the actual Psalter is scanty.[50] The whole is from a form-critical point of view a community lament. Yet despite a lamentable situation it shows no trace of cowering despair but faces the future with assurance and faith in God.

If the historical setting is the early postexilic period,[51] then the piece has been inserted to round off Micah's collection and thus to fit it for use in the worship of the new, young Israel. There are indications elsewhere in the book that serve to confirm this editorial purpose. The artistry of the compiler is revealed in the rhetorical question of v. 18, *What God is there like you?*—evidently an allusion to Micah's name, which means, "Who is like Yahweh?"[52] The very name of the prophet is fittingly taken up and woven into a final poem of praise to God within a communal response to Micah's messages of judgment and salvation.

The piece is held together by a number of themes that run through its constituent parts. All four sections are concerned with the past sin of the community or its consequences in their present distress. The first three parts depict the coming triumph of Israel in terms of the discomfiture of enemy nations, while the second and third join in representing their triumph as an opportunity for territorial enlargement.[53] All four relate the fortunes of the community to the will of Yahweh, their covenant God.

The constituent parts display a greater degree of metrical regularity than most of the pieces in the book. The first, third, and fourth, all spoken

49. B. Stade, "Micha 7, 7–20 ein Psalm," *ZAW* 23(1903), pp. 164–171, demonstrated the close parallels with the terminology of the Psalms. H. Gunkel, in *What Remains of the OT and Other Essays* (E.T. 1928), pp. 115–149, laid down valuable form-critical guidelines to the passage. B. Reicke, *HTR* 60 (1967), pp. 349–367, regards the whole of ch. 7 as a unit, composed for the ritual of the New Year Festival or designed as a prophetic imitation of such a composition.

50. For OT examples see the comment and note on Joel 2:19.

51. See the Introduction.

52. Cf. "Michael," which means "Who is like God?"

53. Parts one and three are linked by a striking soundplay: *rā'â*, vv. 9f., 10f.—*'ôr*, vv. 8f.—*rā'â*, v. 14—*yārē'*, v. 17.

by the community, consist substantially of a 3+2 meter, varied with 2+2. The second stanza stands metrically apart, as is fitting with the change of speaker: its four lines consist of a chiastic arrangement of the heavier 3+3 and 4+4 rhythms, solemn measures in keeping with the character of the section as a divine oracle.

8–10 The speaker is evidently Zion, which stands for the community of God's people at worship. The feminine form used in the original for *your God* at v. 10 reveals that it is not an individual person who is speaking. There are parallels in the book of Lamentations: for instance, Lam. 1:10–16, 18–22 are laments spoken by Zion. Indeed a similar air of catastrophe looms in the backgrounds of both those poems and this section. But whereas there the disaster has demoralized the community, here they have nearly traversed their dark tunnel of despair and can glimpse light at its other end, the future reversal of their fortunes by Yahweh. As in the later chapters of Lamentations, they can, if not smile through their tears, at least look upward and ahead through their tear-filled eyes instead of being morbidly engrossed in their past affliction. It is most probable that the same situation underlies both pieces, namely, the tragic fall of Jerusalem in 587 B.C. Theologically it spelled Yahweh's revoking of the covenant, which his people had broken before so repeatedly. Now all they could do was to accept the tragedy as merited punishment, to seek his face in repentance, and to plead with him to renew his covenant.

This communal lament opens when these measures have already been taken. This later generation had evidently taken to heart Micah's dual message concerning the sin and judgment of God's people and also the salvation that lay beyond. The first section of the closing passage of response is imbued with a penitential spirit and with the confidence that Yahweh will resume his role as senior partner of the covenant and rescue his people.[54] It is this assurance that bids those who mock at Jerusalem's downfall to stop their mocking. In Lam. 3:14 an individual representing the community mourns that he has become "the laughingstock of all peoples," while in 4:21 the rejoicing of Edom is said to be premature: Zion's fate is soon to become their own. Here it is uncertain whether "my enemy" is a collective term[55] or refers to a specific counterpart to the lamenting community at their worship in Jerusalem. In the latter case Edom is most likely in view, since it tended to be singled out as a mocking spectator of the fall of Jerusalem.[56]

The community has regained its morale. Like Paul, according to J. B. Phillips' paraphrase of 2 Cor. 4:9, they are "knocked down but not knocked out." Their future rise to renewed stability is anticipated in the mood of resilience that they possess already. At the moment they *sit in the*

54. Cf. K. Baltzer, *The Covenant Formulary* (E.T. 1970), p. 56.
55. It is feminine: cf. *yôšheḇet,* a feminine collective in 1:11–15.
56. Cf. Ps. 137:7; Isa. 34:5–17; Obadiah.

dark. This is a figure that is also applied to the fate of Jerusalem in Lam. 3:6. It is borrowed from the experience of imprisonment.[57] Darkness and light are universal symbols of calamity and prosperity. For those who speak, prosperity is essentially linked with God. As the psalmist could call Yahweh "my light and my salvation" (Ps. 27:1), so the community could look to him to turn their long night of suffering into the dawn of new light and life. Yet they do not kick against their suffering and plaintively bemoan it. They have reached the point of being able to have a healthy attitude of acceptance. It had been instilled into them by the law and the prophets that it was God's nature to punish their sin. This was his *wrath,* a concept that also dominates the book of Lamentations. It is the reaction of a moral God to the breaking of his covenant stipulations. Suffering Israel has not stood alone in asking the instinctive question, "What have I done to deserve this?" but for Israel it was a genuine question and not a complaint. The generation who speak have come to understand that they are bearing the backlog of their forefathers' sins. The nation's past has caught up with them; in a conscious attitude of solidarity with former generations they confess their national sin. They realize that the troops of Nebuchadnezzar were sent by God to quell their spiritual rebellion against him, their Overlord in the covenant.[58]

Prisoners in their dark dungeon of desolation and disfavor, they had to serve their just sentence; but they could depend on God for their eventual release. They have the assurance that the covenant would be renewed. In his own good time Yahweh would take their part. Imagery is used that is derived from the lawcourt. It is often not appreciated that the idea of God's judgment was for Israel a doctrine of comfort as well as of warning.[59] Just as the victimized looked to the judge for help and redress, so the divine Judge was viewed as the champion of those who suffered in this unjust world. God judged not only one's own sins but the sins of others against oneself. This note is frequently struck in laments, with reference to unfair treatment at the hands of enemies:

> "*You have taken up my cause, Yahweh, . . .*
> *you have seen the wrong done to me, Yahweh.*
> *Judge my case.*" (Lam. 3:58, 59)[60]

The community are conscious of being not only sinners but sinned against. The issue mentioned at the outset is still much in mind: the malicious laughter at Zion's disaster was like kicking a man when he was down. The worshippers are sure they can depend on God to repay their foes by vindicating them, his people. *Right* has the connotation of salvation, just as

57. Cf. Ps. 107:10–16; Isa. 42:7.
58. Cf. 2 K. 18:14, where Hezekiah describes his rebellion against Sennacherib with the phrase "I have sinned."
59. See C. S. Lewis, *Reflections on the Psalms* (1958), ch. 2.
60. Cf. Ps. 35:1; 43:1.

Yahweh's "righteous acts" in 6:8 are his saving deeds for his oppressed people.

Again the hearts of the community savor the prospect of light and liberation at God's hand, a theme Charles Wesley applied so finely to the Christian experience of conversion:

Long my imprisoned spirit lay
fast bound in sin and nature's night.
Thine eye diffused a quickening ray,
I woke, the dungeon flamed with light.
My chains fell off, my heart was free,
I rose, went forth and followed thee.

The people of God resent the mocking of their enemies not only for the natural and human reason of damaged self-esteem. It can hardly be denied that Zion's "cheeks flush for a moment with the hate of the enemy and the assurance of revenge" (G. A. Smith). But the people are even more concerned because Yahweh himself was included in their taunts: Zion's foes have doubted the reality of the power of Israel's patron and blasphemed his name. It is his own honor that is at stake,[61] and he can be trusted to vindicate his glory and might. They whose cause is ultimately identical with that of Yahweh look forward to the time when his supremacy can be clearly seen in the triumph of his human representatives and the defeat of their common enemies. This victory is described in dramatic terms which allude to the ancient Near Eastern custom of a conqueror's placing his foot on the enemy's neck.[62] This triumph of Israel will bring glory to their Lord. In their eyes it is poetic justice that they should eventually come to the position of gloating over those who had treated them maliciously.

11–13 A new voice breaks in to take up the note of triumph and to confirm it. The assertions of the community are affirmed in this passage of promise. A feature of Israel's worship was the welcome interruption of petition and prayer with an answer from God delivered by prophet or priest. This two-way communion continued in the worship of the early Church, which also had its prophets.[63] It is this living intimacy of fellowship between God and his congregation that is reflected here. The worshipping community of Jerusalem are addressed with news that their rehabilitation is imminent.[64] Since Zion is addressed,[65] it is apparently the literal walls of Jerusalem that are meant here. It is significant that a term is used that refers to the enclosure of a vineyard, a traditional metaphor for

61. Cf. Deut. 32:26f.; Ps. 42:3, 10(4, 11); 74:22; 79:10.
62. Cf. Josh. 10:24; Ps. 110:1.
63. Cf. 1 Cor. 14:26–32; 1 John 4:1.
64. Cf. Ps. 102:13, 16(14, 17).
65. A feminine pronominal suffix is used.

Israel in their enjoyment of a healthy relationship with Yahweh.[66] The rebuilding of Jerusalem's walls is invested with theological meaning as the signal for a change of Israel's fortunes, the experience of God's grace after enduring his wrath.[67] It was Nehemiah who during his first term as governor of Judah, which began in 445 B.C., accomplished the crucial task of rebuilding the walls.[68] This material goes back to a period before that time.

A parallel promise is given that the territorial boundaries of the little, struggling community will be flung far and wide. The next two lines surely reinforce and elaborate this promise. They are generally taken as a reference to the return of Jewish exiles and refugees to their native land or the pilgrimage of pagan nations to worship at Yahweh's shrine. But there are difficulties in the way of this understanding of the text.[69] A more natural interpretation is to take the lines as a definition of the area the new Israel is to embrace.[70] This view is suggested by the parallels between the geographical horizons presented here and the ideal limits of Israel stated elsewhere. Zech. 9:10 takes up the promise of the royal psalm, Ps. 72:8, in predicting the arrival of a king at Jerusalem whose

dominion will be from sea to sea
and from the River to the ends of the earth.

The Euphrates is frequently called *the River* par excellence. Yahweh's covenant affirmation to Abraham concerning the gift of the land of promise to his descendants envisaged an area ranging "from the river of Egypt to the great river, the river Euphrates" (Gen. 15:18). It seems to be with some reference to the keeping of this promise that Solomon's empire is said to have extended "from the Euphrates to Philistine country and to the Egyptian border" (1 K. 4:21[5:1]),[71] while in Ps. 80:11(12) Israel's former vineyard is wistfully mentioned as stretching "to the sea," i.e., the Mediterranean, and "to the River."[72] Here the traditional promise is renewed to the theocratic community living in cramped conditions around Jerusalem. Zion was once more to become capital of a vast domain.

The reference to Egypt and Assyria apparently means that Israel's territory was to extend up to the Assyrian border, regarded as the Euphrates, in the northeast and down to the Egyptian border in the

66. Cf. Ps. 80:13; 89:40(41); Isa. 5:5.
67. Cf. Ezra 9:9; Ps. 51:18(20).
68. Evidently an attempt was also made some years earlier in the reign of Artaxerxes I, only to be nullified by destruction (cf. Ezra 4:23).
69. Heb. *yāḇô'* must be taken as an indefinite singular or, as is usually done, changed with G to a plural *yāḇô'û,* "they will come"; *from . . . to* should be "from . . . and from."
70. Cf., e.g., Josh. 1:4. Then the *frontier* of v. 11 is the subject of the verb. For *bô' 'aḏ,* "come to," in the sense of territory coming into one's control, cf. 4:8 and Num. 32:19.
71. In Josh. 15:4, 47 Judah's territory reaches to the Brook of Egypt, probably Wadi el-'Arish, as does Israel's in Num. 34:5 (cf. Ezek. 47:19; 48:28).
72. The links between vv. 11f. and Ps. 80:11f.(12f.) suggest some relationship between these passages; cf. too the reference to "mountains" in Ps. 80:10(11).

southwest. *From sea to sea* is evidently a diameter drawn from the Mediterranean to the Persian Gulf, presumably skirting Babylonia. *Mountain to mountain* is less easily explained. It probably indicates the northern and southern axis. The northern boundary may be the Lebanon range in Syria, which conforms with the ideal limit in Deut. 11:24; Josh. 1:4, and then the mountainous counterpart to "the wilderness" in those texts is perhaps Mount Sinai.[73] The promise concerns not worldwide dominion, as Zech. 9:10 does, but a wide area bounded by the frontiers of Israel's traditional enemies, Mesopotamia and Egypt. These supremely comprise *the outside world.*[74] For these areas nothing good is promised. Their denizens are to reap the fruit of age-old enmity and exploitation of God's people. As Israel's territory has been the scarred battlefield of successive foreign armies, so by way of compensation their territory is to suffer desolation. Whether or not they themselves are to be annihilated is not clear from the text.

The oracle is the counterpart to the Christian doctrine of the Last Judgment. In traditional language which Israel could understand it expresses the assurance that deficits in the moral balance sheet of the world are eventually to be paid, while the kingdom of God is to be established in triumph. Would God's people of the OT have come closer to enjoying the promise if they had been more faithful?

14–17 The congregation speak again, in a prayer of supplication. It expresses how ardent their desire is that the divine oracle should come true. The promises of territorial expansion and of enemy defeat are echoed with a fervent "please." They pray in the spirit of David's prayer in 2 Sam. 7:25 that Yahweh will make his word come true.[75]

Their appeal is so couched as to touch Yahweh's heart. Was it not daring presumption to remind him of his covenant commitments to Israel? Indeed not. The shepherd imagery is mentioned in all three sections of hope in the book.[76] The motif is a not uncommon one in the supplications of laments,[77] but it is significant that hitherto in the book it has featured in divine promises. The congregation are building on the basis of God's own pledges this pinnacle of prayer. Yahweh, as their kingly Overlord, is their Shepherd: he has pledged himself already to care for his human flock and to rescue them from danger and deprivation. Now in their time of need they yearn for Yahweh to keep his promise. They describe their straitened circumstances in pastoral terms. The green grass they could see lay beyond the confines of their own poor grazing land. Other peoples had commandeered the choice pastures Israel had once enjoyed, while they were cooped

73. Cheyne, Wade.
74. Lit. "the earth, world," here excluding the promised land.
75. Vuilleumier aptly compares Rev. 22:20.
76. Previously in 2:12; 4:6f.
77. Cf. Ps. 28:9; 74:1; 79:13; 80:1(2).

up in a tiny area[78] around a Jerusalem that was a shadow of its former glory. With plaintive pathos they lay their forlorn condition before their God. It is significant that in 3:12 Micah had predicted that Jerusalem would become a hilltop of *ya'ar,* the Hebrew word used here for *scrubland.*[79] God's word had come tragically true. In A.D. 70 Rabbi Akiba saw a fox coming out of the temple and smiled, because he looked for the fulfilment of prophetic promises of good now that Micah's prediction of woe had come to pass.[80] In similar vein the repetition of this term indicates a yearning among the struggling postexilic community for the fulfilment of God's other word.

Israel lays claim to the areas of the northern Transjordan that once were theirs. The pastoral figure is maintained, since both *Bashan* and *Gilead* were known for their rich pastures.[81] Jeroboam II had won the area for the Northern Kingdom from the Arameans, but it had remained in Israelite hands for only a few decades until the Assyrians wrested it from them. Since then it had belonged to the successive empires of Assyria, Babylon, and Persia. Here the community nostalgically look back to an earlier period, the glorious age of David and Solomon when this Transjordanian territory had come under the dominion of Israel. Their prayer is that God may grant to their nation the achievements their illustrious ancestors had accomplished with divine aid. Here again the plea is not presumptuous, for they are building upon the rock of God's promise in 4:8 concerning the restoration of Jerusalem's former realm. The past, which showed what God could do for his people, is used as the standard and measure of their future blessing.

One reference to past splendor triggers off another. They look back further, to the Exodus, when God had stormed[82] out of Egypt, victoriously leading his oppressed people to liberation and the land of promise. As he had then miraculously intervened to save his people from their peril, so now when they are again reduced to circumstances of hardship, they look to him to work another miracle on their behalf. Such appeals to God's mighty acts of salvation in former days are characteristic of the lament.[83] They are viewed as the prototype of what God is able to do for Israel in the future. The acute tension between his display of extraordinary might in

78. "Stretching less than twenty-five miles in a straight line along the watershed-ridge from north of Jerusalem to south of Beth-zur" (W. F. Albright, *BA* 9[1946], p. 8).

79. Eissfeldt, *loc. cit.,* pp. 260–62, relates the phrase to Yahweh as occupying a shrine within a wood set amid the mountain range of Carmel, although no such sanctuary is known. For the editor at least, *ya'ar* referred back to Jerusalem's fate. *Alone* seems contextually better as a description of the community than of Yahweh. Heb. *karmel* and *ya'ar* are contrasted also in Isa. 29:17; 32:15.

80. Babylonian Talmud, *Maccoth* 24b.

81. Num. 32:1–5; Deut. 32:14.

82. Cf. 2 Sam. 5:24; Ps. 60:10(12).

83. Cf. Ps. 44:1f.(2f.); 74:2, 12–15; 77:5, 11, 14–20(6, 12, 15–21); 80:8–11(9–12).

their past history and their present distress is resolved in the hope that burns in their hearts, kindled by the traditions of the past, and sustains them while the wind of present harsh reality blows with bitter cold.

The prayer moves on to sound a note struck twice earlier, in vv. 10 and 13, concerning the humiliation of the now triumphant nations. Probably there lingers in the mind, after the Exodus reference, a reminiscence of its regular corollary, Yahweh's subjugation of the nations of Canaan when he brought Israel to the haven of the promised land. Once again his people were threatened by giant nations and prevented from entering into their destined heritage. To them had descended the divine pledges of deliverance from surrounding enemies given earlier in the book.[84] They are therefore emboldened to pray that their encroaching neighbors may be confronted by God's renewed displays of might, and accordingly may derive no joy from the contemplation of their own *power,* so puny by comparison. Those who had been so brazen in their taunts need to be taught a lesson in demoralization. The prayer is that God will make them speechless and dumbfounded by a sensational turning of the tables for Israel's benefit, and that they will be reduced to a state of shock, deafened by the thunder of his might.[85] The congregation revel in the prospect of this discomfiture, for it would spell the vindication of Yahweh over the forces of evil that frustrate his purposes for his people.

Their desire is that these foes may come in humble submission and grovel before him in enforced homage. The figure of licking *the dust* alludes to the traditional custom of defeated enemies kissing the feet of their new overlord in token of vassalage.[86] They crave for their foes' prostration as the token of Yahweh's demonstration of his supremacy, as Paul in his prison was to yearn for the time when "every knee would bow at the name of Jesus" (Phil. 2:10). This triumph Paul attributed to the Cross, where in effect the "principalities and powers" were already subjugated (Col. 2:16); but he looked forward to its manifestation whereby none would remain outside the sway of his Lord. Similarly the desire of this Jewish community is, in the words of another communal lament:

> *May they know that you alone,*
> *whose name is Yahweh, are Most High over the whole world.*
> (Ps. 83:18[19])

This is the lofty ideal to which the people's hearts aspire.

The final line is a conscious echo of an expression found in the psalm attributed to David that celebrates his victories over his enemies (Ps. 18:45[47]). But it is most significant that whereas there they "came trembling out of their strongholds" to the king, here it is not to Israel but to Israel's God that their foes are to present themselves in submission. Divine

84. 4:11–13; 5:7f.(8f.).
85. For the gesture of placing the hand over the mouth cf. Judg. 18:19; Job 21:5.
86. Cf. Ps. 72:9.

glory rather than vainglory, divine vindication rather than selfish vindictiveness are the prime motives that drive God's oppressed people to their knees. They ask for their hope to be realized that:

The nations will fear the name of Yahweh
and all the kings in the world your glory.
When Yahweh rebuilds Zion,
he will be revealed in his glory. (Ps. 102:15f.[16f.])

18–20 The fourth and last movement of this liturgical symphony is a choral piece of devotion and doxology. It begins in the style of a hymn, extolling the compassionate nature of God. A theme from the opening movement is taken up and developed, the burden of God's wrath resting upon the sin-conscious hearts of the community. They have come in repentance, but that is not enough to win back the blessing of God. He is no petulant princeling to be wooed away from a fit of capricious temper. Nothing they can do will avail of itself to secure God's acceptance. The sole ground of their hope lies in the noble character of God as one who forgives, forgets, and offers a fresh beginning. Superficially this claim sounds like the one made in 2:7 and categorically denied by Micah. But the respective attitudes of heart are poles apart. The complacency that shrugged off prophetic warnings in the spirit of *pardonner—c'est son métier* had given way to a deep sense of the seriousness of sin. The heartfelt appreciation of divine grace that impassions this finale is an emotion that can be experienced only by those who have come to see sin through God's eyes.

The community rise in spirit far above their doleful environment in joyful, lilting contemplation of the grace of God. Their rhetorical question concerning God's matchlessness is usually reserved for a consideration of Yahweh's mighty acts, as for instance in Exod. 15:11.[87] There were many nations around who claimed power for their gods; Israel was always glad when their own God, whom they believed to be invested with universal omnipotence, was proved to be so in a manner convincing to those to whom seeing was believing. But with an insight born of richer experience, God's people have come to see that his majesty is most evident in his grace.

Countless acts of pardoning grace
beyond Thine other wonders shine.
Who is a pardoning God like Thee
or who has grace so rich and free? (Samuel Davies)

In the term *remnant* they glance briefly but poignantly back along the path they have trodden. It is a term that sounds a persistent echo through the hope sections of the book with deliberate emphasis on the harrowing losses

87. Cf. Ps. 71:19; 79:14; 89:9. Cf. C. J. Labuschagne, *The Incomparability of Yahweh in the OT*. Pretoria Oriental Series 5 (1966), p. 21f., 91, 104.

suffered by Israel.[88] Paradoxically it opens a door of hope, since they have the pledge that after judgment is to come salvation.

But if the people of God find themselves in a new and awesome situation, the language they use is hallowed by long tradition. It echoes the classic characterization of Yahweh in Exod. 34:6f. as the God "who forgives wrong, rebellion, and sin," who is "slow to anger and full of constant love."[89] The God of ancient Israel has not changed; he has remained the same down to the present. A new generation take up the old formulation and make it their own by faith. They look away from their wrath-laden situation and affirm again, as they had at the outset in vv. 8f., that this must be a temporary phenomenon. Now they argue from the character of God: it is grace that better reveals his very heart:

For his anger lasts a moment,
but his favor a lifetime.
Weeping may stay the night,
but with the morning comes joy. (Ps. 30:5[6])

Believers know that the purpose of God's dealings with them is to train them in the ways of righteousness and harmony with himself. To this end chastisement may play a part, but over and beyond it lies the mystery of grace.

It is this vital truth concerning the revealed nature of God that they apply to themselves, treasuring it as the guarantee of their future blessing. Standing on the promise inherent in God's character, they make an attestation of faith concerning their prospects. They can glimpse the certainty of a renewed demonstration of divine goodwill toward them in the forgiveness of their sins. They know that their lives must remain unblessed as long as they are separated from God by the guilt of sin. They rejoice therefore in the assurance that the heritage of sin, which dogs their steps[90] and has cast over them its disastrous shadow, will be thrown off for good and all. Has the Song of Moses in Exod. 15, echoed at the beginning of the section, influenced the piece again? Just as once God's incomparable power shook off the pursuing Egyptians and overcame them, so now God's incomparable grace is to triumph over sin. Thus would the second Exodus prayed for in v. 15 be realized. No longer would his people be slaves to sin and its consequences. No longer would they be held captive to the frustration of its thraldom. Paul echoed this very theme in Rom. 5f.

The wonder of it whirls the worshippers from meditation to a

88. 2:12; 4:6; 5:7f.(8f.). On metrical grounds the last phrase of v. 18 has sometimes been regarded as a gloss (cf. *BHK*). *BHS* is right to retain it: it contains a hallmark of the hope sections.

89. Heb. *ḥeseḏ,* as here in v. 18 and also in v. 20: cf. the comments on 6:8; 7:2. It is significant that Lam. 3:22f., 32 likewise looks forward confidently to a demonstration of this divine attribute.

90. Cf. 1:5; 3:8; 6:7.

renewed intimacy of prayer.[91] They confront God with their heartfelt conviction that he would drown their sins forever, just as Pharaoh's charioteers were "hurled" into *the sea* and sank "down into the depths like a stone" (Exod. 15:5). The black shadow of guilt for past sin that had dominated their experience would disappear from their lives, never to threaten them again. Another psalmist sang in similar vein:

> *As far as the east is from the west*
> *he removes from us our guilt as rebels.* (Ps. 103:12)

But as yet the cloud is still there for this congregation; they look forward to its future removal. Then the way would lie open for unbroken harmony with their covenant God. Their community would become strong and healthy both in spiritual relationships and in their social and political outworking. It is this corollary of divine forgiveness that is the closing melody of the passage. Further echoes of Exod. 34:6 may be heard in the joint reference to *faith,* i.e., faithfulness, and *constant love*. The traditional attributes of the God of the covenant, of which the phrase "grace and truth" in John 1:7 is the descendant, are borrowed for inclusion in a larger canvas than that of the covenant of Sinai. The community delve further back into their religious past to find an even deeper foundation for their confidence. They lay claim to patriarchal promises.[92] At the moment they languish in a corner of the promised land, numerically a vestige of what the nation once had been and spiritually victims of divine indignation. Their situation is the very opposite of that envisaged in God's sworn pledges to the patriarchs concerning the land of promise, posterity as numerous as stars, sand, and dust, and the fullness of divine blessing.[93] In a sense the patriarchs lived on in their descendants: *Jacob* stands for the people of God to whom the ancient voice of blessing comes afresh, as at Bethel of old. Even *Abraham* is a bold individualization of the community in whom the patriarch survives to remind God of his solemn promises. The present congregation profess the ties of solidarity binding them to the great heroes of the past, around whom clustered even greater expectations. This oneness is fittingly portrayed in order to stress that these folk, weak and feeble as

91. The change from third person to second in v. 19b has troubled ancient versions and modern commentators alike and has induced many attempts at amelioration: (1) to substitute an easier third person *wᵉhishlîḵ* for MT *wᵉṯashlîḵ* (G S V T, *BHS,* Willi-Plein); (2) to revocalize as a Hophal or passive Qal *wᵉṯushlaḵ* (G. R. Driver, *JTS* 39[1938], p. 268; Dahood, *CBQ* 20[1958], p. 46); (3) to condemn vv. 18b–19a as secondary (Stade, J. M. P. Smith); or (4) to rewrite as a second person in v. 19a (Robinson, George). MT can stand as a quite natural distortion of perspective. Verse 18 after a second person address passes into a third person description of God's attributes. Logically v. 19a, passing from general characterization to future event, should have reverted to the second person, but by a natural attraction continues with the third. The passage reverts later, in v. 19b, and maintains the direct address till the end.

92. Cf. Ps. 105:8–11.

93. Gen. 12:2f.; 15:5f.; 22:16–18; 28:13f.

they are, yet are heirs to promised glory. Therefore tightly they cling to God's ancient word of grace.[94] The Christian Church is no stranger to this assurance, for the same theme of laying claim to the heritage of promised grace reappears in Acts 3:25; Gal. 3:6–29.

Martin Luther provided what amounts to a remarkable summary of the whole passage, vv. 8–20:

Though great our sins and sore our wounds
and deep and dark our fall,
his helping mercy hath no bounds,
his love surpasseth all.
Our trusty loving Shepherd he,
who shall at last set Israel free
from all their sin and sorrow.

(E.T. by Catharine Winkworth)

The piece forms a worthy climax to the book of Micah. It builds upon the prophetic word with the assurance and tone of spiritual reality that marked Micah's own ministry. It is a monument to the faith of men who transcended their earthly woes and climbed to a spiritual vantage point. From there they could survey the present in the reassuring light of God's past and future dealings with his covenant people. As Micah's prophesying was marked by a holy boldness that enabled him to confront a corrupt society as fearlessly as Peter, John, and Paul in a later age, so here is an earnest of boldness toward God in approaching "the throne of grace to receive mercy and find grace in the form of timely help" (Heb. 4:16). It exudes a confidence akin to that of which Charles Wesley testified:

Bold I approach the eternal throne
and claim the crown, through Christ my own.

94. "The Abrahamic covenant stood as a witness to the primacy of grace in all God's dealings with his people Israel and testified to the belief that election was an act of God and not a state to which men could attain by their obedience to a law" (R. E. Clements, *Abraham and David*. SBT 2:5 [1967], p. 88).

INDEX OF CHIEF SUBJECTS

INDEX OF AUTHORS

INDEX OF SCRIPTURE REFERENCES